D1497273

*The Making of*

# AMERICAN DEMOCRACY

## READINGS AND DOCUMENTS

EDITED BY

## RAY ALLEN BILLINGTON

William Smith Mason Professor of History,
Northwestern University

## BERT JAMES LOEWENBERG

Professor of American History,
Sarah Lawrence College

## SAMUEL HUGH BROCKUNIER

Professor of History, Wesleyan University

VOLUME TWO

New York · Toronto

RINEHART AND COMPANY · INC ·

Carl A. Rudisill Library
LENOIR RHYNE COLLEGE

973.082
B49m

28314
Jan '53

First Printing May, 1950
Second Printing November, 1950
Third Printing June, 1951
Fourth Printing January, 1952

Copyright, 1950, by Ray Allen Billington,

Bert James Loewenberg, and Samuel Hugh Brockunier

Designed by Stefan Salter

Printed in the United States of America

All Rights Reserved

# PREFACE

The purpose of this book is to present a continuous documentary account of American history. The sequence of chapters and topics centers attention on critical periods in the nation's growth. The connective tissue of narrative introductions provides an integrated account of major trends and relates the documentary excerpts to their larger social context. It is hoped that such a book, weaving documents into a narrative of general history, will be more significant and useful than an ordinary compilation of readings.

In view of the broadening historical horizon and the growth of interest in social, economic, and intellectual history, the editors have sought not only to include "standard" documents, but to balance them with other types of materials. The readings range from public and official documents to contemporary impressions and eye-witness accounts, contemporary statements of critical problems and ideas, and modern evaluations.

The documents are reproduced as originally written. Necessarily, excisions have been made, in order to delete extraneous material and to make room for additional documents. All omissions are indicated by ellipses. A few minor changes in punctuation and abbreviation have been made in the interest of clarity and uniformity.

The Constitution of the United States, including the Bill of Rights and all subsequent amendments, has been included as an appendix in both volumes; the Declaration of Independence, which appears as a document in the first volume, has also been included as an appendix in the second. Selected and annotated bibliographies for each chapter of the readings appear at the end of each volume.

The editors wish to acknowledge special indebtedness to the following: to Professor Chester M. Destler for his several readings and many suggestions, as well as for his aid in obtaining documents; to Professors Edwin B. Coddington, Gilbert C. Fite, James B. Hedges, and Rodman W. Paul for their readings and helpful suggestions; and to Mr. Edward Lurie for his aid in checking various documents.

R.A.B.
B.J.L.
February, 1950                                                                                    S.H.B.

# CONTENTS

## XV

# WESTWARD EXPANSION AND RURAL DISLOCATION

### 1865–1890

XXIII

# THE WORLD'S ILLUSION

1900–1917

## THE FALL OF LIBERAL NATIONALISM

## AMERICAN EXPANSION AND POWER POLITICS

XXIV

# NATIONALISM AND NORMALCY

1918–1932

## SOVEREIGNTY TRIUMPHANT

## CONSERVATISM AND CONSTITUTIONAL LAW

## NATIONALISM AND NORMALCY

## XXV

# THE ROOSEVELT REVOLUTION

### 1933–1940

### SOCIAL TENSIONS AND REFORM

### SOCIAL PLANNING AND PRIVATE ENTERPRISE

### THE REVOLUTION IN CONSTITUTIONAL LAW

### DEMOCRACY AND PARTY LOYALTY

## XXVI

# DEMOCRACY VERSUS NATIONALISM

### 1933–1945

### RECESSION FROM NATIONALISM

# THE ROAD TO REUNION

## 1865–1876

Appomattox failed to bring peace to the United States. The guns were silenced, but, as in all wars, peace could not simply be declared; it had to be made. And, as in every major conflict, the social tensions bred by war intensified the problems of peace. Tensions were everywhere apparent in 1865; America was divided by sectional hatreds, by political conflicts, and by economic antagonisms. Men were often confused and sometimes blinded, and lacked strong and intelligent leadership. Instead, lesser men sat in the White House, inadequate to stem the tide of hatred, helpless to bring order and peace to the nation. The years between 1865 and 1876 were not truly years of reconstruction, for reconstruction implied long-term plans. Of these there were none; there was only weariness and confusion, hatred and fear.

## STAGES OF RECONSTRUCTION

### 1

With the close of the war, northern attention turned to the defeated South. On the ruins of the Confederacy, some Northerners hoped to build a new America in which Negroes and whites, given opportunities for education and economic betterment, would work side by side to remove the scars of war. Few realized that the complexity of the issues and the intensity of hatreds ruled out simple solutions. One of these was Carl Schurz, a liberal statesman, whose report to Congress in 1866 strikingly revealed the difficulties awaiting those who attempted to reconstruct the South:[1]

I regret to say that views and intentions so reasonable I found confined to a small minority. Aside from the assumption that the negro will not work without physical compulsion, there appears to be another popular notion prevalent in the south, which stands as no less serious an obstacle in the way of a successful solution of the problem. It is that the negro exists for the special object of raising cotton, rice and sugar *for the whites,* and that it is illegitimate for him to indulge, like other people, in the pursuit of his own happiness in his own way. Although it is admitted that he

has ceased to be the property of a master, it is not admitted that he has a right to become his own master. . . . An ingrained feeling like this is apt to bring forth that sort of class legislation which produces laws to govern one class with no other view than to benefit another. This tendency can be distinctly traced in the various schemes for regulating labor which here and there see the light. . . .

In seeking remedies for such disorders we ought to keep in view, above all, the nature of the problem to be solved. As to what is commonly termed "reconstruction," it is not only the political machinery of the States and their constitutional relations to the general government, but the whole organism of southern society that must be reconstructed, or rather constructed anew, so as to bring it in harmony with the rest of American society. The difficulties of this task are not to be considered overcome when the people of the south take the oath of allegiance and elect governors and legislatures and members of Congress, and militia captains. . . .

The true nature of the difficulties of the situation is this: The general government of the republic has, by proclaiming the emancipation of the slaves, commenced a great social revolution in the south, but has, as yet, not completed it. Only the negative part of it is accomplished. The slaves are emancipated in point of form, but free

---

[1] Carl Schurz, "An Impartial View," *United States Senate Executive Documents,* 39 Cong., 1st Sess., pp. 20-40.

labor has not yet been put in the place of slavery in point of fact. . . .

In my despatches from the south I repeatedly expressed the opinion that the people were not yet in a frame of mind to legislate calmly and understandingly upon the subject of free negro labor. . . . When the rebellion was put down they found themselves not only conquered in a political and military sense, but economically ruined. The planters, who represented the wealth of the southern country, are partly laboring under the severest embarrassments, partly reduced to absolute poverty. Many who are stripped of all available means, and have nothing but their land, cross their arms in gloomy despondency, incapable of rising to a manly resolution. Others, who still possess means, are at a loss how to use them, as their old way of doing things is, by the abolition of slavery, rendered impracticable, at least where the military arm of the government has enforced emancipation. Others are still trying to go on in the old way, and that old way is in fact the only one they understand, and in which they have any confidence. Only a minority is trying to adopt the new order of things. A large number of the plantations, probably a considerable majority of the more valuable estates, is under heavy mortgages, and the owners know that, unless they retrieve their fortunes in a comparatively short space of time, their property will pass out of their hands. Almost all are, to some extent, embarrassed. The nervous anxiety which such a state of things produces extends also to those classes of society which, although not composed of planters, were always in close business connexion with the planting interest, and there was hardly a branch of commerce or industry in the south which was not directly or indirectly so connected. Besides, the southern soldiers, when returning from the war, did not, like the northern soldiers, find a prosperous community which merely waited for their arrival to give them remunerative employment. They found, many of them, their homesteads destroyed, their farms devastated, their families in distress; and those that were less unfortunate found, at all events, an impoverished and exhausted community which had but little to offer them. Thus a great many have been thrown upon the world to shift as best they can. They must do something honest or dishonest, and must do it soon, to make a living, and their prospects are, at present, not very bright. Thus that nervous anxiety to hastily repair broken fortunes, and to prevent still greater ruin and distress, embraces nearly all classes, and imprints upon all the movements of the social body a morbid character.

In which direction will these people be most apt to turn their eyes? Leaving the prejudice of race out of the question, from early youth they have been acquainted with but one system of labor, and with that one system they have been in the habit of identifying all their interests. They know of no way to help themselves but the one they are accustomed to. Another system of labor is presented to them, which, however, owing to circumstances which they do not appreciate, appears at first in an unpromising light. To try it they consider an experiment which they cannot afford to make while their wants are urgent. They have not reasoned calmly enough to convince themselves that the trial must be made. It is, indeed, not wonderful that, under such circumstances, they should study, not how to introduce and develop free labor, but how to avoid its introduction, and how to return as much and as quickly as possible to something like the old order of things. Nor is it wonderful that such studies should find an expression in their attempts at legislation. But the circumstance that this tendency is natural does not render it less dangerous and objectionable. The practical question presents itself: Is the immediate restoration of the late rebel States to absolute self-control so necessary that it must be done even at the risk of endangering one of the great results of the war, and of bringing on in those States insurrection or anarchy, or would it not be better to postpone that restoration until such dangers are past? If, as long as the change from slavery to free labor is known to the southern people only by its destructive results, these people must be expected to throw obstacles in its way, would it not seem necessary that the movement of social "reconstruction" be kept in the right channel by the hand of the power which originated the change, until that change can have disclosed some of its beneficial results? . . .

One reason why the southern people are slow in accommodating themselves to the new order of things is, that they confidently expect soon to be permitted to regulate matters according to their own notions. Every concession made to them by the government has been taken as an encouragement to persevere in this hope, and, unfortunately for them, this hope is nourished by influences from other parts of the country. Hence their anxiety to have their State governments restored *at once,* to have the troops withdrawn, and the Freedmen's Bureau abolished, although a good many discerning men know well that, in view of the lawless spirit still prevailing, it would be far better for them to have the general order of society firmly maintained by the federal power until things have arrived at a final settlement. . . . If, therefore, the national government firmly and unequivocally announces its policy not to give up the control of the free-labor reform until it is finally accomplished, the progress of that reform will undoubtedly be far more rapid and far less difficult than it will be if the attitude of the government is such as to permit contrary hopes to be indulged in.

## 2

Yet those who helped to solve the problems of war regarded the problems of peace as soluble, if not simple. Abraham Lincoln be-

lieved that the southern states should be returned to the Union as speedily as possible. With the Thirteenth Amendment assuring political rights for Negroes, whites and blacks in the South could then work together to rebuild the shattered economy of the section. This was his purpose when he issued a proclamation outlining the steps necessary before the rebellious states could resume their former place in the Union:[2]

I, Abraham Lincoln, President of the United States, do proclaim. . . . to all persons who have, directly or by implication, participated in the existing rebellion, except as hereinafter excepted, that a full pardon is hereby granted to them and each of them, with restoration of all rights of property, except as to slaves and in property cases where rights of third parties shall have intervened, and upon the condition that every such person shall take and subcribe an oath and thenceforward keep and maintain said oath inviolate, and which oath shall be registered for permanent preservation and shall be of the tenor and effect following, to wit:

I, ———— ————, do solemnly swear, in presence of Almighty God, that I will henceforth faithfully support, protect, and defend the Constitution of the United States and the Union of the States thereunder; and that I will in like manner abide by and faithfully support all acts of Congress passed during the existing rebellion with reference to slaves, so long and so far as not repealed, modified, or held void by Congress or by decision of the Supreme Court; and that I will in like manner abide by and faithfully support all proclamations of the President made during the existing rebellion having reference to slaves, so long and so far as not modified or declared void by decision of the Supreme Court. So help me God.

The persons excepted from the benefits of the foregoing provisions are all who are or shall have been civil or diplomatic of-

[2] J. D. Richardson (comp.), *Messages and Papers of the Presidents, 1789-1897* (Washington, 1897, 1909; taken from the 1909 vol.), VI, 213-215.

ficers or agents of the so-called Confederate Government; all who have left judicial stations under the United States to aid the rebellion; all who are or shall have been military or naval officers of said so-called Confederate Government above the rank of colonel in the army or of lieutenant in the navy; all who left seats in the United States Congress to aid the rebellion; all who resigned commissions in the Army or Navy of the United States and afterwards aided the rebellion; and all who have engaged in any way in treating colored persons, or white persons in charge of such, otherwise than lawfully as prisoners of war, and which persons may have been found in the United States service as soldiers, seamen, or in any other capacity.

And I do further proclaim, declare, and make known that whenever, in any of the States of Arkansas, Texas, Louisiana, Mississippi, Tennessee, Alabama, Georgia, Florida, South Carolina, and North Carolina, a number of persons, not less than one-tenth in number of the votes cast in such State at the Presidential election of the year A.D. 1860, each having taken oath aforesaid, and not having since violated it, and being a qualified voter by the election law of the State existing immediately before the so-called act of secession, and excluding all others, shall re-establish a State government which shall be republican and in nowise contravening said oath, such shall be recognized as the true government of the State, and the State shall receive thereunder the benefits of the constitutional provision which declares that "the United States shall guarantee to every State in this Union a republican form of government and shall protect each of them against invasion, and, on application of the legislature, or the executive (when the legislature can not be convened), against domestic violence."

And I do further proclaim, declare, and make known that any provision which may be adopted by such State government in relation to the freed people of such State which shall recognize and declare their permanent freedom, provide for their education, and which may yet be consistent as a temporary arrangement with their present condition as a laboring, landless, and homeless class, will not be objected to by the National Executive.

And it is suggested as not improper that in constructing a loyal State government in any State the name of the State, the boundary, the subdivisions, the constitution, and the general code of laws as before the rebellion be maintained, subject only to the modifications made necessary by the conditions hereinbefore stated, and such others, if any, not contravening said conditions and which may be deemed expedient by those framing the new State government.

To avoid misunderstanding, it may be proper to say that this proclamation, so far as it relates to State governments, has no reference to States wherein loyal State governments have all the while been maintained. And for the same reason it may be proper to further say that whether members sent to Congress from any State shall be admitted to seats constitutionally rests exclusively with the respective Houses, and not to any extent with the Executive. And, still further, that this proclamation is intended to present the people of the States wherein the national authority has been suspended and loyal State governments have been subverted a mode in and by which the national authority and loyal State governments may be re-established within said States or in any of them; and while the mode presented is the best the Executive can suggest, with his present impressions, it must not be understood that no other possible mode would be acceptable.

## 3

Although Lincoln's Reconstruction Plan was welcomed by most Northerners and led to the immediate return of three rebel states—Tennessee, Louisiana, and Arkansas—it failed to satisfy Republican leaders in Congress. Long resentful of Lincoln's wartime powers, they insisted that Congress should resume its "normal" direction of national affairs. Moreover, they regarded the lenient presidential plan as an encouragement to further treason because it promised clemency to traitors. Radical Republican policy, first proclaimed in the Wade-Davis Bill (July 2, 1864), not only proposed a harsher formula but directly challenged the President:[3]

*Be it enacted* . . . That in the states declared in rebellion against the United States, the President shall, by and with the advice and consent of the Senate, appoint for each a provisional governor. . . . who shall be charged with the civil administration of such state until a state government therein shall be recognized as hereinafter provided.

SECTION 2. That so soon as the military resistance to the United States shall have been suppressed in any such state, and the people thereof shall have sufficiently returned to their obedience to the constitution and the laws of the United States, the provisional governor shall direct the marshal of the United States, as speedily as may be, to name a sufficient number of deputies, and to enroll all white male citizens of the United States, resident in the state in their respective counties, and to request each one to take the oath to support the constitution of the United States, and in his enrolment to designate those who take and those who refuse to take that oath, which rolls shall be forthwith returned to the provisional governor; and if the persons taking that oath shall amount to a majority of the persons enrolled in the state, he shall, by proclamation, invite the loyal people of the state to elect delegates to a convention charged to declare the will of the people of the state relative to the reëstablishment of a state government subject to, and in conformity with, the constitution of the United States.

SEC. 3. That the convention shall consist of as many members as both houses of the last constitutional state legislature, apportioned by the provisional governor among the counties, parishes, or districts of the state, in proportion to the white population, returned as electors, by the marshal, in compliance with the provisions of this act. The provisional governor shall . . . provide an adequate force to keep the peace during the election.

SEC. 4. That the delegates shall be elected by the loyal white male citizens of the United States of the age of twenty-one years, and resident at the time in the county, parish, or district in which they shall offer to vote, and enrolled as aforesaid, or absent in the military service of the United States, and who shall take and subscribe the oath of allegiance to the United States in the form contained in the act of July 2, 1862; and all such citizens of the United States who are in the military service of the United States shall vote at the headquarters of their respective commands, under such regulations as may be prescribed by the provisional governor for the taking and return of their votes; but no person who has held or exercised any office, civil or military, state or confederate, under the rebel usurpation, or who has voluntarily borne arms against the United States, shall vote, or be eligible to be elected as delegate, at such election.

SEC. 5. That the said commissioners . . . shall proceed in the manner used in the state prior to the rebellion. The oath of allegiance shall be taken and subscribed on the poll-book by every voter in the form above prescribed, but every person known by, or proved to, the commissioners to have held or exercised any office, civil or military, state or confederate, under the rebel usurpation, or to have voluntarily borne arms against the United States, shall be excluded, though he offer to take the oath; and in case any person who shall have borne arms against the United States shall offer to vote he shall

[3] *Ibid.*, pp. 223-226.

be deemed to have borne arms voluntarily unless he shall prove the contrary by the testimony of a qualified voter. . . .

Sec. 6. That the provisional governor shall, by proclamation, convene the delegates elected as aforesaid, at the capital of the state, on a day not more than three months after the election, giving at least thirty days' notice of such day. In case the said capital shall in his judgment be unfit, he shall in his proclamation appoint another place. He shall preside over the deliberations of the convention, and administer to each delegate, before taking his seat in the convention, the oath of allegiance to the United States in the form above prescribed.

Sec. 7. That the convention shall declare, on behalf of the people of the state, their submission to the constitution and laws of the United States, and shall adopt the following provisions, hereby prescribed by the United States in the execution of the constitutional duty to guarantee a republican form of government to every state, and incorporate them in the constitution of the state, that is to say:

*First.* No person who has held or exercised any office, civil or military, except offices merely ministerial, and military offices below the grade of colonel, state or confederate, under the usurping power, shall vote for or be a member of the legislature, or governor.

*Second.* Involuntary servitude is forever prohibited, and the freedom of all persons is guaranteed in said state.

*Third.* No debt, state or confederate, created by or under the sanction of the usurping power, shall be recognized or paid by the state.

Sec. 8. That when the convention shall have adopted those provisions, it shall proceed to reëstablish a republican form of government, and ordain a constitution containing those provisions, which, when adopted, the convention shall by ordinance provide for submitting to the people of the state, entitled to vote under this law, at an election to be held in the manner prescribed by the act for the election of delegates; but at a time and place named by the convention, at which election the said electors, and none others, shall vote directly for or against such constitution and form of state government, and the returns of said election shall be made to the provisional governor, who shall canvass the same in the presence of the electors, and if a majority of the votes cast shall be for the constitution and form of government, he shall certify the same, with a copy thereof, to the President of the United States, who, after obtaining the assent of congress, shall, by proclamation, recognize the government so established, and none other, as the constitutional government of the state, and from the date of such recognition, and not before, Senators and Representatives, and electors for President and Vice-President may be elected in such state, according to the laws of the state and of the United States.

Sec. 9. That if the convention shall refuse to reëstablish the state government on the conditions aforesaid, the provisional governor shall declare it dissolved; but it shall be the duty of the President, whenever he shall have reason to believe that a sufficient number of the people of the state entitled to vote under this act, in number not less than a majority of those enrolled, as aforesaid, are willing to reestablish a state government on the conditions aforesaid, to direct the provisional governor to order another election of delegates to a convention for the purpose. . . .

Sec. 10. That, until the United States shall have recognized a republican form of state government, the provisional governor in each of said states shall see that this act, and the laws of the United States, and the laws of the state in force when the state government was overthrown by the rebellion, are faithfully executed within the state; but no law or usage whereby any person was heretofore held in involuntary servitude shall be recognized or enforced by any court or officer in such state, and the laws for the trial and punishment of white persons, and jurors shall have the qualifications of voters under this law for delegates to the convention. . . .

SEC. 12. That all persons held to involuntary servitude or labor in the states aforesaid are hereby emancipated and discharged therefrom, and they and their posterity shall be forever free. And if any such persons or their posterity shall be restrained of liberty, under pretence of any claim to such service or labor, the courts of the United States shall, on habeas corpus, discharge them.

SEC. 13. That if any person declared free by this act, or any law of the United States, or any proclamation of the President, be restrained of liberty, with intent to be held in or reduced to involuntary servitude or labor, the person convicted before a court of competent jurisdiction of such act shall be punished by fine of not less than fifteen hundred dollars, and be imprisoned not less than five nor more than twenty years.

SEC. 14. That every person who shall hereafter hold or exercise any office, civil or military, except offices merely ministerial, and military offices below the grade of colonel, in the rebel service, state or confederate, is hereby declared not to be a citizen of the United States.

## 4

Abraham Lincoln responded to the Wade-Davis Bill by a pocket veto. Yet he demonstrated his political acumen by agreeing to recognize any southern states that re-entered the Union under its provisions. This was far from acceptable to congressional Republicans, and they answered by a sharp manifesto which not only rebuked the President but widened the growing breach between the executive and legislative branches:[4]

We have read without surprise, but not without indignation, the Proclamation of the President of the 8th of July. . . .

The President, by preventing this bill from becoming a law, holds the electoral votes of the rebel States at the dictation of his personal ambition. If those votes turn the balance in his favor, is it to be supposed that his competitor, defeated by such means, will acquiesce?

If the rebel majority assert their supremacy in those States, and send votes which elect an enemy of the Government, will we not repel his claims?

And is not that civil war for the Presidency inaugurated by the votes of rebel States?

Seriously impressed with these dangers, Congress, *"the proper constituted authority,"* formally declared that there are no State governments in the rebel States, and provided for their erection at a proper time; and both the Senate and the House of Representatives rejected the Senators and Representatives chosen under the authority of what the President calls the free constitution and government of Arkansas.

The President's proclamation *"holds for naught"* this judgment, and discards the authority of the Supreme Court, and strides headlong toward the anarchy his proclamation of the 8th of December inaugurated.

If electors for President be allowed to be chosen in either of those States, a sinister light will be cast on the motives which induced the President to "hold for naught" the will of Congress rather than his government in Louisiana and Arkansas.

That judgment of Congress which the President defies was the exercise of an authority exclusively vested in Congress by the Constitution to determine what is the established government in a State, and in its own nature and by the highest judicial authority binding on all other departments of the government. . . .

A more studied outrage on the legislative authority of the people has never been perpetrated.

Congress passed a bill; the President re-

[4] New York *Tribune*, August 5, 1864, p. 5.

fused to approve it, and then by proclamation puts as much of it in force as he sees fit, and proposes to execute those parts by officers unknown to the laws of the United States and not subject to the confirmation of the Senate!

The bill directed the appointment of Provisional Governors by and with the advice and consent of the Senate.

The President, after defeating the law, proposes to appoint without law, and without the advice and consent of the Senate, *Military* Governors for the rebel States!

He has already exercised this dictatorial usurpation in Louisiana, and he defeated the bill to prevent its limitation. . . .

The President has greatly presumed on the forbearance which the supporters of his Administration have so long practiced, in view of the arduous conflict in which we are engaged, and the reckless ferocity of our political opponents.

But he must understand that our support is of a cause and not of a man; that the authority of Congress is paramount and must be respected; that the whole body of the Union men of Congress will not submit to be impeached by him of rash and unconstitutional legislation; and if he wishes our support, he must confine himself to his executive duties,—to obey and execute, not make the laws—to suppress by arms armed rebellion, and leave political reorganization to Congress.

If the supporters of the Government fail to insist on this, they become responsible for the usurpations which they fail to rebuke, and are justly liable to the indignation of the people whose rights and security, committed to their keeping, they sacrifice.

Let them consider the remedy for these usurpations, and, having found it, fearlessly execute it.

## 5

The objectives of Radical Republicans who sponsored the Wade-Davis manifesto were best expressed by Representative Thaddeus Stevens of Pennsylvania. Opposed to all caste and aristocracy and sincerely concerned with the welfare of the freedmen, Stevens believed Lincoln's mild reconstruction policy would never alter the bond-labor system of the South. He regarded military rule as necessary; the confiscation of plantation estates, the punishment of unreconstructed rebels, and the rehabilitation of unprotected freedmen required the supervision of federal troops. Stevens's vindictive hatred of southern aristocrats was revealed in an address delivered at Lancaster, Pennsylvania, on September 7, 1865:[5]

. . . We hold it to be the duty of the Government to inflict condign punishment on the rebel belligerents, and so weaken their hands that they can never again endanger the Union; and so reform their municipal institutions as to make them republican in spirit as well as in name.

We especially insist that the property of the chief rebels should be seized and appropriated to the payment of the National debt, caused by the unjust and wicked war which they instigated.

How can such punishments be inflicted and such forfeitures produced without doing violence to established principles?

Two positions have been suggested.

1st—To treat those States as never having been out of the Union, because the Constitution forbids secession, and, therefore, a fact forbidden by law could not exist.

2nd—To accept the position in which they placed themselves as severed from the union; an independent government *de facto,* and an alien enemy to be dealt with according to the laws of war.

It seems to me that while we do not aver that the United States are bound to treat them as an alien enemy, yet they have a right to elect so to do if it be for the in-

---

[5] Thaddeus Stevens, "Reconstruction." Printed by the Lancaster (Pa.), *Examiner and Herald,* 1865. In collection of speeches and documents bound by the New York Public Library, entitled *U. S. History, 1866-1908* (Ford Collection), pp. 2-6. (Pages not numbered consecutively.)

terest of the nation; and that the "Confederate States" are estopped from denying that position. . . . The Confederate States were for four years what they claimed to be, an alien enemy in all their rights and liabilities. To say that they were states under the protection of that constitution which they were assaulting with bloody defeats, simply because they became belligerents through crime, is making theory over-rule fact to an absurd degree. It will I suppose at least be conceded that the United States if not obliged so to do, have a right to treat them as an alien enemy now conquered, and subject to all the liabilities of a vanquished foe. . . .

All writers agree that the victor may inflict punishment upon the vanquished enemy even to the taking of his life, liberty, or the confiscation of all his property; but that this extreme right is never exercised, except upon a cruel, barbarous, obstinate, or dangerous foe who has waged an unjust war.

Upon the character of the belligerent, and the justice of the war, and the manner of conducting it, depends our right to take the lives, liberty, and property of the belligerent. This war had its origin in treason without one spark of justice. It was prosecuted before notice of it, by robbing our forts and armories, and our navy-yards; by stealing our money from the mints and depositories, and by surrendering our forts and navies by perjurers who had sworn to support the Constitution. In its progress our prisoners, by the authority of their government were slaughtered in cold blood. Ask Fort Pillow and Fort Wagner. Sixty thousand of our prisoners have been deliberately starved to death because they would not enlist in the rebel armies. The graves at Andersonville have each an accusing tongue. The purpose and avowed object of the enemy "to found an empire whose corner-stone should be slavery," render its perpetuity or revival dangerous to human liberty.

Surely, these things are sufficient to jus-tify the exercise of the extreme rights of war—"to execute, to imprison, to confiscate." How many captive enemies it would be proper to execute, as an example to nations, I leave others to judge. I am not fond of sanguinary punishments, but surely some victims must propitiate the *manes* of our starved, murdered, slaughtered martyrs. A court martial could do justice according to law.

But we propose to confiscate all the estate of every rebel belligerent whose estate was worth $10,000, or whose land exceeded two hundred acres in quantity. Policy if not justice would require that the poor, the ignorant, and the coerced should be forgiven. They followed the example and teachings of their wealthy and intelligent neighbors. The rebellion would never have originated with them. Fortunately those who would thus escape form a large majority of the people though possessing but a small portion of the wealth. The proportion of those exempt compared with the punished would be I believe about nine tenths.

There are about six millions of freemen in the South. The number of acres of land is 465,000,000. Of this those who own above two hundred acres each, number about 70,000 persons, holding in the aggregate (together with the States) about 394,-000,000 acres, leaving for all the others below 200 each about 71,000,000 of acres. By thus forfeiting the estates of the leading rebels, the Government would have 394,-000,000 of acres beside their town property, and yet nine tenths of the people would remain untouched. Divide this land into convenient farms. Give if you please forty acres to each adult male freedman. Suppose there are one million of them. That would require 40,000,000 of acres, which deducted from 394,000,000 leaves three hundred and fifty-four millions of acres for sale. Divide it into suitable farms and sell it to the highest bidders. I think it, including town property, would average at least ten dollars per acre. That would produce $3,540,000,000,—Three billions, five hundred and forty millions of dollars.

Let that be applied as follows to wit:

1. Invest $300,000,000 in six per cent. government bonds, and add the interest semi-annually to the pensions of those who have become entitled by this villanous war.

2. Appropriate $200,000,000 to pay the damages done to loyal men North and South by the rebellion.

3. Pay the residue being $3,040,000,000 towards the payment of the National debt.

What loyal man can object to this? Look around you, and everywhere behold your neighbors, some with an arm, some with a leg, some with an eye carried away by rebel bullets. Others horribly mutilated in every form. And yet numerous others wearing the weeds which mark the death of those on whom they leaned for support. Contemplate these monuments of rebel perfidy, and of patriotic suffering, and then say if too much is asked for our valiant soldiers. . . .

The whole fabric of southern society *must* be changed and never can it be done if this opportunity is lost. Without this, this Government can never be, as it never has been, a true republic. Heretofore, it had more the features of aristocracy than of democracy.—The Southern States have been despotisms, not governments of the people. It is impossible that any practical equality of rights can exist where a few thousand men monopolize the whole landed property. The larger the number of small proprietors the more safe and stable the government. As the landed interest must govern, the more it is subdivided and held by independent owners, the better. What would be the condition of the State of New York if it were not for her independent yeomanry? She would be overwhelmed and demoralized by the Jews, Milesians and vagabonds of licentious cities. How can republican institutions, free schools, free churches, free social intercourse exist in a mingled community

of nabobs and serfs; of the owners of twenty thousand acre manors with lordly palaces, and the occupants of narrow huts inhabited by "low white trash?"—If the south is ever to be made a safe republic let her lands be cultivated by the toil of the owners or the free labor of intelligent citizens. This must be done even though it drive her nobility into exile. If they go, all the better.

It will be hard to persuade the owner of ten thousand acres of land, who drives a coach and four, that he is not degraded by sitting at the same table, or in the same pew, with the embrowned and hard-handed farmer who has himself cultivated his own thriving homestead of 150 acres. This subdivision of the lands will yield ten bales of cotton to one that is made now, and he who produced it will own it and *feel himself a man*.

It is far easier and more beneficial to exile 70,000 proud, bloated, and defiant rebels, than to expatriate four millions of laborers, native to the soil and loyal to the Government. . . .

Let us forget all parties, and build on the broad platform of "reconstructing the Government out of the conquered territory, converted into new and free States, and admitted into the Union by the sovereign power of Congress, with another plank,"—THE PROPERTY OF THE REBELS SHALL PAY OUR NATIONAL DEBT, *and indemnify freed-men and loyal sufferers.*—and that under no circumstances will we suffer the National debt to be repudiated, or the interest scaled below the contract rates; nor permit any part of the rebel debt to be assumed by the nation.

Let all who approve of these principles tarry with us. Let all others go with Copperheads and rebels. Those will be the opposing parties. Young men, this duty devolves on you. Would to God, if only for that, I were still in the prime of life, that I might aid you to fight through this last and greatest battle of Freedom.

## 6

Had Abraham Lincoln lived, his great popularity and his remarkable political insight might have altered the plans of congressional Republicans. But Lincoln's assassination was a national tragedy. Andrew Johnson, the Tennessee Democrat who ascended to the presidency, had no love for the southern planter class, but he lacked Lincoln's faith in the future of the former slaves. He appealed neither to Republicans who advocated immediate social equality for Negroes nor to Democrats who urged mildness in the treatment of southern whites. Moreover, he lacked both the humility and the political skill that made Lincoln a master of men. Yet his first Reconstruction Plan, issued as a proclamation on May 29, 1865, outlined a program remarkably like that sponsored by President Lincoln save in the following two important particulars:[6]

*Thirteenth.* All persons who have voluntarily participated in said rebellion and the estimated value of whose taxable property is over $20,000.

*Fourteenth.* All persons who have taken the oath of amnesty as prescribed in the President's proclamation of December 8, A.D. 1863, or an oath of allegiance to the Government of the United States since the date of said proclamation and who have not thenceforward kept and maintained the same inviolate.

## 7

Taking advantage of the fact that Congress was not in session during the summer, President Johnson applied his Reconstruction Plan so successfully that by December 4, 1865, all the ex-slave states save Texas, Kentucky, and Delaware were ready to take their accustomed places in the Union. When congressmen reassembled on that day, the Radical Republicans started at once to undo all the President had accomplished, if for no other reason than to dispute the right of the executive to govern. Refusing to seat the representatives of the southern states, they began work on a re-

construction plan of their own. Their first step was an act of February, 1866, which extended the life of the wartime Freedmen's Bureau, at the same time authorizing the agency to use troops in protecting Negro rights. Johnson's straightforward veto of the measure revealed the gulf between Congress and the President:[7]

I have examined with care the bill, which originated in the Senate and has been passed by the two Houses of Congress, to amend an act entitled "An act to establish a bureau for the relief of freedmen and refugees," and for other purposes. Having with much regret come to the conclusion that it would not be consistent with the public welfare to give my approval to the measure, I return the bill to the Senate with my objections. . . .

I share with Congress the strongest desire to secure to the freedmen the full enjoyment of their freedom and property and their entire independence and equality in making contracts for their labor, but the bill before me contains provisions which in my opinion are not warranted by the Constitution and are not well suited to accomplish the end in view.

The bill proposes to establish by authority of Congress military jurisdiction over all parts of the United States containing refugees and freedmen. It would by its very nature apply with most force to those parts of the United States in which the freedmen most abound, and it expressly extends the existing temporary jurisdiction of the Freedmen's Bureau, with greatly enlarged powers, over those States "in which the ordinary course of judicial proceedings has been interrupted by the rebellion." The source from which this military jurisdiction is to emanate is none other than the President . . . acting through the War Department and the Commissioner of the Freedmen's Bureau. The agents to carry out this military jurisdiction are to be selected either from the

---

[6] J. D. Richardson (comp.), *Messages and Papers of the Presidents, 1789-1897* (Washington, 1897, 1909; taken from the 1909 vol.), VI, 312.

[7] *Ibid.*, pp. 398-405.

Army or from civil life; the country is to be divided into districts and sub-districts, and the number of salaried agents to be employed may be equal to the number of counties or parishes in all the United States where freedmen and refugees are to be found.

The subjects over which this military jurisdiction is to extend in every part of the United States include protection to "all employees, agents, and officers of this bureau in the exercise of the duties imposed" upon them by the bill. In eleven States it is further to extend over all cases affecting freedmen and refugees discriminated against "by local law, custom, or prejudice." In those eleven States the bill subjects any white person who may be charged with depriving a freedman of "any civil rights or immunities belonging to white persons" to imprisonment or fine, or both, without, however, defining the "civil rights and immunities" which are thus to be secured to the freedmen by military law. This military jurisdiction also extends to all questions that may arise respecting contracts. The agent who is thus to exercise the office of a military judge may be a stranger, entirely ignorant of the laws of the place, and exposed to the errors of judgment to which all men are liable. The exercise of power over which there is no legal supervision by so vast a number of agents as is contemplated by the bill must, by the very nature of man, be attended by acts of caprice, injustice, and passion.

The trials having their origin under this bill are to take place without the intervention of a jury and without any fixed rules of law or evidence. The rules on which offenses are to be "heard and determined" by the numerous agents are such rules and regulations as the President, through the War Department, shall prescribe. No previous presentment is required nor any indictment charging the commission of a crime against the laws; but the trial must proceed on charges and specifications. The

punishment will be, not what the law declares, but such as a court-martial may think proper; and from these arbitrary tribunals there lies no appeal, no writ of error to any of the courts in which the Constitution . . . vests exclusively the judicial power of the country.

While the territory and the classes of actions and offenses that are made subject to this measure are so extensive, the bill itself, should it become a law, will have no limitation in point of time, but will form a part of the permanent legislation of the country. I can not reconcile a system of military jurisdiction of this kind with the words of the Constitution which declare that "no person shall be held to answer for a capital or otherwise infamous crime unless on a presentment or indictment of a grand jury, except in cases arising in the land or naval forces, or in the militia when in actual service in time of war or public danger," and that "in all criminal prosecutions the accused shall enjoy the right to a speedy and public trial by an impartial jury of the State and district wherein the crime shall have been committed." The safeguards which the experience and wisdom of ages taught our fathers to establish as securities for the protection of the innocent, the punishment of the guilty, and the equal administration of justice are to be set aside, and for the sake of a more vigorous interposition in behalf of justice we are to take the risks of the many acts of injustice that would necessarily follow from an almost countless number of agents established in every parish or county in nearly a third of the States of the Union, over whose decisions there is to be no supervision or control by the Federal courts. The power that would be thus placed in the hands of the President is such as in time of peace certainly ought never to be intrusted to any one man.

If it be asked whether the creation of such a tribunal within a State is warranted as a measure of war, the question immediately presents itself whether we are still engaged in war. Let us not unnecessarily disturb the commerce and credit and industry of the country by declaring to the American people and to the world that the United States are still in a condition of civil war. At present there is no part of , our country in which the authority of the United States is disputed. Offenses that may be committed by individuals should not work a forfeiture of the rights of whole communities. The country has returned, or is returning, to a state of peace and industry, and the rebellion is in fact at an end. The measure, therefore, seems to be as inconsistent with the actual condition of the country as it is at variance with the Constitution of the United States. . . .

I can not but add another very grave objection to this bill. The Constitution imperatively declares, in connection with taxation, that each State *shall* have at least one Representative, and fixes the rule for the number to which, in future times, each State shall be entitled. It also provides that the Senate . . . *shall* be composed of two Senators from each State, and adds with peculiar force "that no State, without its consent, shall be deprived of its equal suffrage in the Senate." The original act was necessarily passed in the absence of the States chiefly to be affected, because their people were then contumaciously engaged in the rebellion. Now the case is changed, and some, at least, of those States are attending Congress by loyal representatives, soliciting the allowance of the constitutional right for representation. At the time, however, of the consideration and the passing of this bill there was no Senator or Representative in Congress from the eleven States which are to be mainly affected by its provisions. The very fact that reports were and are made against the good disposition of the people of that portion of the country is an additional reason why they need and should have representatives of their own in Congress to explain their condition, reply to accusations, and assist by their local knowledge in the perfecting

of measures immediately affecting themselves. While the liberty of deliberation would then be free and Congress would have full power to decide according to its judgment, there could be no objection urged that the States most interested had not been permitted to be heard. The principle is firmly fixed in the minds of the American people that there should be no taxation without representation. Great burdens have now to be borne by all the country, and we may best demand that they shall be borne without murmur when they are voted by a majority of the representatives of all the people. I would not interfere with the unquestionable right of Congress to judge, each House for itself, "of the elections, returns, and qualifications of its own members"; but that authority can not be construed as including the right to shut out in time of peace any State from the representation to which it is entitled by the Constitution. . . .

In accordance with the Constitution, I return the bill to the Senate, in the earnest hope that a measure involving questions and interests so important to the country will not become a law, unless upon deliberate consideration by the people it shall receive the sanction of an enlightened public judgment.

## THE FOURTEENTH AMENDMENT

### 8

When a jubilant Congress overrode Johnson's veto of the Freedmen's Bureau Bill, the stage was set for the triumph of the congressional reconstruction plan. Step by step, during the next months, the Radical Republicans adopted a series of laws designed to punish Confederates, secure equal rights for Negroes, and perpetuate the national supremacy of the Republican party. Of these none was more significant than the Civil Rights Act of April 9, 1866, which guaranteed former slaves the equal protection of the laws:[8]

*Be it enacted,* That all persons born in the United States and not subject to any

---

[8] *United States Statutes at Large,* XIV, 27-29.

foreign power, excluding Indians not taxed, are hereby declared to be citizens of the United States; and such citizens, of every race and color, without regard to any previous condition of slavery or involuntary servitude, except as a punishment for crime whereof the party shall have been duly convicted, shall have the same right, in every State and Territory in the United States, to make and enforce contracts, to sue, be parties, and give evidence, to inherit, purchase, lease, sell, hold, and convey real and personal property, and to full and equal benefit of all laws and proceedings for the security of person and property, as is enjoyed by white citizens, and shall be subject to like punishment, pains, and penalties, and to none other, any law, statute, ordinance, regulation, or custom, to the contrary notwithstanding.

SECTION 2. *And be it further enacted,* That any person who, under color of any law, statute, ordinance, regulation, or custom, shall subject, or cause to be subjected, any inhabitant of any State or Territory to the deprivation of any right secured or protected by this act, or to different punishment, pains, or penalties on account of such person having at any time been held in a condition of slavery or involuntary servitude, except as a punishment for crime whereof the party shall have been duly convicted, or by reason of his color or race, than is prescribed for the punishment of white persons, shall be deemed guilty of a misdemeanor, and, on conviction, shall be punished by fine not exceeding one thousand dollars, or imprisonment not exceeding one year, or both, in the discretion of the court.

SEC. 3. *And be it further enacted,* That the district courts . . . shall have, exclusively of the courts of the several States, cognizance of all crimes and offences committed against the provisions of this act, and also, concurrently with the circuit courts of the United States, of all causes, civil and criminal, affecting persons who

are denied or cannot enforce in the courts or judicial tribunals of the State or locality where they may be any of the rights secured to them by the first section of this act. . . .

SEC. 4. *And be it further enacted,* That the district attorneys, marshals, and deputy marshals of the United States, the commissioners appointed by the circuit and territorial courts of the United States, with powers of arresting, imprisoning, or bailing offenders against the laws of the United States, the officers and agents of the Freedmen's Bureau, and every other officer who may be specially empowered by the President of the United States, shall be, and they are hereby, specially authorized and required, at the expense of the United States, to institute proceedings against all and every person who shall violate the provisions of this act, and cause him or them to be arrested and imprisoned, or bailed, as the case may be, for trial before such court of the United States or territorial court as by this act has cognizance. . . .

SEC. 8. *And be it further enacted,* That whenever the President of the United States shall have reason to believe that offences have been or are likely to be committed against the provisions of this act within any judicial district, it shall be lawful for him, in his discretion, to direct the judge, marshal, and district attorney of such district to attend at such place within the district, and for such time as he may designate, for the purpose of the more speedy arrest and trial of persons charged with a violation of this act; and it shall be the duty of every judge or other officer, when any such requisition shall be received by him, to attend at the place and for the time therein designated.

SEC. 9. *And be it further enacted,* That it shall be lawful for the President of the United States, or such person as he may empower for that purpose, to employ such part of the land or naval forces of the

United States, or of the militia, as shall be necessary to prevent the violation and enforce the due execution of this act.

SEC. 10. *And be it further enacted,* That upon all questions of law arising in any cause under the provisions of this act a final appeal may be taken to the Supreme Court of the United States.

## 9

No sooner was the Civil Rights Act adopted than Republican leaders, fearful that this was not enough, began casting about for additional means to assure permanent protection for Negroes. A constitutional amendment was the obvious device. The Fourteenth Amendment, adopted at the time and ratified in July, 1868, not only defined citizenship but granted federal protection against an invasion of individual rights by the states—a historic reversal in federal relations:[9]

SECTION I. All persons born or naturalized in the United States, and subject to the jurisdiction thereof, are citizens of the United States and of the State wherein they reside. No State shall make or enforce any law which shall abridge the privileges or immunities of citizens of the United States; nor shall any State deprive any person of life, liberty, or property, without due process of law; nor deny to any person within its jurisdiction the equal protection of the laws.

SEC. 2. Representatives shall be apportioned among the several States according to their respective numbers, counting the whole number of persons in each State, excluding Indians not taxed. But when the right to vote at any election for the choice of electors for President and Vice-President of the United States, Representatives in Congress, the Executive and Judicial officers of a State, or the members of the Legislature thereof, is denied to any of the male inhabitants of such State, being twenty-one years of age, and citizens of the United States, or in any way abridged,

except for participation in rebellion, or other crime, the basis of representation therein shall be reduced in the proportion which the number of such male citizens shall bear to the whole number of male citizens twenty-one years of age in such State.

SEC. 3. No person shall be a Senator or Representative in Congress, or elector of President and Vice-President, or hold any office, civil or military, under the United States, or under any State, who, having previously taken an oath, as a member of Congress, or as an officer of the United States, or as a member of any State legislature, or as an executive or judicial officer of any State, to support the Constitution of the United States, shall have engaged in insurrection or rebellion against the same, or given aid or comfort to the enemies thereof. But Congress may by a vote of two-thirds of each House, remove such disability.

SEC. 4. The validity of the public debt of the United States, authorized by law, including debts incurred for payment of pensions and bounties for services in suppressing insurrection or rebellion, shall not be questioned. But neither the United States nor any State shall assume or pay any debt or obligation incurred in aid of insurrection or rebellion against the United States, or any claim for the loss or emancipation of any slave; but all such debts, obligations and claims shall be held illegal and void.

SEC. 5. The Congress shall have power to enforce, by appropriate legislation, the provisions of this article.

## 10

The motives governing the framers of the Fourteenth Amendment were admirably summarized by Representative Thaddeus Stevens, one of the chief architects of the measure, in a speech to Congress on May 8, 1866:[10]

---

[9] *Ibid.,* XV, 708-709.

[10] Thaddeus Stevens, "The Fourteenth Amendment," *Congressional Globe,* 39th Cong., 1st Sess., XXXVI, Pt. 3, pp. 2459-2460.

This proposition is not all that the committee desired. It falls far short of my wishes, but it fulfills my hopes. I believe it is all that can be obtained in the present state of public opinion. Not only Congress but the several States are to be consulted. Upon a careful survey of the whole ground, we did not believe that nineteen of the loyal States could be induced to ratify any proposition more stringent than this. I say nineteen, for I utterly repudiate and scorn the idea that any State not acting in the Union is to be counted on the question of ratification. It is absurd to suppose that any more than three fourths of the States that propose the amendment are required to make it valid; that States not here are to be counted as present. Believing then, that this is the best proposition that can be made effectual, I accept it. . . .

The first section prohibits the States from abridging the privileges and immunities of citizens of the United States, or unlawfully depriving them of life, liberty, or property, or of denying to any person within their jurisdiction the "equal" protection of the laws.

I can hardly believe that any person can be found who will not admit that every one of these provisions is just. They are all asserted, in some form or other, in our DECLARATION or organic law. But the Constitution limits only the action of Congress, and is not a limitation on the States. This amendment supplies that defect, and allows Congress to correct the unjust legislation of the States, so far that the law which operates upon one man shall operate *equally* upon all. Whatever law punishes a white man for a crime shall punish the black man precisely in the same way and to the same degree. Whatever law protects the white man shall afford "equal" protection to the black man. Whatever means of redress is afforded to one shall be afforded to all. Whatever law allows the white man to testify in court shall allow the man of color to do the same. These are great advantages over their present codes. Now different degrees of punishment are inflicted, not on account of the magnitude of the crime, but according to the color of the skin. Now color disqualifies a man from testifying in courts, or being tried in the same way as white men. I need not enumerate these partial and oppressive laws. Unless the Constitution should restrain them, those States will all, I fear, keep up this discrimination, and crush to death the hated freedmen. Some answer, "Your civil rights bill secures the same things." That is partly true, but a law is repealable by a majority. And I need hardly say that the first time that the South with their copperhead allies obtain the command of Congress it will be repealed. The veto of the President and their votes on the bill are conclusive evidence of that. And yet I am amazed and alarmed at the impatience of certain well-meaning Republicans at the exclusion of the rebel States until the Constitution shall be so amended as to restrain their despotic desires. This amendment once adopted cannot be annulled without two thirds of Congress. That they will hardly get. And yet certain of our distinguished friends propose to admit State after State before this becomes a part of the Constitution. What madness! Is their judgment misled by their kindness; or are they unconsciously drifting into the haven of power at the other end of the avenue? I do not suspect it, but others will.

The second section I consider the most important in the article. It fixes the basis of representation in Congress. If any State shall exclude any of her adult male citizens from the elective franchise, or abridge that right, she shall forfeit her right to representation in the same proportion. The effect of this provision will be either to compel the States to grant universal suffrage or so to shear them of their power as to keep them forever in a hopeless minority in the national Government, both legislative and executive. If they do not enfranchise the freedmen, it would give to the rebel States but thirty-seven Representatives. Thus shorn of their power, they would soon become restive. Southern pride would not long brook a hopeless minority. True, it will take two, three, possibly five years before they conquer their prejudices sufficiently to allow their late slaves to become their equals at the polls. That short delay would not be injurious. In the mean time the freedmen would become more enlightened, and more fit to discharge the high duties of their new condition. In that time, too, the loyal Congress could mature their laws and so amend the Constitution as to secure the rights of every human being, and render disunion impossible. Heaven forbid that the southern States, or *any one of them,* should be represented on this floor until such muniments of freedom are built high and firm. Against our will they have been absent for four bloody years; against our will they must not come back until we are ready to receive them. Do not tell me that there are loyal representatives waiting for admission —until their States are loyal they can have no standing here. They would merely *mis*represent their constituents.

I admit that this article is not as good as the one we sent to death in the Senate. In my judgment, we shall not approach the measure of justice until we have given every adult freedman a homestead on the land where he was born and toiled and suffered. Forty acres of land and a hut would be more valuable to him than the immediate right to vote. Unless we give them this we shall receive the censure of mankind and the curse of Heaven. That article referred to provided that if *one* of the injured race was excluded the State should forfeit the right to have any of them represented. That would have hastened their full enfranchisement. This section allows the States to discriminate among the same class, and receive proportionate credit in representation. This I dislike. But it is a short step forward. The large stride which we in vain proposed is

dead; the murderers must answer to the suffering race. I would not have been the perpetrator. A load of misery must sit heavy on their souls.

The third section may encounter more difference of opinion here. Among the people I believe it will be the most popular of all the provisions; it prohibits rebels from voting for members of Congress and electors of President until 1870. My only objection to it is that it is too lenient. I know that there is a morbid sensibility, sometimes called mercy, which affects a few of all classes, from the priest to the clown, which has more sympathy for the murderer on the gallows than for his victim. I hope I have a heart as capable of feeling for human woe as others. I have long since wished that capital punishment were abolished. But I never dreamed that all punishment could be dispensed with in human society. Anarchy, *treason,* and violence would reign triumphant. Here is the mildest of all punishments ever inflicted on traitors. I might not consent to the extreme severity denounced upon them by a provisional governor of Tennessee—I mean the late lamented Andrew Johnson of blessed memory—but I would have increased the severity of this section. I would be glad to see it extended to 1876, and to include all State and municipal as well as national elections. In my judgment we do not sufficiently protect the loyal men of the rebel States from the vindictive persecutions of their victorious rebel neighbors. Still I will move no amendment, nor vote for any, lest the whole fabric should tumble to pieces.

I need say nothing of the fourth section, for none dare object to it who is not himself a rebel. To the friend of justice, the friend of the Union, of the perpetuity of liberty, and the final triumph of the rights of man and their extension to every human being, let me say, sacrifice as we have done your peculiar views, and instead of vainly insisting upon the instantaneous operation of all that is right accept what is possible, and "all these things shall be added unto you."

## 11

Having disposed of the troublesome question of Negro rights, Congress turned to the admission of former Confederate states to the Union. One thing was clear: the rebellious commonwealths must be treated more harshly than under the President's Reconstruction Plan. Moreover, congressmen agreed that any alternative plan must be presented to the people before the elections of 1866, for they were confident that northern voters would rebuff Andrew Johnson decisively if the issue were clearly drawn. The Radical Republicans, therefore, created a Joint Committee on Reconstruction which on June 20, 1866, laid its recommendations before the nation:[11]

It is the opinion of your committee—

I. That the States lately in rebellion were, at the close of the war, disorganized communities, without civil government, and without constitutions or other forms, by virtue of which political relation could legally exist between them and the federal government.

II. That Congress cannot be expected to recognize as valid the election of representatives from disorganized communities, which, from the very nature of the case, were unable to present their claim to representation under those established and recognized rules, the observance of which has been hitherto required.

III. That Congress would not be justified in admitting such communities to a participation in the government of the country without first providing such constitutional or other guarantees as will tend to secure the civil rights of all citizens of the republic; a just equality of representation; protection against claims founded in rebellion and crime; a temporary restoration of the right of suffrage to those who have not actively participated in the efforts

to destroy the Union and overthrow the government, and the exclusion from position of public trust of, at least, a portion of those whose crimes have proved them to be enemies of the Union, and unworthy of public confidence. . . .

We now propose to re-state, as briefly as possible, the general facts and principles applicable to all the States recently in rebellion: . . .

*Third.* Having voluntarily deprived themselves of representation in Congress for the criminal purpose of destroying the Union, and having reduced themselves, by the act of levying war, to the condition of public enemies, they have no right to complain of temporary exclusion from Congress; but . . . the burden now rests upon them, before claiming to be reinstated in their former condition, to show that they are qualified to resume federal relations. . . .

*Fourth.* Having . . . forfeited all civil and political rights and privileges under the federal Constitution, they can only be restored thereto by the permission and authority of that constitutional power against which they rebelled and by which they were subdued.

*Fifth.* These rebellious enemies were conquered by the people of the United States acting through all the co-ordinate branches of the government, and not by the executive department alone. The powers of conqueror are not so vested in the President that he can fix and regulate the terms of settlement and confer congressional representation on conquered rebels. . . . The authority to restore rebels to political power in the federal Government can be exercised only with the concurrence of all the departments in which political power is vested. . . .

*Eighth.* As has been shown in this report, and in the evidence submitted, no proof has been afforded to Congress of a constituency in any one of the so-called Confederate States, unless we except the State of Tennessee, qualified to elect sena-

---

[11] *United States Reports of the Committees of the House of Representatives,* 39th Cong., 1st Sess., Report No. 30, Pt. I, II, pp. xvii-xxi.

tors and representatives in Congress. No
State Constitution, or amendment to a
State Constitution, has had the sanction of
the people. All the so-called legislation of
State conventions and legislatures has been
had under military dictation. If the President may, at his will and under his own
authority, whether as military commander
or chief executive, qualify persons to appoint senators and elect representatives,
and empower others to appoint and elect
them, he thereby practically controls the
organization of the legislative department.
The constitutional form of government
is thereby practically destroyed, and its
power absorbed in the Executive. . . .

*Ninth.* The necessity of providing adequate safeguards for the future, before
restoring the insurrectionary States to a
participation in the direction of public affairs, is apparent from the bitter hostility
to the government and people of the
United States yet existing throughout the
conquered territory. . . .

*Tenth.* The conclusion of your committee therefore is, that the so-called Confederate States are not, at present, entitled to
representation in the Congress of the
United States: that, before allowing such
representation, adequate security for future peace and safety should be required;
that this can only be found in such changes
of the original law as shall determine the
civil rights and privileges of all citizens
in all parts of the republic, shall place
representation on an equitable basis, shall
fix a stigma upon treason, and shall protect the loyal people against future claims
for the expenses incurred in support of
rebellion and for manumitted slaves, together with an express grant of power in
Congress to enforce these provisions. To
this end they offer a joint resolution for
amending the Constitution of the United
States, and two several bills designed to
carry the same into effect, being referred
to.

Before closing this report your committee begs leave to state that the specific

recommendations submitted by them are
the result of mutual concession, after a
long and careful comparison of conflicting opinions. Upon a question of such
magnitude, infinitely important as it is to
the future of the republic, it was not expected that all should think alike. Sensible
of the imperfections of the scheme, your
committee submits it to Congress, as the
best they could agree upon in the hope
that its imperfections may be cured, and
its deficiencies supplied by legislative wisdom; and that, when finally adopted, it
may tend to restore peace and harmony to
the whole country, and to place our republican institutions on a more stable
foundation.

## THE CRITICAL YEAR

### 12

Had the militant leaders of conservative
southern opinion shown some moderation,
they might have swung the North to Johnson's
milder reconstruction policy. Instead, events
played directly into the hands of the Radical
Republicans. Each state seeking readmittance
under the Presidential Reconstruction Plan
insisted on two steps that caused great indignation in the North. One was the return of
prominent Confederates to important governmental office; the other was the adoption of
a "Black Code" that virtually returned
Negroes to slavery. Of the latter, the code
adopted by Alabama on December 15, 1865,
was typical:[12]

. . . SECTION 1. . . . That the commissioners' court of any county in this State
may purchase, rent, or provide such lands,
buildings and other property as may be
necessary for a poor-house, or house of
correction for any such county, and may
appoint suitable officers for the management thereof, and make all necessary by-
laws, rules and regulations for the government of the inmates thereof, and cause
the same to be enforced; but in no case

---

[12] *Acts of the Session of 1865-1866 of the General
Assembly of Alabama* (Montgomery, 1866), pp.
119-121.

shall the punishment inflicted exceed hard labor, either in or out of said house; the use of chain-gangs, putting in stocks, if necessary, to prevent escapes; such reasonable correction as a parent may inflict upon a stubborn, refractory child; and solitary confinement for not longer than one week, on bread and water; and may cause to be hired out such as are vagrants, to work in chain-gangs or otherwise, for the length of time for which they are sentenced; and the proceeds of such hiring must be paid into the county treasury, for the benefits of the helpless in said poorhouse, or house of correction.

SEC. 2. . . . That the following persons are vagrants in addition to those already declared to be vagrants by law, or that may hereafter be so declared by law; a stubborn or refractory servant; a laborer or servant who loiters away his time, or refuses to comply with any contract for a term of service, without just cause; and such person may be sent to the house of correction in the county in which such offense is committed; and for want of such house of correction, the common jail of the county may be used for that purpose.

SEC. 3. . . . That when a vagrant is found, any justice of the peace of the county must, upon complaint made upon oath, or on his own knowledge, issue his warrant to the sheriff or any constable of the county, to bring such person before him; and if, upon examination and hearing of testimony, it appears to the justice, that such person is a vagrant, he shall assess a fine of fifty dollars and costs against such vagrant; and in default of payment, he must commit such vagrant to the house of correction; or if no such house, to the common jail of the county, for a term not exceeding six months, and until such fine, costs and charges are paid, or such party is otherwise discharged by law; *Provided,* That when committed to jail under this section, the commissioners' court may cause him to be hired out in like manner as in section one of this act.

SEC. 4. . . . That when any person shall be convicted of vagrancy, as provided for in this act, the justice of the peace, before whom such conviction is had, may, at his discretion, either commit such person to jail, to the house of correction, or hire such person to any person who will hire the same, for a period not longer than six months, for cash, giving three days' notice of the time and place of hiring; and the proceeds of such hiring, after paying all costs and charges, shall be paid into the county treasury for the benefit of the helpless in the poor-house.

SEC. 5. . . . That all fines received by any justice of the peace under the provisions of this act, shall be paid into the county treasury for the purposes as set forth in section one of this act.

SEC. 6. . . . That it shall be the duty of the justice of the peace to settle with the county treasurer at least once a month, for all fines received by him under this act, and for a wilful default so to do, he shall be guilty of a misdemeanor; and upon conviction in any court having jurisdiction, shall be fined in double the amount so received or collected by him, and all costs of suit.

SEC. 7. . . . That the court of county commissioners of each county shall have full and complete control of the public works and public highways therein, and shall make all contracts in relation thereto; and shall have power to appoint a superintendent of said public works and highways, under such rules and regulations as said court shall determine; and any justice of the peace trying any cause under this act, on conviction, shall have power to sentence such vagrant to work on said public works and highways, under the supervision of such superintendent, for not more than forty days.

## 13

This southern attitude strengthened the case of congressional policy makers. News of the "Black Codes," combined with an inept campaign by President Johnson on behalf of his moderate candidates, race riots in New Orleans, and an adroit appeal to northern patriotism permitted a Radical Republican sweep at the polls in the fall elections of 1866. Convinced that the returns were a mandate for its policy, the group began work on a reconstruction program deliberately designed to humble prideful Southerners and to perpetuate the rule of the Republican party. The First Reconstruction Act (March 2, 1867) outlined the methods it proposed to follow:[13]

Whereas, No legal State governments or adequate protection for life or property now exists in the rebel States of Virginia, North Carolina, South Carolina, Georgia, Mississippi, Alabama, Louisiana, Florida, Texas, and Arkansas; and whereas it is necessary that peace and good order should be enforced in said States until loyal and republican State governments can be legally established: Therefore,

Be it enacted, That said rebel States shall be divided into military districts and made subject to the military authority of the United States as hereinafter prescribed, and for that purpose Virginia shall constitute the first district; North Carolina and South Carolina the second district; Georgia, Alabama, and Florida the third district; Mississippi and Arkansas the fourth district; and Louisiana and Texas the fifth district.

Section 2. That it shall be the duty of the President to assign to the command of each of said districts an officer of the army, not below the rank of brigadier-general, and to detail a sufficient military force to enable such officer to perform his duties and enforce his authority within the district to which he is assigned.

Sec. 3. That it shall be the duty of each officer assigned as aforesaid, to protect all persons in their rights of persons and property, to suppress insurrection, disorder, and violence, and to punish, or cause to be punished, all disturbers of the public peace and criminals; and to this end he may

allow local civil tribunals to take jurisdiction of and to try offenders, or, when in his judgment it may be necessary for the trial of offenders, he shall have power to organize military commissions or tribunals for that purpose, and all interference under color of State authority with the exercise of military authority under this act, shall be null and void.

Sec. 4. That all persons put under military arrest by virtue of this act shall be tried without unnecessary delay, and no cruel or unusual punishment shall be inflicted, and no sentence of any military commission or tribunal hereby authorized, affecting the life or liberty of any person, shall be executed until it is approved by the officer in command of the district, and the laws and regulations for the government of the army shall not be affected by this act, except in so far as they conflict with its provisions: Provided, That no sentence of death under the provisions of this act shall be carried into effect without the approval of the President.

Sec. 5. That when the people of any one of said rebel States shall have formed a constitution of government in conformity with the Constitution of the United States in all respects, framed by a convention of delegates elected by the male citizens of said State, twenty-one years old and upward, of whatever race, color, or previous condition, who have been resident in said State for one year previous to the day of such election, except such as may be disfranchised for participation in the rebellion or for felony at common law, and when such constitution shall provide that the elective franchise shall be enjoyed by all such persons as have the qualifications herein stated for electors of delegates, and when such constitution shall be ratified by a majority of the persons voting on the question of ratification who are qualified as electors for delegates, and when such constitution shall have been submitted to Congress for examination and approval, and Congress shall have approved the

[13] *United States Statutes at Large*, XIV, 428-429.

same, and when said State, by a vote of its legislature elected under said constitution, shall have adopted the amendment to the Constitution of the United States, proposed by the Thirty-ninth Congress, and known as article fourteen, and when said article shall have become a part of the Constitution of the United States said State shall be declared entitled to representation in Congress, and senators and representatives shall be admitted therefrom on their taking the oath prescribed by law, and then and thereafter the preceding sections of this act shall be inoperative in said State: *Provided,* That no person excluded from the privilege of holding office by said proposed amendment to the Constitution of the United States, shall be eligible to election as a member of the convention to frame a constitution for any of said rebel States, nor shall any such person vote for members of such convention.

Sec. 6. That, until the people of said rebel States shall be by law admitted to representation in the Congress of the United States, any civil governments which may exist therein shall be deemed provisional only, and in all respects subject to the paramount authority of the United States at any time to abolish, modify, control, or supersede the same; and in all elections to any office under such provisional governments all persons shall be entitled to vote, and none others, who are entitled to vote, under the provisions of the fifth section of this act; and no persons shall be eligible to any office under any such provisional governments who would be disqualified from holding office under the provisions of the third *article* of said constitutional amendment.

## 14

Andrew Johnson once more accepted the challenge. Undaunted by defeat at the polls, and undismayed by the prospect of a hostile congressional majority capable of overriding his veto, he was still unwilling to abandon his moderate policy. His answer to the Republican Radicals was a lengthy veto message emphasizing the disparity between the two reconstruction plans:[14]

The bill places all the people of the ten States therein named under the absolute domination of military rulers; and the preamble undertakes to give . . . the ground upon which it is justified. It declares that there exists in those States no legal governments and no adequate protection for life or property, and asserts the necessity of enforcing peace and good order within their limits. Is this true as matter of fact?

It is not denied that the States in question have each of them an actual government, with all the powers—executive, judicial, and legislative—which properly belong to a free state. They are organized like the other States of the Union, and, like them, they make, administer, and execute the laws which concern their domestic affairs. An existing *de facto* government, exercising such functions as these, is itself the law of the state upon all matters within its jurisdiction. To pronounce the supreme law-making power of an established state illegal is to say that law itself is unlawful.

The provisions which these governments have made for the preservation of order, the suppression of crime, and the redress of private injuries are in substance and principle the same as those which prevail in the Northern States. . . .

The bill, however, would seem to show upon its face that the establishment of peace and good order is not its real object. . . .

All these conditions must be fulfilled before the people of any of these States can be relieved from the bondage of military domination; but when they are fulfilled, then immediately the pains and penalties of the bill are to cease, no matter whether there be peace and order or not,

---

[14] J. D. Richardson (comp.), *Messages and Papers of the Presidents, 1789-1897* (Washington, 1897, 1909; taken from the 1909 vol.), VI, 498-511.

and without any reference to the security of life or property. The excuse given for the bill in the preamble is admitted by the bill itself not to be real. The military rule which it establishes is plainly to be used, not for any purpose of order or for the prevention of crime, but solely as a means of coercing the people into the adoption of principles and measures to which it is known that they are opposed, and upon which they have an undeniable right to exercise their own·judgment.

I submit to Congress whether this measure is not in its whole character, scope, and object without precedent and without authority, in palpable conflict with the plainest provisions of the Constitution. . . .

The ten States named in the bill are divided into five districts. For each district an officer of the Army, not below the rank of a brigadier-general, is to be appointed to rule over the people; and he is to be supported with an efficient military force to enable him to perform his duties and enforce his authority. Those duties and that authority, as defined by the third section of the bill, are "to protect all persons. in their rights of person and property, to suppress insurrection, disorder, and violence, and to punish or cause to be punished all disturbers of the public peace or criminals." The power thus given to the commanding officer over all the people of each district is that of an absolute monarch. His mere will is to take the place of all law. The law of the States is now the only rule applicable to the subjects placed under his control, and that is completely displaced by the clause which declares all interference of State authority to be null and void. He alone is permitted to determine what are rights of person or property, and he may protect them in such way as in his discretion may seem proper. It places at his free disposal all the lands and goods in his district, and he may distribute them without let or hindrance to whom he pleases. Being bound by no State law, and there being no other law to regulate

the subject, he may make a criminal code of his own; and he can make it as bloody as any recorded in history, or he can reserve the privilege of acting upon the impulse of his private passions in each case that arises. He is bound by no rules of evidence; there is, indeed, no provision by which he is authorized or required to take any evidence at all. Everything is a crime which he chooses to call so, and all persons are condemned whom he pronounces to be guilty. He is not bound to keep and record or make any report of his proceedings. He may arrest his victims wherever he finds them, without warrant, accusation, or proof of probable cause. If he gives them a trial before he inflicts the punishment, he gives it of his grace and mercy, not because he is commanded so to do. . . .

It is also provided that "he shall have power to organize military commissions or tribunals"; but this power he is not commanded to exercise. . . . Instead of mitigating the harshness of his single rule, such a tribunal would be used much more probably to divide the responsibility of making it more cruel and unjust. . . .

It is plain that the authority here given to the military officer amounts to absolute despotism. But to make it still more unendurable, the bill provides that it may be delegated to as many subordinates as he chooses to appoint, for it declares that he shall "punish or cause to be punished." Such a power has not been wielded by any monarch in England for more than five hundred years. In all that time no people who speak the English language have borne such servitude. It reduces the whole population of the ten States—all persons, of every color, sex, and condition, and every stranger within their limits—to the most abject and degrading slavery. . . .

I come now to a question which is, if possible, still more important. Have we the power to establish and carry into execution a measure like this? I answer, Certainly not, if we derive our authority from the

Constitution and if we are bound by the limitations which it imposes.

This proposition is perfectly clear, that no branch of the Federal Government— executive, legislative, or judicial—can have any just powers except those which it derives through and exercises under the organic law of the Union. Outside of the Constitution we have no legal authority more than private citizens, and within it we have only so much as that instrument gives us. This broad principle limits all our functions and applies to all subjects. It protects not only the citizens of States which are within the Union, but it shields every human being who comes or is brought under our jurisdiction. . . . If, therefore, the Southern States were in truth out of the Union, we could not treat their people in a way which the fundamental law forbids.

Some persons assume that the success of our arms in crushing the opposition which was made in some of the States to the execution of the Federal laws reduced those States and all their people—the innocent as well as the guilty—to the condition of vassalage and gave us a power over them which the Constitution does not bestow or define or limit. No fallacy can be more transparent than this. Our victories subjected the insurgents to legal obedience, not to the yoke of an arbitrary despotism. . . .

Invasion, insurrection, rebellion, and domestic violence were anticipated when the Government was framed, and the means of repelling and suppressing them were wisely provided for in the Constitution; but it was not thought necessary to declare that the States in which they might occur should be expelled from the Union. Rebellions, which were invariably suppressed, occurred prior to that out of which these questions grow; but the States continued to exist and the Union remained unbroken. . . . It is true that in these earlier cases there was no formal expression of a determination to withdraw from the Union, but it is also true that in the Southern States the ordinances of secession were treated by all the friends of the Union as mere nullities and are now acknowledged to be so by the States themselves. If we admit that they had any force or validity or that they did in fact take the States in which they were passed out of the Union, we sweep from under our feet all the grounds upon which we stand in justifying the use of Federal force to maintain the integrity of the Government.

This is a bill passed by Congress in time of peace. There is not in any one of the States brought under its operation either war or insurrection. The laws of the States and of the Federal Government are all in undisturbed and harmonious operation. The courts, State and Federal, are open and in the full exercise of their proper authority. Over every State comprised in these five military districts, life, liberty, and property are secured by State laws and Federal laws, and the National Constitution is everywhere in force and everywhere obeyed. What, then, is the ground on which this bill proceeds? The title of the bill announces that it is intended "for the more efficient government" of these ten States. It is recited by way of preamble that no legal State governments "nor adequate protection for life or property" exist in those States, and that peace and good order should be thus enforced. The first thing which arrests attention upon these recitals, which prepare the way for martial law, is this, that the only foundation upon which martial law can exist under our form of government is not stated or so much as pretended. Actual war, foreign invasion, domestic insurrection—none of these appear; and none of these, in fact, exist. It is not even recited that any sort of war or insurrection is threatened. . . .

I need not say to the representatives of the American people that their Constitution forbids the exercise of judicial power in any way but one—that is, by the ordained and established courts. It is equally well known that in all criminal cases a trial by jury is made indispensable by the express words of that instrument. I will not enlarge on the inestimable value of the right thus secured to every freeman or speak of the danger to public liberty in all parts of the country which must ensue from a denial of it anywhere or upon any pretense. A very recent decision of the Supreme Court has traced the history, vindicated the dignity, and made known the value of this great privilege so clearly that nothing more is needed. To what extent a violation of it might be excused in time of war or public danger may admit of discussion, but we are providing now for a time of profound peace, when there is not an armed soldier within our borders except those who are in the service of the Government. It is in such a condition of things that an act of Congress is proposed which, if carried out, would deny a trial by the lawful courts and juries to 9,000,000 American citizens and to their posterity for an indefinite period. It seems to be scarcely possible that anyone should seriously believe this consistent with a Constitution which declares in simple, plain, and unambiguous language that all persons shall have that right and that no person shall ever in any case be deprived of it. The Constitution also forbids the arrest of the citizen without judicial warrant, founded on probable cause. This bill authorizes an arrest without warrant, at the pleasure of a military commander. The Constitution declares that "no person shall be held to answer for a capital or otherwise infamous crime unless on presentment by a grand jury." This bill holds every person not a soldier answerable for all crimes and all charges without any presentment. The Constitution declares that "no person shall be deprived of life, liberty, or property without due process of law." This bill sets aside all process of law, and makes the citizen answerable in his person and property to the will of one man, and as to his life to the will of two. Finally, the Constitution

declares that "the privilege of the writ of *habeas corpus* shall not be suspended unless when, in case of rebellion or invasion, the public safety may require it"; whereas this bill declares martial law (which of itself suspends this great writ) in time of peace, and authorizes the military to make the arrest, and gives to the prisoner only one privilege, and that is a trial "without unnecessary delay." He has no hope of release from custody, except the hope, such as it is, of release by acquittal before a military commission.

The United States are bound to guarantee to each State a republican form of government. Can it be pretended that this obligation is not probably broken if we carry out a measure like this, which wipes away every vestige of republican government in ten States and puts the life, property, liberty, and honor of all the people in each of them under the domination of a single person clothed with unlimited authority?

The purpose and object of the bill—the general intent which pervades it from beginning to end—is to change the entire structure and character of the State governments and to compel them by force to the adoption of organic laws and regulations which they are unwilling to accept if left to themselves. The negroes have not asked for the privilege of voting; the vast majority of them have no idea what it means. This bill not only thrusts it into their hands, but compels them, as well as the whites, to use it in a particular way. If they do not form a constitution with prescribed articles in it and afterwards elect a legislature which will act upon certain measures in a prescribed way, neither blacks nor whites can be relieved from the slavery which the bill imposes upon them. Without pausing here to consider the policy or impolicy of Africanizing the southern part of our territory, I would simply ask the attention of Congress to that manifest, well-known, and universally acknowledged rule of constitutional law which declares that the Federal Government has no jurisdiction, authority, or power to regulate such subjects for any State. To force the right of suffrage out of the hands of the white people and into the hands of the negroes is an arbitrary violation of this principle. . . .

The bill also denies the legality of the governments of ten of the States which participated in the ratification of the amendment to the Federal Constitution abolishing slavery forever within the jurisdiction of the United States and practically excludes them from the Union. If this assumption of the bill be correct, their concurrence can not be considered as having been legally given, and the important fact is made to appear that the consent of three-fourths of the States—the requisite number—has not been constitutionally obtained to the ratification of that amendment, thus leaving the question of slavery where it stood before the amendment was officially declared to have become a part of the Constitution. . . .

It is a part of our public history which can never be forgotten that both Houses of Congress, in July, 1861, declared in the form of a solemn resolution that the war was and should be carried on for no purpose of subjugation, but solely to enforce the Constitution and laws, and that when this was yielded by the parties in rebellion the contest should cease, with the constitutional rights of the States and of individuals unimpaired. This resolution was adopted and sent forth to the world unanimously by the Senate and with only two dissenting voices in the House. It was accepted by the friends of the Union in the South as well as in the North as expressing honestly and truly the object of the war. On the faith of it many thousands of persons in both sections gave their lives and their fortunes to the cause. To repudiate it now by refusing to the States and to the individuals within them the rights which the Constitution and laws of the Union would secure to them is a breach of our

plighted honor for which I can imagine no excuse and to which I can not voluntarily become a party.

The evils which spring from the unsettled state of our Government will be acknowledged by all. Commercial intercourse is impeded, capital is in constant peril, public securities fluctuate in value, peace itself is not secure, and the sense of moral and political duty is impaired. To avert these calamities from our country it is imperatively required that we should immediately decide upon some course of administration which can be steadfastly adhered to. I am thoroughly convinced that any settlement or compromise or plan of action which is inconsistent with the principles of the Constitution will not only be unavailing, but mischievous; that it will but multiply the present evils, instead of removing them. The Constitution, in its whole integrity and vigor, throughout the length and breadth of the land, is the best of all compromises. Besides, our duty does not, in my judgment, leave us a choice between that and any other. I believe that it contains the remedy that is so much needed, and that if the coordinate branches of the Government would unite upon its provisions they would be found broad enough and strong enough to sustain in time of peace the nation which they bore safely through the ordeal of a protracted civil war. Among the most sacred guarantees of that instrument are those which declare that "each State shall have at least one Representative," and that "no State, without its consent, shall be deprived of its equal suffrage in the Senate." Each House is made the "judge of the elections, returns, and qualifications of its own members," and may, "with the concurrence of two-thirds, expel a member." Thus, as heretofore urged, "in the admission of Senators and Representatives from any and all of the States there can be no just ground of apprehension that persons who are disloyal will be clothed with the powers of legislation, for this could not happen when the Constitution and the laws are enforced by a vigilant and faithful Congress." "When a Senator or Representative presents his certificate of election, he may at once be admitted or rejected: or, should there be any question as to his eligibility, his credentials may be referred for investigation to the appropriate committee. If admitted to a seat, it must be upon evidence satisfactory to the House of which he thus becomes a member that he possesses the requisite constitutional and legal qualifications. If refused admission as a member for want of due allegiance to the Government, and returned to his constituents, they are admonished that none but persons loyal to the United States will be allowed a voice in the legislative councils of the nation, and the political power and moral influence of Congress are thus effectively exerted in the interests of loyalty to the Government and fidelity to the Union." And is it not far better that the work of restoration should be accomplished by simple compliance with the plain requirements of the Constitution than by recourse to measures which in effect destroy the States and threaten the subversion of the General Government? All that is necessary to settle this simple but important question without further agitation or delay is a willingness on the part of all to sustain the Constitution and carry its provisions into practical operation. If tomorrow either branch of Congress would declare that upon the presentation of their credentials members constitutionally elected and loyal to the General Government would be admitted to seats in Congress, while all others would be excluded and their places remain vacant until the selection by the people of loyal and qualified persons, and if at the same time assurance were given that this policy would be continued until all the States were represented in Congress, it would send a thrill of joy throughout the entire land, as indicating the inauguration of a system which must

speedily bring tranquillity to the public mind.

While we are legislating upon subjects which are of great importance to the whole people, and which must affect all parts of the country, not only during the life of the present generation, but for ages to come, we should remember that all men are entitled to at least a hearing in the councils which decide upon the destiny of themselves and their children. At present ten States are denied representation, and when the Fortieth Congress assembles on the 4*th* day of the present month sixteen States will be without a voice in the House of Representatives. This grave fact, with the important question before us, should induce us to pause in the course of legislation which, looking solely to the attainment of political ends, fails to consider the rights it transgresses, the law which it violates, or the institutions which it imperils.

## MAKING THE SOUTH SOLID

### 15

While Congress and President battled for power in Washington, reconstruction in the South went slowly on. By the spring of 1868 seven of the ten southern states had re-entered the Union under the congressional formula, and were operating efficiently with legislatures composed of Negroes, northern carpetbaggers, and southern Republicans, or Scalawags. Historians have delighted in ridiculing the conduct of the Negro legislators, picturing them as reckless spenders whose fraudulent acts set a new standard in corruption. Such a judgment ignores the significant social progress for which they were responsible. In every state educational systems were installed, public works were begun, roads were built, sanitation was improved, and life made better for rich and poor alike. The progressive nature of laws passed by the so-called black-and-tan legislatures was illustrated by the South Carolina Constitution of 1868:[15]

[15] *The Constitution of South Carolina* (Charleston, 1868), pp. 2-6. (Pages not numbered consecutively.) Collection entitled *State Constitutions*, collected and bound by the New York Public Library.

*We, the People of the State of South Carolina, in Convention assembled,* Grateful to Almighty God for this opportunity, deliberately and peaceably of entering into an explicit and solemn compact with each other, and forming a new Constitution of civil government for ourselves and posterity, recognizing the necessity of the protection of the people in all that pertains to their freedom, safety and tranquillity, and imploring the direction of the Great Legislator of the Universe, do agree upon, ordain and establish the following

*Declaration of Rights and Form of Government as the Constitution of the Commonwealth of South Carolina*

Article I: Declaration of Rights

Section 1. All men are born free and equal—endowed by their Creator with certain inalienable rights, among which are the rights of enjoying and defending their lives and liberties, of acquiring, possessing and protecting property, and of seeking and obtaining their safety and happiness.

Sec. 2. Slavery shall never exist in this State; neither shall involuntary servitude, except as a punishment for crime, whereof the party shall have been duly convicted.

Sec. 3. All political power is vested in and derived from the people only; therefore they have the right, at all times, to modify their form of government in such manner as they may deem expedient, when the public good demands.

Sec. 4. Every citizen of this State owes paramount allegiance to the Constitution and Government of the United States, and no law or ordinance of this State in contravention or subversion thereof can have any binding force.

Sec. 5. This State shall ever remain a member of the American Union, and all attempts, from whatever source, or upon whatever pretext, to dissolve the said Union, shall be resisted with the whole power of the State.

Sec. 6. The right of the people peaceably to assemble to consult for the common good, and to petition the Government, or any department thereof, shall never be abridged.

Sec. 7. All persons may freely speak, write and publish their sentiments on any subject, being responsible for the abuse of that right; and no laws shall be enacted to restrain or abridge the liberty of speech or of the press.

Sec. 8. In prosecutions for the publication of papers investigating the official conduct of officers or men in public capacity, or when the matter published is proper for public information, the truth thereof may be given in evidence; and in all indictments for libel, the jury shall be the judges of the law and the facts.

Sec. 9. No person shall be deprived of the right to worship God according to the dictates of his own conscience; *Provided,* That the liberty of conscience hereby declared shall not justify practices inconsistent with the peace and moral safety of society.

Sec. 10. No form of religion shall be established by law; but it shall be the duty of the General Assembly to pass suitable laws to protect every religious denomination in the peaceable enjoyment of its own mode of worship.

Sec. 11. The right of trial by jury shall remain inviolate.

Sec. 12. No person shall be disqualified as a witness, or be prevented from acquiring, holding and transmitting property, or be hindered in acquiring education, or be liable to any other punishment for any offence, or be subjected in law to any other restraints or disqualifications in regard to any personal rights than such as are laid upon others under like circumstances.

Sec. 13. No person shall be held to answer for any crime or offence until the same is fully, fairly, plainly, substantially and formally described to him; or be compelled to accuse or furnish evidence against himself; and every person shall have a right to produce all proofs that may be favorable to him, to meet the witnesses against him face to face, to have a speedy and public trial by an impartial jury, and to be fully heard in his defence by himself or by his counsel, or by both, as he may elect.

Sec. 14. No person shall be arrested, imprisoned, despoiled or dispossessed of his property, immunities or privileges, put out of the protection of the law, exiled or deprived of his life, liberty, or estate, but by the judgment of his peers or the law of the land. And the General Assembly shall not enact any law that shall subject any person to punishment without trial by jury; nor shall he be punished but by virtue of a law already established, or promulgated prior to the offence, and legally applied.

Sec. 15. All Courts shall be public, and every person, for any injury that he may receive in his lands, goods, person or reputation, shall have remedy by due course of law and justice administered without unnecessary delay.

Sec. 16. All persons shall, before conviction, be bailable by sufficient sureties, except for capital offences, when the proof is evident or the presumption great; and excessive bail shall not, in any case, be required, nor corporal punishment inflicted.

Sec. 17. The privilege of the writ of *Habeas Corpus* shall not be suspended, except when, in case of insurrection, rebellion or invasion, the public safety may require it.

Sec. 18. No person, after having been once acquitted by a jury, shall again, for the same offence, be put in jeopardy of his life or liberty.

Sec. 19. All offences less than felony, and in which the punishment does not exceed a fine of one hundred dollars, or imprisonment for thirty days, shall be tried summarily before a Justice of the Peace, or other officer authorized by law, on information under oath, without indictment or intervention of a Grand Jury, saving to the defendant the right of appeal;

and no person shall be held to answer for any higher crime or offence unless on presentment of a Grand Jury, except in cases arising in the land and naval service, or in the militia when in actual service in time of war or public danger.

Sec. 20. No person shall be imprisoned for debt, except in cases of fraud; and a reasonable amount of property, as a homestead, shall be exempted from seizure or sale for the payment of any debts or liabilities, except for the payment of such obligations as are provided for in this Constitution.

Sec. 21. No bill of attainder, *ex post facto* law, nor any law impairing the obligation of contracts, shall ever be enacted; and no conviction shall work corruption of blood or forfeiture of estate.

Sec. 22. All persons have a right to be secure from unreasonable searches or seizures of their persons, houses, papers or possessions. All warrants shall be supported by oath or affirmation, and the order of the warrant to a civil officer to make search or seizure in suspected places, or to arrest one or more suspected persons, or to seize their property, shall be accompanied with a special designation of the persons or objects of search, arrest or seizure; and no warrant shall be issued but in the cases and with the formalities prescribed by the laws.

Sec. 23. Private property shall not be taken or applied for public use, or for the use of corporations, or for private use, without the consent of the owner or a just compensation being made therefore; *Provided, however,* That laws may be made securing to persons or corporations the right of way over the lands of either persons or corporations, and, for works of internal improvement, the right to establish depots, stations, turnouts, etc.; but a just compensation, shall, in all cases, be first made to the owner.

Sec. 24. The power of suspending the laws, or the execution of the laws, shall never be exercised but by the General Assembly, or by authority derived therefrom; to be exercised in such particular cases only as the General Assembly shall expressly provide for.

Sec. 25. No person shall, in any case, be subject to martial law, or to any pains or penalties by virtue of that law, except those employed in the army or navy of the United States, and except the militia in actual service, but by authority of the General Assembly.

Sec. 26. In the government of this Commonwealth, the Legislative, Executive and Judicial powers of the Government shall be forever separate and distinct from each other, and no person or persons exercising the functions of one of said departments shall assume or discharge the duties of any other.

Sec. 27. The General Assembly ought frequently to assemble for the redress of grievances and for making new laws as the common good may require.

Sec. 28. The people have a right to keep and bear arms for the common defence. As in times of peace, armies are dangerous to liberty, they ought not to be maintained without the consent of the General Assembly. The military power ought always to be held in an exact subordination to the civil authority and be governed by it. . . .

## Article VIII: Right of Suffrage

Section 1. In all elections by the people the electors shall vote by ballot.

Sec. 2. Every male citizen of the United States, of the age of twenty-one years and upwards, not laboring under the disabilities named in this Constitution, without distinction of race, color, or former condition, who shall be a resident of this State at the time of the adoption of this Constitution, or who shall thereafter reside in this State one year, and in the County in which he offers to vote, sixty days next preceding any election, shall be entitled to vote for all officers that are now, or hereafter may be, elected by the people, and upon all questions submitted to the electors

at any elections; *Provided,* That no person shall be allowed to vote or hold office who is now or hereafter may be disqualified therefor by the Constitution of the United States, until such disqualification shall be removed by the Congress of the United States; *Provided further,* That no person, while kept in any alms house or asylum, or of unsound mind, or confined in any public prison, shall be allowed to vote or hold office.

Sec. 3. It shall be the duty of the General Assembly to provide from time to time for the registration of all electors.

Sec. 4. For the purpose of voting no person shall be deemed to have lost his residence by reason of absence while employed in the service of the United States, nor while engaged upon the waters of this State or the United States, or of the high seas, nor while temporarily absent from the State.

Sec. 5. No soldier, seaman or marine in the army or navy of the United States shall be deemed a resident of this State in consequence of having been stationed therein.

Sec. 6. Electors shall, in all cases, except treason, felony or breach of the peace, be privileged from arrest and civil process during their attendance at elections, and in going to and returning from the same.

Sec. 7. Every person entitled to vote at any election shall be eligible to any office which now is or hereafter shall be elective by the people in the County where he shall have resided sixty days previous to such election, except as otherwise provided in this Constitution or the Constitution and laws of the United States.

Sec. 8. The General Assembly shall never pass any law that will deprive any of the citizens of this State of the right of suffrage except for treason, murder, robbery, or duelling, whereof the persons shall have been duly tried and convicted.

Sec. 9. Presidential electors shall be elected by the people.

Sec. 10. In all elections held by the people under this Constitution, the person or persons who shall receive the highest number of votes shall be declared elected.

Sec. 11. The provision of this Constitution concerning the term of residence necessary to enable persons to hold certain offices therein mentioned, shall not be held to apply to officers chosen by the people at the first election, or by the General Assembly at its first session.

Sec. 12. No person shall be disfranchised for felony, or other crimes committed while such person was a slave.

Article IX: Finance and Taxation

Section 1. The General Assembly shall provide by law for a uniform and equal rate of assessment and taxation, and shall prescribe such regulations as shall secure a just valuation for taxation of all property, real, personal and possessory, except mines and mining claims, the proceeds of which alone shall be taxed; and also excepting such property as may be exempted by law for municipal, educational, literary, scientific, religious or charitable purposes.

Sec. 2. The General Assembly may provide annually for a poll tax not to exceed one dollar on each poll, which shall be applied exclusively to the public school fund. And no additional poll tax shall be levied by any municipal corporation.

Sec. 3. The General Assembly shall provide for an annual tax sufficient to defray the estimated expenses of the State for each year; and whenever it shall happen that such ordinary expenses of the State for any year shall exceed the income of the State for such year, the General Assembly shall provide for levying a tax for the ensuing year sufficient, with other sources of income, to pay the deficiency of the preceding year, together with the estimated expenses of the ensuing year.

Sec. 4. No tax shall be levied except in pursuance of a law, which shall distinctly state the object of the same; to which object such tax shall be applied.

Sec. 5. It shall be the duty of the General Assembly to enact laws for the exemption from taxation of all public schools, colleges, and institutions of learning, all charitable institutions in the nature of asylums for the infirm, deaf and dumb, blind, idiotic and indigent persons, all public libraries, churches and burying grounds; but property of associations and societies, although connected with charitable objects, shall not be exempt from State, County or Municipal taxation; *Provided,* That this exemption shall not extend beyond the buildings and premises actually occupied by such schools, colleges, institutions of learning, asylums, libraries, churches and burial grounds, although connected with charitable objects. . . .

Article X: Education

Section 1. The supervision of public instruction shall be vested in a State Superintendent of Education, who shall be elected by the qualified electors of the State in such manner and at such time as the other State officers are elected; his powers, duties, term of office and compensation shall be defined by the General Assembly.

Sec. 2. There shall be elected biennially, in each County, by the qualified electors thereof, one School Commissioner, said Commissioners to constitute a State Board of Education, of which the State Superintendent shall, by virtue of his office, be Chairman; the powers, duties, and compensation of the members of said Board shall be determined by law.

Sec. 3. The General Assembly shall, as soon as practicable after the adoption of this Constitution, provide for a liberal and uniform system of free public schools throughout the State, and shall also make provision for the division of the State into suitable School Districts. There shall be kept open at least six months in each year one or more schools in each School District.

Sec. 4. It shall be the duty of the General Assembly to provide for the compulsory attendance, at either public or private schools, of all children between the ages of six and sixteen years, not physically or mentally disabled, for a term equivalent to twenty-four months, at least: *Provided,* That no law to that effect shall be passed until a system of public schools has been thoroughly and completely organized, and facilities afforded to all the inhabitants of the State for the free education of their children.

SEC. 5. The General Assembly shall levy at each regular session after the adoption of this Constitution an annual tax on all taxable property throughout the State for the support of public schools, which tax shall be collected at the same time and by the same agents as the general State levy, and shall be paid into the Treasury of the State. There shall be assessed on all taxable polls in the State an annual tax of one dollar on each poll, the proceeds of which tax shall be applied solely to educational purposes. *Provided,* That no person shall ever be deprived of the right of suffrage for the non-payment of said tax. No other poll or capitation tax shall be levied in the State, nor shall the amount assessed on each poll exceed the limit given in this section. The School Tax shall be distributed among the several School Districts of the State, in proportion to the respective number of pupils attending the public schools. No religious sect or sects shall have exclusive right to, or control of any part of the school funds of the State, nor shall sectarian principles be taught in the public schools.

SEC. 6. Within five years after the first regular session of the General Assembly, following the adoption of this Constitution, it shall be the duty of the General Assembly to provide for the establishment and support of a State Normal School, which shall be open to all persons who may wish to become teachers.

SEC. 7. Educational institutions for the benefit of all the blind, deaf and dumb, and such other benevolent institutions, as the public good may require, shall be established and supported by the State, sub-ject to such regulations as may be prescribed by law.

SEC. 8. Provisions shall be made by law, as soon as practicable, for the establishment and maintenance of a State Reform School for juvenile offenders.

SEC. 9. The General Assembly shall provide for the maintenance of the State University, and as soon as practicable, provide for the establishment of an Agricultural College, and shall appropriate the land given to this State, for the support of such a college, by the Act of Congress, passed July second, one thousand eight hundred and sixty-two, or the money or scrip, as the case may be arising from the sale of said lands, or any lands which may hereafter be given or appropriated for such purpose, for the support and maintenance of such college, and may make the same a branch of the State University, for instruction in Agriculture, the Mechanic Arts, and the Natural Sciences connected therewith.

SEC. 10. All the public schools, colleges, and universities of this State supported in whole or in part by the public funds, shall be free and open to all the children and youths of the State, without regard to race or color.

SEC. 11. The proceeds of all lands that have been or hereafter may be given by the United States to this State for educational purposes, and not otherwise appropriated by this State or the United States, and of all lands or other property given by individuals, or appropriated by the State for like purpose, and of all estates of deceased persons who have died without leaving a will or heir, shall be securely invested and sacredly preserved as a State School Fund, and the annual interest and income of said fund, together with such other means as the General Assembly may provide, shall be faithfully appropriated for the purpose of establishing and maintaining free public schools, and for no other purposes or uses whatever.

ARTICLE XI: CHARITABLE AND PENAL IN-
STITUTIONS

SECTION I. Institutions for the benefit of
the insane, blind, deaf and dumb, and the
poor, shall always be fostered and supported by this State, and shall be subject
to such regulations as the General Assembly may enact.

## 16

The significant social contributions of the
Negro legislatures have been recognized by
comparatively few modern scholars. Among
those who have done so is W. E. B. DuBois,
a leading student of reconstruction, whose
important book, *Black Reconstruction,* sheds
new light on the results obtained by Negro
politicians and their northern allies:[16]

It is fair to say that the Negro carpetbag
governments established the public schools
of the South. Although recent researches
have shown many germs of a public school
system in the South before the war, there
can be no reasonable doubt that common
school instruction in the South . . . was
founded by the Freedmen's Bureau and
missionary societies, and that the state public school system was formed mainly by
Negro Reconstruction governments. . . .

From the beginning of the public school
system under Reconstruction, and after,
the fight between local and state control
and supervision has been bitter. Local control meant the control of property and racial particularism. It stood for reaction
and prejudice; and wherever there was retrogression, particularly in Negro schools,
it can be traced to the increased power
of the county and district administrators. . . .

For the first success of the Negro schools,
the South deserved little praise. From the
beginning, most of the Southern states
made the Negro schools just as bad as they

dared to in the face of national public opinion, and every cent spent on them was
taken from Negro rents and wages, and
came back to the property-holders tenfold
in increased opportunities for exploitation.

It is said, for instance, in one state:
"There were to be free public schools. The
blacks were to be the chief beneficiaries of
the new system, but the whites would
pay the taxes. Whites considered such education either useless or positively dangerous to society." Of free, self-sacrificing
gifts for the sake of Negro uplift and intelligence, the vast majority of Southern
white people contributed almost nothing. . . .

Finally, the movement that saved the
Negro public school system was not enlightened Southern opinion, but rather
that Northern philanthropy which at the
very beginning of the Negro education
movement contributed toward the establishment of Negro colleges. The reason for
them at first was to supply the growing
demand for teachers, and was also a concession to Southern prejudice, which so
violently disliked the white teacher in the
Negro school.

This led to the establishment by 1879 of
eighty-four normal and high schools and
sixteen colleges, with over twelve thousand
students. But these institutions soon saw
a higher mission. In the midst of reaction and disfranchisement, of poverty and
growing caste, they became the centers of
a training in leadership and ideals for the
whole Negro race, and the only fine and
natural field of contact between white and
black culture. . . .

Howard University and Freeman's Hospital are survivals of the Freedmen's Bureau. Howard University was chartered in
1867 and General O. O. Howard, head of
the Freedmen's Bureau, was made its first
president. Succeeding as presidents were
W. W. Patton, J. E. Rankin, who wrote
"God Be with You Until We Meet
Again," and John Gordon, a lineal de-

---

[16] From *Black Reconstruction* by W. E. Burghardt
DuBois, pp. 664-667. Copyright, 1935, by Harcourt, Brace and Company, Inc.

scendant of Jonathan Edwards. On its governing board have been Douglass, Langston and Bruce; it has the largest Negro medical center in the United States, and has furnished about half of the Negro lawyers.

Berea College was started by John G. Fee, a Kentuckian, who became an abolitionist. After the war, colored students were admitted, and a brother of the President of Oberlin was at the head of the school. For forty years, colored students attended Berea, but finally, in 1904, the institution was by law closed to Negroes.

Hampton Institute was founded by General S. C. Armstrong, near where the Negroes were first made "contraband of war," and where a colored woman founded the first colored school. Among its trustees were Mark Hopkins, Phillips Brooks, and John G. Whittier.

Atlanta University was founded by Edmund Ware in 1867. "To have gone on as President Ware did during those early years there must have been in his heart deathless love and pity for men who needed what he could give them—a faith in the gospel and eternal righteousness that never wavered, and a love for God that made work easy and suffering joy."

Add to this the picture of DeForrest at Talledega, Cravath at Fisk, and others at Biddle, Knoxville, New Orleans, and Central Tennessee. There were those two influential schools at the edge of the South, Lincoln in Pennsylvania, and Wilberforce in Ohio.

Nearly all of these educational leaders were either nominated by Howard, head of the Freedmen's Bureau, as in the case of General S. C. Armstrong, or received from him the most thorough-going cooperation. There is no greater tribute to the Freedmen's Bureau than this.

Propaganda has centered the attention of the world upon these Northerners who took part in . . . political reconstruction . . . and particularly upon those who were charged with dishonesty, while of the history of this astonishing movement to plant the New England college in the South, and to give the Southern black man a leadership based on scholarship and character, almost nothing has been said. And yet this was the salvation of the South and the Negro. These "carpetbaggers" deserve to be remembered and honored. Without them there can be no doubt that the Negro would have rushed into revolt and vengeance and played into the hands of those determined to crush him. As it was, when reaction triumphed in 1876, there was already present a little group of trained leadership which grew by leaps and bounds until it gripped and held the mass of Negroes at the beginning of the twentieth century.

Had it not been for the Negro school and college, the Negro would, to all intents and purposes, have been driven back to slavery. His economic foothold in land and capital was too slight in ten years of turmoil to effect any defense or stability. His reconstruction leadership had come from Negroes educated in the North, and white politicians, capitalists and philanthropic teachers. The counter-revolution of 1876 drove most of these, save the teachers, away. But already, through establishing public schools and private colleges, and by organizing the Negro church, the Negro had acquired enough leadership and knowledge to thwart the worst designs of the new slave drivers. They avoided the mistake of trying to meet force by force. They bent to the storm of beating, lynching and murder, and kept their souls in spite of public and private insult of every description; they built an inner culture which the world recognizes in spite of the fact that it is still half-strangled and inarticulate.

## 17

The Negro governors of the reconstructed southern states became the victims of their own progressivism. With each new law that promised to elevate the members of their race, the opposition of southern Bourbons mounted. As long as federal troops patrolled the South, legal redress was impossible, but extralegal methods might be employed. A small band of men in May, 1867, organized a secret society known as the Ku Klux Klan. Garbed in sheets and mounted on swift horses, Klansmen soon terrorized Negroes all over the South, forcing them to abstain from voting or office holding, to give up profitable jobs, and to accept an inferior social position. The purposes of this organization were described in the "Principles of the Ku Klux Klan":[17]

### Appellation

This Organization shall be styled and denominated, the Order of the * * *

### Creed

We, the Order of the * * * , reverentially acknowledge the majesty and supremacy of the Divine Being, and recognize the goodness and providence of the same. And we recognize our relation to the United States Government, the supremacy of the Constitution, the Constitutional Laws thereof, and the Union of States thereunder.

### Character and Objects of the Order

This is an institution of Chivalry, Humanity, Mercy, and Patriotism; embodying in its genius and its principles all that is chivalric in conduct, noble in sentiment, generous in manhood, and patriotic in purpose; its peculiar objects being

*First:* To protect the weak, the innocent, and the defenseless, from the indignities, wrongs, and outrages of the lawless, the violent, and the brutal; to relieve the injured and oppressed; to succor the suffering and unfortunate, and especially the widows and orphans of Confederate soldiers.

*Second:* To protect and defend the Constitution of the United States, and all laws passed in conformity thereto, and to pro-

tect the States and the people thereof from all invasion from any source whatever.

*Third:* To aid and assist in the execution of all constitutional laws, and to protect the people from unlawful seizure, and from trial except by their peers in conformity to the laws of the land.

### ARTICLE I: *Titles*

SECTION 1. The officers of this Order shall consist of a Grand Wizard of the Empire, and his ten Genii; a Grand Dragon of the Realm, and his eight Hydras; a Grand Titan of the Dominion, and his six Furies; a Grand Giant of the Province, and his four Goblins; a Grand Cyclops of the Den, and his two Night Hawks; a Grand Magi, a Grand Monk, a Grand Scribe, a Grand Exchequer, a Grand Turk, and a Grand Sentinel.

SEC. 2. The body politic of this Order shall be known and designated as "Ghouls." . . .

### Interrogations to Be Asked

1st. Have you ever been rejected, upon application for membership in the * * * , or have you ever been expelled from the same?

2d. Are you now, or have you ever been, a member of the Radical Republican party, or either of the organizations known as the "Loyal League" and the "Grand Army of the Republic?"

3d. Are you opposed to the principles and policy of the Radical party, and to the Loyal League, and the Grand Army of the Republic, so far as you are informed of the character and purposes of those organizations?

4th. Did you belong to the Federal army during the late war, and fight against the South during the existence of the same?

5th. Are you opposed to negro equality, both social and political?

6th. Are you in favor of a white man's government in this country?

7th. Are you in favor of Constitutional liberty, and a Government of equitable laws instead of a Government of violence and oppression?

8th. Are you in favor of maintaining the Constitutional rights of the South?

9th. Are you in favor of the reenfranchisement and emancipation of the white men of the South, and the restitution of the Southern people to all their rights, alike proprietary, civil, and political?

10th. Do you believe in the inalienable right of self-preservation of the people against the exercise of arbitrary and unlicensed power?

## 18

Congressional Republicans did their best to stamp out the Klan. Sincerely concerned with the rights of the ex-slaves, and aware that white intimidation of Negroes would deprive the Republican party of southern votes, they were anxious to outlaw the secret society. The result was a series of laws designed to guarantee freedmen the civil and political rights promised in the Thirteenth, Fourteenth, and Fifteenth amendments. The most important was the Ku Klux Klan Act of April 20, 1871:[18]

SECTION 2. That if two or more persons within any State or Territory of the United States shall conspire together to overthrow, or to put down, or to destroy by force the government of the United States, or to levy war against the United States, or to oppose by force the authority of the government of the United States, or by force, intimidation, or threat to prevent, hinder, or delay the execution of any law of the United States, or by force to seize, take, or possess any property of the United States contrary to the authority thereof, or by force, intimidation, or threat to prevent any person from accepting or holding any office or trust or place of confidence under the United States, or from discharging the duties thereof, . . . or by force, intimidation, or threat to deter any party or witness in any court of the United States from attending such court, or from testifying in

any matter pending in such court fully, freely, and truthfully, or to injure any such party or witness in his person or property on account of his having so attended or testified, or by force, intimidation, or threat to influence the verdict, presentment, or indictment, of any juror or grand juror in any court of the United States, or to injure such juror in his person or property on account of any verdict, presentment, or indictment lawfully assented to by him, or on account of his being or having been such juror, or shall conspire together, or go in disguise upon the public highway or upon the premises of another for the purpose, either directly or indirectly, of depriving any person or any class of persons of the equal protection of the laws, or of equal privileges or immunities under the laws, or for the purpose of preventing or hindering the constituted authorities of any State from giving or securing to all persons within such State the equal protection of the laws, or shall conspire together for the purpose of in any manner impeding, hindering, obstructing, or defeating the due course of justice in any State or Territory, with intent to deny to any citizen of the United States the due and equal protection of the laws . . . or by force, intimidation, or threat to prevent any citizen of the United States lawfully entitled to vote from giving his support or advocacy in a lawful manner towards or in favor of the election of any lawfully qualified person as an elector of President or Vice-President of the United States, or as a member of the Congress of the United States, or to injure any such citizen in his person or property on account of such support or advocacy, each and every person so offending shall be deemed guilty of a high crime, and, upon conviction thereof in any district or circuit court of the United States or district or supreme court of any Territory of the United States having jurisdiction of similar offences, shall be punished by a fine not less than five hundred nor more than five thou-

---

[18] *United States Statutes at Large,* XVII, 13-15.

sand dollars, or by imprisonment, with or without hard labor, as the court may determine, for a period of not less than six months nor more than six years, as the court may determine, or by both such fine and imprisonment as the court shall determine. . . .

SEC. 3. That in all cases where insurrection, domestic violence, unlawful combinations, or conspiracies in any State shall so obstruct or hinder the execution of the laws thereof, and of the United States, as to deprive any portion or class of the people of such State of any of the rights, privileges, or immunities, or protection, named in the Constitution and secured by this act, and the constituted authorities of such State shall either be unable to protect, or shall, from any cause, fail in or refuse protection of the people in such rights, such facts shall be deemed a denial by such State of the equal protection of the laws to which they are entitled under the Constitution of the United States; and in all such cases . . . it shall be lawful for the President, and it shall be his duty to take such measures, by the employment of the militia or the land and naval forces of the United States, or of either, or by other means, as he may deem necessary for the suppression of such insurrection, domestic violence, or combinations. . . .

SEC. 4. That whenever in any State or part of a State the unlawful combinations named in the preceding section of this act shall be organized and armed, and so numerous and powerful as to be able, by violence, to either overthrow or set at defiance the constituted authorities of such State, and of the United States within such State, or when the constituted authorities are in complicity with, or shall connive at the unlawful purposes of, such powerful and armed combinations; and whenever, by reason of either or all of the causes aforesaid, the conviction of such offenders and the preservation of the public safety shall become in such district impracticable, in every such case such combinations shall be

deemed a rebellion against the government of the United States, and during the continuance of such rebellion, and within the limits of the district which shall be so under the sway thereof, such limits to be prescribed by proclamation, it shall be lawful for the President of the United States, when in his judgment the public safety shall require it, to suspend the privileges of the writ of habeas corpus, to the end that such rebellion may be overthrown: *Provided,* That all the provisions of the second section of [the Habeas Corpus Act of March 3, 1863], which relate to the discharge of prisoners other than prisoners of war, and to the penalty for refusing to obey the order of the court, shall be in full force so far as the same are applicable to the provisions of this section: *Provided further,* That the President shall first have made proclamation, as now provided by law, commanding such insurgents to disperse: *And provided also,* That the provisions of this section shall not be in force after the end of the next regular session of Congress.

## 19

Even more important than the Ku Klux Klan Act was the second Civil Rights Act of March 1, 1875, which sought to assure social equality for the southern Negroes:[19]

*Be it enacted,* That all persons within the jurisdiction of the United States shall be entitled to the full and equal enjoyment of the accommodations, advantages, facilities, and privileges of inns, public conveyances on land or water, theaters, and other places of public amusement; subject only to the conditions and limitations established by law, and applicable alike to citizens of every race and color, regardless of any previous condition of servitude.

SECTION 2. That any person who shall violate the foregoing section by denying to any citizen, except for reasons by law applicable to citizens of every race and color,

[19] *Ibid.,* XVIII, Pt. 3, pp. 335-336.

and regardless of any previous condition of servitude, the full enjoyment of any of the accommodations, advantages, facilities, or privileges in said section enumerated, or by aiding or inciting such denial, shall, for every such offense, forfeit and pay the sum of five hundred dollars to the person aggrieved thereby, . . . and shall also, for every such offense, be deemed guilty of a misdemeanor, and, upon conviction thereof, shall be fined not less than five hundred nor more than one thousand dollars, or shall be imprisoned not less than thirty days nor more than one year. . . .

Sec. 3. That the district and circuit courts of the United States shall have, exclusively of the courts of the several States, cognizance of all crimes and offenses against, and violations of, the provisions of this act. . . .

Sec. 4. That no citizen possessing all other qualifications which are or may be prescribed by law shall be disqualified for service as grand or petit juror in any court of the United States, or of any State, on account of race, color, or previous condition of servitude; and any officer or other person charged with any duty in the selection or summoning of jurors who shall exclude or fail to summon any citizen for the cause aforesaid shall, on conviction thereof, be deemed guilty of a misdemeanor, and be fined not more than five thousand dollars.

## 20

Although Republican architects planned their reconstruction policy well, they faced an insurmountable obstacle. The justices of the Supreme Court held that the wartime amendments gave Congress no power over southern whites, who were still free as individual citizens to deprive Negroes of civil rights. The new constitutional restrictions, the Court maintained, applied only to the states, which could make no laws denying freedmen the privileges guaranteed them in the amendments. This doctrine, on which the "Jim Crow" civilization of the South was to rest, was advanced in the Civil Rights Cases

(1883), which arose when Negroes were denied access to accommodations solely on the grounds of color:[20]

It is true that slavery cannot exist without law any more than property in lands and goods can exist without law, and therefore the Thirteenth Amendment may be regarded as nullifying all state laws which establish or uphold slavery. But it has a reflex character also, establishing and decreeing universal civil and political freedom throughout the United States; and it is assumed that the power in Congress to enforce the articles by appropriate legislation, clothes Congress with power to pass all laws necessary and proper for abolishing all badges and incidents of slavery in the United States; and upon this assumption it is claimed that this is sufficient authority for declaring by law that all persons shall have equal accommodations and privileges in all inns, public conveyances, and places of public amusement; the argument being that the denial of such equal accommodations and privileges is in itself a subjection to a species of servitude within the meaning of the amendment. Conceding the major prosposition to be true, that Congress has a right to enact all necessary and proper laws for the obliteration and prevention of slavery with all its badges and incidents, is the minor proposition also true, that the denial to any person of admission to the accommodations and privileges of an inn, a public conveyance, or a theatre, does subject that person to any form of servitude, or tend to fasten upon him any badge of slavery? If it does not, then power to pass the law is not found in the Thirteenth Amendment. . . .

But is there any similarity between such servitudes and a denial by the owner of an inn, a public conveyance, or a theatre, of its accommodations and privileges to an individual, even though the denial be founded on the race or color of that individual? Where does any slavery or ser-

[20] *United States Reports,* 109 U.S. 20-25.

vitude, or badge of either, arise from such an act of denial? Whether it might not be a denial of a right which, if sanctioned by the state law, would be obnoxious to the prohibitions of the Fourteenth Amendment, is another question. But what has it to do with the question of slavery? . . .

The long existence of African slavery in this country gave us very distinct notions of what it was, and what were its necessary incidents. Compulsory service of the slave for the benefit of the master, restraint of his movements except by the master's will, disability to hold property, to make contracts, to have a standing in court, to be a witness against a white person, and such like burdens and incapacities were the inseparable incidents of the institution. . . . Can the act of a mere individual, the owner of the inn, the public conveyance, or place of amusement, refusing the accommodation, be justly regarded as imposing any badge of slavery or servitude upon the applicant, or only as inflicting an ordinary civil injury, properly cognizable by the laws of the State, and presumably subject to redress by those laws until the contrary appears?

After giving to these questions all the consideration which their importance demands, we are forced to the conclusion that such an act of refusal has nothing to do with slavery or involuntary servitude, and that if it is violative of any right of the party, his redress is to be sought under the laws of the State; or, if those laws are adverse to his rights and do not protect him, his remedy will be found in the corrective legislation which Congress has adopted, or may adopt, for counteracting the effect of state laws, or state action, prohibited by the Fourteenth Amendment. It would be running the slavery argument into the ground to make it apply to every act of discrimination which a person may see fit to make as to the guests he will entertain, or as to the people he will take into his coach or cab or car, or admit to his concert or theatre, or deal with in other matters of intercourse or business. . . .

When a man has emerged from slavery, and by the aid of beneficent legislation has shaken off the inseparable concomitants of that state, there must be some stage in the progress of his elevation when he takes the rank of a mere citizen, and ceases to be the special favorite of the laws, and when his rights as a citizen, or a man, are to be protected in the ordinary modes by which other men's rights are protected. There were thousands of free colored people in this country before the abolition of slavery, enjoying all the essential rights of life, liberty and property the same as white citizens; yet no one, at that time, thought that it was any invasion of his personal status as a freeman because he was not admitted to all the privileges enjoyed by white citizens, or because he was subjected to discriminations in the enjoyment of accommodations in inns, public conveyances and places of amusement. Mere discriminations on account of race or color were not regarded as badges of slavery. If, since that time, the enjoyment of equal rights in all these respects has become established by constitutional enactment, it is not by force of the Thirteenth Amendment (which merely abolishes slavery), but by force of the Fourteenth and Fifteenth Amendments.

On the whole we are of the opinion that no countenance of authority for the passage of the law in question can be found in either the Thirteenth or Fourteenth Amendment of the Constitution; and no other ground of authority for its passage being suggested, it must necessarily be declared void, at least so far as its operation in the several States is concerned.

## THE LEGACY OF RECONSTRUCTION

### 21

Reconstruction bequeathed a legacy of hatred, fear, and bigotry to America. The brief period of Republican rule in the South convinced Bourbons that Negroes must be perpetually repressed if white rule was to be established below Mason and Dixon's line. This could be done only by voting for the party of the whites—the Democratic party—and systematically stripping away political privileges of Negroes who might vote the Republican ticket. The tragic result was the emergence of the Solid South, which for generations never strayed from the Democratic column. The effects have been assessed by a modern student of politics, Arthur N. Holcombe, in his study of *The Political Parties of Today*:[21]

The extent of this advantage which the South and the Democratic party gained through the failure of negro suffrage is reflected in the figures showing the distribution of the Congressmen between the sections under the successive apportionments. By the apportionment based on the census of 1850, New England and the three Middle Atlantic states had 92 representatives in the Congress of the United States and the Northeast was the leading section of the country. The fifteen slave states . . . came next with 90 representatives. The old Northwest, comprising the present Central and North Central sections, followed with 52 representatives. The Far West had two representatives. During the succeeding forty years the Central, North Central, and West Central sections grew more rapidly than any other part of the country and steadily advanced in population until in 1890, if the Fifteenth Amendment had not been adopted, it would have been easily in first place, on the basis of representation in Congress, and the South would have been in third place. But actually the South jumped into first place after 1870 and in 1890 had 127 representatives, while the Northeast had only 99 and the Central, North Central, and West Central sections had 113. The Mountain and Pacific sections had 18 representatives. The additional representation which the

Southern states received under the Fifteenth Amendment fell largely to the Lower South. There were between 25 and 30 of these additional representatives under the apportionment based on the census of 1870, and probably as many as 35 under the apportionment based on the census of 1890. At least two-thirds of these additional representatives went to the eight states of the Lower South, the balance to the other states in which slavery had formerly existed. The corresponding increase of Southern representation in the electoral college did not affect the result of any presidential election during this period, but without these additional Congressmen the Democrats more than once would have had to yield the control of the Congress to the Republicans.

The indirect effects of the failure of negro suffrage in the South were more important to the Republicans than the direct. The solidification of the South in support of the Democratic party compelled the Republican leaders to fall back on sectional appeals such as had been the original justification of the party before the Civil War. But now the war was over, and the conscience of the North and West responded to Grant's magnanimous plea, "Let us have peace." People wearied of "waving the bloody shirt". . . . Though freely indulged in by Republican politicians during the political campaigns of this period, it was discountenanced by the better elements of the party. At Republican national conventions, too, Southern delegates demanded that something be done to protect the political rights of the freedmen, and, despite the reluctance of prudent politicians to stir up old animosities, it was difficult to resist these appeals. In 1890, when for the first time since 1875 the Republicans had a working majority in both branches of the Congress and also controlled the Presidency, a so-called Force Bill was introduced into the Congress for the purpose of establishing effective federal supervision of presidential

[21] *The Political Parties of Today* by Arthur N. Holcombe, pp. 190-195. Copyright, 1929, by Harper & Brothers.

and congressional elections. The popular outcry against this measure throughout the country doubtless contributed to the Republican defeat in the congressional elections of that year, the worst the party has ever suffered. Despite the popular criticism, the measure passed the House, but failed in the Senate through the defection of eight Silver Republicans from the Far West. Since that time the Republican party has made no further attempt to use the authority of the federal government to secure the right to vote for negroes in the Southern states.

The most far-sighted Republican leaders had foreseen the failure of negro suffrage in the South unless something more were done for the freedmen than merely to give them the franchise. They recognized that without economic independence and political intelligence the vote alone is worth little. The expression, "forty acres and a mule," indicates the kind of foundation some of them deemed essential for the free development of the negro. But nothing substantial was done by the federal government during the period of reconstruction to set the negro upon his feet. He was left to find his way for himself as best he could. Later, wise leaders advocated federal aid to education in the South with a view to encouraging the intellectual development of the negro. President Garfield was especially interested in such plans. . . . One of the unfortunate results of his assassination was the loss of his leadership in this promising enterprise. Doubtless it will be a great advantage to this country in the long run that no state can ever make any civil or political discrimination against any class of citizens on account of their race, or color, or previous condition. In a country like ours, where racial differences are great and racial animosities can be easily aroused by unscrupulous politicians, it is well that racial discrimination should be made as difficult as possible. The individual must be dealt with as far as possible on his individual merits. Hence the adoption of the Fifteenth Amendment should prove in the end a great service to the American people. But the immediate consequences were disappointing, both to the Southern negro and to the Republican party. It did not secure the vote for the former, and it did not secure political supremacy for the latter.

Although the Fifteenth Amendment failed to accomplish what had been expected from it at the elections which followed the period of reconstruction, it was not without important effects upon the internal organization of the party itself. The suppression of most of the negro vote in the South threw the party organization in the Southern states into the hands of a few local leaders and bosses, who found ways of turning their partisan activities to account, even if they could not hope to win public elections. When the Republicans controlled the Presidency, these Southern politicians enjoyed the federal patronage and other perquisites in their section of the country. Whether the Republicans were in or out of power at Washington, the federal officeholders and would-be officeholders at the South controlled the delegations from that section to the national nominating conventions. They held the balance of power in all contests among Northern Republicans for the presidential nominations and had little incentive to consult any interests but their own in the disposition of their votes. At every national convention since 1876 the struggle for the votes of the Southern delegates has exercised a demoralizing influence. When the party has been in power at Washington, the administration candidate has always had an advantage over his competitors. That advantage was not great enough to enable Secretary Sherman to win over Grant and Blaine in 1880, nor to enable President Arthur to renominate himself against the opposition of powerful Blaine delegations from the big Republican states of the North in 1884. But it was a very disturbing factor in the convention of 1888, and it enabled President Harrison to defeat Blaine and McKinley in 1892. The greatest mischief, however, did not arise until a later period in the history of the party.

The creation of the Solid South had an unfortunate effect also on the Democratic party. Since there was no substantial opposition to the Democratic party in the eight states of the Lower South, and not enough in the eight other states, where slavery had formerly existed, to make the success of Democratic candidates very doubtful, there was little need for the Democratic party to consider the opinions of the people in those sections on questions of national concern. The national policy of the Democratic party, as defined by the national conventions, was determined by the Northern Democrats. But when the party got into power, the execution of the policy, so far as it was dependent on Acts of Congress, was largely in the hands of the Senators and Representatives from the South who under the rule of seniority generally dominated the important committees and controlled the course of business. The Democrats who wrote the party platforms were not the ones who would carry them into effect. Moreover, since the electoral votes of sixteen states were almost certain to be cast for the Democratic presidential candidate, whoever he might be, it was not necessary to give much consideration to the aspirations of Democratic leaders from that part of the country. No man of Southern birth received the Democratic nomination for the Presidency until 1912, and no active politician from a Southern state has yet been nominated. Doubtless much of the unavailability of Southern politicians was the result of the sectional jealousies caused by the Civil War, but the complete exclusion of Southern Democrats from the lists of candidates considered by the national conventions would have been much less likely if the South had been less solid in its support of the Democratic party. The attempt to establish

negro suffrage, and the concentration of the white voters in one party in order to maintain white supremacy in local politics, were the direct causes of the practical abdication by Southern leaders of their legitimate authority in national politics. In effect they traded their influence in the councils of the party at Washington for the privilege of unrestricted home rule in the state and local governments.

## 22

But the tragedy of reconstruction can be found in the souls of men as well as in columns of election figures. For these Langston Hughes, poet of equality, spoke in "I, Too, Sing America":[22]

### I, TOO, SING AMERICA

I am the darker brother.
They send me to eat in the kitchen
When company comes,
But I laugh,
And eat well,
And grow strong.

Tomorrow,
I'll sit at the table
When company comes.
Nobody'll dare
Say to me,
"Eat in the kitchen,"
Then.

Besides,
They'll see how beautiful I am
And be ashamed,—

I, too, am America.

Langston Hughes's simple words suggest one aspect of the tragedy of reconstruction. To heal the wounds of war, to unite a separated people, and to secure equality for the freed slaves could not be achieved in a single generation. Division rather than unity was the result. In 1876, North and South were still

[22] From *The Dream Keeper and Other Poems* by Langston Hughes, by permission of Alfred A. Knopf, Inc. Copyright 1932 by Alfred A. Knopf, Inc.

wide apart; class conflicts were sharpened, whites and Negroes as divided as they had been when the guns of war were stilled. Yet those who dreamed of better things did not dream wholly in vain. The industrialization of the United States, advancing swiftly as politicians wrangled over reconstruction policies, was to recast society. Ultimately the problems of the Civil War were to be succeeded by other and newer problems.

# THE BANKRUPTCY OF POLITICS

## 1865–1884

Appomattox marked the end of a civilization as well as the end of an era. During the forty years after Lee's tattered troops laid down their arms, an industrial expansion without parallel in the world's history occurred. The factory finally displaced the farm as the typical economic unit; the city ultimately became the dwelling place of most Americans. The revolutions in production, transportation, and manner of living provided spectacular wealth for the fortunate few, and introduced undreamed-of comforts for the many. Yet the results were not all beneficial. For the New World was not created solely by the tangible and visual alterations that changed the face of the land—the cities, factories, and machines. There were intangible and invisible alterations that reshaped attitudes, values, and ways of behavior. Adjustment to the new mechanized environment was terrifyingly difficult, and for generations men suffered no less than they gained from the process of industrialization. In the realm of politics, as elsewhere, the consequences were sooner or later apparent.

## THE PROGRAM OF BUSINESS

### 1

Politically speaking, the years from 1865 to 1884 were marked by drabness, corruption, and lack of democratic gain. The most efficient device yet worked out for registering majorities—the two-party system—still operated effectively; competition between Democrats and Republicans for power was bitter, intense, and constant. The failure of the parties to serve as creative instruments of popular rule was due to two factors. One was the attitude of most politicians; dazzled by the wealth of the industrial titans, they consciously or unconsciously truckled to the demands of industry until the platforms of both parties reflected the wishes of business rather than those of the people. The other was the rise of pressure groups; in effect the parties abdicated after each election, leaving Congress in the hands of powerful minorities bent on securing legislation for special interests. The achievement of a political program dear to the hearts of business leaders was the result. A Homestead Act to assure expanding markets as well as an opportunity to profit from engrossing the national domain, a centralized banking system, a "sound" currency, advantageous labor laws, and a steadily rising tariff were all demanded and achieved. Of these measures, the first to be adopted was the Homestead Act, passed by Congress in 1862 after the southern states had withdrawn from the Union:[1]

[1] *United States Statutes at Large,* XII, 392-412.

AN ACT *to secure homesteads to actual settlers on the public domain.*

*Be it enacted,* That any person who is the head of a family, or who has arrived at the age of twenty-one years, and is a citizen of the United States, or who shall have filed his declaration of intention to become such, as required by the naturalization laws of the United States, and who has never borne arms against the United States Government or given aid and comfort to its enemies, shall, from and after the first of January, eighteen hundred and sixty-three, be entitled to enter one quarter-section or a less quantity of unappropriated public lands, upon which said person may have filed a pre-emption claim, or which may, at the time the application is made, be subject to pre-emption at one dollar and twenty-five cents, or less, per acre; or eighty acres or less of such unappropriated lands, at two dollars and fifty cents per acre, to be located in a body, in conformity to the legal subdivisions of the public lands, and after the same shall have been surveyed: *Provided,* That any person owning or residing on land may, under the provisions of this act, enter other land lying contiguous to his or her said land, which shall not, with the land so already owned and occupied, exceed in the aggregate one hundred and sixty acres. . . .

SECTION 2. That the person applying for the benefit of this act shall, upon application to the register of the land office in which he or she is about to make such entry, make affidavit before the said register or receiver that he or she is the head of a family, or is twenty-one or more years of age, or shall have performed service in the Army or Navy of the United States, and that he has never borne arms against the Government of the United States or given aid and comfort to its enemies, and that such application is made for his or her exclusive use and benefit, and that said entry is made for the purpose of actual settlement and cultivation, and not, either directly or indirectly, for the use or benefit of any other person or persons whomsoever; and upon filing the said affidavit with the register or receiver, and on payment of ten dollars, he or she shall thereupon be permitted to enter the quantity of land specified: *Provided, however,* That no certificate shall be given or patent issued therefor until the expiration of five years from the date of such entry; and if, at the expiration of such time, or at any time within two years thereafter, the person making such entry—or if he be dead, his widow; or in case of her death, his heirs or devisee; or in case of a widow making such entry, her heirs or devisee, in case of her death—shall prove by two credible witnesses that he, she, or they have resided upon or cultivated the same for the term of five years immediately succeeding the time of filing the affidavit aforesaid, and shall make affidavit that no part of said land has been alienated, and that he has borne true allegiance to the Government of the United States; then, in such case, he, she, or they, if at that time a citizen of the United States, shall be entitled to a patent, as in other cases provided for by law: *And provided, further,* That in case of the death of both father and mother, leaving an infant child or children under twenty-one years of age, the right and fee shall inure to the benefit of said infant child or children; and the executor, administrator, or guardian may, at any time within two years after the death of the surviving parent, and in accordance with the laws of the State in which such children for the time being have their domicile, sell said land for the benefit of said infants, but for no other purpose; and the purchaser shall acquire the absolute title by the purchase, and be entitled to a patent from the United States, on payment of the office fees and sum of money herein specified. . . .

## 2

To Americans of the generation after the Civil War, the Homestead Act seemed a humanitarian measure: a generous government offered fertile acres to the poor of the world. And this was indeed the purpose behind the law. Yet the act was so loosely drawn that its laudable objectives were soon negated; speculators found ways to engross the best lands, leaving to the homesteaders only the poorer regions far removed from transportation. Modern scholars estimate that for every acre obtained free by an actual settler, ten passed into the hands of jobbers for resale at exorbitant profits. This process was described by William A. J. Sparks, a sincere reformer who in 1885 became Commissioner of the General Land Office. His first report expressed both incredulity and disgust:[2]

The widespread belief of the people of this country that the land department has been very largely conducted to the advantage of speculation and monopoly, private and corporate, rather than in the public interest, I have found supported by developments in every branch of the service. It seems that the prevailing idea running through this office and those subordinate to it was that the government had no distinctive rights to be considered and no special interests to protect; hence, as between the government and spoilers of the public domain, the government usually had the

[2] "Report of the Commissioner of the General Land Office," *House Executive Documents,* 49th Cong., 1st Sess., XI, 155-156, 217-218.

worst of it. I am satisfied that thousands of claims without foundation in law or equity, involving millions of acres of public land, have been annually passed to patent upon the single proposition that nobody but the government had any *adverse* interest.

The vast machinery of the land department appears to have been devoted to the chief result of conveying the title of the United States to public lands upon fraudulent entries under strained constructions of imperfect public land laws and upon illegal claims under public and private grants. I shall endeavor in this report to point out some of the evidences which illustrate the truth of these general statements. . . .

The pre-emption law provides that all assignments and transfers of the pre-emption right "prior to the issuing of the patent shall be null and void." The homestead laws require proof that the party has not alienated the land, and provide that no land acquired under those laws shall be liable to the satisfaction of any debt contracted prior to the issue of patent. But it is notorious that pre-emption and commuted homestead entries are almost invariably sold, and with equal invariability are made for the purpose of being sold. The most common method by which the transfer is effected is by a power of sale mortgage running for one month or some other brief period of time, which is promptly foreclosed as a matter of course and arrangement. Yet the transferees and mortgagees appear before this office in the attitude of "innocent purchasers" and claim the right to show the "good faith" of the entryman. A hearing is ordered, witnesses for the government tampered with or intimidated, the special agent impeded, threatened, or sought to be influenced or his removal or assignment to another locality attempted through the numerous and varied means of effecting results, or an endeavor is made to swear down ascertained facts by obvious falsehood and well-understood bribery and subornation of perjury. Scores of a class of men known as "cowboys" have been brought up to swear to the residence and improvement of each other on lands uninhabited except by the cattle of their employers; gangs of men hired to cut timber are also hired to swear that logging-camps are "homes" and the timber trespass an "improvement"; and settlers who have appeared as witnesses for the government against entries fraudulently covering up agricultural lands near their homes have had their crops destroyed, and others have been warned to leave the country by "regulators" employed by the procurers of the fraudulent entries. High financial and professional influences have been brought to bear to discredit agents honest enough to do their duty and for the purpose of causing re-examinations and re-hearings to be made or conducted under more pliant auspices. If, after all the machinations, hindrances, evasions, and delays that can be resorted to for obstructing or defeating the reproduction, at a formal hearing, of facts originally discovered by the personal examination of a special agent and testimony taken by him under oath, including the testimony of entrymen, if they could be found, a decision is ultimately rendered against the entry, the assignee takes technical appeals to this office and to the Secretary, and two or three years are consumed in an effort to cancel the most palpably fraudulent and worst classes of collusive, procured, and perjured entries, even those made in names well known to be fictitious. It is my opinion that assignees or mortgagees of homestead, pre-emption, and other entries, conditional upon acts of settlement or improvement and not transferable under the law, have no right to be heard either in place of the alleged entrymen or in their own behalf, and that to permit their intervention or to recognize in any manner their assumed interest is to promote violations of law. But the rulings of the Department, I regret to say, have been to allow them.

Pre-emption and homestead entries are allowed for the purpose of enabling entrymen to establish homes on the public domain. Such entries are not authorized for sale and speculation. A party who makes an entry under these laws, and punctually at the expiration of six months pays up, sells the land, and moves away, leaving the future issue of patent to inure to the benefit of an assignee or mortgagee, proves by his act, even if he has ostensibly "resided" on his claim for the conventional six months, that his entry was not made in good faith for the purpose of a home, but in bad faith, for the purpose of selling it to somebody else, as he has done. It is one of the anomalies in the operation of the homestead and pre-emption laws that deficient residence and meager improvements are always sought to be excused on plea of poverty, but the alleged settler making these hasty proofs is never too poor to pay $200 to $400 to the government, as the case may be, at the first moment of time he is permitted to do it, and long before the laws require him to do so.

It is impossible to execute the laws if violations and evasions of them are systematically permitted or condoned, and it is impossible to protect the public domain from fraudulent appropriation if the government is to be put to protracted trials, under the forms and rules of criminal procedure, . . . to reach a determination by the Commissioner whether an entry is made to his satisfaction, as it is required to be before he is authorized to certify for the issue of a patent upon it. Land office proceedings to ascertain whether an entryman is entitled to a patent for land are not in the nature of indictments for criminal offenses. The government has land to donate and also to sell. The question is whether the party seeking the donation or offering to purchase has brought himself within the law and is entitled to the donation or to make the purchase. The Commissioner is to judge. He may obtain his facts by the most direct methods available.

No method can be more direct, and none more conclusive, than a personal examination. The Commissioner cannot in person make that examination; he must have agencies to do it. Sworn officers of the government are provided him for that purpose. I think nothing else is required except that a sufficient number of agents should be authorized to inspect all claims and investigate all entries before patent is issued on any of them.

That the abuses of the public land laws are largely due to inefficient administration, to the conduct of weak or corrupt officials, and to erratic and fanciful decisions, is undeniable; but that the laws themselves are defective in want of adequate safeguards is also true. That they are improvident in providing so many different forms of appropriation is more palpable still. The pre-emption law has outlived its usefulness; the timber-culture and desert-land laws have not met the purposes for which they were designed; the timber-land act of 1878 has proved available to scarcely any honest purpose; and the commutation feature of the homestead law has undermined the homestead system, while various minor provisions applicable to different laws, such as allowing credit for time before entry, legalizing traffic in relinquishments, and permitting *ex-parte* affidavits to be taken as proofs before a multitude of officers not responsible to the United States, have made fraud easy and prevention difficult. If the rapidly disappearing lands of the nation are to be preserved for actual settlement—not in the distant future, but by the present generation only—a reformation of the public land laws is essential as a basis for the reform of the evil systems that have grown up under them as they now exist.

### 3

The Homestead Act, even though passed with mixed motives and corruptly administered, helped to open the West. Yet something more was needed to satisfy the business interests of the East. A railroad to the Pacific was also on the agenda. An American dream since the 1840's, it was not until the Civil War period that the dream could be fulfilled. The debate over the charter of the Union Pacific Railroad illustrated the close connection between manufacturing and commerce. Virtually every congressional orator from the East who spoke in behalf of the road stressed its benefits to American business. Typical of the views on the West Coast was the speech delivered before the House of Representatives on April 9, 1862, by Timothy G. Phelps of California:[3]

There are, then, two good reasons why we should pass this bill, either one of which is sufficient to justify its passage, namely: it is a military necessity; and, secondly, it is absolutely essential to our internal development. But there is another reason, which would be sufficient of itself to induce any European Government, under similar circumstances, not only to give the aid proposed, but to wholly construct the road in the speediest possible way; and that is, sir, the fact that beyond its western terminus lie Japan, China, and the East Indies, with their more than four hundred millions of industrial inhabitants, whose commerce, the most tempting prize ever within the reach of any country, may be secured thereby. To secure this commerce would not only add vastly to our national wealth, but it would build up, through individual enterprise and the currents of trade opened by it, such a fleet of steam and sail vessels, and give us such a naval predominance upon the Pacific, as would enable us to defy the maritime Powers of the world on that ocean, and would render our Pacific possessions safe within themselves for all time to come. And not only would we derive the advantages of an increased trade and national security, but we would save in the present condition of our commerce, as may be learned from facts within the reach of all, on freight, interest, and insurance on

our precious metals, and on our money exchanges, an amount every ten years equal to the entire cost of the road. As this source of drainage upon our national wealth does not appear to have been much examined into, I beg the indulgence of the House for a few moments to present some facts in relation to it.

Our imports from China, in the year 1857, amounted to $8,356,932, and our domestic exports to China amounted to $3,019,900, leaving a balance of trade against us of $5,337,032. In 1858, our imports from that country amounted to $10,570,536, and our domestic exports to only $2,467,645, leaving a balance against us of $8,102,891. In 1860, the amount of our imports from the same source was $13,566,641, and that of our domestic exports $7,170,784, leaving a balance against us of $6,395,802. These figures exclude the exports of gold and silver. For the years 1859 and 1861 I have been unable to obtain the statistics.

It will be observed that our trade with this nation is rapidly increasing, our imports having increased from 1857 to 1860 about sixty per cent., while our exports of domestic produce show the gratifying increase of more than one hundred and thirty-three per cent. This commerce, so rapidly increasing in importance, needs facilities which it does not now possess; and by giving the facilities necessary to its prospective growth, such as England and all other nations so willingly extend to interests of like magnitude, it may be extended and increased, until at an early day it will profitably absorb annually millions of dollars' worth of our manufactured goods, and all of the gold and silver taken from the mines of California, Oregon, Washington, and Nevada, and give remunerative employment to a merchant fleet as large as that which we now possess.

It is not reasonable to suppose, under any circumstances, that the balance against us in our trade with China, will, at any time, be less than in the year 1860—

[3] *Congressional Globe*, 37th Cong., 2nd Sess., p. 1592.

say $6,400,000 in round numbers. This amount of indebtedness is now mostly paid through English houses, at a cost to us of about twenty per cent. At the present rates of exchange, then, the balance against us, to be paid by remittances of money or bills of credit, will cost us annually the sum of $1,280,000; that is to say, the $6,400,000 purchased by us in excess of our exports, will really cost us $7,680,000. This exchange, of course, is paid in part by every person who consumes a dollar's worth of Chinese goods, as it becomes a part of their cost; and one section of the country is as much interested in reducing the amount as another, it being placed upon the people of the entire country as equally as the duty on imports or any other tax. If we can by the construction of this road open a new channel of commerce which will turn this treasure current to direct shipments, which can be made from San Francisco in twenty-three days, saving from the present specie route at least sixty days in time, reducing the cost of shipment, including exchange, freight, interest, and insurance, to not exceeding four per cent., it would make, annually, a net saving to our people of $984,000. To the sum thus saved should be added the cost of shipment of the same amount of treasure from San Francisco to New York, which cannot be done at less rates than three and one half per cent., and would amount to $259,000. I may very properly add, that the entire balance of trade against us, in what is known in mercantile parlance as the "East India trade," will not fall short of $18,000,000 per annum. On this sum the saving in exchange would amount to $3,600,000.

But, sir, these are but a small portion of the benefits the country would derive from changing the specie route of the world into American channels of trade. It is estimated that the annual balance of trade against Europe and America, and in favor of the Mongolian race, reaches an aggregate of less than $50,000,000. This vast sum should be met by the shipment of gold and silver from San Francisco; and our merchants on the Atlantic sea-board, instead of buying exchange in England to pay for purchases in China, should themselves sell to England and all Europe the exchange to pay their balances. When we reflect that almost the whole of the silver shipped to China and the East Indies is collected on the Pacific coasts of North and South America, and shipped thence across the Isthmus of Panama, via London and Suez, to the point of its destination, thus traversing three fourths of the circumference of the globe, we may well marvel that our Government has failed for the last ten years to appreciate fully the importance of changing these currents of trade by building a continental road, to direct shipments from our own ports by our own people, and by so doing have made New York, instead of London, the point at which the world's balance should be settled. We have probably paid to Europe for exchange or credits in the East, during the last ten years, not less than $14,000,000; and to pay our European balance, our merchants have paid for exchange and freight from the Atlantic sea-board to Europe probably not less than $10,000,000. The gold to pay these balances during that time has been drawn from San Francisco, and has been shipped to New York, at a cost to our miners and merchants of not less than the sum of $20,000,000—making, in the aggregate, $44,000,000, which has been paid for *freight* on gold and silver and exchange, which might have been saved, almost wholly, by building this road and the establishment of steam communication between San Francisco and the East, which its construction would have immediately caused to be done ten years ago.

Nor is this all, sir. A profit on this freight and the world's exchange, which now goes to England, amounting to nearly as much more, would have been realized by our commerce and people. Thus the country is sixty or, perhaps, seventy-five millions of dollars poorer to-day because of our failure to discern and improve our opportunities in this direction.

I am aware, sir, these are startling figures, but they are, nevertheless, correct, being made up from actual computation of our trade and balances, and the rates of exchange as they have existed. For the last half century China has been the silver market of the world; thither have flowed and converged the silver currents of the globe. Within the last two years, and while our attention has been particularly directed to the subject of Asiatic commerce, we have discovered almost upon our western borders the silver mines of Washoe and Esmeralda, abounding in wealth in this metal beyond the ability of man to compute. It is estimated by those competent to judge, that the yield of Washoe alone, for the coming year, will amount to $20,000,000, and this, too, in the very infancy of those mines. When a sufficiency of proper machinery is introduced, probably within two or three years, the yield will not be less than thirty or forty millions of dollars per annum. The question, sir, is, shall we take such steps as will lead to the sending of this silver to its natural market directly, and reap all the advantages to be gained by so doing, or shall we pursue the old narrow-minded policy which has governed us so long, and allow it to take the route via Panama, New York, London, and Suez, a distance of twenty-five thousand miles from our shores, ourselves losing the freight, interest, and exchange, and giving to another and a rival nation the profits which should be our own? In other words, shall we avail ourselves of our own resources and apply them to our own benefit, or shall we continue to be in this respect, at least, a mere tributary, serving to swell the current of a rival's wealth, commerce, and power?

This subject is not one which concerns the Pacific coast alone, but is eminently national; New York, Boston, and the whole country being quite as much inter-ested as the Pacific States. If any one section, in fact, is more interested than another, it is the great cities of the East, for it is there the balances of trade would be settled, and the profits of exchange would be paid. California has, however, an interest peculiar to herself in changing the present specie route. The balance of trade against her, and in favor of her Atlantic sisters with whom she deals, is about forty millions of dollars per annum. This amount she pays by shipments of gold, at a cost in freight, interest, and insurance, of little less than two millions of dollars per annum. If trade was changed, as it would be by a continental road, this balance against her would be adjusted by shipments to China, at the expense and to the credit of the merchants of New York, Boston, and Philadelphia, thus saving California this large item of expense, and largely benefiting them, as the money thus placed to her credit would settle their balances due China and the Indies, and form the basis of exchange to be sold to English and European merchants. I should not fail to notice in this connection, as a matter of great commercial importance, the fact that the Chinese are beginning to receive with much favor gold and silver bullion, and it is probable that hereafter gold will be as acceptable to them as silver, and we may use as much of it in our trade with them as may be desirable.

## 4

Business leaders yearned for more than lands and resources to exploit; they also wanted tariff protection for industry. Between the Civil War and the close of the century (with rare exceptions), the tariff levels moved smoothly upward as pressure groups vied with docile politicians in catering to the demands of American manufacturers. Some of the congressmen who cried "aye" for each new increase were the tools of the steel or textile interests; more, however, sincerely believed that protection would benefit workers and farmers as well as producers. The speech of Justin S. Morrill of Vermont on December 8,

1881, displayed conviction and endeared him to the hearts of businessmen:[4]

As a protective measure this tariff [Morrill tariff of 1861], with all its increasing amendments, has proven more satisfactory to the people than any other on record. The jury of the country has so recorded its verdict. Agriculture has made immense strides forward. The recent exports of food products, though never larger, is not equal by twenty-fold to home consumption, and prices are everywhere more remunerative, agricultural products being higher and manufactures lower. Of wheat, corn and oats there was produced 1,184,540,849 bushels in 1860, but in 1880 the crop had swelled to 2,622,200,030 bushels, or had much more than doubled. Since 1860 lands in many of the Western States have risen from 100 to 175 per cent. The production of rice, during the same time, rose from 11,000,000 pounds to 117,000,000. The fires of the tall chimneys have everywhere been lighted up; and while we made only 987,559 tons of pig iron in 1860, in 1880 we made 4,295,414 tons; and of railroad iron the increase was from 235,107 tons to 1,461,837 tons. In twenty years the production of salt rose from 12,717,200 bushels to 29,800,298 bushels. No previous crop of cotton equalled the 4,861,000 bales of 1860; but the crop of 1880 was larger, and that of 1881 is reported at 6,606,000 bales. The yield of cotton from 1865 to 1881 shows an increase over the fifteen years from 1845 to 1861 of 14,029,000 bales, or almost an average gain of a million bales a year.

The giant water-wheels have revolved more briskly, showing the manufacture of 1,797,000 bales of cotton in 1880 against only 979,000 bales in 1860, and this brought up the price of raw cotton to higher figures than in 1860. . . .

The length of our railroads has been trebled, rising from 31,185 miles in 1860 to 94,000 miles in 1881, and possibly to one-half of all in the world. For commercial purposes the wide area of our country has been compressed within narrow limits, and transportation in time and expense, from New York to Kansas, or from Chicago to Baltimore, is now less formidable than it was from Albany or Pittsburgh to Philadelphia prior to the era of railroads. . . . Workingmen, including every shipload of emigrants, have found acceptable employment. Our aggregate wealth in 1860 was 19,089,156,289, but is estimated to have advanced in 1880 to over forty billions. Further examination will show that the United States are steadily increasing in wealth, and increasing, too, much more rapidly than free trade England, notwithstanding all her early advantages of practical experience and her supremacy in accumulated capital. The increase of wealth in France is twice as rapid as in England, but in the United States it is more rapid than even in France. . . .

Many American productions sustain the character they have won by being the best in the world. Our carpenters and joiners cannot be hired to handle any other than American tools; and there are no foreign agricultural implements, from a spade to a reaper, that an American farmer would accept as a gift. There is no saddlery hardware nor house-furnishing, equal in quality and style to American. Watches and jewelry and the electric gold and silver plated ware of American workmanship as to quality have the foremost place in the marts of the world. The superiority of our staple cotton goods is indisputable, as is proven by the tribute of frequent counterfeits displayed abroad. The city of Philadelphia alone makes many better carpets and more in quantity than the whole of Great Britain. These are notable achievements, which should neither be obscured nor lost by the sinister handling and industrious vituperation of free trade monographists. . . .

---

[4] *Congressional Record*, 47th Cong., 1st Sess., XIII, 55-63.

In six years, ending June 30, 1881, our exports of merchandise exceeded imports by over $1,175,000,000—a large sum in itself, largely increasing our stock of gold, filling the pockets of the people with more than two hundred and fifty millions not found in the treasury or banks, making the return to specie payments easy, and arresting the painful drain of interest so long paid abroad. It is also a very conclusive refutation of the wild free trade chimeras that exports are dependent upon imports, and that comparatively high duties are invariably less productive of revenue than low duties. . . .

## 5

Efforts of business leaders to secure a "sound" currency were complicated by the inflationary "greenbacks" in circulation at the close of the Civil War. These paper dollars, backed only by the credit of the government, fluctuated violently under speculative pressure during the presidential years of Ulysses S. Grant. The President, although alarmed, hesitated to abolish the greenbacks, fearing the business effects of currency contraction. When the Supreme Court, in the case of *Hepburn* v. *Griswold* (1870), decided that greenbacks were not legal tender for obligations entered into before the time they were issued, the President acted. Grant filled two convenient vacancies on the Supreme Court bench with men known to favor his point of view, and ordered his attorney general to move for a rehearing of the issue. In the second Legal Tender Case, *Knox* v. *Lee* (1871), by reversing themselves and sustaining the constitutionality of the greenbacks, the justices indicated that they were not immune to growing business pressure:[5]

The controlling questions in these cases are the following: Are the acts of Congress, known as the legal tender acts, constitutional when applied to contracts made before their passage; and, secondly, Are they valid as applicable to debts contracted

[5] 12 WALLACE 529-553.

since their enactment? . . . It would be difficult to overestimate the consequences which must follow our decision. They will affect the entire business of the country, and take hold of the possible continued existence of the government. If it be held by this court that Congress has no constitutional power, under any circumstances, or in any emergency, to make treasury notes a legal tender for the payment of all debts (a power confessedly possessed by every independent sovereignty other than the United States), the government is without those means of self-preservation which, all must admit, may, in certain contingencies, become indispensable, even if they were not when the acts of Congress now called in question were enacted. . . .

The consequences of which we have spoken, serious as they are, must be accepted, if there is a clear incompatibility between the Constitution and the legal tender acts. But we are unwilling to precipitate them upon the country unless such incompatibility plainly appears. A decent respect for a co-ordinate branch of the government demands that the judiciary should presume, until the contrary is clearly shown, that there has been no transgression of power by Congress—all the members of which act under the obligation of an oath of fidelity to the Constitution. . . .

Nor can it be questioned that, when investigating the nature and extent of the powers conferred by the Constitution upon Congress, it is indispensable to keep in view the objects for which those powers were granted. This is the universal rule of construction applied alike to statutes, wills, contracts, and constitutions. If the general purpose of the instrument is ascertained, the language of its provisions must be construed with reference to that purpose and so as to subserve it. In no other way can the intent of the framers of the instrument be discovered. And there are more urgent reasons for looking to the ultimate purpose in examining the powers conferred by a constitution than there are in construing a statute, a will, or a contract. We do not expect to find in a constitution minute details. It is necessarily brief and comprehensive. It prescribes outlines, leaving the filling up to be deduced from the outlines. . . .

If these are correct principles, if they are proper views of the manner in which the Constitution is to be understood, the powers conferred upon Congress must be regarded as related to each other, and all means for a common end. Each is but part of a system, a constituent of one whole. No single power is the ultimate end for which the Constitution was adopted. It may, in a very proper sense, be treated as a means for the accomplishment of a subordinate object, but that object is itself a means designed for an ulterior purpose. Thus the powers to levy and collect taxes, to coin money and regulate its value, to raise and support armies, or to provide for and maintain a navy, are instruments for the paramount object, which was to establish a government, sovereign within its sphere, with capability of self-preservation, thereby forming a union more perfect than that which existed under the old Confederacy.

The same may be asserted also of all the non-enumerated powers included in the authority expressly given "to make all laws which shall be necessary and proper for carrying into execution the specified powers vested in Congress, and all other powers vested by the Constitution in the government of the United States, or in any department or officer thereof." It is impossible to know what those non-enumerated powers are, and what is their nature and extent, without considering the purposes they were intended to subserve. Those purposes, it must be noted, reach beyond the mere execution of all powers definitely intrusted to Congress and mentioned in detail. They embrace the execution of

all other powers vested by the Constitution in the government of the United States, or in any department or officer thereof. It certainly was intended to confer upon the government the power of self-preservation. . . .

That would appear, then, to be a most unreasonable construction of the Constitution which denies to the government created by it, the right to employ freely every means, not prohibited, necessary for its preservation, and for the fulfillment of its acknowledged duties. Such a right, we hold, was given by the last clause of the eighth of its first article. The means or instrumentalities referred to in that clause, and authorized, are not enumerated or defined. In the nature of things enumeration and specification were impossible. But they were left to the discretion of Congress, subject only to the restrictions that they be not prohibited, and be necessary and proper for carrying into execution the enumerated powers given to Congress, and all other powers vested in the government of the United States, or in any department or officer thereof.

And here it is to be observed it is not indispensable to the existence of any power claimed for the federal government that it can be found specified in the words of the Constitution, or clearly and directly traceable to some one of the specified powers. Its existence may be deduced fairly from more than one of the substantive powers expressly defined, or from them all combined. It is allowable to group together any number of them and infer from them all that the power claimed has been conferred. . . . And it is of importance to observe that Congress has often exercised, without question, powers that are not expressly given nor ancillary to any single enumerated power. Powers thus exercised are what are called by Judge Story, in his Commentaries on the Constitution, resulting powers, arising from the aggregate powers of the government. He instances the right to sue and make contracts. Many others might be given. The oath required by law from officers of the government is one. So is building a capitol or a presidential mansion, and so also is the penal code. . . .

Indeed, the whole history of the government and of congressional legislation has exhibited the use of a very wide discretion, even in times of peace and in the absence of any trying emergency, in the selection of the necessary and proper means to carry into effect the great objects for which the government was framed, and this discretion has generally been unquestioned, or, if questioned, sanctioned by this court. . . .

Before we can hold the Legal Tender Acts unconstitutional, we must be convinced they were not appropriate means, or means conducive to the execution of any or all of the powers of Congress, or of the government, not appropriate in any plain degree (for we are not judges of the degree of appropriateness), or we must hold that they were prohibited. This brings us to the inquiry whether they were, when enacted, appropriate instrumentalities for carrying into effect, or executing any of the known powers of Congress, or of any department of the government. Plainly, to this inquiry, a consideration of the time when they were enacted, and of the circumstances in which the government then stood, is important. It is not to be denied that acts may be adapted to the exercise of lawful power, and appropriate to it, in seasons of exigency, which would be inappropriate at other times.

We do not propose to dilate at length upon the circumstances in which the country was placed, when Congress attempted to make treasury notes a legal tender. They are of too recent occurrence to justify enlarged description. Suffice it to say that a civil war was then raging which seriously threatened the overthrow of the government and the destruction of the Constitu-

tion itself. It demanded the equipment and support of large armies and navies, and the employment of money to an extent beyond the capacity of all ordinary sources of supply. Meanwhile the public treasury was nearly empty, and the credit of the government, if not stretched to its utmost tension, had become nearly exhausted. . . .

It was at such a time and in such circumstances that Congress was called upon to devise means for maintaining the army and navy, for securing the large supplies of money needed, and, indeed, for the preservation of the government created by the Constitution. It was at such a time and in such an emergency that the Legal Tender Acts were passed. Now, if it were certain that nothing else would have supplied the absolute necessities of the treasury, that nothing else would have enabled the government to maintain its armies and navy, that nothing else would have saved the government and the Constitution from destruction, while the Legal Tender Acts would, could any one be bold enough to assert that Congress transgressed its powers? . . .

But if it be conceded that some other means might have been chosen for the accomplishment of these legitimate and necessary ends, the concession does not weaken the argument. . . . At best this is mere conjecture. But admitting it to be true, what does it prove? Nothing more than that Congress had the choice of means for a legitimate end, each appropriate and adapted to that end, though, perhaps, in different degrees. What then? Can this court say that it ought to have adopted one rather than the other? . . .

We hold the acts of Congress constitutional as applied to contracts made either before or after their passage. In so holding we overrule so much of what was decided in *Hepburn* v. *Griswold,* 8 Wallace, 603, as ruled the acts unwarranted by the Constitution so far as applied to contracts made before their enactment. . . .

## 6

With the legality of the greenbacks established, it remained only to place them on a thoroughly "sound" basis. This seemed particularly pressing to industrialists in the early 1870's, since debtors, farmers, and even some men of business began demanding that the United States redeem its wartime bonds in inflated dollars. Moreover, the panic of 1873 and the Democratic victory in the mid-term elections of 1874 sharpened the problem for the President and the retiring Republican Congress. To hard-money men there was but one way to meet the danger and at the same time to keep greenbacks in circulation: to make them redeemable in gold. President Grant, reflecting current business attitudes, recommended such a step to the lameduck Congress in his annual message of December 7, 1874:[6]

In view of the pledges of the American Congress when our present legal-tender system was adopted, and debt contracted, there should be no delay—certainly no unnecessary delay—in fixing by legislation a method by which we will return to specie. To the accomplishment of this end I invite your special attention. I believe firmly that there can be no prosperous and permanent revival of business and industries until a policy is adopted—with legislation to carry it out—looking to a return to a specie basis. It is easy to conceive that the debtor and speculative classes may think it of value to them to make so-called money abundant until they can throw a portion of their burdens upon others. But even these, I believe, would be disappointed in the result if a course should be pursued which will keep in doubt the value of the legal-tender medium of exchange. A revival of productive industry is needed by all classes; by none more than the holders of property, of whatever sort, with debts to liquidate from realization upon its sale. But admitting that these two classes of citizens are to be benefited

by expansion, would it be honest to give it? Would not the general loss be too great to justify such relief? Would it not be just as honest and prudent to authorize each debtor to issue his own legal-tenders to the extent of his liabilities? Than to do this, would it not be safer, for fear of overissues by unscrupulous creditors, to say that all debt obligations are obliterated in the United States, and now we commence anew, each possessing all he has at the time free from incumbrance? These propositions are too absurd to be entertained for a moment by thinking or honest people. Yet every delay in preparation for final resumption partakes of this dishonesty, and is only less in degree as the hope is held out that a convenient season will at last arrive for the good work of redeeming our pledges to commerce. It will never come, in my opinion, except by positive action by Congress, or by national disasters which will destroy, for a time at least, the credit of the individual and the State at large. A sound currency might be reached by total bankruptcy and discredit of the integrity of the nation and of individuals. I believe it is in the power of Congress at this session to devise such legislation as will renew confidence, revive all the industries, start us on a career of prosperity to last for many years and to save the credit of the nation and of the people. Steps toward the return to a specie basis are the great requisites to this devoutly to be sought for end. There are others which I may touch upon hereafter.

A nation dealing in a currency below that of specie in value labors under two great disadvantages: first, having no use for the world's acknowledged medium of exchange, gold and silver, these are driven out of the country because there is no need for their use; second, the medium of exchange in use being of a fluctuating value—for, after all, it is only worth just what it will purchase of gold and silver, metals having an intrinsic value just in proportion to the honest labor it takes to produce

---

[6] J. D. Richardson (comp.), *Messages and Papers of the Presidents, 1789-1897* (Washington, 1897, 1909; taken from the 1909 vol.), VII, 285-287.

them—a larger margin must be allowed for profit by the manufacturer and producer. It is months from the date of production to the date of realization. Interest upon capital must be charged, and risk of fluctuation in the value of that which is to be received in payment added. Hence high prices, acting as a protection to the foreign producer, who receives nothing in exchange for the products of his skill and labor except a currency good, at a stable value, the world over. It seems to me that nothing is clearer than that the greater part of the burden of existing prostration, for the want of a sound financial system, falls upon the working man, who must after all produce the wealth, and the salaried man, who superintends and conducts business. The burden falls upon them in two ways—by the deprivation of employment and by the decreased purchasing power of their salaries. It is the duty of Congress to devise the method of correcting the evils which are acknowledged to exist, and not mine. But I will venture to suggest two or three things which seem to me as absolutely necessary to a return to specie payments, the first great requisite in a return to prosperity. The legal-tender clause to the law authorizing the issue of currency by the National Government should be repealed, to take effect as to all contracts entered into after a day fixed in the repealing act—not to apply, however, to payments of salaries by Government, or for other expenditures now provided by law to be paid in currency, in the interval pending between repeal and final resumption. Provision should be made by which the Secretary of the Treasury can obtain gold as it may become necessary from time to time from the date when specie redemption commences. To this might and should be added a revenue sufficiently in excess of expenses to insure an accumulation of gold in the Treasury to sustain permanent redemption.

I commend this subject to your careful consideration, believing that a favorable solution is attainable, and if reached by this Congress that the present and future generations will ever gratefully remember it as their deliverer from a thraldom of evil and disgrace.

An expiring Republican Congress responded to President Grant's plea with the Resumption Act of 1875. The Act provided that after January 1, 1879, all greenbacks should be redeemable in gold or silver. Plank by plank, the program of business was realized. An expanding population created new markets, railroads tapped the trading areas of the West, steadily mounting tariffs furnished protection for healthy profits, and a stabilized currency assured safety for investment. The industrialists had achieved their goal.

## THE RULE OF THE STALWARTS

### 7

Excessive tariffs, the rape of the public domain, and a currency system tailored to the needs of investors evoked political protest and popular complaint. But the scandals which came to light during the Grant administrations produced a furor. An unholy alliance of corrupt business leaders and Republican "Stalwarts" in both state and national governments plundered the public treasury with such uninhibited flagrancy that the nation and the world were staggered. Of these enterprises, the Crédit Mobilier—a construction company organized by the backers of the Union Pacific Railroad to take advantage both of private investors and of government aid to transcontinental railways so as to divert an undue share of the building profits into their own pockets—was the most nefarious. The company succeeded, for the Mobilier's first dividend almost equaled the sum invested in it; subsequent dividends climbed to nearly 350 per cent a year. Fearful that Congress might investigate their profitable enterprise, its backers distributed stock judiciously among members of that body. These fraudulent practices were exposed by a congressional committee headed by Luke P. Poland of Vermont, which reported in February, 1873. Particularly startling were its revelations concerning Oakes Ames, a member of Congress:[7]

---

[7] *House Report*, 42nd Cong., 3rd Sess., Doc. No. 77, pp. ii-iv.

On the 16th day of August, 1867, a contract was executed between the Union Pacific Railroad Company and Oakes Ames, by which Mr. Ames contracted to build six hundred and sixty-seven miles of the Union Pacific road at prices ranging from $42,000 to $96,000 per mile, amounting in the aggregate to $47,000,000. Before the contract was entered into it was understood that Mr. Ames was to transfer it to seven trustees, who were to execute it, and the profits of the contract were to be divided among the stockholders in the Crédit Mobilier Company, who should comply with certain conditions set out in the instrument transferring the contract to the trustees. The Ames contract and the transfer to trustees are incorporated in the evidence submitted, and therefore further recital of their terms is not deemed necessary.

Substantially, all the stockholders of the Crédit Mobilier complied with the conditions named in the transfer, and thus became entitled to share in any profits said trustees might make in executing the contract.

All the large stockholders in the Union Pacific were also stockholders in the Crédit Mobilier, and the Ames contract and its transfer to trustees were ratified by the Union Pacific, and received the assent of the great body of stockholders, but not of all.

After the Ames contract had been executed, it was expected by those interested that by reason of the enormous prices agreed to be paid for the work very large profits would be derived from building the road, and very soon the stock of the Crédit Mobilier was understood by those holding it to be worth much more than its par value. The stock was not in the market and had no fixed market value, but the holders of it, in December, 1867, considered it worth at least double the par value, and in January and February, 1868, three or four times the par value, but it does not appear that these facts were generally or publicly known, or that the holders of the stock desired they should be.

The foregoing statement the committee think gives enough of the historic details, and condition and value of the stock, to make the following detailed facts intelligible.

Mr. Oakes Ames was then a member of the House of Representatives, and came to Washington at the commencement of the session, about the beginning of December, 1867. During that month Mr. Ames entered into contracts with a considerable number of members of Congress, both Senators and Representatives, to let them have shares of stock in the Crédit Mobilier Company at par, with interest thereon from the first day of the previous July. It does not appear that in any instance he asked any of these persons to pay a higher price than the par value and interest, nor that Mr. Ames used any special effort or urgency to get these persons to take it. In all these negotiations Mr. Ames did not enter into any details as to the value of the stock or the amount of dividend that might be expected upon it, but stated generally that it would be good stock, and in several instances said he would guarantee that they should get at least 10 per cent. on their money.

Some of these gentlemen, in their conversations with Mr. Ames, raised the question whether becoming holders of this stock would bring them into any embarrassment as members of Congress in their legislative action. Mr. Ames quieted such suggestions by saying it could not, for the Union Pacific had received from Congress all the grants and legislation it wanted, and they should ask for nothing more. In some instances those members who contracted for stock paid to Mr. Ames the money for the price of the stock, par and interest; in others, where they had not the money, Mr. Ames agreed to carry the stock for them until they could get the money or it should be met by the dividends.

Mr. Ames was at this time a large stockholder in the Crédit Mobilier, but he did not intend any of these transactions to be sales of his own stock, but intended to fulfill all these contracts from stock belonging to the company.

At this time there were about six hundred and fifty shares of the stock of the company, which had for some reason been placed in the name of Mr. T. C. Durant, one of the leading and active men of the concern.

Mr. Ames claimed that a portion of this stock should be assigned to him to enable him to fulfill engagements he had made for stock. Mr. Durant claimed that he had made similar engagements that he should be allowed stock to fulfill. Mr. McComb, who was present at the time, claimed that he had also made engagements for stock which he should have stock given him to carry out. This claim of McComb was refused, but after the stock was assigned to Mr. Ames, McComb insisted that Ames should distribute some of the stock to his (McComb's) friends, and named Senators Bayard and Fowler, and Representatives Allison and Wilson, of Iowa.

It was finally arranged that three hundred and forty-three shares of the stock of the company should be transferred to Mr. Ames to enable him to perform his engagements, and that number of shares were set over on the books of the company to Oakes Ames, trustee, to distinguish it from the stock held by him before. Mr. Ames at the time paid to the company the par of the stock and interest from the July previous, and this stock still stands on the books in the name of Oakes Ames, trustee, except thirteen shares which have been transferred to parties in no way connected with Congress. The committee do not find that Mr. Ames had any negotiation whatever with any of these members of Congress on the subject of this stock prior to the commencement of the session of December, 1867, except Mr. Scofield, of Pennsylvania, and it was not claimed

that any obligation existed from Mr. Ames to him as the result of it.

In relation to the purpose and motives of Mr. Ames in contracting to let members of Congress have Crédit Mobilier stock at par, which he and all other owners of it considered worth at least double that sum, the committee, upon the evidence taken by them and submitted to the House, cannot entertain doubt. When he said he did not suppose the Union Pacific Company would ask or need further legislation, he stated what he believed to be true. But he feared the interests of the road might suffer by adverse legislation, and what he desired to accomplish was to enlist strength and friends in Congress who would resist any encroachment upon or interference with the rights and privileges already secured, and to that end wished to create in them an interest identical with his own. This purpose is clearly avowed in his letters to McComb, copied in the evidence. He says he intends to place the stock "where it will do most good to us." And again, "we want more friends in this Congress." In his letter to McComb, and also in his statement prepared by counsel, he gives the philosophy of his action, to wit, "That he has found there is no difficulty in getting men to look after their own property." The committee are also satisfied that Mr. Ames entertained a fear that, when the true relations between the Crédit Mobilier Company and the Union Pacific became generally known, and the means by which the great profits expected to be made were fully understood, there was danger that congressional investigation and action would be invoked.

The members of Congress with whom he dealt were generally those who had been friendly and favorable to a Pacific Railroad, and Mr. Ames did not fear or expect to find them favorable to movements hostile to it; but he desired to stimulate their activity and watchfulness in opposition to any unfavorable action by giving them a personal interest in the success of the enterprise, especially so far as it affected the interest of the Crédit Mobilier Company. On the 9th day of December, 1867, Mr. C. C. Washburn, of Wisconsin, introduced in the House a bill to regulate by law the rates of transportation over the Pacific Railroad.

Mr. Ames, as well as others interested in the Union Pacific road, was opposed to this, and desired to defeat it. Other measures apparently hostile to that company were subsequently introduced into the House by Mr. Washburn of Wisconsin, and Mr. Washburne of Illinois. The committee believe that Mr. Ames, in his distributions of stock, had specially in mind the hostile efforts of the Messrs. Washburn, and desired to gain strength to secure their defeat. The reference in one of his letters to "Washburn's move" makes this quite apparent.

# 8

Revelations of plunder during Grant's first administration led Liberal Republicans to rebel. They rebelled against the corruption of the Stalwarts and against continuation of Republican Reconstruction policies. The American Free Trade League induced liberals to support the program of tariff reform; exposure of the Tweed Ring and other scandals convinced Carl Schurz and like-minded Republicans of the need for higher standards in public life. The Liberal Republicans called a convention in 1872, and placed their own candidate in the field. A split on the tariff resulted in the nomination of Horace Greeley, venerable editor of the New York *Tribune* and a high-tariff man, to run against Grant; but in other respects the platform echoed the old democratic spirit of the days before the Civil War:[8]

We, the Liberal Republicans of the United States, in National Convention assembled at Cincinnati, proclaim the following principles as essential to just government:

1. We recognize the equality of all men before the law, and hold that it is the duty of Government, in its dealings with the people to mete out equal and exact justice to all, of whatever nativity, race, color, or persuasion, religious or political.

2. We pledge ourselves to maintain the union of these States, emancipation and enfranchisement, and to oppose any reopening of the questions settled by the Thirteenth, Fourteenth, and Fifteenth Amendments to the Constitution.

3. We demand the immediate and absolute removal of all disabilities imposed on account of the Rebellion, which was finally subdued seven years ago, believing that universal amnesty will result in complete pacification in all sections of the country.

4. Local self-government, with impartial suffrage, will guard the rights of all citizens more securely than any centralized power. The public welfare requires the supremacy of the civil over the military authority, and freedom of person under the protection of the *habeas corpus*. We demand for the individual the largest liberty consistent with public order; for the State self-government, and for the nation a return to the methods of peace and the constitutional limitations of power.

5. The Civil Service of the Government has become a mere instrument of partisan tyranny and personal ambition, and an object of selfish greed. It is a scandal and reproach upon free institutions, and breeds a demoralization dangerous to the perpetuity of republican government. We therefore regard such thorough reforms of the Civil Service as one of the most pressing necessities of the hour; that honesty, capacity, and fidelity, constitute the only valid claims to public employment; that the offices of the Government cease to be a matter of arbitrary favoritism and pa-

---

[8] Edward Stanwood, *A History of Presidential Elections* (Boston, 1892), pp. 287-288.

tronage, and that public station become again a post of honor. To this end it is imperatively required that no President shall be a candidate for re-election.

6. We demand a system of Federal taxation which shall not unnecessarily interfere with the industry of the people, and which shall provide the means necessary to pay the expenses of the Government economically administered, the pensions, the interest on the public debt, and a moderate reduction annually of the principal thereof; and, recognizing that there are in our midst honest but irreconcilable differences of opinion with regard to the respective systems of Protection and Free Trade, we remit the discussion of the subject to the people in their Congressional Districts, and to the decision of Congress thereon, wholly free of Executive interference or dictation.

7. The public credit must be sacredly maintained, and we denounce repudiation in every form and guise.

8. A speedy return to specie payment is demanded alike by the highest considerations of commercial morality and honest government.

9. We remember with gratitude the heroism and sacrifices of the soldiers and sailors of the republic, and no act of ours shall ever detract from their justly-earned fame, or the full reward of their patriotism.

10. We are opposed to all further grants of land to railroads or other corporations. The public domain should be held sacred to actual settlers.

11. We hold that it is the duty of the Government, in its intercourse with foreign nations, to cultivate the friendship of peace, by treating with all on fair and equal terms, regarding it alike dishonorable either to demand what is not right, or to submit to what is wrong.

12. For the promotion and success of these vital principles, and the support of the candidates nominated by this convention we invite and cordially welcome the cooperation of all patriotic citizens, without regard to previous affiliations.

## 9

After Greeley's futile campaign the Liberal Republican movement died swiftly; but its liberalism lived in the Republican left wing that co-operated with liberal Democrats. Meanwhile popular insistence upon reform obviously increased during the second Grant administration, as fresh evidence of fraud was presented to the nation. Indignation was so apparent that the President himself felt called upon to apologize; his last annual message to Congress on December 5, 1876, is a document remarkable for its admissions as well as for its naïveté:[9]

In submitting my eighth and last annual message to Congress it seems proper that I should refer to and in some degree recapitulate the events and official acts of the past eight years.

It was my fortune, or misfortune, to be called to the office of Chief Executive without any previous political training. From the age of 17 I had never even witnessed the excitement attending a Presidential campaign but twice antecedent to my own candidacy, and at but one of them was I eligible as a voter.

Under such circumstances it is but reasonable to suppose that errors of judgment must have occurred. Even had they not, differences of opinion between the Executive, bound by an oath to the strict performance of his duties, and writers and debaters must have arisen. It is not necessarily evidence of blunder on the part of the Executive because there are these differences of views. Mistakes have been made, as all can see and I admit, but it seems to me oftener in the selections made of the assistants appointed to aid in carrying out the various duties of administering the Government—in nearly every case selected without a personal acquaintance

---

[9] J. D. Richardson (comp.), *Messages and Papers of the Presidents, 1789-1897* (Washington, 1897, 1909; taken from the 1909 vol.), VII, 399-400.

with the appointee, but upon recommendations of the representatives chosen directly by the people. It is impossible, where so many trusts are to be allotted, that the right parties should be chosen in every instance. History shows that no Administration from the time of Washington to the present has been free from these mistakes. But I leave comparisons to history, claiming only that I have acted in every instance from a conscientious desire to do what was right, constitutional, within the law, and for the very best interests of the whole people. Failures have been errors of judgment, not of intent.

## THE BANKRUPTCY OF PARTIES

### 10

With the Republicans discredited and divided, Democrats looked toward the election of 1876 with unaccustomed hope. To capitalize on Republican corruption, they chose Samuel J. Tilden, a militant reformer from New York, as their candidate. The Republicans, however, were wise enough to pass over the Stalwart leader, James G. Blaine of Maine, nominating instead a man with a less offensive political record, Rutherford B. Hayes of Ohio. Tilden's strenuous advocacy of reform during the spirited campaign that followed apparently won the election for the Democrats; when the first returns were announced he lacked only one electoral vote of a majority, although the vote of three states remained disputed. The Electoral Commission named to decide the fate of these controversial votes eventually awarded all of them, and the presidency, to Rutherford B. Hayes. The action of the Commission was described by Abram S. Hewitt, national Democratic chairman:[10]

The struggle resulted in the triumphant election of Mr. Tilden, not merely by a majority of all the votes cast, but by a majority of all the states in the Union. It was not until two days after the election that any doubt was expressed as to the result. The country, however, was then astounded by the claim of the Republican National Committee that Hayes had secured 185 electoral votes and would therefore be declared President by a majority of one vote. As soon as this claim was made, based upon the votes of South Carolina, Florida, and Louisiana, I caused letters to be sent to the leading men of the North—Democrats and Republicans alike —inviting them to proceed to South Carolina, Florida, and Louisiana for the purpose of seeing that a fair count was made and the returns honestly canvassed. The next day President Grant, who was in Philadelphia, issued a similar request to leading Republicans only, and thus it happened that two sets of "visiting statesmen" repaired to the several states in doubt, one selected by General Grant acting as partisans and the other selected by me for their standing and character without reference to their political affiliation.

The result is known to all men. The returning boards of the several states referred to gave the votes of these states to Hayes, although it was then known and is now universally admitted that the states of Florida and Louisiana were carried for Tilden. In this emergency the state of Oregon seemed to offer an antidote to the fraud thus perpetrated. Oregon had been carried by the Republicans, but one of the electors was disqualified from acting by a Constitutional provision forbidding Federal office holders to act as electors. One of the Republican electors was a postmaster, and hence the Governor, who was a Democrat, refused his certificate and gave it to the highest candidate on the Democratic ticket. Thus one vote was secured for Tilden giving him 185 votes against 184 votes for Hayes, including all the votes from the three Southern states fraudulently secured through corrupt returning boards. . . .

The question of counting the votes was . . . relegated to the provision of the Constitution that "The President of the Senate

[10] Reprinted from Allan Nevins, editor, *Selected Writings of Abram S. Hewitt*, pp. 162-180. Copyright 1937 by Columbia University Press.

shall in the presence of the Senate and the House of Representatives open all the certificates, and the votes shall then be counted."

In view of the claim made by leading Republicans that the President of the Senate under this clause was invested with authority not only to open the certificates but to count the votes, it was evident that there would be a conflict of authority between the Senate and the House unless some mode of procedure as to the counting of the votes and the declaration of the result should be reached by the two Houses in advance of the date prescribed by the Constitution for the opening of the certificates and the counting of the votes.

Hence, after much consultation and the consideration of the question by a joint caucus of the Democratic members of the Senate and House, the House of Representatives on the 14th December, 1876, appointed a committee of seven to act in conjunction with any similar committee of the Senate "To prepare and report without delay a measure for the removal of difference of opinion as to the proper mode of counting the electoral votes for President and Vice-President which might arise as to the legality and validity of the returns of such votes made by the several states *to the end that the votes should be counted and the result declared by a tribunal whose authority none can question and whose decision all will accept.*" . . .

On the 18th December the Senate resolved to create a special committee of seven Senators "with power to prepare and report without unnecessary delay such a measure either of a legislative or other character as may in their judgment be best calculated to accomplish the counting of the Electoral votes and best disposition of all questions connected therewith and the true declaration of the result." And this committee was instructed to confer and act with the committee of the House of Representatives. . . .

The House committee lost no time in holding a meeting at which Mr. Springer was appointed a committee to collate the proceedings for counting the electoral votes in all the preceding elections of President and Vice-President of the United States. Singularly enough this action was taken in ignorance of the fact that Mr. Tilden had already undertaken to prepare a similar compilation. The two documents appeared almost simultaneously; but in the meantime the House committee proceeded to discuss the questions submitted to it at the very first meeting on the 23d day of December, 1876. Mr. McCrary produced a printed draft of a bill providing for the constitution of an Electoral Commission showing that thus early the matter had been under consideration by the Republican managers and leaders. . . .

. . . On the morning of the 17th of January, therefore, I recommended to the House committee to reject "the original Four Senior Justice Plan—Clifford, Swayne, Davis, and Miller—which had been approved at the consultation in the Speakers' room the night before, and to insist upon the plan finally adopted, by which Clifford and Field, Miller and Strong, two Democrats and two Republicans, were named by their districts with the power to choose the fifth judge—it being generally conceded that Davis must be selected, thus securing the original Five Judge Plan except that Strong was substituted for Swayne, to whom Mr. Tilden had expressed to me some personal objection. This suggestion met with the approval of the Democrats on the House committee and was particularly acceptable to the especial friends of Mr. Tilden who were on the spot, as being far more favorable to Mr. Tilden's interests than the Four Judge Plan.

It was accordingly proposed to the Senate committee as an ultimatum, and after some hours of discussion it was adopted on the 17th of January against the vigorous opposition and protesting vote of Senator Morton, who said to me that it was equivalent to the abandonment of the contest on the Republican side. . . .

The general feeling, however, was that the victory was won, because no one doubted for a moment that Judge Davis would be selected as the fifth member of the commission. . . .

An analysis of the vote proves that the Bill was regarded as a Democratic measure and that a large majority of the Republicans in Congress were opposed to its passage.

I thought at the time, and I still think, that the division of parties on this measure was largely controlled by the conviction that Judge Davis would have the casting vote, and that he could be relied upon to see that the will of the people as expressed in the election of Mr. Tilden should not be thwarted.

The surprise and disappointment, therefore, of the Democrats may be imagined when immediately after the passage of the bill the Democratic members of the legislature of the state of Illinois, reinforced by 7 Republican votes, at once elected Judge Davis to the Senate of the United States without consultation with the National Democratic Committee.

This surprise and disappointment was intensified by the immediate refusal of Judge Davis to be a nominee for the vacant position on the Commission, although his election as Senator in no respect disqualified him for the performance of the duty which he was expected to discharge.

Whether rightly or wrongly, the conviction was general that a bargain had been made by the Republicans by which Judge Davis in consideration of his being made Senator should decline a position upon the Electoral Commission. Certainly if such an arrangement were made it was the last move by which in the long game which had been played between the two parties the final triumph was probably assured to the Republican Party. I can only say that Senator Morton, who had regarded the game as lost, showed as much surprise at this achievement as I felt and could not restrain the expression of his satisfaction.

It now only remained to arrange for the choice of the fifth judge, which was limited to Hunt and Bradley because, as stated above, Mr. Tilden advised against the selection of Swayne. On consultation with Senator Conkling, I was advised not to press the choice of Judge Hunt because, as Mr. Conkling believed that Mr. Tilden had been elected and as he was the personal friend of Judge Hunt, he feared that in his desire to prove his freedom from personal influence he might lean backward and thus unconsciously be unjust to Mr. Tilden.

Practically, therefore, the choice was limited to Justice Bradley, whom I had personally known for many years in New Jersey as a very able lawyer and a man of the highest integrity. The confidence which I felt in him was shared by Mr. Tilden, but in order to make assurance doubly sure I requested a mutual friend of Judge Bradley and myself, the late John G. Stevens, of Trenton, N.J., to confer with Judge Bradley and to ascertain whether he felt that he could decide the questions which would come before the commission without prejudice or party feeling. The report of Mr. Stevens was entirely satisfactory. Judge Bradley was therefore selected with the distinct approval of the Democratic representatives, reinforced by the favorable judgment of Judge Clifford and Judge Field, who assured me that absolute reliance could be placed upon the judicial fairness of Judge Bradley. In fact they both stated that it was absurd to fear that any Justice of the Supreme Court would be governed by partisan feeling or influence, and this was in accordance with the general feeling in Congress and throughout the country.

The other members of the commission under the provisions of the Act consisted of three Republicans and two Democrats from the Senate and three Democrats and two Republicans from the House. The commission, therefore, was composed so far as political preference was concerned of eight Republicans and seven Democrats, practically giving the casting vote to Judge Bradley, in whose freedom from partisan influence absolute confidence was reposed.

The omission of Senator Conkling, whose preferences were supposed to be for Mr. Tilden and who was the putative author of the bill creating the commission, was remarked as tending to show the Republican animus in reference to the commission. The choice by the House of General Garfield who had opposed the bill was also regarded as significant, but the feeling was general that substantial justice would be done by the commission, as declared by Judge Abbott in the address prepared by him for the Democratic members of the commission after its work had been done, "The conscience of this whole people approved the law establishing the Commission, nay, hailed it with joy, because it established as all believed, a fair tribunal, to examine, to inquire into, and determine the charges of fraud and corruption in three States."

This illusion was, however, rudely dispelled when Judge Bradley pronounced his decision in the Florida case by which the vote of this state was unjustly counted for Hayes. The history of this opinion forms an important feature in the final outcome of the electoral count. As stated above, Mr. Stevens was the intimate friend of Judge Bradley. He passed the night previous to the rendition of the judgment in the Florida case at my house. About midnight he returned from a visit to Judge Bradley and reported to General Richard Taylor, who was also staying with me, and to Senator Gibson who was awaiting his return, that he had just left Judge Bradley after reading his opinion in favor of counting the vote of the Democratic electors of the state of Florida. Such a judgment insured the election of Tilden to the Presidency with three votes to spare above the necessary majority. We parted, therefore,

with the assurance that all further doubt as to the Presidency was at rest. I attended the delivery of the judgment the next day without the slightest intimation from any quarter that Judge Bradley had changed his mind. In fact, the reading of the opinion, until the few concluding paragraphs were reached, was strictly in accordance with the report of Mr. Stevens. The change was made between midnight and sunrise. Mr. Stevens afterward informed me that it was due to a visit to Judge Bradley by Senator Frelinghuysen and Secretary Robeson, made after his departure. Their appeals to Judge Bradley were said to have been reinforced by the persuasion of Mrs. Bradley. Whatever the fact may have been, Judge Bradley himself in a subsequent letter addressed to the Newark *Daily Advertiser* admitted that he had written a favorable opinion which on subsequent reflection he saw fit to modify.

The decision in the Florida case produced a feeling of profound disappointment among the Democrats, but not of dismay. It was evident that the principle laid down in this case would necessarily secure one vote from Oregon, enough to ensure the election of Mr. Tilden even if the votes of Louisiana and South Carolina should be awarded to Hayes. Besides these states, there were cases of disqualified electors in other states and particularly one in Illinois cast by a Republican elector who, under the provisions of the Constitution, was disqualified in consequence of holding the office of postmaster. It was decided in view of the decision in the Florida case to object to the counting of this vote, although both sides conceded that Illinois had given a large majority for the Republican candidates. Before the two Houses met, however, on the morning of the next day after, the Florida decision was rendered; Senator Conkling with whom I had had very intimate and confidential relations, leading me to suppose that as he had already taken ground against the claim of the President of the Senate to count the votes and declare the result and had practically demolished this pretense in a speech of remarkable range and power, he would also when a contested case was reached in which the vote clearly belonged to Tilden, not hesitate to take the responsibility of defeating the plans of the Republican leaders to count in Hayes at all hazards.

Senator Conkling asked me whether it was the intention of the Democrats to object to the vote of the Illinois postmaster; on receiving my reply in the affirmative, he said that he would advise us to refrain from this action, because it would be construed into a disposition on the part of the Democrats to claim a vote to which in justice they were not entitled, and that this would be quoted against us when the Oregon case should come up for decision. He added that there was a much stronger reason why we could make no claim in Illinois. He said that the Louisiana case, in which there could be no doubt as to the election having been in favor of Tilden by a large majority, would come up after the Illinois case, and that he would be met in the contention that Tilden was entitled to the electoral votes of Louisiana by the statement that the Democrats had not hesitated to claim a vote in Illinois to which they were not in justice entitled.

I replied that I would submit his views to the committee in charge of the objections and accordingly proceeded at once to confer with J. Randolph Tucker, of Virginia, who had the matter in charge. On full consideration by the committee Mr. Tucker informed me that in view of Mr. Conkling's position they had decided to pass over the state of Illinois without objection. It is proper here to state that no one on our side entertained a doubt of the Constitutional disqualification of this elector, but we all felt that our case would be weakened by the claim and that the Electoral Commission would find some way to defeat it on account of its admitted want of equity.

The Louisiana case was reached on the same day, and the returns were duly opened in the presence of both Houses; one return gave the vote of the state to Hayes, another return gave the vote to Tilden. To the surprise of everybody a third return was presented giving the vote of the state to Peter Cooper. This last return was supposed to be the work of a crank and was after some discussion omitted from the proceedings as having no validity whatever. Mr. Conkling was present at the joint meeting but took no part in the discussions. It was expected, however, that at the meeting of the Senate on the next morning Mr. Conkling would take ground against counting the certificate of the returning board of Louisiana in favor of the Hayes electors. My conference with him in the Illinois case led me to this conclusion, and in the evening Senator Barnum, who was in constant intercourse with Mr. Conkling, assured me that the latter would on the following morning denounce the action of the returning board and show that the vote of Louisiana belonged to Tilden.

But when the session of the Senate was opened on the next morning, Senator Conkling was not in his seat. On inquiry it was stated that he had been seen earlier in the day making his way to the railway station and had said that he was going to Baltimore. It is certain that he did not return until the next day, and in the interval the Louisiana case was, under the provisions of the law, sent to the Electoral Commission for decision, because the two Houses had disagreed as to the counting of the vote.

I do not propose to give any account of the proceedings before the commission in this case, but it is proper to state that the return actually approved by the commission appears to have been a forged return, and that this fact was known not only to the President of the Senate, but to General Garfield, who was sitting as a member of the Electoral Commission. At this date I can now understand why the Peter Cooper return was interjected when the certificates were opened. Attention was thus distracted from the discrepancy which undoubtedly existed between the two sets of the Republican returns opened and submitted by the president of the Senate.

The votes of Louisiana were thus counted for Hayes, and those of South Carolina were also, under the decision of the commission, counted for him and probably justly so in view of the facts afterward developed by the inquiries of the Thompson Committee. . . .

It is not necessary to go into any further details as to the completion of the electoral count. There was much excitement and doubtless scenes of violence would have been witnessed but for the firmness of Speaker Randall, to whose patriotic action the country owes a debt of gratitude for the peaceful issue of this long, exciting, and humiliating controversy, upon which the attention of the country had been concentrated for many months with painful anxiety. In fact, on this late day, eighteen years after these occurrences, it is almost impossible to form any adequate idea of the excitement and the apprehension which prevailed throughout the country. Business was arrested, the wheels of industry ceased to move, and it seemed as if the terrors of civil war were again to be renewed. Petitions from chambers of commerce and from all the centers of trade had deluged Congress in favor of a peaceful settlement of the controversy. Personally, I was satisfied that it would be better for the country to have four years of Republican administration based upon fraudulent returns, than to have four years of civil war. In this view I had the hearty concurrence of Speaker Randall, who was recognized as the firm friend of Mr. Tilden and the unyielding upholder of his rights under the law. To his action in concurrence with my advice as chairman of the National Democratic Committee was due in my opinion the escape from

civil war. To this dread issue we were much nearer than was even at that time supposed. The Democratic forces had been organized in fifteen states and were composed chiefly of the veterans of the war who were quite ready once more to take up arms and move on Washington in defense of what they regarded as the rightful claims of Governor Tilden to the Presidency. In this communication I do not wish to use names, but even the commander-in-chief had been selected, and the governors of many states had declared their willingness to act, in case an emergency should arise demanding the inauguration of Tilden, by military force. . . . The habit of Mr. Tilden's mind was to criticize and postpone, not to decide or approve, but that he accepted the result as the only possible solution of the controversy, other than by the dread arbitrament of arms cannot be doubted. When the latter alternative was presented he did not hesitate to declare to Mr. Randall, as he had previously declared to Judge Thurman and myself, that nothing could justify the resort to physical force. Upon this conclusion both Mr. Randall and I acted. The result was the completion of the count, the inauguration of President Hayes, and the salvation of the country from the perils of civil war. . . .

I have stated above that the pledges given in behalf of President Hayes as to the recognition of the Democratic government in Louisiana and South Carolina were fully kept. He also kept other pledges which must have been made by the Republican visiting statesmen to the three contested states, because in all of them, the active participants in the frauds were promptly rewarded with public office, although in Florida, McLin, feeling aggrieved by the amount of recognition which he received subsequently, made disclosures which were not very agreeable to the Republican managers.

It has also been stated that the vote of Louisiana prior to the final count of the

Returning Board was offered for sale. The price named to me was $200,000, and it was stated that the larger portion of the money would go to Wells and Anderson and a lesser amount of their colleagues on the Returning Board. I declined to make the purchase and notified Mr. Tilden personally of the fact on the Sabbath day when the offer was made. Long after the completion of the count I was informed that other Democrats less scrupulous than I was actually completed the arrangements for the purchase and provided the amount of money required to be paid in New Orleans. This transaction fortunately came to the knowledge of Governor Tilden before the money had been paid over and was arrested by his prompt intervention. As in the first instance he was not willing to raffle for the Presidency, so in the last event he showed that he was equally unwilling to purchase an office to which he was justly entitled. I record this fact because the country ought to know that Governor Tilden at no time ever descended to the low plane of corrupting the electoral functions even for the purpose of defeating a fraud.

Subsequent events, however, made it clear to me that the Republican managers were not governed by the same standard of rectitude. I had it from the mouth of Governor Wells himself that the offer rejected by the Democrats had been accepted by the Republican managers, and that they had agreed after the inauguration of President Hayes to raise the money and pay the amount in cash. In consequence of the failure to redeem this promise Governor Wells subsequently came to Washington and threatened to expose the whole transaction. Whereupon, as I was informed upon good authority, a considerable portion of the money was raised and paid over to Wells in Washington in order to quiet the immediate clamor, with the promise that the remainder should be paid in time. Whether it was paid or not I do not know. Possibly Wells was quieted by

his appointment to the office of Collector of the Customs for the Port of New Orleans; his confederates were also provided for, some by offices and some by money.

With President Hayes I refused to have any intercourse, and although upon the floor of the House of Representatives I took occasion to declare that he held office by his sacred title, for which I was much criticized, I felt that he knew, as I knew, that it had been secured by frauds which ought to have led him to resign his high place and to appeal to the people in a new election for such decision as the sense of public justice might require.

Mr. Conkling never made any public declaration upon the subject, but he never concealed in private his opinion as to the iniquity of these transactions and habitually referred to the President as Rutherfraud B. Hayes. In the House, on the contrary, President Seelye, of Amherst College, and Henry L. Pierce, both representatives for the state of Massachusetts, refused to approve of the Louisiana fraud and finally recorded themselves against counting the vote of that state for Hayes. With these honorable exceptions the Republican Party approved the result, and the country, anxious for peace and repose, cheerfully acquiesced in the decision.

## 11

Hayes proved to be even more courageous than his most ardent supporters had hoped. Defying the Stalwarts within his own party, he officially ended the Reconstruction period; federal troops were removed from the South in 1877. His most enduring contribution, however, was the re-establishment of the presidency as an effective force in American government. Between 1867 and 1877 Congress had stripped away so many presidential powers that the office seemed certain to lose its effectiveness. The practice of attaching "riders" to essential bills became one of Hayes's chief targets. By this device the legislature had repeatedly forced presidents to accept distasteful measures rather than veto the entire act. President Hayes, confronted with such a choice in 1879, vetoed an Army Appropriation Act containing a Democratic "rider" which would have repealed two earlier laws authorizing the use of federal troops in elections:[11]

This section is, however, not presented to me as a separate and independent measure, but is, as has been stated, attached to the bill making the usual annual appropriations for the support of the Army. It makes a vital change in the election laws of the country, which is in no way connected with the use of the Army. It prohibits, under heavy penalties, any person engaged in the civil service of the United States from having any force at the place of any election, prepared to preserve order, to make arrests, to keep the peace, or in any manner to enforce the laws. This is altogether foreign to the purpose of an Army appropriation bill. The practice of tacking to appropriation bills measures not pertinent to such bills did not prevail until more than forty years after the adoption of the Constitution. It has become a common practice. All parties when in power have adopted it. Many abuses and great waste of public money have in this way crept into appropriation bills. The public opinion of the country is against it. The States which have recently adopted constitutions have generally provided a remedy for the evil by enacting that no law shall contain more than one subject, which shall be plainly expressed in its title. The constitutions of more than half of the States contain substantially this provision. The public welfare will be promoted in many ways by a return to the early practice of the Government and to the true principle of legislation, which requires that every measure shall stand or fall according to its own merits. If it were understood that to attach to an appropriation bill a measure irrelevant to the general object of the bill would imperil and probably pre-

vent its final passage and approval, a valuable reform in the parliamentary practice of Congress would be accomplished. The best justification that has been offered for attaching irrelevant riders to appropriation bills is that it is done for convenience' sake, to facilitate the passage of measures which are deemed expedient by all the branches of Government which participate in legislation. It can not be claimed that there is any such reason for attaching this amendment of the election laws to the Army appropriation bill. The history of the measure contradicts this assumption. . . .

Upon the assembling of this Congress, in pursuance of a call for an extra session, which was made necessary by the failure of the Forty-fifth Congress to make the needful appropriations for the support of the Government, the question was presented whether the attempt made in the last Congress to ingraft by construction a new principle upon the Constitution should be persisted in or not. This Congress has ample opportunity and time to pass the appropriation bills, and also to enact any political measures which may be determined upon in separate bills by the usual and orderly methods of proceeding. But the majority of both Houses have deemed it wise to adhere to the principles asserted and maintained in the last Congress by the majority of the House of Representatives. That principle is that the House of Representatives has the sole right to originate bills for raising revenue, and therefore has the right to withhold appropriations upon which the existence of the Government may depend unless the Senate and the President shall give their assent to any legislation which the House may see fit to attach to appropriation bills. To establish this principle is to make a radical, dangerous, and unconstitutional change in the character of our institutions. The various departments of the Government and the Army and the Navy are established by the Constitution or by laws passed in pursuance thereof. Their duties

[11] J. D. Richardson (comp.), *Messages and Papers of the Presidents, 1789-1897* (Washington, 1897, 1909; taken from the 1909 vol.), X, 4475-4484.

are clearly defined and their support is carefully provided for by law. The money required for this purpose has been collected from the people and is now in the Treasury, ready to be paid out as soon as the appropriation bills are passed. Whether appropriations are made or not, the collection of the taxes will go on. The public money will accumulate in the Treasury. It was not the intention of the framers of the Constitution that any single branch of the Government should have the power to dictate conditions upon which this treasure should be applied to the purpose for which it was collected. Any such intention, if it had been entertained, would have been plainly expressed in the Constitution. . . .

The new doctrine, if maintained, will result in a consolidation of unchecked and despotic power in the House of Representatives. A bare majority of the House will become the Government. The Executive will no longer be what the framers of the Constitution intended—an equal and independent branch of the Government. It is clearly the constitutional duty of the President to exercise his discretion and judgment upon all bills presented to him without constraint or duress from any other branch of the Government. To say that a majority of either or both of the Houses of Congress may insist upon the approval of a bill under the penalty of stopping all of the operations of the Government for want of the necessary supplies is to deny to the Executive that share of the legislative power which is plainly conferred by the second section of the seventh article of the Constitution. It strikes from the Constitution the qualified negative of the President. It is said that this should be done because it is the peculiar function of the House of Representatives to represent the will of the people. But no single branch or department of the Government has exclusive authority to speak for the American people. The most authentic and solemn expression of their will is contained in the Constitution of the United States. By that Constitution they have ordained and established a Government whose powers are distributed among coordinate branches, which, as far as possible consistently with a harmonious coöperation, are absolutely independent of each other. The people of this country are unwilling to see the supremacy of the Constitution replaced by the omnipotence of any one department of the Government.

The enactment of this bill into a law will establish a precedent which will tend to destroy the equal independence of the several branches of the Government. Its principle places not merely the Senate and the Executive, but the judiciary also, under the coercive dictation of the House. The House alone will be the judge of what constitutes a grievance, and also of the means and measures of redress.

## 12

Hayes also sought to restore the executive power over appointments, for here, too, Congress had encroached during the administrations of Johnson and of Grant. The Stalwarts, who hoped to select federal officeholders during his administration, were thwarted, and in addition a normal constitutional relationship between the legislative and executive branches of the government was re-established. Hayes's message to Congress on the subject of appointments in December, 1880, was virtually a plea for a civil service law that would place officeholding above politics:[12]

Competitive examinations in aid of impartial appointments and promotions have been conducted for some years past in several of the Executive Departments. . . . The results of these practical trials have been very satisfactory, and have confirmed my opinion in favor of this system of selection. All are subjected to the same tests, and the result is free from prejudice by personal favor or partisan influence. It secures for the position applied for the best qualifications attainable among the competing applicants. It is an effectual pro-

---

[12] *Ibid.*, pp. 4555-4557.

tection from the pressure of importunity, which under any other course pursued largely exacts the time and attention of appointing officers, to their great detriment in the discharge of other official duties, preventing the abuse of the service for the mere furtherance of private or party purposes, and leaving the employee of the Government, freed from the obligations imposed by patronage, to depend solely upon merit for retention and advancement, and with this constant incentive to exertion and improvement.

These invaluable results have been attained in a high degree in the offices where the rules for appointment by competitive examination have been applied.

A method which has so approved itself by experimental tests at points where such tests may be fairly considered conclusive should be extended to all subordinate positions under the Government. I believe that a strong and growing public sentiment demands immediate measures for securing and enforcing the highest possible efficiency in the civil service and its protection from recognized abuses, and that the experience referred to has demonstrated the feasibility of such measures.

The examinations in the custom-houses and post-offices have been held under many embarrassments and without provision for compensation for the extra labor performed by the officers who have conducted them, and whose commendable interest in the improvement of the public service has induced this devotion of time and labor without pecuniary reward. A continuance of these labors gratuitously ought not to be expected, and without an appropriation by Congress for compensation it is not practicable to extend the system of examinations generally throughout the civil service. It is also highly important that all such examinations should be conducted upon a uniform system and under general supervision. Section 1753 of the Revised Statutes authorizes the President to prescribe the regulations for admission to the civil service of the United States, and for this purpose to employ suitable persons to conduct the requisite inquiries with reference to "the fitness of each candidate, in respect to age, health, character, knowledge, and ability for the branch of service into which he seeks to enter"; but the law is practically inoperative for want of the requisite appropriation.

I therefore recommend an appropriation of $25,000 per annum to meet the expenses of a commission, to be appointed by the President in accordance with the terms of this section, whose duty it shall be to devise a just, uniform, and efficient system of competitive examinations and to supervise the application of the same throughout the entire civil service of the Government. I am persuaded that the facilities which such a commission will afford for testing the fitness of those who apply for office will not only be as welcome a relief to members of Congress as it will be to the President and heads of Departments, but that it will also greatly tend to remove the causes of embarrassment which now inevitably and constantly attend the conflicting claims of patronage between the legislative and executive departments. The most effectual check upon the pernicious competition of influence and official favoritism in the bestowal of office will be the substitution of an open competition of merit between the applicants, in which everyone can make his own record with the assurance that his success will depend upon this alone.

I also recommend such legislation as, while leaving every officer as free as any other citizen to express his political opinions and to use his means for their advancement, shall also enable him to feel as safe as any private citizen in refusing all demands upon his salary for political purposes. A law which should thus guarantee true liberty and justice to all who are engaged in the public service, and likewise contain stringent provisions against the use of official authority to coerce the political action of private citizens or of official subordinates, is greatly to be desired.

The most serious obstacle, however, to an improvement of the civil service, and especially to a reform in the method of appointment and removal, has been found to be the practice, under what is known as the spoils system, by which the appointing power has been so largely encroached upon by members of Congress. The first step in the reform of the civil service must be a complete divorce between Congress and the Executive in the matter of appointments. The corrupting doctrine that "to the victors belong the spoils" is inseparable from Congressional patronage as the established rule and practice of parties in power. It comes to be understood by applicants for office and by the people generally that Representatives and Senators are entitled to disburse the patronage of their respective districts and States. It is not necessary to recite at length the evils resulting from this invasion of the Executive functions. The true principles of Government on the subject of appointments to office, as stated in the national conventions of the leading parties of the country, have again and again been approved by the American people, and have not been called in question in any quarter. These authentic expressions of public opinion upon this all-important subject are the statement of principles that belong to the constitutional structure of the Government.

Under the Constitution the President and heads of Departments are to make nominations for office. The Senate is to advise and consent to appointments, and the House of Representatives is to accuse and prosecute faithless officers. The best interest of the public service demands that these distinctions be respected; that Senators and Representatives, who may be judges and accusers, should not dictate appointments to office.

To this end the cooperation of the legislative department of the Government is required alike by the necessities of the case and by public opinion. Members of Congress will not be relieved from the demands made upon them with reference to appointments to office until by legislative enactment the pernicious practice is condemned and forbidden.

It is therefore recommended that an act be passed defining the relations of members of Congress with respect to appointment to office by the President. . . .

Believing that to reform the system and methods of the civil service in our country is one of the highest and most imperative duties of statesmanship, and that it can be permanently done only by the cooperation of the legislative and executive departments of the Government, I again commend the whole subject to your considerate attention.

## 13

The reaction to Hayes's forward-looking suggestions illustrated the degree of party bankruptcy. Democratic and Republican leaders denounced his efforts with equal vehemence. The Republican Stalwarts repudiated him, and in 1880 they nominated another Ohio dark horse, James A. Garfield, whose record was without the slightest taint of reform. The Democrats selected General Winfield Scott Hancock of Pennsylvania as their standard-bearer, a genial veteran whose great physical bulk in no way matched his ability. Politicians of both parties preferred to raise up the dead issues of a twenty-year-old war rather than face the immediate problems induced by the revolutions in economics. Republican campaign tactics consisted largely of damning Democrats, the party of rebellion— a practice known as "waving the bloody shirt." Senator James G. Blaine was a past master of the art:[13]

. . . If you elect General Hancock you inevitably, within the space of a twelvemonth—I am not sure that it would not be within the space of ninety days—hand over to the Democratic party, led by Southern men, the control of the Supreme Court

[13] New York *Tribune,* September 24, 1880.

of the United States absolutely. Five of those Judges are today beyond seventy, or in that neighborhood. They may accept retirement at full pay. If they are reluctant to do so, a Democratic President backed by a Democratic Senate and House would swamp that Court by superior numbers; and by way of advice to the North let me say that a bill is pending on the calendar of the Senate to make that Court consist of twenty members. . . .

I will tell you another thing that will happen if Hancock is elected. We shall have a thorough overhauling of the whole revenue and financial system of the United States. . . . I ask you to look back at the prosperity of the last twenty years and then say if you are willing to put the whole of it to the hazard of an experiment of trying a new theory with new men? I could detain you until morning in recording instances of how the prosperity of the American people has been so enormously developed by reason of a protective tariff, but it is useless at this late date to ask the value of protection.

Another thing that will happen if Hancock is elected—and I only speak of those things publicly vouched as the policy of the party—will arise from a vindication of the theory of States Rights, the underlying principle and guiding inspiration of the Democratic party. If he comes into power, in accordance with bills that have been perpetually renewed in Congress for the last eight years, the old State bank system will be renewed, and the "shin-plaster" currency will be revived. If, outside of the humanitarian achievement of the Republican party there was but this one thing—the abolition of State banks—upon which the party could pride itself, that should be sufficient to entitle it to the country's gratitude. In abolishing this system the Republican party abolished bad money. There has not been a bad bill in circulation since the National Bank system was established. . . .

Now take four and a half millions of negroes in the South who don't have anything more to do with the Government of the United States than they do with the Government of Great Britain; endowed with American citizenship and yet as capable of exercising the right of franchise as if they were in the moon. Take four and a half millions of these men, and what do we see? . . . In Mississippi there are 225,000 coloured men to 100,000 white men—that is nine to four. In Mississippi today four soldiers of the Confederate army will exercise as much power in electing Hancock, by throwing their votes for him, as nine Union soldiers in New-York or New-Jersey will exercise by voting for Garfield; I don't know whether you relish that or not; I don't. And now on the top of the four and a half millions of actual men of flesh and blood deprived entirely of their power as a political element in the Government, we have a million [and] a half of imaginary men to overcome: there are seven millions which are counted on the other side before we start in the race. I say that this sort of thing must be stopped. . . .

We shall not fight over this tomorrow, or next day or next year, but I repeat in another form what I have said, that you cannot continue the Government of the United States when the party in power bases itself on the joint operation of fraud and violence.

Now, gentlemen . . . if you comprehend these issues as coming to your own doors and firesides, that you throw your Supreme Court and your tariff and your financial system and your currency all into the scale of a new experiment to be wrought out by incompetent and dangerous men, I have no doubt of the result. If you believe, as believe every reflecting man must, that the safe thing for this people to do is to stand still while we stand well; that the wise thing for this people to do is to stand by that which has proved itself so stable and true; if you believe in the policy of the Republican party, which has brought the country through a great revolution of blood and through another great revolution of distress and finance; if you believe that party is to be trusted again, it is for New-Jersey as much as that of any State in the Union, upon this great industrial and financial system, to do her duty.

## 14

James A. Garfield was elected in 1880, but four months after his inauguration he was assassinated by a disappointed office seeker who boasted: "I am a Stalwart: Arthur is now President of the United States." Chester A. Arthur, the vice-president unexpectedly elevated to the presidency, was a Stalwart indeed, an intimate of the corrupt Republican clique that had blocked Hayes's mild attempts at reform. Yet so vocal was popular enthusiasm for change that Arthur denounced the corrupt patronage system then in vogue by which federal offices were filled. His first message to Congress boldly urged a civil service system and the legislature responded in January, 1883, with the Pendleton Act:[14]

*Be it enacted* . . . , That the President is authorized to appoint, by and with the advice and consent of the Senate, three persons, not more than two of whom shall be adherents of the same party, as Civil Service Commissioners, and said three commissioners shall constitute the United States Civil Service Commission. Said commissioners shall hold no other official place under the United States.

SECTION 2. That it shall be the duty of said commissioners:

*First.* To aid the President, as he may request, in preparing suitable rules for carrying this act into effect, and when said rules shall have been promulgated it shall be the duty of all officers of the United States in the departments and offices to which any such rules may relate to aid, in all proper ways, in carrying said rules, and any modifications thereof, into effect.

*Second.* And, among other things, said rules shall provide and declare, as nearly as the conditions of good administration will warrant, as follows:

First, for open, competitive examinations for testing the fitness of applicants for the public service now classified or to be classified hereunder. Such examinations shall be practical in their character, and so far as may be shall relate to those matters which will fairly test the relative capacity and fitness of the persons examined to discharge the duties of the service into which they seek to be appointed.

Second, that all the offices, places, and employments so arranged or to be arranged in classes shall be filled by selections according to grade from among those graded highest as the results of such competitive examinations.

Third, appointments to the public service aforesaid in the departments at Washington shall be apportioned among the several States and Territories and the District of Columbia upon the basis of population as ascertained at the last preceding census. . . .

Fifth, that no person in the public service is for that reason under any obligations to contribute to any political fund, or to render any political service, and that he will not be removed or otherwise prejudiced for refusing to do so.

Sixth, that no person in said service has any right to use his official authority or influence to coerce the political action of any person or body.

Seventh, there shall be non-competitive examinations in all proper cases before the commission, when competent persons do not compete, after notice has been given of the existence of the vacancy, under such rules as may be prescribed by the commissioners as to the manner of giving notice. . . .

SEC. 3. . . . The commission shall, at Washington, and in one or more places in each State and Territory where examinations are to take place, designate and se-

---

[14] *United States Statutes at Large,* XXII, 403-406.

lect a suitable number of persons, not less than three, in the official service of the United States, residing in said State or Territory, after consulting the head of the department or office in which such persons serve, to be members of boards of examiners. . . . Such boards of examiners shall be so located as to make it reasonably convenient and inexpensive for applicants to attend before them; and where there are persons to be examined in any State or Territory, examinations shall be held therein at least twice in each year. . . .

Sec. 6. That within sixty days after the passage of this act it shall be the duty of the Secretary of the Treasury, in as near conformity as may be to the classification of certain clerks now existing under . . . the Revised Statutes, to arrange in classes the several clerks and persons employed by the collector, naval officer, surveyor, and appraisers, or either of them, or being in the public service, at their respective offices in each customs district where the whole number of said clerks and persons shall be all together as many as fifty. And thereafter, from time to time, on the direction of the President, said Secretary shall make the like classification or arrangement of clerks and persons so employed, in connection with any said office or offices, in any other customs district. And, upon like request, and for the purposes of this act, said Secretary shall arrange in one or more of said classes, or of existing classes, any other clerks, agents, or persons employed under his department in any said district not now classified; and every such arrangement and classification upon being made shall be reported to the President.

*Second.* Within said sixty days it shall be the duty of the Postmaster-General . . . to separately arrange in classes the several clerks and persons employed, or in the public service, at each post-office, or under any postmaster of the United States, where the whole number of said clerks and persons shall together amount to as many as fifty. And thereafter, from time to time,

on the direction of the President, it shall be the duty of the Postmaster-General to arrange in like classes the clerks and persons so employed in the postal service in connection with any other post-office; and every such arrangement and classification upon being made shall be reported to the President.

*Third.* That from time to time said Secretary, the Postmaster-General, and each of the heads of departments . . . and each head of an office, shall, on the direction of the President, and for facilitating the execution of this act, respectively revise any then existing classification or arrangement of those in their respective departments and offices, and shall, for the purposes of the examination herein provided for, include in one or more of such classes, so far as practicable, subordinate places, clerks, and officers in the public service pertaining to their respective departments not before classified for examination.

Sec. 7. That after the expiration of six months from the passage of this act no officer or clerk shall be appointed, and no person shall be employed to enter or be promoted in either of the said classes now existing, or that may be arranged hereunder pursuant to said rules, until he has passed an examination, or is shown to be specially exempted from such examination in conformity herewith. But nothing herein contained shall be construed to take from those honorably discharged from the military or naval service any preference conferred by . . . the Revised Statutes, nor to take from the President any authority not inconsistent with this act conferred by . . . said statutes; nor shall any officer not in the executive branch of the government, or any person merely employed as a laborer or workman, be required to be classified hereunder; nor, unless by direction of the Senate, shall any person who has been nominated for confirmation by the Senate be required to be classified or to pass an examination.

Sec. 8. That no person habitually using

intoxicating beverages to excess shall be appointed to, or retained in, any office, appointment, or employment to which the provisions of this act are applicable.

Sec. 9. That whenever there are already two or more members of a family in the public service in the grades covered by this act, no other member of such family shall be eligible to appointment to any of said grades.

Sec. 10. That no recommendation of any person who shall apply for office or place under the provisions of this act which may be given by any Senator or member of the House of Representatives, except as to the character or residence of the applicant, shall be received or considered by any person concerned in making any examination or appointment under this act.

Sec. 11. That no Senator, or Representative, or Territorial Delegate of the Congress, or Senator, Representative, or Delegate elect, or any officer or employee of either of said houses, and no executive, judicial, military, or naval officer of the United States, and no clerk or employee of any department, branch or bureau of the executive, judicial, or military or naval service of the United States, shall, directly or indirectly, solicit or receive, or be in any manner concerned in soliciting or receiving, any assessment, subscription, or contribution for any political purpose whatever, from any officer, clerk, or employee of the United States, or any department, branch, or bureau thereof, or from any person receiving any salary or compensation from moneys derived from the Treasury of the United States.

## 15

The unexpected stand taken by President Arthur on the tariff was as disconcerting to Stalwarts as his attitude toward civil service reform. Since the beginning of the Civil War, smoothly functioning Republican majorities in Congress, in response to jabbing from manufacturers' pressure groups, had pushed

levels higher and higher. Opposition to protection was confined to a few meek protests from Republican liberals until 1880, when the Democrats endorsed a "tariff for revenue only." President Arthur felt called upon to appoint a commission to study the whole question. But honest advocates of tariff reform despaired when the names of its members were made public; all were avowed protectionists, and the chairman was the paid secretary and lobbyist of the National Association of Wool Manufacturers. Yet the need for change was so patent that even this board, weighted though it was, recommended, in 1882, a downward revision of at least 20 per cent:[15]

Early in its deliberations the Commission became convinced that a substantial reduction of tariff duties is demanded, not by a mere indiscriminate popular clamor, but by the best conservative opinion of the country, including that which has in former times been most strenuous for the preservation of our national industrial defenses. Such a reduction of the existing tariff the Commission regards not only as a due recognition of public sentiment and a measure of justice to consumers, but one conducive to the general industrial prosperity, and which, though it may be temporarily inconvenient, will be ultimately beneficial to the special interests affected by such reduction. No rates of defensive duties, except for the establishment of new industries, which more than equalize the conditions of labor and capital with those of foreign competitors can be justified. Excessive duties, or those above such standard of equalization, are positively injurious to the interest which they are supposed to benefit. They encourage the investment of capital in manufacturing enterprise by rash and unskilled speculators, to be followed by disaster to the adventurers and their employes, and a plethora of commodities which deranges the operations of skilled and prudent enterprise. Numerous

[15] United States Tariff Commission, *Report*, I, 5-7. (*House Miscellaneous Documents*, 47th Cong., 2nd Sess., Doc. No. 6.)

examples of such disasters and derangements occurred during and shortly after the excessively protective period of the late war, when tariff duties were enhanced by the rates of foreign exchange and premiums upon gold. Excessive duties generally, or exceptionally high duties in particular cases, discredit our whole national economic system and furnish plausible arguments for its complete subversion. They serve to increase uncertainty on the part of industrial enterprise, whether it shall enlarge or contract its operations, and take from commerce, as well as production, the sense of stability required for extended undertakings. It would seem that the rates of duties under the existing tariff—fixed, for the most part, during the war under the evident necessity at that time of stimulating to its utmost extent all domestic production—might be adapted, through reduction, to the present condition of peace requiring no such extraordinary stimulus. And in the mechanical and manufacturing industries, especially those which have been long established, it would seem that the improvements in machinery and processes made within the last twenty years, and the high scale of productiveness which has become a characteristic of their establishments, would permit our manufacturers to compete with their foreign rivals under a substantial reduction of existing duties.

Entertaining these views, the Commission has sought to present a scheme of tariff duties in which substantial reduction should be the distinguishing feature. The average reduction in rates, including that from the enlargement of the free list and the abolition of the duties on charges and commissions, at which the Commission has aimed is not less on the average than 20 per cent.; and it is the opinion of the Commission that the reduction will reach 25 per cent. The reduction, slight in some cases, in others not attempted, is in many cases from 40 to 50 per cent. The actual amount of the total reduction cannot be

stated with precision, partly from want of time to make the calculations required for such details in the brief period intervening between the final determination in particular cases and the preparation of this report; and there is no exact standard by which to estimate the amount of reduction in revenue, on account of the varying character, amount, and prices of commodities in the importations of different years. If the reduction reaches the amount at which the Commission has aimed, and if there is any truth in the allegation of the opponents of the present economic system, that a duty on articles such as are produced in this country, whether in manufactures or agriculture, enhances the price to the consumer, not only of what is imported, but of the whole domestic production, to an amount of which the duty is a measure, the reduction proposed by the Commission would benefit consumers to the extent of hundreds of millions of dollars. As the amount of reduction cannot be stated with precision, it follows that no statement can be safely made as to the effect of the proposed reduction upon the total volume of the revenue from import duties. The amount of the reduction in the total volume of the revenue could be stated absolutely only by showing the income that would be lost by the enlargement of the free list. Although the free list is considerably enlarged in the scheme proposed, this list has already been so enlarged by previous legislation (to such an extent as to embrace nearly one-third in value of the merchandise imported in 1881) that little room is left for reform in this direction. It is probable that the reduction of the total volume of the revenue would not be proportionate to the reduction of the duties, for the reason that the reduction may, temporarily at least, increase importations, and greater revenue for a time may result from the lower duties.

The adoption of an inflexible rule of horizontal reduction would have made the work of the Commission in this direction comparatively easy; but such a method would have been unskillful, timid, and unjust. The essential feature of our existing tariff system for generations has been discrimination, and nothing but disaster has attended the temporary · departures from this rule. A horizontal reduction would have been a violation of the injunction in the law creating the Commission to make the revision upon a scale of justice to all interests. In the exercise of this discrimination the Commission has found its most responsible, delicate, and difficult task. In the use of its best discretion, and in the light of the testimony upon which it was authorized by law to found its conclusions, it has not hesitated to withhold the application of the general rule of reduction in many cases, and in some, though comparatively few, cases to recommend an increase of duties where such increase seemed to be required to preserve the "scale of justice." It has been the effort of the Commission to make the reduction apply to commodities of necessary general consumption, and to diminish or withhold the reduction upon commodities of high cost, requiring more labor, and which being consumed principally by the more wealthy classes could bear higher duties, at the same time supplying revenue and encouraging the higher arts without being oppressive in their operation. Some of the proposed discriminations are made without reference to considerations of revenue, as that in the duty on books, reduced in the interests of the diffusion of knowledge, and the advance in the duties on works of art, made for the encouragement of original American art. It has been sought invariably to make a discrimination in the rate of the duties imposed upon a manufactured product and the raw material or partially manufactured product of which it is made, the object being to impose a higher duty upon the latter. With but a few exceptions a less reduction has been applied to the products of agriculture than to those of the mechanical and manufacturing industries, for the reason that the former are less benefited than the latter by the improvements in machinery and processes, and the economies resulting from a high scale of productiveness. In the reduction applied to the latter, however, it has been earnestly kept in view not to make it so great in any case as to diminish the compensation of labor.

## 16

When advocates of tariff reform in Congress introduced a measure embodying the commission's recommendations, they met with determined resistance. One center of opposition was composed of the manufacturers' pressure groups and their docile servants in the legislature—men such as "Pig Iron" Kelly of Pennsylvania, a Republican, and S. J. Randall or William Mahone, Democratic senators. The other was made up of congressmen who accepted reform in principle but not in practice; thus the chairman of the commission, while sincerely believing in lowered duties, fought doggedly to retain protection for the woolen interests he represented. Senator John Sherman of Ohio, a Republican, left an account of his own confused thinking on this topic in his *Recollections:*[16]

If the committee had embodied, in this bill, the recommendations of the tariff commission, including the schedules without amendment or change, the tariff would have been settled for many years. Unfortunately this was not done, but the schedules prescribing the rates of duty and their classification were so radically changed by the committee that the scheme of the tariff commission was practically defeated. Many persons wishing to advance their particular industries appeared before the committee and succeeded in having their views adopted. The Democratic members seemed to take little interest in the proceeding, as they were opposed to the adoption of the tariff as a part of the bill. I did all I could to prevent these changes, was very much

---

[16] John Sherman, *Recollections of Forty Years in the House, Senate and Cabinet* (Chicago, 1895), II, 851-853.

discouraged by the action of the committee, and doubted the propriety of voting for the bill with the tariff provisions as proposed by the committee and adopted by the Senate. I have always regretted that I did not defeat the bill, which I could readily have done by voting with the Democrats against the adoption of the conference report, which passed the Senate by the vote of yeas 32, nays 30. However, the propriety and necessity of a reduction of internal taxes proposed by the bill were so urgent that I did not feel justified in denying relief from burdensome and unnecessary taxes on account of provisions in the bill that I did not approve. With great reluctance I voted for it.

One reduction made by the committee against my most strenuous efforts was by a change in the classification and rates of duty on wool. When I returned to Ohio I was violently assailed by the Democratic newspapers for voting for a bill that reduced the existing duty on wool about twenty per cent., and I had much difficulty in explaining to my constituents that I opposed the reduction, but, when the Senate refused to adopt my view, did not feel justified, on account of my opposition to this one item, in voting against the bill as a whole. The conference report was agreed to by the House of Representatives on the 2nd of March, and the bill was approved by the President on the 3rd.

I did not conceal my opposition to the tariff sections of the revenue bill. I expressed it in debate, in interviews and in letters. When the bill was reported to the Senate it was met by two kinds of opposition, one the blind party opposition of free traders, led by Senators Beck and Vance, the other (much more dangerous), the conflict of selfish and local interests, mainly on the part of manufacturers, who regarded all articles which they purchased as raw material, on which they wished the lowest possible rate of duty, or none at all, and their work, as the finished article, on which they wished the highest

rate of duty. In other words, what they had to buy they called raw material to be admitted without protection, and what they had to sell they wanted protected. It was a combination of the two kinds of opposition that made the trouble.

The Democratic Senators, with a few exceptions, voted steadily and blindly for any reduction of duty proposed; but they alone could not carry their amendments, and only did so when reënforced by Republican Senators, who, influenced by local interest, could reduce any duty at their pleasure. In this way, often by a majority of one, amendments were adopted that destroyed the harmony of the bill. In this way iron ore, pig iron, scrap iron and wool were sacrificed in the Senate. They were classed as raw materials for manufactures and not as manufactures. For selfish and local reasons tin plates, cotton, ties and iron and steel rods for wire were put at exceptionally low rates, and thus were stricken from the list of articles that could be manufactured in this country. This local and selfish appeal was the great defect of the tariff bill. I do not hesitate to say that the iron and wool sections of the bill, as it passed the Senate, were unjust, incongruous and absurd. They would have reduced the iron and steel industries of the United States to their condition before the war, and have closed up two-thirds of the furnaces and rolling mills in this country. They were somewhat changed in committee of conference, but if they had not been, the only alternative to the manufacturers would have been to close up or largely reduce the wages of labor.

Another mistake made in the Senate was to strike out all the carefully prepared legislative provisions simplifying the mode of collecting customs duties, and the provisions for the trial of customs cases. The tariff commission proposed to repeal the *ad valorem* duty on wool, and leave on it only the specific duty of ten and twelve cents per pound. The chairman of the tariff commission was himself the president or agent of the woolen manufacturers and made the report. The manufacturers of woolens, however, were dissatisfied, and demanded an entire change in the classification of woolens, and, on some important grades, a large increase of rates, but insisted upon a reduction of the duty on wool.

## 17

Party degradation reached a disgraceful low in the campaign of 1884. Republican Stalwarts, forgetting the scare of 1876, nominated James G. Blaine, a Maine politician whose name was regarded in many quarters as synonymous with corruption. Openly courting the industrialists, Blaine waged an inept campaign. Despite his dubious record and questionable associates he would in all likelihood have won but for two colossal blunders just before election: an ill-advised remark by a supporter, and a dinner party that set the tongues of half the population wagging. A newspaper reporter who was present later described them:[17]

I could cite half a dozen incidents of that campaign, any one of which adversely influenced enough votes to have carried New York for Blaine, and New York would have elected him. . . . The historic incident, of course, and the one that cost Blaine most votes, was the Rev. Dr. Burchard's "Rum, Romanism and Rebellion" sentence in an address of welcome to Blaine in the old Fifth Avenue Hotel in New York city. I heard that speech. It had been crowded into a forenoon reception because Blaine was to review a Business Men's parade in the afternoon and the night had been set aside for a banquet tendered by the "captains of industry" destined to become known as "Belshazzar's Feast."

I do not know whether Presidential candidates were "trailed" earlier than 1884 by

agents of their rivals, instructed to watch for "breaks," but a Democratic sleuth followed Blaine in that campaign, took stenographic notes of all he said and reported every incident to William C. Whitney and Senator Arthur Pue Gorman. This trailer was present at the Burchard meeting with eyes and ears alert. He heard the alliterative phrase and realized its damaging possibilities. He hastened to the Cleveland headquarters just one block away—and by late afternoon the city was flooded with sensational circulars intended to arouse the Catholic voters.

Following the meeting a dozen or more newspaper correspondents sat on the famous "Amen Corner" benches in the old Fifth Avenue Hotel discussing its news features. Not one of us gave heed to the utterance that was soon to become a national sensation. Our group included Cleveland men, Blaine men and Butler men but regardless of our politics we were presumed to be wide-awake news-gatherers. Imagine the shock to our pride a few hours later when the deluge of circulars came, sensationalizing a story that every one of us had seen, heard and *missed!*

I say that we had seen and heard. That is only half true—actually we saw, but did not hear Dr. Burchard. I doubt whether many persons heard him. He stood atop the corridor stairway leading from the street level to the first floor. A noisy crowd filled the place. The clergyman's voice was poor, his delivery uninspiring. Thoughts and eyes were centered on Blaine, who faced him listening indifferently.

Blaine, I am sure, was correct in his subsequent statement that he did not hear the damaging words. But neither Blaine nor the correspondents, inasmuch as we had responsibilities in the matter, can be excused on that plea. It was our duty to know what he said. A clergyman's speech, however, seemed to us the last thing to be followed closely for a sensation; it was assumed to be non-explosive. Yet dynamite

[17] From *As I Knew Them* by Henry L. Stoddard, pp. 131-135. Copyright, 1927, by Harper & Brothers.

was there!—dynamite that cost a Presidency!

In all my subsequent campaign experiences, I have not heard such an uproar as that which broke out everywhere as the Burchard sentence became known. Instantly appeals were made to Blaine to repudiate the utterance. But Blaine never liked to answer attacks; he was not a man to take the defensive, preferring always to battle on ground of his own choosing. All that he would say was the brief truth that he had not heard much of Burchard's address and in particular had not heard the unfortunate expression. Next day he continued on his way home to Maine, speaking at different cities according to schedule; but until Saturday night he gave no further heed to Burchard. Then he learned that Catholic churches were to be flooded with circulars on Sunday. This information led him to act—too late, unfortunately, to repair the damage done.

Indisputably, Blaine would have been elected President by a heavy popular vote had there been no Burchard speech. It was estimated then that in New York alone he lost 50,000 votes. My estimate in the Philadelphia Press fixed the loss at more than 50,000, but whatever the actual figure may have been it was large enough to have insured the State and the Presidency to Blaine by a substantial plurality.

However, Burchard's speech was not the only vote-losing incident of that fateful last week of the campaign. Some "captains of industry," as they were called, with unwisdom characteristic of business men that mix in politics, had persuaded Blaine to accept a banquet at Delmonico's, then New York City's most famous restaurant. Cyrus Field, Jay Gould, Andrew Carnegie and men of their type were the sponsors. The dinner was fixed for the same date as the Burchard meeting. It was served on the finest dinner plate Delmonico possessed; the quality of guests and service made it truly "a swagger affair." The only banquet rivalling it that I ever attended was James Hazen Hyde's anniversary of the Equitable Life Assurance Society at the Waldorf about 20 years ago. The Democrats promptly characterized it as "Belshazzar's Feast"—pictured it with all-gold dinner plate, waiters in livery and knee breeches, the banqueters with be-diamonded shirt-fronts.

The New York *World's* headlines next day were:

MAMMON'S HOMAGE
Blaine Hobnobbing With the
Mighty Money Kings
The Banquet in His Honor at
Delmonico's Last Night
Millionaires and Monopolists Seal
Their Allegiance

Blaine had questioned the wisdom of the dinner. His secretary, Thomas H. Sherman, still living in Gorham, Maine, confirms my recollection that Blaine had written and telegraphed objections, but at last good naturedly had set aside his own reaction to it. Next day, even before criticism had reached its volume, he declared the dinner would cost him votes. He seemed more concerned about its effect than about Burchard's "Rum, Romanism and Rebellion"—both appearing in the same day's papers.

## 18

The Democrats were less obtuse in conducting the 1884 election campaign. As their candidate they selected Grover Cleveland, whose record as the reform governor of New York had made him nationally famous. But the Democratic crusade for morality in public life was imperiled when a Buffalo newspaper charged that if Blaine's public career was besmirched, Cleveland's private life was not unsullied. Cleveland, it was alleged, had fathered an illegitimate child. The reaction of Cleveland's supporters—in both Democratic and liberal Republican circles—was recorded by Moorfield Storey, who had been attending a political conference in July, 1884, when the news broke:[18]

The proceedings of the Conference were characterized by great enthusiasm, and we adjourned thoroughly well satisfied with the day's work, but as we were leaving the hall there was placed in our hands copies of a Buffalo newspaper containing the story about Mr. Cleveland's relations with Mrs. Halpine which afterwards played so important a part in the campaign.

A number of us went to the University Club and dined together, and among them was Carl Schurz who sat at the head of the table, next to him was a man from Chicago and I sat next. Just as we were finishing dinner the door opened and George William Curtis, Charles R. Codman, Theodore Lyman and General Barlow with possibly another, whom at this moment I do not recall, came in. Mr. Curtis's face was the picture of woe and he asked us whether we had seen this Buffalo paper. We said that we had and he said: "What are we going to do? We have begun by saying that the issue of the present campaign is moral, not political, and here we are confronted with this scandal. How can we possibly continue our support of Mr. Cleveland?" It was pointed out to him in reply that, since the occurrences described had taken place, Mr. Cleveland had been elected mayor of Buffalo and afterward Governor of New York by an unprecedented majority and that during the campaigns which preceded these elections no allusion had been made to any story of the sort. It was suggested that had this story been true something might have been said about it in these campaigns, and it was also suggested that it was not safe to believe everything that we saw written in the newspaper during a political cam-

paign, especially when feeling ran as high as it did at that time.

Mr. Curtis, however, was not entirely satisfied and the discussion was proceeding when the gentleman on my left, who, I think came from Chicago and who had been silently listening spoke up. He said "Do you want to know how this matter strikes me?" We answered, "Yes." "Well," said he, "from what I hear I gather that Mr. Cleveland has shown high character and great capacity in public office but that in private life his conduct has been open to questions, while, on the other hand, Mr. Blaine in public life has been weak and dishonest while he seems to have been an admirable husband and father. The conclusion that I draw from these facts is that we should elect Mr. Cleveland to the public office which he is so admirably qualified to fill and remand Mr. Blaine to the private life which he is so eminently fitted to adorn."

When Grover Cleveland went to the White House, those who expected any radical change were disappointed. Actually there was little difference between the parties: both were manipulated by the leaders of business. Desire for private gain rather than concern for the public good shaped the conduct of politicians; there could be no basic reform. There was an allied factor: the political process had itself been shaped to reward such conduct, and it obstructed any leaders who tried to reform and reorganize a party.

## DEMOCRACY AND PARTY THEORY

### 19

The crucial problem of parties was recognized by a few scholars, both American and foreign. Two penetrating analyses of politics in this era not only revealed the failures of the American system but pointed the way to a better future. The disparity between democracy in theory and practice was the concern of a celebrated Englishman, James Bryce, whose *American Commonwealth* (1888) became one of the most discussed books of the generation. An equally competent American

[18] Cited as not previously published by James Ford Rhodes in his *History of the United States* (New York, 1920), VIII, 221-223. Copyright 1919 by The Macmillan Company and used with their permission.

scholar, young Woodrow Wilson, reviewed Lord Bryce's book for the *Political Science Quarterly*:[19]

Mr. Bryce divided his work into six parts. In Part I he discusses "The National Government," going carefully over the ground made almost tediously familiar to American constitutional students by commentaries without number. But he gives to his treatment a freshness of touch and a comprehensiveness which impart to it a new and first-rate interest. This he does by combining in a single view both the legal theory and interpretation and the practical aspects and operation of the federal machinery. More than that, he brings that machinery and the whole federal arrangement into constant comparison with federal experiments and constitutional machinery elsewhere. There is a scope and an outlook here such as render his critical expositions throughout both impressive and stimulating. Congress, the presidency, and the federal courts are discussed in every point of view that can yield instruction. The forms and principles of the federal system are explained both historically and practically and are estimated with dispassionate candor. Perhaps the most emphasized point made in this part is one which is derived from comparative politics. It is the separation of the executive from Congress, a separation which deprives the executive of all voice in the formation of administrative and financial policy, and which deprives Congress of such leadership as would give its plans coherency and make available for its use that special and intimate knowledge of administrative possibilities without which much well meant legislation must utterly miscarry. This is of course the particular in which our government differs most conspicuously from all the other governments of the world. Everywhere else there

is one form or another of ministerial leadership in the legislature. A body of ministers constitutes, as it were, a nerve centre, or rather a sensitive presiding brain, in the body politic, taking from the nation such broad suggestions as public opinion can unmistakably convey touching the main ends to be sought by legislation and policy, but themselves suggesting in turn, in the light of their own special knowledge and intimate experience of affairs, the best means by which those ends may be attained. Because we are without such legislative leadership we remain for long periods of embarrassment without any solution of some of the simplest problems that await legislation. To this absence of cabinet government in America, and the consequent absence of party government in the European sense of the term, Mr. Bryce again and again returns as to a salient feature, full of significance both for much evil and for some good. The evil consists in slipshod, haphazard, unskilled and hasty legislation; the good, so far as it may be stated in a single sentence, consists in delaying the triumphs of public opinion and thereby, perhaps, rendering them safer triumphs. . . .

Part III, on "The Party System," is the crowning achievement of the author's method. Here in a learned systematic treatise which will certainly for a long time be a standard authority on our institutions, a much used hand-book for the most serious students of politics, we have a careful, dispassionate, scientific description of the "machine," an accurately drawn picture of "bosses," a clear exposition of the way in which the machine works, an analysis of all the most practical methods of "practical politics," as well as what we should have expected, a sketch of party history, an explanation of the main characteristics of the parties of today, a discussion of the conditions of public life in the United States, those conditions which help to keep the best men out of politics and produce certain distinctively American types of

---

[19] "Bryce's American Commonwealth," by Woodrow Wilson, *Political Science Quarterly*, Vol. IV, No. 1 (March, 1889), 153-169.

politicians, and a complete study of the nominating convention. One can well believe that that not supersensitive person, the practical politician, much as he pretends to scorn the indignant attacks made upon him by "pious" reformers, would be betrayed into open emotion should he read this exact and passionless, this discriminating and scientific digest of the methods by which he lives, of the motives by which he is moved. And certainly those who are farthest removed from the practical politician's point of view will gain from these chapters a new and vital conception of what it is to study constitutions in the life. The wholesome light of Mr. Bryce's method shines with equal ray alike upon the just and upon the unjust.

Mr. Bryce very happily describes our system of nomination by convention as

an effort of nature to fill the void left in America by the absence of the European parliamentary or cabinet system, under which an executive is called into being out of the legislature by the majority of the legislature. In the European system no single act of nomination is necessary, because the leader of the majority comes gradually to the top in virtue of his own strength.

But what, in view of this, are we to say of his judgment that "a system for selecting candidates is not a mere contrivance for preventing party dissensions, but an essential feature of matured democracy"? Clearly no system for nominating candidates can touch the leading places in a democracy, however matured that democracy may be, if those places be filled under the parliamentary or cabinet system, as they are in England and France. . . . Have not the exceeding multiplicity of elective officers and that pernicious principle that no one may be chosen state or national representative except from the district in which he lives—a principle whose history runs back to insignificant Governor Phips of colonial Massachusetts —been more to blame than anything that

can be regarded as essential to democracy? Above all is not that complete obscuration of individual responsibility which results from the operation of the "checks and balances" of our system chiefly chargeable? It prevents any man from selecting himself for leadership by conspicuous service and makes the active part of politics turn upon selecting men rather than selecting measures. Men are not identified with measures; there must, consequently, be some artificial way of picking them out.

In enumerating the causes why the best men do not enter politics, Mr. Bryce seems to me to omit one of the most important, although he elsewhere repeatedly gives evidence that he is in full view of it, namely, the absence of all great prizes of legislative leadership to be won by sheer strength of persuasive mind and constructive skill. He sums up the reasons he does give with admirable point, however, by saying that "in America, while politics are relatively less interesting than in Europe, and lead to less, other careers are relatively more interesting and lead to more"; but he omits to state, in this connection, one of the most patent reasons why politics are relatively less interesting, why they lead to less, here than elsewhere.

## 20

While Lord Bryce dissected the federal system and the particularism of the parties, Woodrow Wilson diagnosed the pathology of democracy. Long famed as a student of political science at the Johns Hopkins and Princeton universities before he entered politics himself, Wilson's principal contribution was *Congressional Government* (1885), a classic that went through fifteen editions before 1900. Many of the ideas of that larger work were conveniently summarized in an address, "Leaderless Government," delivered before the Virginia Bar Association in 1897:[20]

[20] *The Public Papers of Woodrow Wilson, College and State* (Harper & Brothers, New York, 1925), I, 335-359. Quotation by permission of Mrs. Woodrow (Edith Bolling) Wilson, owner of the copyright.

. . . By the words "Leaderless Government" I mean to describe the government of the United States. I do not utter the words with the least touch of censoriousness or cynicism or even discouragement. In using them I am simply speaking a careful and, if I may say so, a dispassionate judgment. I do not believe it a necessary feature of our government that we should be without leaders; neither do I believe that we shall continue to be without them; but as a matter of fact we are without them, and we ought to ask ourselves, Why? I mean, of course, that we are without official leaders—without leaders who can be held immediately responsible for the action and policy of the government, alike upon its legislative and upon its administrative side. Leaders of some sort we, of course, always have; but they come and go like phantoms, put forward as if by accident, withdrawn, not by our choice, but as if upon some secret turn of fortune . . . which we neither anticipate nor as a nation control—some local quarrel, some obscure movement of politics within a single district, some manipulation of a primary or some miscarriage in a convention. . . .

Look at the familiar system for a little with this matter in view, and you shall see that, as we now use it, it seems devised as if to prevent official and responsible leadership. The President cannot lead. . . . He makes it his study to use only a private influence and never to seem a maker of resolutions. And even when the occasion is extraordinary and his own mind definitely made up, he argues and urges—he cannot command. . . . The President can make his message a means of concentrating public opinion upon particular topics of his own choosing, and so force those topics upon the attention of the House. But that is all; and under ordinary circumstances it is not much.

It was not so in the early years of the government. Roughly speaking, Presidents were leaders until Andrew Jackson went home to the "Hermitage." Sometimes they have been leaders since; but in the old days it was a matter of course that they should be. . . . It was taken for granted at the first that the real leaders of the nation would be put into the presidential chair. For a little while Vice-Presidents succeeded Presidents, as if of course; and then for a season Presidents were allowed to name their own successors in their appointment to the office of Secretary of State—or, rather, were expected to fill that great office with men whom their party accepted as second only to the Presidents themselves in weight and influence, their natural successors. The management of these things was left in that day to well-known groups of men which all the country knew to constitute, each for its own party, a sort of unofficial ministry. Nominations were arranged in Congressional caucus, by men in whose hands rested not only the conduct of these matters, but the whole shaping of party policies as well; and they naturally chose according to some recognized plan, compatible with the immediate objects of their organization, putting those in authority who were their actual leaders, and to whom they looked for guidance whether in office or not. . . .

. . . Roger Sherman declared very bluntly, in the Constitutional Convention of 1787, that "he considered the executive magistracy as nothing more than an institution for carrying the will of the Legislature into effect"; and, although we may not be willing to go to the length of saying quite so much as that, we see even more clearly now than Roger Sherman did at the beginning that, in the last resort, it lies with Congress, and not with the executive, to choose what the government shall be and do. And we know that it is a serious matter that the intimate relations which once existed between Congress and the President should have been so completely broken.

The men who are sent to our nominating conventions are men, for the most part, little known—and in other matters little regarded; men who have nothing to do with legislation, and who are without any responsible part whatever in the choice of policies for the nation. An incalculable number of local influences, utterly obscure to the country at large, and unconnected, as we know, with any general party purpose or policy of which the country can know anything, determine the instructions with which delegates are sent. They run together to press the claims of a score of candidates, selected, not by the general voice of any party, but upon grounds of preference which only their special friends and partisans can explain. . . . Some "dark horse"; some man hitherto little thought of; some one whom his friends have astutely known how to push in the secret conferences of separate delegations; some man whose personal tact of force has caught of a sudden the enthusiasm of the convention itself and of the crowds in its galleries; some man unheralded and untried, it may be, catches the drift of the vote and is nominated. A good man he may be, and a fair President—Providence has been kind to us much beyond the encouragement we have given it; but he is not always a man whom we know, and he is seldom a man accepted in Washington as of course a leader and maker of affairs. . . .

. . . Seasoned Congressmen smile in their beards, no doubt, to see the new man come radiant to Washington, beaming authority on every side; but they court him for a brief space, as one who has the ear of the President in the making of appointments; and then, when the appointments are made and the President has found his place, they draw aside to see whether this crack coach will slip into oblivion or not. And so each man has his entry and his exit. . . .

. . . Plainly the nominating convention has separated legislature and executive much more sharply than the makers of the Constitution intended; has brought utterly incalculable forces into play for the choice of our Presidents; and has cut us off once and for all from the old traditions of party leadership. We must take our Presidents somewhat at haphazard and by a special, clumsy, machinery out of the general body of the nation; and the Houses must provide themselves with purposes and leaders of their own.

And yet the Houses show a notable lack of efficient organization; for I take it for granted that when one is speaking of a representative legislature he must mean by "an efficient organization," an organization which provides for deliberate, and deliberative, action, and which enables the nation to affix responsibility for what is done and what is not done. . . . The House of Representatives is neither deliberate nor deliberative. We have not forgotten that one of the most energetic of its recent Speakers thanked God, in his frankness, that the House was not a deliberative body. It has not time for the leadership of argument; it has not time, therefore, to disclose the individual weight of its members. Debate takes time. It also lets the nation hear the prevailing voices and the reasons for action. For debate and leadership in that sort the House must have a party organization and discipline such as it has never had. . . .

. . . The Senate unquestionably . . . stands unique among legislative bodies in the modern time. Whether we relish its uniqueness in the present generation quite as much as it was relished among our fathers is an open question, but its individuality is indubitable. This singular body has assumed of late what I may, perhaps, be allowed to call a sort of Romo-Polish character. Like the Roman Senate, it has magnified its administrative powers and its right of negative in the great fields of finance and foreign affairs, as well as in all ordinary legislation; and, following Polish precedents, it has seemed to arrogate to its members the right of individual veto. Each Senator, like each prince of ancient

Poland, insists, it would seem, upon consulting his own interests and preferences before he will allow measures to reach their final consideration and passage. In the field of administration, it seems plain, the Senate expects the executive very generally to submit to its oversight and suggestion, as Roman magistrates submitted to the Senate of their singular republic. . . .

. . . Who leads the Senate? Can any one say? It, too, has its standing committees, to which all of its business is in the first place sent, as to the committees of the House; but it accords them no such mastery as is accorded the committees of the House. Debate and amendment make free with committee reports, as with any other matter, and upon the open floor of the Senate no man is master. The Vice-President is an outsider, not the leader of his party—even if his party have the majority in the Senate—and generally not a very influential outsider—timid about asserting even the natural powers of a parliamentary moderator. Among the Senators themselves there is an equality as absolute as the equality of the sovereign states which they represent. . . . The Senate as a whole is jealous of its dignity and of its prerogatives; and its members severally stand out distinct units in every matter of controversy. Who shall say who leads and who obeys amongst them?

And so we have the composite thing which we call the Government of the United States. Its several parts are severally chosen; it is no unified and corporate whole. Its President is chosen, not by proof of leadership among the men whose confidence he must have if he is to play an effective part in the making of affairs, but by management—the management of obscure men—and through the uncertain chances of an ephemeral convention which has no other part in politics. Its popular chamber shapes its affairs, not by conference with those who must execute the laws, and show them feasible, nor yet by any clarifying process of debate, but chiefly by means

of the silent management of its moderator, whose office is fixed for a two years' term, and who represents, not the country, but a single constituency. Its Senate is a band of individuals, amongst whom it is impossible to maintain leadership, and to whom it is difficult to extend the discipline of party organization. This is not a government of systematic checks and balances,— a *system* of checks and balances would enable you to distinguish causes and calculate effects. It is a government without definite order, showing a confident interplay of forces, in which no man stands at the helm to steer, whose course is beaten out by the shifting winds of personal influence and popular opinion. . . .

My studies have taught me this one thing with a definiteness which cannot be mistaken: Successful governments have never been conducted safely in the midst of complex and critical affairs except when guided by those who were responsible for carrying out and bringing to an issue the measures they proposed; and the separation of the right to plan from the duty to execute has always led to blundering and inefficiency; and modern representative bodies cannot of themselves combine the two. . . . If you would have the present error of our system in a word, it is this, that Congress is the motive power in the government and yet has in it nowhere any representative of the nation as a whole. Our Executive, on the other hand, is national: at any rate may be made so, and yet has no longer any place of guidance in our system. It represents no constituency, but the whole people; and yet, though it alone is national, it has no originative voice in domestic national policy.

The sum of the matter is, that we have carried the application of the notion that the powers of government must be separated to a dangerous and unheard-of length by thus holding our only national representative, the Executive, at arm's length from Congress, whose very commission it seems to be to represent, not the people, but the communities into which the people are divided. We should have Presidents and Cabinets of a different calibre were we to make it their bounden duty to act as a committee for the whole nation to choose and formulate matters for the consideration of Congress in the name of a party and an Administration; and then, if Congress consented to the measures, what they are already—a committee to execute them—make them work and approve themselves practicable and wise.

And that is exactly what we ought to do. We should have not a little light thrown daily, and often when it was least expected, upon the conduct of the Departments, if the heads of the Departments had daily to face the representatives of the people, to propose, defend, explain administrative policy, upon the floor of the Houses, where such a plan would put them: and heads of departments would be happy under such a system only when they were very straightforward and honest and able men. I am not suggesting that initiative in legislation be by any means confined to the Administration—that would be radical, indeed—but only that they be given a free, though responsible, share in it—and that, I conceive, would bring the government back very nearly to the conception and practice of Washington. It would be a return to our first models of statesmanship and political custom. . . .

. . . I do not suggest methods—this is not the place or the occasion; I suggest an idea—a way out of chaos: the nationalization of the motive power of the government, to offset the economic sectionalization of the country; I suggest the addition to Congress, which represents us severally, of a power, constituted how you will, which shall represent us collectively in the proposing of laws; which shall have the right as of course to press national motives and courses of action to a vote in the Congress. This will not subordinate Congress; it may accept the proposals of the Administration or not, as it pleases (it once took

a scolding from Washington himself for not accepting them); but the country will at least have a mouthpiece and not all of policy will lurk with committees and in executive sessions of the Senate.

## 21

The investigations of Bryce and Wilson framed the basic questions: democratic government meant responsible government; modern government required the use of power adequate to the tasks of industrial urban society; the exercise of power in a democracy implied a strict accountability for its use. The primal question, therefore, was an operational one: how could power, sufficient for social ends, be effectively employed and yet made responsible to majority will? Both Bryce and Wilson agreed that centrally organized parties provided the only method of achieving democratic goals; the failure of the parties between 1865 and 1884 can be explained by their internal breakdown. With leadership lacking, they became tools of pressure groups rather than instruments of popular government. A modern student of the subject, E. E. Schattschneider, might have been writing specifically of those dismal years in his penetrating analysis of the failure of our party system:[21]

The roll calls in the House and the Senate show that party votes are relatively rare. On difficult questions, usually the most important questions, party lines are apt to break badly, and a straight party vote, aligning one party against the other, is the exception rather than the rule. The vote is sometimes unanimous or nearly unanimous; that is, the parties are occasionally in substantial agreement. Often both parties split into approximately equal halves. In this case the party alightment is zero. At other times one party votes as a unit but is joined by a substantial fraction of the other. Finally, a predominant portion of one party may be opposed by a predominant portion of the other party, while

[21] From E. E. Schattschneider, *Party Government,* pp. 130-137. Copyright, 1942, by E. E. Schattschneider. Reprinted by permission of Rinehart & Company, publishers.

minorities, more or less numerous, on each side cross party lines to join their opponents. In general, the last-mentioned case is the nearest approximation to a party vote on an important issue likely to be encountered, aside from routine partisan business. The tendency to cross party lines appears even in legislation sponsored by the president as party leader, though it is true that a popular and able leader in the White House can do something to rally the party behind his program. If the leadership of the president is strong and successful, it is likely, however, to win substantial support from *both* parties. In this case, the opposition tends to play safe and votes for the president's bills if it thinks that he has the country with him, later disclaiming responsibility if the president's policies turn out badly. From the standpoint of presidential leadership it is worthy of note that the president is sometimes able to appeal to the opposition party for support almost as successfully as he can appeal to his own party and, on the other hand, that most of his troubles are likely to be made for him by his own partisans in Congress. This is not the whole story. The need of leadership at times is stronger than the centrifugal forces at work in the party. Moreover, the president is not without his resources. Yet, when all is said, it remains true that the roll calls demonstrate that *the parties are unable to hold their lines in a controversial public issue when the pressure is on.*

The condition described in the foregoing paragraph constitutes *the most important single fact concerning the American parties*. He who knows this fact, and knows nothing else, knows more about American parties than he who knows everything except this fact. What kind of party is it that, having won control of the government, is unable to govern? Surely this is the unmistakable mark of a decentralized party. (Decentralized in the special sense of American politics.) If a party were *never* able to agree in Congress, it would seem

to be no party at all. How can a party disagree so much and still be a party? Apparently, the special form of decentralization existing in American parties requires that the congressional party agree on *some* matters but leaves the members free to do as they please about others. The American major party is, to repeat the definition, a loose confederation of state and local bosses *for limited purposes.*

What are the limited purposes upon which the party oligarchs must agree? The answer will determine what the party is. The state and local party bosses want patronage and that is nearly all they want. As instruments for the extraction of patronage from American government at all levels the parties display none of the indecision and confusion they exhibit when voting on controversial *public* issues. The attitude of the parties toward the private business of politics is to be distinguished sharply from their attitude toward the public business of the parties.

The action of Congress is definitely partisan in the "organization" of the houses (that is, the appointment of the officers of the houses), the appointment of the standing committees, the distribution of the patronage of Congress, certain matters of party tactics, the final votes on the passage of tariff bills (but not in the votes on the significant items in these bills), and some public bills. As a matter of fact, the caucus, the classical instrumentality for party action in Congress, meets hardly at all. In the House, the party leadership, not necessarily in harmony with the presidential leadership, uses a labyrinthine procedure to block legislative projects to which it is opposed before the bills reach the floor. That is, the party leadership is able to say what the majority may *not* do in many instances, but it cannot easily force them to take positive action.

In the Senate, party discipline on *public* issues is notoriously ineffective. If we compare the weakness of party discipline in the Senate on public questions with the extraordinary effectiveness of the support given the rule of senatorial courtesy for the extraction of patronage from the government, the character of the system becomes evident. The party knows its private mind better than it knows its public mind. In private matters (patronage, and so on), vacillation in the alignment of the parties is approximately zero. Obviously, we have here two different things, distinct and separate, and it serves no good purpose to ignore the distinction and to formulate our conceptions of party politics as if the difference did not exist. As an extractive enterprise for the extortion of patronage and plunder from the government, the party acts with great precision. The party as the formulator of public issues is something else altogether. This dualism in the American major party is fundamental. . . .

Why is there a conflict between presidential leadership on issues and the private schemes of the local bosses? The conflict does not, probably, arise because the local bosses have strong views on matters of public policy. Generally the bosses are not interested in public affairs; they read no books, have vague ideas on public business, and are indifferent to conflicts of policy as far as personal prejudice is con-cerned. In the voting on bills the vacillation of congressmen is due as much to the relaxation of the discipline of local bosses on public issues as it is to the fact that local bosses force them to move in divergent directions. On the other hand, it is safe to assume that party lines on public issues will hold only if the central leadership is strong enough to control congressmen effectively. This is true because congressmen escape from discipline of the local bosses only to fall prey to the pressures of organized special interests. The central-local conflict within the parties does not grow out of irreconcilable differences between central and local party leaders over public policy. It arises out of the fact that *a national leadership strong enough to control party majorities in Congress would also be strong enough to cut off the flow of patronage to the local bosses.* Here the conflict is real.

Without responsible leadership, both major parties ignored their obligations to the majority, responding instead to the pressure groups of business. The result was disastrous, for while fortunes multiplied in the hands of the few, the masses of the population sank deeper into a poverty that threatened the very basis of the democratic experiment.

# WESTWARD EXPANSION AND RURAL DISLOCATION

## 1865–1890

The political triumph of business brought the American farmer face to face with a bewildering problem: how could he survive in a nation dedicated to industry rather than to agriculture? Traditionally the most numerous element of the population, agrarians had dominated national politics, and were scarcely prepared to surrender to the representatives of shop and factory. Such a reversal was certain to breed a political clash, and dissatisfaction was accentuated by events in the West during the decades after the Civil War. The frontier moved westward so rapidly that by 1890 the conquest of the continent was a fact. The difficulties of adjusting to the unique environment of the trans-Mississippi country, together with low agricultural prices created by the competition of farmers for markets, did not improve the situation. Agrarian unrest in rural America was the result.

## THE ADVANCING FRONTIER

### 1

When the Civil War ended, tawny Indians and shaggy buffalo roamed over most of the trans-Mississippi West. During the next quarter century the pioneers surged westward—miners, cattlemen, Indian fighters, railroad builders, homesteaders—until by 1890 the director of the census announced that an unbroken frontier line no longer existed. The miners came first, and during the 1860's and 1870's they panned the streams of Colorado, Nevada, the Inland Empire, and South Dakota in their feverish search for dull yellow dust and gleaming silver metal. Something of the excitement that attended each new rush was captured by Mark Twain, who described his own adventures in the Nevada silver fields:[1]

By and by I was smitten with the silver fever. "Prospecting parties" were leaving for the mountains every day, and discovering and taking possession of rich silver-bearing lodes and ledges of quartz. Plainly this was the road to fortune. The great "Gould and Curry" mine was held at three or four hundred dollars a foot when we arrived; but in two months it had sprung up to eight hundred. The "Ophir" had been worth only a mere trifle, a year gone by, and now it was selling at *four thousand dollars a foot!* Not a mine could

be named that had not experienced an astonishing advance in value within a short time. Everybody was talking about these marvels. Go where you would, you heard nothing else, from morning till far into the night. Tom So-and-So had sold out of the "Amanda Smith" for $40,000— hadn't a cent when he "took up" the ledge six months ago. John Jones had sold half his interest in the "Bald Eagle and Mary Ann" for $65,000, gold coin, and gone to the States for his family. The widow Brewster had "struck it rich" in the "Golden Fleece" and had sold ten feet for $18,000 —hadn't money enough to buy a crape bonnet when Sing-Sing Tommy killed her husband at Baldy Johnson's wake last spring. The "Last Chance" had found a "clay casing" and knew they were "right on the ledge"—consequence, "feet" that went begging yesterday were worth a brick house apiece today, and seedy owners who could not get trusted for a drink at any bar in the country yesterday were roaring drunk on champagne today and had hosts of warm personal friends in a town where they had forgotten how to bow or shake hands from long-continued want of practice. Johnny Morgan, a common loafer, had gone to sleep in the gutter and waked up worth a hundred thousand dollars, in consequence of the decision in the "Lady Franklin and Rough and Ready" lawsuit.

[1] Samuel L. Clemens, *Roughing It* (New York, 1899), pp. 210-215.

And so on—day in and day out the talk pelted our ears and the excitement waxed hotter and hotter around us.

I would have been more or less than human if I had not gone mad like the rest. Cart-loads of solid silver bricks, as large as pigs of lead, were arriving from the mills every day, and such sights as that gave substance to the wild talk about me. I succumbed and grew as frenzied as the craziest.

Every few days news would come of the discovery of a brand-new mining region; immediately the papers would teem with accounts of its richness, and away the surplus population would scamper to take possession. By the time I was fairly inoculated with the disease, "Esmeralda" had just had a run and "Humboldt" was beginning to shriek for attention. "Humboldt! Humboldt!" was the new cry, and straightway Humboldt, the newest of the new, the richest of the rich, the most marvelous of the marvelous discoveries in silver-land, was occupying two columns of the public prints to "Esmeralda's" one. I was just on the point of starting to Esmeralda, but turned with the tide and got ready for Humboldt. That the reader may see what moved me, and what would as surely have moved him had he been there, I insert here one of the newspaper letters of the day. It and several other letters from the same calm hand were the main means of converting me. I shall not garble the extract, but put it in just as it appeared in the *Daily Territorial Enterprise:*

"But what about our mines? I shall be candid with you. I shall express an honest opinion, based upon a thorough examination. Humboldt county is the richest mineral region upon God's footstool. Each mountain range is gorged with the precious ores. Humboldt is the true Golconda.

"The other day an assay of mere *croppings* yielded exceeding *four thousand dollars to the ton*. A week or two ago an assay of just such surface developments made returns of *seven thousand* dollars to the ton. Our mountains are full of rambling prospectors. Each day and almost every hour reveals new and more startling evidences of the profuse and intensified wealth of our favored county. The metal is not silver alone. There are distinct ledges of auriferous ore. A late discovery plainly evinces cinnabar. The coarser metals are in gross abundance. Lately evidences of bituminous coal have been detected. My theory has ever been that coal is a ligneous formation. I told Col. Whitman, in times past, that the neighborhood of Dayton (Nevada) betrayed no present or previous manifestations of a ligneous foundation, and that hence I had no confidence in his lauded coal mines. I repeated the same doctrine to the exultant coal discoverers of Humboldt. I talked with my friend Captain Burch on the subject. My pyrhanism vanished upon his statement that in the very region referred to he had seen petrified trees of the length of two hundred feet. Then is the fact established that huge forests once cast their grim shadows over this remote section. I am firm in the coal faith. Have no fears of the mineral resources of Humboldt county. They are immense—incalculable."

Let me state one or two things which will help the reader to better comprehend certain items in the above. At this time, our near neighbor, Gold Hill, was the most successful silver-mining locality in Nevada. It was from there that more than half the daily shipments of silver bricks came. "Very rich" (and scarce) Gold Hill ore yielded from $100 to $400 to the ton; but the usual yield was only $20 to $40 per ton—that is to say, each hundred pounds of ore yielded from one dollar to two dollars. But the reader will perceive by the above extract, that in Humboldt from one-fourth to nearly half the mass was silver! That is to say, every one hundred pounds of the ore had from *two hundred* dollars up to about *three hundred and fifty* in it. Some days later this same correspondent wrote:

"I have spoken of the vast and almost fabulous wealth of this region—it is incredible. The intestines of our mountains are gorged with precious ore to plethora. I have said that nature has so shaped our mountains as to furnish most excellent facilities for the working of our mines. I have also told you that the country about here is pregnant with the finest mill sites in the world. But what is the mining history of Humboldt? The Sheba mine is in the hands of energetic San Francisco capitalists. It would seem that the ore is combined with metals that render it difficult of reduction with our imperfect mountain machinery. The proprietors have combined the capital and labor hinted at in my exordium. They are toiling and probing. Their tunnel has reached the length of one hundred feet. From primal assays alone, coupled with the development of the mine and public confidence in the continuance of effort, the stock had reared itself to eight hundred dollars market value. I do not know that one ton of the ore has been converted into current metal. I do know that there are many lodes in this section which surpass the Sheba in primal assay value. Listen a moment to the calculations of the Sheba operators. They purpose transporting the ore concentrated to Europe. The conveyance from Star City (its locality) to Virginia City will cost seventy dollars per ton; from Virginia to San Francisco, forty dollars per ton; from thence to Liverpool, its destination, ten dollars per ton. Their idea is that its conglomerate metals will reimburse them their cost of original extraction, the price of transportation, and the expense of reduction, and that then a ton of the raw ore will net them twelve hundred dollars. The estimate may be extravagant. Cut it in twain, and the product is enormous, far transcending any previous developments of our racy Territory.

"A very common calculation is that many of our mines will yield five hundred dollars to the ton. Such fecundity

throws the Gould & Curry, the Ophir and the Mexican, of your neighborhood, in the darkest shadow. I have given you the estimate of the value of a single developed mine. Its richness is indexed by its market valuation. The people of Humboldt county are *feet* crazy. As I write, our towns are near deserted. They look as languid as a consumptive girl. What has become of our sinewy and athletic fellow-citizens? They are coursing through ravines and over mountain tops. Their tracks are visible in every direction. Occasionally a horseman will dash among us. His steed betrays hard usage. He alights before his adobe dwelling, hastily exchanges courtesies with his townsmen, hurries to an assay office and from thence to the District Recorder's. In the morning, having renewed his provisional supplies, he is off again on his wild and unbeaten route. Why, the fellow numbers already his feet by thousands. He is the horse-leech. He has the craving stomach of the shark or anaconda. He would conquer metallic worlds."

This was enough. The instant we had finished reading the above article, four of us decided to go to Humboldt. We commenced getting ready at once. And we also commenced upbraiding ourselves for not deciding sooner—for we were in terror lest all the rich mines would be found and secured before we got there, and we might have to put up with ledges that would not yield more than two or three hundred dollars a ton, maybe. An hour before, I would have felt opulent if I had owned ten feet in a Gold Hill mine whose ore produced twenty-five dollars to the ton; now I was already annoyed at the prospect of having to put up with mines the poorest of which would be a marvel in Gold Hill.

## 2

The mining frontier produced the mine towns that symbolized the romance of the "wild West" to millions of Easterners. Jammed into narrow streets, dance halls, saloons, gambling dens, and dives of every description guaranteed to satisfy the most discriminating taste in debauchery. Lawless cutthroats attracted to the "mining camps" forced the sober majority among the miners to adopt extralegal means to curb banditry, claim jumping, and assorted crimes; and the vigilance committees formed in every camp added only to the excitement. A contemporary, N. P. Langford, recalls these turbulent times in a colorful book, *Vigilante Days and Ways,* one section of which described conditions in Virginia City, Montana, during a gold rush:[2]

Of the settlements in Alder Gulch, Virginia City was the principal, though Nevada, two miles below, at one time was of nearly equal size and population. A stranger from the Eastern States entering the gulch for the first time, two or three months after its discovery, would be inspired by the scene and its associations with reflections of the most strange and novel character. This human hive, numbering at least ten thousand people, was the product of ninety days. Into it were crowded all the elements of a rough and active civilization. Thousands of cabins and tents and brush wakiups, thrown together in the roughest form, and scattered at random along the banks, and in the nooks of the hills, were seen on every hand. Every foot of the gulch, under the active manipulations of the miners, was undergoing displacement, and it was already disfigured by huge heaps of gravel, which had been passed through the sluices, and rifled of their glittering contents. In the gulch itself all was activity. Some were removing the superincumbent earth to reach the pay-dirt, others who had accomplished that were gathering up the clay and gravel upon the surface of the bedrock, while by others still it was thrown into the sluice boxes. This exhibition of mining industry was twelve miles long. Gold was abundant, and every possible device was employed by the gamblers, the

traders, the vile men and women that had come with the miners to the locality, to obtain it. Nearly every third cabin in the towns was a saloon where vile whiskey was peddled out for fifty cents a drink in gold dust. Many of these places were filled with gambling tables and gamblers, and the miner who was bold enough to enter one of them with his day's earnings in his pocket, seldom left until thoroughly fleeced. Hurdy-gurdy dance-houses were numerous, and there were plenty of camp beauties to patronize them. There too, the successful miner, lured by siren smiles, after an evening spent in dancing and carousing at his expense, steeped with liquor, would empty his purse into the lap of his charmer for an hour of license in her arms. Not a day or night passed which did not yield its full fruition of fights, quarrels, wounds, or murders. The crack of the revolver was often heard above the merry notes of the violin. Street fights were frequent, and as no one knew when or where they would occur, every one was on his guard against a random shot.

Sunday was always a gala day. The miners then left their work and gathered about the public places in the towns. The stores were all open, the auctioneers specially eloquent on every corner in praise of their wares. Thousands of people crowded the thoroughfares, ready to rush in any direction of promised excitement. Horseracing was among the most favored amusements. Prize rings were formed, and brawny men engaged at fisticuffs until their sight was lost and their bodies pommelled to a jelly, while hundreds of onlookers cheered the victor. Hacks rattled to and fro between the several towns, freighted with drunken and rowdy humanity of both sexes. Citizens of acknowledged respectability often walked, more often perhaps rode side by side on horseback, with noted courtesans in open day through the crowded streets, and seemingly suffered no harm in reputation. Pistols flashed, bowie-knives flourished,

[2] N. P. Langford, *Vigilante Days and Ways* (New York, 1893), I, 377-380.

and braggart oaths filled the air, as often as men's passions triumphed over their reason. This was indeed the reign of unbridled license, and men who at first regarded it with disgust and terror, by constant exposure soon learned to become part of it, and forget that they had ever been aught else. All classes of society were represented at this general exhibition. Judges, lawyers, doctors, even clergymen, could not claim exemption. Culture and religion afforded feeble protection, where allurement and indulgence ruled the hour.

## 3

Scarcely less romantic than the miners were the cowboys who followed prospectors into the Far West. Their domain was the giant grassland region known as the Great Plains, stretching from the tier of states along the Mississippi to the Rocky Mountains. Unsettled when the Civil War closed, this immense pasture was free to all who could scrape together a herd, appropriate a likely camp site along a stream, and defend it with six-shooters. When beef prices, inflated by wartime demands, first called attention to lush profits, longhorns were driven northward from Texas, where cattle were plentiful, to stock the northern plains or to be sold at "cow towns" that sprang up along the railroads of Kansas. Thus was born the "long drive." A modern historian of the Southwest, Edward E. Dale, has vividly described the methods of Texan drovers:[3]

The customary procedure was to gather the herd and pass the animals through a chute where each received the "road brand." Each cowboy furnished his own saddle and bedding, but horses were supplied by the owner of the cattle. The bedding, food, and camp equipment were loaded in the chuck wagon driven by the cook, while a "horse wrangler," often a boy, was employed to look after the band of horses usually called the "saddle band,"

"remuda," or "caballado." Cowboys were commonly paid twenty-five to forty dollars a month, and the cook about five dollars a month more, while the trail boss, who had full responsibility of the herd on the drive, would receive a monthly salary of about $125.

The cattle were moved very slowly at first, in order to get them accustomed to travel on the trail, and were watched closely at night. After a few days or weeks, they could be pushed along a little more rapidly and two men at a time were usually sufficient for night duty. These usually stood guard in three shifts, the first until about eleven o'clock, the second from eleven until two, and the third from two until daylight.

It was most important to move slowly and carefully at first, or until the cattle were "road broken." Herds that became frightened and stampeded once or twice early in the drive did not recover from the experience for a long time. The cattle became "spoiled" and in the future would stampede upon the slightest provocation, and so give the drivers endless trouble. When camp was broken early in the morning the herd was drifted slowly away from the bedding ground toward the north, grazing as it went for an hour or two. By this time it was well "strung out" on the trail and moved along at a good rate of speed until noon. In the meantime, the cook had driven on ahead to a place agreed upon, usually on some stream, where he had formed camp and prepared dinner. When the herd arrived the animals were thrown along the stream in loose herd or "at ease" for a couple of hours. When the drive was resumed the cook again pushed on ahead with the chuck wagon to establish camp at a point designated by the trail boss. . . .

The post of honor was the "point" covered by two men who were usually old and experienced hands and whose duty it was to direct the herd, to prevent a mixup with other herds, and to check instantly

---

[3] Reprinted from Edward Everett Dale, *The Range Cattle Industry*, pp. 65-68, copyright 1930 by the University of Oklahoma Press. Reprinted by kind permission of the publisher.

any tendency to run. In the rear was always a group of lazy, slow or lame cattle and this post of "bringing up the drag" was the most disagreeable of all since the riders here were exposed to the dust raised by the entire herd and frequently had their patience sorely tried by the slow or perverse animals that fell back to that position in the herd. Young and inexperienced men were often placed at drag.

At the end of the drive the men were paid, and usually returned to Texas with the wagon and a part or all of the remuda. In many cases the horses were also sold except one for each man who wished to ride back to Texas. Some drovers who also owned ranches in the North would send two or three men with a remuda of horses from the northern ranch to meet the herd halfway up the trail. The Texas horses would then be returned to the home ranch in the South.

## INDIANS AND WHITE MEN

### 4

The advance of the mining and cattle frontiers brought the United States face to face with the recurring Indian problem. For two centuries, pioneers had pushed the red men backward or cast them aside on unwanted lands; now the Indians had either to accept the fate meted out by the "superior" race or to resist. The federal government, seeking a solution, set aside reservations where Indians could be supported while they recast their lives in the white man's mold. The largest reservations were in Oklahoma for the southern tribes and in western Dakota for the Sioux. Many refused to accept; they realized that the reservation implied the end of ancient traditions; it also implied ill-treatment from incompetent and corrupt government agents. The writings of Charles A. Eastman, a well-educated Sioux who served for a time as physician at the Pine Ridge Agency in South Dakota, suggest that such fears were not unjustified:[4]

The Indian of the Northwest came into reservation life reluctantly, very much like a man who has dissipated his large inheritance and is driven out by foreclosure. One morning he awoke to the fact that he must give up his freedom and resign his vast possessions to live in a squalid cabin in the backyard of civilization. For the first time his rovings were checked by well-defined boundaries, and he could not hunt or visit neighboring tribes without a passport. He was practically a prisoner, to be fed and treated as such; and what resources were left him must be controlled by the Indian Bureau through its resident agent.

Who is this Indian agent, or superintendent, as he is now called? He is the supreme ruler on the reservation, responsible directly to the Commissioner of Indian Affairs; and all requests or complaints must pass through his office. The agency doctor, clerks, farmers, superintendents of agency schools, and all other local employees report to him and are subject to his orders. Too often he has been nothing more than a ward politician of the commonest stamp, whose main purpose is to get all that is coming to him. His salary is small, but there are endless opportunities for graft.

If any appeal from the agent's decisions, they are "kickers" and "insubordinate." If they are Indians, he can easily deprive them of privileges, or even imprison them on trumped-up charges; if employees, he will force them to resign or apply for transfers; and even the missionaries may be compelled, directly or indirectly, to leave the reservation for protesting too openly against official wrongdoing. The inspector sent from Washington to investigate finds it easy to "get in with" the agent and very difficult to see or hear anything that the agent does not wish him to hear or see. Many Indians now believe sincerely in Christ's teachings as explained to them by their missionaries, but they find it impossible to believe that this Gov-

---

[4] Charles A. Eastman, *The Indian Today* (Boston, 1915), pp. 41-45. Used by permission of Elaine Goodale Eastman.

ernment is Christian, or the average official an honest man.

Any untutored people, however, are apt imitators, and so these much-exploited natives become politicians in spite of themselves. The most worthless of the tribe are used as the agent's spies and henchmen; a state of affairs demoralizing on the face of it. As long as the Indian Bureau is run in the interest of the politicians, and Indian civilization is merely an incident, the excellent and humanitarian policies approved by the American people will not be fully carried into effect.

It is true that good men and especially good women have gone into the Indian service with a genuine desire to deal justly and kindly by the Indian and to serve the Government honorably and efficiently. Such people often become disgusted with the system and find it impossible to stay, or else are forced out by methods familiar to the experienced. When you clear your American cities of grafters, and purify your politics, then perhaps you will be in a position to redeem the Indian service, and only then. Alas! the skirts of the Goddess of Liberty have never yet been quite clean!

The Indian is no fool; on the other hand, he is a keen observer and an apt student. Although an idealist by nature, many of the race have proved themselves good business men. But under the reservation system they have developed traits that are absolutely opposed to the racial type. They become time-serving, beggarly, and apathetic. Some of their finest characters, such as Chief Joseph, have really died of a broken heart. These are men who could not submit to be degraded; the politicians call them "incorrigible savages."

The distribution of rations to the Plains Indians was, as I have explained, originally a peace measure, and apparently a necessity in place of their buffalo which the white man had exterminated. For many years Texas beef was issued monthly "on the hoof"; that is, the cattle were driven

out one by one upon the plain, and there surrounded and shot down by representatives of the groups to which they belonged. Bacon, flour, sugar, and coffee were doled out to the women, usually as often as once in two weeks, thus requiring those who lived at a considerable distance from the agency to spend several days of each month on the road, neglecting their homes and gardens, if they had any. Once a year there was a distribution of cheap blankets and shoddy clothing. The self-respect of the people was almost fatally injured by these methods. This demoralizing ration-giving has been gradually done away with as the Indians progressed toward self-support, but is still found necessary in many cases.

Not all features of reservation life are bad; for while many good things are shut out and some evils flourish, others are excluded. Liquor traffic among Indians has been forbidden by law since the colonial period; and the law is fairly well enforced by a number of special officers; yet in a few tribes there has been in recent years much demoralization through liquor. It is generally admitted that there is more crime and rowdyism on the reservation than in civilized communities of equal size. In 1878 a force of native police was authorized to keep order, eject intruders, act as truant officers, and perform other duties under the direction of the agent. Though paid only ten or twelve dollars a month, these men have been faithful and efficient in the performance of duties involving considerable hardship and sometimes danger. Their loyalty and patriotism are deserving of special praise. In making arrests and bringing in desperate prisoners, as in the case of Pretty Elk the Brule Sioux murderer, and of the chief, Sitting Bull, the faithful police have sometimes lost their lives.

## 5

Tribes refusing to accept reservation life were left with war as the only alternative.

Between 1864 and 1890 the West was seldom at peace. Troops ranged over the plains in pursuit of Indian bands, who had either refused to become government wards or had broken away from the agency, an environment alien to their needs and habits. Usually the natives were driven to the warpath in retaliation, then hunted down and cruelly slaughtered. The heartless spirit characteristic of Indian warfare was nowhere better illustrated than in the Chivington Massacre. On November 29, 1864, militiamen under Colonel J. M. Chivington surprised a band of five hundred Cheyenne and Arapaho on the Sand Creek Reservation in Colorado. Even the hardened soldiers who witnessed the event were horrified. Two of them testified before a congressional investigating committee:[5]

Personally appeared before me Lieutenant James Connor First New Mexico Volunteer Infantry, who, after being duly sworn, says: That on the 28th day of November, 1864, I was ordered by Major General Scott J. Anthony to accompany him on an expedition (Indian) as his battalion adjutant; the object of that expedition was to be a thorough campaign against hostile Indians, as I was led to understand. I referred to the fact of there being a friendly camp of Indians in that immediate neighborhood and remonstrated against simply attacking that camp, as I was aware that they were resting there, in fancied security under promises held out to them of safety from Major E. W. Wynkoop, former Commander of the post of Fort Lyon, as well as by Major J. S. Anthony, then in command.

Our battalion was attached to the command of Colonel J. M. Chivington, and left Fort Lyon on the night of the 28th of November, 1864; about daybreak on the morning of the 29th of November we came in sight of the camp of the friendly Indians aforementioned, and were ordered by Colonel Chivington to attack the same, which was accordingly done. The command of Colonel Chivington was com-

posed of about one thousand men; the village of the Indians consisted of from one hundred to one hundred and thirty lodges, and, as far as I am able to judge, of from five hundred to six hundred souls, the majority of which were women and children; in going over the battle-ground the next day I did not see a body of man, woman, or child but was scalped, and in many instances their bodies were mutilated in the most horrible manner—men, women, and children's privates cut out, &c; I heard one man say that he had cut out a woman's private parts and had them for exhibition on a stick; I heard another man say that he had cut the fingers off an Indian to get the rings on the hand; occording to the best of my knowledge and belief these atrocities that were committed were with knowledge of J. M. Chivington, and I do not know of his taking any measures to prevent them; I heard of one instance of a child a few months old being thrown in the feed-box of a wagon, and after being carried some distance left on the ground to perish; I also heard of numerous instances in which men had cut out the private parts of females and stretched them over the saddle-bows, and wore them over their hats while riding in the ranks. All these matters were a subject of general conversation, and could not help being known by Colonel J. M. Chivington.

Lieutenant Cramer Sworn: I am stationed at this post, First lieutenant, Company C, veteran battalion, Colorado Cavalry. I was at this post when Colonel Chivington arrived here, and accompanied him on his expedition. He came into the post with a few officers and men, and threw out pickets, with instructions to allow no one to go beyond the line. I was then in command of company K. He brought some eight or nine hundred men with him, and took from this post over a hundred men, all being mounted. My company was ordered along to take part. We arrived at the Indian village about

[5] *Reports of Committees,* 39th Cong., 2nd Sess., Doc. No. 156, pp. 53, 73-74.

daylight. On arriving in sight of the village a battalion of the 1st cavalry and the Fort Lyon battalion were ordered on a charge to surround the village and the Indian herd. After driving the herd towards the village, Lieutenant Wilson's battalion of the 1st took possession of the northeast side of the village, Major Anthony's battalion took position on the south, Colonel Chivington's 3d regiment took position in our rear, dismounted, and after the fight had been commenced by Major Anthony and Lieutenant Wilson, mounted, and commenced firing through us and over our heads. About this time Captain John Smith, Indian interpreter, attempting to come to our troops, was fired on by our men, at the command of some one in our rear, "To shoot the damned old son of a bitch." One of my men rode forward to save him, but was killed. To get out of the fire from the rear, we were ordered to the left. About this time Colonel Chivington moved his regiment to the front, the Indians retreating up the creek, and hiding under the banks. There seemed to be no organization among our troops; every one on his own hook, and shots flying between our own ranks. White Antelope ran towards our columns unarmed, and with both arms raised, but was killed. Several other of the warriors were killed in like manner. The women and children were huddled together, and most of our fire was concentrated on them. Sometimes during the engagement I was compelled to move my company to get out of the fire of our own men. Captain Soule did not order his men to fire when the order was given to commence the fight. During the fight, the battery on the opposite side of the creek kept firing at the bank while our men were in range. The Indian warriors, about one hundred in number, fought desperately; there were about five hundred all told. I estimated the loss of the Indians to be from one hundred and twenty-five to one hundred and seventy-five killed; no

wounded fell into our hands, and all the dead were scalped. The Indian who was pointed out as White Antelope had his fingers cut off. Our force was so large that there was no necessity of firing on the Indians. They did not return the fire until after our troops had fired several rounds. We had the assurance from Major Anthony that Black Kettle and his friends should be saved, and only those Indians who had committed depredations should be harmed. During the fight no officer took any measures to get out of the fire of our own men. Left Hand stood with his arms folded, saying he would not fight the white men, as they were his friends. I told Colonel Chivington of the position in which the officers stood from Major Wynkoop's pledges to the Indians, and also Major Anthony's, and that it would be murder, in every sense of the word, if he attacked those Indians. His reply was, bringing his fist down close to my face, "Damn any man who sympathizes with Indians." I told him what pledges were given the Indians. He replied, "That he had come to kill Indians, and believed it to be honorable to kill Indians under any and all circumstances"; all this at Fort Lyon. Lieutenant Dunn went to Colonel Chivington and wanted to know if he could kill his prisoner, young Smith. His reply was, "Don't ask me; you know my orders; I want no prisoners." Colonel Chivington was in position where he must have seen the scalping and mutilation going on. One of the soldiers was taking a squaw prisoner across the creek, when other soldiers fired on him, telling him they would kill him if he did not let her go. On our approach to the village I saw some one with a white flag approaching our lines, and the troops fired upon it; and at the time Captain Smith was fired upon, some one wearing a uniform coat was fired upon approaching our lines. Captain Smith was wearing one. After the fight I saw the United States flag in the Indian camp. It is a mistake that there were any white scalps found in the village. I saw one, but it was very old, the hair being much faded. I was ordered to burn the village, and was through all the lodges. There was not any snow on the ground, and no rifle-pits. . . .

## 6

The history of Indian wars following the Chivington Massacre has been written from the only records available—diaries and reports of soldiers who mercilessly hunted down the red men during the next two decades. Neither then nor since have white men bothered to ascertain the Indian point of view. This fact adds meaning to a brief speech delivered by Chief Joseph, a Nez Percé warrior, who surrendered to the American Army late in 1877 after a year of warfare. Asking for peace, his simple words suggest the tragedy of a people:[6]

Tell General Howard I know his heart. What he told me before—I have it in my heart. I am tired of fighting. Too-hul-hil-sit is dead. Looking Glass is dead. He-who-led-the-young-men-in-battle is dead. The chiefs are all dead. It is the young men now who say "yes" or "no." My little daughter has run away upon the prairie. I do not know where to find her—perhaps I shall find her too among the dead. It is cold and we have no fire; no blankets. Our little children are crying for food but we have none to give. Hear me, my chiefs. From where the sun now stands, Joseph will fight no more forever.

## 7

Eventually popular resentment against the brutal Indian policy of the Army led to a period of national soul searching. Was the United States dealing fairly with its red-skinned stepchildren? Were not Indians entitled to humane treatment? As these questions were asked in the 1870's and 1880's, Washington officials began to examine the whole question. President Chester A. Arthur,

in his annual message to Congress on December 6, 1881, summed up the results of humanitarian thinking and advanced a practical solution:[7]

It has been easier to resort to convenient makeshifts for tiding over temporary difficulties than to grapple with the great permanent problem, and accordingly the easier course has almost invariably been pursued.

It was natural, at a time when the national territory seemed almost illimitable and contained many millions of acres far outside the bounds of civilized settlements, that a policy should have been initiated which more than aught else has been the fruitful source of our Indian complications.

I refer, of course, to the policy of dealing with the various Indian tribes as separate nationalities, of relegating them by treaty stipulations to the occupancy of immense reservations in the West, and of encouraging them to live a savage life, undisturbed by any earnest and well-directed efforts to bring them under the influences of civilization.

The unsatisfactory results which have sprung from this policy are becoming apparent to all.

As the white settlements have crowded the borders of the reservations, the Indians, sometimes contentedly and sometimes against their will, have been transferred to other hunting grounds, from which they have again been dislodged whenever their newfound homes have been desired by the adventurous settlers.

These removals and the frontier collisions by which they have often been preceded have led to frequent and disastrous conflicts between the races.

It is profitless to discuss here which of them has been chiefly responsible for the disturbances whose recital occupies so large a space upon the pages of our history.

---

[6] Chester A. Fee, *Chief Joseph* (New York, 1936), p. 330. (Transcript prepared by Charles E. S. Wood.)

[7] J. D. Richardson (comp.), *Messages and Papers of the Presidents, 1789-1897* (Washington, 1897, 1909; taken from the 1909 vol.), VII, 55-56.

We have to deal with the appalling fact that though thousands of millions of dollars have been expended in the attempt to solve the Indian problem, it has until within the past few years seemed scarcely nearer a solution than it was half a century ago. But the Government has of late been cautiously but steadily feeling its way to the adoption of a policy which has already produced gratifying results, and which, in my judgment, is likely, if Congress and the Executive accord in its support, to relieve us ere long from the difficulties which have hitherto beset us.

For the success of the efforts now making to introduce among the Indians the customs and pursuits of civilized life and gradually to absorb them into the mass of our citizens, sharing their rights and holden to their responsibilities, there is imperative need for legislative action.

My suggestions in that regard will be chiefly such as have been already called to the attention of Congress and have received to some extent its consideration.

*First.* I recommend the passage of an act making the laws of the various States and Territories applicable to the Indian reservations within their borders and extending the laws of the State of Arkansas to the portion of the Indian Territory not occupied by the Five Civilized Tribes.

The Indian should receive the protection of the law. He should be allowed to maintain in court his rights of person and property. He has repeatedly begged for this privilege. Its exercise would be very valuable to him in his progress toward civilization.

*Second.* Of even greater importance is a measure which has been frequently recommended by my predecessors in office, and in furtherance of which several bills have been from time to time introduced in both Houses of Congress. The enactment of a general law permitting the allotment in severalty, to such Indians, at least, as desire it, of a reasonable quantity of land secured to them by patent, and for

their own protection made inalienable for twenty or twenty-five years, is demanded for their present welfare and their permanent advancement.

In return for such considerate action on the part of the Government, there is reason to believe that the Indians in large numbers would be persuaded to sever their tribal relations and to engage at once in agricultural pursuits. Many of them realize the fact that their hunting days are over and that it is now for their best interests to conform their manner of life to the new order of things. By no greater inducement than the assurance of permanent title to the soil can they be led to engage in the occupation of tilling it.

The well-attested reports of their increasing interest in husbandry justify the hope and belief that the enactment of such a statute as I recommend would be at once attended with gratifying results. A resort to the allotment system would have a direct and powerful influence in dissolving the tribal bond, which is so prominent a feature of savage life, and which tends so strongly to perpetuate it.

*Third.* I advise a liberal appropriation for the support of Indian schools, because of my confident belief that such a course is consistent with the wisest economy.

## 8

President Arthur's suggestion resulted in the passage of the Dawes Severalty Act of February 8, 1887. Henry L. Dawes, humanitarian senator from Massachusetts, sponsored the measure which carried the principle of Indian assimilation into landownership. Reformers hoped it would convert the red men into "civilized" Americans, earning their living through trade or agriculture, attending schools and eventually being absorbed into society:[8]

*Be it enacted,* That in all cases where any tribe or band of Indians has been, or shall hereafter be, located upon any reservation created for their use, either by treaty

[8] *United States Statutes at Large,* XXIV, 338-391.

stipulation or by virtue of an act of Congress or executive order setting apart the same for their use, the President of the United States be, and he hereby is, authorized, whenever in his opinion any reservation or any part thereof of such Indians is advantageous for agriculture and grazing purposes to cause said reservation, or any part thereof, to be surveyed, or resurveyed if necessary, and to allot the lands in said reservation in severalty to any Indian located thereon in quantities as follows:

To each head of a family, one-quarter of a section;

To each single person over eighteen years of age, one-eighth of a section;

To each orphan child under eighteen years of age, one-eighth of a section; and,

To each other single person under eighteen years now living, or who may be born prior to the date of the order of the President directing an allotment of the lands embraced in any reservation, one-sixteenth of a section. . . .

SECTION 5. That upon the approval of the allotments provided for in this act by the Secretary of the Interior, he shall . . . declare that the United States does and will hold the land thus allotted, for the period of twenty-five years, in trust for the sole use and benefit of the Indian to whom such allotment shall have been made . . . and that at the expiration of said period the United States will convey the same by patent to said Indian, or his heirs as aforesaid. . . .

SEC. 6. That upon the completion of said allotments and the patenting of the lands to said allottees, each and every member of the respective bands or tribes of Indians to whom allotments have been made shall have the benefit of and be subject to the laws, both civil and criminal, of the State or Territory in which they may reside. . . . And every Indian born within the territorial limits of the United States to whom allotments shall have been made under the provisions of this act, or under any law or treaty, and every Indian born within the territorial limits of the United States who has voluntarily taken up, within said limits, his residence separate and apart from any tribe of Indians therein, and has adopted the habits of civilized life, is hereby declared to be a citizen of the United States, and is entitled to all the rights, privileges, and immunities of such citizens, whether said Indian has been or not, by birth or otherwise, a member of any tribe of Indians within the territorial limits of the United States without in any manner impairing or otherwise affecting the right of any such Indian to tribal or other property.

## THE FARMERS' FRONTIER

### 9

The Indians were followed by legions of small farmers whose plows broke the plains of the West. Held back by the unfamiliar environment of the Great Plains until the 1870's, the pioneers moved westward with such speed during the next two decades that the continent was occupied by 1890. Their advance was made possible by improved agricultural machinery, fencing, and well-drilling equipment, and particularly by the building of the railroads. The first to span the continent was the Union Pacific, built in the 1860's with the aid of bountiful land grants and generous loans from the federal government. W. A. Bell, an English traveler, watched construction crews push the tracks westward, and described their feverish activities:[9]

One can see all along the line of the now completed road the evidences of ingenious self-protection and defence which our men learned during the war. The same curious huts and underground dwellings which were a common sight along our army lines then, may now be seen burrowed into the sides of the hills, or built up with ready adaptability in sheltered spots. The whole organisation of the

[9] W. A. Bell, *New Tracks in North America* (New York and London, 1869), II, 253.

Carl A. Rudisill Library
LENOIR RHYNE COLLEGE

force engaged in the construction of the road is, in fact, semi-military. The men who go ahead, locating the road, are the advance guard. Following these is the second line, cutting through the gorges, grading the road, and building bridges. Then comes the main line of the army, placing the sleepers, laying the track, spiking down the rails, perfecting the alignment, ballasting the rail, and dressing up and completing the road for immediate use. This army of workers has its base, to continue the figure, at Omaha, Chicago, and still farther eastward, from whose markets are collected the material for constructing the road. Along the line of the completed road are construction trains constantly "pushing forward to the front" with supplies. The company's grounds and workshops at Omaha are the arsenal, where these purchases, amounting now to millions of dollars in value, are collected and held ready to be sent forward. The advanced limit of the rail is occupied by a train of long box cars, with hammocks swung under them, bunks built within them, in which the sturdy, broad-shouldered pioneers of the great iron highway sleep at night and take their meals. Close behind this train come loads of ties and rails and spikes, &c., which are being thundered off upon the roadside, to be ready for the track-layers. The road is graded a hundred miles in advance. The ties are laid roughly in place, then adjusted, gauged, and levelled. Then the track is laid.

Track-laying on the Union Pacific is a science, and we pundits of the Far East stood upon that embankment, only about a thousand miles this side of sunset, and backed westward before that hurrying corps of sturdy operatives with mingled feelings of amusement, curiosity, and profound respect. On they came. A light car, drawn by a single horse, gallops up to the front with its load of rails. Two men seize the end of the rail and start forward, the rest of the gang taking hold by twos until

it is clear of the car. They come forward at a run. At the word of command the rail is dropped in its place, right side up, with care, while the same process goes on at the other side of the car. Less than thirty seconds to a rail for each gang, and so four rails go down to the minute! Quick work, you say, but the fellows on the U. P. are tremendously in earnest. The moment the car is empty it is tipped over on the side of the track to let the next loaded car pass it, and then it is tipped back again; and it is a sight to see it go flying back for another load, propelled by a horse at full gallop at the end of 60 or 80 feet of rope, ridden by a young Jehu, who drives furiously. Close behind the first gang come the gaugers, spikers, and bolters, and a lively time they make of it. It is a grand Anvil Chorus that those sturdy sledges are playing across the plains. It is in triple time, three strokes to a spike. There are ten spikes to a rail, four hundred rails to a mile, eighteen hundred miles to San Francisco. That's the sum, what is the quotient? Twenty-one million times are those sledges to be swung—twenty-one million times are they to come down with their sharp punctuation, before the great work of modern America is complete!

## 10

Over the gleaming rails of the Union Pacific and other transcontinental lines came the farmers who settled the Far West. Their migration dwarfed all population movements of the American past; between 1870 and 1900 more land was settled and placed under cultivation than in the whole history of the earlier frontier. Wherever they went in the Dakotas, or Kansas, or Nebraska, or Colorado—the pioneers staked out claims and built sod houses as close as possible to a railroad. The all-important influence of the Iron Horse in the peopling of the West was recognized by Robert Louis Stevenson, literary English traveler, whose comments were recorded in *Across the Plains:*[10]

[10] Robert Louis Stevenson, *Across the Plains* (New York, 1892), pp. 48-50, 59-61.

And yet when day came, it was to shine upon the same broken and unsightly quarter of the world. Mile upon mile, and not a tree, a bird, or a river. Only down the long, sterile cañons, the train shot hooting and awoke the resting echo. That train was the one piece of life in all the deadly land; it was the one actor, the one spectacle fit to be observed in this paralysis of man and nature. And when I think how the railroad has been pushed through this unwatered wilderness and haunt of savage tribes, and now will bear an emigrant for some £12 from the Atlantic to the Golden Gates; how at each stage of the construction, roaring, impromptu cities, full of gold and lust and death, sprang up and then died away again, and are now but wayside stations in the desert; how in these uncouth places pigtailed Chinese pirates worked side by side with border ruffians and broken men from Europe, talking together in a mixed dialect, mostly oaths, gambling, drinking, quarrelling and murdering like wolves; how the plumed hereditary lord of all America heard, in this last fastness, the scream of the "bad medicine waggon" charioting his foes; and then when I go on to remember that all this epical turmoil was conducted by gentlemen in frock coats, and with a view to nothing more extraordinary than a fortune and a subsequent visit to Paris, it seems to me, I own, as if this railway were the one typical achievement of the age in which we live, as if it brought together into one plot all the ends of the world and all the degrees of social rank, and offered to some great writer the busiest, the most extended, and the most varied subject for an enduring literary work. If it be romance, if it be contrast, if it be heroism that we require, what was Troy town to this? But, alas! it is not these things that are necessary— it is only Homer.

Here also we are grateful to the train, as to some god who conducts us swiftly through these shades and by so many hidden perils. Thirst, hunger, the sleight and ferocity of Indians are all no more feared, so lightly do we skim these horrible lands; as the gull, who wings safely through the hurricane and past the shark. . . .

The rest were all American born, but they came from almost every quarter of that Continent. All the States of the North had sent out a fugitive to cross the plains with me. From Virginia, from Pennsylvania, from New York, from far western Iowa and Kansas, from Maine that borders on the Canadas, and from the Canadas themselves—some one or two were fleeing in quest of a better land and better wages. The talk in the train, like the talk I heard on the steamer, ran upon hard times, short commons, and hope that moves ever westward. I thought of my shipful from Great Britain with a feeling of despair. They had come 3000 miles, and yet not far enough. Hard times bowed them out of the Clyde, and stood to welcome them at Sandy Hook. Where were they to go? Pennsylvania, Maine, Iowa, Kansas? These were not places for immigration, but for emigration, it appeared; not one of them, but I knew a man who had lifted up his heel and left it for an ungrateful country. And it was still westward that they ran. Hunger, you would have thought, came out of the east like the sun, and the evening was made of edible gold. And, meantime, in the car in front of me, were there not half a hundred emigrants from the opposite quarter? Hungry Europe and hungry China, each pouring from their gates in search of provender, had here come face to face. The two waves had met; east and west had alike failed; the whole round world had been prospected and condemned; there was no El Dorado anywhere; and till one could emigrate to the moon, it seemed as well to stay patiently at home. Nor was there wanting another sign, at once more picturesque and disheartening; for, as we continued to steam westward toward the land of gold, we were continually passing other emigrant trains upon the journey east; and these were as crowded as our own. Had all these return voyagers made a fortune in the mines? Were they all bound for Paris, and to be in Rome by Easter? It would seem not, for, whenever we met them, the passengers ran on the platform and cried to us through the windows, in a kind of wailing chorus, to "Come back." On the plains of Nebraska, in the mountains of Wyoming, it was still the same cry, and dismal to my heart, "Come back!" That was what we heard by the way "about the good country we were going to." And at that very hour the Sandlot of San Francisco was crowded with the unemployed, and the echo from the other side of Market Street was repeating the rant of demagogues.

If, in truth, it were only for the sake of wages that men emigrate, how many thousands would regret the bargain! But wages, indeed, are only one consideration out of many; for we are a race of gipsies, and love change and travel for themselves.

## 11

The eager land seekers who filled the West were drawn from all over the world, but the majority came either from the Mississippi Valley or from Europe. Those from Missouri or Illinois or Arkansas were seasoned farmers whose ancestors had pursued illusive fortune halfway across the continent; those from Europe were peasants in quest of new opportunity. From the Scandinavian countries, from Germany, from Ireland, from the lands bordering the Mediterranean they added numbers and strength to western society. Some were lured to the frontier by the advertising of land-grant railroads, but the strongest persuasive force were the "America Letters" written by successful immigrants. Every new arrival wrote of his good fortune to European friends, and as these accounts were snatched from hand to hand in Old World villages, or read to eager listeners by the local minister, they decided others to embark on the grand adventure. The following "America Letter"

was written by Gjert Gregoriussen Hovland to friends in Norway:[11]

I must take this opportunity to let you know that we are in the best of health, and that we—both my wife and I—find ourselves exceedingly satisfied. Our son attends the English school, and talks English as well as the native-born. Nothing has made me more happy and contented than the fact that we left Norway and journeyed to this country. We have gained more since our arrival here than I did during all the time that I lived in Norway, and I have every prospect of earning a livelihood here for myself and my family —even if my family were larger—so long as God gives me good health.

Such excellent plans have been developed here that, even though one be infirm, no one need suffer want. Competent men are elected whose duty it is to see that no needy persons, either in the cities or in the country, shall have to beg for their living. If a man dies and is survived by a widow and children who are unable to support themselves—as is so often the case—they have the privilege of petitioning these officials. To each one will then be given every year as much as is needed of clothes and food, and no discrimination will be shown between the native-born and those from foreign countries. These things I have learned through daily observation, and I do not believe there can be better laws and arrangements . . . in the whole world. I have talked with a sensible person who has traveled in many countries, who has lived here twenty-six years, and has a full knowledge of the matter; both of him and of other reliable persons I have made inquiries, for I wish to let everyone know the truth.

When assemblies are held to elect officials who are to serve the country, the

[11] Theodore C. Blegen (ed.), "A Typical America Letter," in *Mississippi Valley Historical Review*, IX (June, 1922), 71-72. Reprinted by permission of the *Mississippi Valley Historical Review*.

vote of the common man carries just as much authority and influence as does that of the rich and powerful man. Neither in the matter of clothes nor in seats are distinctions to be observed, whether one be a farmer or a clerk. The freedom which one enjoys is just as good as that of the other. So long as he comports himself honestly he will be subjected to no interference. Everybody has the liberty to travel about in the country, wherever he wishes, without any passports or papers. Everyone is permitted to engage in whatever business he finds most desirable, in trade or commerce, by land or by water. But if anyone is found guilty of crime, he will be prosecuted and severely punished for it.

No duties are levied upon goods which are produced in the country and brought to the city by water or by land. In case of death, no registration is required; the survivor, after paying the debts, is free to dispose of the property for himself and his family just as he desires. . . . It would heartily please me if I could learn that every one of you who are in need and have little chance of gaining support for yourselves and your families would make up your mind to leave Norway and come to America, for, even if many more were to come, there would still be room here for all. For all those who are willing to work there is no lack of employment and business here. It is possible for all to live in comfort and without suffering want. I do not believe that any of those who suffer under the oppression of others and who must rear their children under straightened circumstances could do better than to help the latter to come to America. But alas, many persons, even though they want to come, lack the necessary means and many others are so stupid as to believe that it is best to live in the country where they have been brought up even if they have nothing but hard bread to satisfy their hunger. It is as if they should say that those who move to a better land,

where there is plenty, commit a wrong. But I can find no place where our Creator has forbidden one to seek one's food in an honorable manner. I should like to talk to many persons in Norway for a little while, but we do not wish to live in Norway. We lived there altogether too long. Nor have I talked with any immigrant in this country who wished to return.

## 12

The rush to the West was so swift that by the 1880's good lands were becoming increasingly scarce. Panic swept the frontiersmen; they must find farms while opportunity still remained. The result was a "boomer" psychology best expressed by the peopling of Oklahoma. Long an Indian preserve, Oklahoma was gradually opened to settlement after 1889 as reservation after reservation was made available to homesteaders. Each new opening was the occasion for a wild rush of "boomers." The first and most dramatic occurred when President Benjamin Harrison proclaimed that the Oklahoma District, a triangle of land in the center of the territory, could be homesteaded after noon on April 22, 1889. A hundred thousand people were camped along the edges of the district when the deadline arrived. The wild scenes that followed were described by a contemporary:[12]

Those who were arranging the Territory for the entrance of the white settlers located imaginary towns at various points; and these districts were surveyed for town sites. No deviation was permitted from the law of right angles; but a section was cut into square blocks, which, in turn, were subdivided into city lots. In the case of Guthrie, one square was set apart for municipal buildings and another for a university. In the heart of the town a tract was reserved for the "Government Acre," on which was erected the crude, one-story, wooden building of the landoffice. At different points throughout the Territory an

[12] Helen C. Candee, "Social Conditions in Our Newest Territory," *The Forum*, XXV (June, 1898), 427-429.

entire section was also reserved by the Government for the benefit of the school fund, which land it was intended to lease; using the money thus obtained for the maintenance of the fine public-school system which is one of the best features of our Western civilization.

For several weeks before the opening, the country, then being ready for the reception of homesteaders, was cleared of all individuals except the soldiers stationed there to prevent the arrival of "sooners." The latter, however, ingeniously effaced themselves for the time only; for, when the signal gun was fired, they seemed to rise from the ground, as though Cadmus had been on earth again sowing the fabled dragon's teeth. Men who had herded cattle, and those who had traded with the Indians for years, were not to be outdone by the vigilance of soldiers ignorant of sheltering "draws," hidden "dug-outs," and obscuring fastnesses of scrub-oak and blue-stem. "A feller had to keep mighty quiet until the marshal's gun fired," said a successful "sooner," "every draw kept fillin' with men all night long; an' it was hard to keep from seein' and bein' seen."

With everything cleared for action, the crowd was lined up on the border of the new country awaiting the hour of noon, April 22, 1889. It was a crowd of determined, almost desperate, men and women, many of whom, having failed in the fight for prosperity, had gathered here for a fresh trial. Every man's hand was against his fellow. His neighbor on the right, placed there by accident, might be the one who would beat him in the race. The men who stood in line were composed of two classes: (1) those who had failed in every undertaking, and (2) others so young that this was their first bout with fortune. Some were mounted on ponies, which they had ridden from distant states; others were in farm-wagons in which they had journeyed from Kansas, Missouri, and even from Tennessee. The failure of Western Kansas after its period of booming

was accountable for a large part of the enormous crowd that gathered at the Oklahoma border. The opportunity to try again so near home could not be neglected.

It was with difficulty that the crowd was restrained by the marshals; and, when finally the signal was given, a mad race began the results of which make interesting history. All men started as enemies. The reward was to the selfish and to the bully; and greed and strength were the winners. The number of homesteaders exceeded the number of claims; and more than one man pitched upon the same quarter section. In some cases as many as four or five insisted on the right of possession. Thus on the very first day began the contests which have ever since been a harvest to the lawyers, and have produced an unhappy condition of society unknown elsewhere. As an example, two families built their rude homes simultaneously on opposite corners of the same quarter-section; each family being positive of its own right. The help of the law was sought; decisions and reversed decisions resulted, harassing the contestants, until one, more unscrupulous and desperate than the other, shot his enemy through the window or among the outbuildings at twilight. This is not an exception, but a common condition of things. All over the Territory are claimants who dare not live upon their property until the contest is finally settled. They take refuge in the nearest town; and the case goes on through the local courts until it reaches Washington, and the Secretary of the Interior gives his ultimatum. So much litigation is an expense which all cannot bear; and many a rightful contestant loses his claim for want of money to defend it. This condition of injustice and criminality is passing away as the time allotted by the Government for "proving up" approaches expiration; but the hatred engendered in each man's breast was an unhappy handicap in the settlement of a new country. Besides this, the uncertainty, whether a man is or is not the permanent possessor of the land, robs him of ambition to improve it; for he may be working for the good of one whom he would rather kill than benefit.

## 13

The "boomer" rushes into Oklahoma symbolized the end of an era. The continent was settled; America had henceforth to adjust to existence within closed borders. Thoughtful men recognized the magnitude of the problem, and perceived, too, that readjustment required a thorough understanding of the unique forces shaping American civilization. The foremost student concerned with these unique factors was Frederick Jackson Turner, a young historian at the University of Wisconsin. In 1893, in his important essay, "The Significance of the Frontier in American History," he made his countrymen aware of the importance of the frontier as a molding force:[13]

In a recent bulletin of the Superintendent of the Census for 1890 appear these significant words: "Up to and including 1880 the country had a frontier of settlement, but at present the unsettled area has been so broken into by isolated bodies of settlement that there can hardly be said to be a frontier line. In the discussion of its extent, its westward movement, etc., it can not, therefore, any longer have a place in the census reports." This brief official statement marks the closing of a great historic movement. Up to our own day American history has been in a large degree the history of the colonization of the Great West. The existence of an area of free land, its continuous recession, and the advance of American settlement westward, explain American development. . . .

Behind institutions, behind constitutional forms and modifications, lie the vital forces that call these organs into life and shape them to meet changing conditions. The peculiarity of American institutions is, the fact that they have been compelled to adapt themselves to the changes of an expanding people—to the changes involved in crossing a continent, in winning a wilderness, and in developing at each area of this progress out of the primitive economic and political conditions of the frontier into the complexity of city life. . . . All peoples show development; the germ theory of politics has been sufficiently emphasized. In the case of most nations, however, the development has occurred in a limited area; and if the nation has expanded, it has met other growing peoples whom it has conquered. But in the case of the United States we have a different phenomenon. Limiting our attention to the Atlantic coast, we have the familiar phenomenon of the evolution of institutions in a limited area, such as the rise of representative government; the differentiation of simple colonial governments into complex organs; the progress from primitive industrial society, without division of labor, up to manufacturing civilization. But we have in addition to this a recurrence of the process of evolution in each western area reached in the process of expansion. Thus American development has exhibited not merely advance along a single line, but a return to primitive conditions on a continually advancing frontier line, and a new development for that area. American social development has been continually beginning over again on the frontier. This perennial rebirth, this fluidity of American life, this expansion westward with its new opportunities, its continuous touch with the simplicity of primitive society, furnish the forces dominating American character. The true point of view in the history of this nation is not the Atlantic coast, it is the Great West. . . .

In the settlement of America we have to observe how European life entered the continent, and how America modified and developed that life and reacted on Europe.

[13] From *The Frontier in American History* by Frederick Jackson Turner, pp. 1-4, 22-25, 27, 30-32, 37-38. Copyright, 1920 by Frederick J. Turner. By permission of Henry Holt and Company, Inc.

Our early history is the study of European germs developing in an American environment. Too exclusive attention has been paid by institutional students to the Germanic origins, too little to the American factors. The frontier is the line of most rapid and effective Americanization. The wilderness masters the colonist. It finds him a European in dress, industries, tools, modes of travel, and thought. It takes him from the railroad car and puts him in the birch canoe. It strips off the garments of civilization and arrays him in the hunting shirt and the moccasin. It puts him in the log cabin of the Cherokee and Iroquois and runs an Indian palisade around him. Before long he has gone to planting Indian corn and plowing with a sharp stick; he shouts the war cry and takes the scalp in orthodox Indian fashion. In short, at the frontier the environment is at first too strong for the man. He must accept the conditions which it furnishes, or perish, and so he fits himself into the Indian clearings and follows the Indian trails. Little by little he transforms the wilderness, but the outcome is not the old Europe, not simply the development of Germanic germs. . . . The fact is, that here is a new product that is American. At first, the frontier was the Atlantic coast. It was the frontier of Europe in a very real sense. Moving westward, the frontier became more and more American. As successive terminal moraines result from successive glaciations, so each frontier leaves its traces behind it, and when it becomes a settled area the region still partakes of the frontier characteristics. Thus the advance of the frontier has meant a steady movement away from the influence of Europe, a steady growth of independence on American lines. . . .

First, we note that the frontier promoted the formation of a composite nationality for the American people. The coast was preponderantly English, but the later tides of continental immigration flowed across to the free lands. This was the case from the early colonial days. The Scotch-Irish and the Palatine Germans, or "Pennsylvania Dutch," furnished the dominant element in the stock of the colonial frontier. With these peoples were also the freed indented servants, or redemptioners, who at the expiration of their time of service passed to the frontier. . . . Very generally these redemptioners were of non-English stock. In the crucible of the frontier the immigrants were Americanized, liberated, and fused into a mixed race, English in neither nationality nor characteristics. The process has gone on from the early days to our own. Burke and other writers in the middle of the eighteenth century believed that Pennsylvania was "threatened with the danger of being wholly foreign in language, manners, and perhaps even inclinations." The German and Scotch-Irish elements in the frontier of the South were only less great. In the middle of the present century the German element in Wisconsin was already so considerable that leading publicists looked to the creation of a German state out of the commonwealth by concentrating their colonization. Such examples teach us to beware of misinterpreting the fact that there is a common English speech in America into a belief that the stock is also English.

In another way the advance of the frontier decreased our dependence on England. The coast, particularly of the South, lacked diversified industries, and was dependent on England for the bulk of its supplies. In the South there was even a dependence on the Northern colonies for articles of food. . . . Before long the frontier created a demand for merchants. As it retreated from the coast it became less and less possible for England to bring supplies directly to the consumer's wharfs, and carry away staple crops, and staple crops began to give way to diversified agriculture for a time. The effect of this phase of the frontier action upon the northern section is perceived when we realize how the advance of the frontier aroused seaboard cities like Boston, New York, and Baltimore, to engage in rivalry for what Washington called "the extensive and valuable trade of a rising empire."

The legislation, which most developed the powers of the national government, and played the largest part in its activity, was conditioned on the frontier. Writers have discussed the subjects of tariff, land, and internal improvement, as subsidiary to the slavery question. . . .

This is a wrong perspective. The pioneer needed the goods of the coast, and so the grand series of internal improvement and railroad legislation began, with potent nationalizing effects. Over internal improvements occurred great debates, in which grave constitutional questions were discussed. Sectional groupings appear in the votes, profoundly significant for the historian. Loose construction increased as the nation marched westward. But the West was not content with bringing the farm to the factory. Under the lead of Clay— "Harry of the West"—protective tariffs were passed, with the cry of bringing the factory to the farm. The disposition of the public lands was a third important subject of national legislation influenced by the frontier. . . .

It is safe to say that the legislation with regard to land, tariff, and internal improvements—the American system of the nationalizing Whig party—was conditioned on frontier ideas and needs. But it was not merely in legislative action that the frontier worked against the sectionalism of the coast. The economic and social characteristics of the frontier worked against sectionalism. The men of the frontier had closer resemblances to the Middle region than to either of the other sections. Pennsylvania had been the seedplot of frontier emigration, and, although she passed on her settlers along the Great Valley into the west of Virginia and the Carolinas, yet the industrial society of these Southern frontiersmen was always more like that of the Middle region than like that of the tide-water portion of the South, which later came to spread its industrial type throughout the South.

The Middle region, entered by New York harbor, was an open door to all Europe. The tide-water part of the South represented typical Englishmen, modified by a warm climate and servile labor, and living in baronial fashion on great plantations; New England stood for a special English movement—Puritanism. The Middle region was less English than the other sections. It had a wide mixture of nationalities, a varied society, the mixed town and county system of local government, a varied economic life, many religious sects. In short, it was a region mediating between New England and the South, and the East and the West. It represented that composite nationality which the contemporary United States exhibits, that juxtaposition of non-English groups, occupying a valley or a little settlement, and presenting reflections of the map of Europe in their variety. It was democratic and nonsectional, if not national; "easy, tolerant, and contented"; rooted strongly in material prosperity. It was typical of the modern United States. It was least sectional, not only because it lay between North and South, but also because with no barriers to shut out the frontiers from its settled region, and with a system of connecting waterways, the Middle region mediated between East and West as well as between North and South. Thus it became the typically American region. Even the New Englander, who was shut out from the frontier by the Middle region, tarrying in New York or Pennsylvania on his westward march, lost the acuteness of his sectionalism on the way. . . .

But the most important effect of the frontier has been in the promotion of democracy here and in Europe. As has been indicated, the frontier is productive of individualism. Complex society is precipitated by the wilderness into a kind of primitive organization based on the family. The tendency is anti-social. It produces antipathy to control, and particularly to any direct control. The tax-gatherer is viewed as a representative of oppression. . . . Frontier conditions prevalent in the colonies are important factors in the explanation of the American Revolution, where individual liberty was sometimes confused with absence of all effective government. The same conditions aid in explaining the difficulty of instituting a strong government in the period of the confederacy. The frontier individualism has from the beginning promoted democracy.

The frontier States that came into the Union in the first quarter of a century of its existence came in with democratic suffrage provisions, and had reactive effects of the highest importance upon the older States whose peoples were being attracted there. An extension of the franchise became essential. It was *western* New York that forced an extension of suffrage in the constitutional convention of that State in 1821; and it was *western* Virginia that compelled the tide-water region to put a more liberal suffrage provision in the constitution framed in 1830, and to give to the frontier region a more nearly proportionate representation with the tide-water aristocracy. The rise of democracy as an effective force in the nation came in with western preponderance under Jackson and William Henry Harrison, and it meant the triumph of the frontier. . . .

So long as free land exists, the opportunity for a competency exists, and economic power secures political power. But the democracy born of free land, strong in selfishness and individualism, intolerant of administrative experience and education, and pressing individual liberty beyond its proper bounds, has its dangers as well as its benefits. Individualism in America has allowed a laxity in regard to governmental affairs which has rendered possible the spoils system and all the manifest evils that follow from the lack of a highly developed civic spirit. In this connection may be noted also the influence of frontier conditions in permitting lax business honor, inflated paper currency and wild-cat banking. The colonial and revolutionary frontier was the region whence emanated many of the worst forms of an evil currency. The West in the War of 1812 repeated the phenomenon on the frontier of that day, while the speculation and wild-cat banking of the period of the crisis of 1837 occurred on the new frontier belt of the next tier of States. Thus each one of the periods of lax financial integrity coincides with periods when a new set of frontier communities had arisen, and coincides in area with these successive frontiers, for the most part. The recent Populist agitation is a case in point. Many a State that now declines any connection with the tenets of the Populists, itself adhered to such ideas in an earlier stage of the development of the State. A primitive society can hardly be expected to show the intelligent appreciation of the complexity of business interests in a developed society. The continual recurrence of these areas of paper-money agitation is another evidence that the frontier can be isolated and studied as a factor in American history of the highest importance. . . .

From the conditions of frontier life came intellectual traits of profound importance. The works of travelers along each frontier from colonial days onward describe certain common traits, and these traits have, while softening down, still persisted as survivals in the place of their origin, even when a higher social organization succeeded. The result is that to the frontier the American intellect owes its striking characteristics. That coarseness and strength combined with acuteness and inquisitiveness; that practical, inventive turn of mind, quick to find expedients;

that masterful grasp of material things, lacking in the artistic but powerful to effect great ends; that restless, nervous energy; that dominant individualism, working for good and for evil, and withal that buoyancy and exuberance which comes from freedom—these are traits of the frontier, or traits called out elsewhere because of the existence of the frontier. Since the days when the fleet of Columbus sailed into the waters of the New World, America has been another name for opportunity, and the people of the United States have taken their tone from the incessant expansion which has not only been open but has even been forced upon them. He would be a rash prophet who should assert that the expansive character of American life has now entirely ceased. Movement has been its dominant fact, and, unless this training has no effect upon a people, the American energy will continually demand a wider field for its exercise. But never again will such gifts of free land offer themselves. For a moment, at the frontier, the bonds of custom are broken and unrestraint is triumphant. There is not *tabula rasa*. The stubborn American environment is there with its imperious summons to accept its conditions; the inherited ways of doing things are also there; and yet, in spite of environment, and in spite of custom, each frontier did indeed furnish a new field of opportunity, a gate of escape from the bondage of the past; and freshness, and confidence, and scorn of older society, impatience of its restraints and ideas, and indifference to its lessons, have accompanied the frontier. What the Mediterranean Sea was to the Greeks, breaking the bond of custom, offering new experiences, calling out new institutions and activities, that, and more, the ever retreating frontier has been to the United States directly, and to the nations of Europe more remotely. And now, four centuries from the discovery of America, at the end of a hundred years of life under the Constitution, the frontier has gone, and with its

going has closed the first period of American history.

## CAPITALISM CAPTURES THE FARMER

### 14

Hundreds of thousands of farmers in the West after the Civil War lived in a new and different world. No longer independent producers, no longer self-sufficient, they had become mere adjuncts to the industrialized, urbanized East. Physically the farmers were forced to adjust to a system of specialization in cash crops, produced with the aid of machinery, and sold in the world's markets for money that went to purchase the necessities of life. They were also required to accommodate themselves to a social order of complex interrelationships in which national legislation was geared to the needs of industry rather than to those of agriculture. Yearly profits seemed to depend less on a fortunate climate and hard work than on the price of wheat in Russia or the size of the world cotton crop. Readjustment was difficult, and underlay much of the agrarian discontent of the latter nineteenth century. A modern student of social psychology, John M. Williams, has cogently analyzed the problem:[14]

Stolidity was an attitude that pervaded rural behaviour. A man who "showed his feelings" while listening to a sermon or to music, or even in bereavement, was disapproved of because he did not "control his feelings better." Thus repression, due primarily to the strenuous economic life, left its mark on behaviour generally. Though restrained, emotions were powerful when they did break forth.

Self-restraint caused an uncompromising attitude toward self-indulgence. This attitude of self-denial extended over the whole range of behaviour. There was a denial of impulses for "luxuries" in food and drink. The farmer lived well but confined his

[14] *Our Rural Heritage: The Social Psychology of Rural Development* by James Mickel Williams, pp. 88-92, 100-101. Copyright 1925; used by permission of the Appleton-Century-Crofts Co., Inc.

diet as far as possible to what he produced and did not find a ready market for. One who "hankered after dainties" was ridiculed. So was the fellow who was at all particular in his dress. Farmer boys often took pride in showing by their dress that they "didn't care how they looked." Self-denial was particularly emphasized in connection with forbidden amusements. Amusements were forbidden because of their "evil tendency." Dancing and theatre-going were associated with licentiousness, card-playing and billiard and pool-playing with gambling, liquor-drinking with intoxication. These vices unfitted the farmer for that "sober, righteous and godly life" that was necessary for a successful struggle with nature. But self-denial was carried further than this, and there was a tendency to think of any pleasure as somehow bad. It was contrary to the strenuous economic attitudes and the serious religious attitudes. There was danger that people by enjoying themselves might get carried away, to the neglect of their work and their church. The church gave self-denial a variety of sanctions and prescribed certain customary expressions of it, which caused it to be carried to an extreme that the common sense of the individual, uninfluenced, never would have permitted. For instance, extremely religious people observed the custom called tithing, that is, gave one-tenth of their income to the church, and many of them thereby were forced to unreasonable self-denial.

Because of the rigorous self-denial, there was a tendency to go to an extreme in the few satisfactions that were not socially tabooed. The farmer allowed no man to tell him what he should not eat, for the sake of his health, and this was one reason for the immoderate eating that characterized the rural districts, with its train of bodily ills and the resulting vogue of patent medicines. Similarly he had his will in sex relations, as the large families show. Men felt that their lives were narrowed by hard work and they did not propose to scrimp themselves on the few pleasures within their reach, though they did deny themselves expensive foods.

Self-denial accentuated also the farmer's grip on his property. The deep-seated attitude for private property in rural America cannot be understood without keeping in mind the sacrifice incurred in wringing wealth from the soil. So much has been said about the money made in land speculation that we sometimes forget the great mass of plodding farmers who never made any money in that way. They worked for what they got. As the child was dear to the mother because of what she had to endure to give it birth and bring it up, so was his property dear to the farmer because of the sacrifice he had to undergo in order to accumulate it.

The farmer was secretive in this his main interest. He did not want anyone to know how much he was worth and sometimes did not even tell his family. He did not want people to know of his business dealings or how he had made his will. So when he needed advice he was accustomed to go to some man who was known to be "close-mouthed" and in whose judgment he had confidence, often the community doctor. This absorption in property and secrecy in accumulation and bequest is characteristic of the farmer to the present day. An editor of a rural paper who has the confidence of thousands of farmers gets many letters each year asking his advice on a variety of subjects, particularly about property and its bequest. In spite of all the "reasons" that may be given for this secrecy there seems to have been something instinctive in it, something akin to the dislike of having mere acquaintances come in just when the family was eating. The secrecy urge was powerful and it continues to this day. . . .

The second condition that emphasized thrift was the fact that the farmer was independent. Everything he saved in the course of work was his own. Wherefore, both he and his wife developed shrewdness in the saving of materials. He would "tinker up" an old tool rather than buy a new one and she would "get along" with her old kitchen utensils. They were saving also in the steps they took, and in planning their work so as to accomplish most with least effort. In driving the team the boy was taught to drive in a way to accomplish most with least effort. Thus the farmer often built up an organization of high efficiency. When the question arose of the expenditure of money for a new building or a new piece of furniture it was discussed by husband and wife over a long period and the money was spent in a way to "go the farthest." Thrift insinuated itself even into the period of the year when people are naturally most lavish, the Christmas season; the family emphasized the buying of useful presents or the giving of home-made presents. A too generous husband was upbraided by his wife for presenting her with an object of her heart's desire, to which he replied that he got it on his own account; he did not want to have to hear constantly how much she wished she had it.

On the other hand when, in the second period, the farmer came to produce more largely for the market, and came to live off his bank account the habit of thrift weakened. But it continued stronger among the rural population, generally speaking, than among those living in villages and cities. There wages came regularly at short intervals and this encourages spending on the expectation of a regular income. As contrasted with this, the income of the farmer is less certain and regular, and this has caused him to realize that he cannot spend all the money on hand. He must save and this necessity fosters the saving habit. There is another important difference between farmers' and factory workers' social incentives to thrift. The latter live in villages and cities which are replete with stimuli to spend—the show windows, the social life on the street

and in the social circles and organizations —while farmers are less subjected to these temptations.

The essential tendency of human nature is to satisfy impulses thoughtlessly so that spending is a stronger tendency than saving. Spending means to satisfy impulses while saving means to restrain them. When restraint is compelled by the existing conditions there develops a social attitude of self-restraint which is strengthened by various sanctions. But it is apt to pass as soon as hard necessity no longer compels restraint. As we say, to spend is "more natural than to save." Thought for the future is an intellectual process of which few people are capable to any extent, hence, under easy economic conditions, the natural tendency to spend becomes a social attitude. So the saving person who still reacts according to the attitude of restraint of the past is apt to be ridiculed. The ridicule of thrift is due not only to the fact that it is unusual but also to the spendthrift's sense of superiority over him whom necessity compels to save. Among the early farmers it was hard necessity that compelled restraint of impulses. Life was intolerable as a hired man and to escape this fate a man must acquire land and save in order to pay for it. He restrained impulses to spend for the sake of making those payments. He carefully saved his produce for the sake of selling the produce saved. So the habit of looking to the future was an everyday habit. It was not a matter altogether of foresight but a habit. . . .

The attitudes described . . . were those of a settled agricultural population. They implied a sense of permanence of their relations on the part of the farmers of a neighbourhood. If a farmer felt that his neighbour was there permanently he would be more anxious for his goodwill, more willing to help him, more careful, in his conversation, of his neighbour's honour than if the neighbour was "here today, gone tomorrow." When the sense of solidarity of the neighbourhood weakened, because of the increasing migration from the rural districts to the villages and cities and from one neighbourhood to another, the attitudes began to change. Take, for instance, the attitude of helpfulness. The reciprocity of helpfulness was at first undetermined as to the time given and the exertion required. That is, an act of help did not necessarily create an expectation of an exact return in time worked or kind of work but simply strengthened the habitual expectation of help when needed—whatever help a situation might require. But when the sense of solidarity began to weaken, the particular act of help became important as an economic service return of which might be expected, while it had little social value as a means of strengthening the habitual expectation. This change came when the inhabitants of the neighbourhood were less permanently settled and families were less thoroughly friendly.

The farmer's relation with neighbours thus began to have something of the aspect of a business relation. But it was in relations with dealers in farm produce that the business relation had its extreme development. In selling the tendency was to bargain up to the last and the farmer would not sell until he could feel he had the "top price." He demanded an exorbitant price if he thought the dealer much wanted his product. His bargaining was not guided by any rational policy, for instance, to develop the reputation of being a reasonable man to deal with. He liked rather the reputation of being a hard man to deal with for that meant a man whom the dealer could not easily "handle." The farmer realized that he was not shrewd and that he lacked the dealer's knowledge of the market, and this made him suspicious of the dealer. This antagonism between farmer and dealer seems inevitable and the natural solution is the co-operative marketing of farm produce.

The attitudes of the individualistic farmer have proved to be contrary not only to profitable marketing but also to profitable production. The purpose of the settler was to clear the land and exploit the virgin soil. Exploitation continued after the situation began to call for conservation. The land was stripped of its trees and then of its fertility. Extensive instead of intensive farming continued even on into the third period. This was due to hidebound adherence to the customary extensive farming and to lack of agricultural training. In recent years such training has been more sought than formerly by the more capable of the younger farmers.

## 15

The postwar decades provided impressive examples of the truth of these observations. In both West and South, the heart of rural America, farmers struggled blindly against forces they barely understood. Those who lived in the West, where wheat was the principal cash crop, believed that life could be righted only if a decent price could be secured from the monopolistic grain-elevator operators who purchased their crop and from the equally monopolistic railroads that hauled it to market. Whatever the condition of the individual farmer, however, production was high. Thus a traveler in Minnesota, writing in *Harper's New Monthly Magazine* for 1868, described the richness of the land:[15]

As one goes over the country in the fall of the year he sees vast tracts of "new breaking," where the virgin soil, black as ink, and rich almost to glutinousness, has been broken by the plow, and the soil turned bottom upward in long, dark bands or layers as far as the eye can reach. Here it is exposed for months to the wind and weather till it decomposes and becomes fit for agricultural purposes. Every year vast tracts of prairie are thus turned over, or "broken," and with the next the loam is leveled and the seed is cast in; and thus large additions are annually made to the aggregate amount of acres and wheat.

[15] G. W. Schatzel, "Among the Wheat Fields of Minnesota," *Harper's New Monthly Magazine,* XXXVI, No. 212 (January, 1868), 193, 199-200.

Take your stand on one of these "new Breaking pieces," and look perhaps in any direction, and will find yourself inclosed by its dreary strips of black loam; not a blade of grass nor a single leaf will appear. It is a picture of desolation and vacancy. . . . Nothing can exceed the contrasts between this and what these same fields will present a year or two afterward, when they stand yellow with the harvest, an emblem of cheerfulness and prosperity.

Farms are generally 160 acres in extent —a "quarter section" being usually the quantity bought and worked. Under the Homestead Law lands are constantly taken up, the cost being a mere trifle for fees, etc. The settler is required to locate on it, put up a small house, do some fencing and "breaking," and pass a night on it at least once every six months.

Many amusing stories are told how persons of ingenious habits of mind and India-rubber consciences manage to conform to the letter, while they evade the more burdensome intents of the law. The merest apology for a house, and the least possible amount of residence and "improvements" are done. Still this dodging of the law works no serious violation of its contemplated objects. Lands are opened, destitute families are provided with a farm and means of attaining independence and prosperity, and the State is settled up. Some times a family is so constituted as to be able to take four quarters, or a full square mile of land. No single applicant can take out papers for more than one quarter section, and a man and his wife and young children are viewed as one party. But if he has a widowed mother and two unmarried sisters grown up living with him, each is regarded as a legal applicant; and they arrange it often thus: They select four quarter sections lying contiguous to each other, and put up a house right upon the centre where the four quarter sections touch, so that each quarter section of the building stands on a different quarter section. Partitions divide the interior into rooms to correspond; and each party then fulfills his obligations to the law at one-fourth the expense he or she would otherwise incur. . . .

These wild lands thus entered are worth about $5 per acre, and when "improved" rise to $15 or $25 according to circumstances. At the end of five years' residence Government gives a clean deed to the property. Many, however, having the means, prefer to buy the land outright at the start, paying the government price $1.25 per acre. . . .

Every railroad station and steamboat landing is a wheat outlet, and boasts its elevator. As one will stand for all, a few words about that at St. Charles, where I am now writing, will answer for the rest. It is a building 100 feet by 30, and, perhaps 50 feet high. . . . Within it are two elevators which give it its name. These are broad bands, provided with a number of "buckets" or "baskets," which are constantly ascending or descending . . . from the bottom to the top of the building. As the band goes up its baskets are filled with wheat, which is constantly carried aloft, where it is emptied into large bins. At each end of the building are two places for receiving the wheat, called "hoppers," such as are seen in any flour mill. To these the wheat wagons draw up, the sacks are untied, and the wheat is poured down the aperture of the hopper into a large box which rests on a platform scales. Here it is weighed . . . [and hoisted] aloft to the bins.

On the other side of the building the railroad is laid in close proximity; and here there are several spouts, through which the grain is passed down from the bins into the freight-cars, which are brought here alongside.

## 16

The plight of the southern planter was trying. Addicted to specialization as was his western neighbor, he, too, found his life conditioned by events beyond his control: a war in the Far East, a drought in India might mean the difference between prosperity and poverty when he shipped his cotton bales to market. Moreover, he faced the difficult problem of operating with a new labor system in which freedmen took the place of slaves. The problems of plantation owners, using their former slaves as hired hands or as share croppers, were noted by Edward King, a journalist who traveled through the South in 1873 and 1874:[16]

We crossed the field, bordered by noble cypresses and oaks, stopping now and then to watch the negroes as they carefully prepared the ground which an inundation might, in less than a day, reduce to a hopeless wilderness of mud. Entering the house of the overseer, we found that functionary smoking his pipe and reposing after a long ride over the plantation. He was a rough, hearty, good-natured man, accustomed to living alone and faring rudely. I asked what he thought of the negro as a free laborer.

"He works well, mostly, sir. These yer Alabama niggers that's workin' on our plantations now do well on wages. They make some little improvements around their cabins, but mighty little, sir. Ef politics would only let 'em alone, they'd get along well enough, I reckon."

"Do the negroes on this plantation vote?"

"I reckon not (laughing). I don't want my niggers to have anything to do with politics. They can't vote as long as they stay with us, and these Alabama boys don't take no interest in the elections here."

"What do they receive as monthly wages?"

"From ten to sixteen dollars. It costs us about fifteen dollars per head to bring 'em from Alabama. These niggers likes wages better than shares. We keep a store here, and, Saturday nights, most of the money they have earned comes back to us in trade. They're fond o' whisky and good things to eat."

"What is the routine of your work on a large plantation like this, and those adjoining it, throughout the year?"

"Wal, sir, I reckon that's a long story. We don't have much spare time, and mighty little amusement. Wal, sir, the first thing we do, sir, we begin early in January, a few weeks after the old crop is all gathered in, to repair fences and clean out all the ditches, sir. Then we pull down the old stalks, and start the ploughs to throw quadruple furrows in the fields. Then we throw out the 'middles.' "

"What are they?"

"Wal, sir, we throw out soil at the sides so as to leave a slope bed of fresh ground to plant on, and loose earth to cover it with. If the spring freshet breaks on to this yer prepared earth, we've got to begin over again, and that makes the season very late.

"Planting begins about the last of March, or very early in April. Piles of cotton seed are laid along some ways apart on the field, and then the niggers sow it along the beds, a ton of seed to eight acres. Then it is 'barred off'—covered up, that means.

"Ez soon as the cotton stalks begin to peep up, 'scraping' begins. The hands weed every row carefully, and don't leave any weakly plants. That, and looking after the caterpillars, keeps 'em busy till July. Caterpillars ain't the only danger we have to fight against. Thar's a hundred others. Cotton's a ticklish plant to raise. You've got to watch it mighty close, and then the worms and the weather will sometimes ruin the crop.

"Between July and September we keep the hands busy, getting out baskets, and setting things in order; then we pile in new help, and for the rest of the season, employ three times as many hands as thar's in the fields now. Up to Christmas it's picking and ginning, and it's right lively, you can be sure."

From the overseer's conversation I learned that cotton-picking is done quite as thoroughly under the system of free la-

---

[16] Edward King, *The Great South* (Hartford, 1875), pp. 67-78, 279-299, 305-307.

bor as in the days when slave-driving was permissible; but that the "niggers" require constant watching. On many plantations where the yield is abundant, it is difficult to concentrate labor enough at the proper time to get the cotton into the ginhouse the same year that it is planted. I have seen cotton-fields still white with their creamy fleeces late in December, because the negroes were either too lazy or too busily engaged in their annual merry-makings to gather the harvest. But on the large lowland plantations along the Mississippi, the crop is usually gathered early, and the picking is very thorough. I could not discover that there was any system of "forced labor" now in use, and I thought the overseer's statement, that a "good field-hand now-a-days would pick 250 pounds of cotton daily," was excellent testimony in favor of free labor. He added, however, that on many plantations the average hands would not pick more than 100 pounds per day.

The laborers were coming in from the field in a long picturesque procession. As it was spring-time many of them had been ploughing, and were mounted upon the backs of the stout mules which had been their companions all day. Some of the men were singing rude songs, others were shouting boisterously and scuffling as they went their way along the broad pathway bordered by giant cypress and noble oaks. The boys tumbling and wriggling in the grass perpetually exploded into guffaws of contagious laughter. Many of the men were tall and finely formed. They had an intelligent look, and were evidently not so degraded as those born on the Louisiana lowlands. The overseer sat on the veranda of his house, now and then calling out a sharp command or a caution, the negroes looking up obsequiously and touching their hats as they heard his voice. When the mules were stabled the men came lounging back to the cabins, where the women were preparing their homely supper, and an hour afterward we heard the tinkle of

banjos, the pattering of feet and uproarious laughter. The interiors of the negro cabins were of the rudest description. The wretched huts in which the workmen live seem to them quite comfortable, however. I saw no one who appeared discontented with his surroundings. Few of these laborers could read at all. Even those who had some knowledge of the alphabet did not seem to be improving it. . . .

The thing which struck me as most astonishing here, in the cotton-lands, as on the rice plantations of South Carolina, was the absolute subjection of the negro. Those with whom I talked would not directly express any idea. They gave a shuffling and grimacing assent to whatever was suggested; or, if they dissented, would beg to be excused from differing verbally, and seemed to be much distressed at being required to express their opinions openly. Of course, having the most absolute political liberty, because in that section they were so largely in the majority, numerically, that no intimidation could have been practiced, it seemed astonishing that they should be willing to forego the right to vote, and to willingly isolate themselves from their fellows. I could not discover that any of the negroes were making a definite progress, either manifested by a subscription to some newspaper or by a tendency to discussion; and, while the planter gave me the fullest and freest account of the social status of the negroes employed by him, he failed to mention any sign of a definite and intellectual growth. The only really encouraging sign in their social life was the tendency to create for themselves homes, and now and then to cultivate the land about them. . . .

Mr. Robert Somers, in his excellent observations on the labor question, as viewed in Alabama, made during a journey throughout the Southern States in 1870-71, hits upon some truths with regard to the relations of the planter and freedman, in the following manner:

"What the planters are disposed to complain of is, that while they have lost their slaves, they have not got free laborers in any sense common either in the Northern States or in Europe. One cannot but think that the New England manufacturer and the Old England farmer must be equally astonished at a recital of the relations of land, capital and labor, as they exist on the cotton plantations of the Southern States. The wages of the negroes, if such a term can be applied to a mode of remuneration so unusual and anomalous, consist, as I have often indicated, of one-half the crop of corn and cotton, the only crops in reality produced.

"The negro on the semi-communistic basis thus established finds his own rations; but, as these are supplied to him by the planter or the planter's notes of credit on the merchants, and as much more sometimes as he thinks he needs by the merchants on his own credit, from the 1st of January onward throughout the year, in anticipation of crops which are not marketable until the end of December, he can lose nothing by the failures or deficient outcome of the crops, and is always sure of his subsistence. As a permanent economic relation, this would be startling anywhere betwixt any classes of men brought together in the business of life. Applied to agriculture, in any other part of the world, it would be deemed outrageously absurd, but this is only a part of the 'privileges' (a much more accurate term than 'wages') of the negro field-hand. In addition to half the crops, he has a free cottage of the kind he seems to like, and the windows of which he or his wife persistently nail up; he has abundance of wood from the planter's estate for fuel, and for building his corn-cribs and other outhouses, with teams to draw it from the forest. He is allowed to keep hogs and milch cows and young cattle, which roam and feed with the same right of pasture as the hogs and cattle of the planter, free of all charge. Though entitled to one-half the crops, he is not required to con-

tribute any portion of the seed, nor is he called upon to pay any part of the taxes on the plantation. The only direct tax on the negroes is a poll tax." Mr. Somers declares that he found this tax "everywhere in arrear, and, in some places, in a helpless chaos of non-payment. Yet," he adds, "while thus freed from the burden of taxation, the negro has, up to this period of reconstruction, enjoyed the monopoly of representation, and has had all legislative and executive power moulded to his will by Governors, Senators and Deputies, who have been either his tools, or of whom he himself has been the dupe. For five years," he concludes, "the negroes have been kings, lords and commoners, and something more, in the Southern States."

"But to come back," continues Mr. Somers, "to the economic condition of the plantations, the negro field-hand, with his right of half-crop and privileges as described, who works with ordinary diligence, looking only to his own pocket, and gets his crops forward and gathered in due time, is at liberty to go to other plantations and pick cotton, in doing which he may make from two to two and a-half dollars a day. For every piece of work outside the crop that he does even on his own plantation, he must be paid a dollar a day. While the land owner is busy keeping account betwixt himself and his negro hands, ginning their cotton for them, doing all the marketing of produce and supplies, of which they have the lion's share, and has hardly a day he can call his own, the hands may be earning a dollar a day from him for work which is quite as much theirs as his. Yet the negroes, with all their superabounding privilege on the cotton-field, make little of it. A ploughman or a herd in the Old World would not exchange his lot for theirs, as it stands and as it appears in all external circumstances."

I have quoted these excellent remarks, as they afford a glimpse into some of the causes of the discouragement which prevails among large numbers of cotton-planters.

## THE REVOLT OF THE GRANGERS

### 17

Agrarian discontent began to mount in 1868, when the inflationary wartime prices first broke. Rising to dangerous heights after the panic of 1873, depression came to the rural areas. Farmers, recognizing the impotency of individual protest, began to organize in an effort to break the rhythm of diminishing returns, poverty, and uncertainty. Employing a social organization founded in 1867, the Patrons of Husbandry, they joined in such numbers that by 1874 its membership totaled 1,500,000. The objects of the "Grangers" were boldly proclaimed in a declaration of purposes issued that year:[17]

1. PREAMBLE. Profoundly impressed with the truth that the National Grange of the United States should definitely proclaim to the world its general objects, we hereby unanimously make this Declaration of Purposes of the Patrons of Husbandry:

GENERAL OBJECTS. 1. United by the strong and faithful tie of agriculture, we mutually resolve to labor for the good of our Order, our country, and mankind.

2. We heartily indorse the motto: "In essentials, unity; in non-essentials, liberty; in all things, charity."

SPECIFIC OBJECTS. 3. We shall endeavor to advance our cause by laboring to accomplish the following objects:

To develop a better and higher manhood and womanhood among ourselves. To enhance the comforts and attractions of our homes, and strengthen our attachments to our pursuits. To foster mutual understanding and coöperation. To maintain inviolate our laws, and to emulate

each other in labor to hasten the good time coming. To reduce our expenses, both individual and corporate. To buy less and produce more, in order to make our farms self-sustaining. To diversify our crops, and crop no more than we can cultivate. To condense the weight of our exports, selling less in the bushel and more on hoof and in fleece; less in lint, and more in warp and woof. To systematize our work, and calculate intelligently on probabilities. To discountenance the credit system, the mortgage system, the fashion system, and every other system tending to prodigality and bankruptcy.

We propose meeting together, talking together, working together, buying together, selling together, and in general acting together for our mutual protection and advancement, as occasion may require. We shall avoid litigation as much as possible by arbitration in the Grange. We shall constantly strive to secure entire harmony, goodwill, vital brotherhood among ourselves, and to make our order perpetual. We shall earnestly endeavor to suppress personal, local, sectional, and national prejudices, all unhealthy rivalry, all selfish ambition. Faithful adherence to these principles will insure our mental, moral, social, and material advancement.

BUSINESS RELATIONS. 4. For our business interests, we desire to bring producers and consumers, farmers and manufacturers into the most direct and friendly relations possible. Hence we must dispense with a surplus of middlemen, not that we are unfriendly to them, but we do not need them. Their surplus and their exactions diminish our profits.

We wage no aggressive warfare against any other interest whatever. On the contrary, all our acts and all our efforts, so far as business is concerned, are not only for the benefit of the producer and consumer, but also for all other interests that tend to bring these two parties into speedy and economical contact. Hence we hold that transportation companies of every

---

[17] *Proceedings* of the Seventh Session of the Patrons of Husbandry, February 4, 1874. Reprinted by permission of the publishers, The Arthur H. Clark Company, from *Documentary History of American Industrial Society,* edited by Commons and others, X, 100-105.

kind are necessary to our success, that their interests are intimately connected with our interests, and harmonious action is mutually advantageous, keeping in view the first sentence in our declaration of principles of action that "Individual happiness depends upon general prosperity."

We shall, therefore, advocate for every state the increase in every practicable way, of all facilities for transporting cheaply to the seaboard, or between home producers and consumers, all the productions of our country. We adopt it as our fixed purpose to "open out the channels in nature's great arteries that the life-blood of commerce may flow freely."

We are not enemies of railroads, navigable and irrigating canals, nor of any corporation that will advance our industrial interests, nor of any laboring classes.

In our noble Order there is no communism, no agrarianism.

We are opposed to such spirit and management of any corporation or enterprise as tends to oppress the people and rob them of their just profits. We are not enemies to capital, but we oppose the tyranny of monopolies. We long to see the antagonism between capital and labor removed by common consent, and by an enlightened statesmanship worthy of the nineteenth century. We are opposed to excessive salaries, high rates of interest, and exorbitant per cent profits in trade. They greatly increase our burdens, and do not bear a proper proportion to the profits of producers. We desire only self-protection and the protection of every true interest of our land by legitimate transactions, legitimate trade, and legitimate profits.

EDUCATION. We shall advance the cause of education among ourselves and for our children, by all just means within our power. We especially advocate for our agricultural and industrial colleges that practical agriculture, domestic science, and all the arts which adorn the home, be taught in their courses of study.

THE GRANGE NOT PARTISAN. 5. We emphatically and sincerely assert the oft-repeated truth taught in our organic law, that the Grange, National, State, or Subordinate, is not a political or party organization. No Grange, if true to its obligations, can discuss political or religious questions, nor call political conventions, nor nominate candidates, nor even discuss their merits in its meetings.

Yet the principles we teach underlie all true politics, all true statesmanship, and, if properly carried out, will tend to purify the whole political atmosphere of our country. For we seek the greatest good to the greatest number.

We must always bear in mind that no one, by becoming a Patron of Husbandry, gives up that inalienable right and duty which belongs to every American citizen, to take a proper interest in the politics of his country.

On the contrary, it is right for every member to do all in his power legitimately to influence for good the action of any political party to which he belongs. It is his duty to do all he can in his own party to put down bribery, corruption, and trickery; to see that none but competent, faithful, and honest men, who will unflinchingly stand by our industrial interests, are nominated for all positions of trust; and to have carried out the principle which should always characterize every Patron, that the office should seek the man, and not the man the office.

We acknowledge the broad principle that difference of opinion is no crime, and hold that "progress toward truth is made by differences of opinion," while "the fault lies in bitterness of controversy."

We desire a proper equality, equity, and fairness; protection for the weak, restraint upon the strong; in short, justly distributed burdens and justly distributed power. These are American ideas, the very essence of American independence, and to advocate the contrary is unworthy of the sons and daughters of an American republic.

We cherish the belief that sectionalism is, and of right should be, dead and buried with the past. Our work is for the present and the future. In our agricultural brotherhood and its purposes we shall recognize no north, no south, no east, no west.

It is reserved by every Patron, as the right of a freeman, to affiliate with any party that will best carry out his principles.

OUTSIDE COÖPERATION. 6. Ours being peculiarly a farmers' institution, we cannot admit all to our ranks. Many are excluded by the nature of our organization, not because they are professional men, or artisans, or laborers, but because they have not a sufficient direct interest in tilling the soil, or may have some interest in conflict with our purposes. But we appeal to all good citizens for their cordial coöperation to assist in our efforts toward reform, that we may eventually remove from our midst the last vestige of tyranny and corruption. We hail the general desire for fraternal harmony, equitable compromises, and earnest coöperation, as an omen of our future success.

7. It shall be an abiding principle with us to relieve any of our oppressed and suffering brotherhood by any means at our command.

Last, but not least, we proclaim it among our purposes to inculcate a proper appreciation of the abilities and sphere of woman, as is indicated by admitting her to membership and position in our order.

Imploring the continued assistance of our Divine Master to guide us in our work, we here pledge ourselves to faithful and harmonious labor for all future time, to return by our united efforts to the wisdom, justice, fraternity, and political purity of our forefathers.

## 18

The Granger protest rested on a broad social basis, but monopolistic practices of railroads and grain elevators turned it into a political movement. If dealers could be forced by competition to pay a decent price for wheat, they insisted, and if public carriers could be made to lower their rates, food would sell in the East at such low prices that agricultural surpluses would vanish. That the transportation monopoly generated passionate feelings was instanced by the resolutions passed by a group of Illinois farmers who assembled at Springfield on April 2, 1873:[18]

*Resolved,* By the farmers of Illinois, in mass meeting assembled, That all chartered monopolies, not regulated and controlled by law, have proved detrimental to the public prosperity, corrupting in their management, and dangerous to republican institutions.

*Resolved,* That the railways of the world, except in those countries where they have been held under the strict regulation and supervision of the government, have proved themselves arbitrary, extortionate and as opposed to free institutions and free commerce between states as were the feudal barons of the middle ages.

*Resolved,* That we hold, declare and resolve, that this despotism, which defies our laws, plunders our shipers, impoverishes our people, and corrupts our government, shall be subdued and made to subserve the public interest. . . .

*Resolved,* That in view of the present extortions, we look with alarm upon the future of an interest which can combine in the hands of a few men a capital of nearly $250,000,000, and we believe it essential to the prosperity of all classes that this contest continue until these corporations acknowledge the supremacy of law.

*Resolved,* That we regard it as the undoubted power, and the imperative duty of the legislature, to pass laws fixing reasonable maximum rates for freight and passengers, without classification of roads, and that we urge upon our General Assembly the passage of such laws. . . .

*Resolved,* That we urge the passage of a bill enforcing the principle that railroads are public highways, and requiring

[18] Quoted in J. Periam, *The Groundswell* (Cincinnati, 1874), pp. 286-289.

railroads to make connections with all roads whose tracks meet or cross their own, and to receive and transmit cars and trains offered over their roads at reasonable maximum rates, whether offered at such crossings, or at stations along their roads, and empowering the making of connections by municipal corporations for that purpose. . . .

*Resolved,* That we indorse most fully the action of those who tender legal rates of fare upon the railroads, and refuse to pay more; and that it is the duty of the legislature to provide by law for the defense by the State of Illinois of suits commenced, or that hereafter may be commenced by railroad companies against individuals who have in good faith insisted, or hereafter may insist, upon the right to ride in railroads at legal rates.

*Resolved,* That the presentation of railroad passes to our legislators, whatever may be the spirit and intent with which they are accepted, are demoralizing . . . ; and we look to our legislature, now in session, to rise above personal considerations of pecuniary interest or convenience, and to pass a law making it a misdemeanor for any Senator, or other state or county officers, to accept any railroad pass. . . .

WHEREAS, The constitution of 1848, Article X, prohibits the legislature from granting special railroad charters . . . it is extremely doubtful whether any railroad charter granted since April 1, 1848, by the legislature of Illinois, is of any validity, and that the vested rights of railroad monopolies in this state exist only by assumption of the monopolies and the sufferance of the people. . . .

WHEREAS, The Constitution of 1870, Article XI, Section 13, prohibits any railroad company from issuing watered stock . . . and whereas, this article of the constitution has probably been violated by nearly all the railroad companies in the state; therefore, Resolved, that it is the duty of the railroad commissioners to look carefully into this matter, and to commence proceedings in all clear cases . . . against all railroad companies which have disregarded this important provision of the organic law of the state. . . .

*Resolved,* That we are in favor of the immediate repeal of the protective duties on iron, steel, lumber, and all materials which enter into the construction of railroad cars, steamships, sailing vessels, agricultural implements, etc. and that we urge upon Congress immediate action for this purpose, that cheap railroads and cheap ships are necessary to cheap freights, and that we invite the railroad companies to co-operate with us to that end.

## 19

Western discontent was translated into political action when Grangers gained control of the legislatures in several Mississippi Valley states. Recognizing the impracticability of competition as a device to control the price either of storing or of transporting grain, they turned instead to rate regulation. State after state enacted laws setting maximum freight rates for railroads and placing ceilings over fees charged by elevator operators. These were promptly disputed by the road and elevator operators, who insisted that such laws violated the Fourteenth Amendment by depriving them of property without due process of law. They contended, in effect, that such laws abrogated unrestrained freedom of competition. The Supreme Court, in the celebrated case of *Munn* v. *Illinois* (1876), upholding the Grangers, opened a new era in federal-state relationships:[19]

WAITE, C. J. . . . The Constitution contains no definition of the word "deprive," as used in the Fourteenth Amendment. To determine its signification, therefore, it is necessary to ascertain the effect which usage has given it, when employed in the same or a like connection.

While this provision of the amendment is new in the Constitution . . . as a limitation upon the powers of the States, it is

[19] *United States Reports,* 94 U.S., 123-126.

old as a principle of civilized government. It is found in Magna Charta, and, in substance if not in form, in nearly or quite all the constitutions that have been from time to time adopted by the several States of the Union. By the Fifth Amendment, it was introduced into the Constitution of the United States as a limitation upon the powers of the national government, and by the Fourteenth, as a guarantee against any encroachment upon an acknowledged right of citizenship by the legislatures of the States. . . .

When one becomes a member of society, he necessarily parts with some rights or privileges which, as an individual not affected by his relations to others, he might retain. "A body politic," as aptly defined in the preamble of the constitution of Massachusetts, "is a social compact by which the whole people covenants with each citizen, and each citizen with the whole people, that all shall be governed by certain laws for the common good." This does not confer power upon the whole people to control rights which are purely and exclusively private; but it does authorize the establishment of laws requiring each citizen to so conduct himself, and so use his own property, as not unnecessarily to injure another. This is the very essence of government. . . . From this source come the police powers, which, as was said by Mr. Chief Justice Taney in the License Cases, 5 How. 583, "are nothing more or less than the powers of government inherent in every sovereignty, . . . that is to say, . . . the power to govern men and things." Under these powers the government regulates the conduct of its citizens one towards another, and the manner in which each shall use his own property, when such regulation becomes necessary for the public good. In their exercise it has been customary in England from time immemorial, and in this country from its first colonization, to regulate ferries, common carriers, hackmen, bakers, millers, wharfingers, innkeepers, &c., and in so doing to fix a maximum of charge to be made for services rendered, accommodations furnished, and articles sold. To this day, statutes are to be found in many of the States upon some or all these subjects; and we think it has never yet been successfully contended that such legislation came within any of the constitutional prohibitions against interference with private property. With the Fifth Amendment in force Congress, in 1820, conferred power upon the city of Washington "to regulate . . . the rates of wharfage at private wharves, . . . the sweeping of chimneys, and to fix the rates of fees therefor, . . . and the weight and quality of bread," 3 Stat. 587, § 7; and, in 1848, "to make all necessary regulations respecting hackney carriages and the rates of fare of the same, and the rates of hauling by cartmen, wagoners, carmen, and draymen, and the rates of commission of auctioneers," 9 Id. 224, sect. 2.

From this it is apparent that, down to the time of the adoption of the Fourteenth Amendment; it was not supposed that statutes regulating the use, or even the price of the use, of private property necessarily deprived an owner of his property without due process of law. Under some circumstances they may, but not under all. The amendment does not change the law in this particular: it simply prevents the States from doing that which will operate as such a deprivation.

This brings us to inquire as to the principles upon which this power of regulation rests, in order that we may determine what is within and what without its operative effect. Looking, then, to the common law, from whence came the right which the Constitution protects, we find that when private property is "affected with a public interest, it ceases to be *juris privati* only." This was said by Lord Chief Justice Hale more than two hundred years ago, in his treatise *De Portibus Maris,* 1 Harg. Law Tracts, 78, and has been accepted without objection as an essential element in the law of property ever since. Property does become clothed with a public interest when used in a manner to make it of public consequence, and affect the community at large. When, therefore, one devotes his property to a use in which the public has an interest, he, in effect, grants to the public an interest in that use, and must submit to be controlled by the public for the common good, to the extent of the interest he has thus created. He may withdraw his grant by discontinuing the use; but, so long as he maintains the use, he must submit to the control. . . .

Common carriers exercise a sort of public office, and have duties to perform in which the public interested. . . . Their business is, therefore, "affected with a public interest," within the meaning of the doctrine which Lord Hale has so forcibly stated.

But we need not go further. Enough has already been said to show that, when private property is devoted to a public use, it is subject to public regulation. It remains only to ascertain whether the warehouses of these plaintiffs in error, and the business which is carried on there, come within the operation of this principle.

For this purpose we accept as true the statements of fact contained in the elaborate brief of one of the plaintiffs in error. . . .

In this connection it must also be borne in mind that, although in 1874 there were in Chicago fourteen warehouses adapted to this particular business, and owned by about thirty persons, nine business firms controlled them, and that the prices charged and received for storage were such "as have been from year to year agreed upon and established by the different elevators or warehouses in the city of Chicago, and which rates have been annually published in one or more newspapers printed in said city, in the month of January in each year, as the established rates for the year then next ensuing such publication." Thus it is apparent that all the ele-

vating facilities through which these vast productions "of seven or eight great States of the West" must pass on the way "to four or five of the States on the sea-shore" may be a "virtual" monopoly.

Under such circumstances it is difficult to see why, if the common carrier, or the miller, or the ferryman, or the innkeeper, or the wharfinger, or the baker, or the cartman, or the hackney-coachman, pursues a public employment and exercises "a sort of public office," these plaintiffs in error do not. They stand, to use again the language of their counsel, in the very "gateway of commerce," and take toll from all who pass. Their business most certainly "tends to a common charge, and is become a thing of public interest and use." . . . Certainly, if any business can be clothed "with a public interest and cease to be *juris privati* only," this has been. It may not be made so by the operation of the constitution of Illinois or this statute, but it is by the facts. . . .

For our purposes we must assume that if a state of facts could exist that would justify such legislation, it actually did exist when the statute now under consideration was passed. For us the question is one of power, not of expediency. If no state of circumstances could justify such a statute, then we may declare this one void, because in excess of the legislative power of the State. But if it could we must presume it did. Of the propriety of legislative interference within the scope of legislative power, the legislature is the exclusive judge.

Neither is it a matter of any moment that no precedent can be found for a statute precisely like this. It is conceded that the business is one of recent origin, that its growth has been rapid, and that it is already of great importance. And it must also be conceded that it is a business in which the whole public has a direct and positive interest. It presents, therefore, a case for the application of a long-known and well-established principle in social science, and this statute simply extends the law so as to meet this new development of commercial progress. There is no attempt to compel these owners to grant the public an interest in their property, but to decline their obligations, if they use it in this particular manner.

It matters not in this case that these plaintiffs in error had built their warehouses and established their business before the regulations complained of were adopted. What they did was from the beginning subject to the power of the body politic to require them to conform to such regulations as might be established by the proper authorities for the common good. They entered upon their business and provided themselves with the means to carry it on subject to this condition. If they did not wish to submit themselves to such interference, they should not have clothed the public with an interest in their concerns. The same principle applies to them that does to the proprietor of a hackney-carriage, and as to him it has never been supposed that he was exempt from regulating statutes or ordinances because he had purchased his horses and carriage and established his business before the statute or the ordinance was adopted.

It is insisted, however, that the owner of property is entitled to a reasonable compensation for its use, even though it be clothed with a public interest, and that what is reasonable is a judicial and not a legislative question.

As has already been shown, the practice has been otherwise. In countries where the common law prevails, it has been customary from time immemorial for the legislature to declare what shall be a reasonable compensation under such circumstances, or perhaps more properly speaking, to fix a maximum beyond which any charge made would be unreasonable. Undoubtedly in mere private contracts, relating to matters in which the public has no interest, what is reasonable must be ascertained judicially. But this is because the legislature has no control over such a contract. So, too, in matters which do not affect the public interest, and as to which legislative control may be exercised . . . the courts must determine what is reasonable. The controlling fact is the power to regulate at all. If that exists, the right to establish the maximum charge, as one of the means of regulation, is implied. . . .

We know that this is a power which may be abused; but that is no argument against its existence. For protection against abuses by legislatures the people must resort to the polls, not to the courts. . . .

*Munn* v. *Illinois* was an important victory, but the farmers did not long remain satisfied. Railroads and elevator operators might be more reasonable, but the problems of overproduction, of drought, of debt, and of mortgage foreclosure were still unresolved. Agrarian discontent was the consequence of the revolutions in economics that transformed the United States in the years after the Civil War.

# INDUSTRY AND URBAN LIFE

## 1865–1890

Although agrarian unrest in America after the Civil War was based partly on economic griev-ances, the farmers' hostility to city dwellers was almost equally responsible for rural dissatis-faction. The rise of the city had shifted the center of life—economic, political, social, and intellectual—from farm to metropolis. No phenomenon stemming from the revolutions in eco-nomics was more spectacular, or exerted a wider influence on society, than this arresting transition. The United States was recast in an urban mold. Thought patterns were revised, intellectual activity was stimulated, and cultural progress was accelerated. The city altered American civilization, sharpened the conflicts and heightened the contrasts between wealth and poverty marked by the advent of the machine age.

## THE URBAN IMPACT

### 1

Contemporary opinion on the results of urbanization varied greatly. Most of those who witnessed the emergence of the city as a major force in civilization were undisturbed by doubts. The smoke-domed towns sur-rounding each cluster of factories were su-preme achievements of the creative genius of man. The city offered comforts and pleasures unknown to many less fortunate ancestors; and democracy would make new gains as people learned to live side by side. Such views were reflected in the optimistic com-ments of Andrew Carnegie, wealthy steel man and philanthropist, whose frequent pro-nouncements on every aspect of life were also the opinions of the upper and middle classes:[1]

In 1830 only six and a half per cent. of the population lived in towns of eight thousand inhabitants and upwards; in 1880 the proportion had risen to twenty-two per cent. Thus, nearly one person in every four in America is now a member of a hive of more than eight thousand human beings. Fifty years ago this was true of but one in fifteen, for fourteen out of fifteen lived in the country or in small villages.

This is a stupendous change and marks the development of the Republic from the first stage of homogeneity of pastoral pursuits into the heterogeneous occupa-tions of a more highly civilized state. The nation is now complete, as it were, in it-self, and ready for independent action. Its mechanical and inventive genius has full scope in the thousand and one diversified pursuits which a civilized community necessarily creates, and which necessitate the gathering of men together in masses.

The American, however, need not fear the unhealthy or abnormal growth of cities. He need not imitate the example of those who advocated legislative measures to prevent the growth of London, which Cobbett called a wart upon the hand of England. The free play of economic laws is keeping all quite right, for the town gained upon the country population only one-fourth as fast during the last decade (1870 to 1880) as in the previous one.

Oh, these grand, immutable, all-wise laws of natural forces, how perfectly they work if human legislators would only let them alone! But no, they must be tinkering. One day they would protect the balance of power in Europe by keeping weak, small areas apart and independent —an impossible task, for petty States must merge into the greater—political is as certain as physical gravitation; the next day it is silver in America, which our sage rulers would make of greater intrinsic value. So our governors, all over the world, are at Sisyphus's work—ever rolling the

[1] Andrew Carnegie, *Triumphant Democracy* (1886), pp. 47-49. Reprinted by permission of Charles Scribner's sons, publishers.

stone uphill to see it roll back to its proper bed at the bottom.

That the country held its own so well in the competition with the towns during the last decade is partly due to the fact that the enormous profits made under an improved system of agriculture held the rural population to the soil. The general depression of manufactures also checked settlement in towns, and forced population into the country. The commercial panic of 1873 drove hundreds of thousands from the crowded cities of the East to the unoccupied plains of the West. Train-load after train-load of native emigrants were to be seen passing west to become farmers. With a return to normal conditions we may expect to find the towns absorbing much more than an equal share.

It is always a result of industrial depression in America that the towns are relieved of surplus population which in older countries remains in poverty and distress to swell the ranks of the unemployed. Horace Greeley's advice, "Go West, young man!" is followed. One needs however to add to it, "and stay there," to complete the matter. The equilibrium is thus restored between producers and consumers, and prosperity to both follows. If there be too much food it is unprofitable to grow more cereals, and fewer people become farmers; if the market be overstocked with manufactures, manufacturing becomes unprofitable and fewer engage in it. The population, meanwhile increasing at the rate of nearly two millions per annum, soon requires the surplus, be it food or manufactures. America possesses hundreds of thousands of acres of virgin soil ready for the plough. Like the fabled Antæus, her power of recuperation lies in the earth: let her touch but that and her giant strength is restored. This will continue to be so until her population becomes as dense as that of Europe.

## 2

Other observers of urbanization entertained doubts that never clouded Andrew Carnegie's optimism. Changes stemming from the rise of the city were so destructive of long-established modes that Americans were forced to re-evaluate their social mores, their economic habits, and their political institutions. Was the transition possible, and would democratic institutions survive the change? Were older practices and ideas, threatened by destruction, worth saving? These were the questions asked by Reverend Josiah Strong, a Congregational minister and pioneer in the movement for social Christianity. To him the rising city endangered "free institutions":[2]

Two generations ago Alexis De Tocqueville showed that the principle of local self-government is fundamental to our political institutions and to the very spirit of liberty itself. He then wrote: "Local assemblies of citizens constitute the strength of free nations. Municipal institutions are to liberty what primary schools are to science; they bring it within the people's reach, they teach men how to use and how to enjoy it. A nation may establish a system of free government, but without the spirit of municipal institutions it cannot have the spirit of liberty."

At that time the people of the United States enjoyed local self-government, but since then important and significant changes have taken place, not wholly unforeseen by this student of American democracy. He says further: "I look upon the size of certain American cities, and especially upon the nature of the population, as a real danger which threatens the security of the democratic republics of the New World"; that is, the several states of the Union. When this was written, our urban population was less than nine per cent of the whole; in 1900, it was thirty-three per cent., or more than three times as large, relatively.

The American city is becoming a menace to state and nation because, as it grows more powerful, it is becoming less

[2] Josiah Strong, *The Challenge of the City* (New York, 1907), pp. 55-62. Used by permission of the Missionary Education Movement, successor to the Young People's Missionary Movement.

capable of self-government. The maladministration of municipal affairs in our large cities has long since become a national scandal, and the opening up of its rottenness has made municipal democracy a stench in the nostrils of the civilized world. Our friendly but discriminating English critic, the Honorable James Bryce, says that the one conspicuous failure of American institutions is the government of our great cities; and every intelligent man knows this to be true. Professor Franklin H. Giddings, of Columbia University, said a few years ago, in an address before the Nineteenth Century Club: "We are witnessing to-day, beyond question, the decay—perhaps not permanent, but at any rate the decay—of republican institutions. No man in his right mind can deny it."

Not every one is aware to what extent fundamental principles have been abandoned. Our Revolutionary sires thought it worth while to go to war rather than submit to taxation without representation; and as to local self-government, they deemed it the very essence of liberty. What would they have said if they could have foreseen that their grandchildren would—I will not say pusillanimously surrender these precious principles without a struggle, but—actually *thrust them out of their hands?*

Our theory is that of government by the people. The municipal council represented the people and in it was municipal government formerly centered, including, of course, the levying of taxes for municipal expenditure. But as business men became absorbed in private concerns, to the neglect of public interests, and the voters who voted failed in civic intelligence and conscientiousness, incompetent and venal aldermen were elected, and intolerable abuses naturally followed. A large majority of the voters who placed demagogues in control were non-taxpayers and regardless of the burdens laid on property owners. The latter class, instead of arousing themselves to their civic duties

and undertaking the education of public opinion and of the popular conscience, resorted to the easier course of appealing to the state legislature, which afforded them protection from their own representatives by restricting the powers of the municipal council. These powers were transferred to independent boards, which were in no way accountable to the people. Thus our cities, for the most part, lost their autonomy and came to be governed by the state legislature, most of whose members could have little knowledge of local conditions, and would not be held responsible by their own constituents for the mismanagement of municipal affairs, in which the rural districts had but little interest.

The next step was to place the appointment of these boards in the hands of the mayor, that he might be held responsible. Thus, in our larger cities, power has been transferred from the legislative to the executive branch, and so centralized.

The struggle for liberty has been a struggle to wrest power from one, or the few, and to lodge it with the many; that is, to decentralize government. When popular government fails, society is saved from anarchy by the strong man; that is, power is again centralized. The movement, therefore, to centralize government by transferring power from the council to the mayor was a confession that popular government in our large cities had failed.

It has been supposed that it would be safe for the legislature to confer extraordinary powers on the mayor, because in that event the election of a man of ability and integrity would be of such transcendent importance that the intelligence and character of the city would certainly unite to insure a wise choice.

Surely that experiment could not be tried under the stress of more powerful motives than those brought to bear in the first municipal election of Greater New York. Its mayor (or his boss) would have in his gift offices whose salaries amounted to $500,000 a year. This new government would administer municipal property to the value of $1,000,000,000, and control the annual expenditure of $75,-000,000—a sum nearly equal to the annual budget of the Turkish empire, or to that of Holland and Switzerland combined. The citizens who desired good government were in a large majority; nothing was needed to insure success, except intelligent and unselfish devotion to the public good; but that is precisely what was lacking, and the appeal to civic patriotism failed; and it was shown that the Greater New York was as incapable of self-government as was the lesser city.

Evidently democracy in our larger cities has broken down. Let us be thankful that the warning came before the dominating numbers of the urban population rendered that failure final.

So general has become the distrust of our cities, that for years we have relied on the country vote to save the state and nation from the consequences of the city vote. And though our great cities have shown themselves incapable of self-government, they have not brought upon either the country or themselves the full natural consequences of their ignorance and corruption, because in important particulars the state under recent constitutions has controlled and restrained them.

We are now prepared to weigh the gravity of the fact that more than one half of our population will soon be urban, and that in due time we shall be a nation of cities. If the rate of the movement of population from country to city, between 1890 and 1900 continues until 1940, there will then be in the United States 21,000,000 more people in our cities than outside of them. If the rate of growth above referred to is not sustained, it will make a difference of a few years only, as the preponderance of our city population in the near future must be regarded as certain. The cities will then no longer accept limitations from the state, but, when they become fully conscious of their

power, will take into their hands not only their own affairs, but also those of the state and of the nation.

*What if the cities are then incapable of self-government? If their government is then "a conspicuous failure," what will become of our free institutions?*

## 3

A more searching appraisal of the dangers of urbanization was written by Adna F. Weber, who feared that the growing cities would encourage an uneven distribution of wealth, political corruption, and even class conflicts:[3]

The changes in the distribution of population . . . have necessarily effected changes in State and national politics and national power.

In the first place, . . . the causes of concentration are forces which augment national wealth. Compare the distribution of wealth in the United States at the present time and in 1787. In the Constitutional Convention it was held that the distribution of wealth was so even throughout the country, that any system of taxation might safely be based on numbers. How different in 1898! The rural population is not less wealthy now than it was a century since, but the urban population has amassed incalculably greater wealth. . . .

Of even more fundamental importance than national power is national stability. Anything . . . that diminishes the elector's love of country or interest in its preservation must excite distrust. Now land ownership has in the past been recognized as the most important conservative force in politics. . . . But with increasing concentration of population goes an increase of tenancy, both as regards land and dwelling houses. . . .

Thus statistics show that the ownership

[3] Adna F. Weber, *The Growth of Cities in the Nineteenth Century* (New York, 1899), pp. 425-437.

of the home becomes less common in the degree that we leave the farm and village and proceed up (or down) the scale to the great cities. We do not wish to minimize the importance of this fact from the political point of view, and yet we must remember that there are other forms of property than real estate. If a man who rents his home has a good bank account, he is not likely to vote for the overthrow of government. . . .

Nevertheless, the danger of class antagonism is particularly grave in the cities. . . . The chasm created by the industrial system yawns widest in the cities; and the means of bridging it will require careful consideration. . . .

· Aristotle saw the difficulty of governing a vast agglomeration of people, and limited the population of his ideal city-state to 10,000. . . . A dense population engenders problems that are never thought of in a village. Run the eye over a directory of the public officials of a great city and observe how few of them are known to village governments. . . . It would take pages merely to enumerate the officials of New York City, the majority of whom perform functions to which no parallel is found in the village.

The complexity of a city government . . . [makes] it the most difficult kind of government to watch. Even the national government does not under-take to regulate so many details, and the general supervision to which it is mainly limited can be more easily watched. The city is in many respects a great business corporation; it calls for a careful, systematic, business-like administration. Now, administration is a branch of politics in which Americans have hitherto shown more awkwardness than is pleasant to think of. Corruption if not inefficiency has been the characteristic mark of public administration, especially in the cities. And the reason why Americans have submitted to such service, has been its small sphere, as compared with the sphere of local (*i.e.*

rural) government, which has been the strength of our democratic institutions. As Mr. Bryce has said: "Americans constantly reply to the criticisms which Europeans pass on the faults of their State legislatures and the shortcomings of Congress by pointing to the healthful efficiency of their rural administration, which enables them to bear with composure the defects of the higher organs of government." Now it is obvious that with the rapid movement of population from the rural districts to the cities, the sphere of local rural government . . . has been continually narrowed. With only 25 or 35 per cent. of our people residing in the rural districts (Massachusetts), the "healthy efficiency of rural administration" signifies but little.

The difficulties of city government . . . are enhanced by the large floating population which is a necessary accompaniment of a great migratory movement toward the cities. The thousands of new residents are strangers to the city's history and traditions, have no local attachments, and do not readily acquire any civic pride. The vast majority are non-taxpayers, and feel little concern in the city's government. . . .

On top of these obstacles to good government comes the problem of assimilating the foreign nationalities. When the foreign immigrants settle in isolated "quarters," which is the natural tendency, much effort is required to raise them to the city's standard. This is perhaps the one danger of the "movement toward the cities" so far as the United States is concerned: the influx of a shiftless and degraded population from foreign lands, which cannot be readily distributed throughout the country.

Inasmuch as this is not a treatise on municipal government, no discussion of proposed reforms is in place. But one thing is to be strenuously insisted upon, and that is the right of the cities to self-government. The strength of our political institutions has always been in local government, and the only hope for our cities is freedom to work out for themselves a plan of government which shall take the place of that rural local administration that has been our boast in times past. . . . The only hope for the cities is to educate the mass of the propertyless, and this will never be accomplished until the liberal and generous minds of the city have the assurance that their work is not liable to be undone at any moment by the State legislature. . . .

As to the cities themselves, we have just noted how good government and even social solidarity are threatened by class antagonisms. The actual cause of such social antipathies will be found in an exaggerated individualism, which has been developed by an era of industrialism, out of mediaeval militarism. The new industrial forces which transformed the solidified Age of Authority into a liquefied Age of Freedom, have naturally been more predominant in the cities than elsewhere, for the close contact of man with man in a dense population removes prejudices and engenders liberalism. The cities have always been the cradles of liberty, just as they are to-day the centres of radicalism. Every man of the world knows that isolation and solitude are found in a much higher degree in the crowded city than in a country village, where one individual's concerns are the concern of all. The cities, then, are favorable to free thought and the sense of individual responsibility.

But it is a question whether the loosening of the ties of individual responsibility has not gone too far. "The great danger to morality and good government," says Roscher, "is that the individual is lost in the multitude of atoms,—a condition that may abolish the sense of duty and make the great city as insecure as the opposite extreme, the wilderness." Now this extreme individualism of the cities is merely one manifestation of the . . . fluidity of modern society, and its cause is chiefly industrial. Cities vary in their lack of social feeling . . . and those cities have the least portion of it which are most given to

industrial enterprises in which the competitive system has obtained full sway.

It may be said, indeed, that it is our industrial system, and not city life, which engenders the essentially egoistic, self-seeking and materialistic attitude; but so long as the cities remain the results of the competitive industrial regime, they must share the blame. No one can view with equanimity the continual drift of population to the cities where it will be subject to such demoralizing influences. . . .

This separation of classes which has so nearly destroyed social solidarity in all large cities, is especially dangerous in the United States (where, under democratic forms, solidarity is especially indispensable) on account of differences in race and religion, as well as social rank and condition. In American cities the "upper" social ranks—the commercial and professional classes—are predominantly American and Protestant; the "lower" ranks—the hewers of wood and drawers of water—are on the contrary chiefly of foreign origin and of the Roman Catholic faith. The danger of class antagonism is therefore peculiarly great in our cities.

What can be done to wipe out class feelings and unify the community? A brief survey of what has already been done will encourage those who have most clearly perceived the dangers of the competitive system and the concentration of population in modern cities, which have been called the "most impersonal combinations of individuals that have ever been formed in the world's history."

Social observers have for some time been aware that society is emerging from the period of Industrialism, into a period of Humanitarianism. Criticism of Industrialism began as soon as it was discovered that its fundamental idea (Individualism) was not identical with personal welfare. Scepticism, *laissez-faire,* the insistence upon rights as opposed to mediaeval restrictions and obligations, succeeded in freeing the individual from the authority of superiors, but turned him over to the tender mercy of things that society had created and not learned to control. Matter was exalted over mind, and the twin-companion of Individualism was Materialism. The guild-laws had scarcely been abolished in England before factory legislation began— the opening of a new period of Reconstruction. . . . In recent years every enlightened country has enacted laws along the line of *personal welfare*. Some call such legislation Socialism; it is in the spirit of co-operation—Humanitarianism.

Now, it is perfectly natural that the most noticeable traces of the humanitarian movement should be found in the cities, where the greatest abuses of industrialism and materialism existed. Men cannot live long in close contact without acquiring a painful sense of the separateness of individual interests, of the absurdity of identifying the individual's interest with the interest of society and the consequent policy of *laissez-faire*. . . . It may be to my interest to employ poverty-stricken families, living amidst filth and contagious diseases, to make cheap shirts and clothing; but it is not to the interest of my fellow-citizens. In short, there arise a thousand and one conflicts between individual interests and social interests, and in their adjustment selfishness is curbed and a social feeling excited. This explains why Socialism has so far been largely Municipal Socialism. It is easier, and at the same time more necessary, for the people in a city to co-operate.

Political co-operation, however, will not operate to remedy all the evils of an extreme individualism. Accordingly, we see a multitude of philanthropic associations and enterprises in every great city. The guide-book to reform clubs in New York city is a volume of no mean dimensions. All of these associations unite to foster civic pride and a spirit of mutual helpfulness. And still something is lacking to overcome the indifference of the "West Side" to the "East Side" and the lack of neigh-borly feelings expressed in the North Country proverb: "Friends are far when neighbors are near." The poor become hopeless, "the submerged tenth," from want of stimulus and help, and the rich become "charityless" from want of the insight that personal contact gives. To bring together rich and poor is the office of university and other social settlements— Toynbee Hall in London, Hull House in Chicago, and many others. This is perhaps the most promising of all social movements. It signifies charity in the highest sense—not the selfish opening of the pocket to free oneself from the annoyance of a beggar or to buy entrance into Paradise.

## A NEW DESIGN FOR WOMEN

### 4

If the urban process transformed the lives of men, it revolutionized the lives of women. Traditionally creatures of the home, "females" had been denied legal, social, or political equality. Although a few bold reformers lifted their voices in protest just before the Civil War, the condition of women in 1865 was little better than it had been two centuries earlier. Industrialization and urbanization offered the chance for emancipation. Industry not only provided women with laborsaving devices releasing them from household drudgery, but gave them new chances for gainful employment. Cities provided opportunities to organize in behalf of reform. Strengthened and united, they first sought political equality, advancing the claim that the Fourteenth Amendment, which endowed them with citizenship, entitled them to vote. The Supreme Court, however, gave short shrift to this argument in the case of *Minor* v. *Happersett* (1875):[4]

It is contended that the provisions of the Constitution and laws of the State of Missouri, which confine the right of suffrage and registration therefor to men, are in violation of the Constitution of the United

---

[4] 21 WALLACE 165-177.

States, and therefore void. The argument is, that as a woman, born or naturalized in the United States and subject to the jurisdiction thereof, is a citizen of the United States and of the State in which she resides, she has the right of suffrage as one of the privileges and immunities of her citizenship, which the State cannot by its laws or constitution abridge.

There is no doubt that women may be citizens as they are persons, and by the Fourteenth Amendment "all persons born or naturalized in the United States and subject to the jurisdiction thereof" are expressly declared to be "citizens of the United States and of the State wherein they reside." But, in our opinion, it did not need this amendment to give them that position. Before its adoption the Constitution of the United States did not in terms prescribe who should be citizens of the United States or of the several States, yet there were necessarily such citizens without such provision. . . . Sex has never been made one of the elements of citizenship in the United States. In this respect men have never had an advantage over women. The same laws precisely apply to both. The Fourteenth Amendment did not affect the citizenship of women any more than it did of men. In this particular, therefore, the rights of Mrs. Minor do not depend upon the amendment. She has always been a citizen from her birth, and entitled to all the privileges and immunities of citizenship. . . .

If the right of suffrage is one of the necessary privileges of a citizen of the United States, then the constitution and laws of Missouri confining it to men are in violation of the Constitution of the United States, as amended, and consequently void. The direct question is, therefore, presented whether all citizens are necessarily voters.

The Constitution does not define the privileges and immunities of citizens. For that definition we must look elsewhere. In this case we need not determine what they are, but only whether suffrage is necessarily one of them.

It certainly is nowhere made so in express terms. The United States has no voters in the States of its own creation. The elective officers of the United States are all elected directly or indirectly by state voters. . . .

The Amendment did not add to the privileges and immunities of a citizen. It simply furnished an additional guaranty for the protection of such as he already had. No new voters were necessarily made by it. Indirectly it may have had that effect, because it may have increased the number of citizens entitled to suffrage under the constitution and laws of the States, but it operates for this purpose, if at all, through the States and the state laws, and not directly upon the citizen.

It is clear therefore, we think, that the Constitution has not added the right of suffrage to the privileges and immunities of citizenship as they existed at the time it was adopted. This makes it proper to inquire whether suffrage was co-extensive with the citizenship of the States at the time of its adoption. If it was, then it may with force be argued that suffrage was one of the rights which belonged to citizenship, and in the enjoyment of which every citizen must be protected. But if it was not, the contrary may with propriety be assumed. . . .

In this condition of the law in respect to suffrage in the several States it cannot for a moment be doubted that if it had been intended to make all citizens of the United States voters, the framers of the Constitution would not have left it to implication. . . .

It is true that the United States guarantees to every State a republican form of government. . . .

The guaranty is of a republican form of government. No particular government is designated as republican, neither is the exact form to be guaranteed, in any manner especially designated. Here, as in other parts of the instrument, we are compelled to resort elsewhere to ascertain what was intended.

The guaranty necessarily implies a duty on the part of the States themselves to provide such a government. All the States had governments when the Constitution was adopted. In all the people participated to some extent, through their representatives elected in the manner specially provided. These governments the Constitution did not change. They were accepted precisely as they were, and it is, therefore, to be presumed that they were such as it was the duty of the States to provide. Thus we have unmistakable evidence of what was republican in form, within the meaning of that term as employed in the Constitution.

As has been seen, all the citizens of the States were not invested with the right of suffrage. In all, save perhaps New Jersey, this right was only bestowed upon men and not upon all of them. Under these circumstances it is certainly now too late to contend that a government is not republican, within the meaning of this guaranty in the Constitution, because women are not made voters. . . .

Certainly if the courts can consider any question settled, this is one. For nearly ninety years the people have acted upon the idea that the Constitution, when it conferred citizenship, did not necessarily confer the right of suffrage. If uniform practice long continued can settle the construction of so important an instrument as the Constitution of the United States confessedly is, most certainly it has been done here. Our province is to decide what the law is, not to declare what it should be.

We have given this case the careful consideration its importance demands. If the law is wrong, it ought to be changed; but the power for that is not with us. The arguments addressed to us bearing upon such a view of the subject may perhaps be sufficient to induce those having the power

to make the alteration, but they ought not to be permitted to influence our judgment in determining the present rights of the parties now litigating before us. No argument as to woman's need of suffrage can be considered. We can only act upon her rights as they exist. It is not for us to look at the hardship of withholding. Our duty is at an end if we find it within the power of the state to withhold.

Being unanimously of the opinion that the Constitution of the United States does not confer the right of suffrage upon any one, and that the constitutions and laws of the several States which commit that important trust to men alone are not necessarily void, we

AFFIRM THE JUDGMENT.

## 5

Disappointed but not disheartened, American women continued the struggle for equal rights. With efficient organizations, they soon were clamoring at the doors of national and state legislatures, demanding educational facilities, legal equality, and especially political recognition. The campaign for suffrage made little headway in the nineteenth century, although a few western states opened the ballot to women. One of the most effective pleas in their behalf was made in the minority report of the House Judiciary Committee in 1884, although the majority decided that "females" were unworthy of the franchise:[5]

The majority of the committee claim that suffrage is not a right but a privilege to be guarded by those who have it, and to be by them doled out to those who shall become worthy. That every extension of suffrage has been granted in some form or other by those already holding it is probably true. In some countries, however, it has been extended upon the simple basis of expediency, and in others in obedience to a claim of right. If suffrage be a right, if it be true that no man has a claim to gov-

[5] Quoted in Elizabeth Cody Stanton, *et al.*, *The History of Woman Suffrage* (Rochester, 1902), IV, 54-55.

ern any other man except to the extent that the other man has a right to govern him, then there can be no discussion of the question of Woman Suffrage. No reason on earth can be given by those who claim suffrage as a right of manhood which does not make it a right of womanhood also. If the suffrage is to be given man to protect him in his life, liberty and property, the same reasons urge that it be given to woman, for she has the same life, liberty and property to protect. If it be urged that her interests are so bound up in those of man that they are sure to be protected, the answer is that the same argument was urged as to the merging in the husband of the wife's right of property, and was pronounced by the judgment of mankind fallacious in practice and in principle. If the natures of men and women are so alike that for that reason no harm is done by suppressing women, what harm can be done by elevating them to equality? If the natures be different, what right can there be in refusing representation to those who might take juster views about many social and political questions?

Our Government is founded, not on the rule of the wisest and best, but upon the rule of all. The learned and the ignorant, the wise and the unwise, the judicious and the injudicious are all invited to assist in governing, and upon the broad principle that the best government for mankind is not the government which the wisest and best would select, but that which the average of mankind would select. Laws are daily enacted, not because they seem the wisest even to those legislators who pass them, but because they represent what the whole people wish. And, in the long run, it may be just as bad to enact laws in advance of public sentiment as to hold on to laws behind it. Upon what principle in a Government like ours can one-half the minds be denied expression at the polls? Is it because they are untrained in public affairs? Are they more so than the slaves were when the right of suffrage was con-

ferred on them? It is objected that to admit women would be temporarily to lower the suffrage on account of their lack of training in public duties. What is now asked of us is not immediate admission to the right, but the privilege of presenting to the Legislatures of the different States the amendment, which can not become effective until adopted by three-fourths of them. It may be said that the agitation and discussion of this question will, long before its adoption, have made women as familiar with public affairs as the average of men, for the agitation is hardly likely to be successful until after a majority, at least, of women are in favor of it.

We believe in the educating and improving effect of participation in government. We believe that every citizen in the United States is made more intelligent, more learned and better educated by his participation in politics and political campaigns. It must be remembered that education, like all things else, is relative. While the average American voter may not be all that impatient people desire, and is far behind his own future, yet he is incomparably superior to the average citizen of any other land where the subject does not fully participate in the government. Discussions on the stump, and above all the discussions he himself has with his fellows, breed a desire for knowledge which will take no refusal and which leads to great general intelligence. In political discussion, acrimony and hate are not essential, and have of late years quite perceptibly diminished and will more and more diminish when discussions by women, and in the presence of women, become more common. If, then, discussion of public affairs among men has elevated them in knowledge and intelligence, why will it not lead to the same results among women? It is not merely education that makes civilization, but diffusion of education. The standing of a nation and its future depend not upon the education of the few, but of the whole. Every improvement in the status of women in the matter of education has been an improvement to the whole race. Women have by education thus far become more womanly, not less. The same prophecies of ruin to womanliness were made against her education on general subjects that are now made against her participation in politics.

It is sometimes asserted that women now have a great influence in politics through their husbands and brothers. This is undoubtedly true. But that is just the kind of influence which is not wholesome for the community, for it is influence unaccompanied by responsibility. People are always ready to recommend to others what they would not do themselves. If it be true that women can not be prevented from exercising political influence, is not that only another reason why they should be steadied in their political action by that proper sense of responsibility which comes from acting themselves?

We conclude, then, that every reason which in this country bestows the ballot upon man is equally applicable to the proposition to bestow the ballot upon woman, and that in our judgment there is no foundation for the fear that woman will thereby become unfitted for all the duties she has hitherto performed.

## 6

While some reformers advocated militant action, others hoped that better educational opportunities for women would gradually lead to change. To this end, Sophia Smith, a New England spinster, devoted her considerable fortune. The purpose of Smith College, founded in 1875, was clearly expressed in her will:[6]

I hereby make the following provisions for the establishment and maintenance of an Institution for the higher education of young women, with the design of furnishing for my own sex means and facili-

ties for education equal to those which are afforded now in our Colleges to young men.

It is my opinion that by the higher and more thorough Christian education of women, what are called their "wrongs" will be redressed, their wages adjusted, their weight of influence in reforming the evils of society will be greatly increased, as teachers, as writers, as mothers, as members of society, their power for good will be incalculably enlarged.

## INTELLECTUAL AND RELIGIOUS FERMENT

### 7

Urbanization stimulated intellectual as well as social ferment. Theological thought was particularly affected by the rise of the city, for the churches were faced with urban problems just as serious as those confronting other institutions. How could they compete for men's attention in a secular world that enshrined profits as the new god? How could they train men's minds if public schools performed that function so admirably? How could they match the distractive lure of theaters, newspapers, sports, restaurants, and excursions? In other words, the church, like the home, suffered a curtailment of function. This was bad enough, but far worse was the scientific assault on established theologies which coincided with the urban threat. The publication of the *Origin of Species* by Charles Darwin in 1859, followed by the *Descent of Man* in 1871, heralded a scientific upheaval and precipitated a debate in every quarter of the globe. The leading issues were luminously set forth by John Dewey, one of the greatest of American philosophers, who himself in considerable part epitomized them:[7]

The exact bearings upon philosophy of the new logical outlook are, of course, as yet, uncertain and inchoate. We live in the twilight of intellectual transition.

---

[6] *Bulletin of Smith College,* Catalogue Issue, Series 34, No. 3 (Northampton, 1940), p. 34.

[7] John Dewey, "Charles Darwin and His Influence upon Philosophy," *Popular Science Monthly,* July, 1909, pp. 93-98. Reprinted by permission of *Popular Science Monthly.*

One must add the rashness of the prophet to the stubbornness of the partizan to venture a systematic exposition of the influence upon philosophy of the Darwinian method. At best, we can but inquire as to its general bearing—the effect upon mental temper and complexion, upon that body of half-conscious, half-instinctive intellectual aversions and preferences which determine, after all, our more deliberate intellectual enterprises. In this vague inquiry there happens to exist as a kind of touchstone a problem of long historic currency that has also been much discussed in Darwinian literature. I refer to the old problem of design *versus* chance, mind *versus* matter, as the causal explanation, first or final, of things.

As we have already seen, the classic notion of species carried with it the idea of purpose. In all living forms, a specific type is present directing the earlier stages of growth to the realization of its own perfection. Since this purposive regulative principle is not visible to the senses, it follows that it must be an ideal or rational force. Since, however, the perfect form is gradually approximated through the sensible changes, it also follows that in and through a sensible realm a rational ideal force is working out its own ultimate manifestation. These inferences were extended to nature: (a) She does nothing in vain; but all for an ulterior purpose. (b) Within natural sensible events there is therefore contained a spiritual causal force, which as spiritual escapes perception, but is apprehended by an enlightened reason. (c) The manifestation of this principle brings about a subordination of matter and sense to its own realization, and this ultimate fulfilment is the goal of nature and of man. The design argument thus operated in two directions. Purposefulness accounted for the intelligibility of nature and the possibility of science, while the absolute or cosmic character of this purposefulness gave sanction and worth to the moral and religious endeavors of man.

Science was underpinned and morals authorized by one and the same principle, and their mutual agreement was eternally guaranteed.

This philosophy remained, in spite of sceptical and polemic outbursts, the official and the regnant philosophy of Europe for over two thousand years. The expulsion of fixed first and final causes from astronomy, physics, and chemistry had indeed given the doctrine something of a shock. But, on the other hand, increased acquaintance with the details of plant and animal life operated as a counterbalance and perhaps even strengthened the argument from design. The marvelous adaptations of organisms to their environment, of organs to the organism, of unlike parts of a complex organ—like the eye—to the organ itself; the foreshadowing by lower forms of the higher; the preparation in earlier stages of growth for organs that only later had their functioning—these things were increasingly recognized with the progress of botany, zoology, paleontology, and embryology. Together, they added such prestige to the design argument that by the late eighteenth century it was, as approved by the sciences of organic life, the central point of theistic and idealistic philosophy.

The Darwinian principle of natural selection cut straight under this philosophy. If all organic adaptations are due simply to constant variation and the elimination of those variations which are harmful in the struggle for existence that is brought about by excessive reproduction, there is no call for a prior intelligent causal force to plan and preordain them. Hostile critics charged Darwin with materialism and with making chance the cause of the universe.

Some naturalists, like Asa Gray, favored the Darwinian principle and attempted to reconcile it with design. Gray held to what may be called design on the installment plan. If we conceive the "stream of variations" to be itself intended, we may suppose that each successive variation was designed from the first to be selected. In that case, variation, struggle, and selection simply define the mechanism of "secondary causes" through which the "first cause" acts; and the doctrine of design is none the worse off because we know more of its *modus operandi*.

Darwin could not accept this mediating proposal. He admits or rather he asserts that it is "impossible to conceive this immense and wonderful universe including man with his capacity of looking far backwards and far into futurity as the result of blind chance or necessity." But nevertheless he holds that since variations are in useless as well as in useful direction, and since the latter are sifted out simply by the stress of the conditions of struggle for existence, the design argument as applied to living beings is unjustifiable; and its lack of support there deprives it of scientific value as applied to nature in general. If the variations of the pigeon, which under artificial selection give the pouter pigeon, are not preordained for the sake of the breeder, by what logic do we argue that variations resulting in natural species are pre-designed? . . .

So much for some of the more obvious facts of the discussion of design *versus* chance, as causal principles of nature and of life as a whole. We brought up this discussion . . . as a crucial instance. What does our touchstone indicate as to the bearing of Darwinian ideas upon philosophy? In the first place, the new logic outlaws, flanks, dismisses—what you will—one type of problems and substitutes for it another type. Philosophy forswears inquiry after absolute origins and absolute finalities in order to explore specific values and the specific conditions that generate them.

Darwin concluded that the impossibility of assigning the world to chance as a whole and to design in its parts indicated the insolubility of the question. Two radi-

cally different reasons, however, may be given as to why a problem is insoluble. One reason is that the problem is too high for intelligence; the other is that the question in its very asking makes assumptions that render the question meaningless. The latter alternative is unerringly pointed to in the celebrated case of design *versus* chance. Once admit that the sole verifiable or fruitful object of knowledge is the particular set of changes that generate the object of study together with the consequences that then flow from it, and no intelligible question can be asked about what, by assumption, lies outside. To assert—as is often asserted—that specific values of particular truth, social bonds and forms of beauty, if they can be shown to be generated by concretely knowable conditions, are meaningless and in vain; to assert that they are justified only when they and their particular causes and effects have all at once been gathered up into some inclusive first cause and some exhaustive final goal, is intellectual atavism. Such argumentation is reversion to the logic that explained the extinction of fire by water through the formal essence of aqueousness and the quenching of thirst by water through the final cause of aqueousness. Whether used in the case of the special event or that of life as a whole, such logic only abstracts some aspect of the existing course of events in order to reduplicate it as a petrified eternal principle by which to explain the very changes of which it is the formalization.

When Henry Sidgwick casually remarked in a letter that as he grew older his interest in what or who made the world was altered into interest in what kind of a world it is anyway, his voicing of a common experience of our own day illustrates also the nature of that intellectual transformation effected by the Darwinian logic. Interest shifts from the wholesale essence back of special changes to the question of how special changes serve and defeat concrete purposes; shifts from an intelligence that shaped things once and for all to the particular intelligences which things are even now shaping; shifts from an ultimate goal of good to the direct increments of justice and happiness that intelligent administration of existent conditions may beget and that present carelessness or stupidity will destroy or forego.

In the second place, the classic type of logic inevitably set philosophy upon proving that life *must* have certain qualities and values—no matter how experience presents the matter—because of some remote cause and eventual goal. The duty of wholesale justification inevitably accompanies all thinking that makes the meaning of special occurrences depend upon something that once and for all lies behind them. The habit of derogating from present meanings and uses prevents our looking the facts of experience in the face; it prevents serious acknowledgment of the evils they present and serious concern with the goods they promise but do not as yet fulfil. It turns thought to the business of finding a wholesale transcendent remedy for the one and guarantee for the other. One is reminded of the way many moralists and theologians greeted Herbert Spencer's recognition of an unknowable energy from which welled up the phenomenal physical processes without and the conscious operations within. Merely because Spencer labeled his unknowable energy "God," this faded piece of metaphysical goods was greeted as an important and grateful concession to the reality of the spiritual realm. Were it not for the deep hold of the habit of seeking justification for ideal values in the remote and transcendent, surely this reference of them to an unknowable absolute would be despised in comparison with the demonstrations of experience that knowable energies are daily generating about us precious values.

The displacing of this wholesale type of philosophy will doubtless not arrive by sheer logical disproof, but rather by growing recognition of its futility. Were it a thousand times true that opium produces sleep because of its dormitive energy, yet the inducing of sleep in the tired, and the recovery to waking life of the poisoned, would not be thereby one least step forwarded. And were it a thousand times dialectically demonstrated that life as a whole is regulated by a transcendent principle to a final inclusive goal, none the less truth and error, health and disease, good and evil, hope and fear in the concrete, would remain just what and where they now are. To improve our education, to ameliorate our manners, to advance our politics, we must have recourse to specific conditions of generation.

Finally, the new logic introduces responsibility into the intellectual life. To idealize and rationalize the universe at large is after all a confession of inability to master the courses of things that specifically concern us. As long as mankind suffered from this impotency, it naturally shifted a burden of responsibility that it could not carry over to the more competent shoulders of the transcendent cause. But if insight into specific conditions of value and into specific consequences of ideas is possible, philosophy must in time become a method of locating and interpreting the more serious of the conflicts that occur in life, and a method of projecting ways for dealing with them: a method of moral and political diagnosis and prognosis.

The claim to formulate *a priori* the legislative constitution of the universe is by its nature a claim that may lead to elaborate dialectic developments. But it is also one that removes these very conclusions from subjection to experimental test, for, by definition, these results make no differences in the detailed course of events. But a philosophy that humbles its pretensions to the work of projecting hypotheses for the education and conduct of mind, individual and social, is thereby subjected to test by the way in which the ideas it propounds work out in practice. In having modesty forced upon it, philosophy also acquires responsibility.

Doubtless I seem to have violated the implied promise of my earlier remarks and to have turned both prophet and partizan. But in anticipating the direction of the transformations in philosophy to be wrought by the Darwinian genetic and experimental logic, I do not profess to speak for any save those who yield themselves consciously or unconsciously to this logic. No one can fairly deny that at present there are two effects of the Darwinian mode of thinking. On the one hand, there are making many sincere and vital efforts to revise our traditional philosophic conceptions in accordance with its demands. On the other hand, there is as definitely a recrudescence of absolutistic philosophies; an assertion of a type of philosophic knowing distinct from that of the sciences, one which opens to us another kind of reality from that to which the sciences give access; an appeal through experience to something that essentially goes beyond experience. This reaction affects popular creeds and religious movements as well as technical philosophies. The very conquest of the biological sciences by the new ideas has led many to proclaim an explicit and rigid separation of philosophy from science.

Old ideas give way slowly; for they are more than abstract logical forms and categories. They are habits, predispositions, deeply engrained attitudes of aversion and preference. Moreover, the conviction persists—though history shows it to be a hallucination—that all the questions that the human mind has asked are questions that can be answered in terms of the alternatives that the questions themselves present. But in fact intellectual progress usually occurs through sheer abandonment of questions together with both of the alternatives they assume—an abandonment that results from their decreasing vitality and a change of urgent interest. We do not solve them: we get over them. Old questions are solved by disappearing, evaporating, while new questions corresponding to the changed attitude of endeavor and preference take their place. Doubtless the greatest dissolvent in contemporary thought of old questions, the greatest precipitant of new methods, new intentions, new problems, is the one effected by the scientific revolution that found its climax in the "Origin of the Species."

## 8

Men of faith divided sharply on the subject of evolution. Some, representing the conservative creeds, refused to accept the newest "heresy." They argued heatedly that acceptance of Darwin implied the rejection of special creation, and the rejection of the Biblical story of creation implied rejection of the Bible itself. Clergymen who held these views invented the fable that Darwin taught that man descended from monkeys. The fundamentalist point of view was presented in the speeches and writings of Edwin P. Whipple, a well-known contemporary lecturer and critic:[8]

Do you complain that I am speaking in a passion? It seems to me it's about time for all of us to be in a passion. Perhaps, if we show these men of science that there is in us a little righteous wrath, they may be considerate enough to stop with the monkey,—make the monkey "a finality," sir, and not go lower down in the scale of creation to find an ancestor for us. It is our meek submission to the monkey which is now urging them to attempt more desperate outrages still. What if Darwin had been treated as he deserved when he published the original edition of his villainous book? If I had been Chief Justice of England when that high priest of "natural selection" first tried to oust me out of the fee-simple of my species, I would have given him an illustration of "the struggle for existence" he wouldn't have relished. I

---

[8] Edwin P. Whipple, *Outlooks on Society, Literature and Politics* (Boston, 1888), pp. 58-62.

would have hanged him on the highest gallows ever erected on this planet since the good old days of Haman. What has been the result of a mistaken clemency in this case? Why, he has just published a fourth edition of his treatise, and what do you think he now puts forward as our "probable" forefather? "It is probable," he says, "from what we know of the embryos of mammals, birds, fishes, and reptiles, that all the members in these four great classes are the modified descendants of one ancient progenitor, which was furnished in its adult state with branchiæ, had a swim-bladder, four simple limbs, and a long tail fitted for an aquatic life." Probable, indeed! Why, it is also probable, I suppose, that this accounts for the latent tendency in the blood of our best-educated collegians to turn water-men, and abandon themselves with a kind of sacred fury to the fierce delight of rowing-matches. The "long tail fitted for an aquatic life" will also "probably" come in course of time. Student-mammals of Harvard and Yale, what think you of your "one ancient progenitor?" Inheritors of his nature, are you sure you have not yet succeeded in cutting off the entail of the estate?

We have been brought up, sir, in the delusive belief that "revolutions never go backwards." It's a lie, I tell you; for this new revolution in science does nothing else. It is going backwards and backwards and backwards, and it won't stop until it involves the whole of us in that nebulous mist of which, it seems, all things are but the "modified" development. Well, in for a penny, in for a pound. Let us not pause at that "long tail fitted for an aquatic life" which made our one ancient progenitor such an ornament of fluvial society, but boldly strike out into space, and clutch with our thoughts that primitive tail which flares behind the peacock of the heavens,—the comet. There's nebulous matter for your profound contemplation. That is the flimsy material out of which stars, earth, water, plants, jelly-fish, an-

cient progenitor, monkey, man, were all equally evolved. That is the grand original of all origins. We are such stuff as comets' tails are made of,—"third lobe," "hippocampus minor," "posterior cornu of the laterial ventricle," and all the rest. "Children of the Mist," we are made by this "sublime speculation" at home in the universe. Nebuchadnezzar, when he went to grass, only visited a distant connection. The stars over our heads have for thousands of years been winking their relationship with us, and we have never intelligently returned the jocose salutation, until science taught us the use of our eyes. We are now able to detect the giggle, as of feminine cousins, in the grain whose risibilities are touched by the wind. We can now cheer even the dull stone which we kick from our path with a comforting "Hail fellow, well met!" We must not be aristocrats and put on airs. We must hob and nob with all the orders of creation, saying alike to radiates, articulates, and mullusks, "Go ahead, my hearties! don't be shamefaced; you're as good as vertebrates, and only want, like some of our human political lights, a little backbone to have your claims admitted. You are all on your glorious course manward, *via* the ancient progenitor and the chimpanzee. It seems a confounded long journey; for Nature is a slow coach, and thinks nothing of a million of years to effect a little transformation. But one of these days our science may find means to expedite that old sluggard, and hurry you through the intermediate grades in a way to astonish the venerable lady. Liberty, equality, and fraternity,—those are the words which will open the gates of your organized Bastiles, and send your souls on a career of swifter development. Trust in Darwin, and let creation ring with your song of 'A good time coming, Invertebrates!'"

Well, sir, you want logic, and there you have it with a vengeance! I have pitched you back into nebula, where these fellows tell me you belong, and I trust you're satisfied. Now what is my comfort, sir, after making my brain dizzy with this sublime speculation of theirs? Why, it's found in the fact that, by their own concession, the thing will not work, but must end in the biggest "catastrophe" ever heard of. The whole infernal humbug is to explode, sir, and by no exercise of their "hippocampus minor" can they prevent it. This fiery mist, which has hardened and rounded into our sun and planets, and developed into the monkey's "third lobe" and ours, does not lose the memory or the conceit of *its* origin, but is determined to get back into its first condition as quickly as circumstances will admit. It considers itself somehow to have been swindled in every step of the long process it has gone through in arriving at our brains. It doesn't think the speculation pays; prefers its lounging, vagabond, *dolce far niente* existence, loafing through the whole space between the sun and Neptune, to any satisfaction it finds in being concentrated in your thoughts or mine; and accordingly it meditates a *coup d'état* by which the planets are to fall into the sun at such a pace as to knock the whole system into eternal smash, and reduce it to its original condition of nebulous mist, sir. Do you like the prospect? I tell you there is no way of escaping from conclusions, if you are such a greenhorn as to admit premises. I have been over the whole chain of the logic, and find its only weak link is the monkey one. Knock that out, and you save the solar system as well as your own dignity as a man, sir; retain it, and some thousands of generations hence the brains of your descendants will be blown into a texture as gauzy as a comet's tail, and it will be millions of ages before, in the process of a new freak of development in the unquiet nebula, they can hope to arrive again at the honor of possessing that inestimable boon, dear equally to baboons and to men, "the posterior cornu of the lateral ventricle"!

## 9

Other religious thinkers, less intense, realized that doctrines of science could not be dismissed by emotionalism. They examined the works of Darwin and discovered that an "irreconcilable conflict" between science and Christianity did not necessarily exist. God's wonders, they argued, were as apparent in an evolutionary method as in any other creative process. Such apologetics were highly successful among clergy and laity alike. One of the most active preachers of this viewpoint, Rev. Henry Ward Beecher, found the divine hand of Providence in the mutation of species. In a sermon preached on May 31, 1885, he said:[9]

First, then, what is Evolution, and what does it reveal? The theory of Evolution teaches that the creation of this earth was not accomplished in six days of twenty-four hours; that the divine method occupied ages and ages of immense duration; that nothing, of all the treasures of the globe as they now stand, was created at first in its present perfectness; that everything has grown through the lapse of ages into its present condition; that the whole earth, with their development in it, was, as it were, an egg, a germ, a seed; that the forests, the fields, the shrubs, the vineyards, all grasses and flowers, all insects, fishes, and birds, all mammals of every gradation, have had a long history, and that they have come to the position in which they now stand through ages and ages of gradual change and unfolding. Also that the earth itself went through a period of long preparation, passing from ether by condensation to a visible cloud form with increasing solidity, to such a condition as now prevails in the sun; that it condensed and became solid; that cold congealed its vapor; that by chemical action and by mechanical grinding of its surface by ice a soil was prepared fit for vegetation, long before it was fit for ani-

---

[9] Henry Ward Beecher, "The Two Revelations," in *Evolution and Religion* (New York, 1893), pp. 49-54.

mal life; that plants simple and coarse came first and developed through all stages of complexity to the present conditions of the vegetable kingdom; that aquatic, invertebrate animals were the earliest of animals, according to the testimony of fossils in the earth. Fishes came next in order, then amphibians, then reptiles. "All these tribes were represented by species before the earliest of the mammals appeared. The existence of birds before the earliest mammal is not proved, though believed by some paleontologists upon probable evidence. The early mammals were marsupial, like the opossum and the kangaroo, and lived in the same era called by Agassiz, the reptilian period. True mammals came into geologic history in the tertiary era. Very long after the appearance of the first bird came man, the last and grandest of the series, it is doubtful whether in the tertiary period or immediately sequent. It is not established whether his bones or relics occur as far back as the tertiary era."

This is a very brief statement, not my own, but that of Professor Dana, of renown. No man is more trusted, more careful, more cautious than he, and this brief history of the unfolding series I have taken bodily from his writings.

Second.—As thus set forth, it may be said that Evolution is accepted as *the method* of creation by the whole scientific world, and that the period of controversy is passed and closed. A few venerable men yet live, with many doubts; but it may be said that ninety-nine per cent.—as has been declared by an eminent physicist— ninety-nine per cent. of scientific men and working scientists of the world are using this theory without any doubt of its validity. While the scientific world is at agreement upon this *order* of occurrence, it has been much divided as to the *causes* which have operated to bring about these results. There is a diversity of opinion still, but with every decade scientific men are drawing together to a common ground of belief.

Third.—The theory of Evolution is the *working* theory of every department of physical science all over the world. Withdraw this theory, and every department of physical research would fall back into heaps of hopelessly dislocated facts, with no more order or reason or philosophical coherence than exists in a basket of marbles, or in the juxtaposition of the multitudinous sands of the seashore. We should go back into chaos if we took out of the laboratories, out of the dissecting-rooms, out of the fields of investigation, this great doctrine of Evolution.

Fourth.—This science of Evolution is taught in all advanced academies, in all colleges and universities, in all medical and surgical schools, and our children are receiving it as they are the elements of astronomy or botany or chemistry. That in another generation Evolution will be regarded as uncontradictable as the Copernican system of astronomy, or the Newtonian doctrine of gravitation, can scarcely be doubted. Each of these passed through the same contradiction by theologians. They were charged by the Church, as is Evolution now, with fostering materialism, infidelity, and atheism. We know what befell Galileo for telling the truth of God's primitive revelation. We know, or do not know, at least, how Newton stood charged with infidelity and with atheism when he announced the doctrine of gravitation. Who doubts the heliocentric theory to-day? Who doubts whether it is the sun which is moving round the earth or the earth round the sun? Who doubts that the law of attraction, as developed by Newton, is God's material law universally? The time is coming when the doctrine of Evolution, or the method of God in the creation of the world, will be just as universally accepted as either of these great physical doctrines. The whole Church fought them; yet they stand, conquerors.

Fifth.—Evolution is substantially held by men of profound Christian faith: by the now venerable and universally honored scientific teacher, Professor Dana of Yale College, a devout Christian and communicant of a Congregational Church; by Professor Le Conte of the University of California, an elder in the Presbyterian Church; by President McCosh of Princeton College, a Presbyterian of the Presbyterians, and a Scotch Presbyterian at that; by Professor Asa Gray of Harvard University, a communicant of the Christian Church; by increasing numbers of Christian preachers in America, by Catholics like Mivart, in England; by Wallace, a Christian not only, but of the spiritualistic school; by the Duke of Argyle of the Scotch Presbyterian Church; by Ground, an ardent admirer of Herbert Spencer and his whole theory, though rejecting his agnosticism—an eminent and leading divine in the Church of England; and finally, among hundreds of other soundly learned and Christian men, by the Bishop of London, Dr. Williams, whose Bampton Lectures for 1884 contain a bold, frank, and judicial estimate of Evolution, and its relations to Christianity.

Sixth.—To the fearful and the timid let me say, that while Evolution is certain to oblige theology to reconstruct its system, it will take nothing away from the grounds of true religion. It will strip off Saul's unmanageable armor from David, to give him greater power of the giant. Simple religion is the unfolding of the best nature of man towards God, and man has been hindered and embittered by the outrageous complexity of unbearable systems of theology that have existed. If you can change theology, you will emancipate religion; yet men are continually confounding the two terms, religion and theology. They are not alike. Religion is the condition of a man's nature as toward God and toward his fellow-men. That is religion—love that breeds truth, love that breeds justice, love that breeds harmonies

of intimacy and intercommunication, love that breeds duty, love that breeds conscience, love that carries in its hand the scepter of pain, not to destroy and to torment, but to teach and to save. Religion is that state of mind in which a man is related by his emotions, and through his emotions by his will and conduct, to God and to the proper performance of duty in this world. Theology is the philosophy of God, of divine government, and of human nature. The philosophy of these may be one thing; the reality of them may be another and totally different one. Though intimately connected, they are not all the same. Theology is a science; religion, an art.

Evolution will multiply the motives and facilities of righteousness, which was and is the design of the whole Bible. It will not dull the executive doctrines of religion, that is, the forms of them by which an active and reviving ministry arouses men's consciences, by which they inspire faith, repentance, reformation, spiritual communion with God. Not only will those great truths be unharmed, by which men work zealously for the reformation of their fellow-men, but they will be developed to a breadth and certainty not possible in their present philosophical condition. At present the sword of the spirit is in the sheath of a false theology. Evolution, applied to religion, will influence it only as the hidden temples are restored, by removing the sands which have drifted in from the arid deserts of scholastic and medieval theologies. It will change theology, but only to bring out the simple temple of God in clearer and more beautiful lines and proportions.

Seventh.—In every view of it, I think we are to expect great practical fruit from the application of the truths that flow now from the interpretation of Evolution. It will obliterate the distinction between natural and revealed religion, both of which are the testimony of God; one, God's testimony as to what is best for man in his social and physical relations, and the other, what is best for man in his higher spiritual nature. What is called morality will be no longer dissevered from religion. Morals bear to spirituality the same relation which the root bears to the blossom and the fruit. Hitherto a false and imperfect theology has set them in two different provinces. We have been taught that morality will not avail us, and that spirituality is the only saving element: whereas, there is no spirituality itself without morality; all true spirituality is an outgrowth, it is the blossom and fruit on the stem of morality. It is time that these distinctions were obliterated, as they will be, by the progress and application of the doctrine of Evolution.

In every view, then, it is the duty of the friends of simple and unadulterated Christianity to hail the rising light and to uncover every element of religious teaching to its wholesome beams. Old men may be charitably permitted to die in peace, but young men and men in their prime are by God's providence laid under the most solemn obligation to thus discern the signs of the times, and to make themselves acquainted with the knowledge which science is laying before them. And above all, those zealots of the pulpit—who make faces at a science which they do not understand, and who reason from prejudice to ignorance, who not only will not lead their people, but hold up to scorn those who strive to take off the burden of ignorance from their shoulders—these men are bound to open their eyes and see God's sun shining in the heavens.

## 10

The scientific impact on religion was shattering, but the churches were also threatened by industrial and urban changes. "Infidelity" was less the result of scholarly criticism than of the inadequacy of the churches to function meaningfully in the new environment they neither understood nor accepted. Following wealth rather than poverty as society more sharply divided into rich and poor, conventional religious groups had by the 1880's begun to lose touch with the slum-dwelling masses who needed solace most. At this point a number of crusading clergymen began to preach the gospel of Social Christianity, a virile and enlightened movement. Of these one of the most outspoken was Rev. Washington Gladden, a Congregational minister of Columbus, Ohio:[10]

But now comes a harder question. How is this growing wealth divided? Is it rightly or wrongly divided? If it is wrongly divided, has the Christian Moralist anything to say about a better way? Christianity, as we have seen, has much to do with the production of wealth; has it anything to do with its distribution? . . .

Plainly there is something out of joint in our machinery of distribution, or this state of things could not be. During the past fourteen years the wealth of this nation has increased much faster than the population, but the people who work for wages are little if any better off than they were fourteen years ago. It is doubtful whether the average yearly wages of the mechanic, the laborer, or the operative will purchase for him more of the necessaries of life now than at that time. At any rate, the gain, if gain there has been, must be very slight. What is true of the wage-laborer is true, also, of the small trader who subsists upon the laborer's patronage, and also quite largely of clerks and of teachers, as well as of those professional men whose services are chiefly in request among the poorer classes. There is a considerable class in the community whose fortunes are closely linked with those of the wage-laborers.

This, then, is the existing state of things. The production of wealth in the country increases enormously year by year; the workingman's share of what is produced, and the share of those economically affiliated with the workingman, increases very slowly. . . .

[10] Washington Gladden, *Applied Christianity* (Boston, 1886), pp. 8-9, 12-15, 17-20, 22.

What has the Christian moralist to say about this state of things? He is bound to say that it is a bad state of things, and must somehow be reformed. He is bound to declare that "the laborer is worthy of his hire"; that, in the words of the apostle Paul, "the husbandman that laboreth must be the first to partake of the fruits." The broad equities of Christ's rule demand that this great increase of wealth be made, somehow, to inure to the benefit, in a far larger degree, of the people by whose labor it is produced. He will not deny that the capitalist should have a fair reward for his prudence and his abstinence; he will not refuse to the "undertaker," the *entrepreneur*, the organizer of labor, who stands between capitalist and laborer, enabling them to combine in the production of wealth, that large reward to which his superior intelligence and experience entitle him; but he will still insist that the workman ought to have a larger share. . . . And Christianity, by the lips of all its teachers, ought with all its emphasis to say to society: "Your present industrial system, which fosters these enormous inequalities, which permits a few to heap up most of the gains of this advancing civilization, and leaves the many without any substantial share in them, is an inadequate and inequitable system, and needs important changes to make it the instrument of righteousness."

But when this testimony is borne, we shall hear men answering after this fashion: "Suppose it is wrong; what are you going to do about it? Would you have the state take possession of all the property and divide it equally among its citizens?" . . .

First, then, it is undoubtedly the duty of Christians to do what they can by means of law to secure a better industrial system. But this is not saying that Christians should ask the state to take the property of the rich and distribute it among the poor. It is true that the state does something in that direction already. It takes, by taxation, the property of the rich in large amounts, and expends it for the benefit of all, the poor equally with the rich. Thousands who pay no taxes at all have the full benefit of streets, street-lamps, sewers, side-walks, water, police, fire department, and schools, not to speak of important provisions made exclusively for the poor, such as city physicians and dispensaries, alms-houses, insane hospitals, and the like. The destitute classes thus get the benefit of a considerable distribution of property annually enforced by the state. And it is pretty clear that the state is now going quite as far in this direction as it is safe to go. Certainly we want no more eleemosynary distribution of money by the state than we have now. The time may come when the nation will be compelled to take under its control, if not into its ownership, the railroads and the telegraphs, and administer them for the common good. They are falling, in far too large a degree, into the hands of men who use them for the spoiling of our commerce and the corruption of our politics. But the wisdom or the equity of this measure is not yet so clear that it can be demanded as an act of public justice, and therefore the Christian moralist will not yet venture to pronounce upon it.

There are, however, one or two things that he will insist upon as the immediate duty of the state. Certain outrageous monopolies exist that the state is bound to crush. It is an outrage on public justice that half a dozen men should be able to control the entire fuel supply of New York and New England, forbidding the miners to work more than two or three days in a week, lest the operatives of the New England mills or the longshoremen of the New York wharves should get their coal at a little smaller price per ton. This forcible suppression of an industry by which one of the necessaries of life is furnished, this violent interference with the natural laws of trade in the interest of a few monopolists, is so contrary to public justice and public policy that some way must be found of making an end of it. The coal barons must not be permitted to enrich themselves by compelling the miners to starve at one end of their lines and the operatives to freeze at the other. In like manner the great lines of transportation from the West are under the control of three or four men, and although they have not hitherto been able to combine in such a way as greatly to enhance the price of breadstuffs, it is not improbable that combinations will yet take place by which such a levy will be made upon the food of the nation. Even now the oil in the poor man's lamp is heavily taxed by a greedy monopoly. All these iniquitous encroachments upon the rights of the people must be arrested; and it is the duty of every Christian, as the servant of a God of justice and righteousness, to say so in terms that cannot be misunderstood.

Another gigantic public evil that the state must exterminate is that of gambling in stocks and produce. This system of gambling in margins is a system of piracy; by means of it hundreds of millions of dollars are plundered every year from the industrial classes. It is treason to say that it cannot be put down; it must be put down or it will destroy the nation. It is the vampire that is sucking the life-blood of our commerce; it is the dragon that is devouring the moral vigor of our young men. When these monsters of the Stock and Produce Exchanges are killed, and a few of our great monopolies are laid low, the greatest obstructions to a free distribution of wealth will be removed, and the working classes will secure a larger share of the product of their industry than they are getting now. All such violent hindrances to a free and fair exchange of commodities and services—all such hungry parasites of industry—the state is bound to remove, and Christian morality calls on all its professors to enforce this obligation on the state. . . .

All that intelligent Christians will ask the state to do, therefore, toward promoting the distribution of wealth, is to provide for the general welfare, as it now does, by taxation; to protect all classes in the exercise of their rights; to strike down those foes that now clutch our industries by the throat, and then to leave the natural laws of trade and the motives of humanity and good-will to effect a more equitable distribution.

## 11

The nature of American Christianity underwent a gradual change as preachers of the social gospel won converts. "Institutionalized" churches invaded the lower-class sections of the cities. Equipped with clubrooms, gymnasiums, reading rooms, manual training or sewing classes, and young peoples' groups, they offered social relaxation as well as spiritual comfort. But more militant ministers were still unsatisfied. They were led to examine the very nature of society as they observed the poverty and suffering among their charges. The result was the rise of a vigorous school of Christian Socialism, whose clerical members preached the need of reform as energetically as they advocated salvation. An outstanding example was Rev. George D. Herron, a Congregationalist, whose writings castigated the existing social order:[11]

It is hardly disputed that capital, under our modern industrial system, is receiving more than a just share of the fruits of labor, and the laborer is receiving relatively less and less of the profits of his toil. The increase of wealth and wages is in no sense equitable. There is not a progressive economist in America or England who does not say that wealth is growing out of all proportion to the benefits that the laborer derives from his labor. The distribution of wealth is not according to industry or ability; not according to one's worth in society; but according in large measure to the skill of some in appropriating to themselves the fruits of the labor of others by commercial legerdemain. It

[11] George D. Herron, *The New Redemption* (New York, 1893), pp. 25-40.

is thus that while we are the richest nation on the globe our wealth is rapidly being centered in the hands of a few and industrial toilers are being reduced to a condition of practical servitude. "Thoughtful men see and admit," says Judge Walter Q. Gresham, "that our country is becoming less and less democratic and more and more plutocratic," and plutocracy he pronounces the most insidious of all forms of tyranny. "Nothing," says Dr. Theodore Dwight Woolsey, "would lead the mass of men to embrace socialism sooner than the conviction that this enormous accumulation of capital in a few hands was to be not only an evil in fact, if not prevented, but a necessary evil beyond prevention. . . . A revolution, slow or rapid, would certainly bring about a new order of things." Nor can the difference between the working and capitalistic classes be concealed by the fact that wages average better than forty or fifty years ago. It is a waste of time to cite statistics to show that the laboring man has economic goods he did not formerly have. Forty to fifty years ago the mechanic and his master worked side by side; the apprentice was the social equal of his employer. There was not the stratification of society which we now see, and almost every man produced something of his own livelihood. Fuel cost him but the work of bringing it to his door yard. He raised necessities which must now be purchased. The lowest wages of a half a century ago represented a more equitable share in the *social* benefits of civilization than the highest wages of to-day. And the inevitable result of the system of wages and competition will be to increase social inequalities, to increase the wealth of a few and the poverty of the many. It is to the interest of capital, when it releases itself from moral and social obligations, and looks only to its own increase, to keep a huge class of unemployed men, who must work or starve. The present industrial system could not exist were it not for the fact that great

multitudes of the unemployed have been brought to this country, systematically and purposely, for the sake of reducing wages and producing a state of poverty. By this method the clothing trade of the United States thrives upon the sweating system. By pitting the unemployed against the employed, by reducing men and women and children to a condition of poverty, where they must work at any price or starve, competition has prospered by the blood of men and women. In the midst of great wealth, with the glory of its material enterprise, its blind luxury and mad speculation, its disregard for human life, for moral law, there is an increasing poverty and degradation; a deep and angry social discontent; a growing distrust in the reality of our liberties and the sincerity of our Christianity, proving that our competitive system does not belong to a divine order of things. It is unnatural that the strong should prosper at the expense of the weak; that the earning of one's daily bread should be an uncertain strife. It is a violation of nature that prosperity should come through the triumph of cunning over character, and the conflict of selfish interests. Our so-called industrial order is the disordering of nature. It is the disorganization of human life. There is enough in this world for all to have and enjoy in abundance, if there were a system by which there could be an equitable distribution of that abundance upon the principles of the divine economy.

*The social problem is the call of the state to become Christian.* The state can save itself only by believing in the Lord Jesus Christ as the supreme authority in law, politics, and society. The state is the social organ. To meet the strain that will be put upon it by the revolution, *the state must be redeemed from the worship of property and from commercial theories of government.* It can prove its right to be only by procuring a greater measure of social justice and giving a larger recognition to the sacredness of man. The state must have in it the mind that was in Jesus, who is the final political economist. The Sermon on the Mount is the science of society, it is a treatise on political economy; it is a system of justice. It consists of the natural laws which proceed from the heart of God, and operate in the creation and redemption of the world; in the evolution of man and the progressive development of society. It is the constitution of the divine and universal society which John in the Revelation calls a new earth. The establishment of its justice underneath the politics and social structures of man is the new Jerusalem which John saw coming down out of heaven from God. The business of the state is to adopt this social constitution of Jesus as the spirit and justice of the people, and bring every activity into subjection to its authority. It is not primarily the mission of the state to protect property as a thing in itself. *The state is the organization of the life of man in unity with the life of God; its concern is with human beings.* Property is valuable only as it is the instrument of justice between man and man, and a bond of fellowship with God. Property has a right to protection only as it is designedly working out the whole welfare of man. It is the business of the state to develop and shield the common manhood and happiness, the physical and moral health, of men as sons of God. Government has a right to existence and authority for no other end than that for which God sent his only begotten Son into the world. It is the vocation of the state, as the social organ, to so control property, so administer the production and distribution of economic goods, as to give to every man the fruit of his labor, and protect the laborer from the irresponsible tyranny of the passion for wealth. It is the duty of the state to so reconstruct itself as to procure for every man full opportunity to develop all his powers, and to see that no member of society suffers for the want of work and bread.

A baseless assumption which the state must correct is, that employers have an economic right to employ and discharge from the individual standpoint, with only a money obligation to employees, and no responsibility to society. But the Christian state, as the organization of the divine life of man, is bound to deny the existence of any such right in a moral world. The assertion of such a right is the denial of the humanity of man; it is infidelity to Christ; it is substantial atheism. The assumption that capital may discharge and employ solely on the basis of self-interest shuts God out of human affairs and denies the brotherhood of man. It is social anarchism. It is the declaration on the part of capital that it will not submit to law. He who sets himself apart from social relationships, to do what he pleases with his own, upon the ground of pure individualism, asserts the right to do what God himself dare not do. In so far as the state allows the assumption and exercise of such a right, it fails to secure justice. No industrial concern has a right to receive the benefits of society without bearing commensurate responsibilities. It is monstrous and undemocratic, it is the enthronement of industrial despotism, for the state to grant powers and protection to corporate or individual employers, and yet leave them irresponsible for the social welfare. The assertion on the part of capital of a right to exist for the sake of gain, independent of the voice of the people or the welfare of labor, has had its day. It is the last remnant of that absolutism which has been slowly and revengefully yielding to the redemptive forces that have been making men free ever since the Son of man poured out his life upon the Calvary of truth. There was a day when men thought the state could be preserved only by maintaining the absolute authority of the king, and by giving the people no voice in their government. Men once believed that the divine right of kings alone could secure political order and procure social justice. But that day has gone by, and democracy everywhere has the political field, or is gaining it in every civilized nation. *Absolutism of every sort is doomed and cannot hold its own against the purposes of God. It can no more sustain itself in industry than in politics. If democracy is good for the state, it is good for industry.* King George's assertion of a right to tax American colonists without representation, was not half as unjust, as intolerable and despotic, as the assumption that a great corporation can enjoy the nurture and claim the protection of society, and yet deny society all management or voice in its affairs. A man could not have what he calls his own, save through the co-operation of his fellow-men; and they have rights in the management of capital for the social welfare commensurate with the privileges and opportunities which capital receives. If democracy, which is social fellowship and political mutualism, can best procure political justice and preserve the state, then it can also procure the largest economic justice and industrial freedom. Capital is a social creation, and its administration a social responsibility; so that industrial federation lies in the nature of things.

But the initiative in the establishment of a democracy of Jesus in the world of work and wealth must be taken by capital itself, which has in its hands both the power and the responsibility. The commercial dogma that capital has discharged its duty when it has paid its employees the market rate of wages, with the market under the sovereignty of what is known as the law of supply and demand, asserts the supremacy of capital over moral law, and gives to it a worth greater than the worth of human life. *Labor is not a commodity any more than human souls are a commodity; labor is life.* The relation between employer and employee is a sacred relationship; a relationship that must not be sundered by mere caprice or self-interest. It is the utter disregard of the sacredness of this rela-

tionship by both employer and employee treating it as simply a money relationship that is the root of the strife between the two. The union of men in industry is a communion of human lives for divine ends; and the selfish severing of this union is not merely a violation of the Sermon on the Mount; it is economic foolishness and social lawlessness. Capital should recognize that the life of the laborer is a greater matter than the gain of the employer. It was Lincoln's belief that labor should own capital, in opposition to the slave-owner's view that capital should own labor. The history of industry bears out the belief that wherever there has been a recognition of the manhood of labor on the part of capital, with the spirit of social fellowship and Christian democracy, there have been peace and prosperity for both employer and workman. The love that moved God to give his only begotten Son to save the world must be the law that shall govern wealth, and move its possessors to consecrate themselves to the creation of a Christian society and Christian state. It lies within the power of the American capitalists who call themselves Christian, by taking the Sermon on the Mount and patiently working it into the foundations of industry, to be the creators of a new and divine civilization that would surpass all our apprehensions of the Revelation of John. If they would take the Sermon on the Mount as economic law, as a revelation of the nature of things, as the safest basis upon which the market of the world could stand, they would lift the commerce and industry of the world above the chance and strife of competing interests, and make the moving trains of merchandise, the toil of the mills and echo of the mines, the barter and exchange of the markets, all accordant parts of a harmony of divine justice. *I do not believe there can ever be peace between man and man, between interest and interest, between class and class, by any other mode than through the belief of capital, the be-*

*ief of industry, the belief of the market,*
*n the naturalness, in the wisdom, in the*
*afety, of the moral law of Jesus. This the*
*church must teach, and its members must*
*cease to promulgate social atheism. It can-*
*not be stated too plainly that either the*
*people will become atheistic, or the wealth*
*which is in Christian hands must obey the*
*social laws of the Sermon on the Mount.*
*Either its laws are practicable, reasonable,*
and natural, and will give the largest prosperity to all, or men will not believe in an
all-good and all-wise God. Obedience to
Christ's laws would give a new redemption to man that would be the creation of
a new earth, overspread with the healing
wisdom of a new heaven of divine truth,
from which the sea of social troubles
would flee away forever. . . .

It is to-day the one emergent mission of
the church to bring together in a divine
unity the various human interests that are
now at strife. The whole conception of the
necessary antagonism between capital and
labor is not simply an economic and political falsehood, not only a peril to the
state and a denial of justice, but it makes
Christianity an ideal impossible of realization. The church must demand social conditions that shall realize the Christian
gospel. Unto it has been given the message
that the interest of one man is the interest
of all. The interest of labor is the interest
of capital; and the interest of capital is the
interest of labor. When capital keeps from
labor its Christian share of the produce of
labor, it injures itself; and labor injures
itself in destroying capital. The church
must open the eyes of men to see the wisdom and power of living for the common
good, to the practical atheism and anarchism of selfish principles, and declare love
to be the natural law of industrial activity
and social life. Love at the heart of society, love at the heart of the state, love
in the heart of the church, love at the
heart of commerce, will right our economic wrongs, give labor its just rewards,
and diffuse among the people the benefits

of civilization. Only by obedience to the
law of love can society be regenerated and
historic problems be solved. There is in
love alone the power to dispel the clouds
of darkness that now over-gloom the earth
with peril and judgment, calling for a
new earth to rise to meet the descending
heavens of larger truth. And the law of
love can be obeyed only through communion with God and sacrifice for man.

## 12

Meanwhile material growth and rugged
individualism found a new sanction in Darwinian notions of natural evolution and the
supposedly immutable laws of progress. Pro-
tagonists of this philosophy reconciled Darwin
and Spencer with Holy Writ. They deduced
that laissez faire was a "natural" evolution
divine in origin. The impact of the Darwinian ideas, unsettling to older religious beliefs but congenial to a belief in acquisition
and enjoyment, was candidly set forth in the
*Autobiography* of Andrew Carnegie:[12]

Reaction against the theology of past
days comes to many who have been surrounded in youth by church people entirely satisfied that the truth and faith
indispensable to future happiness were derived only through strictest Calvinistic
creeds. The thoughtful youth is naturally
carried along and disposed to concur in
this. He cannot but think, up to a certain
period of development, that what is believed by the best and the highest educated around him—those to whom he
looks for example and instruction—must
be true. He resists doubt as inspired by
the Evil One seeking his soul, and sure
to get it unless faith comes to the rescue.
Unfortunately he soon finds that faith is
not exactly at his beck and call. Original
sin he thinks must be at the root of this
inability to see as he wishes to see, to believe as he wishes to believe. It seems clear

[12] From *Autobiography of Andrew Carnegie*
(1920), pp. 338-340. Reprinted by permission of
and arrangement with Houghton Mifflin Company, the authorized publishers.

to him that already he is little better than one of the lost. Of the elect he surely cannot be, for these must be ministers, elders, and strictly orthodox men.

The young man is soon in chronic rebellion, trying to assume godliness with the others, acquiescing outwardly in the creed and all its teachings, and yet at heart totally unable to reconcile his outward accordance with his inward doubt. If there be intellect and virtue in the man but one result is possible; that is, Carlyle's position after his terrible struggle when after weeks of torment he came forth: "If it be incredible, in God's name, then, let it be discredited." With that the load of doubt and fear fell from him forever.

When I, along with three or four of my boon companions, was in this stage of doubt about theology, including the supernatural element, and indeed the whole scheme of salvation through vicarious atonement and all the fabric built upon it, I came fortunately upon Darwin's and Spencer's works "The Data of Ethics," "First Principles," "Social Statics," "The Descent of Man." Reaching the pages which explain how man has absorbed such mental foods as were favorable to him, retaining what was salutary, rejecting what was deleterious, I remember that light came as in a flood and all was clear. Not only had I got rid of theology and the supernatural, but I had found the truth of evolution. "All is well since all grows better" became my motto, my true source of comfort. Man was not created with an instinct for his own degradation, but from the lower he had risen to the higher forms. Nor is there any conceivable end to his march to perfection. His face is turned to the light; he stands in the sun and looks upward.

Humanity is an organism, inherently rejecting all that is deleterious, that is, wrong, and absorbing after trial what is beneficial, that is, right. If so disposed, the Architect of the Universe, we must assume, might have made the world and man perfect, free from evil and from pain as angels in heaven are thought to be; but although this was not done, man has been given the power of advancement rather than of retrogression. The Old and New Testaments remain, like other sacred writings of other lands, of value as records of the past and for such good lessons as they inculcate. Like the ancient writers of the Bible our thoughts should rest upon this life and our duties here. "To perform the duties of this world well, troubling not about another, is the prime wisdom," says Confucius, great sage and teacher. The next world and its duties we shall consider when we are placed in it. . . .

## 13

Despite the efforts of pacific reformers such as Henry Ward Beecher and social crusaders such as Washington Gladden and George D. Herron, the churches steadily lost ground during the last years of the nineteenth century. Most of those who deserted the cause were simply too immersed in secular affairs to be concerned with divine worship. Others were convinced that religion was outmoded in a rationalistic, scientific age. Robert Green Ingersoll was the prophet of this group. His writings and speeches won international fame; he became the great agnostic. *Mistakes of Moses,* a book that enjoyed a tremendous circulation, expressed the thought of many doubters and explained why Ingersoll was vilified by the orthodox as the most dangerous public enemy of religion:[13]

Now and then some one asks me why I am endeavoring to interfere with the religious faith of others, and why I try to take from the world the consolation naturally arising from a belief in eternal fire. And I answer, I want to do what little I can to make my country truly free, I want to broaden the intellectual horizon of our people. I want it so that we can differ upon all those questions, and yet grasp each other's hands in genuine friend-

[13] Robert G. Ingersoll, *Mistakes of Moses* (New York and London, n.d.), pp. 1-9. (Pages not numbered consecutively.)

hip. I want in the first place to free the clergy. I am a great friend of theirs, but they don't seem to have found it out generally. I want it so that every minister will not be a parrot, not an owl sitting upon a dead limb of the tree of knowledge and hooting the hoots that have been hooted for eighteen hundred years. But I want it so that each one can be an investigator, a thinker; and I want to make his congregation grand enough so that they will not only allow him to think, but will demand that he shall think, and give to them the honest truth of his thought. As it is now, ministers are employed like attorneys—for the plaintiff or the defendant. If a few people know of a young man in the neighborhood maybe who has not a good constitution—he may not be healthy enough to be wicked—a young man who has shown no decided talent—it occurs to them to make him a minister. They contribute and send him to some school. If it turns out that that young man has more of the man in him than they thought, and he changes his opinion, everyone who contributed will feel himself individually swindled—and they will follow that young man to the grave with the poisoned shafts of malice and slander. I want it so that every one will be free—so that a pulpit will not be a pillory. They have in Massachusetts, at a place called Andover, a kind of minister-factory; and every professor in that factory takes an oath once in every five years—that is as long as an oath will last—that not only has he not during the last five years, but so help him God, he will not during the next five years intellectually advance; and probably there is no oath he could easier keep. Since the foundation of that institution there has not been one case of perjury. They believe the same creed they first taught when the foundation stone was laid, and now when they send out a minister they brand him as hardware from Sheffield and Birmingham. And every man who knows where he was educated knows his creed, knows every argument of his creed, every book that he reads, and just what he amounts to intellectually, and knows he will shrink and shrivel, and become solemnly stupid day after day until he meets with death. It is all wrong; it is cruel. Those men should be allowed to grow. They should have the air of liberty and the sunshine of thought.

I want to free the schools of our country. I want it so that when a professor in a college finds some fact inconsistent with Moses, he will not hide the fact, that it will not be worse for him for having discovered the fact. I wish to see an eternal divorce and separation between church and schools. The common school is the bread of life; but there should be nothing taught in the schools except what somebody knows; and anything else should not be maintained by a system of general taxation. I want its professors so that they will tell everything they find; that they will be free to investigate in every direction, and will not be trammeled by the superstitions of our day. What has religion to do with facts? Nothing. Is there any such thing as Methodist mathematics, Presbyterian botany, Catholic astronomy or Baptist biology? What has any form of superstition or religion to do with a fact or with any science? Nothing but to hinder, delay or embarrass. I want, then, to free the schools; and I want to free the politicians, so that a man will not have to pretend he is a Methodist, or his wife a Baptist, or his grandmother a Catholic; so that he can go through a campaign, and when he gets through will find none of the dust of hypocrisy on his knees.

I want the people splendid enough that when they desire men to make laws for them, they will take one who knows something, who has brain enough to prophesy the destiny of the American Republic, no matter what his opinions may be upon any religious subject. Suppose we are in a storm out at sea, and the billows are washing over our ship, and it is necessary that some one should reef the topsail, and a man presents himself. Would you stop him at the foot of the mast to find out his opinion on the five points of Calvinism? What has that to do with it? Congress has nothing to do with baptism or any particular creed, and from what little experience I have had of Washington, very little to do with any kind of religion whatever. Now I hope, this afternoon, this magnificent and splendid audience will forget that they are Baptists or Methodists, and remember that they are men and women. These are the highest titles humanity can bear—man and woman; and every title you add belittles them. Man is the highest; woman is the highest. Let us remember that we are simply human beings, with interests in common. And let us all remember that our views depend largely upon the country in which we happen to live. Suppose we were born in Turkey most of us would have been Mohammedans; and when we read in the book that when Mohammed visited heaven he became acquainted with an angel named Gabriel, who was so broad between his eyes that it would take a smart camel three hundred days to make the journey, we probably would have believed it. If we did not, people would say: "That young man is dangerous; he is trying to tear down the fabric of our religion. What do you propose to give us instead of that angel? We can not afford to trade off an angel of that size for nothing." Or if we had been born in India, we would have believed in a god with three heads. Now we believe in three gods with one head. And so we might make a tour of the world and see that every superstition that could be imagined by the brain of man has been in some place held to be sacred.

Now, some one says, "The religion of my father and mother is good enough for me." Suppose we all said that, where would be the progress of the world? We would have the rudest and most barbaric religion, which no one could believe. I do not believe that it is showing real re-

spect to our parents to believe something simply because they did. Every good father and every good mother wish their children to find out more than they ken; every good father wants his son to overcome some obstacle that he could not grapple with; and if you wish to reflect credit on your father and mother, do it by accomplishing more than they did, because you live in a better time. Every nation has had what you call a sacred record, and the older and more sacred, the more contradictory and the more inspired is the record. We, of course, are not an exception and I propose to talk a little about what is called the Pentateuch, a book, or a collection of books, said to have been written by Moses. And right here in the commencement let me say that Moses never wrote one word of the Pentateuch—not one word was written until he had been dust and ashes for hundreds of years. But as the general opinion is that Moses wrote these books, I have entitled this lecture "The Mistakes of Moses." For the sake of this lecture, we will admit that he wrote it. Nearly every maker of religion has commenced by making the world; and it is one of the safest things to do, because no one can contradict as having been present, and it gives free scope to the imagination. These books, in times when there was a vast difference between the educated and the ignorant, became inspired, and people bowed down and worshipped them.

I saw a little while ago a Bible with immense oaken covers, with hasps and claps large enough almost for a penitentiary, and I can imagine how that book would be regarded by barbarians in Europe when not more than one person in a dozen could read and write. In imagination I saw it carried into the cathedral, heard the chant of the priest, saw the swinging of the censer and the smoke rising; and when the Bible was put on the altar I can imagine the barbarian looking at it and wondering what influence that black book could have on their ives and future. I do not wonder that they imagined it was inspired. None of them could write a book, and consequently when they saw it they adored it; they were stricken with awe; and rascals took advantage of that awe.

Now they say that the book is inspired. I do not care whether it is or not; the question is, Is it true? If it is true it don't need to be inspired. Nothing needs inspiration except a falsehood or a mistake. A fact never went into partnership with a miracle. Truth scorns the assistance of wonders. A fact will fit every other fact in the universe, and that is how you can tell whether it is or is not a fact. A lie will not fit anything except another lie made for the express purpose; and, finally, someone gets tired of lying, and the last lie will not fit the next fact, and then there is a chance for inspiration. Right then and there a miracle is needed. The real question is: In the light of science, in the light of the brain and heart of the nineteenth century, is this book true? The gentleman who wrote it begins by telling us that God made the universe out of nothing. That I can not conceive; it may be so, but I can not conceive it. Nothing, regarded in the light of raw material, is to my mind, a decided and disastrous failure. I can not imagine of nothing being made into something, any more than I can of something being changed back into nothing. I can not conceive of force aside from matter, because force to be force must be active, and unless there is matter there is nothing for force to act upon, and consequently it can not be active. So I simply say I can not comprehend it. I can not believe it. I may roast for this, but it is my honest opinion. The next thing he proceeds to tell us is that God divided the darkness from the light; and right here let me say when I speak about God I simply mean the being described by the Jews. There may be in immensity some being beneath whose wing the universe exists, whose every thought is a glit-

tering star, but I know nothing about Him—not the slightest—and this afternoon I am simply talking about the being described by the Jewish people. When I say God, I mean Him. Moses describes God dividing the light from the darkness. I suppose that at that time they must have been mixed. You can readily see how light and darkness can get mixed. They must have been entities. The reason I think so is because in that same book I find that darkness overspread Egypt so thick that it could be felt, and they used to have on exhibition in Rome a bottle of the darkness that once overspread Egypt. The gentleman who wrote this in imagination saw God dividing light from the darkness. I am sure the man who wrote it believed darkness to be an entity, a something, a tangible thing that can be mixed with light.

The next thing that he informs us is that God divided the waters above the firmament from those below the firmament. The man who wrote that believed the firmament to be a solid affair. And that is what the gods did. You recollect the gods came down and made love to the daughters of men—and I never blamed them for it. I have never read a description of any heaven I would not leave on the same errand. That is where the gods lived. That is where they kept the water. It was solid. That is the reason the people prayed for rain. They believed that an angel could take a lever, raise a window and let out the desired quantity. I find in the Psalms that "He bowed the heavens and came down"; and we read that the children of men built a tower to reach the heavens and climb into the abode of the gods. The man who wrote that believed the firmament to be solid. He knew nothing about the laws of evaporation. He did not know that the sun wooed with amorous kiss the waves of the sea, and that, disappointed, their vaporous sighs changed to tears and fell again as rain. The next thing he tells us is that the grass began to grow, and the branches of the trees laughed into blossom, and the grass ran up the shoulder of the hills, and not a solitary ray of light had left the eternal quiver of the sun. Not a blade of grass had ever been touched by a gleam of light. And I do not think that grass will grow to hurt without a gleam of sunshine. I think the man who wrote that simply made a mistake, and is excusable to a certain degree. The next day he made the sun and moon—the sun to rule the day and the moon to rule the night. Do you think the man who wrote that knew anything about the size of the sun? I think he thought it was about three feet in diameter, because I find in some book that the sun was stopped a whole day, to give a general named Joshua time to kill a few more Amalekites; and the moon was stopped also. Now, it seems to me that the sun would give light enough without stopping the moon; but as they were in the stopping business they did it just for devilment. At another time, we read, the sun was turned ten degrees backward to convince Hezekiah that he was not going to die of a boil. How much easier it would have been to cure the boil! The man who wrote that thought the sun was two or three feet in diameter, and could be stopped and pulled around like the sun and moon in a theatre. Do you know that the sun throws out every second of time as much heat as could be generated by burning eleven thousand million tons of coal? I don't believe he knew that, or that he knew the motion of the earth. I don't believe he knew that it was turning on its axis at the rate of a thousand miles an hour, because if he did, he would have understood the immensity of heat that would have been generated by stopping the world. It has been calculated by one of the best mathematicians and astronomers that to stop the world would cause as much heat as it would take to burn a lump of solid coal three times as big as the globe. And yet we find in that book

that the sun was not only stopped, bu turned back ten degrees, simply to con vince a gentleman that he was not goin; to die of a boil! They may say I will b damned if I do not believe that, and I te] them I will if I do.

## THE MINGLING OF PEOPLES

## 14

The city not only provoked religious con troversies but inspired one of the greates population movements in history. To th underprivileged of the world, the Americar city was an irresistible lure: each new factor meant jobs for the hungry; each new tene ment meant homes for the dispossessed. An so they came by the millions, crowding int cities ill equipped to receive them, filling th slums as they battled for the privilege c working at starvation wages in a land tha still held out more hope than the worn field and inhospitable cities of the Old World. Th contrast between the glittering dreams c those who fled Europe's oppression and th pot of ashes found in the sweatshop and th slum was movingly described by a Russiar born writer, Anzia Yezierska. *How I Foun America* pictured the voyage across the A lantic and disappointment in New York:[14]

Silently, we followed my father bacl into the hut from which the Cossack ha driven us a while before. We childrer looked from mother to father and from father to mother.

"*Gottunieu!* the czar himself is pushin; us to America by this last ukase." M mother's face lighted up the hut like lamp.

"*Meshugeneh Yideneh!*" admonishe my father. "Always your head in th air. What—where—America? With wha money? Can dead people lift themselve up to dance?"

"Dance?" The samovar and the bras pots reëchoed my mother's laughter. "

[14] From *Hungry Hearts* by Anzia Yezierska, pț 258-265. Copyright 1920 and 1948 by Anzi Yezierska. Used by permission of the publisher; Houghton Mifflin Company.

ould dance myself over the waves of the ocean to America."

In amazed delight at my mother's joy, we children rippled and chuckled with her. My father paced the room, his face dark with dread for the morrow.

"Empty hands, empty pockets; yet it dreams itself in you—America," he said.

"Who is poor who has hopes on America?" flaunted my mother.

"Sell my red-quilted petticoat that grandmother left for my dowry," I urged in excitement.

"Sell the feather-beds, sell the samovar," chorused the children.

"Sure, we can sell everything—the goat and all the winter things," added my mother. "It must be always summer in America."

I flung my arms around my brother, and he seized Bessie by the curls, and we danced around the room, crazy with joy.

"Beggars!" said my laughing mother. "Why are you so happy with yourselves? How will you go to America without a shirt on your back, without shoes on your feet?"

But we ran out into the road, shouting and singing:

"We'll sell everything we got; we're going to America. White bread and meat we'll eat every day in America, in America!"

That very evening we brought Berel Zalman, the usurer, and showed him all our treasures, piled up in the middle of the hut.

"Look! All these fine feather-beds, Berel Zalman!" urged my mother. "This grand fur coat came from Nijny itself. My grandfather bought it at the fair."

I held up my red-quilted petticoat, the supreme sacrifice of my ten-year-old life. Even my father shyly pushed forward the samovar.

"It can hold enough tea for the whole village," he declared.

"Only a hundred rubles for them all!" pleaded my mother, "only enough to lift us to America! Only one hundred little rubles!"

"A hundred rubles! *Pfui!*" sniffed the pawnbroker. "Forty is overpaid. Not even thirty is it worth."

But, coaxing and cajoling, my mother got a hundred rubles out of him.

Steerage, dirty bundles, foul odors, seasick humanity; but I saw and heard nothing of the foulness and ugliness about me. I floated in showers of sunshine; visions upon visions of the New World opened before me. From lip to lip flowed the golden legend of the golden country:

"In America you can say what you feel, you can voice your thoughts in the open streets without fear of a Cossack."

"In America is a home for everybody. The land is your land, not, as in Russia, where you feel yourself a stranger in the village where you were born and reared, the village in which your father and grandfather lie buried."

"Everybody is with everybody alike in America. Christians and Jews are brothers together."

"An end to the worry for bread, an end to the fear of the bosses over you. Everybody can do what he wants with his life in America."

"There are no high or low in America. Even the President holds hands with Gedalyah Mindel."

"Plenty for all. Learning flows free, like milk and honey."

"Learning flows free." The words painted pictures in my mind. I saw before me free schools, free colleges, free libraries, where I could learn and learn and keep on learning. In our village was a school, but only for Christian children. In the schools of America I'd lift up my head and laugh and dance, a child with other children. Like a bird in the air, from sky to sky, from star to star, I'd soar and soar.

"Land! land!" came the joyous shout. All crowded and pushed on deck. They strained and stretched to get the first glimpse of the "golden country," lifting their children on their shoulders that they might see beyond them. Men fell on their knees to pray. Women hugged their babies and wept. Children danced. Strangers embraced and kissed like old friends. Old men and old women had in their eyes a look of young people in love. Age-old visions sang themselves in me, songs of freedom of an oppressed people. America! America!

## PART II

Between buildings that loomed like mountains we struggled with our bundles, spreading around us the smell of the steerage. Up Broadway, under the bridge, and through the swarming streets of the Ghetto, we followed Gedalyah Mindel.

I looked about the narrow streets of squeezed-in stores and houses, ragged clothes, dirty bedding oozing out of the windows, ash-cans and garbage-cans cluttering the sidewalks. A vague sadness pressed down my heart, the first doubt of America.

"Where are the green fields and open spaces in America?" cried my heart. "Where is the golden country of my dreams?" A loneliness for the fragrant silence of the woods that lay beyond our mud hut welled up in my heart, a longing for the soft, responsive earth of our village streets. All about me was the hardness of brick and stone, the smells of crowded poverty.

"Here's your house, with separate rooms like a palace," said Gedalyah Mindel, and flung open the door of a dingy, airless flat.

"*Oi weh!*" cried my mother in dismay. "Where's the sunshine in America?" She went to the window and looked out at the blank wall of the next house. "*Gottunieu!* Like in a grave so dark!". . .

"It ain't so dark; it's only a little shady," said Gedalyah Mindel, and lighted the gas. "Look only!"—he pointed with pride to the dim gaslight—"No candles, no kerosene lamps, in America. You turn on a screw, and put to it a match, and you got it light like with sunshine."

Again the shadow fell over me, again the doubt of America. In America were rooms without sunlight; rooms to sleep in, to eat in, to cook in, but without sunshine, and Gedalyah Mindel was happy. Could I be satisfied with just a place to sleep in and eat in, and a door to shut people out, to take the place of sunlight? Or would I always need the sunlight to be happy? And where was there a place in America for me to play? I looked out into the alley below, and saw pale-faced children scrambling in the gutter. "Where is America?" cried my heart.

## 15

Michael Pupin, who left a heart-warming account of his own migration, was an immigrant from Yugoslavia. He became a distinguished scientist and professor at Columbia University. *From Immigrant to Inventor,* his autobiography, suggested that even such arrivals as seemed least likely to succeed in the adopted land actually achieved most:[1]

On the fourteenth day, early in the morning, the flat coast-line of Long Island hove in sight. Nobody in the motley crowd of excited immigrants was more happy to see the promised land than I was. It was a clear, mild and sunny March morning, and as we approached New York Harbor the warm sun-rays seemed to thaw out the chilliness which I had accumulated in my body by continuous exposure to the wintry blasts of the North Atlantic. I felt like a new person, and saw in every new scene presented by the New World as the ship moved into it a new promise that I should be welcome. Life and activity kept blossoming out all along the ship's course, and seemed to reach full bloom as we entered New York Harbor. The scene which was then unfolded before my eyes was most novel and bewildering. The first impres-

---

[15] Michael Pupin, *From Immigrant to Inventor* (1923), pp. 37-40. Reprinted by permission of Charles Scribner's Sons, publishers.

sions of Budapest and of Prague seemed like pale-faced images of the grand realities which New York Harbor disclosed before my eyes. A countless multitude of boats lined each shore of the vast river; all kinds of craft ploughed hurriedly in every direction through the waters of the bay; great masses of people crowded the numerous ferry boats, and gave me the impression that one crowd was just about as anxious to reach one shore of the huge metropolis as the other was to reach the other shore; they all must have had some important thing to do, I thought. The city on each side of the shore seemed to throb with activity. I did not distinguish between New York and Jersey City. Hundreds of other spots like the one I beheld, I thought, must be scattered over the vast territories of the United States, and in these seething pots of human action there must be some one activity, I was certain, which needed me. This gave me courage. The talk which I had listened to during two weeks on the immigrant ship was rather discouraging, I thought. One immigrant was bragging about his long experience as a cabinet-maker, and informed his audience that cabinet-makers were in great demand in America; another one was telling long tales about his skill as a mechanician; a third one was spinning out long yarns about the fabulous agricultural successes of his relatives out West, who had invited him to come there and join them; a fourth confided to the gaping crowd that his brother, who was anxiously waiting for him, had a most prosperous bank in some rich mining-camp in Nevada where people never saw any money except silver and gold and hardly ever a coin smaller than a dollar; a fifth one, who had been in America before, told us in a rather top-lofty way that no matter who you were or what you knew or what you had you would be a greenhorn when you landed in the New World, and a greenhorn has to serve his apprenticeship before he can establish his claim to any recogni-

tion. He admitted, however, that immigrants with a previous practical training, or strong pull through relatives and friends, had a shorter apprenticeship. I had no practical training, and I had no relatives nor friends nor even acquaintances in the New World. I had nothing of any immediate value to offer to the land I was about to enter. That thought had discouraged me as I listened to the talks of the immigrants; but the activity which New York Harbor presented to my eager eyes on that sunny March day was most encouraging.

Presently the ship passed by Castle Garden, and I heard some one say: "There is the Gate to America." An hour or so later we all stood at the gate. The immigrant ship, Westphalia, landed at Hoboken and a tug took us to Castle Garden. We were carefully examined and cross-examined, and when my turn came the examining officials shook their heads and seemed to find me wanting. I confessed that I had only five cents in my pocket and had no relatives here, and that I knew of nobody in this country except Franklin, Lincoln, and Harriet Beecher Stowe, whose "Uncle Tom's Cabin" I had read in translation. One of the officials, who had one leg only, and walked with a crutch, seemed much impressed by this remark, and looking very kindly into my eyes and with a merry twinkle in his eye he said in German: "You showed good taste when you picked your American acquaintances." I learned later than he was a Swiss who had served in the Union army during the Civil War. I confessed also to the examining officials that I had no training in the arts and crafts, but that I was anxious to learn, and that this desire had brought me to America. In answer to the question why I had not stayed at home or in Prague to learn instead of wandering across the sea with so little on my back and nothing in my pocket, I said that the Hungarian and Austrian authorities had formed a strong prejudice against me on account of my sympathies with people, . . . who objected to being cheated out of their ancient rights and privileges which the emperor had guaranteed to them for services which they had been rendering to him loyally for nearly two hundred years. I spoke with feeling, and I felt that I made an impression upon the examiners, who did not look to me like officials such as I was accustomed to see in Austria-Hungary. They had no gold and silver braid and no superior airs but looked very much like ordinary civilian mortals. That gave me courage and confidence, and I spoke frankly and fearlessly, believing firmly that I was addressing human beings who had a heart which was not held in bondage by cast-iron rules invented by their superiors in authority. The Swiss veteran who walked on crutches, having lost one of his legs in the Civil War, was particularly attentive while I was being cross-examined, and nodded approvingly whenever I scored a point with my answers. He whispered something to the other officials, and they finally informed me that I could pass on, and I was conducted promptly to the Labor Bureau of Castle Garden.

## 16

However valuable the immigrant contribution to American life, immigration was not always viewed as an unqualified blessing. Nativists deplored the "Mongolization" of native blood, labor unions resented competition with workers with lower living standards, and professional patriots bemoaned the crime of poverty which, they charged, was to be laid at the alien's door. A New York benevolent society, the Association for the Improvement of the Condition of the Poor, voiced such an opinion in a report setting forth persistent American stereotypes with unconscious frankness:[16]

Foreign immigration for philanthropic considerations, and for its national advan-

tages, has ever been advocated in these Reports. Industry is productive, and labor is here needed to develop the resources and wealth of our almost limitless country; for as these objects are promoted, commerce, manufactures, and the arts flourish, agriculture is encouraged and becomes remunerative and profitable. It is worthy of notice, that the most numerous class of immigrants are laborers; and the next in order are farmers, mechanics, merchants and female servants. The enterprise and skill of some, and the industry of others, wherever they locate, not only increase the numerical strength, but augment the wealth and prosperity of the nation. In following the "Star of Empire" to this Western Hemisphere, who does not discern the guiding hand of Divine Providence in its bearing on their destiny, and on the country of their adoption? How largely this city is indebted to European emigration for its unparalleled growth, is indicated by the fact, that nearly one-half of the population are foreign born; while the addition of some five millions to our native increase, from the same source, satisfactorily accounts for the unprecedented progress of the nation in population, wealth and power.

But immigration is not an unqualified blessing. It presents other less satisfactory aspects which should be well considered, especially in its bearing on the character and condition of our cities. In some there may be stronger counteracting and conservative forces than in others; but its deteriorating effects on morals, as observation and statistics show, are usually in the ratio of the foreign to the native population, in any given locality. . . .

Again, what class of our citizens most strenuously resist the moral restraints of the community, when irreconcilable with their own habits, and factiously combine to defeat the operation of the most benign laws, when they happen to oppose their own demoralizing indulgences, or supposed interests? Who among our popula-

[16] *Twenty-fourth Annual Report of the New York Association for the Improvement of the Condition of the Poor* (New York, 1867), pp. 36-37, 39, 42-45. (Pages not numbered consecutively.)

tion would give unrestricted and unregu-
lated license to the ten thousand drinking
places in the city, which are the chief re-
ceptacles of drunkenness, debauchery, vil-
lainy, and disease? Who is it that would
annihilate the Sabbath—the very citadel of
Christian institutions—the bulwark of private virtue, domestic happiness, national
freedom, and prosperity—by converting it
into a day of profligacy and dissipation?
To these, and similar interrogations, which
might be indefinitely multiplied, let facts
respond, and there is but one answer.

All who are conversant with the social
and moral condition of this city will admit, that there is now, in the lower strata
of the population, a larger mass of ignorance, vice, and heathenism combined,
than was ever before known in our history. Its chief source is familiar to us. It
is the residuum or dregs of four millions
of European immigrants, including paupers, felons, and convicts, that have landed
at this port within the last twenty years.
Uncultured as credulous, they brought
with them the habits, prejudices, passions,
and vices of the Old World. . . .

But the subject presents other aspects
not less important, which in this connection require grave consideration. The fact
is obvious and indisputable, that the social relations of the foreign to the native
population have, in late years, materially
changed. They no longer, as formerly,
melt away, or so blend with the native
stocks as to become incorporated with it.
So large are the aggregations of different
foreign nationalities, that they no longer
conform to our habits, opinions, and manners, but, on the contrary, create for themselves distinct communities, almost as
impervious to American sentiments and
influences, as are the inhabitants of Dub-
lin or Hamburg. This principle or tendency of segregation extends to their private,
social, and public life—which every new
arrival augments in numbers and strength.
They have their own theatres, recreations,

amusements, military and national organizations; to a great extent their own schools,
churches, and trade unions—their own
newspapers and periodical literature. In
further illustration of this tendency to
sever themselves from everything American, we find that they have in this city
seventy-three churches; they publish thirty-
five newspapers and periodicals, in five
different languages, and sustain several
eleemosynary and philanthropic institutions, for the exclusive benefit of their own
people. As these foreign masses, in short,
have little intercourse with the native population, beyond the claims of business, and
read few American papers, they are generally as ignorant of all that is peculiar to
the institutions of the country, as if no
such sources of information existed, or as
if they were still subjects of a foreign
power. . . .

So heterogeneous, however, are these
masses, that they cannot coalesce and har-
monize with each other, much less with
Americans. Even if the exodus from Europe should diminish or cease, as eventually it must from depletion, generations
will elapse before they become thoroughly
Americanized; and, until it does cease, the
difficulty in our large cities of dealing wisely
with the evils of a population so divided
and constituted will continue. . . .

Let it not for a moment be imagined that
the prominence which has been given to
our foreign population is attributable to
prejudice or unkindness. They have, on
the contrary, been specially referred to for
two reasons; first, because of their important relations to this Association and to
the community; and second, to awaken a
deeper social and moral interest in their
welfare. The ignorance, debasement, and
wretchedness of many of them, though
fitted to repel intercourse and repress sympathy, should excite a more active and
earnest concern in their behalf. They have
been led hither by the guiding hand of
Divine Providence for a beneficent end.
They have been thrown upon our care,

not to be neglected, scorned, and depressed, but to be lifted up to a better life. To the Christian benevolence of this city, and, in no considerable degree, to the labors and influence of this Institution, God has intrusted this glorious stewardship. Though their character has been depicted with the fidelity which truth requires, yet toward no other class has the thoughtful solicitude of the Association been more deeply exercised than to them, for their benefit, and for the present and future advantage of the community.

The foreign-born, be it remembered, constitute about three-fourths of the recipients of this charity, and the attention and aid it gives are not grudgingly bestowed, provided they are attended with the desired results. They are, if not the majority, at least the controlling political element in the city. Every day they are increasing in numbers, and they know it. They are not circumstanced like the same classes in the Old World, and they cannot be wisely or safely treated in the same way. Their best interests this Association would conscientiously promote. It believes, however, in no legislative encroachments on capital, nor in diminishing the hours of labor while the pay is increased; for all such class legislation and levelling endeavors will be generally disastrous, and ultimately work out their own defeat. The philosophy of the times, on the contrary, points not to legislative interference, nor yet to violence or to "strikes," but to the increased intelligence and enterprise of labor, to the power of organized industry to redress its own grievances, real or imaginary, and to "co-operative movements," perhaps, which severally recognizing the sanctity of property as well as the rights of labor, are essentially conservative as well as progressive, and will insure the largest recompense which the laws that govern labor will admit. This being the course both of duty and safety, let no unkind opprobrium be cast upon the ignorant poor who need counsel and sympathy, not yet upon the degraded that need pity and help; but rather may they be lifted up to the average level of intelligence and education. This is certainly the spirit of our impartial institutions, and the dictate of practical Christianity, which alike aim at man's highest physical, social, and moral good.

## 17

One group experienced active nativistic oppression during the postwar period. Opposition to Chinese immigration reached such proportions on the Pacific coast that in 1879 an exclusion measure passed Congress, despite a treaty between the two powers that guaranteed reciprocal immigration privileges. President Chester A. Arthur vetoed the act, then ordered the drafting of a new treaty giving Congress a freer hand. In 1882, as a result, a Chinese Exclusion Act suspended immigration for a decade; this was subsequently extended and became permanent:[17]

WHEREAS, In the opinion of the Government of the United States the coming of Chinese laborers to this country endangers the good order of certain localities within the territory thereof: Therefore,

*Be it enacted,* That from and after the expiration of ninety days next after the passage of this act, and until the expiration of ten years next after the passage of this act, the coming of Chinese laborers to the United States be, . . . suspended; and during such suspension it shall not be lawful for any Chinese laborer to come, or, having so come after the expiration of said ninety days, to remain within the United States.

SECTION 2. That the master of any vessel who shall knowingly bring within the United States on such vessel, and land or permit to be landed, any Chinese laborer, from any foreign port or place, shall be deemed guilty of a misdemeanor, and on conviction thereof shall be punished by a fine of not more than five hundred dollars for each and every such Chinese laborer

---

[17] *United States Statutes at Large,* XXII, 58-61.

so brought, and may be also imprisoned for a term not exceeding one year.

SEC. 3. That the two foregoing sections shall not apply to Chinese laborers who were in the United States on the seventeenth day of November, eighteen hundred and eighty, or who shall have come into the same before the expiration of ninety days next. . . .

SEC. 6. That in order to the faithful execution of articles one and two of the treaty in this act before mentioned, every Chinese person other than a laborer who may be entitled by said treaty and this act to come within the United States, and who shall be about to come to the United States, shall be identified as so entitled by the Chinese Government in each case, such identity to be evidenced by a certificate issued under the authority of said government, which certificate shall be in the English language or (if not in the English language) accompanied by a translation into English, stating such right to come, and which certificate shall state the name, title, or official rank, if any, the age, height, and all physical peculiarities, former and present occupation or profession, and place of residence in China of the person to whom the certificate is issued and that such person is entitled conformably to the treaty in this act mentioned to come within the United States. . . .

SEC. 12. That no Chinese person shall be permitted to enter the United States by land without producing to the proper officer of customs the certificate in this act required of Chinese persons seeking to land from a vessel. And any Chinese person found unlawfully within the United States shall be caused to be removed therefrom to the country from whence he came, by direction of the President of the United States, and at the cost of the United States, after being brought before some justice, judge, or commissioner of a court of the United States and found to be one not lawfully entitled to be or remain in the United States.

SEC. 13. That this act shall not apply to diplomatic and other officers of the Chinese Government traveling upon the business of that government, whose credentials shall be taken as equivalent to the certificate in this act mentioned, and shall exempt them and their body and household servants from the provisions of this act as to other Chinese persons.

SEC. 14. That hereafter no State court or court of the United States shall admit Chinese to citizenship; and all laws in conflict with this act are hereby repealed.

SEC. 15. That the words "Chinese laborers," whenever used in this act, shall be construed to mean both skilled and unskilled laborers and Chinese employed in mining.

## 18

The exclusion of Chinese laborers did little to satisfy nativists, who next directed their attention to illiterates among the arrivals from other lands. They advocated the inauguration of a selective process to eliminate aliens likely to become public charges. Actually, however, they desired to restrict the number of new arrivals drastically. A congressional speech by Senator Henry Cabot Lodge of Massachusetts delivered on March 16, 1896, in support of a literacy test for immigrants illustrates this attitude:[18]

Mr. President, this bill is intended to amend the existing law so as to restrict still further immigration to the United States. Paupers, diseased persons, convicts, contract laborers are now excluded. By this bill it is proposed to make a new class of excluded immigrants and add to those which have just been named the totally ignorant. The bill is of the simplest kind. The first section excludes from the country all immigrants who cannot read or write either their own or some other language. The second section merely provides a simple test for determining whether the immigrant can read or write,

---

[18] *Congressional Record*, 54th Cong., 1st Sess. XXVIII, 2817-2820.

and is added to the bill so as to define the duties of the immigrant inspectors, and to assure to all immigrants alike perfect justice and a fair test of their knowledge. . . .

The third method was to exclude all immigrants who could neither read nor write, and this is the plan which was adopted by the committee and which is embodied in this bill. In their report the committee have shown by statistics, which have been collected and tabulated with great care, the emigrants who would be affected by this illiteracy test. It is not necessary for me to do more than summarize the results of the committee's investigation, which have been set forth fully in this report. It is found in the first place that the illiteracy test will bear most heavily upon Italians, Russians, Poles, Hungarians, Greeks and Asiatics, and very lightly, or not at all, upon English-speaking emigrants or Germans, Scandinavians, and French. In other words, the races most affected by the illiteracy test are those whose emigration to this country has begun within the last twenty years and swelled rapidly to enormous proportions, races with which the English-speaking people have never hitherto assimilated, and who are the most alien to the great body of the people of the United States. On the other hand, immigrants from the United Kingdom and of those races which are the most closely related to the English-speaking people, and who with the English-speaking people themselves founded the American colonies and built up the United States, are affected but little by the proposed test. These races would not be prevented by this law from coming to this country in practically undiminished numbers. These kindred races also are those who alone go to the Western and Southern States, where immigrants are desired, and take up our unoccupied lands. The races which would suffer most seriously by exclusion under the proposed bill furnish the immigrants who do not go to the West or South, where immigration is needed, but who remain on the Atlantic Seaboard, where immigration is not needed and where their presence is most injurious and undesirable. . . .

I have said enough to show what the effects of this bill would be, and that if enacted into law it would be fair in its operation and highly beneficial in its results. It now remains for me to discuss the second and larger question, as to the advisability of restricting immigration at all. This is a subject of the greatest magnitude and the most far-reaching importance. It has two sides, the economic and the social. As to the former, but few words are necessary. There is no one thing which does so much to bring about a reduction of wages and to injure the American wage earner as the unlimited introduction of cheap foreign labor through unrestricted immigration. Statistics show that the change in the race character of our immigration has been accompanied by a corresponding decline in its quality. The number of skilled mechanics and of persons trained to some occupation or pursuit has fallen off, while the number of those without occupation or training, that is, who are totally unskilled, has risen in our recent immigration to enormous proportions. This low, unskilled labor is the most deadly enemy of the American wage earner, and does more than anything else towards lowering his wages and forcing down his standard of living. An attempt was made, with the general assent of both political parties, to meet this crying evil some years ago by the passage of what are known as the contract-labor laws. That legislation was excellent in intention, but has proved of but little value in practice. It has checked to a certain extent the introduction of cheap, low-class labor in large masses into the United States. It has made it a little more difficult for such labor to come here, but the labor of this class continues to come, even if not in the same way, and the total amount of it has not been materially reduced. Even if the contract-labor laws were enforced intelligently and thoroughly, there is no reason to suppose that they would have had any adequate effect in checking the evil which they were designed to stop. It is perfectly clear after the experience of several years that the only relief which can come to the American wage earner from the competition of low-class immigrant labor must be by general laws restricting the total amount of immigration and framed in such a way as to affect most strongly those elements of the immigration which furnish the low, unskilled, and ignorant foreign labor.

It is not necessary to enter further into a discussion of the economic side of the general policy of restricting immigration. In this direction the argument is unanswerable. If we have any regard for the welfare, the wages, or the standard of life of American workingmen, we should take immediate steps to restrict foreign immigration. There is no danger, at present at all events, to our workingmen from the coming of skilled mechanics or of trained and educated men with a settled occupation or pursuit, for immigrants of this class will never seek to lower the American standard of life and wages. On the contrary, they desire the same standard for themselves. But there is an appalling danger to the American wage earner from the flood of low, unskilled, ignorant, foreign labor which has poured into the country for some years past, and which not only takes lower wages, but accepts a standard of life and living so low that the American workingman can not compete with it. . . .

Mr. President, more precious even than forms of government are the mental and moral qualities which make what we call our race. While those stand unimpaired all is safe. When those decline all is imperiled. They are exposed to but a single danger, and that is by changing the quality of our race and citizenship by the wholesale infusion of races whose traditions and inheritances, whose thoughts and whose beliefs are wholly alien to ours and with whom we have never assimilated or even been associated in the past. The danger has

begun. It is small as yet, comparatively speaking, but it is large enough to warn us to act while there is yet time and while it can be done easily and efficiently. There lies the peril at the portals of our land; there is pressing in the tide of unrestricted immigration. The time has certainly come, if not to stop, at least to check, to sift, and to restrict those immigrants. In careless strength, with generous hand, we have kept our gates wide open to all the world. If we do not close them, we should at least place sentinels beside them to challenge those who would pass through. The gates which admit men to the United States and to citizenship in the great Republic should no longer be left unguarded.

### 19

The bill advocated by Senator Lodge finally passed Congress, but was vetoed by President Grover Cleveland in a message exposing its faulty logic:[19]

A century's stupendous growth, largely due to the assimilation and thrift of sturdy and patriotic adopted citizens, attests the success of this generous and free-handed policy, which, while guarding the people's interests, exacts from our immigrants only physical and moral soundness and a willingness and ability to work. . . .

The best reason that could be given for this radical restriction of immigration is the necessity of protecting our population against degeneration and saving our national peace and quiet from imported turbulence and disorder.

I can not believe that we would be protected against these evils by limiting immigration to those who can read and write in any language twenty-five words of our Constitution. In my opinion it is infinitely more safe to admit a hundred thousand immigrants who, though unable to read and write, seek among us only a home and opportunity to work, than to admit

---

[19] *United States Senate Documents*, 54th Cong., 2nd Sess., V, Doc. No. 185, pp. 1-3. (Pages not numbered consecutively.)

one of those unruly agitators and enemies of governmental control, who can not only read and write but delights in arousing by inflammatory speech the illiterate and peacefully inclined to discontent and tumult. Violence and disorder do not originate with illiterate laborers. They are rather the victims of an educated agitator. The ability to read and write as required in this bill, in and of itself, affords, in my opinion, a misleading test of contented industry and supplies unsatisfactory evidence of desirable citizenship or a proper apprehension of the benefits of our institutions. If any particular element of our illiterate immigration is to be feared for other causes than illiteracy, these causes should be dealt with directly instead of making illiteracy the pretext for exclusion to the detriment of other illiterate immigrants against whom the real cause of complaint can not be alleged.

## 20

Not even strident voices of superpatriots who adopted the slogan "America for the Americans" could quench the flame in the breasts of Europe's masses. Emma Lazarus, a modern poet, paid tribute to the newcomers and to their faith in America who gazed for the first time on the Statue of Liberty:[20]

---

[20] From Morris U. Schappes (ed.), *Emma Lazarus, Selections from Her Poetry and Prose* (1944), Co-operative Book League, Jewish-American Section, International Workers' Order, p. 40.

Not like the brazen giant of Greek fame,
With conquering limbs astride from land to land;
Here at our sea-washed, sunset gates shall stand
A mighty woman with a torch, whose flame
Is the imprisoned lightning, and her name
Mother of Exiles. From her beacon-hand
Glows world-wide welcome; her mild eyes command
The air-bridged harbor that twin cities frame.
"Keep, ancient lands, your storied pomp!" cries she
With silent lips. "Give me your tired, your poor,
Your huddled masses yearning to breathe free,
The wretched refuse of your teeming shore.
Send these, the homeless, tempest-tost to me,
I lift my lamp beside the golden door!"

The cities of the United States, crowded with immigrants who longed to be free and stirring with intellectual ferment, epitomized the new America. But urbanization was responsible for something more than theological controversies and invigorating additions to the population. If the city symbolized the material and intellectual gains of an industrial civilization, it crystallized the failure of man to solve the social problems of a modern world. The sins of society were most apparent in the cities.

# THE SINS OF SOCIETY

## 1865–1890

The revolutions in economics accentuated American contrasts. In the crowded cities of the United States, colossal fortunes existed side by side with abject poverty, lavish mansions looked down upon ugly slums, and cultured gentlemen fresh from the splendor of Delmonico's rubbed elbows with toilers whose horizon was no broader than the sweatshop where they labored or the hovel where they slept. Accustomed to the middle-class standards of an agrarian society, workers and reformers alike began to express concern for the future of the United States, and envisaged a social order where such extremes could not exist. To assure salvation for the nation and for democracy, the sins of society had to be eradicated.

## THE GOSPEL OF WEALTH

### 1

Vocal defenders of the existing order were few, but their influence was great and their supporters were many. They hoped to demonstrate that an economic system of laissez faire was inevitable, and that actually it brought the greatest number the greatest good. Best known of the spokesmen of the gospel of wealth was Andrew Carnegie, a Scotch immigrant whose ability to transmute iron and steel into gold dramatized the possibilities for those who could transform thrift, energy, and good fortune into riches. Carnegie not only followed the pattern from the insignificance of poverty to the fame of colossal wealth, but elaborated the methods that he employed into a philosophy that became part of the American creed. Nowhere did he more specifically justify the right of acquisition and the obligation of stewardship than in a volume called *The Gospel of Wealth*:[1]

Objections to the foundations upon which society is based are not in order, because the condition of the race is better with these than with any other which has been tried. Of the effect of any new substitutes proposed we cannot be sure. The Socialist or Anarchist who seeks to overturn present conditions is to be regarded as attacking the foundation upon which civilization itself rests, for civilization took its start from the day when the capable, industrious workman said to his incompetent and lazy fellow, "If thou dost not sow, thou shalt not reap," and thus ended primitive Communism by separating the drones from the bees. One who studies this subject will soon be brought face to face with the conclusion that upon the sacredness of property civilization itself depends—the right of the laborer to his hundred dollars in the savings-bank, and equally the legal right of the millionaire to his millions. Every man must be allowed to "sit under his own vine and fig-tree, with none to make afraid," if human society is to advance, or even to remain so far advanced as it is. To those who propose to substitute Communism for this intense Individualism, the answer therefore is: The race has tried that. All progress from that barbarous day to the present time has resulted from its displacement. Not evil, but good, has come to the race from the accumulation of wealth by those who have had the ability and energy to produce it. But even if we admit for a moment that it might be better for the race to discard its present foundation, Individualism, —that it is a nobler ideal that man should labor, not for himself alone, but in and for a brotherhood of his fellows, and share with them all in common . . . even admit all this, and a sufficient answer is, This is not evolution, but revolution. It necessi-

[1] Andrew Carnegie, *The Gospel of Wealth* (New York, 1900), pp. 5–13. Reprinted by permission of the Carnegie Corporation of New York.

tates the changing of human nature itself—a work of eons, even if it were good to change it, which we cannot know.

It is not practicable in our day or in our age. Even if desirable theoretically, it belongs to another and long-succeeding sociological stratum. Our duty is with what is practicable now. . . . It is criminal to waste our energies in endeavoring to uproot, when all we can profitably accomplish is to bend the universal tree of humanity a little in the direction most favorable to the production of good fruit under existing circumstances. We might as well urge the destruction of the highest existing type of man because he failed to reach our ideal as to favor the destruction of Individualism, Private Property, the Law of Accumulation of Wealth, and the Law of Competition; for these are the highest result of human experience, the soil in which society, so far, has produced the best fruit. Unequally or unjustly, perhaps, as these laws sometimes operate, and imperfect as they appear to the Idealist, they are, nevertheless, like the highest type of man, the best and most valuable of all that humanity has yet accomplished.

We start, then, with a condition of affairs under which the best interests of the race are promoted, but which inevitably gives wealth to the few. Thus far, accepting conditions as they exist, the situation can be surveyed and pronounced good. The question then arises,—and if the foregoing be correct, it is the only question with which we have to deal,—What is the proper mode of administering wealth after the laws upon which civilization is founded have thrown it into the hands of the few? And it is of this great question that I believe I offer the true solution. It will be understood that fortunes are here spoken of, not moderate sums saved by many years of effort, the returns from which are required for the comfortable maintenance and education of families. This is not wealth, but only competence,

which it should be the aim of all to acquire, and which it is for the best interests of society should be acquired.

There are but three modes in which surplus wealth can be disposed of. It can be left to the families of the decedents; or it can be bequeathed for public purposes; or, finally, it can be administered by its possessors during their lives. Under the first and second modes most of the wealth of the world that has reached the few has hitherto been applied. Let us in turn consider each of these modes. The first is the most injudicious. In monarchical countries, the estates and the greatest portion of the wealth are left to the first son, that the vanity of the parent may be gratified by the thought that his name and title are to descend unimpaired to succeeding generations. The condition of this class in Europe today teaches the failure of such hopes or ambitions. The successors have become improverished through their follies, or from the fall in the value of land. Even in Great Britain the strict law of entail has been found inadequate to maintain an hereditary class. Its soil is rapidly passing into the hands of the stranger. Under republican institutions the division of property among the children is much fairer; but the question which forces itself upon thoughtful men in all lands is, Why should men leave great fortunes to their children? If this is done from affection, is it not misguided affection? Observation teaches that, generally speaking, it is not well for the children that they should be so burdened. Neither is it well for the State. Beyond providing for the wife and daughters moderate sources of income, and very moderate allowances indeed, if any, for the sons, men may well hesitate; for it is no longer questionable that great sums bequeathed often work more for the injury than for the good of the recipients. Wise men will conclude that, for the best interests of the members of their families, and of the State, such bequests are an improper use of their means.

It is not suggested that men who have failed to educate their sons to earn a livelihood shall cast them adrift in poverty. If any man has seen fit to rear his sons with a view to their living idle lives, or, what is highly commendable, has instilled in them the sentiment that they are in a position to labor for public ends without reference to pecuniary considerations, then, of course, the duty of the parent is to see that such are provided for in moderation. There are instances of millionaires' sons unspoiled by wealth, who, being rich, still perform great services to the community. Such are the very salt of the earth, as valuable as, unfortunately, they are rare. It is not the exception, however, but the rule, that men must regard; and, looking at the usual result of enormous sums conferred upon legatees, the thoughtful man must shortly say, "I would as soon leave my son a curse as the almighty dollar," and admit to himself that it is not the welfare of the children, but family pride, which inspires these legacies.

As to the second mode, that of leaving wealth at death for public uses, it may be said that this is only a means for the disposal of wealth, provided a man is content to wait until he is dead before he becomes of much good in the world. Knowledge of the results of legacies bequeathed is not calculated to inspire the brightest hopes of much posthumous good being accomplished by them. The cases are not few in which the real object sought by the testator is not attained, nor are they few in which his real wishes are thwarted. In many cases the bequests are so used as to become only monuments of his folly. It is well to remember that it requires the exercise of not less ability than that which acquires it, to use wealth so as to be really beneficial to the community. Besides this, it may fairly be said that no man is to be extolled for doing what he cannot help

doing, nor is he to be thanked by the community to which he only leaves wealth at death. Men who leave vast sums in this way may fairly be thought men who would not have left it at all had they been able to take it with them. The memories of such cannot be held in grateful remembrance, for there is no grace in their gifts. It is not to be wondered at that such bequests seem so generally to lack the blessing.

The growing disposition to tax more and more heavily large estates left at death is a cheering indication of the growth of a salutary change in public opinion. The State of Pennsylvania now takes—subject to some exceptions—one tenth of the property left by its citizens. The budget presented in the British Parliament the other day proposes to increase the death duties; and, most significant of all, the new tax is to be a graduated one. Of all forms of taxation this seems the wisest. Men who continue hoarding great sums all their lives, the proper use of which for public ends would work good to the community from which it chiefly came, should be made to feel that the community, in the form of the State, cannot thus be deprived of its proper share. By taxing estates heavily at death the State marks its condemnation of the selfish millionaire's unworthy life.

It is desirable that nations should go much further in this direction. Indeed, it is difficult to set bounds to the share of a rich man's estate which should go at his death to the public through the agency of the State, and by all means such taxes should be graduated, beginning at nothing upon moderate sums to dependents, and increasing rapidly as the amounts swell. . . .

This policy would work powerfully to induce the rich man to attend to the administration of wealth during his life, which is the end that society should always have in view, as being by far the most fruitful for the people. Nor need it be feared that this policy would sap the root of enterprise and render men less anxious to accumulate, for, to the class whose ambition it is to leave great fortunes and be talked about after their death, it will attract even more attention, and, indeed, be a some what nobler ambition, to have enormous sums paid over to the State from their fortunes.

There remains, then, only one mode of using great fortunes; but in this we have the true antidote for the temporary unequal distribution of wealth, the reconciliation of the rich and the poor—a reign of harmony, another ideal, differing, indeed, from that of the Communist in requiring only the further evolution of existing conditions, not the total overthrow of our civilization. It is founded upon the present most intense Individualism, and the race is prepared to put it in practice by degrees whenever it pleases. Under its sway we shall have an ideal State, in which the surplus wealth of the few will become, in the best sense, the property of the many, because administered for the common good; and this wealth, passing through the hands of the few, can be made a much more potent force for the elevation of our race than if distributed in small sums to the people themselves. Even the poorest can be made to see this, and to agree that great sums gathered by some of their fellow citizens and spent for public purposes, from which the masses reap the principal benefit, are more valuable to them than if scattered among themselves in trifling amounts through the course of many years.

## 2

Again and again in voluminous defenses of the gospel of wealth, Andrew Carnegie emphasized the social obligation of the well to do. Endorsing the pseudo-Darwinian doctrine that "lives of poverty and struggle" developed superior beings, he insisted that for a man to die wealthy or to endow his children with a disproportionate share of the world's goods constituted the greatest crime against society. His own lavish philanthropies added weight to the argument advanced in his essay on "The Advantages of Poverty":[2]

The fundamental idea of the gospel of wealth is that surplus wealth should be considered as a sacred trust to be administered by those into whose hands it falls, during their lives, for the good of the community. It predicts that the day is at hand when he who dies possessed of enormous sums, which were his and free to administer during his life, will die disgraced, and holds that the aim of the millionaire should be to die poor. It likewise pleads for modesty of private expenditure.

The most serious obstacle to the spread of such a gospel is undoubtedly the prevailing desire of men to accumulate wealth for the express purpose of bequeathing it to their children, or to spend it in ostentatious living. I have therefore endeavored to prove that at the root of the desire to bequeath to children there lay the vanity of the parents, rather than a wise regard for the good of the children. That the parent who leaves his son enormous wealth generally deadens the talents and energies of the son, and tempts him to lead a less useful and less worthy life than he otherwise would, seems to me capable of proof which cannot be gainsaid. It is many years since I wrote in a rich lady's album, "I should as soon leave to my son a curse as the almighty dollar." Exceptions abound to every general rule, but I think not more exceptions to this rule than to others— namely, that wealth is a curse to young men, and poverty a blessing"; but if these terms seem rather strong, let us state the proposition thus: that wealth left to young men, as a rule, is disadvantageous; that lives of poverty and struggle are advantageous.

---

[2] Andrew Carnegie, "The Advantages of Poverty," *Nineteenth Century Magazine*, XXIX (March, 1891), 370-371.

## 3

The ideal of Andrew Carnegie's writings was a "rags to riches and back to rags" career for every individual with gumption enough to succeed in a dog-eat-dog society. He believed in an economic order in which each man was free to do as he wished, without the restraint of either governmental or social controls. Yet neither Carnegie nor others of his class were willing to practice what they preached. In the business world they aimed to create monopolies, in the form of trusts and combinations, which stifled free competition. Carnegie defended this practice in an article written in 1889:[3]

A demand exists for a certain article beyond the capacity of existing works to supply it. Prices are high and profits tempting. Every manufacturer of that article immediately proceeds to enlarge his works and increase their producing power. In addition to this, the unusual profits attract the attention of his principal managers or those who are interested to a greater or less degree in the factory. These communicate the knowledge of the prosperity of the works to others. New partnerships are formed and new works are erected, and before long the demand for the article is fully satisfied and prices do not advance . . . prices begin to fall. They continue falling until the article is sold at cost to the less-favorably situated or less-ably managed factory, and even until the best managed and best equipped factory is not able to produce the article at the price at which it may be sold. . . . As manufacturing is carried on today, in enormous establishments with five or ten millions of dollars of capital invested and with thousands of workers, it costs much less to run at a loss per ton or yard than to check production. . . . It is in soil thus prepared that anything promising relief is gladly welcome. . . . Combinations, syndicates, trusts—they are willing to try anything. A meeting is called, and in the presence of immediate danger they decide to take united action and form a trust. Each factory is rated as worth a certain amount. Officers are chosen and through those the entire product of the article in question is to be distributed to the public at remunerative prices. Such is the genesis of "trusts" in manufactured articles.

## 4

That Andrew Carnegie's views on trusts were usual among men of his class was constantly demonstrated in both theory and practice. Another businessman who sought to escape the hazards of a free market by devices to control prices was John D. Rockefeller, whose giant Standard Oil Company enjoyed its palmiest days before the advent of the automobile—and of antitrust legislation. Rockefeller explained the virtues of monopoly in his *Random Reminiscences of Men and Events:*[4]

The story of the early history of the oil trade is too well known to bear repeating in detail. The cleansing of crude petroleum was a simple and easy process, and at first the profits were very large. Naturally, all sorts of people went into it; the butcher, the baker, and the candlestick maker began to refine oil, and it was only a short time before more of the finished product was put on the market than could possibly be consumed. The price went down and down until the trade was threatened with ruin. It seemed absolutely necessary to extend the market for oil by exporting to foreign countries, which required a long and most difficult development, and also to greatly improve the processes of refining so that oil could be made and sold cheaply, yet with a profit, and to use as by-products all of the materials which in the less efficient plants were lost or thrown away.

[3] Andrew Carnegie, "The Bugaboo of Trusts," *North American Review,* CXLVIII (January-June, 1889), 141-142.

[4] From *Random Reminiscences of Men and Events,* pp. 81-87, by John D. Rockefeller, copyright 1909 by Doubleday, Doran and Company, Inc., copyright 1937 by John D. Rockefeller. Reprinted by permission.

These were the problems which confronted us almost at the outset, and this great depression led to consultations with our neighbors and friends in the business in the effort to bring some order out of what was rapidly becoming a state of chaos. To accomplish all these tasks of enlarging the market and improving the methods of manufacture in a large way was beyond the power or ability of any concern as then constituted. It could only be done, we reasoned, by increasing our capital and availing ourselves of the best talent and experience.

It was with this idea that we proceeded to buy the largest and best refining concerns and centralize the administration of them with a view to securing greater economy and efficiency. The business grew faster than we anticipated.

This enterprise, conducted by men of application and ability working hard together, soon built up unusual facilities in manufacture, in transportation, in finance, and in extending markets. We had our troubles and setbacks; we suffered from some severe fires; and the supply of crude oil was most uncertain. Our plans were constantly changed by changed conditions. We developed great facilities in an oil center, erected storage tanks, and connected pipe lines; then the oil failed and our work was thrown away. At best it was a speculative trade, and I wonder that we managed to pull through so often, but we were gradually learning how to conduct a most difficult business. . . .

I ascribe the success of the Standard Oil Company to its consistent policy of making the volume of its business large through the merit and cheapness of its products. It has spared no expense in utilizing the best and most efficient method of manufacture. It has sought for the best superintendents and workmen and paid the best wages. It has not hesitated to sacrifice old machinery and old plants for new and better ones. It has placed its manufactories at the points where they could supply markets at the least expense. It has not only sought markets for its principal products but for all possible by-products, sparing no expense in introducing them to the public in every nook and corner of the world. It has not hesitated to invest millions of dollars in methods for cheapening the gathering and distribution of oils by pipe lines, special cars, tank-steamers, and tank-wagons. It has erected tank stations at railroad centers in every part of the country to cheapen the storage and delivery of oil. It has had faith in American oil and has brought together vast sums of money for the purpose of making it what it is and for holding its market against the competition . . . [of] all the countries which are producers of oil and competitors against American products.

5

Rockefeller, extolling the productivity of large-scale combinations and Carnegie suspecting them of less virtuous objects, presented only part of the picture. Methods for market control employed by the great entrepreneurs and their result, the lowered bargaining position of consumers, became the concern of many who looked for preservation of large-scale efficiencies but demanded protection also of the liberty of the individual against combinations. Influential among urban reformers who prophesied the end of unrestrained individualism was Henry Demarest Lloyd, a New York financial writer. His article, "Lords of Industry," was one of a series that helped strengthen the movement for regulation of big business:[5]

When President Gowen, of the Reading Railroad, was defending that company in 1875 before a committee of the Pennsylvania Legislature for having taken part in the combination of the coal companies to cure the evil of "too much coal" by putting up the price and cutting down the amount for sale, he pleaded that there were fifty trades in which the same thing

[5] H. D. Lloyd, "Lords of Industry," *North American Review*, CXXXVIII (June, 1884), 535-553.

was done. He had a list of them to show the committee. . . .

Adam Smith said in 1776: "People of the same trade hardly meet together even for merriment and diversion but the conversation ends in a conspiracy against the public or in some contrivance to raise prices." The expansive ferment of the New Industry, coming with the new science, the new land, and the new liberties of our era, broke up these "conspiracies," and for a century we have heard nothing of them; but the race to overrun is being succeeded by the struggle to divide, and combinations are reappearing on all sides. This any one may see from the reports of the proceedings of the conventions and meetings of innumerable associations of manufacturers and dealers and even producers, which are being held almost constantly. They all do something to raise prices, or hold them up, and they wind up with banquets for which we pay. . . .

The coal combination was investigated by the New York Legislature in 1878, after the combination had raised the prices of coal in New York to double what they had been. The Legislature found that private mine-operators who were not burdened like the great companies with extravagant and often corrupt purchases of coal lands, heavily watered stock, and disadvantageous contracts, forced on them by interested directors, and who have only to pay the actual cost of producing the coal, "can afford to sell at a much less price than the railroad coal-producing companies, and would do so if they could get transportation from the mines to the market." . . . The committee found that coal could be laid down on the dock in New York, after paying all charges, for an average of $3.20 a ton. It was at that time retailing in the city for $4.90 to $5.25 a ton. . . .

One of the sights which this coal side of our civilization has to show is the presence of herds of little children of all ages, from six years upward, at work in the coal breakers, toiling in dirt, and air thick with carbon dust, from dawn to dark, of every day in the week except Sunday. These coal breakers are the only schools they know. A letter from the coal regions in the Philadelphia Press declares that "there are no schools in the world where more evil is learned or more innocence destroyed than in the breakers. It is shocking to watch the vile practices indulged in by these children, to hear the frightful oaths they use, to see their total disregard for religion and humanity." In the upper part of Luzerne County, out of 22,000 inhabitants 3000 are children, between six and fifteen years of age, at work in this way. "There is always a restlessness among the miners," an officer of one of the New York companies said, "when we are working them on half time." The latest news from the region of the coal combination is that the miners are so dissatisfied with the condition in which they are kept, by the suspension of work and the importation of competing Hungarian laborers in droves, that they are forming a combination of their own, a revival of the old Miners' and Laborers' Association, which was broken up by the labor troubles of 1874 and 1875. . . .

There has been since 1872 a national combination of the manufacturers of the stoves into which the combination coal must be put; and its effect, the founder said, in his speech at the annual banquet in Cleveland, last February, had been to change the balance from the wrong to the right side of the ledger. Until lately, at least, combination matches lighted the fire of combination coal in these combination stoves, and it is combination oil which the cook, contrary to orders, puts on the fires to make them burn faster. . . .

When the housemaid strikes a combination match on the wall-paper, she leaves a mark on an article the manufacture, sale, and price of which are rigidly regulated by the American Wall Paper Manufacturers' Association. A recent writer has described this oath-bound monarchy in the United States. When the cook takes the paper from off the express package, the hardware, the dry-goods, the groceries, the candy, the ham, which have been sent home, she is still handling an article the price of which is fixed by private enactments. The Western Wrapping Paper Association, ever since 1880, has, with more or less success, been struggling to keep down the deluge of too much wrapping paper, and to fix the prices of all kinds, from the paper under the carpet to that which is used in roofing. . . . The Western Wooden Ware Asociation discovered, last December, that there were too many pails, tubs, and bowls and ordered its members to manufacture but one fifth of their capacity. In February it gave them permission to increase this to one half. The Western Cracker Bakers' Association met in Chicago in February to consider, among other things, "the reprehensible system of cutting prices." They first had a banquet. After their "merriment and diversion" the revellers, true to Adam Smith's description, turned to consider "some contrivance to raise prices." "The price lists were perfected," said the newspaper report, and then they adjourned. . . .

Every one knows about the thirty-million-dollar steel combination, which has not kept the price of rails from declining from $166 a ton in 1867 to $32 a ton in 1884, but during this decline has kept the price of rails, that is, the price of transportation, that is, the price of everything, higher in this country than anywhere else. Chairman Morrison of the Committee of Ways and Means is a witness to the fact that the chimneys of the Vulcan Mill at St. Louis stood smokeless for years, and meanwhile its owners received a subsidy reported at $400,000 a year from the other mills of the combination for not making rails, with, however, no payment to its men for not working. The steel-rail makers of England, France, Belgium, and Germany are negotiating for an international combination to keep up prices. . . .

On the theory of "too much of everything," our industries, from railroads to working men, are being organized to prevent milk, nails, lumber, freights, labor, soothing syrup, and all these other things from becoming too cheap. The majority have never yet been able to buy enough of anything. The minority have too much of everything to sell. Seeds of social trouble germinate fast in such conditions. Society is letting these combinations become institutions without compelling them to adjust their charges to the cost of production, which used to be the universal rule of price. Our laws and commissions to regulate the railroads are but toddling steps in a path in which we need to walk like men. The change from competition to combination is nothing less than one of those revolutions which march through history with giant strides. It is not likely that this revolution will go backward. Nothing goes backward in this country except reform. When Stephenson said of railroads that where combination was possible competition was impossible, he was unconsciously declaring the law of all industry. . . .

The dream of the French Revolution, that man was good enough to be emancipated from the bonds of association and government by the simple proclamation of Liberty, Fraternity, and Equality, was but the frenzied expression of what was called Freedom of Self-interest in a quieter but not less bloody revolution, if the mortality of the factories, the mines, and the tenements be charged to its account. A rope cannot be made of sand; a society cannot be made of competitive units.

We have given competition its own way, and have found that we are not good enough or wise enough to be trusted with this power of ruining ourselves in the attempt to ruin others. . . . Morals and values rise and fall together. If our combinations have no morals, they can have no values. If the tendency to combination is irresistible, control of it is imperative. Monopoly and anti-monopoly, odious as these words have become to the literary ear, represent the two great tendencies of our time: monopoly, the tendency to combination; anti-monopoly, the demand for social control of it. . . . We cannot hereafter, as in the past, recover freedom by going to the prairies; we must find it in the society of the good.

## 6

To the defenders of the gospel of wealth, reformers were not only impractical idealists but dangerous enemies. They interfered with a social system evolving by Darwinianlike natural processes never clearly understood by man. Meddling would only serve to upset the evolutionary process; a weak government that confined itself to protecting life and property while fostering a laissez-faire economic order seemed far better. The most lucid exponent of this argument was William Graham Sumner, a Yale professor of sociology and economics, whose varied writings attacked socialism, planned society, governmental interference in business, public welfare projects, state-supported education—and especially reformers. Sumner's ideas were cogently defined in his essay entitled "What Social Classes Owe to Each Other":[6]

We are told every day that great social problems stand before us and demand a solution, and we are assailed by oracles, threats, and warnings in reference to those problems. There is a school of writers who are playing quite a *rôle* as the heralds of the coming duty and the coming woe. They assume to speak for a large, but vague and undefined, constituency, who set the task, exact a fulfilment, and threaten punishment for default. The task or problem is not specifically defined. Part of the task which devolves on those who are subject to the duty is to define the problem. They are told only that something is the matter: that it behooves them

to find out what it is, and how to correct it, and then to work out the cure. All this is more or less truculently set forth.

After reading and listening to a great deal of this sort of assertion I find that the question forms itself with more and more distinctness in my mind: Who are those who assume to put hard questions to other people and to demand a solution of them? How did they acquire the right to demand that others should solve their world-problems for them? Who are they who are held to consider and solve all questions, and how did they fall under this duty?

So far as I can find out what the classes are who are respectively endowed with the rights and duties of posing and solving social problems, they are as follows: Those who are bound to solve the problems are the rich, comfortable, prosperous, virtuous, respectable, educated, and healthy; those whose right it is to set the problems are those who have been less fortunate or less successful in the struggle for existence. The problem itself seems to be, How shall the latter be made as comfortable as the former? To solve this problem, and make us all equally well off, is assumed to be the duty of the former class; the penalty, if they fail of this, is to be bloodshed and destruction. If they cannot make everybody else as well off as themselves, they are to be brought down to the same misery as others.

During the last ten years I have read a great many books and articles, especially by German writers, in which an attempt has been made to set up "the State" as an entity having conscience, power, and will sublimated above human limitations, and as constituting a tutelary genius over us all. I have never been able to find in history or experience anything to fit this concept. I once lived in Germany for two years, but I certainly saw nothing of it there then. Whether the State which Bismarck is moulding will fit the notion is at best a matter of faith and hope. My notion of

---

[6] William Graham Sumner, *What Social Classes Owe to Each Other* (New York, 1883), pp. 7-12, 34-40, 166-169.

the State has dwindled with growing experience of life. As an abstraction, the State is to me only All-of-us. In practice—that is, when it exercises will or adopts a line of action—it is only a little group of men chosen in a very hap-hazard way by the majority of us to perform certain services for all of us. The majority do not go about their selection very rationally, and they are almost always disappointed by the results of their own operation. Hence "the State," instead of offering resources of wisdom, right reason, and pure moral sense beyond what the average of us possess, generally offers much less of all those things. Furthermore, it often turns out in practice that "the State" is not even the known and accredited servants of the State, but, as has been well said, is only some obscure clerk, hidden in the recesses of a Government bureau, into whose power the chance has fallen for the moment to pull one of the stops which control the Government machine. In former days it often happened that "the State" was a barber, a fiddler, or a bad woman. In our day it often happens that "the State" is a little functionary on whom a big functionary is forced to depend.

I cannot see the sense of spending time to read and write observations, such as I find in the writings of many men of great attainments and of great influence, of which the following might be a general type: If the statesmen could attain to the requisite knowledge and wisdom, it is conceivable that the State might perform important regulative functions in the production and distribution of wealth, against which no positive and sweeping theoretical objection could be made from the side of economic science; but statesmen never can acquire the requisite knowledge and wisdom.—To me this seems a mere waste of words. The inadequacy of the State to regulative tasks is agreed upon, as a matter of fact, by all. Why, then, bring State regulation into the discussion simply in order to throw it out again? The whole

subject ought to be discussed and settled aside from the hypothesis of State regulation.

The little group of public servants who . . . constitute the State, when the State determines on anything, could not do much for themselves or anybody else by their own force. If they do anything, they must dispose of men, as in an army, or of capital, as in a treasury. But the army, or police, or *posse comitatus,* is more or less All-of-us, and the capital in the treasury is the product of the labor and saving of All-of-us. Therefore, when the State means power-to-do it means All-of-us, as brute force or as industrial force.

If anybody is to benefit from the action of the State it must be Some-of-us. If, then, the question is raised, What ought the State to do for labor, for trade, for manufactures, for the poor, for the learned professions? etc., etc.—that is, for a class or an interest—it is really the question, What ought All-of-us to do for Some-of-us? But Some-of-us are included in All-of-us, and, so far as they get the benefit of their own efforts, it is the same as if they worked for themselves, and they may be cancelled out of All-of-us. Then the question which remains is, What ought Some-of-us to do for Others-of-us? or, What do social classes owe to each other?

I now propose to try to find out whether there is any class in society which lies under the duty and burden of fighting the battles of life for any other class, or of solving social problems for the satisfaction of any other class; also, whether there is any class which has the right to formulate demands on "society"—that is, on other classes; also, whether there is anything but a fallacy and a superstition in the notion that "the State" owes anything to anybody except peace, order, and the guarantees of rights. . . .

. . . The notion of civil liberty which we have inherited is that of *a status created for the individual by laws and institutions, the effect of which is that each man is guaranteed the use of all his own powers exclusively for his own welfare.* It is not at all a matter of elections, or universal suffrage, or democracy. All institutions are to be tested by the degree to which they guarantee liberty. It is not to be admitted for a moment that liberty is a means to social ends, and that it may be impaired for major considerations. Any one who so argues has lost the bearing and relation of all the facts and factors in a free state. A human being has a life to live, a career to run. He is a centre of powers to work, and of capacities to suffer. What his powers may be—whether they can carry him far or not; what his chances may be, whether wide or restricted; what his fortune may be, whether to suffer much or little—are questions of his personal destiny which he must work out and endure as he can; but for all that concerns the bearing of the society and its institutions upon that man, and upon the sum of happiness to which he can attain during his life on earth, the product of all history and all philosophy up to this time is summed up in the doctrine, that he should be left free to do the most for himself that he can, and should be guaranteed the exclusive enjoyment of all that he does. If the society—that is to say, in plain terms, if his fellow-men, either individually, by groups, or in a mass —impinge upon him otherwise than to surround him with neutral conditions of security, they must do so under the strictest responsibility to justify themselves. Jealousy and prejudice against all such interferences are high political virtues in a free man. It is not at all the function of the State to make men happy. They must make themselves happy in their own way, and at their own risk. The functions of the State lie entirely in the conditions or chances under which the pursuit of happiness is carried on, so far as those conditions or chances can be affected by civil organization. Hence, liberty for labor and security for earnings are the ends for which civil institutions exist, not means

which may be employed for ulterior ends.

Now, the cardinal doctrine of any sound political system is, that rights and duties should be in equilibrium. A monarchical or aristocratic system is not immoral, if the rights and duties of persons and classes are in equilibrium, although the rights and duties of different persons and classes are unequal. An immoral political system is created whenever there are privileged classes—that is, classes who have arrogated to themselves rights while throwing the duties upon others. In a democracy all have equal political rights. That is the fundamental political principle. A democracy, then, becomes immoral, if all have not equal political duties. This is unquestionably the doctrine which needs to be reiterated and inculcated beyond all others, if the democracy is to be made sound and permanent. Our orators and writers never speak of it, and do not seem often to know anything about it; but the real danger of democracy is, that the classes which have the power under it will assume all the rights and reject all the duties—that is, that they will use the political power to plunder those-who-have. Democracy, in order to be true to itself, and to develop into a sound working system, must oppose the same cold resistance to any claims for favor on the ground of poverty, as on the ground of birth and rank. It can no more admit to public discussion, as within the range of possible action, any schemes for coddling and helping wage-receivers than it could entertain schemes of restricting political power to wage-payers. It must put down schemes for making "the rich" pay for whatever "the poor" want, just as it tramples on the old theories that only the rich are fit to regulate society. One needs but to watch our periodical literature to see the danger that democracy will be construed as a system of favoring a new privileged class of the many and the poor.

Holding in mind, now, the notions of liberty and democracy as we have defined them, we see that it is not altogether a matter of fanfaronade when the American citizen calls himself a "sovereign." A member of a free democracy is, in a sense, a sovereign. He has no superior. He has reached his sovereignty, however, by a process of reduction and division of power which leaves him no inferior. It is very grand to call one's self a sovereign, but it is greatly to the purpose to notice that the political responsibilities of the free man have been intensified and aggregated just in proportion as political rights have been reduced and divided. Many monarchs have been incapable of sovereignty and unfit for it. Placed in exalted situations, and inheritors of grand opportunities, they have exhibited only their own imbecility and vice. The reason was, because they thought only of the gratification of their own vanity, and not at all of their duty. The free man who steps forward to claim his inheritance and endowment as a free and equal member of a great civil body must understand that his duties and responsibilities are measured to him by the same scale as his rights and his powers. He wants to be subject to no man. He wants to be equal to his fellows, as all sovereigns are equal. So be it; but he cannot escape the deduction that he can call no man to his aid. The other sovereigns will not respect his independence if he becomes dependent, and they cannot respect his equality if he sues for favors. The free man in a free democracy, when he cut off all the ties which might pull him down, severed also all the ties by which he might have made others pull him up. He must take all the consequences of his new status. He is, in a certain sense, an isolated man. The family tie does not bring to him disgrace for the misdeeds of his relatives, as it once would have done, but neither does it furnish him with the support which it once would have given. The relations of men are open and free, but they are also loose. A free man in a free democracy derogates from his rank if he

takes a favor for which he does not render an equivalent.

A free man in a free democracy has no duty whatever toward other men of the same rank and standing, except respect, courtesy, and good-will. We cannot say that there are no classes, when we are speaking politically, and then say that there are classes, when we are telling A what it is his duty to do for B. In a free state every man is held and expected to take care of himself and his family, to make no trouble for his neighbor, and to contribute his full share to public interests and common necessities. If he fails in this he throws burdens on others. He does not thereby acquire rights against the others. On the contrary, he only accumulates obligations toward them; and if he is allowed to make his deficiencies a ground of new claims, he passes over into the position of a privileged or petted person— emancipated from duties, endowed with claims. This is the inevitable result of combining democratic political theories with humanitarian social theories. It would be aside from my present purpose to show . . . that one result of such inconsistency must surely be to undermine democracy, to increase the power of wealth in the democracy, and to hasten the subjection of democracy to plutocracy; for a man who accepts any share which he has not earned in another man's capital cannot be an independent citizen. . . .

We have now seen that the current discussions about the claims and rights of social classes on each other are radically erroneous and fallacious, and we have seen that an analysis of the general obligations which we all have to each other leads us to nothing but an emphatic repetition of old but well-acknowledged obligations to perfect our political institutions. We have been led to restriction, not extension, of the functions of the State, but we have also been led to see the necessity of purifying and perfecting the operation of the State in the functions which properly belong to it. If we refuse to recognize any classes as existing in society when, perhaps, a claim might be set up that the wealthy, educated, and virtuous have acquired special rights and precedence, we certainly cannot recognize any classes when it is attempted to establish such distinctions for the sake of imposing burdens and duties on one group for the benefit of others. The men who have not done their duty in this world never can be equal to those who have done their duty more or less well. If words like wise and foolish, thrifty and extravagant, prudent and negligent, have any meaning in language, then it must make some difference how people behave in this world, and the difference will appear in the position they acquire in the body of society, and in relation to the chances of life. They may, then, be classified in reference to these facts. Such classes always will exist; no other social distinctions can endure. If, then, we look to the origin and definition of these classes, we shall find it impossible to deduce any obligations which one of them bears to the other. The class distinctions simply result from the different degrees of success with which men have availed themselves of the chances which were presented to them. Instead of endeavoring to redistribute the acquisitions which have been made between the existing classes, our aim should be to *increase, multiply, and extend the chances.* Such is the work of civilization. Every old error or abuse which is removed opens new chances of development to all the new energy of society. Every improvement in education, science, art, or government expands the chances of man on earth. Such expansion is no guarantee of equality. On the contrary, if there be liberty, some will profit by the chances eagerly and some will neglect them altogether. Therefore, the greater the chances the more unequal will be the

fortune of these two sets of men. So it ought to be, in all justice and right reason. The yearning after equality is the offspring of envy and covetousness, and there is no possible plan for satisfying that yearning which can do aught else than rob A to give to B; consequently all such plans nourish some of the meanest vices of human nature, waste capital, and overthrow civilization. But if we can expand the chances we can count on a general and steady growth of civilization and advancement of society by and through its best members. In the prosecution of these chances we all owe to each other goodwill, mutual respect, and mutual guarantees of liberty and security. Beyond this nothing can be affirmed as a duty of one group to another in a free state.

## THE CHALLENGE OF POVERTY

### 7

While the fortunate few defended the gospel of wealth, the mass of the American people either experienced the comforts of middle-class living or felt the lash of poverty. Millions in the latter group had little reason to bless the economic conditions under which they existed. Crowded into city slums, eking out a mere living by long hours of labor in sweatshop or factory, they had every reason to question the national boast that America was the land of opportunity. Two forces derived from the revolutions in economics were responsible: the impersonality of human relations in the machine age, and the rise of the city. Edward A. Ross, a sociologist whose humanitarian interests elevated him to front rank among reformers, examined the first factor in his significant study of *Sin and Society:*[7]

Today the sacrifice of life incidental to quick success rarely calls for the actual spilling of blood. How decent are the pale

[7] Edward A. Ross, *Sin and Society* (1907), pp. 7, 9-19. Reprinted by permission of and arrangement with Houghton Mifflin Company, the authorized publishers.

slayings of the quack, the adulterator, and the purveyor of polluted water, compared with the red slayings of the vulgar bandit or assassin! Even if there is blood-letting, the long range, tentacular nature of modern homicide eliminates all personal collision. What an abyss between the knife-play of brawlers and the law-defying neglect to fence dangerous machinery in a mill, or to furnish cars with safety couplers! The providing of unsuspecting passengers with "cork" life-preservers secretly loaded with bars of iron to make up for their deficiency in weight of cork, is spiritually akin to the treachery of Joab, who, taking Amasa by the beard "to kiss him," smote Amasa "in the fifth rib." . . .

The stealings and slayings that lurk in the complexities of our social relations are not deeds of the dive, the dark alley, the lonely road, and the midnight hour. They require no nocturnal prowling with muffled step and bated breath, no weapon or offer of violence. Unlike the old-time villain, the latter-day malefactor does not wear a slouch hat and a comforter, breathe forth curses and an odor of gin, go about his nefarious work with clenched teeth and an evil scowl. In the supreme moment his lineaments are not distorted with rage, or lust, or malevolence. One misses the dramatic setting, the time-honored insignia of turpitude. Fagin and Bill Sykes and Simon Legree are vanishing types. Gamester, murderer, body-snatcher, and kidnapper may appeal to a Hogarth, but what challenge finds his pencil in the countenance of the boodler, the savings-bank wrecker, or the ballot-box stuffer? Among our criminals of greed, one begins to meet the "grand style" of the great criminals of ambition, Macbeth or Richard III. The modern high-power dealer of woe wears immaculate linen, carries a silk hat and a lighted cigar, sins with a calm countenance and a serene soul, leagues or months from the evil he causes. Upon his gentlemanly presence the eventual blood and tears do not obtrude themselves.

This is why good, kindly men let the wheels of commerce and of industry redden and redden, rather than pare or lose their dividend. This is why our railroads yearly injure one employee in twenty-six, and we look in vain for that promised "day of the Lord" that "will make a man more precious than fine gold." . . .

The covenant breaker, the suborned witness, the corrupt judge, the oppressor of the fatherless,—the old-fashioned sinner, in short,—knows his victim, must hearken, perhaps to bitter upbraidings. But the tropical belt of sin we are sweeping into is largely impersonal. Our iniquity is wireless, and we know not whose withers are wrung by it. The hurt passes into that vague mass, the "public," and is there lost to view. Hence it does not take a Borgia to knead "chalk and alum and plaster" into the loaf, seeing one cannot know just who will eat that loaf, or what gripe it will give him. The purveyor of spurious life-preservers need not be a Cain. The owner of rotten tenement houses, whose "pull" enables him to ignore the orders of the health department, foredooms babies, it is true, but for all that he is no Herod.

Often there are no victims. If the crazy hulk sent out for "just one more trip" meets with fair weather, all is well. If no fire breaks out in the theatre, the sham "emergency exits" are blameless. The corrupt inspector who O.K.'s low-grade kerosene is chancing it, that is all. Many sins, in fact, simply augment risk. Evil does not dog their footsteps with relentless and heart-shaking certainty. When the catastrophe does come, the sinner salves his conscience by blasphemously calling it an "accident" or an "act of God."

Still more impersonal is sin when the immediate harm touches beneficent institutions rather than individuals. . . . The blackguarding editor is really undermining the freedom of the press. The policy kings and saloon keepers, who get out to the polls the last vote of the vicious and criminal classes, are sapping manhood suffrage. Striking engineers who spitefully desert passenger trains in mid-career are jeopardizing the right of man to work only when he pleases. The real victim of a lynching mob is not the malefactor, but the law-abiding spirit. School-board grafters who blackmail applicants for a teacher's position are stabbing the free public school. The corrupt bosses and "combines" are murdering representative government. The perpetrators of election frauds unwittingly assail the institution of the ballot. Rarely, however, are such transgressions abominated as are offenses against persons.

Because of the special qualities of the Newer Unrighteousness, because these devastating latter-day wrongs, being comely of look, do not advertise their vileness, . . . it is possible for iniquity to flourish greatly, even while men are getting better. Briber and boodler and grafter are often "good men," judged by the old tests, and would have passed for virtuous in the American community of seventy years ago. Among the chiefest sinners are now enrolled men who are pure and kindhearted, loving in their families, faithful to their friends, and generous to the needy.

One might suppose that an exasperated public would sternly castigate these modern sins. But the fact is, the very qualities that lull the conscience of the sinner blind the eyes of the onlookers. People are sentimental, and bastinado wrongdoing not according to its harmfulness, but according to the infamy that has come to attach to it. Undiscerning, they chastise with scorpions the old authentic sins, but spare the new. They do not see that boodling is treason, that blackmail is piracy, that embezzlement is theft, that speculation is gambling, that tax-dodging is larceny, that railroad discrimination is treachery, that the factory labor of children is slavery, that deleterious adulteration is murder.

It has not come home to them that the fraudulent promoter "devours widows' houses," that the monopolist "grinds the faces of the poor," that mercenary editors and spellbinders "put bitter for sweet and sweet for bitter." The cloven hoof hides in patent leather; and today, as in Hosea's time, the people "are destroyed for lack of knowledge." The mob lynches the red-handed slayer, when it ought to keep a gallows Haman-high for the venal mine inspector, the seller of infected milk, the maintainer of a fire-trap theatre. The child-beater is forever blasted in reputation, but the exploiter of infant toil, or the concocter of a soothing syrup for the drugging of babies, stands a pillar of society. The petty shoplifter is more abhorred than the stealer of a franchise, and the wife-whipper is outcast long before the man who sends his over-insured ship to founder with its crew.

There is a special cause for the condoning of sins committed in the way of business and without personal malice. Business men, as a rule, insist upon a free hand in their dealings, and, since they are conspicuous and influential in the community, they carry with them a considerable part of the non-business world. The leisured, the non-industrial employees, the bulk of professional men, and many public servants, hold to the unmitigated maxim of *caveat emptor,* and accept the chicane of trade as reasonable and legitimate. In England till 1487 any one who knew how to read might commit murder with impunity by claiming "benefit of clergy." There is something like this in the way we have granted quack and fakir and mine operator and railroad company indulgence to commit manslaughter in the name of business.

On the other hand, the active producers, such as farmers and workingmen, think in terms of livelihood rather than of profit, and tend therefore to consider the social bearings of conduct. Intent on well-being rather than on pecuniary success, they are shocked at the lenient judgment of the commercial world. Although they have hitherto deferred to the traders, the producers are losing faith in business men's standards, and may yet pluck up the courage to validate their own ethics against the individualistic, anti-social ethics of commerce.

Still, even if the mass turns vehement, it is not certain the lash of its censure can reach the cuticle of the sinner. A differentiated society abounds in closed doors and curtained recesses. The murmurs of the alley do not penetrate to the boulevard. The shrieks from the blazing excursion steamer do not invade the distant yacht of her owners. If the curses of tricked depositors never rise to the circles of "high finance" that keep the conscience of the savings-bank wrecker, why should the popular hiss stay the commercial buccaneer? All turns on the power of the greater public to astringe the flaccid conscience of business men until they become stern judges of one another. If we have really entered upon the era of jangling classes, it is, of course, idle to hope for a truly public sentiment upon such matters. Nevertheless, in the past, antiseptic currents of opinion have mounted from the healthy base to the yellowing top of the social tree, and they may do so again.

While idealists are dipping their brushes into the sunset for colors bright enough to paint the Utopias that might be if society were quite made over, one may be pardoned for dreaming of what would be possible, even on the plane of existing institutions, if only in this highly articulated society of ours every one were required to act in good faith, and to do what he had deliberately led others to expect of him. . . .

## 8

Urban impersonality in the machine age accentuated the blight of poverty. Huddled together in congested masses, the slum dwellers not only were denied the light of day and

the beauties of nature but were subjected to dangers unknown in the rural past. John Spargo, a conscientious reformer, explained why the poverty of earlier times differed markedly from the poverty of his own day:[8]

An epidemic of measles spreads over the great city. Silently and mysteriously it enters and, unseen, touches a single child in the street or the school, and the result is as the touch of the blazing torch to dry stubble and straw; only it is not stubble but the nation's heart, its future citizenry, that is attacked. From child to child, home to home, street to street, the epidemic spreads; mansion and tenement are alike stricken, and the city is engaged in a fierce battle against the foe which assails its children. In the tenement districts doctors and nurses hurry through the sun-scorched streets and wearily climb the long flights of stairs hour after hour, day after day; in the districts where the rich live, doctors drive in their carriages to the mansions, and nurses tread noiselessly in and out of the sick rooms. Rich and poor alike struggle against the foe, but it is only in the homes of the poor that there is no hope . . . ; only there that the doctors can say no comforting words of assurance. When the battle is over and the victims are numbered, there is rejoicing in the mansion and bitter, poignant sorrow in the tenement. For poor children are practically the only ones ever to die from measles. Nature starts all her children equally, rich and poor, but the evil conditions of poverty create and foster vast inequalities of opportunity to live and flourish. . . .

The yearly loss of these priceless baby lives does not, however, represent the full measure of the awful cost of the poverty which surrounds the cradle. It is not only that 75,000 or 80,000 die, but that as many more of those who survive are irreparably weakened and injured. Not graves alone

---

[8] From John Spargo, *The Bitter Cry of the Children,* pp. 17-18, 23-24, 117-122. Copyright 1906 by The Macmillan Company. By permission of The Macmillan Company, publishers.

but hospitals and prisons are filled with the victims of childhood poverty. They who survive go to school, but are weak, nervous, dull, and backward in their studies. Discouraged, they become morose and defiant, and soon find their way into the "reformatories," for truancy or other juvenile delinquencies. Later they fill the prisons, for the ranks of the vagrant and the criminal are recruited from the truant and juvenile offender. Or if happily they do not become vicious, they fail in the struggle for existence, the relentless competition of the crowded labor mart, and sink into the abysmal depths of pauperism. Weakened and impaired by the privations of their early years, they cannot resist the attacks of disease. . . .

. . . the problem of poverty as it affects school children may be stated in a few lines. All the data available tend to show that not less than 2,000,000 children of school age in the United States are the victims of poverty which denies them common necessities, particularly adequate nourishment. As a result of this privation they are far inferior in physical development to their more fortunate fellows. This inferiority of physique, in turn, is responsible for much mental and moral degeneration. Such children are in very many cases incapable of successful mental effort, and much of our national expenditure for education is in consequence an absolute waste. With their enfeebled bodies and minds we turn these children adrift unfitted for the struggle of life, which tends to become keener with every advance in our industrial development, and because of their lack of physical and mental training they are found to be inefficient industrially and dangerous socially. They become dependent, paupers, and the procreators of a pauper and dependent race.

Here, then, is a problem of awful magnitude. In the richest country on earth hundreds of thousands of children are literally damned to lifelong, helpless, and debasing poverty. They are plunged in the earliest and most important years of character formation into that terrible maelstrom of poverty which casts so many thousands, ay, millions, of physical, mental, and moral wrecks upon the shores of our social life. For them there is little or no hope of escape from the blight and curse of pauperism unless the nation, pursuing a policy of enlightened self-interest and protection, decides to save them. In the main, this vast sum of poverty is due to causes of a purely impersonal nature which the victims cannot control, such as sickness, accident, low wages, and unemployment. Personal causes, such as ignorance, thriftlessness, gambling, intemperance, indolence, wife-desertion, and other vices or weaknesses, are also responsible for a good deal of poverty, though by no means most of it as is sometimes urged by superficial observers. There are many thousands of temperate and industrious workers who are miserably poor, and many of those who are thriftless or intemperate are the victims of poverty's degenerating influences. But whether a child's hunger and privation is due to some fault of its parents or to causes beyond their control, the fact of its suffering remains, and its impaired physical and mental strength tends almost irresistibly to make it inefficient as a citizen. Whatever the cause, therefore, of its privation, society must, as a measure of self-protection, take upon itself the responsibility of caring for the child.

There can be no compromise upon this vital point. Those who say that society should refuse to do anything for those children who are the victims of their parents' vices or weaknesses adopt a singularly indefensible attitude. In the first place it is barbarously unjust to allow the sins of the parents to bring punishment and suffering upon the child, to damn the innocent and unoffending. No more vicious doctrine than this, which so many excellent and well-intentioned persons are fond of preaching, has ever been formulated by human perversity. Carried to its logical end, it would destroy all legislation for the protection of children from cruel parents or guardians. It is strange that the doctrinaire advocates of this brutal gospel should overlook its practical consequences. If discrimination were to be made at all, it should be in favor of, rather than against, the children of drunken and profligate parents. For these children have a special claim upon society for protection from wrongs in the shape of influences injurious to their physical and moral well-being, and tending to lead them into evil and degrading ways. The half-starved child of the inebriate is not less entitled to the protection of society than the victim of inhuman physical torture. . . .

To the contention that society, having assumed the responsibility of insisting that every child shall be educated, and providing the means of education, is necessarily bound to assume the responsibility of seeing that they are made fit to receive that education, so far as possible, there does not seem to be any convincing answer. It will be objected that for society to do this would mean the destruction of the responsibility of the parents. That is obviously true. But it is equally true of education itself, the responsibility for which society has assumed. Some individualists there are who contend that society is wrong in doing this, and their opposition to the proposal that it should undertake to provide the children with food is far more logical than that of those who believe that society should assume the responsibility of educating the child, but not that of equipping it with the necessary physical basis for that education. The fact is that society insists upon the education of the children, not, primarily, in their interests nor in the interests of the parents, but in its own. All legislation upon child labor, education, child guardianship in general, is based upon a denial of proprietary rights to children by their parents. The child belongs to society rather than to its parents.

## 9

The impersonality and congestion of life in urban slums was notorious in New York City. Jam-packed in tenements in the poorer sections lived thousands of miserable souls whose poverty shocked even professional social workers. Slum conditions were the concern of numerous humanitarians, of whom Jacob Riis was outstanding. His description of the lower segments of society, *How the Other Half Lives,* did much to awaken Americans to the responsibilities of citizenship:[9]

. . . A map of the city, colored to designate nationalities, would show more stripes than on the skin of a zebra, and more colors than any rainbow. The city on such a map would fall into two great halves, green for the Irish prevailing in the West Side tenement districts, and blue for the Germans on the East Side. But intermingled with these ground colors would be an odd variety of tints that would give the whole the appearance of an extraordinary crazy-quilt. From down in the Sixth Ward, upon the site of the old Collect Pond that in the days of the fathers drained the hills which are no more, the red of the Italian would be seen forcing its way northward along the line of Mulberry Street to the quarter of the French purple on Bleecker Street and South Fifth Avenue, to lose itself and reappear, after a lapse of miles, in the "Little Italy" of Harlem, east of Second Avenue. Dashes of red, sharply defined, would be seen strung through the Annexed District, northward to the city line. On the West Side the red would be seen overrunning the old Africa of Thompson Street, pushing the black of the negro rapidly up-town, against querulous but unavailing protests, occupying his home, his church, his trade and all, with a merciless impartiality. There is a church in Mulberry Street that has stood for two generations as a sort of milestone of these

[9] Jacob A. Riis, *How the Other Half Lives* (1890), pp. 25-27, 43-44. Reprinted by permission of Charles Scribner's Sons, publishers.

migrations. Built originally for the worship of staid New Yorkers of the "old stock," it was engulfed by the colored tide, when the draft-riots drove the negroes out of reach of Cherry Street and the Five Points. Within the past decade the advance wave of the Italian onset reached it, and today the arms of United Italy adorn its front. The negroes have made a stand at several points along Seventh and Eighth Avenues; but their main body, still pursued by the Italian foe, is on the march yet, and the black mark will be found overshadowing today many blocks on the East Side, with One Hundredth Street as the centre, where colonies of them have settled recently.

Hardly less aggressive than the Italian, the Russian and Polish Jew, having overrun the district between Rivington and Division Streets, east of the Bowery, to the point of suffocation, is filling the tenements of the old Seventh Ward to the river front, and disputing with the Italian every foot of available space in the back alleys of Mulberry Street. The two races, differing hopelessly in much, have this in common: they carry their slums with them wherever they go, if allowed to do it. Little Italy already rivals its parent, the "Bend," in foulness. Other nationalities that begin at the bottom make a fresh start when crowded up the ladder. Happily both are manageable, the one by rabbinical, the other by the civil law. Between the dull gray of the Jew, his favorite color, and the Italian red, would be seen squeezed in on the map a sharp streak of yellow, marking the narrow boundaries of Chinatown. Dovetailed in with the German population, the poor but thrifty Bohemian might be picked out by the sombre hue of his life as of his philosophy, struggling against heavy odds in the big human bee-hives of the East Side. Colonies of his people extend northward, with long lapses of space, from below the Cooper Institute more than three miles. The Bohemian is the only foreigner with any considerable representation in the city who counts no wealthy man of his race, none who has not to work hard for a living, or has got beyond the reach of the tenement.

Down near the Battery the West Side emerald would be soiled by a dirty stain, spreading rapidly like a splash of ink on a sheet of blotting paper, headquarters of the Arab tribe, that in a single year has swelled from the original dozen to twelve hundred, intent, every mother's son, on trade and barter. Dots and dashes of color here and there would show where the Finnish sailors worship their djumala (God), the Greek pedlars the ancient name of their race, and the Swiss the goddess of thrift. And so on to the end of the long register, all toiling together in the galling fetters of the tenement. Were the question raised who makes the most of life thus mortgaged, who resists most stubbornly its levelling tendency—knows how to drag even the barracks upward a part of the way at least toward the ideal plane of the home—the palm must be unhesitatingly awarded the Teuton. The Italian and the poor Jew rise only by compulsion. The Chinaman does not rise at all; here, as at home, he simply remains stationary. The Irishman's genius runs to public affairs rather than domestic life; wherever he is mustered in force the saloon is the gorgeous centre of political activity. The German struggles vainly to learn his trick; his Teutonic wit is too heavy, and the political ladder he raises from his saloon usually too short or too clumsy to reach the desired goal. The best part of his life is lived at home, and he makes himself a home independent of the surroundings, giving the lie to the saying, unhappily become a maxim of social truth, that pauperism and drunkenness naturally grow in the tenements. He makes the most of his tenement, and it should be added that whenever and as soon as he can save up money enough, he gets out and never crosses the threshold of one again. . . ,

. . . Suppose we look into one? No.—
Cherry Street. Be a little careful, please!
The hall is dark and you might stumble
over the children pitching pennies back
there. Not that it would hurt them; kicks
and cuffs are their daily diet. They have
little else. Here where the hall turns and
dives into utter darkness is a step, and
another, and another. A flight of stairs.
You can feel your way, if you cannot see
it. Close? Yes! What would you have?
All the fresh air that ever enters these
stairs comes from the hall-door that is
forever slamming, and from the windows
of dark bedrooms that in turn receive
from the stairs their sole supply of the
elements God meant to be free, but man
deals out with such niggardly hand. That
was a woman filling her pail by the hy-
drant you just bumped against. The sinks
are in the hallway, that all the tenants
may have access—and all be poisoned alike
by their summer stenches. Hear the pump
squeak! It is the lullaby of tenement house
babies. In summer, when a thousand
thirsty throats pant for a cooling drink
in this block, it is worked in vain. But the
saloon, whose open door you passed in the
hall, is always there. The smell of it has
followed you up. Here is a door. Listen!
That short hacking cough, that tiny helpless wail—what do they mean? They
mean that the soiled bow of white you
saw on the door downstairs will have
another story to tell—Oh! a sadly familiar
story—before the day is at an end. The
child is dying with measles. With half a
chance it might have lived; but it had
none. That dark bedroom killed it.

"It was took all of a suddint," says the
mother, smoothing the throbbing little body
with trembling hands. There is no unkindness in the rough voice of the man in the
jumper, who sits by the window grimly
smoking a clay pipe, with the little life
ebbing out in his sight, bitter as his words
sound: "Hush, Mary! If we cannot keep
the baby, need we complain—such as we?"

Such as we! What if the words ring
in your ears as we grope our way up the
stairs and down from floor to floor, listening to the sounds behind the closed doors
—some of quarrelling, some of coarse
songs, more of profanity. They are true.
When the summer heats come with their
suffering they have meaning more terrible than words can tell. Come over here.
Step carefully over this baby—it is a baby,
spite of its rags and dirt—under these
iron bridges called fire-escapes, but loaded
down, despite the incessant watchfulness
of the firemen, with broken household
goods, with wash-tubs and barrels, over
which no man could climb from a fire.
This gap between dingy brick-walls is the
yard. That strip of smoke-colored sky up
there is the heaven of these people. Do
you wonder the name does not attract
them to the churches? That baby's parents
live in the rear tenement here. She is at
least as clean as the steps we are now
climbing. There are plenty of houses with
half a hundred such in. The tenement is
much like the one in front we just left,
only fouler, closer, darker—we will not
say more cheerless. The word is a mockery. A hundred thousand people lived in
rear tenements in New York last year. . . .

## 10

The slum conditions described by Jacob
Riis endured as much because of popular indifference as because Americans were devoted
to the dialectics of laissez faire. The ideology
of unrestrained competition among individuals—if not among corporations—was particularly entrenched in the courts. This judicial
attitude was illustrated in the case of *In re
Jacobs* (1885), when the New York State
Court of Appeals was asked to pass on the
constitutionality of a state law forbidding the
manufacture of cigars in tenement houses.
Initiated as a test by Samuel Gompers, the
labor leader, it convinced Governor Theodore
Roosevelt that judges "knew nothing whatever of the needs, or the life and labor, of
three-fourths of their fellow citizens in great
cities":[10]

[10] *Reports of Cases*, Court of Appeals, State of
New York, 98 SICKELS 110-115.

. . . Generally it is for the legislature to determine what laws and regulations are needed to protect the public health and secure the public comfort and safety, and while its measures are calculated, intended, convenient and appropriate to accomplish these ends, the exercise of its discretion is not subject to review by the courts. But they must have some relation to these ends. Under the mere guise of police regulations, personal rights and private property cannot arbitrarily be invaded, and the determination of the legislature is not final or conclusive. If it passes an Act ostensibly for the public health, and thereby destroys or takes away the property of a citizen, or interferes with his personal liberty, then it is for the courts to scrutinize the Act and see whether it really relates to and is convenient and appropriate to promote the public health. It matters not that the legislature may in the title to the Act, or in its body, declare that it is intended for the improvement of the public health. . . .

. . . What possible relation to the health of the occupants of a large tenement-house could cigar-making in one of its remote rooms have? If the legislature had in mind the protection of the occupants of the tenement houses, why was the Act confined in its operation to the two cities only? It is plain that this is not a health law, and that it has no relation whatever to the public health . . . Such legislation may invade one class of rights to-day and another to-morrow, and if it can be sanctioned under the Constitution, while far removed in time we will not be far away in practical statesmanship from those ages when governmental prefects supervised the building of houses, the rearing of cattle, the sowing of seed and the reaping of grain, and governmental ordinances regulated the movements and labor of artisans, the rate of wages, the price of food, the diet and clothing of the people, and a large range of other affairs long since in all civilized lands regarded as outside of governmental functions. Such governmental interferences disturb the normal adjustments of the social fabric, and usually derange the delicate and complicated machinery of industry and cause a score of ills while attempting the removal of one.

When a health law is challenged in the courts as unconstitutional on the ground that it arbitrarily interferes with personal liberty and private property without due process of law, the courts must be able to see that it has at least in fact some relation to the public health, that the public health is the end actually aimed at, and that it is appropriate and adapted to that end. This we have not been able to see in this law, and we must, therefore, pronounce it unconstitutional and void.

## 11

As the people of the United States seemed to be dividing into two antagonistic classes, some foreign observers professed to see the end of the democratic experiment. The cleavages in society, growing ever wider, might produce the seeds of revolution, ultimately reducing the nation to anarchy. Such a gloomy prediction was made by Thomas Babington Macaulay, the English statesman and historian:[11]

. . . I heartily wish you a good deliverance. But my reason and my wishes are at war, and I cannot help foreboding the worst. It is quite plain that your government will never be able to restrain a distressed and discontented majority. For, with you, the majority is the government, and has the rich, who are always in a minority, absolutely at its mercy. The day will come when, in the State of New York, a multitude of people, none of whom has had more than half a breakfast, or expects to have more than half a dinner, will choose a Legislature. Is it possible to doubt what sort of a Legislature will be chosen? On one side is a statesman

[11] *Harper's New Monthly Magazine,* LIV (February, 1877), 461.

preaching patience, respect for vested rights, strict observance of public faith. On the other is a demagogue, ranting about the tyranny of capitalists and usurers, and asking why anybody should be permitted to drink Champagne and to ride in a carriage while thousands of honest folks are in want of necessaries. Which of the two candidates is likely to be preferred by a work-man who hears his children cry for more bread? I seriously apprehend that you will, in some such season of adversity as I have described, do things which will prevent prosperity from returning; that you will act like people who should, in a year of scarcity, devour all the seed-corn, and thus make the next a year not of scarcity, but of absolute famine. There will be, I fear, spoliation. The spoliation will increase the distress. The distress will produce fresh spoliation. There is nothing to stop you. Your Constitution is all sail and no anchor. As I said before, when a society has entered on this downward progress, either civilization or liberty must perish. Either some Caesar or Napoleon will seize the reins of government with a strong hand, or your republic will be as fearfully plundered and laid waste by barbarians in the twentieth century as the Roman Empire was in the fifth. . . .

## THE POVERTY OF PROGRESS

### 12

Some Americans were no less apprehensive. Sincere believers in democracy, they were fearful lest growing class divisions destroy the economic equalitarianism upon which political freedom rested. Only positive governmental action could stay the trend. Theorists, however, failed to agree on specific plans; each had his own panacea for economic peace. Henry Demarest Lloyd was particularly influential, and his *Wealth against Commonwealth* (1886) was a classic of courage and acumen. If economic opportunity was the correlate of democracy, he argued, the growth

of corporations had all but wiped out th one and made a mockery of the other:[12]

Nature is rich; but everywhere man, the heir of nature, is poor. Never in this happy country or elsewhere—except in the Land of Miracle, where "they did all eat and were filled"—has there been enough o anything for the people. Never since time began have all the sons and daughters of men been all warm, and all filled, and all shod and roofed. Never yet have all the virgins, wise or foolish, been able to fill their lamps with oil.

The world, enriched by thousands of generations of toilers and thinkers, has reached a fertility which can give every human being a plenty undreamed of even in the Utopias. But between this plenty ripening on the boughs of our civilization and the people hungering for it step the "cornerers," the syndicates, trusts, combinations, with the cry of "over-production"—too much of everything. Holding back the riches of earth, sea, and sky from their fellows who famish and freeze in the dark, they declare to them that there is too much light and warmth and food. They assert the right, for their private profit, to regulate the consumption by the people of the necessaries of life, and to control production, not by the needs of humanity, but by the desires of a few for dividends. The coal syndicate thinks there is too much coal. There is too much iron, too much lumber, too much flour—for this or that syndicate.

The majority have never been able to buy enough of anything; but this minority have too much of everything to sell.

Liberty produces wealth, and wealth destroys liberty. "The splendid empire of Charles V.," says Motley, "was erected upon the grave of liberty." Our bignesses,

[12] *Wealth against Commonwealth*, by Henry Demarest Lloyd, pp. 1-7. Copyright, 1894, by Henry Demarest Lloyd. Copyright, 1922, by William Bross Lloyd. Reprinted by permission of Harper & Brothers.

ities, factories, monopolies, fortunes, which are our empires, are the obesities of an age gluttonous beyond its powers of digestion. Mankind are crowding upon each other in the centres, and struggling to keep each other out of the feast set by the new sciences and the new fellowships. Our size has got beyond both our science and our conscience. The vision of the railroad stockholder is not far-sighted enough to see into the office of the General Manager; the people cannot reach across even a ward of a city to rule their rulers; Captains of Industry "do not know" whether the men in the ranks are dying from lack of food and shelter; we cannot clean our cities nor our politics; the locomotive has more manpower than all the ballot-boxes, and mill-wheels wear out the hearts of workers unable to keep up beating time to their whirl. If mankind had gone on pursuing the ideals of the fighter, the time would necessarily have come when there would have been only a few, then only one, and then none left. This is what we are witnessing in the world of livelihoods. Our ideals of livelihood are ideals of mutual deglutition. We are rapidly reaching the stage where in each province only a few are left; that is the key to our times. Beyond the deep is another deep. This era is but a passing phase in the evolution of industrial Cæsars, and these Cæsars will be of a new type—corporate Cæsars.

For those who like the perpetual motion of a debate in which neither of the disputants is looking at the same side of the shield, there are infinite satisfactions in the current controversy as to whether there is any such thing as "monopoly." "There are none," says one side. "They are legion," says the other. "The idea that there can be such a thing is absurd," says one, who with half a dozen associates controls the source, the price, the quality, the quantity of nine-tenths of a great necessary of life. But "There will soon be a trust for every production, and a master to fix the price for every necessity of life," said the Senator who framed the United States Anti-Trust Law. This difference as to facts is due to a difference in the definitions through which the facts are regarded. Those who say "there are none" hold with the Attorney-General of the United States and the decision he quotes from the highest Federal court which has yet passed on this question that no one has a monopoly unless there is a "disability" or "restriction" imposed by law on all who would compete. A syndicate that had succeeded in bottling for sale all the air of the earth would not have a monopoly in this view, unless there were on the statute-books a law forbidding every one else from selling air. No others could get air to sell; the people could not get air to breathe, but there would be no monopoly because there is no "legal restriction" on breathing or selling the atmosphere.

Excepting in the manufacture of postage-stamps, gold dollars, and a few other such cases of a "legal restriction," there are no monopolies according to this definition. It excludes the whole body of facts which the people include in their definition, and dismisses a great public question by a mere play on words. The other side of the shield was described by Judge Barrett, of the Supreme Court of New York. A monopoly he declared to be "any combination the tendency of which is to prevent competition in its broad and general sense, and to control and thus at will enhance prices to the detriment of the public. . . . Nor need it be permanent or complete. It is enough that it may be even temporarily and partially successful. The question in the end is, Does it inevitably tend to public injury?"

Those who insist that "there are none" are the fortunate ones who came up to the shield on its golden side. But common usage agrees with the language of Judge Barrett, because it exactly fits a fact which presses on common people heavily, and will grow heavier before it grows lighter. The committee of Congress investigating trusts in 1889 did not report any list of these combinations to control markets, "for the reason that new ones are constantly forming, and that old ones are constantly extending their relations so as to cover new branches of the business and invade new territories."

It is true that such a list, like a dictionary, would begin to be wrong the moment it began to appear. But though only an instantaneous photograph of the whirlwind, it would give an idea, to be gained in no other way, of a movement shadowing two hemispheres. In an incredible number of the necessaries and luxuries of life, from meat to tombstones, some inner circle of the "fittest" has sought, and very often obtained, the sweet power which Judge Barrett found the sugar trust had: It "can close every refinery at will, close some and open others, limit the purchases of raw material (thus jeopardizing, and in a considerable degree controlling, its production), artificially limit the production of refined sugar, enhance the price to enrich themselves and their associates at the public expense, and depress the price when necessary to crush out and impoverish a foolhardy rival."

Corners are "acute" attacks of that which combinations exhibit as chronic. First a corner, then a pool, then a trust, has often been the genesis. The last stage, when the trust throws off the forms of combination and returns to the simpler dress of corporations, is already well along. Some of the "sympathetical co-operations" on record have no doubt ceased to exist. But that they should have been attempted is one of the signs of the time, and these attempts are repeated again and again until success is reached. . . .

Laws against these combinations have been passed by Congress and by many of the States. There have been prosecutions under them by the State and Federal governments. The laws and the lawsuits have alike been futile.

In a few cases names and form of or-

ganization have been changed, in consequence of legal pursuit. The whiskey, sugar, and oil trusts had to hang out new signs. But the thing itself, the will and the power to control markets, livelihoods and liberties, and the toleration of this by the public—this remains unimpaired; in truth, facilitated by the greater secrecy and compactness which have been the only results of the appeal to law. . . .

What we call Monopoly is Business at the end of its journey. The concentration of wealth, the wiping out of the middle classes, are other names for it. To get it is in the world of affairs, the chief end of man.

There are no solitary truths, Goethe says, and monopoly—as the greatest business fact of our civilization, which gives to business what other ages gave to war and religion—is our greatest social, political, and moral fact.

The men and women who do the work of the world have the right to the floor. Everywhere they are rising to "a point of information." They want to know how our labor and the gifts of nature are being ordered by those whom our ideals and consent have made Captains of Industry over us; how it is that we, who profess the religion of the Golden Rule and the political economy of service for service, come to divide our produce into incalculable power and pleasure for a few, and partial existence for the many who are the fountains of these powers and pleasures. This book is an attempt to help the people answer these questions. It has been quarried out of official records, and it is a venture in realism in the world of realities. Decisions of courts and of special tribunals like the Interstate Commerce Commission, verdicts of juries in civil and criminal cases, reports of committees of the State Legislatures and of Congress, oath-sworn testimony given in legal proceedings and in official inquiries, corrected by rebutting testimony and by cross-examination—such are the sources of information.

## 13

If the activity of Henry Demarest Lloyd was arresting, the work of Henry George was devastating. His classic indictment of society, *Progress and Poverty* (1879), was a product of tremendous research and enjoyed such popularity that two million copies were sold before 1905. George advocated a single tax on land as a principal weapon of social reform, an idea which still influences countless Americans:[13]

And, unpleasant as it may be to admit it, it is at last becoming evident that the enormous increase in productive power which has marked the present century and is still going on with accelerating ratio, has no tendency to extirpate poverty or to lighten the burdens of those compelled to toil. It simply widens the gulf between Dives and Lazarus, and makes the struggle for existence more intense. The march of invention has clothed mankind with powers of which a century ago the boldest imagination could not have dreamed. But in factories where labor-saving machinery has reached its most wonderful development, little children are at work; wherever the new forces are anything like fully utilized, large classes are maintained by charity or live on the verge of recourse to it; amid the greatest accumulations of wealth, men die of starvation, and puny infants suckle dry breasts; while everywhere the greed of gain, the worship of wealth, shows the force of the fear of want. The promised land flies before us like the mirage. The fruits of the tree of knowledge turn as we grasp them to apples of Sodom that crumble at the touch.

It is true that wealth has been greatly increased, and that the average of comfort, leisure and refinement has been raised; but these gains are not general. In them the lowest class do not share. I do not mean that the condition of the lowest class has nowhere nor in anything been improved; but that there is nowhere any improvement which can be credited to increased productive power. I mean that the tendency of what we call material progress is in nowise to improve the condition of the lowest class in the essentials of healthy, happy human life. Nay, more, that it is still further to depress the condition of the lowest class. The new forces, elevating in their nature though they be, do not act upon the social fabric from underneath, as was for a long time hoped and believed, but strike it at a point intermediate between top and bottom. It is as though an immense wedge were being forced, not underneath society, but through society. Those who are above the point of separation are elevated, but those who are below are crushed down.

This depressing effect is not generally realized, for it is not apparent where there has long existed a class just able to live. Where the lowest class barely lives, as has been the case for a long time in many parts of Europe, it is impossible for it to get any lower, for the next lowest step is out of existence, and no tendency to further depression can readily show itself. But in the progress of new settlements to the conditions of older communities it may clearly be seen that material progress does not merely fail to relieve poverty— it actually produces it. In the United States it is clear that squalor and misery, and the vices and crimes that spring from them, everywhere increase as the village grows to the city, and the march of development brings the advantages of the improved methods of production and exchange. It is in the older and richer sections of the Union that pauperism and distress among the working classes are becoming most painfully apparent. If there is less deep poverty in San Francisco than in New York, is it not because San Francisco is yet behind New York in all that both cities are striving for? When San Francisco reaches the point where New York now is, who can doubt that

---

[13] Henry George, *Progress and Poverty* (New York, 1916), pp. 8-11, 531-532, 539-540.

there will also be ragged and barefoot children on her streets?

This association of poverty with progress is the great enigma of our times. It is the central fact from which spring industrial, social and political difficulties that perplex the world, and with which statesmanship and philanthropy and education grapple in vain. From it come the clouds which overhang the future of the most progressive and self-reliant nations. It is the riddle which the Sphinx of Fate puts to our civilization, and which not to answer is to be destroyed. So long as all the increased wealth which modern progress brings goes but to build up great fortunes, to increase luxury and make sharper the contrast between the House of Have and the House of Want, progress is not real and cannot be permanent. The reaction must come. The tower leans from its foundations, and every new story but hastens the final catastrophe. To educate men who must be condemned to poverty, is but to make them restive; to base on a state of most glaring social inequality political institutions under which men are theoretically equal, is to stand a pyramid on its apex.

All-important as this question is, pressing itself from every quarter painfully upon attention, it has not yet received a solution which accounts for all the facts and points to any clear and simple remedy. This is shown by the widely varying attempts to account for the prevailing depression. They exhibit not merely a divergence between vulgar notions and scientific theories, but also show that the concurrence which should exist between those who avow the same general theories breaks up upon practical questions into an anarchy of opinion. Upon high economic authority we have been told that the prevailing depression is due to over-consumption; upon equally high authority, that it is due to over-production; while the wastes of war, the extension of railroads, the attempts of workmen to keep up

wages, the demonetization of silver, the issues of paper money, the increase labor-saving machinery, the opening shorter avenues to trade, etc., are separately pointed out as the cause. . . .

And while professors thus disagree, the ideas that there is a necessary conflict between capital and labor, that machinery is an evil, that competition must be restrained and interest abolished, that wealth may be created by the issue of money, that it is the duty of government to furnish capital or furnish work, are rapidly making way among the great body of the people, who keenly feel a hurt and are sharply conscious of a wrong. Such ideas, which bring great masses of men, the repositories of ultimate political power, under the leadership of charlatans and demagogues, are fraught with danger; but they cannot be successfully combated until political economy shall give some answer to the great question which shall be consistent with all her teachings, and which shall commend itself to the perceptions of the great masses of men.

It must be within the province of political economy to give such an answer. For political economy is not a set of dogmas. It is the explanation of a certain set of facts. It is the science which, in the sequence of certain phenomena, seeks to trace mutual relations and to identify cause and effect, just as the physical sciences seek to do in other sets of phenomena. . . .

In theory we are intense democrats. The proposal to sacrifice swine in the temple would hardly have excited greater horror and indignation in Jerusalem of old than would among us that of conferring a distinction of rank upon our most eminent citizen. But is there not growing up among us a class who have all the power without any of the virtues of aristocracy? We have simple citizens who control thousands of miles of railroad, millions of acres of land, the means of livelihood of great numbers of men; who name the Governors of sovereign States as they name their clerks, choose Senators as they choose attorneys, and whose will is as supreme with Legislatures as that of a French King sitting in bed of justice. The undercurrents of the times seem to sweep us back again to the old conditions from which we dreamed we had escaped. The development of the artisan and commercial classes gradually broke down feudalism after it had become so complete that men thought of heaven as organized on a feudal basis, and ranked the first and second persons of the Trinity as suzerain and tenant-in-chief. But now the development of manufactures and exchange, acting in a social organization in which land is made private property, threatens to compel every worker to seek a master, as the insecurity which followed the final break-up of the Roman Empire compelled every freeman to seek a lord. Nothing seems exempt from this tendency. Industry everywhere tends to assume a form in which one is master and many serve. And when one is master and the others serve, the one will control the others, even in such matters as votes. Just as the English landlord votes his tenants, so does the New England mill owner vote his operatives.

There is no mistaking it—the very foundations of society are being sapped before our eyes, while we ask, *how* is it possible that such a civilization as this, with its railroads, and daily newspapers, and electric telegraphs, should ever be destroyed? While literature breathes but the belief that we have been, are, and for the future must be, leaving the savage state further and further behind us, there are indications that we are actually turning back again toward barbarism. . . .

But there are evidences far more palpable than any that can be given by statistics, of tendencies to the ebb of civilization. There is a vague but general feeling of disappointment; an increased bitterness among the working classes; a widespread feeling of unrest and brooding revolution. If this were accompanied by a definite idea of how relief is to be obtained, it would be a hopeful sign; but it is not. Though the schoolmaster has been abroad some time, the general power of tracing effect to cause does not seem a whit improved. The reaction toward protectionism, as the reaction toward other exploded fallacies of government, shows this. And even the philosophic freethinker cannot look upon that vast change in religious ideas that is now sweeping over the civilized world without feeling that this tremendous fact may have most momentous relations which only the future can develop. For what is going on is not a change in the form of religion, but the negation and destruction of the ideas from which religion springs. Christianity is not simply clearing itself of superstitions, but in the popular mind it is dying at the root, as the old paganisms were dying when Christianity entered the world. And nothing arises to take its place. The fundamental ideas of an intelligent Creator and of a future life are in the general mind rapidly weakening. Now, whether this may or may not be in itself an advance, the importance of the part which religion has played in the world's history shows the importance of the change that is now going on. Unless human nature has suddenly altered in what the universal history of the race shows to be its deepest characteristics, the mightiest actions and reactions are thus preparing. Such stages of thought have heretofore always marked periods of transition. On a smaller scale and to a less depth (for I think any one who will notice the drift of our literature, and talk upon such subjects with the men he meets, will see that it is sub-soil and not surface plowing that materialistic ideas are now doing), such a state of thought preceded the French Revolution. But the closest parallel to the wreck of religious ideas now going on is to be found in that period in which ancient civilization began to pass from splendor to decline. What change may come, no mortal man can tell, but that some great change *must* come, thoughtful men begin to feel. The civilized world is trembling on the verge of a great movement. Either it must be a leap upward, which will open the way to advances yet undreamed of, or it must be a plunge downward which will carry us back toward barbarism.

## 14

Edward Bellamy was the third member of a triumvirate of great reformers. Choosing the novel as his medium, he wrote *Looking Backward, 2000-1887* (1888), to describe the United States as it would be in the year 2000 if the acquisitive spirit was subordinated to the good of mankind. He envisaged a modified socialism which he called "Nationalism." Four hundred thousand copies of *Looking Backward* were sold between 1888 and 1897, and more than 150 "Nationalist Clubs" were organized to help realize Bellamy's dream. One famous passage explained to a reader in the year 2000 what the United States had been like in 1887:[14]

By way of attempting to give the reader some general impression of the way people lived together in those days, and especially of the relations of the rich and poor to one another, perhaps I cannot do better than to compare society as it then was to a prodigious coach which the masses of humanity were harnessed to and dragged toilsomely along a very hilly and sandy road. The driver was hunger, and permitted no lagging, though the pace was necessarily very slow. Despite the difficulty of drawing the coach at all along so hard a road, the top was covered with passengers who never got down, even at the steepest ascents. These seats on top

were very breezy and comfortable. Well up out of the dust, their occupants could enjoy the scenery at their leisure, or critically discuss the merits of the straining team. Naturally such places were in great demand and the competition for them was keen, every one seeking as the first end in life to secure a seat on the coach for himself and to leave it to his child after him. By the rule of the coach a man could leave his seat to whom he wished, but on the other hand there were many accidents by which it might at any time be wholly lost. For all that they were so easy, the seats were very insecure, and at every sudden jolt of the coach persons were slipping out of them and falling to the ground, where they were instantly compelled to take hold of the rope and help to drag the coach on which they had before ridden so pleasantly. It was naturally regarded as a terrible misfortune to lose one's seat, and the apprehension that this might happen to them or their friends was a constant cloud upon the happiness of those who rode.

But did they think only of themselves? you ask. Was not their very luxury rendered intolerable to them by comparison with the loss of their brothers and sisters in the harness, and the knowledge that their own weight added to their toil? Had they no compassion for fellow beings from whom fortune only distinguished them? Oh, yes; commiseration was frequently expressed by those who rode for those who had to pull the coach, especially when the vehicle came to a bad place in the road, as it was constantly doing, or to a particularly steep hill. At such times, the desperate straining of the team, their agonized leaping and plunging under the pitiless lashing of hunger, the many who fainted at the rope and were trampled in the mire, made a very distressing spectacle, which often called forth highly creditable displays of feeling on the top of the coach. At such times the passengers would call down encouragingly to the toilers of the

---

[14] Edward Bellamy, *Looking Backward* (Boston, 1888). Selection taken from the 1890 edition (London), with preface and notes by Thomas Reynolds, pp. 8-11.

rope, exhorting them to patience, and holding out hopes of possible compensation in another world for the hardness of their lot, while others contributed to buy salves and liniments for the crippled and injured. It was agreed that it was a great pity that the coach should be so hard to pull, and there was a sense of general relief when the specially bad piece of road was gotten over. This relief was not, indeed, wholly on account of the team, for there was always some danger at these bad places of a general overturn in which all would lose their seats.

It must in truth be admitted that the main effect of the spectacle of the misery of the toilers at the rope was to enhance the passengers' sense of the value of their seats upon the coach, and to cause them to hold on to them more desperately than before.

If the passengers could only have felt assured that neither they nor their friends would ever fall from the top, it is probable that, beyond contributing to the funds for liniments and bandages, they would have troubled themselves extremely little about those who dragged the coach.

I am well aware that this will appear to the men and women of the twentieth century an incredible humanity, but there are two facts, both very curious, which partly explain it. In the first place, it was firmly and sincerely believed that there was no other way in which Society could get along, except the many pulled at the rope and the few rode, and not only this, but that no very radical improvement even was possible, either in the harness, the coach, the roadway, or the distribution of the toil. It had always been as it was, and it always would be so. It was a pity, but it could not be helped, and philosophy forbade wasting compassion on what was beyond remedy.

The other fact is yet more curious, consisting in a singular hallucination which those on the top of the coach generally shared, that they were not exactly like their brothers and sisters who pulled at the rope, but of finer clay, in some way belonging to a higher order of beings who might justly expect to be drawn. This seems unaccountable, but, as I once rode on this very coach and shared that very hallucination, I ought to be believed. The strangest thing about the hallucination was that those who had but just climbed up from the ground, before they had outgrown the marks of the rope upon their hands, began to fall under its influence. As for those whose parents and grandparents before them had been so fortunate as to keep their seats on the top, the conviction they cherished of the essential difference between their sort of humanity and the common article, was absolute. The effect of such a delusion in moderating fellow feeling for the sufferings of the mass of men into a distant and philosophical compassion, is obvious. To it I refer as the only extenuation I can offer for the indifference which, at the period I write of, marked my own attitude toward the misery of my brothers.

## 15

Utopian dreamers conjured up visions of future perfection, but practical reformers believed that immediate change was needed to ameliorate destitution in the slums. Their contribution was the "settlement house." Led by Jane Addams, whose Hull House on Chicago's Halstead Street became a model for similar enterprises, they raised money from private sources, then established community centers in congested areas where young and old alike could enjoy wholesome relaxation and the benefits of education. The achievements of one settlement house, the South End House in Boston, were described by its leader, Robert A. Woods:[15]

The police recognize, very cordially, the value of our work in reducing the amount of disorder in the neighborhood.

[15] Quoted in Josiah Strong, *The Challenge of the City* (New York, 1907), pp. 294-296. Used by permission of the Missionary Education Movement, successor to the Young People's Missionary Movement.

This Settlement has had a leading share, both in the establishment and in the administration of the Dover Street Bath House and the Ward 9 Gymnasium. It was active in securing for the district the South End Playground and, in its present admirable form, the South End Branch of the Public Library; and it has been making successful efforts toward broadening the usefulness of both. It has also had a considerable part in the whole movement which has led up to the establishment of the Franklin Union, now in process of erection on the borders of the South End House neighborhood. When this great evening technical institute is complete, and taking into account the Evening High School, also located near by, these six progressive municipal institutions will, it is believed, constitute the most remarkable combination in the way of municipal effort for social improvement to be found in any similar city district in the world.

A clear result of all this work is found in the better physical type represented by the young men and young women of the neighborhood as compared with those who were at the same stage in life ten years ago. While statistics for the neighborhood by itself are not available, it is beyond question that it holds its own with other neighborhoods throughout the city in the proved decrease in juvenile law-breaking. There has been a noticeable improvement in the matter of peace and order, and even in the freedom from bad language. The low-grade characters, which were a large company, are dead; and many of their places are not filled. The young men who are coming on have had warnings on the one hand and incitements on the other; a social sense fixed on somewhat better things is alive in them.

In the homes of the neighborhood there is a noticeably better standard as to sanitation, cooking, and the welfare of the children. There is somewhat more intelligent expenditure on food, on clothing and furniture. The habit of thrift has grown, under persistent practical encouragement. Not a few families, becoming involved in the hospitalities of the neighborhood, have moved out of three-room into four-room tenements in order that they might have a parlor. Many new and uplifting interests have arisen which have kindled a more lively and more generous sort of family and neighborhood intercourse.

The Boys' Club has, to a great extent, done away with the boys' gang. The lesson and example of fair and effective association has not been without effect upon independent local clubs of young men. A measure of neighborhood loyalty, cropping out in connection with the success of a dramatic club or an athletic team, or at one of the neighborhood reunions, has come unmistakably into being. The organization of the scattered local forces of good-will is on the way; and this means the moral recuperation of the neighborhood.

The House has been able to render certain distinctive contributions toward municipal reform in Boston. In the first place, it has made plain by its studies the actual underlying nature of local machine politics. Secondly, it has pointed out clearly that local political corruption depends largely upon the leverage which it gains upon the city treasury through the power of the aldermen. In the third place, it took the lead in securing the passage of a bill by which the aldermen are elected at large, a system which has made it possible to concentrate the vote of good citizens throughout the whole city upon certain aldermanic candidates, with distinctly successful results.

## THREATS TO DEMOCRACY

### 16

Influential as the reformers were, they failed to find the key to a better world. Settlement workers could do little more than provide temporary relief for a small segment of the population. On the other hand, the "Nationalism" of Edward Bellamy and the "single tax" of Henry George were too complex for the average American to comprehend. Discouraged intellectuals, surveying the national scene at the close of the century, were doubtful of immediate and affirmative social change. Many tended to emphasize the pretensions of society rather than stress its positive accomplishments. The brilliant thinker, Thorstein Veblen, wrote in *The Theory of the Leisure Class* (1899):[16]

The end of acquisition and accumulation is conventionally held to be the consumption of the goods accumulated—whether it is consumption directly by the owner of the goods or by the household attached to him and for this purpose identified with him in theory. This is at least felt to be the economically legitimate end of acquisition, which alone it is incumbent on the theory to take account of. Such consumption may of course be conceived to serve the consumer's physical wants—his physical comfort—or his so-called higher wants—spiritual, aesthetic, intellectual, or what not; the latter class of wants being served indirectly by an expenditure of goods, after the fashion familiar to all economic readers.

But it is only when taken in a sense far removed from its naïve meaning that consumption of goods can be said to afford the incentive from which accumulation invariably proceeds. The motive that lies at the root of ownership is emulation; and the same motive of emulation continues active in the further development of the institution to which it has given rise and in the development of all those features of the social structure which this institution of ownership touches. The possession of wealth confers honour; it is an invidious distinction. Nothing equally cogent can be said for the consumption of goods, nor

for any other conceivable incentive to acquisition, and especially not for any incentive to the accumulation of wealth.

It is of course not to be overlooked that in a community where nearly all goods are private property the necessity of earning a livelihood is a powerful and ever present incentive for the poorer members of the community. The need of subsistence and of an increase of physical comfort may for a time be the dominant motive of acquisition for those classes who are habitually employed at manual labour, whose subsistence is on a precarious footing, who possess little and ordinarily accumulate little; but it will appear in the course of the discussion that even in the case of these impecunious classes the predominance of the motive of physical want is not so decided as has sometimes been assumed. On the other hand, so far as regards those members and classes of the community who are chiefly concerned in the accumulation of wealth, the incentive of subsistence or of physical comfort never plays a considerable part. Ownership began and grew into a human institution on grounds unrelated to the subsistence minimum. The dominant incentive was from the outset the invidious distinction attaching to wealth, and, save temporarily and by exception, no other motive has usurped the primacy at any later stage of the development. . . .

So soon as the possession of property becomes the basis of popular esteem, therefore, it becomes also a requisite to that complacency which we call self-respect. In any community where goods are held in severalty it is necessary, in order to his own peace of mind, that an individual should possess as large a portion of goods as others with whom he is accustomed to class himself; and it is extremely gratifying to possess something more than others. But as fast as a person makes new acquisitions, and becomes accustomed to the resulting new standard of wealth, the new standard forthwith ceases to afford ap-

[16] From *The Theory of the Leisure Class* by Thorstein Veblen (1899 ed.), pp. 25-32, 75-88, 110-114. Copyright 1899, 1912 by The Macmillan Company. Reprinted by permission of The Viking Press, Inc.

preciably greater satisfaction than the earlier standard did. The tendency in any case is constantly to make the present pecuniary standard the point of departure for a fresh increase of wealth; and this in turn gives rise to a new standard of sufficiency and a new pecuniary classification of one's self as compared with one's neighbours. So far as concerns the present question, the end sought by accumulation is to rank high in comparison with the rest of the community in point of pecuniary strength. So long as the comparison is distinctly unfavorable to himself, the normal, average individual will live in chronic dissatisfaction with his present lot; and when he has reached what may be called the normal pecuniary standard of the community, or of his class in the community, this chronic dissatisfaction will give place to a restless straining to place a wider and ever-widening pecuniary interval between himself and this average standard. The invidious comparison can never become so favourable to the individual making it that he would not gladly rate himself still higher relatively to his competitors in the struggle for pecuniary reputability.

In the nature of the case, the desire for wealth can scarcely be satiated in any individual instance, and evidently a satiation of the average or general desire for wealth is out of the question. However widely, or equally, or "fairly," it may be distributed, no general increase of the community's wealth can make any approach to satiating this need, the ground of which is the desire of every one to excel every one else in the accumulation of goods. If, as is sometimes assumed, the incentive to accumulation were the want of subsistence or physical comfort, then the aggregate economic wants of a community might conceivably be satisfied at some point in the advance of industrial efficiency; but since the struggle is substantially a race for reputability on the basis of an invidious comparison, no approach to a definitive attainment is possible.

What has just been said must not be taken to mean that there are no other incentives to acquisition and accumulation than this desire to excel in pecuniary standing and so gain the esteem and envy of one's fellow-men. The desire for added comfort and security from want is present as a motive at every stage of the process of accumulation in a modern industrial community; although the standard of efficiency in these respects is in turn greatly affected by the habit of pecuniary emulation. To a great extent this emulation shapes the methods and selects the objects of expenditure for personal comfort and decent livelihood. . . .

Conspicuous consumption of valuable goods is a means of reputability to the gentleman of leisure. As wealth accumulates on his hands, his own unaided effort will not avail to sufficiently put his opulence in evidence by this method. The aid of friends and competitors is therefore brought in by resorting to the giving of valuable presents and expensive feasts and entertainments. Presents and feasts probably had another origin than that of naïve ostentation, but they acquired their utility for this purpose very early, and they have retained that character to the present; so that their utility in this respect has now long been the substantial ground on which these usages rest. Costly entertainments . . . are peculiarly adapted to serve this end. The competitor with whom the entertainer wishes to institute a comparison is, by this method, made to serve as a means to the end. He consumes vicariously for his host at the same time that he is a witness to the consumption of that excess of good things which his host is unable to dispose of single-handed, and he is also made to witness his host's facility in etiquette. . . .

From the foregoing survey of the growth of conspicuous leisure and consumption, it appears that the utility of both alike for the purposes of reputability lies in the element of waste that is common to both. In the one case it is a waste of time and effort, in the other it is a waste of goods. Both are methods of demonstrating the possession of wealth, and the two are conventionally accepted as equivalents. The choice between them is a question of advertising expediency simply, except so far as it may be affected by other standards of propriety, springing from a different source. On grounds of expediency the preference may be given to the one or the other at different stages of the economic development. The question is, which of the two methods will most effectively reach the persons whose convictions it is desired to affect. Usage has answered this question in different ways under different circumstances.

So long as the community or social group is small enough and compact enough to be effectually reached by common notoriety alone,—that is to say, so long as the human environment to which the individual is required to adapt himself in respect of reputability is comprised within his sphere of personal acquaintance and neighbourhood gossip,—so long the one method is about as effective as the other. Each will therefore serve about equally well during the earlier stages of social growth. But when the differentiation has gone farther and it becomes necessary to reach a wider human environment, consumption begins to hold over leisure as an ordinary means of decency. This is especially true during the later, peaceable economic stage. The means of communication and the mobility of the population now expose the individual to the observation of many persons who have no other means of judging of his reputability than the display of goods (and perhaps of breeding) which he is able to make while he is under their direct observation.

The modern organisation of industry works in the same direction also by an-

other line. The exigencies of the modern industrial system frequently place individuals and households in juxtaposition between whom there is little contact in any other sense than that of juxtaposition. One's neighbours, mechanically speaking, often are socially not one's neighbours, or even acquaintances; and still their transient good opinion has a high degree of utility. The only practicable means of impressing one's pecuniary ability on these unsympathetic observers of one's everyday life is an unremitting demonstration of ability to pay. In the modern community there is also a more frequent attendance at large gatherings of people of whom one's everyday life is unknown; in such places as churches, theatres, ballrooms, hotels, parks, shops, and the like. In order to impress these transient observers, and to retain one's self-complacency under their observation, the signature of one's pecuniary strength should be written in characters which he who runs may read. It is evident, therefore, that the present trend of the development is in the direction of heightening the utility of conspicuous consumption as compared with leisure.

It is also noticeable that the serviceability of consumption as a means of repute, as well as the insistence on it as an element of decency, is at its best in those portions of the community where the human contact of the individual is widest and the mobility of the population is greatest. Conspicuous consumption claims a relatively larger portion of the income of the urban than of the rural population, and the claim is also more imperative. The result is that, in order to keep up a decent appearance, the former habitually live hand-to-mouth to a greater extent than the latter. So it comes, for instance, that the American farmer and his wife and daughters are notoriously less modish in their dress, as well as less urbane in their manners, than the city artisan's family with an equal income. It is not that the city population is by nature much more eager for the peculiar complacency that comes of a conspicuous consumption, nor has the rural population less regard for pecuniary decency. But the provocation to this line of evidence, as well as its transient effectiveness, are more decided in the city. This method is therefore more readily resorted to, and in the struggle to outdo one another the city population push their normal standard of conspicuous consumption to a higher point, with the result that a relatively greater expenditure in this direction is required to indicate a given degree of pecuniary decency in the city. The requirement of conformity to this higher conventional standard becomes mandatory. The standard of decency is higher, class for class, and this requirement of decent appearance must be lived up to on pain of losing caste.

Consumption becomes a larger element in the standard of living in the city than in the country. Among the country population its place is to some extent taken by savings and home comforts known through the medium of neighbourhood gossip sufficiently to serve the like general purpose of pecuniary repute. These home comforts and the leisure indulged in— where the indulgence is found—are of course also in great part to be classed as items of conspicuous consumption; and much the same is to be said of the savings. The smaller amount of the savings laid by the artisan class is no doubt due, in some measure, to the fact that in the case of the artisan the savings are a less effective means of advertisement, relative to the environment in which he is placed, than are the savings of the people living on farms and in the small villages. Among the latter, everybody's affairs, especially everybody's pecuniary status, are known to everybody else. Considered by itself simply —taken in the first degree—this added provocation to which the artisan and the urban labouring classes are exposed may not very seriously decrease the amount of savings; but in its cumulative action, through raising the standard of decent expenditure, its deterrent effect on the tendency to save cannot but be very great. . . .

With the exception of the instinct of self-preservation, the propensity for emulation is probably the strongest and most alert and persistent of the economic motives proper. In an industrial community this propensity for emulation expresses itself in pecuniary emulation; and this, so far as regards the Western civilised communities of the present, is virtually equivalent to saying that it expresses itself in some form of conspicuous waste. The need of conspicuous waste, therefore, stands ready to absorb any increase in the community's industrial efficiency or output of goods, after the most elementary physical wants have been provided for. Where this result does not follow, under modern conditions, the reason for the discrepancy is commonly to be sought in a rate of increase in the individual's wealth too rapid for the habit of expenditure to keep abreast of it; or it may be that the individual in question defers the conspicuous consumption of the increment to a later date—ordinarily with a view to heightening the spectacular effect of the aggregate expenditure contemplated. As increased industrial efficiency makes it possible to procure the means of livelihood with less labour, the energies of the industrious members of the community are bent to the compassing of a higher result in conspicuous expenditure, rather than slackened to a more comfortable pace. The strain is not lightened as industrial efficiency increases and makes a lighter strain possible, but the increment of output is turned to use to meet this want, which is indefinitely expansible, after the manner commonly imputed in economic theory to higher or spiritual wants. It is owing chiefly to the presence of this element in the standard of living that J. S. Mill was able to say that "hitherto it is questionable if all the mechanical inventions yet made have lightened the day's toil of any human being."

The accepted standard of expenditure in the community or in the class to which a person belongs largely determines what his standard of living will be. It does this directly by commending itself to his common sense as right and good, through his habitually contemplating it and assimilating the scheme of his life in which it belongs; but it does so also indirectly through popular insistence on conformity to the accepted scale of expenditure as a matter of propriety, under pain of disesteem and ostracism. To accept and practise the standard of living which is in vogue is both agreeable and expedient, commonly to the point of being indispensable to personal comfort and to success in life. The standard of living of any class, so far as concerns the element of conspicuous waste, is commonly as high as the earning capacity of the class will permit—with a constant tendency to go higher. The effect upon the serious activities of men is therefore to direct them with great singleness of purpose to the largest possible acquisition of wealth, and to discountenance work that brings no pecuniary gain. At the same time the effect on consumption is to concentrate it upon the lines which are most patent to the observers whose good opinion is sought; while the inclinations and aptitudes whose exercise does not involve a honorific expenditure of time or substance tend to fall into abeyance through disuse.

Through this discrimination in favour of visible consumption it has come about that the domestic life of most classes is relatively shabby, as compared with the éclat of that overt portion of their life that is carried on before the eyes of observers. As a secondary consequence of the same discrimination, people habitually screen their private life from observation. So far as concerns that portion of their consumption that may without blame be carried on in secret, they withdraw from all contact with their neighbours. Hence the exclusiveness of people, as regards their domestic life, in most of the industrially developed communities; and hence, by remoter derivation, the habit of privacy and reserve that is so large a feature in the code of proprieties of the better classes in all communities. The low birthrate of the classes upon whom the requirements of reputable expenditure fall with great urgency is likewise traceable to the exigencies of a standard of living based on conspicuous waste. The conspicuous consumption, and the consequent increased expense, required in the reputable maintenance of a child is very considerable and acts as a powerful deterrent. It is probably the most effectual of the Malthusian prudential checks.

The effect of this factor of the standard of living, both in the way of retrenchment in the obscurer elements of consumption that go to physical comfort and maintenance, and also in the paucity or absence of children, is perhaps seen at its best among the classes given to scholarly pursuits. Because of a presumed superiority and scarcity of the gifts and attainments that characterise their life, these classes are by convention subsumed under a higher social grade than their pecuniary grade should warrant. The scale of decent expenditure in their case is pitched correspondingly high, and it consequently leaves an exceptionally narrow margin disposable for the other ends of life. By force of circumstances, their own habitual sense of what is good and right in these matters, as well as the expectations of the community in the way of pecuniary decency among the learned, are excessively high—as measured by the prevalent degree of opulence and earning capacity of the class, relatively to the non-scholarly classes whose social equals they nominally are. In any modern community where there is no priestly monopoly of these occupations, the people of scholarly pursuits are unavoidably thrown into contact with classes that are pecuniarily their superiors. The high standard of pecuniary decency in force among these superior classes is transfused among the scholarly classes with but little mitigation of its rigour; and as a consequence there is no class of the community that spends a larger proportion of its substance in conspicuous waste than these.

The sins of society still remained even after eloquent protest. Men like Andrew Carnegie and John D. Rockefeller were not individually to blame; they were products of an age and of a philosophy as were Henry George and Henry Demarest Lloyd. Man had yet to realize that the complexities of a machine civilization demanded social controls un-

dreamed of a century before. Man built railroads spanning a continent, but he had no social program for an interdependent nation; he added Diesels to ocean-going ships, but he had no design for a shrinking world; he created crowded cities, but he gave no thought to planning for decent living; he sketched grandiose plans on industrial blueprints, but he let intricate social relationships develop in planless chaos. Human greed could be curbed only by society as a whole, and the government alone was powerful enough to serve the public interest. Those political leaders who realized that machines had outmoded the doctrine of laissez faire prepared the way for the century of the common man.

# XVIII

# DISSENT AND FRUSTRATION

## 1885-1900

The social critics of the 1880's and 1890's were more enthusiastic than practical. Americans were neither ready for the radical tax reform of Henry George nor ready for the socialism of Edward Bellamy. But their words inspired workers, farmers, and middle-class humanitarians who believed that the economic system required large-scale improvement even if they did not believe it should be rebuilt. Such groups brought the influence of numbers to bear on politicians ever conscious of the vote, and Congress began tentatively to respond to the pressures for social betterment. Yet radical improvements were seldom undertaken, and one by one the congressional reform measures were mutilated in committee or subsequently massacred by the conservatism of the courts.

## CLEVELAND AND CONGRESS

### 1

Social progress in America has always been preceded by theoretical analysis or criticism and then initiated by a strong executive. The role of popular leader in the 1880's belonged to Grover Cleveland, the crusading New York governor elected to the presidency in 1884. Cleveland was no radical; his philosophy today would be considered reactionary. His basic political creed was expounded in the veto of a Texas seed bill (1887) appropriating $10,000 to relieve drought sufferers desperately in need of seed grains. The President based his rejection of the measure on the laissez-faire postulate of "every man for himself" and the rural aphorism that individuals afflicted by misfortune should look to their neighbors for help and comfort:[1]

I return without my approval House bill No. 10203, entitled "An act to enable the Commissioner of Agriculture to make a special distribution of seeds in the drought-stricken counties of Texas, and making an appropriation therefor."

It is represented that a long-continued and extensive drought has existed in certain portions of the State of Texas, resulting in a failure of crops and consequent distress and destitution.

Though there has been some difference

in statements concerning the extent of the people's needs in the localities thus affected, there seems to be no doubt that there has existed a condition calling for relief; and I am willing to believe that, notwithstanding the aid already furnished, a donation of seed grain to the farmers located in this region, to enable them to put in new crops, would serve to avert a continuance or return of an unfortunate blight.

And yet I feel obliged to withhold my approval of the plan, as proposed by this bill, to indulge a benevolent and charitable sentiment through the appropriation of public funds for that purpose.

I can find no warrant for such an appropriation in the Constitution, and I do not believe that the power and duty of the General Government ought to be extended to the relief of individual suffering which is in no manner properly related to the public service or benefit. A prevalent tendency to disregard the limited mission of this power and duty should, I think, be steadfastly resisted, to the end that the lesson should be constantly enforced that though the people support the Government the Government should not support the people.

The friendliness and charity of our countrymen can always be relied upon to relieve their fellow-citizens in misfortune. This has been repeatedly and quite lately

[1] J. D. Richardson (comp.), *Messages and Papers of the Presidents, 1789-1897* (Washington, 1897, 1909; taken from the 1909 vol.), VIII, 557-558.

demonstrated. Federal aid in such cases encourages the expectation of paternal care on the part of the Government and weakens the sturdiness of our national character, while it prevents the indulgence among our people of that kindly sentiment and conduct which strengthens the bonds of a common brotherhood.

It is within my personal knowledge that individual aid has to some extent already been extended to the sufferers mentioned in this bill. The failure of the proposed appropriation of $10,000 additional to meet their remaining wants will not necessarily result in continued distress if the emergency is fully made known to the people of the country.

It is here suggested that the Commissioner of Agriculture is annually directed to expend a large sum of money for the purchase, propagation, and distribution of seeds and other things of this description, two-thirds of which are, upon the request of Senators, Representatives, and Delegates in Congress, supplied to them for distribution among their constituents.

The appropriation of the current year for this purpose is $100,000, and it will probably be no less in the appropriation for the ensuing year. I understand that a large quantity of grain is furnished for such distribution, and it is supposed that this free apportionment among their neighbors is a privilege which may be waived by our Senators and Representatives.

If sufficient of them should request the Commissioner of Agriculture to send their shares of the grain thus allowed them to the suffering farmers of Texas, they might be enabled to sow their crops, the constituents for whom in theory this grain is intended could well bear the temporary deprivation, and the donors would experience the satisfaction attending deeds of charity.

## 2

Yet even a man of Cleveland's conservative temperament was not indifferent to the popu-

lar disquiet. His particular interest was the tariff problem. No friend of free trade (protection had become an article of faith for politicians of both parties since 1865), he was nevertheless brought face to face with the issue when high custom duties produced more revenue than the government needed either for expenses or for debt retirement. Cleveland, fearful of corruption if politicians began spending the surplus funds, concluded that drastic tariff reduction provided the only solution. His special message to Congress on the subject, delivered on December 6, 1887, served as a model for reformers of the generation:[2]

You are confronted at the threshold of your legislative duties with a condition of the national finances which imperatively demands immediate and careful consideration.

The amount of money annually exacted, through the operation of present laws, from the industries and necessities of the people largely exceeds the sum necessary to meet the expenses of the Government.

When we consider that the theory of our institutions guarantees to every citizen the full enjoyment of all the fruits of his industry and enterprise, with only such deduction as may be his share toward the careful and economical maintenance of the Government which protects him, it is plain that the exaction of more than this is indefensible extortion and culpable betrayal of American fairness and justice. This wrong inflicted upon those who bear the burden of national taxation, like other wrongs, multiplies a brood of evil consequences. The public Treasury, which should only exist as a conduit conveying the people's tribute to its legitimate objects of expenditure, becomes a hoarding place for money needlessly withdrawn from trade and the people's use, thus crippling our national energies, suspending our country's development, preventing investment in productive enterprise, threatening financial disturbance, and inviting schemes of public plunder. . . .

[2] *Ibid.,* pp. 580-590.

In the present state of legislation the only pretense of any existing executive power to restore at this time any part of our surplus revenues to the people by its expenditure consists in the supposition that the Secretary of the Treasury may enter the market and purchase the bonds of the Government not yet due. . . .

In considering the question of purchasing bonds as a means of restoring to circulation the surplus money accumulating in the Treasury, it should be borne in mind that premiums must of course be paid upon such purchase, that there may be a large part of these bonds held as investments which can not be purchased at any price, and that combinations among holders who are willing to sell may unreasonably enhance the cost of such bonds to the Government. . . .

Our scheme of taxation, by means of which this needless surplus is taken from the people and put into the public Treasury, consists of a tariff or duty levied upon importations from abroad and internal-revenue taxes levied upon the consumption of tobacco and spirituous and malt liquors. . . .

But our present tariff laws, the vicious, inequitable, and illogical source of unnecessary taxation, ought to be at once revised and amended. These laws . . . raise the price to consumers of all articles imported and subject to duty by precisely the sum paid for such duties. Thus the amount of the duty measures the tax paid by those who purchase for use these imported articles. Many of these things, however, are raised or manufactured in our own country, and the duties now levied upon foreign goods and products are called protection to these home manufactures, because they render it possible for those of our people who are manufacturers to make these taxed articles and sell them for a price equal to that demanded for the imported goods that have paid customs duty. So it happens that while comparatively a few use the imported articles, millions of our people, who never used and never saw any of the foreign products, purchase and use things of the same kind made in this country, and pay therefor nearly or quite the same enhanced price which the duty adds to the imported articles. Those who buy imports pay the duty charged thereon into the public Treasury, but the great majority of our citizens, who buy domestic articles of the same class, pay a sum at least approximately equal to this duty to the home manufacturer. This reference to the operation of our tariff laws is not made by way of instruction, but in order that we may be constantly reminded of the manner in which they impose a burden upon those who consume domestic products as well as those who consume imported articles, and thus create a tax upon all our people.

It is not proposed to entirely relieve the country of this taxation. It must be extensively continued as the source of the Government's income; and in a readjustment of our tariff the interests of American labor engaged in manufacture should be carefully considered, as well as the preservation of our manufacturers. It may be called protection or by any other name, but relief from the hardships and dangers of our present tariff laws should be devised with especial precaution against imperiling the existence of our manufacturing interests. But this existence should not mean a condition which, without regard to the public welfare or a national exigency, must always insure the realization of immense profits instead of moderately profitable returns. As the volume and diversity of our national activities increase, new recruits are added to those who desire a continuation of the advantages which they conceive the present system of tariff taxation directly affords them. So stubbornly have all efforts to reform the present condition been resisted by those of our fellow-citizens thus engaged that they can hardly complain of the suspicion . . . that there exists an organized combination all along the line to maintain their advantage. . . .

It is also said that the increase in the price of domestic manufactures resulting from the present tariff is necessary in order that higher wages may be paid to our workingmen employed in manufactories than are paid for what is called the pauper labor of Europe. . . .

By the last census it is made to appear that of the 17,392,099 of our population engaged in all kinds of industries 7,670,-493 are employed in agriculture, 4,074,238 in professional and personal service (2,-934,876 of whom are domestic servants and laborers), while 1,810,256 are employed in trade and transportation and 3,-827,112 are classed as employed in manufacturing and mining.

For present purposes, however, the last number given should be considerably reduced. Without attempting to enumerate all, it will be conceded that there should be deducted from those which it includes 375,143 carpenters and joiners, 285,401 milliners, dressmakers, and seamstresses, 172,726 blacksmiths, 133,756 tailors and tailoresses, 102,473 masons, 76,421 butcherers, 41,309 bakers, 22,083 plasterers, and 4,891 engaged in manufacturing agricultural implements, amounting in the aggregate to 1,214,023, leaving 2,623,089 persons employed in such manufacturing industries as are claimed to be benefited by a high tariff.

To these the appeal is made to save their employment and maintain their wages by resisting a change. There should be no disposition to answer such suggestions by the allegation that they are in a minority among those who labor, and therefore should forego an advantage in the interest of low prices for the majority.

Their compensation, as it may be affected by the operation of tariff laws, should at all times be scrupulously kept in view; and yet with slight reflection they will not overlook the fact that they are consumers with the rest; that they too have their own wants and those of their families to supply from their earnings, and that the price of the necessaries of life, as well as the amount of their wages, will regulate the measure of their welfare and comfort. . . . Nor can the worker in manufactures fail to understand that while a high tariff is claimed to be necessary to allow the payment of remunerative wages, it certainly results in a very large increase in the price of nearly all sorts of manufactures, which, in almost countless forms, he needs. . . .

In speaking of the increased cost to the consumer of our home manufactures resulting from a duty laid upon imported articles of the same description, the fact is not overlooked that competition among our domestic producers sometimes has the effect of keeping the price of their products below the highest limit allowed by such duty. But it is notorious that this competition is too often strangled by combinations quite prevalent at this time, and frequently called trusts, which have for their object the regulation of the supply and price of commodities made and sold by members of the combination. The people can hardly hope for any consideration in the operation of these selfish schemes.

If, however, in the absence of such combination, a healthy and free competition reduces the price of any particular dutiable article of home production below the limit which it might otherwise reach under our tariff laws, and if with such reduced price its manufacture continues to thrive, it is entirely evident that one thing has been discovered which should be carefully scrutinized in an effort to reduce taxation.

The necessity of combination to maintain the price of any commodity to the tariff point furnishes proof that someone is willing to accept lower prices for such commodity and that such prices are remunerative; and lower prices produced by competition prove the same thing. Thus where either of these conditions exists a case would seem to be presented for an easy reduction of taxation.

The considerations which have been presented touching our tariff laws are intended only to enforce an earnest recommendation that the surplus revenues of the Government be prevented by the reduction of our customs duties, and at the same time to emphasize a suggestion that in accomplishing this purpose we may discharge a double duty to our people by granting to them a measure of relief from tariff taxation in quarters where it is most needed and from sources where it can be most fairly and justly accorded. . . .

The difficulty attending a wise and fair revision of our tariff laws is not underestimated. It will require on the part of the Congress great labor and care, and especially a broad and national contemplation of the subject and a patriotic disregard of such local and selfish claims as are unreasonable and reckless of the welfare of the entire country.

Under our present laws more than 4,000 articles are subject to duty. Many of these do not in any way compete with our own manufactures, and many are hardly worth attention as subjects of revenue. A considerable reduction can be made in the aggregate by adding them to the free list. The taxation of luxuries presents no features of hardship; but the necessaries of life used and consumed by all the people, the duty upon which adds to the cost of living in every home, should be greatly cheapened.

The radical reduction of the duties imposed upon raw material used in manufacturies, or its free importation, is of course an important factor in any effort to reduce the price of these necessaries. It would not only relieve them from the increased cost caused by the tariff on such material, but the manufactured product being thus cheapened that part of the tariff now laid upon such product, as a compensation to our manufacturers for the present price of raw material, could be accordingly modified. Such reduction or free importation would serve besides to largely reduce the revenue. It is not apparent how such a change can have any injurious effect upon our manufacturers. On the contrary, it would appear to give them a better chance in foreign markets with the manufacturers of other countries, who cheapen their wares by free material. Thus our people might have the opportunity of extending their sales beyond the limits of home consumption, saving them from the depression, interruption in business, and loss caused by a glutted domestic market and affording their employees more certain and steady labor. . . .

Our progress toward a wise conclusion will not be improved by dwelling upon the theories of protection and free trade. This savors too much of bandying epithets. It is a *condition* which confronts us, not a theory. Relief from this condition may involve a slight reduction of the advantages which we award our home productions, but the entire withdrawal of such advantages should not be contemplated. The question of free trade is absolutely irrelevant, and the persistent claim made in certain quarters that all the efforts to relieve the people from unjust and unnecessary taxation are schemes of so-called free traders is mischievous and far removed from any consideration for the public good.

### 3

Cleveland's attempted tariff reform failed. A Republican victory at the polls in 1888 (despite a majority popular vote in favor of the Democratic candidate) laid the basis for the excessively high McKinley Tariff of 1892. Thus frustrated, he was forced to gain his greatest victory in an area where he believed change was least necessary. Cleveland had little sympathy with governmental interference in business. Yet he, together with most of the people, had accepted the right of states to regulate railroad rates after the doctrine was upheld in *Munn* v. *Illinois* (1876). Hence he was profoundly shocked by the Supreme Court's decision in the case of *Wabash, St. Louis and Pacific Railroad Company* v. *Illinois* (1886); the states, the justices decided, had no power over railroads engaged in interstate commerce—a ruling that exempted every major road in the nation from regulation:[3]

The supreme court of Illinois, in the case now before us, conceding that each of these contracts was in itself a unit, and that the pay received by the Illinois railroad company was the compensation for the entire transportation from the point of departure in the State of Illinois to the city of New York, holds that, while the statute of Illinois is inoperative upon that part of the contract which has reference to the transportation outside of the State, it is binding and effectual as to so much of the transportation as was within the limits of the State of Illinois; and undertaking for itself to apportion the rates charged over the whole route, decides that the contract and the receipt of the money for so much of it as was performed within the State of Illinois violate the statute of the State on that subject.

If the Illinois statute could be construed to apply exclusively to contracts for a carriage which begins and ends within the State, disconnected from a continuous transportation through or into other States, there does not seem to be any difficulty in holding it to be valid. . . .

The supreme court of Illinois does not place its judgment in the present case on the ground that the transportation and the charge are exclusively state commerce, but, conceding that it may be a case of commerce among the States, or interstate commerce, which Congress would have the right to regulate if it had attempted to do so, argues that this statute of Illinois belongs to that class of commercial regulations which may be established by the laws of a State until Congress shall have exercised its power on that subject. . . .

. . . It cannot be denied that the general language of the court . . . may be susceptible of the meaning which the Illinois court places upon it. . . . Whatever may be the instrumentalities by which the trans-

portation from one point to the other is effected, it is but one voyage, as much so as that of the steamboat on the Mississippi River.

It is not the railroads themselves that are regulated by this act of the Illinois legislature so much as the charge for transportation, and . . . if each one of the States through whose territories these goods are transported can fix its own rules for prices, for modes of transit, for times and modes of delivery, and all the other incidents of transportation to which the word "regulation" can be applied, it is readily seen that the embarrassments upon interstate transportation, as an element of interstate commerce, might be too oppressive to be submitted to. "It was," in the language of the court cited above, "to meet just such a case that the commerce clause of the Constitution was adopted."

It cannot be too strongly insisted upon that the right of continuous transportation, from one end of the country to the other, is essential, in modern times, to that freedom of commerce from the restraints which the States might choose to impose upon it, that the commerce clause was intended to secure. This clause, giving to Congress the power to regulate commerce among the States, and with foreign nations, as this court has said before, was among the most important of the subjects which prompted the formation of the Constitution. And it would be a very feeble and almost useless provision, but poorly adapted to secure the entire freedom of commerce among the States which was deemed essential to a more perfect union by the framers of the Constitution, if, at every stage of the transportation of goods and chattels through the country, the State within whose limits a part of this transportation must be done could impose regulations concerning the price, compensation, or taxation, or any other restrictive regulation interfering with and seriously embarrassing this commerce. . . .

We must therefore hold that it is not,

[3] *United States Reports,* 118 U.S. 557-577.

and never has been, the deliberate opinion of a majority of this court that a statute of a State which attempts to regulate the fares and charges by railroad companies within its limits, for a transportation which constitutes a part of commerce among the States, is a valid law.

Let us see precisely what is the degree of interference with transportation of property or persons from one State to another which this statute proposes. A citizen of New York has goods which he desires to have transported by the railroad companies from that city to the interior of the State of Illinois. A continuous line of rail over which a car loaded with these goods can be carried, and is carried habitually, connects the place of shipment with the place of delivery. He undertakes to make a contract with a person engaged in the carrying business at the end of this route from whence the goods are to start, and he is told by the carrier: "I am free to make a fair and reasonable contract for this carriage to the line of the State of Illinois, but when the car which carries these goods is to cross the line of that State, pursuing at the same time this continuous track, I am met by a law of Illinois which forbids me to make a free contract concerning this transportation within that State, and subjects me to certain rules by which I am to be governed as to the charges which the same railroad company in Illinois may make, or has made, with reference to other persons and other places of delivery." So that while that carrier might be willing to carry these goods from the city of New York to the city of Peoria at the rate of fifteen cents per hundred pounds, he is not permitted to do so, because the Illinois railroad company has already charged at the rate of twenty-five cents per hundred pounds for carriage to Gilman, in Illinois, which is eighty-six miles shorter than the distance to Peoria.

So, also, in the present case, the owner of corn, the principal product of the country, desiring to transport it from Peoria,

in Illinois, to New York, finds a railroad company willing to do this at the rate of fifteen cents per hundred pounds for a car-load, but is compelled to pay at the rate of twenty-five cents per hundred pounds, because the railroad company has received from a person residing at Gilman twenty-five cents per hundred pounds for the transportation of a car-load of the same class of freight over the same line of road from Gilman to New York. This is the result of the statute of Illinois, in its endeavor to prevent unjust discrimination, as construed by the supreme court of that State. The effect of it is that whatever may be the rate of transportation per mile charged by the railroad company from Gilman to Sheldon, a distance of twenty-three miles, in which the loading and the unloading of the freight is the largest expense incurred by the railroad company, the same rate per mile must be charged from Peoria to the city of New York.

The obvious injustice of such a rule as this, which railroad companies are by heavy penalties compelled to conform to, in regard to commerce among the States, when applied to transportation which includes Illinois in a long line of carriage through several States, shows the value of the constitutional provision which confides the power of regulating interstate commerce to the Congress of the United States, whose enlarged view of the interests of all the States, and of the railroads concerned, better fits it to establish just and equitable rules.

Of the justice or propriety of the principle which lies at the foundation of the Illinois statute it is not the province of this court to speak. As restricted to a transportation which begins and ends within the limits of the State, it may be very just and equitable, and it certainly is the province of the state legislature to determine that question. But when it is attempted to apply to transportation through an entire series of States a principle of this kind, and each one of the States shall attempt to establish its own rates of transportation, its own methods to prevent discrimination in rates, or to permit it, the deleterious influence upon the freedom of commerce among the States, and upon the transit of goods through those States, cannot be overestimated. That this species of regulation is one which must be, if established at all, of a general and national character, and cannot be safely and wisely remitted to local rules and local regulations, we think is clear from what has already been said. And if it be a regulation of commerce, as we think we have demonstrated it is, and as the Illinois court concedes it to be, it must be of that national character; and the regulation can only appropriately exist by general rules and principles, which demand that it should be done by the Congress of the United States under the commerce clause of the Constitution.

### 4

Popular resentment at the Court's decision in the Wabash Case was a measure of popular resentment toward laissez faire. Irate farmers insisted that they must not be left to the mercy of monopolistic railroads charging all the traffic would bear; urban workers maintained they must be protected from the higher food prices that followed increased freight rates; middle-class spokesmen soberly pointed out that the decision permitted dangerous monopolies in a field of vital public interest. Congress accepted the implications, for if the states had no power over roads engaged in interstate commerce, clearly the federal government must legislate. The result was the Interstate Commerce Act, approved by President Cleveland on February 4, 1887:[4]

. . . [The] provisions of this act shall apply to any common carrier or carriers engaged in the transportation of passengers or property wholly by railroad, or partly by railroad and partly by water when both are used, under a common control, management, or arrangement, for a continuous carriage or shipment, from

one State or Territory of the United States, or the District of Columbia, to any other State or Territory of the United States, or the District of Columbia, or from any place in the United States to an adjacent foreign country, or from any place in the United States through a foreign country to any other place in the United States, . . .

All charges made for any service rendered or to be rendered in the transportation of passengers or property as aforesaid, or in connection therewith, or for the receiving, delivering, storage, or handling of such property, shall be reasonable and just; and every unjust and unreasonable charge for such service is prohibited and declared to be unlawful.

SECTION 2. That if any common carrier subject to the provisions of this act shall, directly or indirectly, by any special rate, rebate, drawback, or other device, charge, demand, collect, or receive from any person or persons a greater or less compensation for any service rendered, or to be rendered, in the transportation of passengers or property, subject to the provisions of this act, than it charges, demands, collects, or receives from any other person or persons for doing for him or them a like and contemporaneous service in the transportation of a like kind of traffic under substantially similar circumstances and conditions, such common carrier shall be deemed guilty of unjust discrimination, which is hereby prohibited and declared to be unlawful.

SEC. 3. That it shall be unlawful for any common carrier subject to the provisions of this act to make or give any undue or unreasonable preference or advantage to any particular person, company, firm, corporation, or locality, or any particular description of traffic, in any respect whatsoever, or to subject any particular person, company, firm, corporation, or locality, or any particular description of traffic, to any undue or unreasonable prejudice or disadvantage in any respect whatsoever. . . .

---

[4] *United States Statutes at Large*, XXVI, 379-387.

Sec. 4. That it shall be unlawful for any common carrier subject to the provisions of this act to charge or receive any greater compensation in the aggregate for the transportation of passengers or of like kind of property, under substantially similar circumstances and conditions, for a shorter than for a longer distance over the same line, in the same direction, the shorter being included within the longer distance; but this shall not be construed as authorizing any common carrier within the terms of this act to charge and receive as great compensation for a shorter as for a longer distance: *Provided, however,* That upon application to the Commission appointed under the provisions of this act, such common carrier may, in special cases, after investigation by the Commission, be authorized to charge less for longer than for shorter distances for the transportation of passengers or property; and the Commission may from time to time prescribe the extent to which such designated common carrier may be relieved from the operation of this section of this act.

Sec. 5. That it shall be unlawful for any common carrier subject to the provisions of this act to enter into any contract, agreement, or combination with any other common carrier or carriers for the pooling of freights of different and competing railroads, or to divide between them the aggregate or net proceeds of the earnings of such railroads, or any portion thereof; and in any case of an agreement for the pooling of freights as aforesaid, each day of its continuance shall be deemed a separate offense.

Sec. 6. That every common carrier subject to the provisions of this act shall print and keep for public inspection schedules showing the rates and fares and charges for the transportation of passengers and property which any such common carrier has established and which are in force at the time upon its railroad, as defined by the first section of this act. . . .

No advance shall be made in the rates, fares, and charges which have been established and published as aforesaid by any common carrier in compliance with the requirements of this section, except after ten days' public notice, which shall plainly state the changes proposed to be made in the schedule then in force, and the time when the increased rates, fares, or charges will go into effect. . . .

Sec. 9. That any person or persons claiming to be damaged by any common carrier subject to the provisions of this act may either make complaint to the Commission as hereinafter provided for, or may bring suit in his or their own behalf for the recovery of the damages for which such common carrier may be liable under the provisions of this act, in any district or circuit court of the United States. . . .

Sec. 10. That any common carrier subject to the provisions of this act, or, whenever such common carrier is a corporation, any director or officer thereof, or any receiver, trustee, lessee, agent, or person acting for or employed by such corporation, who, alone or with any other corporation, company, person, or party, . . . shall be guilty of any infraction of this act, or shall aid or abet therein, shall be deemed guilty of a misdemeanor, and shall, upon conviction thereof in any district court of the United States within the jurisdiction of which such offense was committed, be subject to a fine of not to exceed five thousand dollars for each offense.

Sec. 11. That a Commission is hereby created and established to be known as the Inter-State Commerce Commission, which shall be composed of five Commissioners, who shall be appointed by the President, by and with the advice and consent of the Senate. The Commissioners first appointed under this act shall continue in office for the term of two, three, four, five, and six years, respectively, from January 1, 1887, the term of each to be designated by the President; but their successors shall be appointed for terms of six years. . . . Any Commissioner may be removed by the President for inefficiency, neglect of duty, or malfeasance in office. Not more than three of the Commissioners shall be appointed from the same political party. No person in the employ of or holding any official relation to any common carrier subject to the provisions of this act, or owning stock or bonds thereof, or who is in any manner pecuniarily interested therein, shall enter upon the duties of or hold such office. Said Commissioners shall not engage in any other business, vocation, or employment. No vacancy in the Commission shall impair the right of the remaining Commissioners to exercise all the powers of the Commission.

SEC. 12. That the Commission hereby created shall have authority to inquire into the management of the business of all common carriers subject to the provisions of this act, and shall keep itself informed as to the manner and method in which the same is conducted, and shall have the right to obtain from such common carriers full and complete information necessary to enable the Commission to perform the duties and carry out the objects for which it was created; and for the purposes of this act the Commission shall have power to require the attendance and testimony of witnesses and the production of all books, papers, tariffs, contracts, agreements, and documents relating to any matter under investigation, and to that end may invoke the aid of any court of the United States in requiring the attendance and testimony of witnesses and the production of books, papers, and documents under the provisions of this section. . . .

SEC. 16. That whenever any common carrier, . . . shall violate or refuse or neglect to obey any lawful order or requirement of the Commission in this act named, it shall be the duty of the Commission, and lawful for any company or person interested in such order or requirement, to apply, in a summary way, by petition, to the circuit court of the United States sitting in equity in the judicial district in which the common carrier complained of has its principal office, or in which the violation or disobedience of such order or requirement shall happen, alleging such violation or disobedience, as the case may be; and the said court shall have power to hear and determine the matter, on such short notice to the common carrier complained of as the court shall deem reasonable. . . .

SEC. 20. That the Commission is hereby authorized to require annual reports from all common carriers subject to the provisions of this act, fix the time and prescribe the manner in which such reports shall be made, and to require from such carriers specific answers to all questions upon which the Commission may need information. Such reports shall also contain such information in relation to rates or regulations concerning fares or freights, or agreements, arrangements, or contracts with other common carriers, as the Commission may require; and the said Commission may, within its discretion, for the purpose of enabling it the better to carry out the purposes of this act, prescribe . . . a period of time within which all common carriers subject to the provisions of this act shall have, as near as may be, a uniform system of accounts, and the manner in which such accounts shall be kept.

## 5

The reaction against monopoly responsible for the Interstate Commerce Act did not subside even after Cleveland vacated the White House in favor of his Republican successor, Benjamin Harrison. By this time popular indignation against trusts was so passionate that Congress could no longer ignore it. A carefully framed measure resulted, which was intended, as Senator Orville H. Platt of Connecticut wryly remarked, to curb popular discontent rather than to curb the unpopular trust. In the Sherman Antitrust Act of July 2, 1890, all goods produced by monopolies were banned from interstate commerce, but the measure was so adroitly phrased that ways were soon found to evade it:[5]

SECTION 1. Every contract, combination in the form of trust or otherwise, or conspiracy, in restraint of trade or commerce among the several States, or with foreign nations, is hereby declared to be illegal. Every person who shall make any such contract or engage in any such combination or conspiracy, shall be deemed guilty of a misdemeanor, and, on conviction thereof, shall be punished by fine not exceeding five thousand dollars, or by imprisonment not exceeding one year, or by both said punishments, in the discretion of the court.

SEC. 2. Every person who shall monopolize, or attempt to monopolize, or combine or conspire with any other person or persons, to monopolize any part of the trade or commerce among the several States, or with foreign nations, shall be deemed guilty of a misdemeanor, and, on conviction thereof, shall be punished by fine not exceeding five thousand dollars, or by imprisonment not exceeding one year, or by both said punishments, in the discretion of the court.

SEC. 3. Every contract, combination in form of trust or otherwise, or conspiracy, in restraint of trade or commerce in any Territory of the United States or of the District of Columbia, or in restraint of trade or commerce between any such Territory and another, or between any such Territory or Territories and any State or States or the District of Columbia, or with foreign nations, or between the District of Columbia and any State or States or foreign nations, is hereby declared illegal. Every person who shall make any such contract or engage in any such combination or conspiracy, shall be deemed guilty of a misdemeanor, and, on conviction thereof, shall be punished by fine not exceeding five thousand dollars, or by imprisonment not exceeding one year, or by

both said punishments, in the discretion of the court.

SEC. 4. The several circuit courts of the United States are hereby invested with jurisdiction to prevent and restrain violations of this act; and it shall be the duty of the several district attorneys of the United States, in their respective districts, under the direction of the Attorney-General, to institute proceedings in equity to prevent and restrain such violations. Such proceedings may be by way of petition setting forth the case and praying that such violation shall be enjoined or otherwise prohibited. When the parties complained of shall have been duly notified of such petition the courts shall proceed, as soon as may be, to the hearing and determination of the case; and pending such petition and before final decrees, the court may at any time make such temporary restraining order or prohibition as shall be deemed just in the premises.

SEC. 5. Whenever it shall appear to the court before which any proceeding under Section four of this act may be pending, that the ends of justice require that other parties should be brought before the court, the court may cause them to be summoned, whether they reside in the district in which the court is held or not; and subpœnas to that end may be served in any district by the marshal thereof.

SEC. 6. Any property owned under any contract or by any combination, or pursuant to any conspiracy (and being the subject thereof) mentioned in section one of this act, and being in the course of transportation from one State to another, or to a foreign country, shall be forfeited to the United States, and may be seized and condemned by like proceedings as those provided by law for the forfeiture, seizure, and condemnation of property imported into the United States contrary to law.

SEC. 7. Any person who shall be injured in his business or property by any other person or corporation by reason of anything forbidden or declared to be unlawful

---

[5] *Ibid.,* pp. 209-210.

by this act, may sue therefor in any circuit court of the United States in the district in which the defendant resides or is found, without respect to the amount in controversy, and shall recover threefold the damages by him sustained, and the costs of suit, including a reasonable attorney's fee.

Sec. 8. That the word "person," or "persons," wherever used in this act shall be deemed to include corporations and associations existing under or authorized by the laws of either the United States, the laws of any of the Territories, the laws of any State, or the laws of any foreign country.

## THE PROTEST OF LABOR

### 6

Two pressure groups were largely responsible for wresting the Interstate Commerce Act and the Sherman Antitrust Act from reluctant legislators. One was composed of workers in eastern cities; the other, of western farmers. Laborers began organizing on a national scale just after the Civil War, realizing that only nation-wide unions could give them the strength to win decent wages, hours, and working conditions from nation-wide industries. The Knights of Labor sought to weld workers of every race, color, skill, and craft into "One Big Union." Its broadly humanitarian constitution, adopted on January 1, 1878, helps explain why it attracted 750,000 members by the middle 1880's:[6]

The recent alarming development and aggression of aggregated wealth, which, unless checked, will invariably lead to the pauperization and hopeless degradation of the toiling masses, render it imperative, if we desire to enjoy the blessings of life, that a check should be placed upon its power and upon unjust accumulation, and a system adopted which will secure to the laborer the fruits of his toil; and as this much-desired object can only be accomplished by the thorough unification of

labor, and the united efforts of those who obey the divine injunction that "In the sweat of thy brow shalt thou eat bread," we have formed the ***** with a view of securing the organization and direction, by co-operative effort, of the power of the industrial classes; and we submit to the world the object sought to be accomplished by our organization, calling upon all who believe in securing "the greatest good to the greatest number" to aid and assist us:—

I. To bring within the folds of organization every department of productive industry, making knowledge a standpoint for action, and industrial and moral worth, not wealth, the true standard of individual and national greatness.

II. To secure to the toilers a proper share of the wealth that they create; more of the leisure that rightfully belongs to them; more societary advantages; more of the benefits, privileges, and emoluments of the world; in a word, all those rights and privileges necessary to make them capable of enjoying, appreciating, defending, and perpetuating the blessings of good government.

III. To arrive at the true condition of the producing masses in their educational, moral, and financial condition, by demanding from the various governments the establishment of bureaus of Labor Statistics.

IV. The establishment of co-operative institutions, productive and distributive.

V. The reserving of the public lands— the heritage of the people—for the actual settler;—not another acre for railroads or speculators.

VI. The abrogation of all laws that do not bear equally upon capital and labor, the removal of unjust technicalities, delays, and discriminations in the administration of justice, and the adopting of measures providing for the health and safety of those engaged in mining, manufacturing, or building pursuits.

VII. The enactment of laws to compel

---

[6] Quoted in Terence V. Powderly, *Thirty Years of Labor, 1859-1890* (Columbus, 1890), pp. 243-245.

chartered corporations to pay their employes weekly, in full, for labor performed during the preceding week, in the lawful money of the country.

VIII. The enactment of laws giving mechanics and laborers a first lien on their work for their full wages.

IX. The abolishment of the contract system on national, State, and municipal work.

X. The substitution of arbitration for strikes, whenever and wherever employers and employes are willing to meet on equitable grounds.

XI. The prohibition of the employment of children in workshops, mines, and factories before attaining their fourteenth year.

XII. To abolish the system of letting out by contract the labor of convicts in our prisons and reformatory institutions.

XIII. To secure for both sexes equal pay for equal work.

XIV. The reduction of the hours of labor to eight per day, so that the laborers may have more time for social enjoyment and intellectual improvement, and be enabled to reap the advantages conferred by the labor-saving machinery which their brains have created.

XV. To prevail upon governments to establish a purely national circulating medium, based upon the faith and resources of the nation, and isued directly to the people, without the intervention of any system of banking corporations, which money shall be a legal tender in payment of all debts, public or private.

## 7

The rise of the Knights of Labor was marked by bitter industrial warfare. Resenting any labor organization, employers fought back ruthlessly. They broke strikes, blacklisted organizers, and subjected the whole labor movement to a campaign of vilification obviously aimed at its total suppression. The union cause suffered from the support it received from a small group of radical anarchists. Anarchists preached a fiery gospel of revolution as the only solution to the class war. The position of the group at this period was explained by one of its leaders, Emma Goldman:[7]

Anarchism cannot but repudiate such a method of production; its goal is the freest possible expression of all the latent powers of the individual. Oscar Wilde defines a perfect personality as "one who develops under perfect conditions, who is not wounded, maimed, or in danger." A perfect personality, then, is only possible in a state of society where man is free to choose the mode of work, the conditions of work, and the freedom to work. One to whom the making of a table, the building of a house, or the tilling of the soil, is what the painting is to the artist and the discovery to the scientist,—the result of inspiration, of intense longing, and deep interest in work as a creative force. That being the ideal of Anarchism, its economic arrangements must consist of voluntary productive and distributive associations, gradually developing into free communism, as the best means of producing with the least waste of human energy. Anarchism, however, also recognizes the right of the individual, or numbers of individuals, to arrange at all times for other forms or work, in harmony with their tastes and desires.

Such free display of human energy being possible only under complete individual and social freedom, Anarchism directs its forces against the third and greatest foe of all social equality; namely the State, organized authority, or statutory law,—the dominion of human conduct.

Just as religion has fettered the human mind, and as property, or the monopoly of things, has subdued and stifled man's needs, so has the State enslaved his spirit, dictating every phase of conduct. "All government in essence," says Emerson, "is tyranny." It matters not whether it is

[7] Emma Goldman, *Anarchism* (New York, 1910), pp. 61-64, 72-73.

government by divine right or majority rule. In every instance its aim is the absolute subordination of the individual.

Referring to the American government, the greatest American Anarchist, David Thoreau, said: "Government, what is it but a tradition, though a recent one, endeavoring to transmit itself unimpaired to posterity, but each instance losing its integrity; it has not the vitality and force of a single living man." Law never made man a whit more just; and by means of their respect for it, even the well disposed are daily made agents of injustice.

Indeed, the keynote of government is "injustice." With the arrogance and self-sufficiency of the King who could do no wrong, governments ordain, judge, condemn, and punish the most insignificant offenses, while maintaining themselves by the greatest of all offenses, the annihilation of individual liberty. Thus Ouida is right when she maintains that "the State only aims at instilling those qualities in its public by which its demands are obeyed, and its exchequer is filled. Its highest attainment is the reduction of mankind to clockwork. In its atmosphere all those finer and more delicate liberties, which require treatment and spacious expansion, inevitably dry up and perish. The State requires a taxpaying machine in which there is no hitch, an exchequer in which there is never a deficit, and a public, monotonous, obedient, colorless, spiritless, moving humbly like a flock of sheep along a straight high road between two walls."

Yet even a flock of sheep would resist the chicanery of the State, if it were not for the corruptive, tyrannical, and oppressive methods it employs to serve its purposes. Therefore Bakunin repudiates the State as synonymous with the surrender of the liberty of the individual or small minorities,—the destruction of social relationship, the curtailment, or complete denial even, of life itself, for its own aggrandizement. The State is the altar of political freedom and, like the religious altar, it is main-

tained for the purpose of human sacrifice.

In fact, there is hardly a modern thinker who does not agree that government, organized authority, or the State, is necessary *only* to maintain or protect property and monopoly. It has proven efficient in that function only. . . .

Direct action, having proved effective along economic lines, is equally potent in the environment of the individual. There a hundred forces encroach upon his being, and only persistent resistance to them will finally set him free. Direct action against the authority in the shop, direct action against the authority of the law, direct action against the invasive, meddlesome authority of our moral code, is the logical, consistent method of Anarchism.

Will it not lead to a revolution? Indeed, it will. No real social change has ever come about without a revolution. People are either not familiar with their history, or they have not yet learned that revolution is but thought carried into action.

Anarchism, the great leaven of thought, is today permeating every phase of human endeavor. Science, art, literature, the drama, the effort for economic betterment, in fact every individual and social opposition to the existing disorder of things, is illumined by the spiritual light of Anarchism. It is the philosophy of the sovereignty of the individual. It is the theory of social harmony. It is the great, surging, living truth that is reconstructing the world, and that will usher in the Dawn.

8

Anarchist doctrines had little appeal to the average American workman, but still less acceptable were the tactics of those who followed the anarchist banner. Breathing bloodshed in every sentence, anarchists shouted from soapboxes in city after city that the "bloated" plutocrats must be annihilated at once; one of their most inflammatory publications was *A Manual of Instruction in the Use and Preparation of Nitroglycerine, Dynamite, Gun-Cotton, Fulminating Mercury, Bombs, Fuses, Poisons, Etc. Etc.* And anarch-

st papers bristled with advice such as that
printed in *The Alarm* in 1885:[8]

*Dynamite!* Of all the good stuff, that is
he stuff! Stuff several pounds of this
ublime stuff into an inch pipe (gas or
water pipe), plug up both ends, insert a
ap with a fuse attached, place this in the
immediate vicinity of a lot of rich loafers
who live by the sweat of other people's
brows, and light the fuse. A most cheerful
and gratifying result will follow. In giving
dynamite to the downtrodden millions
of the globe science has done its best
work. The dear stuff can be carried in the
pocket without danger, while it is a formidable weapon against any force of mili-
ia, police, or detectives that may want to
tifle the cry for justice that goes forth
from the plundered slaves. It is something
not very ornamental, but exceedingly use-
ul. It can be used against persons and
hings. It is better to use it against the
ormer than against bricks and masonry.
t is a genuine boon for the disinherited,
while it brings terror and fear to the rob-
bers. A pound of this good stuff beats a
bushel of ballots all hollow—and don't
you forget it! Our lawmakers might as
well try to sit down on the crater of a
volcano or on the point of a bayonet as
to endeavor to stop the manufacture and
use of dynamite. It takes more justice and
right than is contained in laws to quiet the
spirit of unrest.

## 9

Anarchist support of American workers
seriously embarrassed the Knights of Labor.
As industrial conflicts multiplied with union
growth, ill-informed people associated union-
sm with anarchism; the Haymarket riot convinced them. When Chicago workers, on
trike for the eight-hour day, assembled in
Haymarket Square on a May evening in 1886
to protest the killing of several pickets at the
McCormick Harvester plant, a column of
police entered the square. Someone—none today knows who—threw a bomb killing seven

policemen and injuring several more. Although the Knights of Labor had nothing to
do with this disgraceful act, it bore the brunt
of popular revulsion. As public sentiment
swung against unions, employers were encouraged to use black lists, yellow-dog contracts, and iron-clad oaths to break all labor
organizations. The skilled workers, who suffered most severely from these tactics, deserted the Knights of Labor in large numbers.
However, a call was sent out on December 8,
1886, for a new federation of the trades—the
inception of the American Federation of
Labor:[9]

On May 18, 1886, a conference of the
chief officers of the various national and
international trade unions was held in
Philadelphia, Pa., at which twenty national
and international unions were represented
and twelve more sent letters of sympathy
tendering their support to the conference.
This made at that time thirty-two national
and international trades unions with 367,-
736 members in good standing.

Since then quite a number of trades
union conventions have been held, at all
of which the action of the trades union
conference has been emphatically and
fully endorsed and a desire for a closer federation or alliance of all trades unions has
been generally expressed. Not only that
but a great impetus has been given to the
formation of national trades unions and
several new national unions have recently
been formed, while all the trades societies
with national or international heads have
increased in membership and grown
stronger in every respect.

The time has now arrived to draw the
bonds of unity much closer together between all the trades unions of America.
We need an annual Trades Congress that
shall have for its object:

1. The formation of trades unions and
the encouragement of the trades union
movement in America.

2. The organization of trades assem-

---

*The Alarm,* February 21, 1885.

[9] Quoted in Norman J. Ware, *The Labor Movement in the United States, 1860-1895* (New York,
1929), 294-295.

blies, trades councils or central labor unions in every city in America and the further encouragement of such bodies.

3. The founding of state trade assemblies or state labor congresses to influence state legislation in the interest of the working masses.

4. The establishment of national and international trades unions based upon the strict recognition of the autonomy of each trade, and the promotion and advancement of such bodies.

5. An American Federation or Alliance of all national and international trades unions to aid and assist each other and furthermore to secure national legislation in the interest of the working people and influence public opinion by peaceful and legal methods in favor of organized labor.

6. To aid and encourage the labor press of America and to disseminate tracts and literature on the labor movement.

## 10

Even so conservative an organization as the American Federation of Labor could not escape baptism by violence. Between 1881 and the end of the century there were 23,798 strikes involving 6,610,000 workers and the welfare of the nation. Particularly bitter was the Pullman strike (1894), which arrayed the American Railway Union against the Pullman Parlor Car Company in a dispute over wages. When an irresponsible Chicago mob halted a mail train and damaged an engine, Attorney General Richard Olney procured a blanket injunction enjoining the union's head, Eugene V. Debs, from interfering with railroad operations. Debs was jailed for violating the injunction. In the case of *United States* v. *Debs* (1894) the Supreme Court held the injunction valid under the Sherman Antitrust Act. "Combinations are condemned," in the words of the majority opinion, "not only when they take the form of trusts, but in whatever form found, if they be in restraint of trade." When the union pressed its defense of Debs still farther, the Court, in the famous case of *In re Debs* (1895), denied a petition for a writ of habeas corpus on even broader grounds:[10]

The case presented by the bill is this. The United States, finding that the interstate transportation of persons and property, as well as the carriage of the mails, i forcibly obstructed, and that a combinatio and conspiracy exists to subject the control of such transportation to the will c the conspirators, applied to one of thei courts, sitting as a court of equity, for a injunction to restrain such obstruction an prevent carrying into effect such con spiracy. Two questions of importance ar presented: First. Are the relations of th general government to interstate commerc and the transportation of the mails suc as to authorize a direct interference t prevent a forcible obstruction thereof Second. If authority exists, as authorit in governmental affairs implies both powe and duty, has a court of equity jurisdictio to issue an injunction in aid of the per formance of such duty.

*First.* What are the relations of the gen eral government to interstate commerc and the transportation of the mails? The are those of direct supervision, control, an management. While under the dual sys tem which prevails with us the powers o government are distributed between th state and the nation, and while the latte is properly styled a government of enumer ated powers, yet within the limits of suc enumeration it has all the attributes o sovereignty, and, in the exercise of thos enumerated powers, acts directly upon th citizen, and not through the intermediat agency of the state. . . .

"We hold it to be an incontrovertibl principle, that the government of th United States may, by means of physica force, exercised through its official agent execute on every foot of American soil th powers and functions that belong to i This necessarily involves the power t command obedience to its laws, and henc the power to keep the peace to that ex tent. . . ."

Among the powers expressly given t the national government are the contro

[10] *United States Reports,* 158 U.S. 577-600.

f interstate commerce and the creation nd management of the postoffice sys- m. . . .

Obviously these powers given to the ational government over interstate com- erce and in respect to the transportation f the mails were not dormant and unused. Congress had taken hold of these two mat- ers, and by various and specific acts had ssumed and exercised the powers given o it, and was in the full discharge of its uty to regulate interstate commerce and arry the mails. The validity of such exer- ise and the exclusiveness of its control had een again and again presented to this ourt for consideration. It is curious to ote the fact that in a large proportion of he cases in respect to interstate commerce rought to this court the question pre- ented was of the validity of state legisla- ion in its bearings upon interstate com- erce, and the uniform course of decision as been to declare that it is not within he competency of a state to legislate in uch a manner as to obstruct interstate ommerce. If a state with its recognized owers of sovereignty is impotent to ob- truct interstate commerce, can it be that ny mere voluntary association of individ- als within the limits of that state has a ower which the state itself does not ossess?

As, under the Constitution, power over nterstate commerce and the transportation f the mails is vested in the national gov- rnment, and Congress by virtue of such rant has assumed actual and direct con- rol, it follows that the national govern- ent may prevent any unlawful and forci- le interference therewith. But how shall his be accomplished? Doubtless, it is ithin the competency of Congress to rescribe by legislation that any interfer- nce with these matters shall be offenses gainst the United States, and prosecuted nd punished by indictment in the proper ourts. But is that the only remedy? Have he vast interests of the nation in inter- tate commerce, and in the transportation

of the mails, no other protection than lies in the possible punishment of those who interfere with it? To ask the question is to answer it. By article 3, section 2, clause 3, of the federal Constitution it is pro- vided: "The trial of all crimes except in cases of impeachment shall be by jury; and such trial shall be held in the State where the said crime shall have been com- mitted." If all the inhabitants of a state, or even a great body of them, should com- bine to obstruct interstate commerce or the transportation of the mails, prosecu- tions for such offenses had in such a com- munity would be doomed in advance to failure. And if the certainty of such fail- ure was known, and the national govern- ment had no other way to enforce the freedom of interstate commerce and the transportation of the mails than by prose- cution and punishment for interference therewith, the whole interests of the nation in these respects would be at the absolute mercy of a portion of the inhabitants of that single state.

But there is no such impotency in the national government. The entire strength of the nation may be used to enforce in any part of the land the full and free exer- cise of all national powers and the security of all rights entrusted by the Constitution to its care. The strong arm of the national government may be put forth to brush away all obstructions to the freedom of interstate commerce or the transportation of the mails. If the emergency arises, the army of the nation, and all its militia, are at the service of the nation to compel obedience to its laws.

But passing to the second question, is there no other alternative than the use of force on the part of the executive authori- ties whenever obstructions arise to the freedom of interstate commerce or the transportation of the mails? Is the army the only instrument by which rights of the public can be enforced and the peace of the nation preserved? Grant that any public nuisance may be forcibly abated either at the instance of the authorities, or by any individual suffering private damage therefrom, the existence of this right of forcible abatement is not inconsistent with nor does it destroy the right of appeal in an orderly way to the court for a judicial determination, and an exercise of their powers by writ of injunction and otherwise. . . .

It is obvious from these decisions that while it is not the province of the government to interfere in any mere matter of private controversy between individuals, or to use its great powers to enforce the rights of one against another, yet, whenever the wrongs complained of are such as affect the public at large, and are in respect of matters which by the Constitution are entrusted to the care of the nation, and concerning which the nation owes the duty to all the citizens of securing to them their common rights, then the mere fact that the government has no pecuniary interest in the controversy is not sufficient to exclude it from the courts, or prevent it from taking measures therein to fully discharge those constitutional duties.

The national government, given by the Constitution power to regulate interstate commerce, has by express statute assumed jurisdiction over such commerce when carried upon railroads. It is charged, therefore, with the duty of keeping those highways of interstate commerce free from obstruction, for it has always been recognized as one of the powers and duties of a government to remove obstructions from the highway under its control. . . .

We have given to this case the most careful and anxious attention, for we realize that it touches closely questions of supreme importance to the people of this country. Summing up our conclusions, we hold that the government of the United States is one having jurisdiction over every foot of soil within its territory, and acting directly upon each citizen; that while it is a government of enumerated powers, it

has within the limits of those powers a the attributes of sovereignty; that to it committed power over interstate commer and the transmission of the mail; that th powers thus conferred upon the nation government are not dormant, but hav been assumed and put into practical exe cise by the legislation of Congress; that i the exercise of those powers it is comp tent for the nation to remove all obstru tions upon highways, natural or artificia to the passage of interstate commerce the carrying of the mail; that while it ma be competent for the government (throug the executive branch and in the use of th entire executive power of the nation) forcibly remove all such obstructions, is equally within its competency to appe to the civil courts for an inquiry and dete mination as to the existence and charact of any alleged obstructions, and if suc are found to exist, or threaten to occur, t invoke the powers of these courts to r move or restrain such obstruction; that th jurisdiction of courts to interfere in suc matters by injunction is one recognize from ancient times and by indubitabl authority; that such jurisdiction is n ousted by the fact that the obstructions ar accompanied by or consist of acts in them selves violations of the criminal law; tha the proceeding by injunction is of a civ character, and may be enforced by pr ceedings in contempt; that such proceed ings are not in execution of the crimina laws of the land; that the penalty for violation of injunction is no substitute fo and no defense to a prosecution for an criminal offenses committed in the cours of such violation; that the complaint file in this case clearly showed an existin obstruction of artificial highways for th passage of interstate commerce and th transmission of the mail—an obstructio not only temporarily existing, but threa ening to continue; that under such com plaint the circuit court had power to issu its process of injunction; that it havin been issued and served on these defend

nts, the circuit court had authority to
nquire whether its orders had been dis-
beyed, and when it found that they had
een, then to proceed under section 725,
evised Statutes, which grants power "to
unish by fine or imprisonment, . . . dis-
bedience, . . . to any lawful writ, proc-
ss, order, rule, decree or command," and
nter the order of punishment complained
f; and, finally, that, the circuit court, hav-
ng full jurisdiction in the premises, its
nding of the fact of disobedience is not
pen to review on habeas corpus in this
r any other court. . . .

## 11

The Pullman strike broke the American
ailway Union but gave American liberals a
ew leader. Eugene V. Debs, imprisoned for
iolating the federal injunction, had time to
ead widely for the first time in his busy life.
s a result he emerged from jail a socialist,
nd in 1898 founded the American Socialist
arty. The party's phenomenal growth (it
olled almost a million votes fourteen years
ter) is easy to understand. To thousands of
nskilled workers, barred from the American
ederation of Labor by the lack of a skill or
raft, capitalism no longer seemed the ideal
 had been a generation earlier. There ap-
eared to be sense in the words of Eugene
ebs, who carried the campaign even into
e rural areas of Kansas:[11]

There were no capitalists nor was there
uch a thing as capital before the begin-
ing of the present system. Capitalists
ame with machinery. Up to the time that
achinery supplanted the hand tool the
ttle employer was himself a workingman.
No matter what the shop or factory, you
ould find the employer working side by
de with his men. He was a superior
orkman who got more orders than he
ould fill and employed others to help him,
ut he had to pay them the equivalent of
hat they produced because if he did not
ey would pack up their tools and go
to business for themselves.

Speech delivered at Girard, Kans., May 23,
08. In *Debs: His Life, Writings and Speeches*
hicago, 1910), pp. 481-485, 489-491.

Now, the individual tool has become
the mammoth machine. It has multiplied
production by hundreds. The old tool was
individually owned and used. The modern
tool, in the form of a great machine, is
social in every conception of it. Look at
one of these giant machines. Come to the
Appeal Office and look at the press in
operation. Here the progressive conception
of the ages is crystallized. What individual shall put his hand on this social agency
and say, "This is mine! He who would
apply labor here must first pay tribute to
me."

The hand tool has been very largely supplanted by this machine. Not many tools
are left. You are still producing in a very
small way here in Girard, but your production is flickering out gradually. It is but
a question of time until it will expire entirely. In spite of all that can be said or
done to the contrary production is organizing upon a larger and larger scale and
becoming entirely co-operative. This has
crowded out the smaller competitor and
gradually opened the way for a new social
order.

Your material interest and mine in the
society of the future will be the same. Instead of having to fight each other like
animals, as we do today, and seeking to
glorify the brute struggle for existence—
of which every civilized human being
ought to be ashamed—instead of this, our
material interests are going to be mutual.
We are going to jointly own these mammoth machines, and we are going to operate them as joint partners and we are
going to divide all the products among
ourselves.

We are not going to send our surplus
to the Goulds and Vanderbilts of New
York. We are not going to pile up a billion of dollars in John D. Rockefeller's
hands—a vast pyramid from the height of
which he can look down with scorn and
contempt upon the "common herd." John
D. Rockefeller's great fortune is built upon
your ignorance. When you know enough

to know what your interest is you will support the great party that is organized upon the principle of collective ownership of the means of life. This party will sweep into power upon the issue of emancipation just as republicanism swept into power upon the abolition question half a century ago.

You may think you are very comfortable. Let me make you a little comparison. You may not agree with me. I don't expect you to and I don't ask you to. I am going to ask you to remember what I say this afternoon and perhaps before I am elected president of the United States you will believe what I say is true. Now there are those of you who are fairly comfortable under the present standard. Isn't it amazing to you how little the average man is satisfied with? You go out here to the edge of town and you find a small farmer who has a cabin with just room enough to keep himself and wife and two or three children, which has a mortgage on it, and he works early and late and gets just enough in net returns to keep him in working order, and he will deliver a lecture about the wonderful prosperity of the country.

He is satisfied, and that is his calamity.

Now, the majority of you would say that is his good fortune. "It is a blessing that he is satisfied." I want to see if I can show you that it is a curse to him and to society that he is satisfied.

If it had not been for the discontent of a few fellows who have not been satisfied with their condition you would still be living in caves. You never would have emerged from the jungle. Intelligent discontent is the mainspring of civilization.

Progress is born of agitation. It is agitation or stagnation. I have taken my choice.

This farmer works all day long, works hard enough to produce enough to live the life of a man; not of an animal, but of a man. Now there is an essential difference between a man and an animal. I admire a

magnificent animal in any form except i the human form. Suppose you had ever thing that you could possibly desire, s far as your physical wants are concerned Suppose you had a million to your cred in the bank, a palatial home and relation to suit yourself, but no soul capacity fo real enjoyment. If you were denied know ing what sorrow is, what real joy is, wha music is, and literature and sculpture, an all of those subtle influences that touc the heart and quicken the pulses and fii the senses, and so liven and ennoble a ma that he can feel his head among the sta and in communion with God himself— you are denied these, no matter how slee or fat or contented you may be, you ar still as base and as corrupt and as repulsiv a being as walks God's green earth. . .

Now, we Socialists propose that societ in its collective capacity shall produce, no for profit, but in abundance to satisfy hi man wants; that every man shall have th inalienable right to work, and receive th full equivalent of all he produces; tha every man may stand fearlessly erect i the pride and majesty of his own mar hood.

Every man and every woman will the be economically free. They can, withou let or hindrance, apply their labor, wit the best machinery that can be devised, t all the natural resources, do the work c society and produce for all; and then r ceive in exchange a certificate of valu equivalent to that of their productio Then society will improve its institution in proportion to the progress of inventio Whether in the city or on the farm, a things productive will be carried forwar on a gigantic scale. All industry will b completely organized. Society for the firs time will have a scientific foundatio Every man, by being economically fre will have some time for himself. He ca then take a full and perfect breath. He ca enjoy life with his wife and children, be cause then he will have a home.

We are not going to destroy privat

property. We are going to establish private property—all the private property necessary to house man, keep him in comfort and satisfy his wants. Eighty per cent of the people of the United States have no property today. A few have got it all. They have dispossessed the people, and when we get into power we will dispossess them. We will reduce the workday and give every man a chance. We will go to the parks, and we will have music, because we will have time to play music and desire to hear it.

Is it not sad to think that not one in a thousand knows what music is? Is it not pitiable to see the poor, ignorant, dumb human utterly impervious to the divine influences of music? If humanity could only respond to the higher influences! And would if it had time.

Release the animal, throw off his burden; give him a chance and he rises as if by magic to the plane of a man. Man has all of the divine attributes. They are in latent state. They are not yet developed. It does not pay now to love music. Keep your eye on the almighty dollar and your fellowman. Get the dollar and keep him down. Make him produce for you. You are not your brother's keeper. Suppose he is poor! Suppose his wife is forced into prostitution! Suppose his child is deformed! And suppose he shuffles off by destroying himself! What is that to you?

But you ought to be ashamed. Take the standard home and look it in the face. If you know what that standard means, and you are a success, God help the failure!

Our conduct is determined by our economic relations. If you and I must fight each other to exist, we will not love each other very hard. We can go to the same church and hear the same minister tell us with good conscience that we ought to love each other, and the next day we approach some business transaction. Do we remember what the minister told us? No; it is gone until next Sunday. Six days in the

week we are following the Golden Rule reversed. Now, when we approach a business transaction in competition, what is more natural than that we should try to get the better of it?—get the better of our fellowman?—cheat him if we can?

And if you succeed that fixes you as a business man. You have all the necessary qualifications. Don't let your conscience disturb you—that would interfere with business.

Competition was natural enough at one time, but do you think you are competing today? Many of you think you are competing. Against whom? Against Rockefeller? About as I would if I had a wheelbarrow and was competing with the Santa Fé from here to Kansas City. That is about the way you are competing; but your boys will not have even that chance—if capitalism lives that long. You hear of the "late" panic. It is very late. It is going to be very late. This panic will be with us five years from now, and will continue till then.

I am not a prophet. I can no more penetrate the future than you can. I do study the forces that underlie society and the trend of evolution. I can tell by what we have passed through about what we will have in the future; and I know that capitalism can be abolished and the people put in possession. Now, when we have taken possession, and we jointly own the means of production, we will no longer have to fight each other to live; our interests, instead of being competitive, will be co-operative. We will work side by side. Your interest will be mine and mine will be yours. That is the economic condition from which will spring the humane social relation of the future.

When we are in partnership and have stopped clutching each other's throats, when we have stopped enslaving each other, we will stand together, hands clasped, and be friends. We will be comrades, we will be brothers, and we will begin the march to the grandest civilization the human race has ever known.

## URBAN RADICALISM AND THE AGRARIAN CRUSADE

### 12

The strident voice of agrarian dissent during the 1890's was even more vociferous than the protest of labor. Temporarily appeased by the Granger victories, the farmer group resumed activity again a decade later when declining agricultural prices, mounting freight rates, and a grinding burden of debt stimulated the organization of a series of Farmers' Alliances in the South and West. They demanded a less rigid currency to raise prices and to relieve the pressure of debts. To accomplish these objectives, they advocated that the silver flowing from western mines be coined into dollars at the ratio of sixteen to one—sixteen times as much silver in a silver dollar as gold in a gold dollar. Despite conservative eastern fears, Congress bowed slightly before the pressure of the silver and agrarian blocs in 1890 and adopted the Sherman Silver Purchase Act:[12]

. . . [The] Secretary of the Treasury is hereby directed to purchase, from time to time, silver bullion to the aggregate amount of four million five hundred thousand ounces, or so much thereof as may be offered in each month, at the market price thereof, not exceeding one dollar for three hundred and seventy-one and twenty-five hundredths grains of pure silver, and to issue in payment for such purchases of silver bullion Treasury notes of the United States. . . .

SECTION 2. That the Treasury notes issued in accordance with the provisions of this act shall be redeemable on demand, in coin, at the Treasury of the United States, or at the office of any assistant treasurer of the United States, and when so redeemed may be reissued; but no greater or less amount of such notes shall be outstanding at any time than the cost of the silver bullion and the standard silver dollars coined therefrom, then held in the Treasury purchased by such notes; and such Treasury notes shall be a legal tender

in payment of all debts, public and private except where otherwise expressly stipulated in the contract, and shall be receivable for customs, taxes, and all public dues, and when so received may be reissued; and such notes, when held by any national banking association, may be counted as a part of its lawful reserve. That upon demand of the holder of any of the Treasury notes herein provided for the Secretary of the Treasury shall, under such regulations as he may prescribe, redeem such notes in gold or silver coin, at his discretion, it being the established policy of the United States to maintain the two metals on a parity with each other upon the present legal ratio, or such ratio as may be provided by law.

SEC. 3. That the Secretary of the Treasury shall each month coin two million ounces of the silver bullion purchased under the provisions of this act into standard dollars until July 1, 1891, and after that time he shall coin of the silver bullion purchased under the provisions of this act as much as may be necessary to provide for the redemption of the Treasury notes herein provided for, and any gain or seigniorage arising from such coinage shall be accounted for and paid into the Treasury.

### 13

The Sherman Silver Purchase Act, although welcomed by the silver bloc, failed to appease the farmers. As a cycle of drought years withered crops and raised mortgage rates beyond endurance, the demand for "free silver" swept like wildfire over West and South. By 189 delegates assembled at Omaha and welded the discontented into the People's Party. Enthusiasm approached the fervor of a religious crusade. The Populist platform, adopted on July 4, 1892, was a ringing challenge to the gospel of wealth, a rallying cry for liberals everywhere:[13]

The conditions which surround us best justify our co-operation; we meet in the

---

[12] *United States Statutes at Large*, XXVI, 209.

[13] Edward Stanwood, *A History of Presidential Elections* (Boston, 1892), pp. 474-478.

midst of a nation brought to the verge of moral, political, and material ruin. Corruption dominates the ballot-box, the Legislatures, the Congress, and touches even the ermine of the bench. The people are demoralized; most of the States have been compelled to isolate the voters at the polling places to prevent universal intimidation and bribery. The newspapers are largely subsidized or muzzled, public opinion silenced, business prostrated, homes covered with mortgages, labor impoverished, and the land concentrating in the hands of capitalists. The urban workmen are denied the right to organize for self-protection, imported pauperized labor beats down their wages, a hireling standing army, unrecognized by our laws, is established to shoot them down, and they are rapidly degenerating into European conditions. The fruits of the toil of millions are boldly stolen to build up colossal fortunes for a few, unprecedented in the history of mankind; and the possessors of these, in turn, despise the Republic and endanger liberty. From the same prolific womb of governmental injustice we breed the two great classes—tramps and millionaires.

The national power to create money is appropriated to enrich bond-holders; a vast public debt payable in legal-tender currency has been funded into gold-bearing bonds, thereby adding millions to the burdens of the people. Silver, which has been accepted as coin since the dawn of history, has been demonetized to add to the purchasing power of gold by decreasing the value of all forms of property as well as human labor, and the supply of currency is purposely abridged to fatten usurers, bankrupt enterprise, and enslave industry. A vast conspiracy against mankind has been organized on two continents, and it is rapidly taking possession of the world. If not met and overthrown at once it forebodes terrible social convulsions, the destruction of civilization, or the establishment of an absolute despotism.

We have witnessed for more than a quarter of a century the struggles of the two great political parties for power and plunder, while grievous wrongs have been inflicted upon the suffering people. We charge that the controlling influences dominating both these parties have permitted the existing dreadful conditions to develop without serious effort to prevent or restrain them. Neither do they now promise us any substantial reform. They have agreed together to ignore, in the coming campaign, every issue but one. They propose to drown the outcries of a plundered people with the uproar of a sham battle over the tariff, so that capitalists, corporations, national banks, rings, trusts, watered stock, the demonetization of silver and the oppressions of the usurers may all be lost sight of. They propose to sacrifice our homes, lives, and children on the altar of mammon; to destroy the multitude in order to secure corruption funds from the millionaires.

Assembled on the anniversary of the birthday of the nation, and filled with the spirit of the grand general and chief who established our independence, we seek to restore the government of the Republic to the hands of the "plain people," with which class it originated. We assert our purposes to be identical with the purposes of the National Constitution; "to form a more perfect union and establish justice, insure domestic tranquillity, provide for the common defence, promote the general welfare, and secure the blessings of liberty for ourselves and our posterity." We declare that this Republic can only endure as a free government while built upon the love of the people for each other and for the nation; that it cannot be pinned together by bayonets; that the Civil War is over, and that every passion and resentment which grew out of it must die with it, and that we must be in fact, as we are in name, one united brotherhood of freemen.

Our country finds itself confronted by

conditions for which there is no precedent in the history of the world; our annual agricultural productions amount to billions of dollars in value, which must, within a few weeks or months, be exchanged for billions of dollars' worth of commodities consumed in their production; the existing currency supply is wholly inadequate to make this exchange; the results are falling prices, the formation of combines and rings, the impoverishment of the producing class. We pledge ourselves that if given power we will labor to correct these evils by wise and reasonable legislation, in accordance with the terms of our platform. We believe that the powers of government —in other words, of the people—should be expanded (as in the case of the postal service) as rapidly and as far as the good sense of an intelligent people and the teachings of experience shall justify, to the end that oppression, injustice, and poverty shall eventually cease in the land.

While our sympathies as a party of reform are naturally upon the side of every proposition which will tend to make men intelligent, virtuous, and temperate, we nevertheless regard these questions, important as they are, as secondary to the great issues now pressing for solution, and upon which not only our individual prosperity but the very existence of free institutions depend; and we ask all men to first help us to determine whether we are to have a republic to administer before we differ as to the conditions upon which it is to be administered, believing that the forces of reform this day organized will never cease to move forward until every wrong is righted and equal rights and equal privileges securely established for all the men and women of this country.

We declare, therefore—

*First.*—That the union of the labor forces of the United States this day consummated shall be permanent and perpetual; may its spirit enter into all hearts for the salvation of the Republic and the uplifting of mankind!

*Second.*—Wealth belongs to him who creates it, and every dollar taken from industry without an equivalent is robbery. "If any will not work, neither shall he eat." The interests of rural and civil labor are the same; their enemies are identical.

*Third.*—We believe that the time has come when the railroad corporations will either own the people or the people must own the railroads; and should the government enter upon the work of owning and managing all railroads, we should favor an amendment to the constitution by which all persons engaged in the government service shall be placed under a civil-service regulation of the most rigid character, so as to prevent the increase of the power of the national administration by the use of such additional government employes.

We demand

First a national currency, safe, sound, and flexible issued by the general government only, a full legal tender for all debts, public and private, and that without the use of banking corporations; a just, equitable, and efficient means of distribution direct to the people, at a tax not to exceed 2 per cent. per annum, to be provided as set forth in the sub-treasury plan of the Farmers' Alliance, or a better system; also by payments in discharge of its obligations for public improvements.

(a) We demand free and unlimited coinage of silver and gold at the present legal ratio of sixteen to one.

(b) We demand that the amount of circulating medium be speedily increased to not less than $50 per capita.

(c) We demand a graduated income tax.

(d) We believe that the money of the country should be kept as much as possible in the hands of the people, and hence we demand that all State and national revenues shall be limited to the necessary expenses of the government, economically and honestly administered.

(e) We demand that postal savings banks be established by the government for the safe deposit of the earnings of the people and to facilitate exchange.

Second, transportation. Transportation being a means of exchange and a public necessity, the government should own and operate the railroads in the interest of the people.

(a) The telegraph and telephone, like the post-office system, being a necessity for the transmission of news, should be owned and operated by the government in the interest of the people.

Third, land. The land, including all the natural sources of wealth, is the heritage of the people, and should not be monopolized for speculative purposes, and alien ownership of land should be prohibited. All land now held by railroads and other corporations in excess of their actual needs, and all lands now owned by aliens should be reclaimed by the government and held for actual settlers only. . . .

WHEREAS, Other questions have been presented for our consideration, we hereby submit the following, not as a part of the Platform of the People's Party, but as resolutions expressive of the sentiment of this Convention.

1. *Resolved,* That we demand a free ballot and a fair count in all elections, and pledge ourselves to secure it to every legal voter without Federal intervention, through the adoption by the States of the unperverted Australian or secret ballot system.

2. *Resolved,* That the revenue derived from a graduated income tax should be applied to the reduction of the burden of taxation now levied upon the domestic industries of this country.

3. *Resolved,* That we pledge our support to fair and liberal pensions to ex-Union soldiers and sailors.

4. *Resolved,* That we condemn the fallacy of protecting American labor under the present system, which opens our ports to the pauper and criminal classes of the world and crowds out our wage-earners; and we denounce the present ineffective laws against contract labor, and demand the further restriction of undesirable emigration.

5. *Resolved,* That we cordially sympathize with the efforts of organized workingmen to shorten the hours of labor, and demand a rigid enforcement of the existing eight-hour law on Government work, and ask that a penalty clause be added to the said law.

6. *Resolved,* That we regard the maintenance of a large standing army of mercenaries, known as the Pinkerton system, as a menace to our liberties, and we demand its abolition; and we condemn the recent invasion of the Territory of Wyoming by the hired assassins of plutocracy, assisted by Federal officials.

7. *Resolved,* That we commend to the favorable consideration of the people and the reform press the legislative system known as the initiative and referendum.

8. *Resolved,* That we favor a constitutional provision limiting the office of President and Vice-President to one term, and providing for the election of Senators of the United States by a direct vote of the people.

9. *Resolved,* That we oppose any subsidy or national aid to any private corporation for any purpose.

## 14

Hard times on the farm bred Populism; but just as important in the 1890's was urban dissent. As the depression took its toll, even the cautious A.F. of L. began to share agricultural discontent with the old political parties. Seeking an alliance of farmers and workers, labor leaders in Illinois called the

Springfield Industrial Conference in July, 1894. The "Call" and the "Springfield Platform" expressed the industrial unrest of the 1890's and showed the widening support for liberal demands that urban reformers had urged for two decades:[14]

## TO ALL LABOR UNIONS, LABOR ORGANIZATIONS, INDUSTRIAL ASSOCIATIONS AND POLITICAL REFORM SOCIETIES OF THE STATE OF ILLINOIS—GREETING:

The time for independent political action is at hand; the necessity for the same plainly apparent. The treachery of the Republican and Democratic parties to the interest of the masses may no longer be endured. The duty of the voters of the state of Illinois is plain. The membership of our industrial bodies are urgently demanding such action. The American Federation of Labor at its last convention submitted the following political program for discussion and action:

"1. Compulsory education. 2. Direct legislation. 3. A legal eight-hour workday. 4. Sanitary inspection of workshop, mine and home. 5. Liability of employers for injury to health, body or life. 6. The abolition of contract system in all public work. 7. The abolition of the sweating system. 8. The municipal ownership of street cars, and gas and electric plants for public distribution of light, heat and power. 9. The nationalization of telegraphs, telephones, railroads and mines. 10. The collective ownership by the people of all means of production and distribution. 11. The principle of referendum in all legislation."

The Illinois State Federation of Labor therefore issues to representatives of all organizations of the above description this call to meet and confer in the state capitol building, Monday, Tuesday and Wednes-

day, July 2d, 3d and 4th. Said conference to convene at said place at 10 o'clock sharp, Monday, July 2d, 1894, to consider above programs and such other matters of interest as may be deemed essential to success.

Basis of representation: all bona fide industrial and political reform organizations, three delegates. All central bodies of above, five delegates. Each journal of the reform press, one delegate. . . .

On the afternoon and evening of the 4th, delegates, visitors and citizens will be addressed by speakers of national reputation on the necessity of independent political action.

Address all communications to M. H. Madden, President Illinois State Federation of Labor, 148 Monroe Street, Chicago, Illinois.
April 30, 1894
Chicago, Illinois

*Platform adopted by the Springfield Industrial Conference, at Springfield, Illinois, July 5, 1894.*

The wage-earners of the State of Illinois, in convention assembled, at a time when the growing feeling of brotherhood is attended by the heroic efforts of toilers in behalf of their oppressed fellow workers, declare for political action.

Recognizing the beneficent working of the postal system, we demand the immediate nationalization of the telegraph and telephone, to be followed by governmental ownership of the railroads and mines, and we further demand the municipal ownership of street railways, gas and electric plants for the public distribution of light, heat, and power.

The land is the heritage of the people. Therefore we condemn existing laws which permit the alien ownership of large bodies of land held for speculative purposes and declare in favor of such taxation as will compel the using [sic] of land to make ownership profitable and also favor local option in taxation.

Believing that no general prosperity can

[14] The "Call," *Eight-Hour Herald* (Chicago), May 10, 1894. "Springfield Platform," *ibid.,* July 10, 1894; *Searchlight* (Chicago), July 5, 1894; *American Nonconformist* (Indianapolis), July 12, 1894.

be obtained without an adequate supply of money, which cannot be controlled by private corporations, we demand the issuance by the general government of legal tender notes in sufficient volume to meet the requirements of the business of our country.

We unequivocally condemn the policy of issuing interest-bearing bonds in time of peace.

Recognizing education to be the most potent agency for civilization, we favor such laws as will compel the attendance at school of all children of school age.

The great and unusual disturbances in labor circles force upon us the inevitable conviction that the time has now arrived in which encroachment of capital upon labor must cease and that the interests of the general public demand the passage of such laws as will give adequate protection and relief to the oppressed employes of the railways, in the factory, shop and mine; therefore we demand the following:

1. A legal eight-hour work day.

2. Sanitary inspection of workshop, mine, and home.

3. Liability of employers for injury to health, body or life.

4. The abolition of the contract system in all public work.

5. The abolition of the sweating system.

6. Proportional representation.

7. The right to govern resting with the governed, we demand the adoption of the initiative and referendum system of legislation. [This majority report of the Resolutions Committee, presented by A. L. Maxwell, chairman, who was also chairman of the State Central Committee of the People's party, was adopted only after the following supplemental resolutions— drafted and presented by Henry Demarest Lloyd of Chicago—had been grafted on to it by the margin of a single vote:]

1. We recommend independent political action by the bodies represented in this conference.

2. To that purpose we recommend the officials of these bodies to take immediate steps to hold a national convention to perfect plans for such political action.

3. Pending the organization of such a party we recommend those we represent in this conference to vote for those candidates of the People's party at the coming election who will pledge themselves to the principle of the collective ownership by the people of all such means of production and distribution as the people elect to operate for the commonwealth.

[The following resolutions, reported by W. C. Pomeroy, a Chicago labor leader, on behalf of the Organization Committee, became an essential part of the Springfield Platform:]

*Resolved,* That we adopt the name of the People's party, and under the name make our campaign.

*Resolved,* That we will make no state nominations, but support the ticket already named by the People's party; provided the state candidates of that party sign within thirty days the platform of this convention.

*Resolved,* That inasmuch as the People's party as an independent political organization predominates in point of numbers in the districts outside of our cities, it is the purpose and declared object of this convention to make no nomination in opposition to those already made by the Populists, and we declare it is our desire and purpose to co-operate with that party, using present machinery where it already exists, and where not existing to create the same, but in no instance to run separate tickets.

## 15

More than a million voters cast their ballots for James B. Weaver, the Populist presidential candidate in the election of 1892, and for the first time since the Civil War a minor party captured an electoral vote—in this case, twenty-two. Instead of winning support for free silver from the major parties, however, this impressive showing had the opposite effect. A minor panic swept the nation in 1893, and President Cleveland became convinced that fears of inflation on the part of businessmen were responsible. These could best be removed, he believed, by assuring the financial interests that the Democratic party had no faith in free silver. Calling Congress into special session, on August 3, 1893 he recommended repeal of the Sherman Silver Purchase Act:[15]

The existence of an alarming and extraordinary business situation, involving the welfare and prosperity of all our people, has constrained me to call together in extra session the people's representatives in Congress, to the end that through a wise and patriotic exercise of the legislative duty, with which they solely are charged, present evils may be mitigated and dangers threatening the future may be averted.

Our unfortunate financial plight is not the result of untoward events nor of conditions related to our natural resources, nor is it traceable to any of the afflictions which frequently check national growth and prosperity. With plenteous crops, with abundant promise of remunerative production and manufacture, with unusual invitation to safe investment, and with satisfactory assurance to business enterprise, suddenly financial distrust and fear have sprung up on every side. . . . Values supposed to be fixed are fast becoming conjectural, and loss and failure have invaded every branch of business.

I believe these things are principally chargeable to Congressional legislation touching the purchase and coinage of silver by the General Government.

This legislation is embodied in a statute passed on the 14th day of July, 1890, which was the culmination of much agitation on the subject involved, and which may be considered a truce, after a long struggle, between the advocates of free silver coin-

age and those intending to be more conservative. . . .

This law provides that in payment for the 4,500,000 ounces of silver bullion which the Secretary of the Treasury is commanded to purchase monthly there shall be issued Treasury notes redeemable on demand in gold or silver coin, at the discretion of the Secretary of the Treasury, and that said notes may be reissued. It is, however, declared in the act to be "the established policy of the United States to maintain the two metals on a parity with each other upon the present legal ratio or such ratio as may be provided by law." This declaration so controls the action of the Secretary of the Treasury as to prevent his exercising the discretion nominally vested in him if by such action the parity between gold and silver may be disturbed. Manifestly a refusal by the Secretary to pay these Treasury notes in gold if demanded would necessarily result in their discredit and depreciation as obligations payable only in silver, and would destroy the parity between the two metals by establishing a discrimination in favor of gold. . . .

The policy necessarily adopted of paying these notes in gold has not spared the gold reserve of $100,000,000 long ago set aside by the Government for the redemption of other notes, for this fund has already been subjected to the payment of new obligations amounting to about $150,000,000 on account of silver purchases, and has as a consequence for the first time since its creation been encroached upon. . . .

Unless Government bonds are to be constantly issued and sold to replenish our exhausted gold, only to be again exhausted, it is apparent that the operation of the silver-purchase law now in force leads in the direction of the entire substitution of silver for the gold in the Government Treasury, and that this must be followed by the payment of all Government obligations in depreciated silver.

At this stage gold and silver must part

---

[15] J. D. Richardson (comp.), *Messages and Papers of the Presidents, 1789-1897* (Washington, 1897, 1909; taken from the 1909 vol.), IX, 401-405.

company and the Government must fail in its established policy to maintain the two metals on a parity with each other. Given over to the exclusive use of a currency greatly depreciated according to the standard of the commercial world, we could no longer claim a place among nations of the first class, nor could our Government claim a performance of its obligation, so far as such an obligation has been imposed upon it, to provide for the use of the people the best and safest money. . . .

The people of the United States are entitled to a sound and stable currency and to money recognized as such on every exchange and in every market of the world. Their Government has no right to injure them by financial experiments opposed to the policy and practice of other civilized states, nor is it justified in permitting an exaggerated and unreasonable reliance on our national strength and ability to jeopardize the soundness of the people's money.

This matter rises above the plane of party politics. It vitally concerns every business and calling and enters every household in the land. There is one important aspect of the subject which especially should never be overlooked. At times like the present, when the evils of unsound finance threaten us, the speculator may anticipate a harvest gathered from the misfortune of others, the capitalist may protect himself by hoarding or may even find profit in the fluctuations of values; but the wage earner—the first to be injured by a depreciated currency and the last to receive the benefit of its correction —is practically defenseless. He relies for work upon the ventures of confident and contented capital. This failing him, his condition is without alleviation, for he can neither prey on the misfortunes of others nor hoard his labor. . . .

It is of the utmost importance that such relief as Congress can afford in the existing situation be afforded at once. The maxim "He gives twice who gives quickly" is directly applicable. It may be true that the embarrassments from which the business of the country is suffering arise as much from evils apprehended as from those actually existing. We may hope, too, that calm counsels will prevail, and that neither the capitalists nor the wage earners will give way to unreasoning panic and sacrifice their property or their interests under the influence of exaggerated fears. Nevertheless, every day's delay in removing one of the plain and principal causes of the present state of things enlarges the mischief already done and increases the responsibility of the Government for its existence. Whatever else the people have a right to expect from Congress, they may certainly demand that legislation condemned by the ordeal of three years' disastrous experience shall be removed from the statute books as soon as their representatives can legitimately deal with it.

It was my purpose to summon Congress in special session early in the coming September, that we might enter promptly upon the work of tariff reform, which the true interests of the country clearly demand, which so large a majority of the people, as shown by their suffrages, desire and expect, and to the accomplishment of which every effort of the present Administration is pledged. But while tariff reform has lost nothing of its immediate and permanent importance and must in the near future engage the attention of Congress, it has seemed to me that the financial condition of the country should at once and before all other subjects be considered by your honorable body.

I earnestly recommend the prompt repeal of the provisions of the act passed July 14, 1890, authorizing the purchase of silver bullion, and that other legislative action may put beyond all doubt or mistake the intention and the ability of the Government to fulfill its pecuniary obligations in money universally recognized by all civilized countries.

## 16

The repeal of the Sherman Silver Purchase Act set the stage for one of the most dramatic political contests in American history. The issue was clear-cut: a gold currency or free silver. The antagonists were equally well defined. After casting out a contingent of silverites from the mining states, the Republican party in a platform adopted at St. Louis on June 16, 1896, endorsed the gold standard unequivocally:[16]

For the first time since the civil war the American people have witnessed the calamitous consequence of full and unrestricted Democratic control of the government. It has been a record of unparalleled incapacity, dishonor, and disaster. In administrative management it has ruthlessly sacrificed indispensable revenue, entailed an unceasing deficit, eked out ordinary current expenses with borrowed money, piled up the public debt by $262,-000,000, in time of peace, forced an adverse balance of trade, kept a perpetual menace hanging over the redemption fund, pawned American credit to alien syndicates and reversed all the measures and results of successful Republican rule. In the broad effect of its policy it has precipitated panic, blighted industry and trade with prolonged depression, closed factories, reduced work and wages, halted enterprise and crippled American production, while stimulating foreign production for the American market. Every consideration of public safety and individual interest demands that the government shall be wrested from the hands of those who have shown themselves incapable of conducting it without disaster at home and dishonor abroad and shall be restored to the party which for thirty years administered it with unequaled success and prosperity. And in this connection, we heartily endorse the wisdom, patriotism and success of the administration of Benjamin Harrison. We renew and emphasize our allegiance to the policy of protection as the bulwark of American industrial independence and the foundation of American development and prosperity. This true American policy taxes foreign products and encourages home industry. It puts the burden of revenue on foreign goods; it secures the American market for the American producer. It upholds the American standard of wages for the American workingman; it puts the factory by the side of the farm, and makes the American farmer less dependent on foreign demand and price; it diffuses general thrift, and founds the strength of each. In its reasonable application it is just, fair and impartial, equally opposed to foreign control and domestic monopoly, to sectional discrimination and individual favoritism.

We denounce the present tariff as sectional, injurious to the public credit and destructive to business enterprise. We demand such an equitable tariff on foreign imports which come into competition with the American products as will not only furnish adequate revenue for the necessary expense of the Government, but will protect American labor from degradation and the wage level of other lands. We are not pledged to any particular schedules. The question of rates is a practical question, to be governed by the condition of time and of production. The ruling and uncompromising principle is the protection and development of American labor and industries. The country demands a right settlement, and then it wants a rest.

We believe the repeal of the reciprocity arrangements negotiated by the last Republican Administration was a national calamity, and demand their renewal and extension on such terms as will equalize our trade with other nations, remove the restrictions which now obstruct the sale of American products in the ports of other countries, and secure enlarged markets for the products of our farms, forests, and factories,

---

[16] Keith Porter (comp.), *National Party Platforms* (New York, 1924), pp. 201-204.

Protection and Reciprocity are twin measures of American policy and go hand in hand. Democratic rule has recklessly struck down both, and both must be re-established. Protection for what we produce; reciprocal agreement of mutual interests, which gain open markets for us in return for our open markets for others. Protection builds up domestic industry and trade and secures our own market for ourselves; reciprocity builds up foreign trade and finds an outlet for our surplus. . . .

The Republican party is unreservedly for sound money. It caused the enactment of a law providing for the resumption of specie payments in 1879. Since then every dollar has been as good as gold. We are unalterably opposed to every measure calculated to debase our currency or impair the credit of our country. We are therefore opposed to the free coinage of silver, except by international agreement with the leading commercial nations of the earth, which agreement we pledge ourselves to promote, and until such agreement can be obtained the existing gold standard must be maintained. All of our silver and paper currency must be maintained at parity with gold, and we favor all measures designated to maintain inviolable the obligations of the United States, of all our money, whether coin or paper, at the present standard, . . .

We denounce the practice in the pension bureau so recklessly and unjustly carried on by the present Administration of reducing pensions and arbitrarily dropping names from the rolls, as deserving the severest condemnation of the American people.

Our foreign policy should be at all times firm, vigorous and dignified, and all our interests in the western hemisphere should be carefully watched and guarded.

## 17

The Democratic party, gathered in Chicago early in July, 1896, was more deeply split on the currency problem than were the Republicans. Traditionally divided on the subject, the party contained large numbers of eastern conservatives hostile to a free-silver plank, and even larger numbers of western liberals likely to desert to the Populists should the gold standard be endorsed. When a young delegate from Nebraska mounted the rostrum on July 8 to plead the cause of silver and humanity the issue was joined. William Jennings Bryan's "Cross of Gold" speech not only helped him win the nomination but swept the Democrats into the silver camp, and personalized the aspirations of the common man:[17]

. . . I would be presumptuous, indeed, to present myself against the distinguished gentlemen to whom you have listened if this were a mere measuring of abilities; but this is not a contest between persons. The humblest citizen in all the land, when clad in the armor of a righteous cause, is stronger than all the hosts of error. I come to speak to you in defense of a cause as holy as the cause of liberty—the cause of humanity.

When this debate is concluded, a motion will be made to lay upon the table the resolution offered in commendation of the Administration, and also, the resolution offered in condemnation of the Administration. We object to bringing this question down to the level of persons. The individual is but an atom; he is born, he acts, he dies; but principles are eternal; and this has been a contest over a principle.

Never before in the history of this country has there been witnessed such a contest as that through which we have just passed. Never before in the history of American politics has a great issue been fought out as this issue has been, by the voters of a great party. On the fourth of March 1893, a few Democrats, most of them members of Congress, issued an address to the Democrats of the nation, asserting that the money question was the paramount issue of the hour; declaring that a majority

[17] W. J. Bryan, *The First Battle* (Chicago, 1897), pp. 199-205. Used by permission of W. B. Conkey Company, Chicago.

of the Democratic party had the right to control the action of the party on this paramount issue; and concluding with the request that the believers in the free coinage of silver in the Democratic party should organize, take charge of, and control the policy of the Democratic party. Three months later, at Memphis, an organization was perfected, and the silver Democrats went forth openly and courageously proclaiming their belief, and declaring that, if successful, they would crystallize into a platform the declaration which they had made. Then began the struggle. With a zeal approaching the zeal which inspired the Crusaders who followed Peter the Hermit, our silver Democrats went forth from victory unto victory until they are now assembled, not to discuss, not to debate, but to enter up the judgment already rendered by the plain people of this country. In this contest brother has been arrayed against brother, father against son. The warmest ties of love, acquaintance, and association have been disregarded; old leaders have been cast aside when they have refused to give expression to the sentiments of those whom they would lead, and new leaders have sprung up to give direction to this cause of truth. Thus has the contest been waged, and we have assembled here under as binding and solemn instructions as were ever imposed upon representatives of the people.

We do not come as individuals. As individuals we might have been glad to compliment the gentleman from New York, but we know that the people for whom we speak would never be willing to put him in a position where he could thwart the will of the Democratic party. I saw it was not a question of persons; it was a question of principle, and it is not with gladness, my friends, that we find ourselves brought into conflict with those who are now arrayed on the other side. . . .

When you come before us and tell us that we are about to disturb your business interests, we reply that you have disturbed our business interests by your course.

We say to you that you have made the definition of a business man too limited in its application. The man who is employed for wages is as much a business man as his employer; the attorney in a country town is as much a business man as the corporation counsel in a great metropolis; the merchant at the cross-roads store is as much a business man as the merchant of New York; the farmer who goes forth in the morning and toils all day, who begins in the spring and toils all summer, and who by the application of brain and muscle to the natural resources of the country creates wealth, is as much a business man as the man who goes upon the Board of Trade and bets upon the price of grain; the miners who go down a thousand feet into the earth, or climb two thousand feet upon the cliffs, and bring forth from their hiding places the precious metals to be poured into the channels of trade are as much business men as the few financial magnates who, in a back room, corner the money of the world. We come to speak of this broader class of business men.

Ah, my friends, we say not one word against those who live upon the Atlantic Coast, but the hardy pioneers who have braved all the dangers of the wilderness, who have made the desert to bloom as the rose—the pioneers away out there who rear their children near to Nature's heart, where they can mingle their voices with the voices of the birds—out there where they have erected schoolhouses for the education of their young, churches where they praise their Creator, and cemeteries where rest the ashes of their dead—these people, we say, are as deserving of the consideration of our party as any people in this country. It is for these that we speak. We do not come as aggressors. Our war is not a war of conquest; we are fighting in the defense of our homes, our families, and posterity. We have petitioned, and our petitions have been scorned; we have entreated, and our entreaties have been disregarded; we have begged, and they have mocked when our calamity came. We beg no longer; we entreat no more; we petition no more. We defy them.

The gentleman from Wisconsin has said that he fears a Robespierre. My friends, in this land of the free you need not fear that a tyrant will spring up from among the people. What we need is an Andrew Jackson to stand, as Jackson stood, against the encroachments of organized wealth.

They tell us that this platform was made to catch votes. We reply to them that changing conditions make new issues; that the principles upon which Democracy rests are as everlasting as the hills, but they must be applied to new conditions as they arise. Conditions have arisen, and we are here to meet those conditions. They tell us that the income tax ought not to be brought in here; that it is a new idea. They criticize us for our criticism of the Supreme Court of the United States. My friends, we have not criticized; we have simply called attention to what you already know. If you want criticisms read the dissenting opinions of the court. There you will find criticisms. They say that we passed an unconstitutional law; we deny it. The income tax was not unconstitutional when it was passed; it was not unconstitutional when it went before the Supreme Court for the first time; it did not become unconstitutional until one of the judges changed his mind, and we cannot be expected to know when a judge will change his mind. The income tax is just. It simply intends to put the burden of government justly upon the backs of the people. I am in favor of an income tax. When I find a man who is not willing to bear his share of the burdens of the government which protects him, I find a man who is unworthy to enjoy the blessings of a government like ours.

They say that we are opposing national bank currency; it is true. If you will read

what Thomas Benton said, you will find he said that, in searching history, he could find but one parallel to Andrew Jackson; that was Cicero, he destroyed the conspiracy of Cataline and saved Rome. Benton said that Cicero only did for Rome what Jackson did for us when he destroyed the bank conspiracy and saved America. We say in our platform we believe that the right to coin and issue money is a function of government. We believe it. We believe that it is a part of sovereignty, and can no more with safety be delegated to private individuals than we could afford to delegate to private individuals the power to make penal statutes or levy taxes. Mr. Jefferson, who was once regarded as good Democratic authority, seems to have differed in opinion from the gentleman who has addressed us on the part of the minority. Those who are opposed to this proposition tell us that the issue of paper money is a function of the banks, and that the government ought to go out of the banking business. I stand with Jefferson rather than with them, and tell them, as he did, that the issue of money is a function of government, and that the banks ought to go out of the governing business.

They complain about the plank which declares against life tenure in office. They have tried to strain it to mean that which it does not mean. What we oppose by that plank is the life tenure which is being built up in Washington, and which excludes from participation in official benefits the humbler members of society. . . .

And now, my friends, let me come to the paramount issue. If they ask us why it is that we say more on the money question than we say upon the tariff question, I reply that, if protection has slain its thousands, the gold standard has slain its tens of thousands. If they ask us why we do not embody in our platforms all the things that we believe in, we reply that when we have restored the money of the Constitution, all other necessary reform will be possible; but that until this is done, there is no other reform that can be accomplished.

Why is it that within three months such a change has come over the country? Three months ago when it was confidently asserted that those who believed in the gold standard would frame our platform and nominate our candidates, even the advocates of the gold standard did not think that we could elect a President. And they had good reason for their doubt, because there is scarcely a State here today asking for the gold standard which is not in the absolute control of the Republican Party. But note the change. Mr. McKinley was nominated at St. Louis upon a platform which declared for the maintenance of the gold standard until it can be changed into bimetallism by international agreement. Mr. McKinley was the most popular man among the Republicans, and three months ago everybody in the Republican Party prophesied his election. How is it today? Why, the man who was once pleased to think that he looked like Napoleon—that man shudders today when he remembers that he was nominated on the anniversary of the battle of Waterloo. Not only that, but as he listens, he can hear with ever-increasing distinctness the sound of the waves as they beat upon the lonely shores of St. Helena.

Why this change? Ah, my friends, is not the reason for the change evident to any one who will look at the matter? No private character, however pure, no personal popularity, however great, can protect from the avenging wrath of an indignant people a man who will declare that he is in favor of fastening the gold standard upon this country, or who is willing to surrender the right of self-government and place the legislative control of our affairs in the hands of foreign potentates and powers.

We go forth confident that we shall win. Why? Because upon the paramount issue of this campaign there is not a spot of ground upon which the enemy will dare to challenge battle. If they tell us that the gold standard is a good thing, we shall point to their platform and tell them that their platform pledges the party to get rid of the gold standard and substitute bimetallism. If the gold standard is a good thing why try to get rid of it? I call your attention to the fact that some of the very people who are in this Convention today and who tell us that we ought to declare in favor of international bimetallism—thereby declaring that the gold standard is wrong and that the principle of bimetallism is better—these very people four months ago were open and avowed advocates of the gold standard, and were then telling us that we could not legislate two metals together, even with the aid of all the world. If the gold standard is a good thing, we ought to declare in favor of its retention and not in favor of abandoning it; and if the gold standard is a bad thing why should we wait until other nations are willing to help us to let go? Here is the line of battle, and we care not upon which issue they force the fight; we are prepared to meet them on either issue or on both. If they tell us that the gold standard is the standard of civilization, we reply to them that this, the most enlightened of all the nations of the earth, has never declared for a gold standard and that both the great parties this year are declaring against it. If the gold standard is the standard of civilization, why, my friends, should we not have it? If they come to meet us on that issue we can present the history of our nation. More than that; we can tell them that they will search the pages of history in vain to find a single instance where the common people of any land have ever declared themselves in favor of the gold standard. They can find where the holders of fixed investments have declared for a gold standard, but not where the masses have.

Mr. Carlisle said in 1878 that this was a struggle between the "idle holders of idle capital" and "the struggling masses, who produce the wealth and pay the taxes of the country," and, my friends, the question we are to decide is: Upon which side will the Democratic party fight; upon the side of "the idle holders of idle capital" or upon the side of "the struggling masses"? That is the question which the party must answer first, and then it must be answered by each individual hereafter. The sympathies of the Democratic party, as shown by the platform, are on the side of the struggling masses who have ever been the foundation of the Democratic party. There are two ideas of government. There are those who believe that if you will only legislate to make the well-to-do prosperous, their prosperity will leak through on those below. The Democratic idea, however, has been that if you make the masses prosperous, their prosperity will find its way up through every class which rests upon them.

You come to us and tell us that the great cities are in favor of the gold standard; we reply that the great cities rest upon our broad and fertile prairies. Burn down your cities and leave our farms, and your cities will spring up again as if by magic; but destroy our farms and the grass will grow in the streets of every city in the country.

My friends, we declare that this nation is able to legislate for its own people on every question, without waiting for the aid or consent of any other nation on earth; and upon that issue we expect to carry every state in the Union. I shall not slander the inhabitants of the fair state of Massachusetts nor the inhabitants of the state of New York by saying that, when they are confronted with the proposition, they will declare that this nation is not able to attend to its own business. It is the issue of 1776 over again. Our ancestors, when but three million in number, had the courage to declare their political independence of every other nation; shall we, their descendants, when we have grown to seventy millions, declare that we are less independent than our forefathers?

No, my friends, that will never be the verdict of our people. Therefore, we care not upon what lines the battle is fought. If they say bimetallism is good, but that we cannot have it until other nations help us, we reply, that instead of having a gold standard because England has, we will restore bimetallism, and then let England have bimetallism because the United States has it. If they dare to come out in the open field and defend the gold standard as a good thing, we will fight them to the uttermost. Having behind us the producing masses of this nation and the world, supported by the commercial interests, the laboring interests and the toilers everywhere, we will answer their demand for a gold standard by saying to them: You shall not press down upon the brow of labor this crown of thorns, you shall not crucify mankind upon a cross of gold.

## THE GOSPEL OF WEALTH IN CONSTITUTIONAL LAW

### 18

During the nineties—not really very gay—American dissent reached a harsh climax—and American liberals learned the meaning of despair. They had placed their faith for the future in false hopes: Bryan and a flexible currency, the Democrats and the revision of the tariff, the Interstate Commerce Act and lower freight rates, the Sherman Antitrust Act and the end of monopoly. Bryan went down to defeat in 1896, the Democrats failed to live up to their tariff promises, and the Supreme Court disposed of the Interstate Commerce Act and the Sherman Act in a series of devastating decisions. During the 1890's the Court served as the special defender of the gospel of wealth. Justice Brewer, dissenting in *Budd* v. *New York* (1892), unconsciously revealed the conservative outlook:[18]

The paternal theory of government is to me odious. The utmost possible liberty to the individual, and the fullest possible protection to him and his property, is both the limitation and duty of government. If

[18] *United States Reports,* 143 U.S. 551.

it may regulate the price of one service which is not a public service, or the compensation for the use of one kind of property which is not devoted to a public use, why may it not with equal reason regulate the price of all service, and the compensation to be paid for the use of all property? And if so, "Looking Backward" is nearer than a dream.

## 19

The Supreme Court applied this philosophy in a series of decisions virtually nullifying state and national laws designed to impose just carrying charges on railroads. In the first, *Chicago, Milwaukee and St. Paul Railroad Company* v. *Minnesota* (1889), it was held that rates set by legislative commissions must assure the roads a "reasonable" return, and that the reasonableness of rates was a subject for judicial review:[19]

This being the construction of the statute by which we are bound in considering the present case, we are of the opinion, that, so construed, it conflicts with the Constitution of the United States in the particulars complained of by the railroad company. It deprives the company of its right to a judicial investigation, by due process of law, under the forms and with the machinery provided by the wisdom of successive ages for the investigation judicially of the truth of a matter in controversy, and substitutes therefor, as an absolute finality, the action of a railroad commission which, in view of the powers conceded to it by the State court, cannot be regarded as clothed with judicial functions or possessing the machinery of a court of justice. . . .

By the second section of the statute in question, it is provided that all charges made by a common carrier for the transportation of passengers or property shall be equal and reasonable. Under this provision, the carrier has a right to make equal and reasonable charges for such transportation. In the present case, the re-

turn alleged that the rate of charge fixed by the commission was not equal or reasonable, and the Supreme Court held that the statute deprived the company of the right to show that judicially. The question of the reasonableness of a rate of charge for transportation by a railroad company, involving as it does the element of reasonableness both as regards the company and as regards the public, is eminently a question for judicial investigation, requiring due process of law for its determination. If the company is deprived of the power of charging reasonable rates for the use of its property, and thus, in substance and effect, of the property itself, without due process of law and in violation of the Constitution of the United States; and in so far as it is thus deprived, while other persons are permitted to receive reasonable profits upon their invested capital, the company is deprived of the equal protection of the laws.

## 20

While holding in the Minnesota Rate Case that the reasonableness of railroad rates was subject to judicial review, the justices made no attempt to define what was meant by a "reasonable" return. They did so in *Smyth* v. *Ames* (1897), which held that rates must be high enough to yield a fair return on a fair evaluation of the road's property—without, at the same time, explaining what those terms meant:[20]

We are now to inquire whether the Nebraska statute is repugnant to the Constitution of the United States.

By the 14th Amendment it is provided that no state shall deprive any person of property without due process of law nor deny to any person within its jurisdiction the equal protection of the laws. That corporations are persons within the meaning of this Amendment is now settled. What amounts to deprivation of property without due process of law or what is a denial of the equal protection of the laws is often

---

[19] *Ibid.,* 134 U.S. 456-458.

[20] *Ibid.,* 169 U.S. 522-547.

difficult to determine, especially where the question relates to the property of a quasi-public corporation and the extent to which it may be subjected to public control. But this court, speaking by Chief Justice Waite, has said that, while a state has power to fix the charges for railroad companies for the transportation of persons and property within its own jurisdiction, unless restrained by valid contract, or unless what is done amounts to a regulation of foreign or interstate commerce, such power is not without limit; and that "under pretense of regulating fares, and freights, the state cannot require a railroad corporation to carry persons or property without reward; neither can it do that which in law amounts to a taking of private property for public use without just compensation, or without due process of law.". . .

In the discussion of this question the plaintiffs contended that a railroad company is entitled to exact such charges for transportation as will enable it, at all times, not only to pay operating expenses, but also to meet the interest regularly accruing upon all its outstanding obligations, and justify a dividend upon all its stock; and that to prohibit it from maintaining rates or charges for transportation adequate to *all* those ends will deprive it of its property without due process of law, and deny to it the equal protection of the laws. This contention should not be passed without examination.

In our opinion the broad proposition advanced by counsel involves some misconception of the relations between the public and a railroad corporation. It is unsound in that it practically excludes from consideration the fair value of the property used, omits altogether any consideration of the right of the public to be exempt from unreasonable exactions, and makes the interests of the corporation maintaining a public highway the sole test in determining whether the rates established by or for it are such as may be rightfully prescribed as between it and the public. . . .

We hold, however, that the basis of all calculations as to the reasonableness of rates to be charged by a corporation maintaining a highway under legislative sanction must be the fair value of the property being used by it for the convenience of the public. And, in order to ascertain that value, the original cost of construction, the amount expended in permanent improvements, the amount and market value of its bonds and stocks, the present as compared with the original cost of construction, the probable earning capacity of the property, under particular rates prescribed by statute, and the sum required to meet operating expenses, are all matters for consideration, and are to be given such weight as may be just and right in each case. We do not say that there may not be other matters to be regarded in estimating the value of the property. What the company is entitled to ask is a fair return upon the value of that which it employs for the public convenience. On the other hand, what the public is entitled to demand is that no more be exacted from it for the use of a public highway than the services rendered by it are reasonably worth.

## 21

One line of decisions exempted the railroads from rate control; another frustrated the plans of reformers for a more equitable tax system. Sentiment had been growing for a graduated income tax calculated to shift a part of the cost of government to those best able to pay it. The Wilson-Gorman Tariff Act, passed during Cleveland's second administration, contained a memorable provision for a 2 per cent tax on incomes over $4,000. In the case of *Pollock* v. *Farmers' Loan and Trust Company* (1894), the Court effectively disposed of it:[21]

We are now . . . to determine to which of the two great classes a tax upon a person's entire income, whether derived from rents or products, or otherwise, of real estate, or from bonds, stocks, or other forms

[21] *Ibid.*, 158 U.S. 617-637.

of personal property, belongs; and we are unable to conclude that the enforced subtraction from the yield of all the owner's real or personal property, in the manner prescribed, is so different from a tax on the property itself, that it is not a direct, but an indirect, tax in the meaning of the Constitution. . . .

The reasons for the clauses of the Constitution in respect of direct taxation are not far to seek. . . .

The founders anticipated that the expenditures of the States, their counties, cities, and towns, would chiefly be met by direct taxation on accumulated property, while they expected that those of the Federal government would be for the most part met by indirect taxes. And in order that the power of direct taxation by the general government should not be exercised except on necessity, and, when the necessity arose, should be so exercised as to leave the States at liberty to discharge their respective obligations, and should not be so exercised unfairly and discriminatingly, as to particular States or otherwise, by a mere majority vote, possibly of those whose constituents were intentionally not subjected to any part of the burden, the qualified grant was made. . . . Those who made it knew that the power to tax involved the power to destroy, and that, in the language of Chief Justice Marshall, in *McCulloch* v. *Maryland,* "the only security against the abuse of this power is found in the structure of the government itself.". . . And they retained this security by providing that direct taxation and representation in the lower house of Congress should be adjusted on the same measure.

Moreover, whatever the reasons for the consitutional provisions, there they are, and they appear to us to speak in plain language.

It is said that a tax on the whole income of property is not a direct tax in the meaning of the Constitution, but a duty, and, as

a duty, leviable without apportionment, whether direct or indirect. We do not think so. Direct taxation was not restricted in one breath, and the restriction blown to the winds in another. . . .

The Constitution prohibits any direct tax, unless in proportion to numbers as ascertained by the census, and, in the light of the circumstances to which we have referred, is it not an evasion of that prohibition to hold that a general unapportioned tax, imposed upon all property owners as a body for or in respect of their property, is not direct, in the meaning of the Constitution, because confined to the income therefrom?

Whatever the speculative views of political economists or revenue reformers may be, can it be properly held that the Constitution, taken in its plain and obvious sense, and with due regard to the circumstances attending the formation of the government, authorizes a general unapportioned tax on the products of the farm and the rents of real estate, although imposed merely because of ownership, and with no possible means of escape from payment, as belonging to a totally different class from that which includes the property from whence the income proceeds?

There can be but one answer, unless the constitutional restriction is to be treated as utterly illusory and futile, and the object of its framers defeated. We find it impossible to hold that a fundamental requisition deemed so important as to be enforced by two provisions, one affirmative and one negative, can be refined away by forced distinctions between that which gives value to property and the property itself.

Nor can we perceive any ground why the same reasoning does not apply to capital in personalty held for the purpose of income, or ordinarily yielding income, and to the income therefrom. . . .

Personal property of some kind is of general distribution, and so are incomes, though the taxable range thereof might be narrowed through large exemptions. . . .

Nor are we impressed with the contention that, because in the four instances in which the power of direct taxation has been exercised, Congress did not see fit, for reasons of expediency, to levy a tax on personalty, this amounts to such a practical construction of the Constitution that the power did not exist, that we must regard ourselves bound by it. We should regret to be compelled to hold the powers of the general government thus restricted, and certainly we cannot accede to the idea that the Constitution has become weakened by a particular course of inaction under it.

The stress of the argument is thrown, however, on the assertion that an income tax is not a property tax; . . . that rents received, crops harvested, interest collected, have lost all connection with their origin, and, though once not taxable, have become transmuted, in their new form, into taxable subject-matter; in other words, that income is taxable, irrespective of the source. . . .

We have unanimously held in this case that, so far as this law operates on the receipts from municipal bonds, it cannot be sustained, because it is a tax on the power of the States and on their instrumentalities to borrow money, and consequently repugnant to the Constitution. But, if, as contended, the interest, when received, has become merely money in the recipient's pocket, and taxable, as such, without reference to the source from which it came, the question is immaterial whether it could have been originally taxed at all or not. This was admitted by the Attorney General, with characteristic candor; and it follows that if the revenue derived from municipal bonds cannot be taxed, because the source cannot be, the same rule applies to revenue from any other source not subject to the tax, and the lack of power to levy any but an apportioned tax on real

and personal property equally exists as to the revenue therefrom.

Admitting that this act taxes the income of property, irrespective of its source, still we cannot doubt that such a tax is necessarily a direct tax. . . .

The power to tax real and personal property and the income from both, there being an apportionment, is conceded; that such a tax is a direct tax in the meaning of the Constitution has not been, and, in our judgment, cannot be successfully denied; and yet we are thus invited to hesitate in the enforcement of the mandate of the Constitution, which prohibits Congress from laying a direct tax on the revenue from property of the citizen without regard to state lines, and in such manner that the States cannot intervene by payment in regulation of their own resources, lest a government of delegated powers should be found to be, not less powerful, but less absolute, than the imagination of the advocate had supposed.

We are not here concerned with the question whether an income tax be or be not desirable, nor whether such a tax would enable the government to diminish taxes on consumption and duties on imports, and to enter upon what may be believed to be a reform of its fiscal and commercial system. Questions of that character belong to the controversies of political parties, and cannot be settled by judicial decision. In these cases our province is to determine whether this income tax on the revenue from property does or does not belong to the class of direct taxes. If it does, it is, being unapportioned, in violation of the Constitution, . . .

We have considered the act only in respect of the tax on income derived from real estate, and from invested personal property, and have not commented on so much of it as bears on gains or profits from business, privileges, or employments, in view of the instances in which taxation on business, privileges, or employments has assumed the guise of an excise tax and been sustained as such.

. . . Being of opinion that so much of the section of this law as lays a tax on income from real and personal property is invalid, we are brought to the question of the effect of that conclusion upon these sections as a whole.

It is elementary that the same statute may be in part constitutional and in part unconstitutional, and, if the parts are wholly independent of each other, that which is constitutional may stand while that which is unconstitutional will be rejected. And in the case before us there is no question as to the validity of this act, except sections twenty-seven to thirty-seven, inclusive, which relate to the subject which has been under discussion; and, as to them, we think the rule laid down by Chief Justice Shaw in *Warren* v. *Charlestown*, 2 Gray, 84, is applicable, that if the different parts "are so mutually connected with and dependent on each other, as conditions, considerations, or compensations for each other, as to warrant a belief that the legislature intended them as a whole, and that if all could not be carried into effect the legislature would not pass the residue independently, and some parts are unconstitutional, all the provisions which are thus dependent, conditional, or connected must fall with them.". . .

According to the census, the true valuation of real and personal property in the United States in 1890 was $65,037,091, 197, of which real estate with improvements thereon made up $39,544,544,333. Of course, from the latter must be deducted, in applying these sections, all unproductive property and all property whose net yield does not exceed four thousand dollars; but, even with such deductions, it is evident that the income from realty formed a vital part of the scheme for taxation embodied therein. If that be stricken out, and also the income from all invested personal property, bonds, stocks, investments of all

kinds, it is obvious that by far the largest part of the anticipated revenue would be eliminated, and this would leave the burden of the tax to be borne by professions, trades, employments, or vocations; and in that way what was intended as a tax on capital would remain in substance a tax on occupations and labor. We cannot believe that such was the intention of Congress. We do not mean to say that an act laying by apportionment a direct tax on all real estate and personal property, or the income thereof, might not also lay excise taxes on business, privileges, employments, and vocations. But this is not such an act; and the scheme must be considered as a whole. Being invalid as to the greater part, and falling, as the tax would, if any part were held valid, in a direction which could not have been contemplated except in connection with the taxation considered as an entirety, we are constrained to conclude that sections twenty-seven to thirty-seven, inclusive, of the act, which became a law, without the signature of the President, on August 28, 1894, are wholly inoperative and void.

Our conclusions may, therefore, be summed up as follows:

*First.* We adhere to the opinion already announced, that, taxes on real estate being indisputably direct taxes, taxes on the rents or income of real estate are equally direct taxes.

*Second.* We are of opinion that taxes on personal property, or on the income of personal property, are likewise direct taxes.

*Third.* The tax imposed by sections twenty-seven to thirty-seven, inclusive, of the act of 1894, so far as it falls on the income of real estate and of personal property, being a direct tax within the meaning of the Constitution, and, therefore, unconstitutional and void because not apportioned according to representation, all those sections, constituting one entire scheme of taxation, are necessarily invalid.

## 22

The Supreme Court climaxed its defense of the gospel of wealth by reducing the Sherman Antitrust Act to a jumble of meaningless phrases in the statute books. When the American Sugar Refining Company, also known as the E. C. Knight Company, purchased a controlling interest in four competing concerns, thus securing a virtual monopoly over sugar refining in the United States, the government charged that the step created a combination in restraint of trade. The Court, however, in the case of *United States* v. *E. C. Knight Company* (1895), ruled that the purchase of stock was not an act of interstate commerce and hence did not constitute restraint of trade under the terms of the Sherman Act:[22]

In the view which we take of the case, we need not discuss whether because the tentacles which drew the outlying refineries into the dominant corporation were separately put out, therefore there was no combination to monopolize; or, because according to political economists, aggregations of capital may reduce prices, therefore the objection to concentration of power is relieved; or, because others were theoretically left free to go into the business of refining sugar, and the original stockholders of the Philadelphia refineries after becoming stockholders of the American Company might go into competition with themselves, or, parting with that stock, might set up again for themselves, therefore no objectionable restraint was imposed.

The fundamental question is, whether conceding that the existence of a monopoly in manufacture is established by the evidence, that monopoly can be directly suppressed under the act of Congress in the mode attempted by this bill.

It cannot be denied that the power of a State to protect the lives, health, and property of its citizens, and to preserve good order and the public morals, "the power to govern men and things within the limits of its dominion," is a power originally and always belonging to the States, not surrendered by them to the general government, nor directly restrained by the Constitution of the United States, and essentially exclusive. The relief of the citizens of each State from the burden of monopoly and the evils resulting from the restraint of trade among such citizens was left with the States to deal with. . . . On the other hand, the power of Congress to regulate commerce among the several States is also exclusive. . . .

The argument is that the power to control the manufacture of refined sugar is a monopoly over a necessary of life, to the enjoyment of which by a large part of the population of the United States interstate commerce is indispensable, and that, therefore, the general government in the exercise of the power to regulate commerce may suppress such monopoly directly and set aside the instruments which have created it. But this argument cannot be confined to necessaries of life merely, and must include all articles of general consumption. Doubtless the power to control the manufacture of a given thing involves in a certain sense the control of its disposition, but this is a secondary and not the primary sense; and although the exercise of that power may result in bringing the operation of commerce into play, it does not control it, and affects it only incidentally and indirectly. Commerce succeeds to manufacture, and is not a part of it. The power to regulate commerce is the power to prescribe the rule by which commerce shall be governed, and is a power independent of the power to suppress monopoly. But it may operate in repression of monopoly whenever it comes within the rules by which commerce is governed or whenever the transaction is itself a monopoly of commerce.

It is vital that the independence of the commercial power and of the police power, and the delimitation between them, how-

[22] *Ibid.,* 156 U.S. 10-18.

ever sometimes perplexing, should always be recognized and observed, for while the one furnishes the strongest bond of union, the other is essential to the autonomy of the States as required by our dual form of government; and acknowledged evils, however grave and urgent they may appear to be, had better be borne, than the risk be run, in the effort to suppress them, of more serious consequences by resort to expedients of even doubtful constitutionality.

It will be perceived how far-reaching the proposition is that the power of dealing with a monopoly directly may be exercised by the general government whenever interstate or international commerce may be ultimately affected. The regulation of commerce applies to the subjects of commerce, and not to matters of internal police. Contracts to buy, sell, or exchange goods to be transported among the several States, the transportation and its instrumentalities, and articles bought, sold, or exchanged for the purposes of such transit among the States, or put in the way of transit, may be regulated, but this is because they form part of interstate trade or commerce. The fact that an article is manufactured for export to another State does not of itself make it an article of interstate commerce, and the intent of the manufacturer does not determine the time when the article or product passes from the control of the State and belongs to commerce. . . .

And Mr. Justice Lamar remarked: "A situation more paralyzing to the state governments, and more provocative of conflicts between the general government and the States, and less likely to have been what the framers of the Constitution intended, it would be difficult to imagine."

Contracts, combinations, or conspiracies to control domestic enterprise in manufacture, agriculture, mining production in all its forms, or to raise or lower prices or wages, might unquestionably tend to restrain external as well as domestic trade, but the restraint would be an indirect result, however inevitable and whatever its

extent, and such result would not necessarily determine the object of the contract, combination, or conspiracy.

Again, all the authorities agree that in order to vitiate a contract or combination it is not essential that its result should be a complete monopoly; it is sufficient if it really tends to that end and to deprive the public of the advantages which flow from free competition. Slight reflection will show that if the national power extends to all contracts and combinations in manufacture, agriculture, mining, and other productive industries, whose ultimate result may affect external commerce, comparatively little of business operations and affairs would be left for state control.

It was in the light of well-settled principles that the act of July 2, 1890 was framed. Congress did not attempt thereby to assert the power to deal with monopoly directly as such; or to limit and restrict the rights of corporations created by the States or the citizens of the States in the acquisition, control, or disposition of property; or to regulate or prescribe the price or prices at which such property or the products thereof should be sold; or to make criminal the acts of persons in the acquisition and control of property which the States of their residence or creation sanctioned or permitted. Aside from the provisions applicable where Congress might exercise municipal power, what the law struck at was combinations, contracts, and conspiracies to monopolize trade and commerce among the several States or with foreign nations; but the contracts and acts of the defendants related exclusively to the acquisition of the Philadelphia refineries and the business of sugar refining in Pennsylvania, and bore no direct relation to commerce between the States or with foreign nations. The object was manifestly private gain in the manufacture of the commodity, but not through the control of interstate or foreign commerce. It is true that the bill alleged that the products of these refineries were sold and distributed among the several States, and that all the companies were engaged in trade or commerce with the several States and with foreign nations; but this was no more than to say that trade and commerce served manufacture to fulfil its function. . . . There was nothing in the proofs to indicate any intention to put a restraint upon trade or commerce, and the fact, as we have seen, that trade or commerce might be indirectly affected was not enough to entitle complainants to a decree.

## 23

The legal dialectics of the Knight Case have been expertly analyzed by Edward S. Corwin, one of the greatest scholars of constitutional law:[23]

It is vital that the independence of the commercial power and of the police power, and the delimitation between them, however sometimes perplexing, should always be recognized and observed, for while the one furnishes the strongest bond of union, the other is essential to the preservation of the autonomy of the States as required by our dual form of government; and acknowledged evils, however grave and urgent they may appear to be, had better be borne, than the risk be run, in the effort to suppress them, of more serious consequences by resort to expedients of even doubtful constitutionality.

Thus again we encounter the thought that just because Congress's power to regulate commerce among the States *is* supreme over State power, it must be so construed as not to conflict with State power. And pursuing this line of thought, the Court reached the following result:

Contracts [said Chief Justice Fuller], combinations, or conspiracies to control domestic enterprise in manufacture, agriculture, mining, production in all its forms, or to raise or lower prices or wages, might unquestionably

tend to restrain external as well as domestic trade, but the restraint would be an indirect result, however inevitable, and whatever its extent, and such result would not necessarily determine the object of the contract, combination, or conspiracy. . . . Slight reflection will show that, if the national power extends to all contracts and combinations in manufacture, agriculture, mining, and other productive industries, whose ultimate result may affect external commerce, comparatively little of business operations and affairs would be left for State control.

To put the same idea more briefly, the effects of a combination of producers upon commerce among the States in the product must be labelled "indirect" *however inevitable they may be and however extensive,* and with that label affixed such effects are put beyond Congress's power over commerce among the States, because otherwise there would be little in the way of business for the States to regulate. But why would this result follow? The opinion does not say, but the answer would seem to lie in the Court's tacit recognition that *the tie-up between commerce among the States and production is today both inevitable and extensive.* In short, the term "indirect" in this context is a mere *device,* a *formula* pulled out of the judicial hat, for the purpose of "shooing" away what the Court itself appears to recognize as an altogether natural and logical extension of the national commercial power. . . .

The Supreme Court's decisions during the 1890's deflated liberal confidence. Major political events marked impressive triumphs for the gospel of wealth: the defeat of Bryan, the protectionist Wilson-Gorman Tariff, negation of the Interstate Commerce Act, legalization of the antilabor injunction, outlawing of the income tax, the emasculation of the Sherman Antitrust Act. The long struggle of farmers, workers, and middle-class reformers had apparently failed. Yet a new popular assault upon conservatism was soon to emerge in Progressivism.

---

[23] Edward S. Corwin, *The Commerce Power Versus States Rights* (Princeton, 1936), pp. 154-156. Reprinted by permission of Princeton University Press, publishers.

# THE SHRINKING WORLD

## 1865-1900

The shrinking world was the dominant fact of intercontinental relations after 1865. Geographic isolation ended, for mechanical inventions drew the peoples of the world together, and expanding commerce tightened economic bonds; if the myth of isolation continued to exist, it reflected a heightened nationalism rather than the realities of an altered globe. European interests were involved in the Civil War, the imperial designs of France and Germany enmeshed the United States, and American exponents of "manifest destiny" entangled the nation in the international politics of the Caribbean and the Pacific. Even when Americans momentarily cast Europe and Asia out of mind as they busied themselves with internal concerns, they prepared for greater participation in the affairs of both; manufactured goods had to be exported as well as produced, and capital accumulated from profits required outlets for expansion. The very facts that made America forget the rest of the world ultimately drew her closer to it. By the end of the century the United States was irretrievably committed to a global role.

## DIPLOMACY, 1865-1885

### 1

The first expression of American interest in the world after the Civil War was the result of an expansionistic nationalism. Awakened to a new sense of power, statesmen became aware that external possessions had the same advantages for the United States as for other nations. The wave of expansionistic enthusiasm was responsible for the purchase of Alaska from Russia in June, 1867, and for a diligent effort on the part of President Grant to secure the island of Santo Domingo. Having drafted a treaty of annexation, he explained his actions to the Senate on May 31, 1870:[1]

I transmit to the Senate, for consideration with a view to its ratification, an additional article to the treaty of the 29th of November last, for the annexation of the Dominican Republic to the United States, stipulating for an extension of the time for exchanging the ratifications thereof, signed in this city on the 14th instant by the plenipotentiaries of the parties.

It was my intention to have also negotiated with the plenipotentiary of San Domingo amendments to the treaty of annexation to obviate objections which

may be urged against the treaty as it is now worded; but on reflection I deem it better to submit to the Senate the propriety of their amending the treaty as follows: First, to specify that the obligations of this Government shall not exceed the $1,500,000 stipulated in the treaty; secondly, to determine the manner of appointing the agents to receive and disburse the same; thirdly, to determine the class of creditors who shall take precedence in the settlement of their claims; and, finally, to insert such amendments as may suggest themselves to the minds of Senators to carry out in good faith the conditions of the treaty submitted to the Senate of the United States in January last, according to the spirit and intent of that treaty. From the most reliable information I can obtain, the sum specified in the treaty will pay every just claim against the Republic of San Domingo and leave a balance sufficient to carry on a Territorial government until such time as new laws for providing a Territorial revenue can be enacted and put in force.

I feel an unusual anxiety for the ratification of this treaty, because I believe it will redound greatly to the glory of the two countries interested, to civilization, and to the extirpation of the institution of slavery.

The doctrine promulgated by President

[1] J. D. Richardson (comp.), *Messages and Papers of the Presidents, 1789-1897* (Washington, 1897, 1909; taken from the 1909 vol.), VII, 61-63.

Monroe has been adhered to by all political parties, and I now deem it proper to assert the equally important principle that hereafter no territory on this continent shall be regarded as subject of transfer to a European power.

The Government of San Domingo has voluntarily sought this annexation. It is a weak power, numbering probably less than 120,000 souls, and yet possessing one of the richest territories under the sun, capable of supporting a population of 10,000,000 people in luxury. The people of San Domingo are not capable of maintaining themselves in their present condition, and must look for outside support.

They yearn for the protection of our free institutions and laws, our progress and civilization. Shall we refuse them?

I have information which I believe reliable that a European power stands ready now to offer $2,000,000 for the possession of Samana Bay alone. If refused by us, with what grace can we prevent a foreign power from attempting to secure the prize?

The acquisition of San Domingo is desirable because of its geographical position. It commands the entrance to the Caribbean Sea and the Isthmus transit of commerce. It possesses the richest soil, best and most capacious harbors, most salubrious climate, and the most valuable products of the forest, mine, and soil of any of the West India Islands. Its possession by us will in a few years build up a coastwise commerce of immense magnitude, which will go far toward restoring to us our lost merchant marine. It will give to us those articles which we consume so largely and do not produce, thus equalizing our exports and imports.

In case of foreign war it will give us command of all the islands referred to, and thus prevent an enemy from ever again possessing himself of rendezvous upon our very coast.

At present our coast trade between the States bordering on the Atlantic and those bordering on the Gulf of Mexico is cut into by the Bahamas and the Antilles. Twice we must, as it were, pass through foreign countries to get by sea from Georgia to the west coast of Florida.

San Domingo, with a stable government, under which her immense resources can be developed, will give remunerative wages to tens of thousands of laborers not now on the island.

This labor will take advantage of every available means of transportation to abandon the adjacent islands and seek the blessings of freedom and its sequence— each inhabitant receiving the reward of his own labor. Porto Rico and Cuba will have to abolish slavery, as a measure of self-preservation to retain their laborers.

San Domingo will become a large consumer of the products of Northern farms and manufacturers. The cheap rate at which her citizens can be furnished with food, tools, and machinery will make it necessary that the contiguous islands should have the same advantages in order to compete in the production of sugar, coffee, tobacco, tropical fruits, etc. This will open to us a still wider market for our products.

The production of our own supply of these articles will cut off more than one hundred millions of our annual imports, besides largely increasing our exports. With such a picture it is easy to see how our large debt abroad is ultimately to be extinguished. With a balance of trade against us (including interest on bonds held by foreigners and money spent by our citizens traveling in foreign lands) equal to the entire yield of the precious metals in this country, it is not so easy to see how this result is to be otherwise accomplished.

The acquisition of San Domingo is an adherence to the "Monroe doctrine"; it is a measure of national protection; it is asserting our just claim to a controlling influence over the great commercial traffic soon to flow from east to west by way of the Isthmus of Darien; it is to build up our merchant marine; it is to furnish new markets for the products of our farms, shops, and manufactories; it is to make slavery insupportable in Cuba and Porto Rico at once and ultimately so in Brazil; it is to settle the unhappy condition of Cuba, and end an exterminating conflict; it is to provide honest means of paying our honest debts, without overtaxing the people; it is to furnish our citizens with the necessaries of everyday life at cheaper rates than ever before; and it is, in fine, a rapid stride toward that greatness which the intelligence, industry, and enterprise of the citizens of the United States entitle this country to assume among nations.

## 2

Grant's enthusiasm for Caribbean colonies was not shared by his fellow countrymen, even in the Senate. His leading opponent, Senator Charles Sumner of Massachusetts, blended humanitarianism and isolationism into the "Naboth's vineyard" speech of December 21, 1870, an effective argument against imperialistic expansion:[2]

. . . The negotiation for annexion began with a person known as Buenaventura Baez. All the evidence, official and unofficial, shows him to be a political jockey. But he could do little alone; he had about him two other political jockeys, Cazneau and Fabens; and these three together, a precious copartnership, seduced into their firm a young officer of ours, who entitled himself "Aide-de-Camp to the President of the United States." Together they got up what was called a protocol, in which the young officer entitling himself "Aide-de-Camp to the President" proceeds to make certain promises for the President. . . .

Therefore we have here a "protocol," so entitled, signed by a young officer who

entitles himself "Aide-de-Camp to his Excellency, the President of the United States," and who promises for the President that he shall privately use all his influence in order that the idea of annexing the Dominican Republic to the United States may acquire such a degree of popularity among members of Congress as will be necessary for its accomplishment. Such was the promise. Senators about me know how faithfully the President has fulfilled it, how faithfully he has labored, privately and publicly, even beyond the protocol,— the protocol only required that he should work privately,—privately and publicly, in order that the idea of annexing the Dominican Republic should be agreeable to Congress.

The young officer, "Aide-de-Camp to the President of the United States," with this important and unprecedented document in his pocket, returned to Washington. Instead of being called to account for this unauthorized transaction, pledging the Chief Magistrate to use his influence privately with Congress in order to cram down a measure that the confederates justly supposed to be offensive, he was sent back with directions to negotiate a treaty. I would not allude to that treaty, if it had not been made the subject of discussion by the President himself in his Annual Message. . . .

The treaty exists; and now the practical question is, By what means was it negotiated? I have described to you the three confederates who seduced into their company the aide-de-camp of the President; and now I have to aver, and I insist that the evidence will substantiate what I say, that at the time of the signature of the treaty of annexion Baez was sustained in power by the presence of our naval force in the waters of the Dominican Government. Go to the documents, and you will find that what I say is true. Confer with naval officers, confer with honest patriot citizens who know the case, and they will all testify that without the presence of our

[2] *Congressional Globe,* 41st Cong., 3rd Sess., Pt. I, pp. 227-228, 230.

ships-of-war in those waters Baez would have been obliged to flee.

This is not all, Sir; I broaden the allegation. Ever since the signature of the treaty, and especially since its rejection, Baez has been sustained in power by the presence of our naval force. Such I aver to be the fact. I state it with all the responsibility of my position, and with full conviction of its truth. I ask you to read the documents printed confidentially for the use of the Senate, and I feel sure that what I state will be found to be substantially true. I ask you also to confer with any naval officer who has been there, or with any patriot citizen. I have had the privilege during this summer of communicating with two different officers who were there at the signing of the treaty and for some time thereafter, and they made the same report, that without the presence of our navy Baez would have been obliged to flee.

Sir, this is a most serious business. Nothing more important to the honor of the Republic has occurred for long years. How many of us now are hanging with anxiety on the news from Europe! There stand matched in deadly combat two great historic foes, France and Germany, . . . France now pressed to the wall; and what is the daily report? That Bismarck may take Louis Napoleon from his splendid prison and place him again on the throne of France, there to obtain from him that treaty of surrender which the Republic never will sign. Are we not all indignant at the thought? Why, Sir, it was only the other day that a member of the Cabinet, at my own house, in conversation on this question, said that nothing could make him more angry than the thought that Bismarck could play such a part, and that by this device France might be despoiled. And now, Sir, this is the very part played by the American Government. Baez has been treated as you fear Bismarck may treat Louis Napoleon. You call him "President"; they call him there "Dictator"; bet-

ter call him "Emperor," and then the parallel will be complete. He is sustained in power by the Government of the United States that he may betray his country. Such is the fact, and I challenge any Senator to deny it. I submit myself to question, and challenge the Senator from Indiana, who, as I have already said, champions this proposition, to deny it. I challenge him to utter one word of doubt of the proposition which I now lay down, that Baez is maintained in power by the naval force of the United States, and that, being in power, we seek to negotiate with him that he may sell his country. It cannot be denied. . . .

History is often said to, repeat itself. More or less it does. It repeats itself now. This whole measure of annexion, and the spirit with which it is pressed, find a parallel in the Kansas and Nebraska Bill, and in the Lecompton Constitution, by which it was sought to subjugate a distant Territory to Slavery. The Senator from Indiana was not here during those days, although he was acting well his part at home; but he will remember the pressure to which we were then exposed. And now we witness the same things: violence in a distant island, as there was violence in Kansas; also the same Presidential appliances; and shall I add, the same menace of personal assault filling the air?

In other days, to carry his project, a President tried to change a committee. It was James Buchanan. And now we have been called this session to witness a similar endeavor by our President. He was not satisfied with the Committee on Foreign Relations as constituted for years. He wished a change. He asked first for the removal of the Chairman. Somebody told him that this would not be convenient. He then asked for the removal of the Senator from Missouri [Mr. Schurz]; and he was told that this could not be done without affecting the German vote. He then called for the removal of my friend the Senator from New Hampshire, [Mr.

Patterson,] who unhappily had no German votes behind him. It was finally settled that this could not be done.

I allude to these things reluctantly, and only as part of the case. They illustrate the spirit we are called to encounter. They illustrate the extent to which the President has fallen into the line of bad examples.

Sir, I appeal to you, as Vice-President. By official position and by well-known relations of friendship you enjoy opportunities which I entreat you to use for the good of your country, and, may I add, for the benefit of that party which has so justly honored you. Go to the President, I ask you, and address him frankly with the voice of a friend to whom he must hearken. Counsel him to shun all approach to the example of Franklin Pierce, James Buchanan, and Andrew Jackson; tell him not to allow the oppression of a weak and humble people; ask him not to exercise War Powers without authority of Congress; and remind him, kindly, but firmly, that there is a grandeur in Justice and Peace beyond anything in material aggrandizement, beyond anything in war.

Again I return to the pending resolution, which I oppose as a new stage in the long-drawn machination. Am I wrong in holding up this negotiation, which has in it so much of violence,—violence toward Dominica, violence toward Hayti? Of course the proposed treaty assumes and adopts the civil war pending in the territory annexed. This is the terrible incumbrance. No prudent man buys a lawsuit; but we are called to buy a bloody lawsuit. I read now the recent testimony of Mr. Hatch, who, while in favor of annexion, writes as follows, under date of South Norwalk, Connecticut, December 12, 1870:—

"I have not, however, looked with favor upon the project as it has been attempted to be effected; and I firmly believe, if we should receive that territory from the hands of President Baez, while all the leading men of the Cabral party, the most intelligent, and the wealthiest, are in prison, in exile, or in arms against Baez, without their having a voice in the transfer, it would result in a terrible disaster."

Be taught by the experience of Spain, when in 1861 this power, on the invitation of a predecessor of Baez, undertook to play the part we are asked to play. Forts were built and troops were landed. By a document which I now hold in my hand it appears, that, when at last this power withdrew, she had expended forty millions of hard Spanish dollars and "sacrificed sixteen thousand of the flower of her army." From another source I learn that ten thousand Spanish soldiers were buried there. Are we ready to enter upon this bloody dance? Are we ready to take up this bloody lawsuit?

Vain to set forth, as the Message does, all manner of advantages, "commercially and materially." What are these, if Right and Humanity are sacrificed? What are these without that priceless blessing, Peace? I am not insensible to the commercial and material prosperity of my country. But there is something above these. It is the honor and good name of the Republic, now darkened by an act of wrong. If this territory, so much coveted by the President, were infinitely more valuable than it is, I hope the Senate would not be tempted to obtain it by trampling on the weak and humble. Admit all that the advocates of the present scheme assert with regard to the resources of this territory, and then imagine its lofty mountains bursting with the precious metals, its streams flowing with amber over silver sands, while every field is a Garden of the Hesperides, blooming with vegetable gold, and all this is not worth the price we are called to pay.

There is one other consideration, vast in importance and conclusive in character, to which I allude only. The island of San Domingo, situated in tropical waters, and occupied by another race, of another color, never can become a permanent possession of the United States. You may seize it by force of arms or by diplomacy, where a naval squadron does more than the minister; but the enforced jurisdiction cannot endure. Already by a higher statute is that island set apart to the colored race. It is theirs by right of possession, by their sweat and blood mingling with the soil, by tropical position, by its burning sun, and by unalterable laws of climate. Such is the ordinance of Nature, which I am not the first to recognize. San Domingo is the earliest of that independent group destined to occupy the Caribbean Sea, toward which our duty is plain as the Ten Commandments. Kindness, beneficence, assistance, aid, help, protection, all that is implied in good neighborhood,—these we must give, freely, bountifully; but their independence is as precious to them as is ours to us, and it is placed under the safeguard of natural laws which we cannot violate with impunity.

Long ago it was evident that the Great Republic might fitly extend the shelter of its protection to the governments formed in these tropical islands, dealing with them graciously, generously, and in a Christian spirit,—helping them in their weakness, encouraging them in their trials, and being to them always a friend; but we take counsel of our supposed interests rather than theirs, when we seek to remove them from the sphere in which they have been placed by Providence.

I conclude as I began. I protest against this legislation as another stage in a drama of blood. I protest against it in the name of Justice outraged by violence, in the name of Humanity insulted, in the name of the weak trodden down, in the name of Peace imperiled, and in the name of the African race, whose first effort at Independence is rudely assailed.

## 3

That Congress, and probably the nation, agreed with Charles Sumner was indicated

when the Senate thumpingly rejected the treaty for the annexation of Santo Domingo to the United States. Historic isolationism still transcended Civil War nationalism. Yet, willingly or not, America was drawn relentlessly into the current of world affairs. Relations with England illustrated this clearly. One heritage of the Civil War was a number of claims by American shippers against that country; they maintained that Britain's failure to prevent the "Alabama" and other Confederate raiders from attacking American shipping violated international law. Extreme demands by the United States and England's obstinacy delayed settlement of the "Alabama Claims" until June 17, 1871, when the Treaty of Washington was ratified:[3]

ARTICLE I. Whereas differences have arisen between the Government of the United States and the Government of Her Britannic Majesty, and still exist, growing out of the acts committed by the several vessels which have given rise to the claims generically known as the "Alabama Claims":

And whereas Her Britannic Majesty has authorized her High Commissioners and Plenipotentiaries to express, in a friendly spirit, the regret felt by Her Majesty's government for the escape, under whatever circumstances, of the "Alabama" and other vessels from British ports, and for the depredations committed by those vessels:

Now, in order to remove and adjust all complaints and claims on the part of the United States, and to provide for the speedy settlement of such claims which are not admitted by Her Britannic Majesty's Government, the high contracting parties agree that all the said claims, growing out of acts committed by the aforesaid vessels and generically known as the "Alabama Claims," shall be referred to a tribunal of arbitration to be composed of five Arbitrators, to be appointed in the following manner, that is to say: One shall be named

---

[3] *United States Statutes at Large*, XVII, 863-876.

by the President of the United States; one shall be named by Her Britannic Majesty; His Majesty the King of Italy shall be requested to name one; the President of the Swiss Confederation shall be requested to name one; and His Majesty the Emperor of Brazil shall be requested to name one. . . .

Art. II. The Arbitrators shall meet at Geneva, in Switzerland . . . and shall proceed impartially and carefully to examine and decide all questions that shall be laid before them on the part of the Governments of the United States and Her Britannic Majesty respectively. All questions considered by the tribunal, including the final award, shall be decided by a majority of all the Arbitrators. . . .

Art. VI. In deciding the matters submitted to the Arbitrators, they shall be governed by the following three rules . . . and by such principles of international law not inconsistent therewith as the Arbitrators shall determine to have been applicable to the case.

### Rules

A neutral Government is bound—

First, to use due diligence to prevent the fitting out, arming, or equipping, within its jurisdiction, of any vessel which it has reasonable ground to believe is intended to cruise or to carry on war against any Power with which it is at peace; and also to use like diligence to prevent the departure from its jurisdiction of any vessel intended to cruise or carry on war as above, such vessel having been specially adapted, in whole or in part, within such jurisdiction, to warlike use.

Secondly, not to permit or suffer either belligerent to make use of its ports or waters as the base of naval operations against the other, or for the purpose of renewal or augmentation of military supplies or arms, or the recruitment of men.

Thirdly, to exercise due diligence in its own ports and waters, and, as to all persons within its jurisdiction, to prevent any violation of the foregoing obligations and duties.

Her Britannic Majesty has commanded her High Commissioners and Plenipotentiaries to declare that Her Majesty's Government cannot assent to the foregoing rules as a statement of principles of international law which were in force at the time when the claims mentioned in Article I. arose, but that Her Majesty's Government, in order to evince its desire of strengthening the friendly relations between the two countries, and of making satisfactory provision for the future, agrees that in deciding the questions between the two countries arising out of those claims, the Arbitrators should assume that Her Majesty's Government had undertaken to act upon the principles set forth in these rules.

And the high contracting parties agree to observe these rules as between themselves in future, and to bring them to the knowledge of other maritime Powers, and to invite them to accede to them.

Art. VII. . . . The said tribunal shall first determine as to each vessel separately whether Great Britain has, by any act or omission, failed to fulfil any of the duties set forth in the foregoing three rules, or recognized by the principles of international law not inconsistent with such rules. . . . In case the tribunal find that Great Britain has failed to fulfil any duty or duties as aforesaid, it may, if it think proper, proceed to award a sum in gross to be paid by Great Britain to the United States for all the claims referred to it. . . .

### 4

The Treaty of Washington was an important landmark in the history of international co-operation. By agreeing to accept the findings of an impartial commission, England and the United States demonstrated their willingness to arbitrate disputes such as the "Alabama Claims" rather than resort to war. The result was a settlement satisfactory to both countries, handed down by the so-called Geneva Tribunal after careful consideration had been given to the whole problem:[4]

Whereas, Having regard to the VIth and VIIth articles of the said treaty, the arbitrators are bound under the terms of the said VIth article, "in deciding the matters submitted to them, to be governed by the three rules therein specified and by such principles of international law, not inconsistent therewith, as the arbitrators shall determine to have been applicable to the case";

And Whereas, The "due diligence" referred to in the first and third of the said rules ought to be exercised by neutral governments in exact proportion to the risks to which either of the belligerents may be exposed, from a failure to fulfill the obligations of neutrality on their part; . . .

And Whereas, The effects of a violation of neutrality committed by means of the construction, equipment, and armament of a vessel are not done away with by any commission which the government of the belligerent power, benefited by the violation of neutrality, may afterwards have granted to that vessel; and the ultimate step, by which the offense is completed, cannot be admissible as a ground for the absolution of the offender, nor can the consummation of his fraud become the means of establishing this innocence;

And Whereas, The privilege of exterritoriality accorded to vessels of war has been admitted into the law of nations, not as an absolute right, but solely as a proceeding founded on the principle of courtesy and mutual deference between different nations, and therefore can never be appealed to for the protection of acts done in violation of neutrality; . . .

And Whereas, With respect to the vessel called the "Alabama," it clearly results from all the facts relative to the construction of the ship at first designated by the number "290" in the port of Liverpool, and its equipment and armament in the vicinity of Terceira through the agency of the vessels called the "Agrippina" and the "Bahama," dispatched from Great Britain to that end, that the British government failed to use due diligence in the performance of its neutral obligations; and especially that it omitted, notwithstanding the warnings and official representations made by the diplomatic agents of the United States during the construction of the said number "290," to take in due time any effective measures of prevention, and that those orders which it did give at last, for the detention of the vessel, were issued so late that their execution was not practicable; . . .

And Whereas, The government of Her Britannic Majesty cannot justify itself for a failure in due diligence on the plea of insufficiency of the legal means of action which it possessed:

Four of the arbitrators, for the reasons above assigned, and the fifth for reasons separately assigned by him,

Are of the opinion—

That Great Britain has in this case failed, by omission, to fulfill the duties prescribed in the first and the third of the rules established by the VIth article of the Treaty of Washington. . . .

The tribunal, making use of the authority conferred upon it by Article VII of the said treaty, by a majority of four voices to one, awards to the United States a sum of $15,500,000 in gold, as the indemnity to be paid by Great Britain to the United States, for the satisfaction of all the claims referred to the consideration of the tribunal, conformably to the provisions contained in Article VII of the aforesaid treaty.

## 5

A spirit of international co-operation dominated America's relations with her Latin-American neighbors in the period after the Civil War. Interest in the area began to de-

---

[4] United States Department of State, *Papers Relating to the Treaty of Washington* (Washington, 1872, 1884), IV, 50-51, 53.

velop in the 1870's, when a few business-minded statesmen awakened to the potentialities of the South American market for both manufactured goods and capital. James G. Blaine, secretary of state in Garfield's cabinet in 1881, was their principal spokesman. Addressing himself to the task of winning the friendship of the Latin-Americans, he conceived the idea of a Pan-American Conference. Although Garfield's death, and the subsequent removal of Blaine from the cabinet, delayed the meeting until 1889, Blaine's initial invitation of November 29, 1881, summarized the purposes:[5]

SIR: The attitude of the United States with respect to the question of general peace on the American continent is well known through its persistent efforts for years to avert the evils of warfare, or, these efforts failing, to bring positive conflicts to an end through pacific counsels or the advocacy of impartial arbitration.

This attitude has been consistently maintained, and always with such fairness as to leave no room for imputing to our government any motive except the humane and disinterested one of saving the kindred states of the American continent from the burdens of war. The position of the United States as the leading power of the New World might well give its government a claim to authoritative utterance for the purpose of quieting discord among its neighbors, with all of whom the most friendly relations exist. Nevertheless, the good offices of this government are not and have not at any time been tendered with a show of dictation or compulsion, but only as exhibiting the solicitous good-will of a common friend.

For some years past a growing disposition has been manifested by certain states of Central and South America to refer disputes affecting grave questions of inter-

national relationship and boundaries to arbitration rather than to the sword. It has been on several such occasions a source of profound satisfaction to the Government of the United States to see that this country is in a large measure looked to by all the American powers as their friend and mediator. The just and impartial counsel of the President in such cases has never been withheld, and his efforts have been rewarded by the prevention of sanguinary strife or angry contentions between peoples whom we regard as brethren.

The existence of this growing tendency convinces the President that the time is ripe for a proposal that shall enlist the good-will and active coöperation of all the states of the western hemisphere, both north and south, in the interest of humanity and for the common weal of nations. He conceives that none of the governments of America can be less alive than our own to the dangers and horrors of a state of war, and especially of war between kinsmen. He is sure that none of the chiefs of governments on the continent can be less sensitive than he is to the sacred duty of making every endeavor to do away with the chances of fratricidal strife. And he looks with hopeful confidence to such active assistance from them as will serve to show the broadness of our common humanity and the strength of the ties which bind us all together as a great and harmonious system of American commonwealths.

Impressed by these views, the President extends to all the independent countries of North and South America an earnest invitation to participate in a general congress to be held in the city of Washington on the 24th day of November, 1882, for the purpose of considering and discussing the methods of preventing war between the nations of America. He desires that the attention of the congress shall be strictly confined to this one great object; that its sole aim shall be to seek a way of perma-

---

[5] United States Department of State, *Papers Relating to the Foreign Relations of the United States,* Transmitted to Congress, with the Annual Message of the President (Washington, 1861-1893; taken from vol. covering 1881), pp. 13-15.

nently averting the horrors of cruel and bloody combat between countries, oftenest of one blood and speech, or the even worse calamity of internal commotion and civil strife; that it shall regard the burdensome and far-reaching consequences of such struggles, the legacies of exhausted finances, of oppressive debt, of onerous taxation, of ruined cities, of paralyzed industries, of devastated fields, of ruthless conscription, of the slaughter of men, of the grief of the widow and the orphan, of embittered resentment that long survive those who provoked them and heavily afflict the innocent generations that come after.

The President is especially desirous to have it understood that, in putting forth this invitation, the United States does not assume the position of counseling or attempting through the voice of the congress, to counsel any determinate solution of existing questions which may now divide any of the countries of America. Such questions can not properly come before the congress. Its mission is higher. It is to provide for the interest of all in the future, not to settle the individual differences of the present. For this reason especially the President has indicated a day for the assembling of the congress so far in the future as to leave good ground for hope that by the time named the present situation on the South Pacific coast will be happily terminated, and that those engaged in the contest may take peaceable part in the discussion and solution of the general question affecting in an equal degree the well-being of all.

It seems also desirable to disclaim in advance any purpose on the part of the United States to prejudge the issues to be presented to the congress. It is far from the intent of this government to appear before the congress as in any sense the protector of its neighbors or the predestined and necessary arbitrator of their disputes. The United States will enter into the deliberations of the congress on the same footing as the other powers represented, and with the loyal determination to approach any proposed solution, not merely in its own interest, or with a view to asserting its power, but as a single member among many coördinate and coequal states. So far as the influence of this government may be potential, it will be exerted in the direction of conciliating whatever conflicting interests of blood, or government, or historical tradition may necessarily come together in response to a call embracing such vast and diverse elements.

You will present these views to the ministries of foreign relations of the Argentine Republic, enlarging, if need be, in such terms as will readily occur to you, upon the great mission which it is within the power of the proposed congress to accomplish in the interest of humanity, and upon the firm purpose of the United States to maintain a position of the most absolute and impartial friendship towards all. You will thereupon, in the name of the President of the United States, tender to His Excellency the President of the Argentine Republic, a formal invitation to send two commissioners to the congress, provided with such powers and instructions on behalf of their government as will enable them to consider the questions brought before that body within the limit of submission contemplated by their invitation. The United States, as well as the other powers, will, in like manner, be represented by two commissioners, so that equality and impartiality will be amply secured in the proceedings of the congress.

In delivering this invitation through the minister of foreign affairs, you will read this dispatch to him and leave him a copy, intimating that an answer is desired by this government as promptly as the just consideration of so important a proposition will permit.

I am, etc.,

JAMES G. BLAINE

## THE REVIVAL OF "MANIFEST DESTINY"

### 6

America's slow progress toward a larger world role accelerated after 1885. Industrial and capital surpluses required new markets, but more important was the effect of the revolutions in economics on the American mind. Each new set of statistics on the output of farm and factory bolstered the national ego; each new gain in production schedules convinced many Americans they were a superior people. Once more, as in the 1840's, men raised the claim of "manifest destiny"; once more street-corner orators and congressional spokesmen demanded that the blessings of American civilization be extended to the downtrodden of "backward" nations. The Reverend Josiah Strong, a leading Protestant clergyman, expressed this spirit in an influential book, *Our Country* (1885):[6]

Every race which has deeply impressed itself on the human family has been the representative of some great idea—one or more—which has given direction to the nation's life and form to its civilization. Among the Egyptians this seminal idea was life, among the Persians it was light, among the Hebrews it was purity, among the Greeks it was beauty, among the Romans it was law. The Anglo-Saxon is the representative of two great ideas, which are closely related. One of them is that of civil liberty. Nearly all of the civil liberty in the world is enjoyed by Anglo-Saxons: the English, the British colonists, and the people of the United States. To some, like the Swiss, it is permitted by the sufferance of their neighbors; others, like the French, have experimented with it; but, in modern times, the peoples whose love of liberty has won it, and whose genius for self-government has preserved it, have been Anglo-Saxons. The noblest

races have always been lovers of liberty. That love ran strong in early German blood, and has profoundly influenced the institutions of all the branches of the great German family; but it was left for the Anglo-Saxon branch fully to recognize the right of the individual to himself, and formally to declare it the foundation stone of government.

The other great idea of which the Anglo-Saxon is the exponent is that of a pure *spiritual* Christianity. It was no accident that the great reformation of the sixteenth century originated among a Teutonic, rather than a Latin people. It was the fire of liberty burning in the Saxon heart that flamed up against the absolutism of the Pope. Speaking roughly, the peoples of Europe which are Celtic are Catholic, and those which are Teutonic are Protestant; and where the Teutonic race was purest, there Protestantism spread with the greatest rapidity. . . . Protestantism on the continent seems to be about as poor in spiritual life and power as Catholicism. That means that most of the spiritual Christianity in the world is found among Anglo-Saxons and their converts; for this is the great missionary race. . . .

There can be no reasonable doubt that North America is to be the great home of the Anglo-Saxon, the principal seat of his power, the center of his life and influence. Not only does it constitute seven-elevenths of his possessions, but his empire is unsevered, while the remaining four-elevenths are fragmentary and scattered over the earth. Australia will have a great population; but its disadvantages, as compared with North America, are too manifest to need mention. Our continent has room and resources and climate, it lies in the pathway of the nations, it belongs to the zone of power, and already, among Anglo-Saxons, do we lead in population and wealth. . . .

But we are to have not only the larger portion of the Anglo-Saxon race for generations to come, we may reasonably expect

---

[6] Josiah Strong, *Our Country; Its Possible Future and Its Present Crisis* (New York, 1885, 1891; taken from the 1891 vol.), pp. 159-160, 165, 168, 170-177, 178-180. Used by permission of the American Home Missionary Society.

to develop the highest type of Anglo-Saxon civilization. If human progress follows a law of development, if "Time's noblest offspring is the last," our civilization should be the noblest; for we are "The heirs of all the ages in the foremost files of time," and not only do we occupy the latitude of power, but *our land is the last to be occupied in that latitude.* There is no other virgin soil in the North Temperate Zone. If the consummation of human progress is not to be looked for here, if there is yet to flower a higher civilization, where is the soil that is to produce it? Whipple says: "There has never been a great migration that did not result in a new form of national genius." Our national genius is Anglo-Saxon, but not English, its distinctive type is the result of a finer nervous organization, which is certainly being developed in this country. . . .

Mr. Darwin is not only disposed to see, in the superior vigor of our people, an illustration of his favorite theory of natural selection, but even intimates that the world's history thus far has been simply preparatory for our future, and tributary to it. He says: "There is apparently much truth in the belief that the wonderful progress of the United States, as well as the character of the people, are the results of natural selection; for the more energetic, restless, and courageous men from all parts of Europe have emigrated during the last ten or twelve generations to that great country, and have there succeeded best. Looking at the distant future, I do not think that the Rev. Mr. Zincke takes an exaggerated view when he says: 'All other series of events—as that which resulted in the culture of mind in Greece, and that which resulted in the Empire of Rome—only appear to have purpose and value when viewed in connection with, or rather as subsidiary to, the great stream of Anglo-Saxon emigration to the West.' "

There is abundant reason to believe that the Anglo-Saxon race is to be, is, indeed, already becoming, more effective here than in the mother country. The marked superiority of this race is due, in large measure, to its highly mixed origin. Says Rawlinson: "It is a general rule, now almost universally admitted by ethnologists, that the mixed races of mankind are superior to the pure ones"; and adds: "Even the Jews, who are so often cited as an example of a race at once pure and strong, may, with more reason, be adduced on the opposite side of the argument." The ancient Egyptians, the Greeks, and the Romans, were all mixed races. Among modern races, the most conspicuous example is afforded by the Anglo-Saxons. Mr. Green's studies show that Mr. Tennyson's poetic line, "Saxon and Norman and Dane are we," must be supplemented with Celt and Gaul, Welshman and Irishman, Frisian and Flamand, French Huguenot and German Palatine. What took place a thousand years ago and more in England again transpires to-day in the United States. "History repeats itself"; but, as the wheels of history are the chariot wheels of the Almighty, there is, with every revolution, an onward movement toward the goal of his eternal purposes. There is here a new commingling of races; and, while the largest injections of foreign blood are substantially the same elements that constituted the original Anglo-Saxon admixture, so that we may infer the general type will be preserved, there are strains of other bloods being added, which, if Mr. Emerson's remark is true, that "the best nations are those most widely related," may be expected to improve the stock, and aid it to a higher destiny. If the dangers of immigration . . . can be successfully met for the next few years, until it has passed its climax, it may be expected to add value to the amalgam which will constitute the new Anglo-Saxon race of the New World. Concerning our future, Herbert Spencer says: "One great result is, I think, tolerably clear. From biological truths it is to be inferred that the eventual mixture of the allied varieties of the Aryan race, forming the population, will produce a more powerful type of man than has hitherto existed, and a type of man more plastic, more adaptable, more capable of undergoing the modifications needful for complete social life. I think, whatever difficulties they may have to surmount, and whatever tribulations they may have to pass through, the Americans may reasonably look forward to a time when they will have produced a civilization grander than any the world has known."

It may be easily shown, and is of no small significance, that the two great ideas of which the Anglo-Saxon is the exponent are having a fuller development in the United States than in Great Britain. There the union of Church and State tends strongly to paralyze some of the members of the body of Christ. Here there is no such influence to destroy spiritual life and power. Here, also, has been evolved the form of government consistent with the largest possible civil liberty. Furthermore, it is significant that the marked characteristics of this race are being here emphasized most. Among the most striking features of the Anglo-Saxon is his money-making power—a power of increasing importance in the widening commerce of the world's future. We have seen . . . that, although England is by far the richest nation of Europe, we have already outstripped her in the race after wealth, and we have only begun the development of our vast resources.

Again, another marked characteristic of the Anglo-Saxon is what may be called an instinct or genius for colonizing. His unequaled energy, his indomitable perseverance, and his personal independence, made him a pioneer. He excels all others in pushing his way into new countries. It was those in whom this tendency was strongest that came to America, and this inherited tendency has been further developed by the westward sweep of successive generations across the continent. So

noticeable has this characteristic become that English visitors remark it. Charles Dickens once said that the typical American would hesitate to enter heaven unless assured that he could go further west.

Again, nothing more manifestly distinguishes the Anglo-Saxon than his intense and persistent energy; and he is developing in the United States an energy which, in eager activity and effectiveness, is peculiarly American. This is due partly to the fact that Americans are much better fed than Europeans, and partly to the undeveloped resources of a new country, but more largely to our climate, which acts as a constant stimulus. Ten years after the landing of the Pilgrims, the Rev. Francis Higginson, a good observer, wrote: "A sup of New England air is better than a whole flagon of English ale." Thus early had the stimulating effect of our climate been noted. Moreover, our social institutions are stimulating. In Europe the various ranks of society are, like the strata of the earth, fixed and fossilized. There can be no great change without a terrible upheaval, a social earthquake. Here society is like the waters of the sea, mobile; as General Garfield said, and so signally illustrated in his own experience, that which is at the bottom to-day may one day flash on the crest of the highest wave. Every one is free to become whatever he can make of himself; free to transform himself from a rail-splitter or a tanner or a canal-boy, into the nation's President. Our aristocracy, unlike that of Europe, is open to all comers. Wealth, position, influence, are prizes offered for energy; and every farmer's boy, every apprentice and clerk, every friendless and penniless immigrant, is free to enter the lists. Thus many causes cooperate to produce here the most forceful and tremendous energy in the world.

What is the significance of such facts? These tendencies infold the future; they are the mighty alphabet with which God writes his prophecies. May we not, by a careful laying together of the letters, spell out something of his meaning? It seems to me that God, with infinite wisdom and skill, is training the Anglo-Saxon race for an hour sure to come in the world's future. Heretofore there has always been in the history of the world a comparatively unoccupied land westward, into which the crowded countries of the East have poured their surplus populations. But the widening waves of migration, which millenniums ago rolled east and west from the valley of the Euphrates, meet to-day on our Pacific coast. There are no more new worlds. The unoccupied arable lands of the earth are limited, and will soon be taken. The time is coming when the pressure of population on the means of subsistence will be felt here as it is now felt in Europe and Asia. Then will the world enter upon a new stage of its history—*the final competition of races, for which the Anglo-Saxon is being schooled.* Long before the thousand millions are here, the mighty *centrifugal* tendency, inherent in this stock and strengthened in the United States, will assert itself. Then this race of unequaled energy, with all the majesty of numbers and the might of wealth behind it—the representative, let us hope, of the largest liberty, the purest Christianity, the highest civilization—having developed peculiarly aggressive traits calculated to impress its institutions upon mankind, will spread itself over the earth. If I read not amiss, this powerful race will move down upon Mexico, down upon Central and South America, out upon the islands of the sea, over upon Africa and beyond. And can any one doubt that the result of this competition of races will be the "survival of the fittest"? "Any people," says Dr. Bushnell, "that is physiologically advanced in culture, though it be only in a degree beyond another which is mingled with it on strictly equal terms, is sure to live down and finally live out its inferior. Nothing can save the inferior race but a ready and pliant assimilation. Whether the feebler and more abject races are going to be regenerated and raised up, is already very much of a question. What if it should be God's plan to people the world with better and finer material? Certain it is, whatever expectations we may indulge, that there is a tremendous overbearing surge of power in the Christian nations, which, if the others are not speedily raised to some vastly higher capacity, will inevitably submerge and bury them forever. These great populations of Christendom—what are they doing, but throwing out their colonies on every side, and populating themselves, if I may so speak, into the possession of all countries and climes?" To this result no war of extermination is needful; the contest is not one of arms, but of vitality and of civilization. "At the present day," says Mr. Darwin, "civilized nations are everywhere supplanting barbarous nations, excepting where the climate opposes a deadly barrier; and they succeed mainly, though not exclusively, through their arts, which are the products of the intellect?" Thus the Finns were supplanted by the Aryan races in Europe and Asia, the Tartars by the Russians, and thus the aborigines of North America, Australia and New Zealand are now disappearing before the all-conquering Anglo-Saxons. It would seem as if these inferior tribes were only precursors of a superior race, voices in the wilderness crying: "Prepare ye the way of the Lord!" . . . The Anglo-Saxon race would speedily decay but for the salt of Christianity. Bring savages into contact with our civilization, and its destructive forces become operative at once, while years are necessary to render effective the saving influences of Christian instruction. Moreover, the pioneer wave of our civilization carries with it more scum than salt. Where there is one missionary, there are hundreds of miners or traders or adventurers ready to debauch the native. Whether the extinction of inferior races before the advancing Anglo-Saxon seems to the reader sad or otherwise, it certainly appears probable. I know of nothing except climatic conditions to prevent this race from populating Africa as it has peopled North America. And those portions of Africa which are unfavorable to Anglo-Saxon life are less extensive than was once supposed. The Dutch Boers, after two centuries of life there, are as hardy as any race on earth. The Anglo-Saxon has established himself in climates totally diverse—Canada, South Africa, and India—and, through several generations, has preserved his essential race characteristics. He is not, of course, superior to climatic influences; but, even in warm climates, he is likely to retain his aggressive vigor long enough to supplant races already enfeebled. Thus, in what Dr. Bushnell calls "the out-populating power of the Christian stock," may be found God's final and complete solution of the dark problem of heathenism among many inferior peoples. . . .

Is there room for reasonable doubt that this race, unless devitalized by alcohol and tobacco, is destined to dispossess many weaker races, assimilate others, and mold the remainder, until, in a very true and important sense, it has Anglo-Saxonized mankind?. Already "the English language, saturated with Christian ideas, gathering up into itself the best thought of all the ages, is the great agent of Christian civilization throughout the world; at this moment affecting the destinies and molding the character of half the human race." Jacob Grimm, the German philologist, said of this language: "It seems chosen, like its people, to rule in future times in a still greater degree in all the corners of the earth." He predicted, indeed, that the language of Shakespeare would eventually become the language of mankind. . . .

In my own mind, there is no doubt that the Anglo-Saxon is to exercise the commanding influence in the world's future; but the exact nature of that influence is, as yet, undetermined. How far his civilization will be materialistic and atheistic, and

how long it will take thoroughly to Christianize and sweeten it, how rapidly he will hasten the coming of the kingdom wherein dwelleth righteousness, or how many ages he may retard it, is still uncertain; but *it is now being swiftly determined.* Let us weld together in a chain the various links of our logic which we have endeavored to forge. Is it manifest that the Anglo-Saxon holds in his hands the destinies of mankind for ages to come? Is it evident that the United States is to be the home of this race, the principal seat of his power, the great center of his influence? Is it true that the great West is to dominate the nation's future? Has it been shown that this generation is to determine the character, and hence the destiny, of the West? Then may God open the eyes of this generation! . . . Men of this generation, from the pyramid top of opportunity on which God has set us, *we* look down on forty centuries! We stretch our hand into the future with power to mold the destinies of unborn millions.

## 7

Military strategists joined with strategists of "manifest destiny" in the urge for extraterritorial possessions. In a world grown smaller, they argued, the United States could never remain aloof from Europe's squabbles. Resulting wars would be fought either in America, or on the adjacent seas. Hence the need for a larger navy, and the necessity of extending the defensive frontier of the United States to the Hawaiian Islands, the Caribbean, and Central America. Alfred Thayer Mahan was one of the foremost proponents of these views, and *The Influence of Sea Power upon History, 1660-1783* (1890) became one of the most important books on this subject. In a later work, *The Interest of America in Sea Power* (1897), he argued cogently against isolationism:[7]

For nearly the lifetime of a generation, therefore, American industries have been

[7] *The Interest of America in Sea Power,* by Captain Alfred T. Mahan, U.S.N. (Boston, 1897, 1898), pp. 4, 6-16. Used by permission of Lyle Evans Mahan.

thus protected, until the practice has assumed the force of a tradition, and is clothed in the mail of conservatism. In their mutual relations, these industries resemble the activities of a modern ironclad that has heavy armor, but inferior engines and guns; mighty for defence, weak for offence. Within, the home market is secured; but outside, beyond the broad seas, there are the markets of the world, that can be entered and controlled only by a vigorous contest, to which the habit of trusting to protection by statute does not conduce.

At bottom, however, the temperament of the American people is essentially alien to such a sluggish attitude. Independently of all bias for or against protection, it is safe to predict that, when the opportunities for gain abroad are understood, the course of American enterprise will cleave a channel by which to reach them. Viewed broadly, it is a most welcome as well as significant fact that a prominent and influential advocate of protection, a leader of the party committed to its support, a keen reader of the signs of the times and of the drift of opinion, has identified himself with a line of policy which looks to nothing less than such modifications of the tariff as may expand the commerce of the United States to all quarters of the globe. . . .

. . . The interesting and significant feature of this changing attitude is the turning of the eyes outward, instead of inward only, to seek the welfare of the country. To affirm the importance of distant markets, and the relation to them of our own immense powers of production, implies logically the recognition of the link that joins the products and the markets,—that is, the carrying trade; the three together constituting that chain of maritime power to which Great Britain owes her wealth and greatness. Further, is it too much to say that, as two of these links, the shipping and the markets, are exterior to our own borders, the acknowledgment of them carries with it a view of the relations of the

United States to the world radically distinct from the simple idea of self-sufficingness? We shall not follow far this line of thought before there will dawn the realization of America's unique position, facing the older worlds of the East and West, her shores washed by the oceans which touch the one or the other, but which are common to her alone.

Coincident with these signs of change in our own policy there is restlessness in the world at large which is deeply significant, if not ominous. It is beside our purpose to dwell upon the internal state of Europe, whence, if disturbances arise, the effect upon us may be but partial and indirect. But the great seaboard powers there do not stand on guard against their continental rivals only; they cherish also aspirations for commercial extension, for colonies, and for influence in distant regions, which may bring, and, even under our present contracted policy, already have brought them into collision with ourselves. The incident of the Samoa Islands, trivial apparently, was nevertheless eminently suggestive of European ambitions. America then roused from sleep as to interests closely concerning her future. At this moment internal troubles are imminent in the Sandwich Islands, where it should be our fixed determination to allow no foreign influence to equal our own. All over the world German commercial and colonial push is coming into collision with other nations: witness the affair of the Caroline Islands with Spain; the partition of New Guinea with England; the yet more recent negotiation between these two powers concerning their share in Africa viewed with deep distrust and jealousy by France; the Samoa affair; the conflict between German control and American interests in the islands of the western Pacific; and the alleged Progress of German influence in Central and South America. It is noteworthy that, while these various contentions are sustained with the aggressive military spirit characteristic of the German

Empire, they are credibly said to arise from the national temper more than from the deliberate policy of the government, which in this matter does not lead, but follows, the feeling of the people,—a condition much more formidable.

There is no sound reason for believing that the world has passed into a period of assured peace outside the limits of Europe. Unsettled political conditions, such as exist in Haiti, Central America, and many of the Pacific Islands, especially the Hawaiian group, when combined with great military or commercial importance as is the case with most of these positions, involve, now as always, dangerous germs of quarrel, against which it is prudent at least to be prepared. Undoubtedly, the general temper of nations is more averse from war than it was of old. If no less selfish and grasping than our predecessors, we feel more dislike to the discomforts and sufferings attendant upon a breach of peace; but to retain that highly valued repose and the undisturbed enjoyment of the returns of commerce, it is necessary to argue upon somewhat equal terms of strength with an adversary. It is the preparedness of the enemy, and not acquiescence in the existing state of things, that now holds back the armies of Europe.

On the other hand, neither the sanctions of international law nor the justice of a cause can be depended upon for a fair settlement of differences, when they come into conflict with a strong political necessity on the one side opposed to comparative weakness on the other. In our still-pending dispute over the seal-fishing of Bering Sea, whatever may be thought of the strength of our argument, in view of generally admitted principles of international law, it is beyond doubt that our contention is reasonable, just, and in the interest of the world at large. But in the attempt to enforce it we have come into collision not only with national susceptibilities as to the honor of the flag, which we ourselves very strongly share, but also with a state governed by a powerful necessity, and ex-

ceedingly strong where we are particularly weak and exposed. Not only has Great Britain a mighty navy and we a long defenceless seacoast, but it is a great commercial and political advantage to her that her larger colonies, and above all Canada, should feel that the power of the mother country is something which they need, and upon which they can count. . . . These feelings of attachment and mutual dependence supply the living spirit, without which the nascent schemes for Imperial Federation are but dead mechanical contrivances; nor are they without influence upon such generally unsentimental considerations as those of buying and selling, and the course of trade.

This dispute, seemingly paltry yet really serious, sudden in its appearance and dependent for its issue upon other considerations than its own merits, may serve to convince us of many latent and yet unforeseen dangers to the peace of the western hemisphere, attendant upon the opening of a canal through the Central American Isthmus. In a general way, it is evident enough that this canal, by modifying the direction of trade routes, will induce a great increase of commercial activity and carrying trade throughout the Caribbean Sea; and that this now comparatively deserted nook of the ocean will become, like the Red Sea, a great thoroughfare of shipping, and will attract, as never before in our day, the interest and ambition of maritime nations. Every position in that sea will have enhanced commercial and military value, and the canal itself will become a strategic centre of the most vital importance. Like the Canadian Pacific Railroad, it will be a link between the two oceans; but, unlike it, the use, unless most carefully guarded by treaties, will belong wholly to the belligerent which controls the sea by its naval power. In case of war, the United States will unquestionably command the Canadian Railroad, despite the deterrent force of operations by the hostile navy upon our seaboard; but no less unquestionably will she be impotent, as against any of the great maritime powers, to control the Central American canal. Militarily speaking, and having reference to European complications only, the piercing of the Isthmus is nothing but a disaster to the United States, in the present state of her military and naval preparation. It is especially dangerous to the Pacific coast; but the increased exposure of one part of our seaboard reacts unfavorably upon the whole military situation.

Despite a certain great original superiority conferred by our geographical nearness and immense resources,—due, in other words, to our natural advantages, and not to our intelligent preparations,— the United States is wofully unready, not only in fact but in purpose to assert in the Caribbean and Central America a weight of influence proportioned to the extent of her interests. We have not the navy, and, what is worse, we are not willing to have the navy, that will weigh seriously in any disputes with those nations whose interests will conflict there with our own. We have not, and we are not anxious to provide, the defence of the seaboard which will leave the navy free for its work at sea. We have not, but many other powers have, positions, either within or on the borders of the Caribbean which not only possess great natural advantages for the control of that sea, but have received and are receiving that artificial strength of fortification and armament which will make them practically inexpugnable. On the contrary, we have not on the Gulf of Mexico even the beginning of a navy yard which could serve as the base of our operations. Let me not be misunderstood. I am not regretting that we have not the means to meet on terms of equality the great navies of the Old World. I recognize, what few at least say, that despite its great surplus revenue, this country is poor in proportion to its length of seaboard and its exposed points. That which I deplore, and which is a sober, just, and reasonable cause of deep national

concern is that the nation neither has nor cares to have its sea frontier so defended, and its navy of such power, as shall suffice, with the advantages of our position, to weigh seriously when inevitable discussions arise,—such as we have recently had about Samoa and Bering Sea, and which may at any moment come up about the Caribbean Sea or the canal. Is the United States, for instance, prepared to allow Germany to acquire the Dutch stronghold of Curaçao, fronting the Atlantic outlet of both the proposed canals of Panama and Nicaragua? Is she prepared to acquiesce in any foreign power purchasing from Haiti a naval station on the Windward Passage, through which pass our steamer routes to the Isthmus? Would she acquiesce in a foreign protectorate over the Sandwich Islands, that great central station of the Pacific, equidistant from San Francisco, Samoa, and the Marquesas, and an important post on our lines of communication with both Australia and China? Or will it be maintained that any one of these questions, supposing it to arise, is so exclusively one-sided, the arguments of policy and right so exclusively with us, that the other party will at once yield his eager wish, and gracefully withdraw? Was it so at Samoa? Is it so as regards the Bering Sea? The motto seen on so many ancient cannon, *Ultima ratio regum,* is not without its message to republics.

It is perfectly reasonable and legitimate, in estimating our needs of military preparation, to take into account the remoteness of the chief naval and military nations from our shores, and the consequent difficulty of maintaining operations at such a distance. It is equally proper, in framing our policy, to consider the jealousies of the European family of states, and their consequent unwillingness to incur the enmity of a people so strong as ourselves; their dread of our revenge in the future, as well as their inability to detach more than a certain part of their forces to our shores without losing much of their own weight in the councils of Europe. In truth, a careful determination of the force that Great Britain or France could probably spare for operations against our coasts, if the latter were suitably defended, without weakening their European position or unduly exposing their colonies and commerce, is the starting-point from which to calculate the strength of our own navy. If the latter be superior to the force that can thus be sent against it, and the coast be so defended as to leave the navy free to strike where it will we can maintain our rights; not merely the rights which international law concedes, and which the moral sense of nations now supports, but also those equally real rights which, though not supported by law, depend upon a clear preponderance of interest, upon obviously necessary policy, upon self-preservation, either total or partial. . . .

# 8

As popular demand for overseas possessions mounted, attention was increasingly focused on the Hawaiian Islands. Imperialists urged redemption of the "backward" natives; in Hawaii, American sugar planters who had invested $25,000,000 by 1890 demanded annexation to place their crop within the tariff wall. Discouraged by the failure of their home government to act, the planters took matters into their hands in 1893, staged a revolution, deposed the native queen, and asked to be admitted to the Union. President Benjamin Harrison was delighted; on February 13, 1893, he laid a treaty of annexation before the Senate with a strong message urging its adoption:[8]

I transmit herewith, with a view to its ratification, a treaty of annexation concluded on the 14th day of February, 1893, between John W. Foster, Secretary of State . . . and Lorin A. Thurston, W. R. Castle, W. C. Wilder, C. L. Carter, and Joseph Marsden, the commissioners on the part of the Government of the Hawaiian Islands. . . .

I do not deem it necessary to discuss at any length the conditions which have resulted in this decisive action. It has been the policy of the Administration not only to respect but to encourage the continuance of an independent government in the Hawaiian Islands so long as it afforded suitable guaranties for the protection of life and property and maintained a stability and strength that gave adequate security against the domination of any other power. The moral support of this Government has continually manifested itself in the most friendly diplomatic relations and in many acts of courtesy to the Hawaiian rulers.

The overthrow of the monarchy was not in any way promoted by this Government, but had its origin in what seems to have been a reactionary and revolutionary policy on the part of Queen Liliuokalani, which put in serious peril not only the large and preponderating interests of the United States in the islands, but all foreign interests, and indeed, the decent administration of civil affairs and the peace of the islands. It is quite evident that the monarchy had become effete and the Queen's Government so weak and inadequate as to be the prey of designing and unscrupulous persons. The restoration of Queen Liliuokalani to her throne is undesirable, if not impossible, and unless actively supported by the United States would be accompanied by serious disaster and the disorganization of all business interests. The influence and interest of the United States in the islands must be increased and not diminished.

Only two courses are now open—one the establishment of a protectorate by the United States, and the other annexation full and complete. I think the latter course, which has been adopted in the treaty, will be highly promotive of the best interests of the Hawaiian people, and is the only one that will adequately secure the interests of the United States. These interests are not wholly selfish. It is essential

[8] J. D. Richardson (comp.), *Messages and Papers of the Presidents, 1789-1897* (Washington, 1897, 1909; taken from 1909 vol.), IX, 345-349.

hat none of the other great powers shall
ecure these islands. Such a possession
vould not consist with our safety and with
he peace of the world. This view of the
ituation is so apparent and conclusive that
.o protest has been heard from any gov-
rnment against proceedings looking to an-
exation. Every foreign representative at
Honolulu promptly acknowledged the
Provisional Government, and I think there
s a general concurrence in the opinion
hat the deposed Queen ought not to be
estored.

Prompt action on this treaty is very
desirable. If it meets the approval of the
Senate, peace and good order will be se-
ured in the islands under existing laws
until such time as Congress can provide
by legislation a permanent form of government for the islands. This legislation
hould be, and I do not doubt will be, not
only just to the natives and all other residents and citizens of the islands, but
hould be characterized by great liberality
and a high regard to the rights of all
people and all foreigners domiciled there.
The correspondence which accompanies
his treaty will put the Senate in possession of all facts known to the Executive.

## 9

Unfortunately for the sugar planters, the
Hawaiian annexation treaty was still pending
before the Senate in 1893, when Harrison re-
inquished the presidency to Grover Cleve-
and. Humanitarian by nature and anti-imperi-
alistic by conviction, Cleveland sensed that the
revolution hardly represented the will of the
native majority on the islands. After a special
agent investigated events on the spot and confirmed these suspicions, Cleveland immediately reversed his predecessor's policy. In a
message to the Senate on December 18, 1893,
he withdrew the treaty of annexation:[9]

I suppose that right and justice should
determine the path to be followed in treating this subject. If national honesty is to be
disregarded and a desire for territorial ex-

tension or dissatisfaction with a form of
government not our own ought to regulate
our conduct, I have entirely misappre-
hended the mission and character of our
Government and the behavior which the
conscience of our people demands of their
public servants.

When the present Administration entered upon its duties, the Senate had under
consideration a treaty providing for the
annexation of the Hawaiian Islands to the
territory of the United States. Surely under
our Constitution and laws the enlargement
of our limits is a manifestation of the
highest attribute of sovereignty, and if
entered upon as an Executive act all things
relating to the transaction should be clear
and free from suspicion. Additional importance attached to this particular treaty
of annexation because it contemplated a
departure from unbroken American tradition in providing for the addition to our
territory of islands of the sea more than
2,000 miles removed from our nearest
coast.

These considerations might not of themselves call for interference with the completion of a treaty entered upon by a previous Administration, but it appeared from
the documents accompanying the treaty
when submitted to the Senate that the
ownership of Hawaii was tendered to us
by a Provisional Government set up to succeed the constitutional ruler of the islands,
who had been dethroned, and it did not
appear that such Provisional Government
had the sanction of either popular revolution or suffrage. Two other remarkable
features of the transaction naturally attracted attention. One was the extraordinary haste, not to say precipitancy, characterizing all the transactions. . . . Thus
between the initiation of the scheme for a
Provisional Government in Hawaii, on the
14th day of January, and the submission to
the Senate of the treaty of annexation concluded with such Government the entire
interval was thirty-two days, fifteen of
which were spent by the Hawaiian com-

[9] *Ibid.,* pp. 461-463, 469-470.

missioners in their journey to Washington. . . .

But a protest also accompanied said treaty, signed by the Queen and her ministers at the time she made way for the Provisional Government, which explicitly stated that she yielded to the superior force of the United States, whose minister had caused United States troops to be landed at Honolulu and declared that he would support such Provisional Government.

The truth or falsity of this protest was surely of the first importance. If true, nothing but the concealment of its truth could induce our Government to negotiate with the semblance of a government thus created, nor could a treaty resulting from the acts stated in the protest have been knowingly deemed worthy of consideration by the Senate. Yet the truth or falsity of the protest had not been investigated.

I conceived it to be my duty, therefore, to withdraw the treaty from the Senate for examination, and meanwhile to cause an accurate, full, and impartial investigation to be made of the facts attending the subversion of the constitutional Government of Hawaii. . . .

The report, with its accompanying proofs and such other evidence as is now before the Congress or is herewith submitted, justifies, in my opinion, the statement that when the President was led to submit the treaty to the Senate with the declaration that "the overthrow of the monarchy was not in any way promoted by this Government," and when the Senate was induced to receive and discuss it on that basis, both President and Senate were misled. . . .

I believe that a candid and thorough examination of the facts will force the conviction that the Provisional Government owes its existence to an armed invasion by the United States. Fair-minded people, with the evidence before them, will hardly claim that the Hawaiian Government was overthrown by the people of the islands or that the Provisional Government had ever

existed with their consent. I do not understand that any member of this Government claims that the people would uphold it by their suffrages if they were allowed to vote on the question.

While naturally sympathizing with every effort to establish a republican form of government, it has been the settled policy of the United States to concede to people of foreign countries the same freedom and independence in the management of their domestic affairs that we have always claimed for ourselves, and it has been our practice to recognize revolutionary governments as soon as it became apparent that they were supported by the people. . . .

As I apprehend the situation, we are brought face to face with the following conditions:

The lawful Government of Hawaii was overthrown without the drawing of a sword or the firing of a shot by a process every step of which, it may safely be asserted, is directly traceable to and dependent for its success upon the agency of the United States acting through its diplomatic and naval representatives.

But for the notorious predilections of the United States minister for annexation the committee of safety, which should be called the committee of annexation, would never have existed.

But for the landing of the United States forces upon false pretexts respecting the danger to life and property the committee would never have exposed themselves to the pains and penalties of treason by undertaking the subversion of the Queen's Government.

But for the presence of the United States forces in the immediate vicinity and in position to afford all needed protection and support the committee would not have proclaimed the Provisional Government from the steps of the Government building.

And finally, but for the lawless occupation of Honolulu under false pretexts by the United States forces, and but for Minister Stevens's recognition of the Provisional Government when the United States forces were its sole support and constituted its only military strength, the Queen and her Government would never have yielded to the Provisional Government, even for a time and for the sole purpose of submitting her case to the enlightened justice of the United States.

Believing, therefore, that the United States could not, under the circumstances disclosed, annex the islands without justly incurring the imputation of acquiring them by unjustifiable methods, I shall not again submit the treaty of annexation to the Senate for its consideration, and in the instructions of Minister Willis, a copy of which accompanies this message, I have directed him to so inform the Provisional Government. . . .

## 10

Although jolted by Cleveland's action, budding imperialists were not discouraged. Militant confidence in the strength of America was voiced again during the Venezuelan boundary controversy. A long-standing conflict between England and Venezuela over the boundary of British Guiana reached a boiling point in 1887, and Venezuela broke off diplomatic relations with Britain. Maintaining that the Monroe Doctrine was involved, Cleveland determined to intervene in 1895. On his instructions, Secretary of State Richard Olney penned an inflammatory note to the British government, which reflected a growing sense of strength although it did not register prevailing American opinion:[10]

That America is in no part open to colonization, though the proposition was not universally admitted at the time of its first enunciation, has long been universally conceded. We are now concerned, therefore, only with that other practical application of the Monroe doctrine the disregard of which by an European power

[10] *United States House Documents,* 54th Cong., 1st Sess., Doc. No. 1, Pt. 1, I, 554-555, 557-558.

is to be deemed an act of unfriendliness towards the United States. The precise scope and limitations of this rule cannot be too clearly apprehended. It does not establish any general protectorate by the United States over other American states. It does not relieve any American state from its obligations as fixed by international law nor prevent any European power directly interested from enforcing such obligations or from inflicting merited punishment for the breach of them. It does not contemplate any interference in the internal affairs of any American state or in the relations between it and other American states. It does not justify any attempt on our part to change the established form of government of any American state or to prevent the people of such state from altering that form according to their own will and pleasure. The rule in question has but a single purpose and object. It is that no European power or combination of European powers shall forcibly deprive an American state of the right and power of self-government and of shaping for itself its own political fortunes and destinies. . . .

It is true, then, that the safety and welfare of the United States are so concerned with the maintenance of the independence of every American state as against any European power as to justify and require the interposition of the United States whenever that independence is endangered? The question can be candidly answered in but one way. The states of America, South as well as North, by geographical proximity, by natural sympathy, by similarity of governmental constitutions, are friends and allies, commercially and politically, of the United States. To allow the subjugation of any of them by an European power is, of course, to completely reverse that situation and signifies the loss of all the advantages incident to their natural relations to us. But that is not all. The people of the United States have a vital interest in the cause of popular self-government. They have secured the right for themselves and their posterity at the cost of infinite blood and treasure. They have realized and exemplified its beneficent operation by a career unexampled in point of national greatness or individual felicity. They believe it to be for the healing of all nations, and that civilization must either advance or retrograde accordingly as its supremacy is extended or curtailed. Imbued with these sentiments, the people of the United States might not impossibly be wrought up to an active propaganda in favor of a cause so highly valued both for themselves and for mankind. But the age of the Crusades has passed, and they are content with such assertion and defense of the right of popular self-government as their own security and welfare demand. It is in that view more than in any other that they believe it not to be tolerated that the political control of an American state shall be forcibly assumed by an European power.

The mischiefs apprehended from a source are none the less real because not immediately imminent in any specific case, and are none the less to be guarded against because the combination of circumstances that will bring them upon us cannot be predicted. The civilized states of Christendom deal with each other on substantially the same principles that regulate the conduct of individuals. The greater its enlightenment, the more surely every state perceives that its permanent interests require it to be governed by the immutable principles of right and justice. Each, nevertheless, is only too liable to succumb to the temptations offered by seeming special opportunities for its own aggrandizement, and each would rashly imperil its own safety if it were not to remember that for the regard and respect of other states it must be largely dependent upon its own strength and power. Today the United States is practically sovereign on this continent, and its fiat is law upon the subjects to which it confines its inter-

position. Why? It is not because of the pure friendship or good will felt for it. It is not simply by reason of its high character as a civilized state, nor because wisdom and justice and equity are the invariable characteristics of the dealings of the United States. It is because, in addition to all other grounds, its infinite resources combined with its isolated position render it master of the situation and practically invulnerable as against any or all other powers.

All the advantages of this superiority are at once imperiled if the principle be admitted that European powers may convert American states into colonies or provinces of their own. The principle would be eagerly availed of, and every power doing so would immediately acquire a base of military operations against us. What one power was permitted to do could not be denied to another, and it is not inconceivable that the struggle now going on for the acquisition of Africa might be transferred to South America. If it were, the weaker countries would unquestionably be soon absorbed, while the ultimate result might be the partition of all South America between the various European powers. The disastrous consequences to the United States of such a condition of things are obvious. The loss of prestige, of authority, and of weight in the councils of the family of nations, would be among the least of them. Our only real rivals in peace as well as enemies in war would be found located at our very doors. Thus far in our history we have been spared the burdens and evils of immense standing armies and all the other accessories of huge warlike establishments, and the exemption has largely contributed to our national greatness and wealth as well as to the happiness of every citizen. But, with the powers of Europe permanently encamped on American soil, the ideal conditions we have thus far enjoyed can not be expected to continue. We too must be armed to the teeth, we too must convert the lower of our male population into soldiers and sailors, and by withdrawing them from the various pursuits of peaceful industry we too must practically annihilate a large share of the productive energy of the nation. . . .

## 11

Olney's demand that the Venezuelan dispute be submitted to arbitration met a cold response at the Court of St. James's. Instead, England held that the Monroe Doctrine did not apply, and insisted that its boundary claim was just. When President Cleveland laid this correspondence before Congress on December 17, 1895, with a request for an independent commission to settle the controversy, war between the two countries seemed imminent. That England finally backed down was due to the outbreak of the Boer War in Africa and hostile pressure from Germany rather than to any moderation in Cleveland's congressional message of December 17:[11]

In my annual message addressed to the Congress on the 3d instant I called attention to the pending boundary controversy between Great Britain and the Republic of Venezuela and recited the substance of a representation made by this Government to Her Britannic Majesty's Government suggesting reasons why such dispute should be submitted to arbitration for settlement and inquiring whether it would be so submitted.

The answer of the British Government, which was then awaited, has since been received, and, together with the despatch to which it is a reply, is hereto appended.

Such reply is embodied in two communications addressed by the British prime minister to Sir Julian Pauncefote, the British ambassador at this capital. It will be seen that one of these communications is devoted exclusively to observations upon the Monroe doctrine, and claims that in the present instance a new and strange exten-

sion and development of this doctrine is insisted on by the United States; that the reasons justifying an appeal to the doctrine enunciated by President Monroe are generally inapplicable "to the state of things in which we live at the present day," and especially inapplicable to a controversy involving the boundary line between Great Britain and Venezuela.

Without attempting extended argument in reply to these positions, it may not be amiss to suggest that the doctrine upon which we stand is strong and sound, because its enforcement is important to our peace and safety as a nation and is essential to the integrity of our free institutions and the tranquil maintenance of our distinctive form of government. It was intended to apply to every stage of our national life and can not become obsolete while our Republic endures. If the balance of power is justly a cause for jealous anxiety among the Governments of the Old World and a subject for our absolute noninterference, none the less is an observance on the Monroe doctrine of vital concern to our people and their Government.

Assuming, therefore, that we may properly insist upon this doctrine without regard to "the state of things in which we live" or any changed conditions here or elsewhere, it is not apparent why its application may not be invoked in the present controversy.

If a European power by an extension of its boundaries takes possession of the territory of one of our neighboring Republics against its will and in derogation of its rights, it is difficult to see why to that extent such European power does not thereby attempt to extend its system of government to that portion of this continent which is thus taken. This is the precise action which President Monroe declared to be "dangerous to our peace and safety," and it can make no difference whether the European system is extended by an advance of frontier or otherwise.

It is also suggested in the British reply

---

[11] J. D. Richardson (comp.), *Messages and Papers of the Presidents, 1789-1897* (Washington, 1897, 1909; taken from 1909 vol.), IX, 655-658.

that we should not seek to apply the Monroe doctrine to the pending dispute because it does not embody any principle of international law which "is founded on the general consent of nations," and that "no statesman, however eminent, and no nation, however powerful, are competent to insert into the code of international law a novel principle which was never recognized before and which has not since been accepted by the government of any other country."

Practically the principle for which we contend has peculiar, if not exclusive, relation to the United States. It may not have been admitted in so many words to the code of international law, but since in international councils every nation is entitled to the rights belonging to it, if the enforcement of the Monroe doctrine is something we may justly claim it has its place in the code of international law as certainly and as securely as if it were specifically mentioned; and when the United States is a suitor before the high tribunal that administers international law the question to be determined is whether or not we present claims which the justice of that code of law can find to be right and valid.

The Monroe doctrine finds its recognition in those principles of international law which are based upon the theory that every nation shall have its rights protected and its just claims enforced.

Of course this Government is entirely confident that under the sanction of this doctrine we have clear rights and undoubted claims. Nor is this ignored in the British reply. The prime minister, while not admitting that the Monroe doctrine is applicable to present conditions, states:

In declaring that the United States would resist any such enterprise if it was contemplated, President Monroe adopted a policy which received the entire sympathy of the English Government of that date.

He further declares:

Though the language of President Monroe is directed to the attainment of objects which most Englishmen would agree to be salutary, it is impossible to admit that they have been inscribed by any adequate authority in the code of international law.

Again he says:

They fully concur with the view which President Monroe apparently entertained, that any disturbance of the existing territorial distribution in that hemisphere by any fresh acquisitions on the part of any European State would be a highly inexpedient change.

In the belief that the doctrine for which we contend was clear and definite, that it was founded upon substantial considerations and involved our safety and welfare, that it was fully applicable to our present conditions and to the state of the world's progress, and that it was directly related to the pending controversy, and without any conviction as to the final merits of the dispute, but anxious to learn in a satisfactory and conclusive manner whether Great Britain sought under a claim of boundary to extend her possessions on this continent without right, or whether she merely sought possession of territory fairly included within her lines of ownership, this Government proposed to the Government of Great Britain a resort to arbitration as the proper means of settling the question, to the end that a vexatious boundary dispute between the two contestants might be determined and our exact standing and relation in respect to the controversy might be made clear.

It will be seen from the correspondence herewith submitted that this proposition has been declined by the British Government upon grounds which in the circumstances seem to me to be far from satisfactory. It is deeply disappointing that such an appeal, actuated by the most friendly feelings toward both nations directly concerned, addressed to the sense of justice and to the magnanimity of one of the great powers of the world, and touching its reations to one comparatively weak and small, should have produced no better results.

The course to be pursued by this Government in view of the present condition does not appear to admit of serious doubt. Having labored faithfully for many years to induce Great Britain to submit this dispute to impartial arbitration, and having been now finally apprised of her refusal to do so, nothing remains but to accept the situation, to recognize its plain requirements, and deal with it accordingly. Great Britain's present proposition has never thus far been regarded as admissible by Venezuela, though any adjustment of the boundary which that country may deem for her advantage and may enter into of her own free will can not of course be objected to by the United States.

Assuming, however, that the attitude of Venezuela will remain unchanged, the dispute has reached such a stage as to make it now incumbent upon the United States to take measures to determine with sufficient certainty for its justification what is the true divisional line between the Republic of Venezuela and British Guiana. The inquiry to that end should of course be conducted carefully and judicially, and due weight should be given to all available evidence, records, and facts in support of the claims of both parties.

In order that such an examination should be prosecuted in a thorough and satisfactory manner, I suggest that the Congress make an adequate appropriation for the expenses of a commission, to be appointed by the Executive, who shall make the necessary investigation and report upon the matter with the least possible delay. When such report is made and accepted it will, in my opinion, be the duty of the United States to resist by every means in its power, as a wilful aggression upon its rights and interests, the appropriation by Great Britain of any lands or the exercise of governmental jurisdiction over any territory which after investigation we have determined of right belongs to Venezuela.

In making these recommendations I am fully alive to the responsibility incurred and keenly realize all the consequences that may follow.

I am, nevertheless, firm in my conviction that while it is a grievous thing to contemplate the two great English-speaking peoples of the world as being otherwise than friendly competitors in the onward march of civilization and strenuous and worthy rivals in all the arts of peace, there is no calamity which a great nation can invite which equals that which follows a supine submission to wrong and injustice and the consequent loss of national self-respect and honor, beneath which are shielded and defended a people's safety and greatness.

## THE GLITTER OF EMPIRE

### 12

The Spanish-American War, three years after the Venezuelan crisis, was the culmination of the newer nationalistic tendencies. A Cuban revolution against Spain in 1895 provided the immediate background. American opinion, always emotionally identified with movements for political freedom, was profoundly stirred. In addition, Cuba's geographical position was of real concern to a people cultivating Latin-American trade, while a $100,000,000 annual commerce with the island and heavy investments there did not lessen the interest. Spain, anxious to avoid war, agreed to give the Cubans a larger measure of independence and to cure the evils with which she was charged. The sinking of the battleship "Maine" in a Cuban harbor (February 15, 1898) made a peaceful solution difficult, but President McKinley, defying popular pressure intensified by an irresponsible press, strove to achieve it. Spain was equally anxious for peace as a message to McKinley from Stewart L. Woodford, American minister to Madrid, written on April 5, 1898, demonstrates:[12]

---

[12] *United States House Documents*, 55th Cong., 3rd Sess., Doc. No. 1, Pt. 1, I, 741-742.

Should the Queen proclaim the following before 12 o'clock noon of Wednesday, April 6, will you sustain the Queen, and can you prevent hostile action by Congress?

At the request of the Holy Father, in this Passion Week and in the name of Christ, I proclaim immediate and unconditional suspension of hostilities in the island of Cuba.

This suspension is to become immediately effective so soon as accepted by the insurgents in that island, and is to continue for the space of six months, to the 5th day of October, eighteen ninety-eight.

I do this to give time for passions to cease, and in the sincere hope and belief that during this suspension permanent and honorable peace may be obtained between the insular government of Cuba and those of my subjects in that island who are now in rebellion against the authority of Spain.

I pray the blessing of Heaven upon this Truce of God, which I now declare in His name and with the sanction of the Holy Father of all Christendom.

April 5, 1898

Please read this in the light of all my previous telegrams and letters. I believe that this means peace, which the sober judgment of our people will approve long before next November, and which must be approved at the bar of final history.

I permit the papal nuncio to read this telegram, upon my own responsibility and without committing you in any manner. I dare not reject this last chance for peace. I will show your reply to the Queen in person, and I believe that you will approve this last conscientious effort for peace.

### 13

Spain's willingness to accept every American demand made little difference. Perverted accounts of Spanish atrocities in the "yellow press" produced a sentiment for intervention so insistent that compromise was difficult. Nor could McKinley stem the tide. On April 11, 1898, he called upon Congress to declare war, basing his argument on a distorted picture of the whole Cuban situation, and neglecting to

state that he had received a note from Spain promising an immediate end of hostilities in Cuba:[13]

Obedient to that precept of the Constitution which commands the President to give from time to time to the Congress information of the state of the Union and to recommend to their consideration such measures as he shall judge necessary and expedient, it becomes my duty to now address your body with regard to the grave crisis that has arisen in the relations of the United States to Spain by reason of the warfare that for more than three years has raged in the neighboring island of Cuba. . . .

Our trade has suffered, the capital invested by our citizens in Cuba has been largely lost, and the temper and forbearance of our people have been so sorely tried as to beget a perilous unrest among our own citizens, which has inevitably found its expression from time to time in the National Legislature, so that issues wholly external to our own body politic engross attention and stand in the way of that close devotion to domestic advancement that becomes a self-contained commonwealth whose primal maxim has been the avoidance of all foreign entanglements. All this must needs awaken, and has, indeed, aroused, the utmost concern on the part of this Government, as well during my predecessor's term as in my own. . . .

The war in Cuba is of such a nature that, short of subjugation or extermination, a final military victory for either side seems impracticable. The alternative lies in the physical exhaustion of the one or the other party, or perhaps of both—a condition which in effect ended the ten years' war by the truce of Zanjon. The prospect of such a protraction and conclusion of the present strife is a contingency hardly to be contemplated with equanim-

[13] J. D. Richardson (comp.), *Messages and Papers of the Presidents, 1789-1897* (Washington, 1897, 1909; taken from 1909 vol.), X, 56-57, 60-61, 64-67.

ity by the civilized world, and least of all by the United States, affected and injured as we are, deeply and intimately, by its very existence.

Realizing this, it appeared to be my duty, in a spirit of true friendliness, no less to Spain than to the Cubans, who have so much to lose by the prolongation of the struggle, to seek to bring about an immediate termination of the war. To this end I submitted on the 27th ultimo, as a result of much representation and correspondence, through the United States minister at Madrid, propositions to the Spanish Government looking to an armistice until October 1 for the negotiation of peace with the good offices of the President.

In addition I asked the immediate revocation of the order of reconcentration, so as to permit the people to return to their farms and the needy to be relieved with provisions and supplies from the United States, co-operating with the Spanish authorities, so as to afford full relief.

The reply of the Spanish cabinet was received on the night of the 31st ultimo. It offered, as the means to bring about peace in Cuba, to confide the preparation thereof to the insular parliament, inasmuch as the concurrence of that body would be necessary to reach a final result, it being, however, understood that the powers reserved by the constitution to the central Government are not lessened or diminished. As the Cuban parliament does not meet until the 4th of May next, the Spanish Government would not object for its part to accept at once a suspension of hostilities if asked for by the insurgents from the general in chief, to whom it would pertain in such case to determine the duration and conditions of the armistice. . . .

With this last overture in the direction of immediate peace, and its disappointing reception by Spain, the Executive is brought to the end of his effort.

In my annual message of December last I said:

Of the untried measures there remain only: recognition of the insurgents as belligerents; recognition of the independence of Cuba; neutral intervention to end the war by imposing a rational compromise between the contestants, and intervention in favor of one or the other party. I speak not of forcible annexation, for that can not be thought of. That, by our code of morality, would be criminal aggression.

Thereupon I reviewed these alternatives in the light of President Grant's measured words, uttered in 1875, when, after seven years of sanguinary, destructive, and cruel hostilities in Cuba, he reached the conclusion that the recognition of the independence of Cuba was impracticable and indefensible and that the recognition of belligerence was not warranted by the facts according to the tests of public law. I commented especially upon the latter aspect of the question, pointing out the inconveniences and positive dangers of a recognition of belligerence, which, while adding to the already onerous burdens of neutrality within our own jurisdiction, could not in any way extend our influence or effective offices in the territory of hostilities.

Nothing has since occurred to change my view in this regard, and I recognize as fully now as then that the issuance of a proclamation of neutrality, by which process the so-called recognition of belligerents is published, could of itself and unattended by other action accomplish nothing toward the one end for which we labor—the instant pacification of Cuba. . . .

There remain the alternative forms of intervention to end the war, either as an impartial neutral, by imposing a rational compromise between the contestants, or as the active ally of the one party or the other.

As to the first, it is not to be forgotten that during the last few months the relation of the United States has virtually been one of friendly intervention in many ways, each not of itself conclusive, but all tending to the exertion of a potential influence toward an ultimate pacific result, just and honorable to all interests concerned. The spirit of all our acts hitherto has been an earnest, unselfish desire for peace and prosperity in Cuba, untarnished by differences between us and Spain and unstained by the blood of American citizens.

The forcible intervention of the United States as a neutral to stop the war, according to the large dictates of humanity and following many historical precedents where neighboring states have interfered to check the hopeless sacrifices of life by internecine conflicts beyond their borders, is justifiable on rational grounds. It involves, however, hostile constraint upon both the parties to the contest, as well to enforce a truce as to guide the eventual settlement.

The grounds for such intervention may be briefly summarized as follows:

*First.* In the cause of humanity and to put an end to the barbarities, bloodshed, starvation, and horrible miseries now existing there, and which the parties to the conflict are either unable or unwilling to stop or mitigate. It is no answer to say this is all in another country, belonging to another nation, and is therefore none of our business. It is specially our duty, for it is right at our door.

*Second.* We owe it to our citizens in Cuba to afford them that protection and indemnity for life and property which no government there can or will afford, and to that end to terminate the conditions that deprive them of legal protection.

*Third.* The right to intervene may be justified by the very serious injury to the commerce, trade, and business of our people and by the wanton destruction of property and devastation of the island.

*Fourth,* and which is of the utmost importance. The present condition of affairs in Cuba is a constant menace to our peace and entails upon this Government an enormous expense. With such a conflict waged

for years in an island so near us and with which our people have such trade and business relations; when the lives and liberty of our citizens are in constant danger and their property destroyed and themselves ruined; where our trading vessels are liable to seizure and are seized at our very door by war ships of a foreign nation; the expeditions of filibustering that we are powerless to prevent altogether, and the irritating questions and entanglements thus arising—all these and others that I need not mention, with the resulting strained relations, are a constant menace to our peace and compel us to keep on a semi-war footing with a nation with which we are at peace.

These elements of danger and disorder already pointed out have been strikingly illustrated by a tragic event which has deeply and justly moved the American people. I have already transmitted to Congress the report of the naval court of inquiry on the destruction of the battle ship *Maine* in the harbor of Havana during the night of the 15th of February. The destruction of that noble vessel has filled the national heart with inexpressible horror. Two hundred and fifty-eight brave sailors and marines and two officers of our Navy, reposing in the fancied security of a friendly harbor, have been hurled to death, grief and want brought to their homes and sorrow to the nation.

The naval court of inquiry, which, it is needless to say, commands the unqualified confidence of the Government, was unanimous in its conclusion that the destruction of the *Maine* was caused by an exterior explosion—that of a submarine mine. It did not assume to place the responsibility. That remains to be fixed.

In any event, the destruction of the *Maine,* by whatever exterior cause, is a patent and impressive proof of a state of things in Cuba that is intolerable. That condition is thus shown to be such that the Spanish Government can not assure safety and security to a vessel of the American Navy in the harbor of Havana on a mission of peace. . . .

The long trial has proved that the object for which Spain has waged the war can not be attained. The fire of insurrection may flame or may smolder with varying seasons, but it has not been and it is plain that it can not be extinguished by present methods. The only hope of relief and repose from a condition which can no longer be endured is the enforced pacification of Cuba. In the name of humanity, in the name of civilization, in behalf of endangered American interests which give us the right and the duty to speak and to act, the war in Cuba must stop.

In view of these facts and of these considerations I ask the Congress to authorize and empower the President to take measures to secure a full and final termination of hostilities between the Government of Spain and the people of Cuba, and to secure in the island the establishment of a stable government, capable of maintaining order and observing its international obligations, insuring peace and tranquillity and the security of its citizens as well as our own, and to use the military and naval forces of the United States as may be necessary for these purposes.

And in the interest of humanity and to aid in preserving the lives of the starving people of the island I recommend that the distribution of food and supplies be continued and that an appropriation be made out of the public Treasury to supplement the charity of our citizens.

The issue is now with the Congress. It is a solemn responsibility. I have exhausted every effort to relieve the intolerable condition of affairs which is at our doors. Prepared to execute every obligation imposed upon me by the Constitution and the law, I await your action.

Yesterday, and since the preparation of the foregoing message, official information was received by me that the latest decree of the Queen Regent òf Spain directs General Blanco, in order to prepare and facilitate peace, to proclaim a suspension of hostilities, the duration and details of which have not yet been communicated to me.

This fact, with every other pertinent consideration, will, I am sure, have your just and careful attention in the solemn deliberations upon which you are about to enter. If this measure attains a successful result, then our aspirations as a Christian, peace-loving people will be realized. If it fails, it will be only another justification for our contemplated action.

## 14

Actually, American motives leading to the Spanish-American War were more idealistic than imperialistic. Some people certainly entertained visions of empire, but most were honestly concerned with the fate of the Cubans. Blood was worth spilling, in the terms of a respected American tradition, to water the tree of liberty. The so-called Teller Amendment, adopted by Congress on April 20, 1898, five days before the formal declaration of war, suggests this spirit of humanitarianism:[14]

WHEREAS, The abhorrent conditions which have existed for more than three years in the Island of Cuba, so near our own borders, have shocked the moral sense of the people of the United States, have been a disgrace to Christian civilization, culminating, as they have, in the destruction of a United States battle ship, with two hundred and sixty-six of its officers and crew, while on a friendly visit in the harbor of Havana, and can not longer be endured, as has been set forth by the President of the United States in his message to Congress of April eleventh, eighteen hundred and ninety-eight, upon which the action of Congress was invited: Therefore,

*Resolved, . . . First.* That the people of

---

[14] *United States Statutes at Large,* XXX, 738-739.

the Island of Cuba are, and of right ought to be, free and independent.

*Second.* That it is the duty of the United States to demand, and the Government of the United States does hereby demand, that the Government of Spain at once relinquish its authority and government in the Island of Cuba and withdraw its land and naval forces from Cuba and Cuban waters.

*Third.* That the President of the United States be, and he hereby is, directed and empowered to use the entire land and naval forces of the United States, and to call into the actual service of the United States the militia of the several States, to such extent as may be necessary to carry these resolutions into effect.

*Fourth.* That the United States hereby disclaims any disposition or intention to exercise sovereignty, jurisdiction, or control over said Island except for the pacification thereof, and asserts its determination, when that is accomplished, to leave the government and control of the Island to its people.

## 15

The Spanish-American War was short and decisive. With its close, an ancient empire disintegrated and a new empire emerged. Defeated, Spain gave up Puerto Rico and Guam to the United States, but the question of the Philippines posed a moral problem of greater magnitude. The islands had been conquered by American arms, but could a nation that championed the freedom of subject peoples take colonists under its own wing? Before the war, a majority of Americans would have answered "No" emphatically, but the easy victory over Spanish arms bolstered imperialistic sentiment in the United States. A sage commentator, Finley Peter Dunne, illustrated the shift in opinion in a conversation between his two beloved characters, the genial bartender Mr. Dooley, and his patient stooge, Mr. Hennessey:[15]

[15] Reprinted from *Mr. Dooley in Peace and War*, by Peter Finley Dunne (Boston, 1898, 1899), pp. 43-37. Used by permission of the publishers, Charles Scribner's Sons.

"I know what I'd do if I was Mack," said Mr. Hennessy. "I'd hist a flag over th' Ph'lippeens, an' I'd take in th' whole lot iv them."

"An' yet," said Mr. Dooley, "'tis not more thin two months since ye larned whether they were islands or canned goods. Ye'er back yard is so small that ye'er cow can't turn r-round without buttin' th' woodshed off th' premises, an' ye wudden't go out to th' stock yards without takin' out a policy on yer life. Suppose ye was standin' at th' corner iv State Sthreet an' Archey R-road, wud ye know what car to take to get to th' Ph'lippeens? If yer son Packy was to ask ye where th' Ph'lippeens is, cud ye give him anny good idea whether they was in Rooshia or jus' west iv th' thracks?"

"Mebbe I cudden't," said Mr. Hennessy, haughtily, "but I'm f'r takin' thim in, annyhow."

"So might I be," said Mr. Dooley, "if I cud on'y get me mind on it. Wan iv the worst things about this here war is th' way it's makin' puzzles f'r our poor, tired heads. Whin I wint into it, I thought all I'd have to do was to set up here behind th' bar with a good tin-cint see-gar in me teeth, an' toss dinnymite bombs into th' hated city iv Havana. But look at me now. Th' war is still goin' on; an' ivry night, when I'm countin' up the cash, I'm askin' mesilf will I annex Cubia or lave it to the Cubians? Will I take Porther Ricky or put it by? An' what shud I do with the Ph'lippeens? Oh, what shud I do with thim? I can't annex thim because I don't know where they ar-re. I can't let go iv thim because some wan else'll take thim if I do. They are eight thousan' iv thim islands, with a popylation iv wan hundherd millyon naked savages; an' me bedroom's crowded now with me an' th' bed. How can I take thim in, an' how on earth am I goin' to cover th' nakedness iv thim savages with me wan shoot iv clothes? An' yet 'twud break me heart to think iv givin' people I niver see or heerd tell iv back to other people I don't know. An', if I don't take thim, Schwartzmeister down th' sthreet, that has half me thrade already, will grab thim sure.

"It ain't that I'm afraid iv not doin' th' r-right thing in th' end, Hinnissy. Some mornin' I'll wake up an' know jus' what to do, an' that I'll do. But 'tis th' annoyance in th' mane time. I've been r-readin' about th' counthry. 'Tis over beyant ye'er left shoulder whin ye're facin' east. Jus' throw ye'er thumb back, an' ye have it as ac'rate as anny man in town. 'Tis farther thin Boohlgahrya an' not so far as Blewchoochoo. It's near Chiny, an' it's not so near; an', if a man was to bore a well through fr'm Goshen, Indianny, he might sthrike it, an' thin again he might not. It's a poverty-sthricken counthry, full iv goold an' precious stones, where th' people can pick dinner off th' threes an' ar-re starvin' because they have no stepladders. Th' inhabitants is mostly naygurs an' Chinnymen, peaceful, industhrus, an' lawabidin', but savage an' bloodthirsty in their methods. They wear no clothes except what they have on, an' each woman has five husbands an' each man has five wives. Th' r-rest goes into th' discard, th' same as here. Th' islands has been ownded be Spain since befure th' fire; an' she's threated thim so well they're now up in ar-rms again her, except a majority iv thim which is thurly loyal. Th' natives seldom fight, but whin they get mad at wan another they r-run-a-muck. Whin a man r-runs-a-muck, sometimes they hang him an' sometimes they discharge him an' hire a new motorman. Th' women ar-re beautiful, with languishin' black eyes, an' they smoke see-gars, but ar-re hurried an' incomplete in their dhress. I see a pitcher iv wan th' other day with nawthin' on her but a basket of cocoanuts an' a hoop-skirt. They're no prudes. We import juke, hemp, cigar wrappers, sugar, an' fairy tales fr'm th' Ph'lippeens, an' export six-inch shells an' th' like. Iv late th' Ph'lippeens has awaked to th' fact

they're behind th' times, an' has received much American amminition in their midst. They say th' Spanyards is all tore up about it.

"I larned all this fr'm th' papers, an' I know 'tis sthraight. An' yet, Hinnissy, I dinnaw what to do about th' Ph'lippeens. An' I'm all alone in th' wurruld. Ivrybody else has made up his mind. Ye ask anny con-ducthor on Ar-rchy R-road, an' he'll tell ye. Ye can find out fr'm th' papers; an', if ye really want to know, all ye have to do is to ask a prom'nent citizen who can mow all th' lawn he owns with a safety razor. But I don't know."

"Hang on to thim," said Mr. Hennessy, stoutly. "What we've got we must hold."

"Well," said Mr. Dooley, "if I was Mack, I'd lave it to George. I'd say: 'George,' I'd say, 'if ye're f'r hangin' on, hang on it is. If ye say, lave go, I dhrop thim.' 'Twas George won thim with th' shells, an' th' question's up to him."

## 16

President McKinley's views shifted with those of the people. When he recommended war to Congress he had no intention of adding the Philippines to the growing American empire, but he could no more resist the changing climate of opinion than could Mr. Hennessy. Later he explained his conversion to imperialism in a talk to a group of Methodist clergymen. It is important to note that his four arguments were based on (1) honor of the nation, (2) economic nationalism, (3) superiority of race, and (4) the "white man's burden":[16]

When next I realized that the Philippines had dropped into our laps I confess I did not know what to do with them. I sought counsel from all sides—Democrats as well as Republicans—but got little help. I thought first we would take only Manila; then Luzon; then other islands perhaps also.

[16] *The Life of William McKinley* by Charles S. Olcott (1916), II, 110-111. Used by permission of the publishers, Houghton Mifflin Company.

I walked the floor of the White House night after night until midnight; and I am not ashamed to tell you, gentlemen, that I went down on my knees and prayed Almighty God for light and guidance more than one night. And one night late it came to me this way—I don't know how it was, but it came:

(1) That we could not give them back to Spain—that would be cowardly and dishonorable;

(2) That we could not turn them over to France or Germany—our commercial rivals in the Orient—that would be bad business and discreditable;

(3) That we could not leave them to themselves—they were unfit for self-government—and they would soon have anarchy and misrule worse than Spain's *war;*

(4) That there was nothing left for us to do but to take them all, and to educate the Filipinos, and uplift and civilize and Christianize them as our fellow-men for whom Christ also died.

And then I went to bed and slept soundly, and the next morning I sent for the chief engineer of the War Department (our map-maker), and I told him to put the Philippines on the map of the United States (pointing to a large map on the wall of his office), and there they are, and there they will stay while I am President!

## 17

Translated into slightly less pious language, President McKinley's views were transmitted to the American peace commissioners on September 16, 1898:[17]

It is my earnest wish that the United States in making peace should follow the same high rule of conduct which guided it in facing war. It should be as scrupulous and magnanimous in the concluding settlement as it was just and humane in its original action. The luster and the moral strength attaching to a cause which can

be confidently rested upon the considerate judgment of the world should not under any illusion of the hour be dimmed by ulterior designs which might tempt us into excessive demands or into an adventurous departure on untried paths. It is believed that the true glory and the enduring interests of the country will most surely be served if an unselfish duty conscientiously accepted and a signal triumph honorably achieved shall be crowned by such an example of moderation, restraint, and reason in victory as best comports with the traditions and character of our enlightened Republic.

Our aim in the adjustment of peace should be directed to lasting results and to the achievement of the common good under the demands of civilization, rather than to ambitious designs. The terms of the protocol were framed upon this consideration. The abandonment of the Western Hemisphere by Spain was an imperative necessity. In presenting that requirement, we only fulfilled a duty universally acknowledged. It involves no ungenerous reference to our recent foe, but simply a recognition of the plain teachings of history, to say that it was not compatible with the assurance of permanent peace on and near our own territory that the Spanish flag should remain on this side of the sea. This lesson of events and of reason left no alternative as to Cuba, Porto Rico, and the other islands belonging to Spain in this hemisphere.

The Philippines stand upon a different basis. It is none the less true, however, that, without any original thought of complete or even partial acquisition, the presence and success of our arms at Manila imposes upon us obligations which we can not disregard. The march of events rules and overrules human action. Avowing unreservedly the purpose which has animated all our effort, and still solicitous to adhere to it, we can not be unmindful that, without any desire or design on our part, the war has brought us new duties

---

[17] *United States House Documents,* 55th Cong., 3rd Sess., Doc. No. 1, I, 907, 908.

and responsibilities which we must meet and discharge as becomes a great nation on whose growth and career from the beginning the Ruler of Nations has plainly written the high command and pledge of civilization.

Incidental to our tenure in the Philippines is the commercial opportunity to which American statesmanship can not be indifferent. It is just to use every legitimate means for the enlargement of American trade; but we seek no advantages in the Orient which are not common to all. Asking only the open door for ourselves, we are ready to accord the open door to others. The commercial opportunity which is naturally and inevitably associated with this new opening depends less on large territorial possession than upon an adequate commercial basis and upon broad and equal privileges. . . .

In view of what has been stated, the United States can not accept less than the cession in full right and sovereignty of the island of Luzon. It is desirable, however, that the United States shall acquire the right of entry for vessels and merchandise belonging to citizens of the United States into such ports of the Philippines as are not ceded to the United States upon terms of equal favor with Spanish ships and merchandise, both in relation to port and customs charges and rates of trade accorded to citizens of one country within the territory of another. You are therefore instructed to demand such concession, agreeing on your part that Spain shall have similar rights as to her subjects and vessels in the ports of any territory in the Philippines ceded to the United States. . . .

McKinley's altered attitude followed the alteration in American opinion. Awakened to a new-found might, Americans cheered the President as he grabbed off the Philippines, annexed Puerto Rico and Guam, and retained such a tight hold over Cuba that the bewildered natives wondered if they had simply exchanged one colonial master for another. Yet not all Americans were infected with the imperialistic fever. A healthy minority, which grew steadily over the course of the years, insisted that a nation dedicated to the cause of freedom had no place in the race for empire. Americans gradually awakened to their international responsibilities. Isolation, however powerful it remained as a myth, was outmoded as a fact. Global responsibility was frequently confused with selfish imperialism, but Americans were preparing for the larger world role that the United States was to play in the twentieth century.

# THE RISE OF PROGRESSIVISM

## 1900–1912

The wave of conservatism after the Civil War reached its peak in the 1890's. The imperialism of the Spanish-American War, the negation of the Interstate Commerce and Sherman acts by the Supreme Court, the defeat of the income-tax bill, the judicial blessing given the labor injunction, and the downfall of the free silverites at the polls all marked triumphs for the forces of reaction. In the end, however, the conservatives went too far. Farmers, workers, and especially middle-class progressives, raising the banners of revolt and reform, demanded an end to the era of exploitation. The result was the Progressive Period, which lasted from the beginning of the twentieth century to the outbreak of World War I. During those years reformers and their political allies labored to restore democracy—political, social, and economic—to its traditional place in American life.

## THE IDEA OF PROGRESS

### 1

The first task of reformers who launched the Progressive Era was to refute the generally accepted arguments of defenders of the gospel of wealth. Spokesmen for industrialism had maintained that material progress could best be achieved by adherence to a philosophy of laissez faire; society, they insisted, was evolving along natural lines not clearly comprehensible to ordinary mortals. Any interference would not only upset the divine plan but lower the standard of living for all. "Progress," wrote Herbert Spencer, the English champion of laissez faire, "is not an accident, not a thing within human control, but a beneficent necessity." Humanitarians recognized that they could do nothing until they shattered popular complacency by revealing the ugly disparity between the boast of progress and the realities of daily life. From John Dewey, "philosopher of the common man," came, in an article first published in 1916, a frontal attack upon the naïve if comfortable dream of "automatic uninterrupted progress":[1]

Two things are apparent. First, progress depends not on the existence of social change but on the direction which human beings deliberately give that change. Secondly, ease of social change is a condition of progress. Side by side with the fact that the mere substitution of a dynamic or readily changing social structure for a static society does not accomplish progress, stands the fact that this substitution furnishes the opportunity for progress. We cannot too much insist upon the fact that until men got control of natural forces civilization was a local accident. It depended upon the ability of a small number of men to command, with assurance, the labor and services of other men. Any civilization based mainly upon ability to exploit the energies of men is precarious; it is at the mercy of internal revolt and external overflow. By exploring the heaps of rubbish scattered over the face of the earth, we are just beginning to learn how many civilizations have arisen in the past only to sink into rubbish heaps. The dominion of man over the labor of other men is a shaky basis for civilization. And civilization never attained stability upon such a basis. The scientific conquest of nature has at least given us another basis. . . . While the modern man was deceived about the automatic certainty of progress, he was right in thinking that for the first time in history mankind is in command of the possibility of progress. The rest is for us to say. . . .

[1] From *Characters and Events* by John Dewey and edited by Joseph Ratner, II, 820-830. Copyright, 1929, by Henry Holt and Company, Inc.

. . . Progress is not automatic; it depends upon human intent and aim and upon acceptance of responsibility for its production. It is not a wholesale matter, but a retail job, to be contracted for and executed in sections. I doubt if the whole history of mankind shows any more vicious and demoralizing ethic than the recent widespread belief that each of us, as individuals and as classes, might safely and complacently devote ourselves to increasing our own possessions, material, intellectual, and artistic, because progress was inevitable anyhow.

In dwelling upon the need of conceiving progress as a responsibility and not as an endowment, I put primary emphasis upon responsibility for intelligence, for the power which foresees, plans and constructs in advance. We are so overweighted by nature with impulse, sentiment and emotion, that we are always tempted to rely unduly upon the efficacy of these things. Especially do we like to entrust our destiny to them when they go by eulogistic names—like altruism, kindliness, peaceful feelings. But spite of the dogma which measures progress by increase in these sentiments, there is no reason that I know of to suppose that the basic fund of these emotions has increased appreciably in thousands and thousands of years. Man is equipped with these feelings at birth as well as with emotions of fear, anger, emulation and resentment. What appears to be an increase in one set and a decrease in the other set is, in reality, a change in their social occasions and social channels. Civilized man has not a better endowment of ear and eye than savage man; but his social surroundings give him more important things to see and hear than the savage has, and he has the wit to devise instruments to reinforce his eye and ear—the telegraph and telephone, the microscope and telescope. But there is no reason for thinking that he has less natural aggressiveness or more natural altruism—or will ever have—than the bar-

barian. But he may live in social conditions that create a relatively greater demand for the display of kindliness and which turn his aggressive instincts into less destructive channels. There is at any time a sufficient amount of kindly impulses possessed by man to enable him to live in amicable peace with all his fellows; and there is at any time a sufficient equipment of bellicose impulses to keep him in trouble with his fellows. An intensification of the exhibition of one may accompany an intensification of the display of the other, the only difference being that social arrangements cause the kindly feelings to be displayed toward one set of fellows and the hostile impulses toward another set. Thus, as everybody knows, the hatred toward the foreigner characterizing peoples now at war is attended by an unusual manifestation of mutual affection and love within each warring group. So characteristic is this fact that that man was a good psychologist who said that he wished that this planet might get into war with another planet, as that was the only effective way he saw of developing a world-wide community of interest in this globe's population.

I am not saying this to intimate that all impulses are equally good or that no effective control of any of them is possible. My purpose is, in lesser part, to suggest the futility of trying to secure progress by immediate or direct appeal to even the best feelings in our makeup. In the main, there is an adequate fund of such feelings. What is lacking is adequate social stimulation for their exercise as compared with the social occasions which evoke less desirable emotions. In greater part, my purpose is to indicate that since the variable factor, the factor which may be altered indefinitely, is the social conditions which call out and direct the impulses and sentiments, the positive means of progress lie in the application of intelligence to the construction of proper social devices. Theoretically, it is possible to have social arrangements which will favor the friendly tendencies of human nature at the expense of the bellicose and predatory ones, and which will direct the latter into channels where they will do the least harm or even become means of good. Practically this is a matter of the persistent use of reflection in the study of social conditions and the devising of social contrivances. . . .

We are living still under the dominion of a laissez-faire philosophy. I do *not* mean by this an individualistic as against a socialistic philosophy. I mean by it a philosophy which trusts the direction of human affairs to nature, or Providence, or evolution, or manifest destiny—that is to say, to accident—rather than to a contriving and constructive intelligence. To put our faith in the collective state instead of in individual activity is quite as laissez-faire a proceeding as to put it in the results of voluntary private enterprise. The only genuine opposite to a go-as-you-please let-alone philosophy is a philosophy which studies specific social needs and evils with a view to constructing the special social machinery for which they call.

So far I have avoided any contrast of the so-called progressive attitude with the so-called conservative attitude. I cannot maintain that reserve any longer. While in general, the opposite of the progressive attitude is not so much conservatism as it is disbelief in the possibility of constructive social engineering, the conservative mind is a large factor in propagating this disbelief. The hard and fast conservative is the man who cannot conceive that existing constitutions, institutions and social arrangements are mechanisms for achieving social results. To him, *they* are the results; they are final. If he could once cure himself of this illusion, he would be willing to admit that they grew up at haphazard and cross purposes, and mainly at periods quite unlike the present. Admitting this, he would be ready to conceive the possibility that they are as poor mechanisms for accomplishing

needed social results as were the physical tools which preceded the mastery of nature by mind. He would then be free: Not freed just to get emotionally excited about something called progress in general, but to consider what improved social mechanisms or contrivances are demanded at the present day.

## 2

John Dewey, by calling attention to the social imbalance caused by the impersonal drive of the machine, drove home the fact that modern men were more helpless as individuals than at any time since the era of arrogant monarchy. Clearly a new concept of progress was called for, one built on the vision of a general welfare state dedicated to a faith in democracy and the dignity of the individual personality. This could be achieved only by awakening the public to its social responsibilities, while demonstrating at the same time the evils of irresponsible power and self-seeking individualism. The methods employed by Progressives in this educational campaign were recalled by Frances Perkins, a young social worker in the 1900's, much later Secretary of Labor:[2]

Out of our first century of national life we evolved the ethical principle that it was not right or just that an honest and industrious man should live and die in misery. He was entitled to some degree of sympathy and security. Our conscience declared against the honest workman's becoming a pauper, but our eyes told us that he very often did.

The beginning of our second century of national sympathy and life found us with concern toward the problems of those who worked for wages. We had not much actual information regarding industrial conditions—nothing so extensive as the statistics which are available now—but we did have a point of view. Charles Booth's study of the causes of pauperism in London made during the previous decade came with a startling impact to the gen-

[2] Frances Perkins, *People at Work*, John Day Company, New York, 1934, pp. 38-44.

eration that was maturing in the nineteen hundreds. It was such a piling up of case records that no one could be at ease after the reading.

Time after time the cause was, directly or indirectly, the ills that were gathered around machine production. There were men suffering from lead poisoning, their wives working in factories and their children cared for in asylums; there were ballast heavers broken down at the age of thirty-two, bottle workers who burst blood-vessels carrying heavy loads—a whole series of horrors one after another, through which the wageworker sank into dependence. . . .

Early in this century we in America became conscious of two things which linked us to the London which Charles Booth had showed—two things which had not been problems for our grandfathers. One of these was a vast population—in our case largely foreign born—whose standards of living were not the old standards. The other was the existence of slums in which the people who worked herded together in order to be near their work under living conditions that had nothing to do with the American standard. "The words 'East Side' called up a vague and alarming picture of something strange and alien," wrote Lillian Wald of the time when she established the Nurses' Settlement in Henry Street, "a vast crowded area, a foreign city within our own, for whose conditions we had no concern. Aside from its exploiters, political and economic, few people had any definite knowledge of it, and its literary discovery had just begun."

This "literary discovery" of the conditions under which the wageworkers were living in our own cities, was an effective follow-up on Charles Booth's book on London. Magazine readers were lured on by the humor of Myra Kelley and Josephine Daskam Bacon to read about what living in the slums was like. There could be no more gripping piece of preaching than O. Henry's "Unfinished Story.". . .

Over on the West Side of Chicago, Jane Addams had established Hull House, and was beginning to build up for those whose needs and temptations and aspirations and beauty and strength she understood, walls of protection, and to open pathways to sound solutions of their problems. It was she who taught us to take all elements of the community into conference for the solution of any human problem— the grasping landlord, the corner saloonkeeper, the policeman on the beat, the president of the university, the head of the railroad, the labor leader—all co-operating through that latent desire for association which is characteristic of the American genius. She has become a symbol of that period in our national life when we passed from a highly individualistic to a brotherly service conception of human relations in a democracy.

It was in 1906 that Upton Sinclair through "The Jungle" made the literary discovery of the Chicago stockyards and the packing houses. He wrote about the labor conditions, as Myra Kelley had written about the living conditions of the New York East Side, and as Alice Hegan Rice had written about the Cabbage Patch in St. Louis, but he made such a direct and personal appeal to every one who ate meat, that there was a sudden popular revulsion, and instead of an effective change in the laws regulating labor in the packing houses, Senator Beveridge sponsored laws directed against adulterated and impure food, drugs and meat, which were enacted amid a great clamor of popular approval.

We were deeply stirred by all these things. The feeling was growing up that all was not right with a civilization that produced such contrasts, and that some obligation rested somewhere to make the blessings of modern science available for easing the lives of the under dogs of the world. But we had not yet any great body of facts on which to form public opinion as a basis for action. If there was exhausting, unpleasant and dangerous work to be done; if a large part of our people felt their world always quivering under them with uncertainty—we knew this economic misery was not just, that it was not right, but it seemed eternally necessary. We did, however, put it fairly and squarely to ourselves as a question, and we set out to find the answer in terms of such things as wages, hours, safety and security. We asked ourselves what it meant when a girl on the Eighth Street crosstown car lost her transfer and said when the conductor asked for her fare:

"Why, I can't pay another nickel. This is Saturday and I haven't got another cent."

An analysis of the budgets of girls earning six dollars a week showed that only ten cents was left after the bare necessities were paid for.

The average annual earnings of wageworkers in the United States as computed by the National Bureau of Economic Research for the year 1911 was $540. This estimate takes account of unemployment, and represents the net income of the average wage-earner.

In terms of specific industries, the figures run as follows:

| | |
|---|---|
| Manufacturing | $519 |
| Mines, quarries and oil wells | 565 |
| Construction | 644 |
| Transportation | 646 |
| Mercantile | 585 |

In 1909 Professor Robert Coit Chapin who had made a study of the standard of workingmen's families in New York City wrote:

"Families having between $900 and $1000 a year are able in general to get food enough to keep body and soul together and clothing and shelter enough to meet the most urgent demands of decency."

Slowly we gathered facts like these, and began to ask ourselves what was the basic cause of the present unlovely pattern of American life. It was becoming increasingly clear that the rôle of the charitable who established soup kitchens and crèches was the rôle of the well-meaning spectator. Where did we have to begin on the problem in order to solve it?

### 3

Philosophers and social workers did not labor alone in the vineyard of reform. Churchmen, too, lifted their voices in behalf of social justice. One by one, in the opening years of the century, the liberal churches accepted a new creed, eloquently outspoken in its defense of the dignity and worth of the individual. No more significant deepening of the democratic faith had ever appeared in religious thought than the concept of a "social gospel." A statement adopted by the General Conference of the Methodist Episcopal Church in May, 1908, summarized the aspirations of forward-looking religious leaders:[3]

The Methodist Episcopal Church stands:

For equal rights and complete justice for all men in all stations of life.

For the principle of conciliation and arbitration in industrial dissensions.

For the protection of the worker from dangerous machinery, occupational disease, injuries and mortality.

For the abolition of child labor.

For such regulation of the conditions of labor for women as shall safeguard the physical and moral health of the community.

For the suppression of the "sweating system."

For the gradual and reasonable reduction of the hours of labor to the lowest practical point, with work for all; and for that degree of leisure for all which is the condition of the highest human life.

For a release from employment one day in seven.

[3] H. F. Ward (ed.), *A Year Book of the Church and Social Service in the United States* (New York, 1914), pp. 148-149.

For a living wage in every industry.

For the highest wage that each industry can afford, and for the most equitable division of the products in industry that can ultimately be devised.

For the recognition of the Golden Rule, and the mind of Christ as the supreme law of society and the sure remedy for all social ills.

## THE LITERATURE OF PROTEST

### 4

Before advocates of a welfare state could gain political backing, they had to translate their arguments into a language understandable to the common man. This task was performed by a legion of writers who set out in the early 1900's to convince the United States that something was wrong with its economic system. Derisively labeled "muckrakers" by Theodore Roosevelt, they directed their barbs against monopolistic trusts, government corruption, industrial exploitation of labor, and all the other ills that had multiplied in the machine age. Speaking in a language that all could understand, and basing their arguments on irrefutable facts rather than high-flown theories, the muckrakers did more to arouse zeal for reform than any other group. Best known among them was Upton Sinclair, whose novel, *The Jungle* (1906), helped secure passage of the first pure food and drug law by its gruesome picture of conditions in the meat-packing industry:[4]

This was the first time in his life that he had ever really worked, it seemed to Jurgis; it was the first time that he had ever had anything to do which took all he had in him. Jurgis had stood with the rest up in the gallery and watched the men on the killing-beds, marvelling at their speed and power as if they had been wonderful machines; it somehow never occurred to one to think of the flesh-and-blood side of it—that is, not until he actually got down into the pit and took off

---

[4] Upton Sinclair, *The Jungle* (New York, 1906), pp. 66-74. Reprinted by permission of Upton Sinclair.

his coat. Then he saw things in a different light, he got at the inside of them. The pace they set here, it was one that called for every faculty of a man—from the instant the first steer fell till the sounding of the noon whistle, and again from half-past twelve till heaven only knew what hour in the late afternoon or evening, there was never one instant's rest for a man, for his hand or his eye or his brain. Jurgis saw how they managed it; there were portions of the work which determined the pace of the rest, and for these they had picked men whom they paid high wages, and whom they changed frequently. You might easily pick out these pace-makers, for they worked under the eye of the bosses, and they worked like men possessed. This was called "speeding up the gang," and if any man could not keep up with the pace, there were hundreds outside begging to try.

Yet Jurgis did not mind it; he rather enjoyed it. It saved him the necessity of flinging his arms about and fidgeting as he did in most work. He would laugh to himself as he ran down the line, darting a glance now and then at the man ahead of him. It was not the pleasantest work one could think of, but it was necessary work; and what more had a man the right to ask than a chance to do something useful, and to get good pay for doing it?

So Jurgis thought, and so he spoke, in his bold, free way; very much to his surprise, he found that it had a tendency to get him into trouble. For most of the men here took a fearfully different view of the thing. He was quite dismayed when he first began to find it out—that most of the men *hated* their work. It seemed strange, it was even terrible, when you came to find out the universality of the sentiment; but it was certainly the fact— they hated their work. They hated the bosses and they hated the owners; they hated the whole place, the whole neighborhood—even the whole city, with an all-inclusive hatred, bitter and fierce. Women and little children would fall to cursing about it; it was rotten, rotten as hell—everything was rotten. When Jurgis would ask them what they meant, they would begin to get suspicious, and content themselves with saying, "Never mind, you stay here and see for yourself."

One of the first problems that Jurgis ran upon was that of the unions. He had had no experience with unions, and he had to have it explained to him that the men were banded together for the purpose of fighting for their rights. Jurgis asked them what they meant by their rights, a question in which he was quite sincere, for he had not any idea of any rights that he had, except the right to hunt for a job, and do as he was told when he got it. Generally, however, this harmless question would only make his fellow-workingmen lose their tempers and call him a fool. There was a delegate of the butcher-helpers' union who came to see Jurgis to enroll him; and when Jurgis found that this meant that he would have to part with some of his money, he froze up directly, and the delegate, who was an Irishman and only knew a few words of Lithuanian, lost his temper and began to threaten him. In the end Jurgis got into a fine rage, and made it sufficiently plain that it would take more than one Irishman to scare him into a union. Little by little he gathered that the main thing the men wanted was to put a stop to the habit of "speeding-up"; they were trying their best to force a lessening of the pace, for there were some, they said, who could not keep up with it, whom it was killing. But Jurgis had no sympathy with such ideas as this—he could do the work himself, and so could the rest of them, he declared, if they were good for anything. If they couldn't do it, let them go somewhere else. Jurgis had not studied the books, and he would not have known how to pronounce *"laissez-faire";* but he had been round the world enough to know

that a man has to shift for himself in it, and that if he gets the worst of it, there is nobody to listen to him holler.

Yet there have been known to be philosophers and plain men who swore by Malthus in the books, and would, nevertheless, subscribe to a relief fund in time of a famine. It was the same with Jurgis, who consigned the unfit to destruction, while going about all day sick at heart because of his poor old father, who was wandering somewhere in the yards begging for a chance to earn his bread. Old Antanas had been a worker ever since he was a child; he had run away from home when he was twelve, because his father beat him for trying to learn to read. And he was a faithful man, too; he was a man you might leave alone for a month, if only you had made him understand what you wanted him to do in the meantime. And now here he was, worn out in soul and body, and with no more place in the world than a sick dog. He had his home, as it happened, and some one who would care for him if he never got a job; but his son could not help thinking, suppose this had not been the case. Antanas Rudkus had been into every building in Packingtown by this time, and into nearly every room; he had stood mornings among the crowd of applicants till the very policemen had come to know his face and to tell him to go home and give it up. He had been likewise to all the stores and saloons for a mile about, begging for some little thing to do; and everywhere they had ordered him out, sometimes with curses, and not once even stopping to ask him a question.

So, after all, there was a crack in the fine structure of Jurgis' faith in things as they are. The crack was wide while Dede Antanas was hunting a job—and it was yet wider when he finally got it. For one evening the old man came home in a great state of excitement, with the tale that he had been approached by a man in one of the corridors of the pickle-rooms of Durham's, and asked what he would pay to get a job. He had not known what to make of this at first; but the man had gone on with matter-of-fact frankness to say that he could get him a job, provided that he were willing to pay one-third of his wages for it. Was he a boss? Antanas had asked; to which the man had replied that that was nobody's business, but that he could do what he said.

Jurgis had made some friends by this time, and he sought one of them and asked what this meant. The friend, who was named Tamoszius Kuszleika, was a sharp little man who folded hides on the killing-beds, and he listened to what Jurgis had to say without seeming at all surprised. They were common enough, he said, such cases of petty graft. It was simply some boss who proposed to add a little to his income. After Jurgis had been there awhile he would know that the plants were simply honeycombed with rottenness of that sort—the bosses grafted off the men, and they grafted off each other; and some day the superintendent would find out about the boss, and then he would graft off the boss. Warming to the subject, Tamoszius went on to explain the situation. Here was Durham's, for instance, owned by a man who was trying to make as much money out of it as he could, and did not care in the least how he did it; and underneath him, ranged in ranks and grades like an army, were managers and superintendents and foremen, each one driving the man next below him and trying to squeeze out of him as much work as possible. And all the men of the same rank were pitted against each other; the accounts of each were kept separately, and every man lived in terror of losing his job, if another made a better record than he. So from top to bottom the place was simply a seething cauldron of jealousies and hatreds; there was no loyalty or decency anywhere about it, there was no place in it where a man counted for anything against a dollar. And worse than

there being no decency, there was not even any honesty. The reason for that? Who could say? It must have been old Durham in the beginning; it was a heritage which the self-made merchant had left to his son, along with his millions.

Jurgis would find out these things for himself, if he stayed there long enough; it was the men who had to do all the dirty jobs, and so there was no deceiving them; and they caught the spirit of the place, and did like all the rest. Jurgis had come there, and thought he was going to make himself useful, and rise and become a skilled man; but he would soon find out his error—for nobody rose in Packingtown by doing good work. You could lay that down for a rule—if you met a man who was rising in Packingtown, you met a knave. That man who had been sent to Jurgis's father by the boss, *he* would rise; the man who told tales and spied upon his fellows would rise; but the man who minded his own business and did his work—why, they would "speed him up" till they had worn him out, and then they would throw him into the gutter.

Jurgis went home with his head buzzing. Yet he could not bring himself to believe such things—so, it could not be so. Tamoszius was simply another of the grumblers. He was a man who spent all his time fiddling; and he would go to parties at night and not get home till sunrise, and so of course he did not feel like work. Then, too, he was a puny little chap, and so he had been left behind in the race, and that was why he was sore. And yet so many strange things kept coming to Jurgis's notice every day!

He tried to persuade his father to have nothing to do with the offer. But old Antanas had begged until he was worn out, and all his courage was gone; he wanted a job, any sort of a job. So the next day he went and found the man who had spoken to him, and promised to bring him a third of all he earned; and that same day he was put to work in Durham's cellars. It was a "pickle-room," where there was never a dry spot to stand upon, and so he had to take nearly the whole of his first week's earnings to buy him a pair of heavy-soled boots. He was a "squeedgie" man; his job was to go about all day with a long-handled mop, swabbing up the floor. Except that it was damp and dark, it was not an unpleasant job, in summer.

Now Antanas Rudkus was the meekest man that God ever put on earth; and so Jurgis found it a striking confirmation of what the men all said, that his father had been at work only two days before he came home as bitter as any of them, and cursing Durham's with all the power of his soul. For they had set him to cleaning out the traps; and the family sat round and listened in wonder while he told them what that meant. It seemed that he was working in the room where the men prepared the beef for canning, and the beef had lain in vats full of chemicals, and men with great forks speared it out and dumped it into trucks, to be taken to the cooking rooms. When they had speared out all they could reach, they emptied the vat on the floor, and then with shovels scraped up the balance and dumped it into the truck. This floor was filthy, yet they set Antanas with his mop slopping the "pickle" into a hole that connected with a sink, where it was caught and used over again forever; and if that were not enough, there was a trap in the pipe, where all the scraps of meat and odds and ends of refuse were caught, and every few days it was the old man's task to clean these out, and shovel their contents into one of the trucks with the rest of the meat.

This was the experience of Antanas; and then there came also Jonas and Marija with tales to tell. Marija was working for one of the independent packers, and was quite beside herself and outrageous with triumph over the sums of money she was making as a painter of cans. But one day she walked home with a pale-faced little woman who worked opposite to her,

Jadvyga Marcinkus by name, and Jadvyga told her how she, Marija had chanced to get her job. She had taken the place of an Irish woman who had been working in the factory ever since any one could remember, for over fifteen years, so she declared. Mary Dennis was her name, and a long time ago she had been seduced, and had a little boy; he was a cripple, and an epileptic, but still he was all that she had in the world to love, and they had lived in a little room alone somewhere back of Halsted Street, where the Irish were. Mary had had consumption, and all day long you might hear her coughing as she worked; of late she had been going all to pieces, and when Marija came, the "forelady" had suddenly decided to turn her off. The forelady had to come up to a certain standard herself, and could not stop for sick people, Jadvyga explained. The fact that Mary had been there so long had not made any difference to her—it was doubtful if she even knew that, for both the forelady and the superintendent were new people, having only been there two or three years themselves. Jadvyga did not know what had become of the poor creature; she would have gone to see her, but had been sick herself. She had pains in her back all the time, Jadvyga explained, and feared that she had womb trouble. It was not fit work for a woman, handling fourteen-pound cans all day.

It was a striking circumstance that Jonas, too, had gotten his job by the misfortune of some other person. Jonas pushed a truck loaded with hams from the smoke-rooms on to an elevator, and thence to the packing-rooms. The trucks were all of iron, and heavy, and they put about three-score hams on each of them, a load of more than a quarter of a ton. On the uneven floor it was a task for a man to start one of these trucks, unless he was a giant; and when it was once started he naturally tried his best to keep it going. There was always the boss prowling about, and if there was a second's delay he would fall to cursing; Lithuanians and Slovaks and such, who could not understand what was said to them, the bosses were wont to kick about the place like so many dogs. Therefore these trucks went for the most part on the run; and the predecessor of Jonas had been jammed against the wall by one and crushed in a horrible and nameless manner.

All of these were sinister incidents; but they were trifles compared to what Jurgis saw with his own eyes before long. One curious thing he had noticed, the very first day, in his profession of shoveller of guts; which was the sharp trick of the floor-bosses whenever there chanced to come a "slunk" calf. Any man who knows anything about butchering knows that the flesh of a cow that is about to calve, or has just calved, is not fit for food. A good many of these came every day to the packing-houses—and, of course, if they had chosen, it would have been an easy matter for the packers to keep them till they were fit food. But for the saving of time and fodder, it was the law that cows of that sort came along with the others, and whoever noticed it would tell the boss, and the boss would start up a conversation with the government inspector, and the two would stroll away. So in a trice the carcass of the cow would be cleaned out, and the entrails would have vanished. It was Jurgis's task to slide them into the trap, calves and all, and on the floor below they took out these "slunk" calves, and butchered them for meat, and used even the skins of them.

One day a man slipped and hurt his leg; and that afternoon, when the last of the cattle had been disposed of, and the men were leaving, Jurgis was ordered to remain and do some special work which this injured man had usually done. It was late, almost dark, and the government inspectors had all gone, and there were only a dozen or two of men on the floor. That day they had killed about four thousand cattle, and these cattle had come in freight trains from far states, and some of them had got hurt. There were some with broken legs, and some with gored sides; there were some that had died, from what cause no one could say; and they were all to be disposed of, here in darkness and silence. "Downers," the men called them; and the packing-house had a special elevator upon which they were raised to the killing-beds, where the gang proceeded to handle them, with an air of businesslike nonchalance which said plainer than any words that it was a matter of everyday routine. It took a couple of hours to get them out of the way, and in the end Jurgis saw them go into the chilling-rooms with the rest of the meat, being carefully scattered here and there so that they could not be identified. When he came home that night he was in a very sombre mood, having begun to see at last how those might be right who had laughed at him for his faith in America.

## 5

While Upton Sinclair almost persuaded half the population never to eat meat again, other muckrakers championed the cause of labor. Their concern was the alarmingly large number of strikes that marked the opening years of the Progressive Era; industrial disputes, they pointed out, that cost the workers, management, and the public heavily. Seeking a cause for unrest, they found the answer in the attitude of employers and the legislative stooges who did their bidding in state and national legislatures. Their conclusion was that equitable laws, properly enforced, would assure labor peace. One who argued this point effectively was Ray Stannard Baker, a brilliant young journalist whose *The Reign of Lawlessness* first appeared in *McClure's Magazine* in 1904 and was later published in book form:[5]

One of the great underlying reasons for the existing struggle, as I have said, was the demand for an eight-hour day in the

[5] Ray Stannard Baker, "The Reign of Lawlessness," *McClure's Magazine*, XXIII (May, 1904), 52-54. Reprinted by permission of Rachel Baker Napier.

smelters and mills of Colorado. The eight-hour agitation has been long-continued and bitter. Several years ago the unions began a systematic effort to secure legislation limiting the hours of work in reduction mills, in underground mine workings, and in smelters—all occupations more or less dangerous and injurious to health—where the employees now work from nine to twelve hours a day. And twelve hours a day in the often poisonous atmosphere of a smelter, any one will admit, is not humanizing toil. In 1899 the Legislature passed an eight-hour law restricting employment in these occupations. When an attempt to enforce it was made, the Smelter Trust, the Coal Operators, and other interests fought it before the State Supreme Court, which finally declared the law unconstitutional, although the United States Supreme Court had already approved a similar law passed in Utah. Such legislation, indeed, now exists in Kansas, Utah, Montana, Nevada, Arizona, British Columbia, and elsewhere. . . .

The unions then began the work of getting an amendment to the Constitution. In November, 1902, the question was submitted to the people of Colorado, and an amendment carried by the tremendous majority of 46,714 votes. Both Democratic and Republican parties solemnly pledged themselves in their platforms to execute the will of the people and make laws to enforce this amendment in the Legislature of 1902-3.

Well, the Legislature met, and at once a powerful lobby appeared, such prominent citizens of Colorado as J. B. Grant, representing the American Smelting and Refining Company (the Smelter Trust), Crawford Hill of the Boston Smelting Company, Caldwell Yeaman of the Victor Coal and Coke Company, and J. C. Osgood of the Colorado Fuel and Iron Company, one of the greatest corporations in the West—these were the same interests that had fought the former eight-hour law. They now appeared before the Legis-

lature, they and others, confusing the issue with multitudinous suggestions, disagreeing, "jockeying"—but all the time really endeavoring to prevent the passage of the laws necessary to make the amendment effective. It was nothing to them that the people of Colorado had declared such a law to be their will by an immense majority; it interfered with their business interests! And they had a lawless Legislature to deal with. At the very beginning of the session the House, which was Republican, unseated a number of the Democratic minority, in order to get a majority in the joint conference which was to elect a United States Senator. Then the Senate, largely Democratic, retaliated by expelling some of its Republican members. Both Senate and House sat for days guarded by armed men. General Sherman Bell, afterwards in command at Cripple Creek, protected the Republican House with members of the state troops! . . .

When the eight-hour bill came up, neither party wanted to pass it; each sought to throw the odium for its rejection upon the other. And all the while the lobby experts were working silently underneath, as such lobbies know how to work. By the wording of the amendment it was made mandatory on the Legislature to pass the eight-hour law—"The General Assembly *shall* provide by law"—and yet they *adjourned without passing it*.

Rarely, indeed, has there been in this country a more brazen, conscienceless defeat of the will of the people, plainly expressed, not only at the ballot, but by the pledges of both parties. And the great corporations of Colorado continued smugly with their nine, ten, and twelve hour days —earning a little more profit.

J. B. Grant, of the Smelter Trust, in a published statement, asserted that the additional cost involved in granting an eight-hour day, the establishment of three shifts instead of two, would render it impossible for his company to conduct a profitable business in Colorado.

Let us look at the Smelter Trust. Born in the period of inflated corporate enterprises, it was capitalized at $100,000,000, about $50,000,000 of which was water. Here, then, we have a condition not dissimilar to the cause underlying Parksism in New York—the managers of the Smelter Trust trying to squeeze out dividends on a capitalization half of which had no existence in values. Indeed, no dividends have yet been paid on the $50,000,-000 of common stock. Is it surprising that they should squeeze their working-men; that they should fight an eight-hour day, bring pressure to bear on a pledged Legislature, and defeat the will of the people? Compare this lawlessness which, beginning with watered stock, must undermine the honor of a state in order to earn dividends, with the lawlessness that knocks a "scab" on the head. Which is worse? Who is the greater anarchist, the millionaire magnate or the Italian miner who goes out in the night and shoots a fellow workman in the back? . . .

The effect of this defeat upon the unions may well be imagined. They had worked long and hard to secure this legislation, they had voted for pledged legislators only to see the plainly expressed will of the people deliberately defeated! Is it a wonder that they were discouraged, even desperate? Here they were compelled to strike to enforce what should have been a state law! It is just such doings as these that drive men to Socialism. We preach to the agitators: "Your remedy is the ballot: vote and get your rights."

Here voting did no good. In nearly all the strike speeches I heard in Colorado, this defeat of the will of the people was the strongest argument that could be used. I heard President Moyer say in a speech at Pueblo:

"What is the use of your ballots anyway? You might as well tear them up and throw them in the gutter."

The conclusion drawn by the leaders is that union men must vote the Socialist ticket: and the logic is not unconvincing.

No doubt the Smelter Trust and the Coal Operators called the defeat of the eight-hour law in the Legislature a great victory, as the union spoke of the former strikes in Cripple Creek and Telluride as victories. But it was not a victory. It was a defeat. The present scourge in Colorado, which has not spared these great money interests, found one of its chief sources there in the State-house in the definite place where the lobby and the Legislature met, where the legislator considered his political and private interests above the sacred interests of his state. . . .

These dark deeds of the lobby are no more definitely provable and punishable than the dynamitings and assassinations in the strike districts, and yet no one in Colorado has any more doubt that the corporations and political corruption were behind the defeat of the eight-hour law than that the unions and their political sheriffs and other officers are responsible for the violence in the gold camps. Each sort of lawlessness, darkly planned, secretly executed, comes oozing to the surface in loss of dividends, in destruction of property, in hunger and want, in assassination. And when mines and mills are tied up, business suffering, banks failing, industry paralyzed, we hear a cry of horror going up, not unhumorously, that Capital is being frightened away from Colorado! The great god Business has been disturbed! We cannot defend for a moment the lawless methods of unionism—anarchy by bludgeon; but neither can we excuse that other sort of lawlessness—anarchy by finesse: that crawling, underhanded lawlessness that corrupts legislators and breaks the greater laws. . . .

I asked several officials of the coal-mining corporations why these laws were not obeyed, why the unions must strike to enforce state laws, and the answer was to this effect:

"Nobody observes those laws; they're unconstitutional anyway.". . .

The excuse of these corporations for disregarding the law is only a little different from that of the union in excusing the slugging of "scabs." Why are the laws not enforced in both cases? Because the State must be prosecutor, and both sides *really hold the State in contempt.* The corporations have the best and shrewdest lawyers that money can hire to fight the enforcement of such laws; they find legal fees cheaper than obedience. The unions on their side threaten the State's attorney, or the sheriff, or the coroner, with a withdrawal of votes. So both sides escape.

Here is the bed-rock fact as to the situation in Colorado: if the laws on the statute books, including the eight-hour law, which should have been enacted, had been obeyed, there would have been no disturbance last year.

## 6

The muckrakers' attack on trusts was rivaled by their assault on governmental corruption. The principal cause for popular unrest, they believed, was the alliance between business and government; legislatures were so dominated by lobbyists that the nation was ruled by the "interests" rather than by the people. These must be weeded out of every legislative branch, from Congress to city council, to restore popular rule. The spotlight of indignation was turned on the Senate particularly, for business interests were commonly believed to exert complete control there. David Graham Phillips, in his well-read "The Treason of the Senate," laid bare the methods employed by industrialists to frustrate democracy:[6]

These articles have been attacked but their facts—the facts of the treason of the Senate, taken from the records—have not been attacked. Abuse is not refutation; it is confession. New to this democratic republic, and more than suspicious, is the doctrine that the people must not be shown

the public records of their public servants; that the people may not learn how the "merged" senators, with Joe Cannon's "merged" House concurring, license and protect the "high financiers" in piling up vast fortunes for the few and in multiplying for the many the difficulties of getting a livelihood and a competence; that the people must not be told how the Senate has never moved to use its ample Constitutional powers to protect the people until public anger compelled; how it has then merely passed some deliberately ineffective measure, like the Cullom interstate commerce act of 1887; and how, by killing reciprocity treaties and by injecting robber schedules into tariff laws, it has penned the people in from even such slight relief as might have come from abroad. . . .

We have noted the "merger" of the two national political machines, and have watched it in operation, its Republicans and its Democrats playing into one another's hands. We have examined the records of its leaders. We have seen that they, the avowed chief men of the two political parties, the chosen arrangers of campaigns and legislative programmes, are of, by and for "the interests." We have seen, beneath the dust of senatorial debates, measures in the popular interest maimed or assassinated, so-called Democrats cooperating with so-called Republicans, each crowd of the sham battlers wearing an angry front toward the other—to fool and confuse the people. . . .

Philander C. Knox, a graduate of Mount Union College, Ohio, in the class of 1872, became a lawyer and, in 1875, United States district attorney at Pittsburg. "The interests" are always alert to annex the bright young men who enter public service and who show capacity for mischief—and for usefulness. Knox graduated from the office of people's prosecutor into the service of those whom the people most wish and most need to have prosecuted; he has been in that service without a break ever since. His most profitable client for

[6] David Graham Phillips, "The Treason of the Senate," *Cosmopolitan Magazine,* XLI (July and August, 1906), 368, 374-376.

many years was the scandalously corrupt Carnegie Steel Company, as to whose vast rebating crimes President Cassatt of the Pennsylvania has lately "peached." He had the Pittsburg, Bessemer & Lake Erie, the Pittsburg, Fort Wayne & Chicago, the Pittsburg and Birmingham Traction, and other powerful corporate clients, several of them always in need of the skill of an adroit lawyer, because, like the Carnegie Company, they were engaged in wholesale law breaking and law-dodging. . . .

The Carnegie Company was manufacturing armor-plate at a cost of less than two hundred dollars a ton, was selling it to the Russian government for two hundred and forty-nine dollars a ton, and to the United States government at from five hundred and twenty dollars to seven hundred dollars a ton. These are all official figures. The difference in price was not in value but in "patriotism"—our Carnegies with their "blow-hole" plate for the navy and our Armours with their "embalmed beef" for the army are nothing if not "patriots"; to criticise them or their agents in public life is "anarchy," is "pessimistic," is "muck-raking." A Congressional committee, after examining thoroughly into the Carnegie Company's methods of manufacturing for American warships, reported (House Report No. 1468, 53d Congress, 2d session):

"The company was hired to make the best possible armor-plate and was paid an enormous price. Resting under these obligations the company or its servants have perpetrated manifold frauds, the natural tendency of which was to palm off upon the government an *inferior armor whose inferiority might perchance appear only in the shock of battle and with incalculable damage to the country.*

"The efforts of the company, and of its superintendents Cline, Corey, and Schwab, have been to satisfy your committee that the armor is up to the requirements of the contract, notwithstanding the false reports to inspectors, doctoring of specimens, plug-

ging of plates, fraudulent re-treating of test-plates and 'jockeying' of the testing-machine. The *unblushing character of the frauds to which these men have been parties and the disregard for truth and honesty* which they have shown in testifying before your committee render them unworthy of credence."

The committee made charts showing the exact location of many bad plates upon thirteen American warships and specifying the defects so far as they could be ascertained. Did Knox throw up his retainer of fifty thousand dollars a year from this company, thus convicted? No! Did he refuse to defend it? No! Did he demand the dismissal of the men who had been detected and branded as untruthful and dishonest, parties to crimes against their and his country? Not he; not Patriot Knox. On the contrary, he continued as chief lawyer for them, continued intimately to associate with them, continued to grow rich out of fees and dividends earned from and by them. And when the Carnegie Company entered the United States Steel Corporation, with first Schwab and then Corey as president, Knox was made one of the legal sponsors of that gigantic tax upon industries and fraud upon investors. And to that same crowd he owes a large part of the money which makes him a millionaire. As we shall see, he also owes it his seat in the Senate.

March 22, 1901, J. Pierpont Morgan, the big man of the steel corporation, called, in the evening, upon President McKinley, at the White House. The next morning Mr. McKinley announced that the attorney-general, the head of the national Department of Justice, the legal guardian of the people against the common enemy, "the interests," would be—Philander Knox! And Mr. Roosevelt, charmed by his engaging personality and manifest abilities, impulsively retained him. . . .

During Knox's custody of the national Department of Justice the expected happened. Nothing was done to reestablish justice, to drive off or even seriously hamper the insolent thieves of "high finance." Mr. Roosevelt ordered Knox to proceed against the notorious Northern Securities Company which Morgan, Jim Hill, Harriman, the Rothschilds, and the Rockefellers had had cooked up by their lawyer lackeys. And what did Knox do? Let the answer come from the United States Supreme Court, from the opinion delivered by Mr. Justice Holmes, on March 14, 1904:

"It is vain to insist that this is not a criminal proceeding. The words cannot be read one way in a suit which is to end in fine and imprisonment, and another in one which seeks an injunction. I am no friend of *artificial interpretations*. . . . So I say we must read the words before us as if the question were whether two small exporting grocers should go to jail."

That is, Mr. Justice Holmes, in judicial language, exposed and rebuked Knox's sly betrayal of the President and the people in bringing a *civil* action against men who, as the justice said, were guilty of crime, if guilty at all. The court held that they were guilty; but the faithful Knox had seen to it that there could be no "running amuck," no jailing of rich lawbreakers as if they were poor devils with no education and with their poverty in extenuation of their crimes.

## 7

David Graham Phillips's exposures of graft in the national government were matched by Lincoln Steffens's revelations of corruption in the cities. A well-known journalist, Steffens served as editor of the leading muckraking journal, *McClure's Magazine,* between 1902 and 1906. There he published serially his *Shame of the Cities,* which also appeared in book form in 1904:[7]

Other American cities, no matter how bad their own condition may be, all point

with scorn to Philadelphia as worse—"the worst-governed city in the country." St. Louis, Minneapolis, Pittsburgh submit with some patience to the jibes of any other community; the most friendly suggestion from Philadelphia is rejected with contempt. The Philadelphians are "supine," "asleep"; hopelessly ring-ruled, they are "complacent." "Politically benighted," Philadelphia is supposed to have no light to throw upon a state of things that is almost universal.

This is not fair. Philadelphia is, indeed, corrupt; but it is not without significance. Every city and town in the country can learn something from the typical experience of this great representative city. New York is excused for many of its ills because it is the metropolis, Chicago because of its forced development; Philadelphia is our "third largest" city and its growth has been gradual and natural. Immigration has been blamed for our municipal conditions; Philadelphia, with 47 per cent. of its population native-born of native-born parents, is the most American of our greater cities. It is "good," too, and intelligent. I don't know just how to measure the intelligence of a community, but a Pennsylvania college professor who declared to me his belief in education for the masses as a way out of political corruption, himself justified the "rake-off" of preferred contractors on public works on the ground of a "fair business profit." Another plea we have made is that we are too busy to attend to public business, and we have promised, when we come to wealth and leisure, to do better. Philadelphia has long enjoyed great and widely distributed prosperity; it is the city of homes; there is a dwelling house for every five persons —men, women, and children,—of the population; and the people give one a sense of more leisure and repose than any community I have ever dwelt in. Some Philadelphians account for their political state on the ground of their ease and comfort. There is another class of opti-

[7] Lincoln Steffens, *The Shame of the Cities* (New York, 1904), pp. 193-201. Reprinted by permission of the copyright owner, Ella Winter.

mists whose hope is in an "aristocracy" that is to come by and by; Philadelphia is surer that it has a "real aristocracy" than any other place in the world, but its aristocrats, with few exceptions, are in the ring, with it, or of no political use. Then we hear that we are a young people and that when we are older and "have traditions," like some of the old countries, we also will be honest. Philadelphia is one of the oldest of our cities and treasures for us scenes and relics of some of the noblest traditions of "our fair land." Yet I was told once, "for a joke," a party of boodlers counted out the "divvy" of their graft in unison with the ancient chime of Independence Hall.

Philadelphia is representative. This very "joke," told, as it was, with a laugh, is typical. All our municipal governments are more or less bad, and all our people are optimists. Philadelphia is simply the most corrupt and the most contented. Minneapolis has cleaned up, Pittsburgh has tried to, New York fights every other election, Chicago fights all the time. Even St. Louis has begun to stir (since the elections are over), and at its worst was only shameless. Philadelphia is proud; good people there defend corruption and boast of their machine. My college professor, with his philosophic view of "rake-offs," is one Philadelphia type. Another is the man, who, driven to bay with his local pride, says: "At least you must admit that our machine is the best you have ever seen."

Disgraceful? Other cities say so. But I say that if Philadelphia is a disgrace, it is a disgrace not to itself alone, nor to Pennsylvania, but to the United States and to American character. For this great city, so highly representative in other respects, is not behind in political experience, but ahead, with New York. Philadelphia is a city that has had its reforms. Having passed through all the typical stages of corruption, Philadelphia reached the period of miscellaneous loot with a boss for chief thief, under James McManes and

the Gas Ring 'way back in the late sixties and seventies. This is the Tweed stage of corruption from which St. Louis, for example, is just emerging. Philadelphia, in two inspiring popular revolts, attacked the Gas Ring, broke it, and in 1885 achieved that dream of American cities—a good charter. The present condition of Philadelphia, therefore, is not that which precedes, but that which follows reform, and in this distinction lies its startling general significance. What has happened since the Bullitt Law or charter went into effect in Philadelphia may happen in any American city "after reform is over."

For reform with us is usually revolt, not government, and is soon over. Our people do not seek, they avoid self-rule, and "reforms" are spasmodic efforts to punish bad rulers and get somebody that will give us good government or something that will make it. A self-acting form of government is an ancient superstition. We are an inventive people, and we think that we shall devise some day a legal machine that will turn out good government automatically. The Philadelphians have treasured this belief longer than the rest of us and have tried it more often. Throughout their history they have sought this wonderful charter and they thought they had it when they got the Bullitt Law, which concentrates in the mayor ample power, executive and political, and complete responsibility. Moreover, it calls for very little thought and action on the part of the people. All they expected to have to do when the Bullitt Law went into effect was to elect as mayor a good business man, who, with his probity and common sense, would give them that good business administration which is the ideal of many reformers.

The Bullitt Law went into effect in 1887. A committee of twelve—four men from the Union League, four from business organizations, and four from the bosses—picked out the first man to run under it on the Republican ticket, Edwin H. Fitler, an able, upright business man, and he was elected. Strange to say, his administration was satisfactory to the citizens, who speak well of it to this day, and to the politicians also; Boss McManes (the ring was broken, not the boss) took to the next national convention from Philadelphia a delegation solid for Fitler for President of the United States. It was a farce, but it pleased Mr. Fitler, so Matthew S. Quay, the State boss, let him have a complimentary vote on the first ballot. The politicians "fooled" Mr. Fitler, and they "fooled" also the next business mayor, Edwin S. Stuart, likewise a most estimable gentleman. Under these two administrations the foundation was laid for the present government of Philadelphia, the corruption to which the Philadelphians seem so reconciled, and the machine which is "at least the best you have ever seen."

The Philadelphia machine isn't the best. It isn't sound, and I doubt if it would stand in New York or Chicago. The enduring strength of the typical American political machine is that it is a natural growth—a sucker, but deep-rooted in the people. The New Yorkers vote for Tammany Hall. The Philadelphians do not vote; they are disfranchised, and their disfranchisement is one anchor of the foundation of the Philadelphia organization.

This is no figure of speech. The honest citizens of Philadelphia have no more rights at the polls than the negroes down South. Nor do they fight very hard for this basic privilege. You can arouse their Republican ire by talking about the black Republican votes lost in the Southern States by white Democratic intimidation, but if you remind the average Philadelphian that he is in the same position, he will look startled, then say, "That's so, that's literally true, only I never thought of it in just that way." And it is literally true.

The machine controls the whole process of voting, and practices fraud at every stage. The assessor's list is the voting list, and the assessor is the machine's man.

"The assessor of a division kept a disorderly house; he padded his list with fraudulent names registered from his house; two of these names were used by election officers. . . . The constable of the division kept a disreputable house; a policeman was assessed as living there. . . . The election was held in the disorderly house maintained by the assessor. . . . The man named as judge had a criminal charge for a life offense pending against him. . . . Two hundred and fifty-two votes were returned in a division that had less than one hundred legal votes within its boundaries." These extracts from a report of the Municipal League suggest the election methods. The assessor pads the list with the names of dead dogs, children, and non-existent persons. One newspaper printed the picture of a dog, another that of a little four-year-old negro boy, down on such a list. A ring orator in a speech resenting sneers at his ward as "low down" reminded his hearers that that was the ward of Independence Hall, and, naming the signers of the Declaration of Independence, he closed his highest flight of eloquence with the statement that "these men, the fathers of American liberty, voted down here once. And," he added, with a catching grin, "they vote here yet." Rudolph Blankenburg, a persistent fighter for the right and the use of the right to vote (and, by the way, an immigrant), sent out just before one election a registered letter to each voter on the rolls of a certain selected division. Sixty-three per cent. were returned marked "not at," "removed," "deceased," etc. From one four-story house where forty-four voters were addressed, eighteen letters came back undelivered; from another of forty-eight voters, came back forty-one letters; from another sixty-one out of sixty-two; from another forty-four out of forty-seven. Six houses in one division were assessed at one hundred and seventy-two voters, more than the votes cast in the previous election in any one of two hundred entire divisions.

The repeating is done boldly, for the machine controls the election officers, often choosing them from among the fraudulent names; and when no one appears to serve, assigning the heeler ready for the expected vacancy. The police are forbidden by law to stand within thirty feet of the polls, but they are at the box and they are there to see that the machine's orders are obeyed and that repeaters whom they help to furnish are permitted to vote without "intimidation" on the names they, the police, have supplied. The editor of an anti-machine paper who was looking about for himself once told me that a ward leader who knew him well asked him into a polling place. "I'll show you how it's done," he said, and he had the repeaters go round and round voting again and again on the names handed them on slips. "But," as the editor said, "that isn't the way it's done." The repeaters go from one polling place to another, voting on slips, and on their return rounds change coats, hats, etc. The business proceeds with very few hitches; there is more jesting than fighting. Violence in the past has had its effect; and is not often necessary nowadays, but if it is needed the police are there to apply it. Several citizens told me that they had seen the police help to beat citizens or election officers who were trying to do their duty, then arrest the victim. . . .

## ROOSEVELT AND GOVERNMENT REGULATION

## 8

Muckraking revelations of business corruption laid the basis for an attack on the gospel of wealth, but the swing to Progressivism was stimulated by developments in Europe. There nation after nation, faced with the problem of reconciling industrial greed with the public welfare, had enacted laws setting a standard of decency in business conduct undreamed of in the United States. Congressional committees and outside experts repeatedly studied the methods employed to regulate industry in Germany, France, England, and other na-

tions; their findings were embodied in many of the laws passed during the Progressive Period. The fact that German legislation was imitated especially was due to the advanced attitudes of that country, which were reflected in its laws governing stock transactions:[8]

The American policy in reference to the organization of corporations has become that of permitting the incorporators to arrange pretty nearly everything, except the fees and taxes they must pay to the government, as may suit their purposes. Germany, on the other hand, in the law enacted for the whole country in 1884, rigidly limits what the incorporators may do, especially as regards the relation between capitalization and *bona-fide* assets, and holds promoters, incorporators, and boards of directors strictly responsible for compliance with its provisions. This law was not hastily adopted. The country had experienced the ill effects of a lax corporation law in the early 'seventies after the Franco-Prussian war. An unusually representative and competent commission was then created to study the subject, and every aspect was carefully considered before it submitted the recommendations to the Reichstag which were embodied in the statute. Since 1884 numerous occasions for reconsidering the law have arisen. The subject was discussed preceding the enactment of the German Stock Exchange law in 1896 and the adoption of the revised commercial code in 1897. After the war the modification of this as of other laws to conform to the views of the socialist government which came into power was considered, but it, with the whole commercial code, was continued in full force in accordance with Article 178 of the Constitution adopted in 1919. The uncertainties of the period of inflation made necessary the temporary suspension of some of the provisions in regard to the compul-

[8] From *Trust and Corporation Problems* by Henry R. Seager and Charles A. Gulick, Jr., pp. 576-578. Copyright, 1929, by Harper & Brothers.

sory liquidation of a company which had become insolvent, but the only change of importance that has resulted from the substitution of a liberal republican for the earlier monarchical form of government has been the requirement that wage-earners shall have representation on the supervising boards of directors of the corporations which employ them. This would seem to indicate a conviction on the part of all classes interested in German corporations that the law is in essentials wise and that it has not unduly hampered the expansion of German business. That it has had much to do with the absence in Germany of the distrust and hostility toward large corporations with which we are familiar is beyond question. . . .

Under the German law every corporation must have two boards of directors, a supervising board (*Aufsichtsrat*) and a managing board (*Vorstand*). No one may be at the same time a member of both of these boards. Before a corporation can be admitted to registry the members of these boards must be chosen and they must examine and report under oath upon all the organization proceedings, becoming personally liable if they make statements which are untrue and which result in subsequent loss to others which cannot be recovered from those principally responsible. Such liability attaches even when the deception was not deliberate, unless the offender can prove that he exercised the diligence of a prudent business man in verifying the accuracy of the statements to which he has subscribed.

## 9

With muckrakers enflaming public opinion, and Europe serving as a model for reformers, the stage was set for the rise of Progressivism. Those who hoped for improvement were far from optimistic when the century began; President McKinley was an acknowledged friend of the trusts and an outspoken enemy of the Sherman Act. Nor did they anticipate a change when McKinley's assassination elevated Theodore Roosevelt to the presidency.

Roosevelt's violent nationalism and sympathetic attitude toward large-scale business made him hospitable to American corporations that were extending economic controls over other nations. His first annual message to Congress (December 3, 1901), although urging protection for investors, stamped him as a champion of corporations rather than consumers:[9]

The tremendous and highly complex industrial development which went on with ever-accelerated rapidity during the latter half of the nineteenth century brings us face to face, at the beginning of the twentieth, with very serious social problems. . . .

The growth of cities has gone on beyond comparison faster than the growth of the country, and the upbuilding of the great industrial centres has meant a startling increase, not merely in the aggregate of wealth, but in the number of very large individual, and especially of very large corporate, fortunes. The creation of these great corporate fortunes has not been due to the tariff nor to any other governmental action, but to natural causes in the business world, operating in other countries as they operate in our own.

The process has aroused much antagonism, a great part of which is wholly without warrant. . . . The captains of industry who have driven the railway systems across this continent, who have built up our commerce, who have developed our manufactures, have on the whole done great good to our people. Without them the material development of which we are so justly proud could never have taken place. Moreover, we should recognize the immense importance of this material development by leaving as unhampered as is compatible with the public good the strong and forceful men upon whom the success of business operations inevitably rests. The slightest study of business conditions will satisfy any one capable of forming a judg-

[9] *Congressional Record*, 57th Cong., 1st Sess., pp. 81-92.

ment that the personal equation is the most important factor in a business operation; that the business ability of the man at the head of any business concern, big or little, is usually the factor which fixes the gulf between striking success and hopeless failure.

An additional reason for caution in dealing with corporations is to be found in the international commercial conditions of today. The same business conditions which have produced the great aggregations of corporate and individual wealth have made them very potent factors in international commercial competition. Business concerns which have the largest means at their disposal and are managed by the ablest men are naturally those which take the lead in the strife for commercial supremacy among the nations of the world. America has only just begun to assume that commanding position in the international business world which we believe will more and more be hers. It is of the utmost importance that this position be not jeopardized, especially at a time when the overflowing abundance of our own natural resources and the skill, business energy, and mechanical aptitude of our people make foreign markets essential. Under such conditions it would be most unwise to cramp or to fetter the youthful strength of our nation. . . .

The mechanism of modern business is so delicate that extreme care must be taken not to interfere with it in a spirit of rashness or ignorance. Many of those who have made it their vocation to denounce the great industrial combinations which are popularly, although with technical inaccuracy, known as "trusts," appeal especially to hatred and fear. These are precisely the two emotions, particularly when combined with ignorance, which unfit men for the exercise of cool and steady judgment. In facing new industrial conditions, the whole history of the world shows that legislation will generally be both unwise and ineffective unless undertaken after calm inquiry and with sober self-restraint. . . .

All this is true; and yet it is also true that there are real and grave evils, one of the chief being overcapitalization because of its many baleful consequences; and a resolute and practical effort must be made to correct these evils.

There is a widespread conviction in the minds of the American people that the great corporations known as trusts are in certain of their features and tendencies hurtful to the general welfare. This . . . is based upon sincere conviction that combination and concentration should be, not prohibited, but supervised and within reasonable limits controlled; and in my judgment this conviction is right.

It is no limitation upon property rights or freedom of contract to require that when men receive from government the privilege of doing business under corporate form, which frees them from individual responsibility, and enables them to call into their enterprises the capital of the public, they shall do so upon absolutely truthful representations as to the value of the property in which the capital is to be invested. Corporations engaged in interstate commerce should be regulated if they are found to exercise a license working to the public injury. . . .

The first essential in determining how to deal with the great industrial combinations is knowledge of the facts—publicity. In the interest of the public, the government should have the right to inspect and examine the workings of the great corporations engaged in interstate business. Publicity is the only sure remedy which we can now invoke. What further remedies are needed in the way of governmental regulation, or taxation, can only be determined after publicity has been obtained, by process of law, and in the course of administration. . . .

The large corporations, commonly called trusts, though organized in one State, always do business in many States, often doing very little business in the State where they are incorporated. There is utter lack of uniformity in the State laws about them; and as no State has any exclusive interest in or power over their acts, it has in practice proved impossible to get adequate regulation through State action. Therefore, in the interest of the whole people, the nation should, without interfering with the power of the States in the matter itself, also assume power of supervision and regulation over all corporations doing an interstate business. This is especially true where the corporation derives a portion of its wealth from the existence of some monopolistic element or tendency in its business.

## 10

Yet the Theodore Roosevelt who entered the White House promising to carry out McKinley's policies soon changed; wits of the day remarked that he not only carried out McKinley's policies—he buried them as well. His transition from conservative to progressive was the product of many influences: pressure from reformers, the rising popular demand for change, the appalling need for reform, and the uncompromising attitude of business leaders. The President's education on the latter point began in 1902, when he tried to end a coal-mine strike that threatened to leave the nation without fuel in the winter. The unions responded to his pressure, but the managers, led by George F. Baer of the Reading Railway, aggressively asserted there was nothing to negotiate. An impudent letter of Baer's, suggestive of a curious transmutation of the divine right of kings into the divine right of property, became known to the public, contributing to the pressure on managers to meet union leaders:[10]

PHILADELPHIA & READING RAILWAY
COMPANY
*President's Office*
*Reading Terminal, Philadelphia*
17th July 1902

MY DEAR MR. CLARK:—
I have your letter of the 16th instant.

I do not know who you are. I see that you are a religious man; but you are evidently biased in favor of the right of the working man to control a business in which he has no other interest than to secure fair wages for the work he does.

I beg of you not to be discouraged. The rights and interests of the laboring man will be protected and cared for—not by the labor agitators, but by the Christian men to whom God in His infinite wisdom has given the control of the property interests of the country, and upon the successful Management of which so much depends.

Do not be discouraged. Pray earnestly that right may triumph, always remembering that the Lord God Omnipotent still reigns, and that His reign is one of law and order, and not of violence and crime.

Yours truly,
GEO. F. BAER
President

## 11

President Roosevelt's slowly growing conviction of the evils of monopoly was reinforced by Progressives with whom he associated. Of these none was more influential than Senator Robert M. La Follette of Wisconsin, who took office just as Roosevelt commenced his battle for a law that would resuscitate the Interstate Commerce Commission. A sincere liberal, La Follette threw himself so wholeheartedly into the fight for government regulation of railroad rates that he became an inspiration to fellow reformers. The President refused to back him completely in his demand for strong regulatory measures, settling, instead, on the mild Hepburn Act that was passed in 1906. The extraordinary resistance in Congress even to this innocuous measure was revealed by Senator La Follette in his *Autobiography:*[11]

Senator Dolliver was a member of the committee that had framed this bill, and when I began to attack what was called the Hepburn-Dolliver bill, naturally he felt

---

[10] Reprinted from a photostatic copy in Mark Sullivan *Our Times, The United States 1900-1925* (1927), II, 425. Reprinted by permission of Charles Scribner's Sons.

[11] *La Follette's Autobiography: A Personal Narrative of Political Experiences* by Robert M. La Follette, pp. 413-419. The Robert M. La Follette Company, Madison, Wisconsin, 1913.

compelled to defend it. He had been for six or seven years a member of the Committee on Interstate Commerce and he did not seem to understand what I was talking about when I suggested the radical defect in the bill—that it was not possible for the commission to make and enforce reasonable rates, even if this bill passed. . . . I do not believe that Dolliver or any other man in the Senate at that time had ever seriously considered the idea of determining the value of the property, the cost of maintenance and the cost of operation as a necessary basis for fixing the reasonableness of rates. The thing seemed to break upon the Senate as a startling idea, and yet most of them as business men would never have thought of fixing a price on a commodity or for a service without knowing definitely what that service cost. . . .

I pointed out to Senator Dolliver in the course of the debate that there were no means by which the commission could ascertain what was a reasonable rate; that under the law of 1887, as proposed to be amended by the pending bill, it would be possible for the commission to determine whether rates were *relatively reasonable,* but not that they were *reasonable per se;* that one rate could be compared with another, but that the commission had no means of determining whether either rate so compared was itself a reasonable rate. And then I proceeded to lay down the basis for determining reasonable rates, and we had a running debate for about an hour, when Dolliver, who had come down until he stood squarely in front of my desk, said:

"Mr. President, I am disposed to sympathize with the views of the Senator from Wisconsin; I believe that the bill ought to be amended."

And he was one of five other Senators besides myself on the Republican side who voted for the amendment to authorize the Interstate Commerce Commission to ascertain the value of the railroad property of the country. . . .

I do not think the "stand-patters" of the Senate understood what I was talking about when I discussed the Hepburn-Dolliver bill. They did not follow me closely enough to understand. But on the Democratic side of the Senate chamber I had excellent attention, and before I finished I had a goodly number on the other side. . . .

In offering each amendment I made perhaps a five or ten minute statement, and then demanded the yeas and nays. On the amendment for the valuation of railways engaged in interstate commerce I demonstrated conclusively the over-capitalization of the railroads of the country. I argued that if the same system were applied which we were then applying in Wisconsin—that is, the true value of the property ascertained together with the cost of maintaining the property and the cost of operating the property, and the rates so adjusted as to make a fair return to the railroads upon the actual investment made by the roads and not upon capitalization —that it would be working a saving in transportation charges of something more than $400,000,000 to the people of this country every twelve months. In support of that amendment I used the reports of the Interstate Commerce Commission, the decisions of the Supreme Court of the United States, and the demonstration made in Wisconsin. And yet, when the roll was called, my amendment was beaten 40 to 27, the only Republicans voting for it being Burkett, Dolliver, Elkins, Gamble, La Follette, Warner. . . .

Coming home on the street car one day, I wondered how far they would go. And I took a tab out of my pocket and outlined an amendment to the effect that any federal judge should be disqualified from hearing, trying or determining any case for the regulation of railway rates against any road in which he was a stockholder, or whose bonds he owned, or upon which he used free passes. And that amendment was lost 40 to 27. There were only three Republicans who thought that a federal judge ought not to own stock in a road and then hear, try and determine a case involving its interests!

Formerly, record votes on delicate questions were always avoided in the Senate, if possible; but I had a purpose in thus committing the Senators on these phases of railroad control. I wanted to show exactly where they stood and why.

During the summer which followed I made a speaking tour that covered nearly all the states from New York to California, and everywhere I went I used these roll-call records of the Senate. I made twenty-one speeches in which I showed the record of Dryden of New Jersey, and I have no doubt that the proof which these roll calls furnished of the true attitude of Senators served to retire not a few of them. There were twenty-four "stand-pat" members of the Senate at that time (1906) who are not there today.

## 12

President Roosevelt wrested from a reluctant Congress laws that gave the public partial protection against railroad abuses. He was less successful in his effort to conserve natural resources. Both the President's Inland Waterways Commission (1907) and the Conference of Governors (1908) issued reports urging the government to check costly floods, soil erosion, and the denudation of once-proud forest lands. Yet Roosevelt was limited to withdrawing millions of acres of the public domain from despoilers by executive orders creating national forests. Beyond this he could not go, for his messages, such as the following, calling attention to America's lag in adopting conservation policies, encountered only hostility from congressional majorities:[12]

I recommended [in a previous message] to Congress the enactment of such legislation as would provide for title to and development of the surface land as separate and distinct from the right to the underlying mineral fuels in regions where these may occur, and the disposal of these

mineral fuels under a leasing system on conditions which would inure to the benefit of the public as a whole. I again call the attention of Congress to the importance of enacting such legislation. I care little for the details; the prime need is that the system should be established, that from henceforth the nation should retain its title to its fuel resources, and its right to supervise their development in the interest of the public as a whole. Such a leasing system as that proposed represents by no means an untried policy. In the Australian countries during the last fifteen years coal has been mined under a system of government leases, and on conditions so favorable for development that their coal and coke are to-day being sold on the Pacific Coast of both the American continents. In all the great coal producing European countries, except Great Britain, coal is being mined under government leases. In Great Britain, leases are granted almost entirely by the private land owners, but there as in other countries, the surface culture and the mining operations are conducted independently of each other. In Nova Scotia, British Columbia, India, and other British colonies a government leasing system has been adopted, and is working satisfactorily. . . .

Mineral fuels, like the forests and navigable streams, should be treated as public utilities. This is generally recognized abroad. In some foreign countries, practical control of a large portion of the fuel resources was allowed years ago to pass into private hands; but the existing governments are endeavoring to regain this control in order that the diminishing fuel supply may be safeguarded for the common good, instead of being disposed of for the benefit of a few—though the mistake of the preceding generation in disposing of these fuels for a nominal return, cannot always be corrected by the present generation as the cost may be so enormous as to be prohibitory.

In our own Western States and Terri-

---

[12] *Senate Documents*, 59th Cong., 2nd Sess., Doc. No. 310, pp. 1-4.

tories, the scarcity of both the water and forests has rendered necessary their preservation as public utilities; and the preservation of the forests for the purpose of conserving both the water and the timber supply has come to be recognized as the wise and proper policy of the Federal Government.

The quantity of high grade mineral fuels in the West is relatively much smaller than that of the forests; and the proper conservation of these fuels is a matter of far-reaching importance. This government should not now repeat the mistakes of the past. Let us not do what the next generation cannot undo. We have a right to a proper use of both the forests and the fuel during our lifetime but we should not dispose of the birthright of our children. If this government sells its remaining fuel lands, they pass out of its future control. If it now leases them we retain control and a future Congress will be at liberty to decide whether it will continue or change this policy. Meanwhile the government can inaugurate a system which will encourage the separate and independent development of the surface lands for agricultural purposes and the extraction of the mineral fuels in such manner as will best meet the needs of the people and best facilitate the development of manufacturing industries. . . .

Already probably one half of the total area of the high-grade coals in the West has passed under private control. Including both the lignite and the coal areas, these private holdings probably aggregate not less than 30,000,000 acres of coal fields. With the remainder of the lands containing mineral fuels reserved at least by the government, there will be ample opportunity to determine in the near future which of the two systems—private ownership or the leasing system with general government supervision—will best protect the interests of the people and thus promote the permanent development of the West. The necessity for care in the future

management of these fuel supplies is further illustrated by the rapid rate at which use of such fuels is increasing in the United States. The amount of coal used in this country during the last ten years is practically equal to that used during the preceding fifty years of its history. During each decade of this period the coal used was practically equal to the sum of that used during all the preceding decades. This remarkable development and the certain continuity of this prodigious growth compels us to recast all estimates as to the life of our "inexhaustible resources." We can foresee the time when the eastern industries will be much more largely taxed for supplying foreign markets. Then the West will also be largely engaged in varying manufacturing enterprises and this will require the intelligent use of every ton of available fuel in that region. The grave importance of conserving the fuel supplies in the West still remaining under the control of the Government, with a view to the accomplishment of these important purposes, impels me again to bring this matter to the attention of Congress. . . .

## REFORM AND THE DOCTRINE OF VESTED RIGHTS

### 13

Timid as were President Roosevelt's actual efforts for reform, they still aroused the usual storm of protest and controversy. Everywhere conservatives raised their voices to proclaim that governmental interference was ruining business or that private property was no longer safe in America. Their defensive tactics were well planned, for the sanctity of property was part of the traditional American creed. That even the Progressives themselves were hesitant when treading on this holy ground was indicated by Arthur Twining Hadley, the president of Yale University, in a speech explaining American affairs to an audience at Berlin University in 1908:[13]

[13] Arthur Twining Hadley, "The Constitutional Position of Property in America," *The Independent,* LXIV (April 18, 1908), 834-838.

European observers who study either the specific industrial questions which have come before the American people for their solution, or the general relation between the industrial activity of the Government and that of private individuals, are surprised at a certain weakness of public action in all these matters. Our legislatures are often ready to pass drastic measures of regulation; they are rarely willing to pursue a consistent and carefully developed policy for the attainment of an industrial end. The people often declaim against the extent of the powers of private capital; they are seldom willing to put that capital under the direct management of the government itself. The man who talks loudest of the abuses of private railroad management shrinks from the alternative of putting railroads into the direct control and ownership of the State.

The fact is, that private property in the United States, in spite of all the dangers of unintelligent legislation, is constitutionally in a stronger position, as against the Government and the Government authority, than is the case in any country of Europe. However much public feeling may at times move in the direction of socialistic measures, there is no nation which by its constitution is so far removed from socialism or from a socialistic order. This is partly because the governmental means provided for the control or limitation of private property are weaker in America than elsewhere, but chiefly because the rights of private property are more formally established in the Constitution itself.

This may seem a startling proposition; but I think a very brief glance at the known facts of history will be sufficient to support and sustain it. For property in the modern sense was a comparatively recent development in the public law of European communities. In the United States, on the contrary, property in the modern sense represents the basis on which the whole social order was established and built up. . . .

The delegates to the convention of 1787 were concerned with questions of constitutional law in the narrower sense. They were not thinking of the legal position of private property. But it so happened that in making mutual limitations upon the powers of the Federal and the State government they unwittingly incorporated into the Constitution itself certain very extraordinary immunities to the property holders as a body.

It was in the first place provided that there should be no taking of private property without due process of law. The States Rights men feared that the Federal Government might, under the stress of military necessity, pursue an arbitrary policy of confiscation. The Federalists, or national party, feared that under the influence of sectional jealousy one or more of the States might pursue the same policy. This constitutional provision prevented the legislature or executive, either of the nation or of the individual States from taking property without judicial inquiry as to the necessity, and without making full compensation even in case the result of such inquiry was favorable to the government. No man foresaw the subsequent effect of this provision in preventing a majority of voters, acting in the legislature or thru the executive, from disturbing existing arrangements with regard to railroad building or factory operation until the railroad stockholders or factory owners had had the opportunity to have their case tried in the courts.

There was another equally important clause in the Constitution providing that no State should pass a law impairing the obligation of contracts. In this case also a provision which was at first intended to prevent sectional strife and to protect the people of one locality against arbitrary legislation in another became a means of strengthening vested rights as a whole against the possibility of legislative or executive interference. Nor was the direct effect of these two clauses in preventing specific acts on the part of the legislature the most important result of their existence. They were a powerful means of establishing the American courts in that position of supremacy which they enjoy under the Constitution. For whenever an act of the legislature or the executive violated, or even seemed to violate, one of these clauses, it came before the courts for review. If the Federal courts said that the act of a legislature violated one of these provisions it was blocked—rendered powerless by a dictum of the judges. . . .

The rights of individual owners against legislative interference were thus most fully protected. But how was it when property was in the hands of corporations?

Here also the power of control by the Government was weakened and the rights and immunities of the property holders correspondingly strengthened by two events, whose effect upon the modern industrial situation may be fairly characterized as fortuitous. One of these was the decision in the celebrated Dartmouth College case in 1819; the other was the passage of the Fourteenth Amendment to the Constitution of the United States in 1868.

I call their effect fortuitous, because neither the judges who decided the Dartmouth College case nor the legislators who past [sic] the Fourteenth Amendment had any idea how these things would affect the modern industrial situation. The Dartmouth College case dealt with an educational institution, not with an industrial enterprise. The Fourteenth Amendment was framed to protect the negroes from oppression by the whites, not to protect corporations from oppression by the legislature. It is doubtful whether a single one of the members of Congress who voted for it had any idea that it would touch the question of corporate regulation at all. Yet the two together have had the effect of placing the modern industrial corporation in an almost impregnable constitutional position.

In 1816 the New Hampshire Legislature attempted to take away the charter rights of Dartmouth College. Daniel Webster was employed by the college in its defense, and his reasoning so impressed the court that they committed themselves to the position that a charter was a contract; that a State, having induced people to invest money by certain privileges and immunities, could not at will modify those privileges and immunities thus granted. Whether the court would have taken so broad a position if the matter had come before it thirty or forty years later, when the abuses of ill-judged industrial charters had become more fully manifest, is not sure; but, having once taken this position and maintained it in a series of decisions, the court could not well recede from it. Inasmuch as many of the corporate charters granted by State legislation had an unlimited period to run, the theory that these instruments were contracts binding the State for all time had a very important bearing in limiting the field within which a legislature could regulate the activity of such a body, or an executive interfere with it.

Again, by the Fourteenth Amendment to the Constitution of the United States every State was forbidden to interfere with the civil rights of any person or to treat different persons in an unequal way. This amendment to the Constitution, past just after the close of the Civil War, was intended to prevent the Southern States readmitted, or on the point of being readmitted, to the Union from abridging the rights of the negro members of the commonwealth. A number of years elapsed before the effect of this amendment upon the constitutional position of railroad and industrial corporations seems to have been fully realized. But in 1882 the Southern Pacific Railway Company, having been, as it conceived, unfairly taxed by the assessors of a certain county in California, took the position that a law of the State of California taxing the property of a corporation at a different rate from that under which similar property of an individual would be taxed was in effect a violation of the Fourteenth Amendment to the Constitution, because a corporation was a person and therefore entitled to equal treatment. This view, after careful consideration, was upheld by the Federal courts. A corporation, therefore, under the law of the United States, is entitled to the same immunities as any other person; and, since the charter creating it is a contract, whose obligation cannot be impaired by the one-sided act of the legislature, its constitutional position as a property holder is much stronger than anywhere in Europe.

Under these circumstances, it is evident that large powers and privileges have been constitutionally delegated to private property in general and to corporate property in particular. I do not mean that property owners, and specifically the owners of corporate property, have more *practical* freedom from interference in the United States than they do in some other countries, notably in England. Probably they do not have as much. But their theoretical position —the sum of the conditions which affect their standing for the long future and not for the immediate present—is far stronger in the United States. The general status of the property owner under the law cannot be changed by the action of the legislature or the executive, or the people of a State voting at the polls, or all three put together. It cannot be changed without either a consensus of opinion among the judges, which should lead them to retrace their old views, or an amendment of the Constitution of the United States by the slow and cumbersome machinery provided for that purpose, or, last—and I hope most improbable—a revolution.

When it is said, as it commonly is, that the fundamental division of powers in the modern State is into legislative, executive and judicial, the student of American institutions may fairly note an exception. The fundamental division of powers in the Constitution of the United States is between voters on the one hand and property owners on the other. The forces of democracy on one side, divided between the executive and the legislature, are set over against the forces of property on the other side, with the judiciary as arbiter between them; the Constitution itself not only forbidding the legislature and executive to trench upon the rights of property, but compelling the judiciary to define and uphold those rights in a manner provided by the Constitution itself.

This theory of American politics has not often been stated. But it has been universally acted upon. One reason why it has not been more frequently stated is that it has been acted upon so universally that no American of earlier generations ever thought it necessary to state it. It has had the most fundamental and far-reaching effects upon the policy of the country. To mention but one thing among many, it has allowed the experiment of universal suffrage to be tried under conditions essentially different from those which led to its ruin in Athens or in Rome. The voter was omnipotent—within a limited area. He could make what laws he pleased, as long as those laws did not trench upon property right. He could elect what officers he pleased, as long as those officers did not try to do certain duties confided by the Constitution to the property holders. Democracy was complete as far as it went, but constitutionally it was bound to stop short of social democracy. . . .

## 14

Encouraged by the American tendency to enshrine property rights, industrialists increasingly resorted to the courts to protect their holdings against social controls. That they were successful was attested by the long line of Supreme Court decisions during the Progressive Era, nearly all of them negating or weakening congressional measures designed to protect the people from unethical business practices. As reformers watched the slaughter of their brain children, anti-Court sentiment mounted rapidly. Some brought the compe-

tence of judges into question; others of philosophical bent doubted the extent of democracy
in a system where nine men could frustrate
the will of popular majorities. Forthright
among the critics was Theodore Roosevelt,
who echoed Lincoln in contending that the
courts should be subject to the force of public opinion:[14]

On August 29, at Denver, before the
Colorado Legislature, I made an address
dwelling partly upon the necessity of good
government, and specifically upon the
need of more coherent work between the
state and the national governments, and of
action on the part of the legislative, executive, and judicial officers of the country,
both national and state, which would prevent the growth and extension of a neutral
territory or borderland of ill-defined limits
in which neither the nation nor any state
should be able to exercise effective control,
especially over big corporations, in their
relations to the public at large and to their
own employees. I spoke in part as follows:—

The courts occupy a position of importance
in our government such as they occupy in no
other government, because, instead of dealing
only with the rights of one man face to face
with his fellow-men, as is the case with other
governments, they here pass upon the fundamental governmental rights of the people as
exercised through their legislative and executive officers. Unfortunately, the courts, instead
of leading in the recognition of the new conditions, have lagged behind, and, as each case
has presented itself, have tended by a series of
negative decisions to create a sphere in which
neither nation nor state has effective control,
and where the great business interests that can
call to their aid the ability of the greatest corporation lawyers escape all control whatsoever. Let me illustrate what I mean by a
reference to two concrete cases. Remember
that I believe in states' rights wherever states'
rights mean the people's rights. On the other
hand, I believe in national rights wherever
national rights mean the people's rights; and,

above all, I believe that in every part of our
complicated social fabric there must be either
national or state control, and that it is ruinous
to permit governmental action, and especially
judicial action, which prevents the exercise of
such control.

The first case to which I shall refer is the
Knight Sugar Trust case. In that case the
Supreme Court of the United States handed
down a decision which rendered it exceedingly difficult for the people to devise any
method of controlling and regulating the
business use of great capital in interstate
commerce. It was a decision nominally against
national rights, but really against popular
rights, against the democratic principle of
government by the people.

The second case is the so-called New York
Bakeshop case. In New York City, as in most
large cities, the baking business is likely to
be carried on under unhygienic conditions,
conditions which tell against the welfare of
the general public. The New York Legislature
passed, and the New York Governor signed,
a bill remedying these unhealthy conditions.
New York State was the only body which
could deal with them; the nation had no
power whatever in the matter. Acting on evidence which to them seemed ample and sufficient, acting in the interest of the public and
in accordance with the demand of the public,
the only governmental authority having affirmative power in the matter, the Governor
and the Legislature of the State of New York
took the action which they deemed necessary,
after what inquiry and study were needed to
satisfy them as to the conditions, and as to the
remedy. The Governor and the Legislature
alone had the power to remedy the abuse.
But the Supreme Court of the United States
possessed, and unfortunately exercised, the
negative power of not permitting the abuse to
be remedied. By a five-to-four vote they declared the action of the State of New York
unconstitutional, because, forsooth, men must
not be deprived of their "liberty" to work
under unhealthy conditions. All who are acquainted with the effort to remedy industrial
abuses know the type of mind (it may be
perfectly honest, but is absolutely fossilized),
which declines to allow us to work for the
betterment of conditions among the wage
earners on the ground that we must not interfere with the "liberty" of a girl to work under
conditions which jeopardize life and limb, or
the "liberty" of a man to work under condi-

[14] Theodore Roosevelt, "Criticism of the Courts,"
*The Outlook*, XCVI (September 24, 1910), 149-
153.

tions which ruin his health after a limited number of years.

Such was the decision. The Court was of course absolutely powerless to make the remotest attempt to provide a remedy for the wrong which undoubtedly existed, and its refusal to permit action by the state did not confer any power upon the nation to act. The decision was nominally against states' rights, but really against popular rights.

Much exception was taken in the East to this speech as an "attack" on the Supreme Court, some of the critics going so far as to call it an attack upon the judiciary as a whole, an incitement to riot, and an appeal to the passions of the mob. The gloom caused by the "attack" was naturally deepest in that section of the metropolitan press which is owned and edited in the shadow of Wall Street; but many good and honest people were misled into a feeling of uneasiness on the subject. . . .

. . . Now as to the question whether it is ever proper to criticize a court. My views on this point have been set forth at length in the Message I sent to Congress when I was President, on December 3, 1906, which runs in part as follows:—

All honor cannot be paid to the wise and fearless judge if we permit the growth of an absurd convention which would forbid any criticism of the judge of another type, who shows himself timid in the presence of arrogant disorder, or who on insufficient grounds grants an injunction that does grave injustice, or who in his capacity as a construer, and therefore in part a maker, of the law, in flagrant fashion thwarts the cause of decent government. The judge has a power over which no review can be exercised; he himself sits in review upon the acts of both the executive and legislative branches of the Government; save in the most extraordinary cases he is amenable only at the bar of public opinion; and it is unwise to maintain that public opinion in reference to a man with such power shall neither be expressed nor led.

The best judges have ever been foremost to disclaim any immunity from criticism. This has been true since the days of the great English Lord Chancellor Parker, who said:

"Let all people be at liberty to know what I found my judgment upon; that, so when I have given it in any cause, others may be at liberty to judge of me." . . . There is one consideration which should be taken into account by the good people who carry a sound proposition to an excess in objecting to any criticism of a judge's decision. The instinct of the American people as a whole is sound in this matter. They will not subscribe to the doctrine that any public servant is to be above all criticism. If the best citizens, those most competent to express their judgment in such matters, and above all those belonging to the great and honorable profession of the bar, so profoundly influential in American life, take the position that there shall be no criticism of a judge under any circumstances, their view will not be accepted by the American people as a whole. In such event the people will turn to, and tend to accept as justifiable, the intemperate and improper criticism uttered by unworthy agitators. Surely it is a misfortune to leave [to] such critics a function, right in itself, which they are certain to abuse. Just and temperate criticism, when necessary, is a safeguard against the acceptance by the people as a whole of that intemperate antagonism toward the judiciary which must be combated by every right-thinking man, and which, if it became widespread among the people at large, would constitute a dire menace to the Republic.

I cannot state my position now more clearly than I stated it then. I continue to uphold the doctrine enunciated fifty-three years ago by Abraham Lincoln as regards criticism of the action of the courts. . . .

## 15

President Roosevelt's criticism of the courts did not arouse universal support among Progressives, and elicited no support from conservatives. Elihu Root, leading lawyer, speaking in 1912 on "Judicial Decisions and Public Feeling" in his presidential address to the New York Bar Association, squarely took issue with the view espoused by Roosevelt and the Progressives:[15]

I must believe also that proposals, in whatever form, to subordinate the decisions

---

[15] *Senate Documents*, 62nd Cong., 2nd Sess., Doc. No. 271, pp. 7-10.

of the courts to the decision of a popular majority, whether it be by punishing the judges for an unsatisfactory decision through removing them from office or by reviewing their decisions at the polls as distinct from reviewing and revising the law upon which they are to decide, proceed upon a failure to realize that this involves an abandonment of the most essential feature of our system of constitutional government.

We may grant that inconvenience frequently arises from decisions of courts finding that constitutional provisions are contravened by legislative action designed to express the popular will in particular cases. We may assume that some of these decisions are erroneous. It is impossible that there should not be some errors among fallible men under any system of government and any distribution of powers, although there are probably by no means as many errors as the ardent advocates of particular views suppose. But under every system and in every field of governmental action it is necessary to submit to inconveniences. . . .

One of the fundamental ideas of our Government is that all the officers to whom the people, whether of the nation or of the State, entrust the powers of government shall be subject to certain definite prescribed limitations upon their power. These limitations are of two kinds. First, those which relate to the distribution of powers. The National Government and the respective State Governments are each to keep within its own prescribed field of action. The legislative, executive, and judicial officers are to be confined to their own departments of government. Within those departments particular officers, wherever it is found expedient, have specific lines of limitation upon their power. If an officer undertakes to do something which is not within the prescribed limits of his authority his action is void and without legal effect. No matter how able and patriotic a President or a Governor may be,

no matter how wise a congress or a legislature may be, no matter how much they may deem it to be for the public good that they should invade the field of action of another department, they are denied the right to do it, not because it might not be a very good thing in the particular case, but because the prevention of unlimited power is of such vast importance to liberty that no particular case can possibly be important enough to justify abandoning the maintenance and the observance of the general rule of prescribed limitations. The door opened for the well-meaning and far-seeing lover of country to exercise power without regard to the limitations set upon it is also a door opened for the self-seeking and ambitious to disregard the same limitations for their own advantage. It is impossible to maintain a rule of limitation upon power which is to be observed when it seems wise and ignored when it seems unwise.

The other kind of prescribed limitation is for the protection of the individual citizen against the power of government. Our fathers had experienced some and observed many invasions of individual liberty and individual right of which governments had been guilty. They realized that the nature of men is not greatly changed by a change in the form of government and that the possession of overwhelming power affords a constant temptation to override the rights of the weak. Accordingly, both in the nation and in the State, they prescribed certain general rules which prohibited all officers to whom they entrusted the powers of government from doing certain things, such as inflicting cruel and unusual punishments, abridging freedom of speech or of the press, prohibiting the free exercise of religion, putting any person twice in jeopardy for the same offense, compelling any one to be a witness against himself in a criminal case, taking private property for public use without just compensation, depriving any one of life, liberty or property without due process of law. It frequently happens that inconvenience results from the application of these rules. Criminals escape because they cannot be tried twice or cannot be compelled to testify; public improvements are hindered because property cannot be taken except by due process of law; the liberty of the press and of speech often degenerates into license and many poor people are misled to their harm by the doctrine of strange and irrational religious sects. Nevertheless the maintenance of these rules is the bulwark which protects the weak individual citizen in the possession of those rights which constitute liberty; and it is because these rules with all their inconveniences, if maintained at all must be always maintained, that the public officer who oversteps them, with however good intentions and for whatever benefit to the public, becomes a trespasser without authority and without protection of the law.

A second and equally necessary feature of our system is that these limitations, both those which distribute official powers and those which declare the great rules of right conduct, must be prescribed abstractly and impersonally rather than with reference to particular cases or particular exigencies or particular individuals. The difference is generic, essential, world wide. The very fact of making a constitution which is to be binding upon legislatures and executives and judges when they come to deal with particular cases exhibits the rules prescribed in the constitution in sharp distinction from the determination of official power when particular cases arise. It is not possible for any human power to make the determination of a legislature or executive at the time of action the same thing as an obligatory general rule of conduct prescribed beforehand. The difference between a constitutional convention prescribing constitutional limitations and a legislature dealing with particular exigencies is not that one represents the people any more truly than the other, or is of any higher character than the other, but it is that one

deals with justice, with right conduct, with the requirements of liberty, with a due balance and distribution of the powers of government impersonally and in the abstract without reference to individuals or the interests or prejudices or inconveniences of particular cases; while the other deals with the particular cases to which the general impersonal rule applies. So it is that at almost every session of our legislative bodies we find attempts made to evade or to appear to evade constitutional rules in order to accomplish specific purposes, when beyond a doubt the very body which attempts the evasion would refuse to abandon the rule as a guide to conduct except in the particular case under consideration. Indeed if it were not for the fact that legislatures and executives would fail to apply the impartial and universal rules of our constitutions to the particular case with which they deal if left free at the time there would be no occasion for constitutions. . . .

A third feature of our system which is a necessary corollary to the other two and essential to them, is the vesting of power in the judicial branch to determine when the action of the legislative and executive branches or any officer of them oversteps the limitations which have been prescribed. Without this all our bills of rights and limitations upon official power would be idle forms of words. If the law-making body of the moment, whether it be a representative legislature or a majority at the polls, is to determine at the time of action either what shall be the rules to control its conduct or the question whether its conduct conforms to the rules already prescribed, that conduct is controlled only by the will of the law-making body at the moment of action, and our whole system of prescribed limitations upon power disappears. The necessary result is that the barriers we have set up from the beginning of our government against official usurpation of power and against official invasion of the liberty and rights of the individual, are broken down, and the power of the majority according to the will of the moment is supreme and uncontrolled. . . .

We must choose between having prescribed rules of right conduct, binding in every case so long as they exist, even though there may be occasional inconvenience through their restraint upon our freedom of action, and having no rules at all to prevent us from doing in every case whatever we wish to do at the time. We cannot maintain one system in part and the other system in part. The gulf between the two systems is not narrowed, but greatly widened by the proposal to dispense with the action of a representative legislature and to substitute direct popular action at the polls. A sovereign people which declares that all men have certain inalienable rights, and imposes upon itself the great impersonal rules of conduct deemed necessary for the preservation of those rights, and at the same time declares that it will disregard those rules whenever, in any particular case, it is the wish of a majority of its voters to do so, establishes as complete a contradiction to the fundamental principles of our Government as it is possible to conceive. It abandons absolutely the conception of a justice which is above majorities, of a right in the weak which the strong are bound to respect. It denies the vital truth taught by religion and realized in the hard experience of mankind, and which has inspired every constitution America has produced and every great declaration for human freedom since Magna Charta—the truth that human nature needs to distrust its own impulses and passions and to establish for its own control the restraining and guiding influence of declared principles of action.

## 16

Neither the hue and cry raised by the anti-Court faction, nor the championing of judicial review by such legalistic minds as Elihu Root greatly affected the nine justices who sat as arbiters over the popular will. Undeterred

by the clamor their decisions aroused, they conscientiously defended the sanctity of property rights. Their most important decisions gave new meaning—and less authority—to the Sherman Antitrust Act, on which both Theodore Roosevelt and William Howard Taft based their trust-busting activities. Of these the most significant was *Standard Oil Company of New Jersey et al.* v. *the United States* (1911). After holding the Standard Oil Company of New Jersey to be a combination in restraint of trade and ordering its dissolution, the justices laid down a "rule of reason" under which a combination was illegal only when—in the personal opinion of the majority of the judges—it was engaged in "undue restraint of trade":[16]

In substance, the propositions urged by the government are reducible to this: That the language of the statute embraces every contract, combination, etc., in restraint of trade, and hence its text leaves no room for the exercise of judgment, but simply imposes the plain duty of applying its prohibitions to every case within its literal language. The error involved lies in assuming the matter to be decided. . . . The merely generic enumeration which the statute makes of the acts to which it refers, and the absence of any definition of restraint of trade as used in the statute, leaves room for but one conclusion, which is, that it was expressly designed not to unduly limit the application of the act by precise definition, but, while clearly fixing a standard, that is, by defining the ulterior boundaries which could not be transgressed with impunity, to leave it to be determined by the light of reason. . . .

If the criterion by which it is to be determined in all cases whether every contract, combination, etc., is a restraint of trade within the intendment of the law, is the direct or indirect effect of the acts involved, then of course the rule of reason becomes the guide.

## 17

The "rule of reason" did not escape denunciation. One of the most effective attacks upon

---

[16] *United States Reports,* 221 U.S. 63, 66.

it was Justice Harlan's dissenting opinion in the Standard Oil Case:[17]

I confess to no little surprise as to what has occurred in the present case. . . . It is more than once intimated, if not suggested, that if the Anti-Trust Act is to be construed as prohibiting *every* contract or combination, of whatever nature, which is in fact in restraint of commerce, regardless of the reasonableness or unreasonableness of such restraint, that fact would show that the court had not proceeded, in its decision, according to "the light of reason," but had disregarded the "rule of reason.". . . Now this court is asked to do that which it has distinctly declared it could not and would not do, and has now done what it then said it could not constitutionally do. It has, by mere interpretation, modified the act of Congress, and deprived it of practical value as a defensive measure against the evils to be remedied. . . . In effect, the court says, that it will now, for the first time, bring the discussion under the "light of reason" and apply the "rule of reason" to the questions to be decided. I have the authority of this court for saying that such a course of proceeding on its part would be "judicial legislation.". . .

But my brethren, in their wisdom, have deemed it best to pursue a different course. They have now said to those who condemn our former decisions and who object to all legislative prohibitions of contracts, combinations, and trusts in restraint of interstate commerce, "You may *now* restrain such commerce, provided you are reasonable about it; only take care that the restraint is not undue.". . .

When Congress prohibited *every* contract, combination, or monopoly in restraint of commerce, it prescribed a simple, definite rule that all could understand. . . . But now, it is to be feared, we are to have, in cases without number, the constantly recurring inquiry—difficult to solve

by proof—whether the particular contract, combination or trust involved in each case is or is not an "unreasonable" or "undue" restraint of trade. . . .

It remains for me to refer, more fully than I have heretofore done, to another, and, in my judgment—if we look to the future—the most important aspect of this case. That aspect concerns the usurpation by the judicial branch of the Government of the functions of the legislative department. . . . I said at the outset that the action of the court in this case might well alarm thoughtful men who revered the Constitution. I meant by this that many things are intimated and said in the court's opinion which will not be regarded otherwise than as sanctioning an invasion by the judiciary of the constitutional domain of Congress—an attempt by interpretation to soften or modify what some regard as a harsh public policy. This court, let me repeat, solemnly adjudged many years ago that it could not, except by *"judicial legislation"* read words into the Anti-Trust Act, not put there by Congress, and which, being inserted, give it a meaning which the words of the act, as passed, if properly interpreted, would not justify. The court has decided that it could not thus change a public policy formulated and declared by Congress; that Congress has paramount authority to regulate interstate commerce, and that it alone can change a policy once inaugurated by legislation. The courts have nothing to do with the wisdom or policy of an act of Congress. Their duty is to ascertain the will of Congress, and if the statute embodying the expression of that will is constitutional, the courts must respect it. They have no function to declare a public policy, nor to *amend legislative enactments*. . . . Nevertheless, if I do not misapprehend its opinion, the court has now read into the act of Congress words which are not to be found there, and has thereby done that which it adjudged in 1896 and in 1898 could not be done without violating the Constitution, namely, by

---

[17] *Ibid.*, pp. 98-106.

interpretation of a statute, changed a public policy declared by the legislative department.

Tangible progressive gains were few during the administrations of Theodore Roosevelt and William Howard Taft. A few industrial combinations were broken down into competing units, a few trusts dissolved, a few new laws placed on the statute books to curb the railroads. Reformers failed to realize their ambitions because Roosevelt had not found—and Taft had not sought—a solution of the problem of a party discipline strong enough to prod into action a Congress dominated by pressure groups. Yet a new day was dawning for believers in popular rule. With the election of Woodrow Wilson, the people found a champion equipped to bring the Progressive Era to its logical development.

# WILSONIAN DEMOCRACY

## 1912-1916

Progressivism reached a triumphant climax during Woodrow Wilson's administration. Wielding a big stick against trusts, goading Congress into passing effective laws, and prodding the courts into accepting the principle that human rights should occasionally transcend property rights, the scholarly President from Princeton's ivied halls brought a semblance of order to the nation's chaotic economic system. That he succeeded where his predecessors failed was due partly to popular support for his program, partly to his political acumen, and partly to his better understanding of the fundamental problem. Wilson's panacea was not a complete destruction of Big Business; mere size, he felt, was not an evil in a corporation that sought to pass on the benefits of large-scale production in the form of lower prices and higher wages. The Federal Trade Commission Act and the Clayton Antitrust Act, by recognizing this principle, made governmental regulation of business more in accord with new trends in American thought.

## CRITICAL REALISM: THE PARTY SYSTEM

### 1

Wilson owed much of his success as President to his training in political science. An astute observer of the deficiencies of his country's political system, he was aware that strong leadership was needed if the will of the majority was to prevail over the influence of pressure groups in Congress. Political parties, if organized under strong leadership and loyal to the mandate received at elections, could carry out the will of the majority. Their failure to equip themselves to do so was one of the tragedies of the age. Wilson had long ago analyzed the reasons for their failure and was familiar with the works of other scholars who had made similar findings. Of these the most penetrating was J. Allen Smith, whose vigorous book, *The Spirit of American Government,* was published in 1907:[1]

The political party, it is true, has come to play an important role under our constitutional system; but its power and influence are of a negative rather than a positive character. It professes, of course, to stand for the principle of majority rule, but in practice it has become an additional

[1] From J. Allen Smith, *The Spirit of American Government,* pp. 208-218, 350-355. Copyright 1907 by The Macmillan Company. Used by permission of The Macmillan Company, publishers.

and one of the most potent checks on the majority.

To understand the peculiar features of the American party system one must bear in mind the constitutional arrangements under which it has developed. The party is simply a voluntary political association through which the people seek to formulate the policy of the government, select the officials who are to carry it out in the actual administration of public affairs, and hold them to strict accountability for so doing. Under any government which makes full provision for the political party, as in the English system of to-day, the party has not only the power to elect but the power to remove those who are entrusted with the execution of its policies. Having this complete control of the government, it can not escape responsibility for failure to carry out the promises by which it secured a majority at the polls. This is the essential difference between the English system on the one hand and the party under the American constitutional system on the other. The one well knows that if it carries the election it will be expected to make its promises good. The other makes certain promises with the knowledge that after the election is over it will probably have no power to carry them out.

It is this lack of power to shape the entire policy of the government which, more than anything else, has given form and character to the party system of the United States. To the extent that the Constitution has deprived the majority of the power to mold the policy of the government through voluntary political associations, it has defeated the main purpose for which the party should exist.

The fact that under the American form of government the party can not be held accountable for failure to carry out its ante-election pledges has had the natural and inevitable result. When, as in England, the party which carries the election obtains complete and undisputed control of the government, the sense of responsibility is ever present in those who direct it. If in the event of its success it is certain to be called upon to carry out its promises, it can not afford for the sake of obtaining votes to make promises which it has no intention of keeping. But when the party, even though successful at the polls may lack the power to enforce its policy, it can not be controlled by a sense of direct responsibility to the people. Promises may be recklessly and extravagantly made merely for the sake of getting votes. The party platform from the point of view of the party managers ceases to be a serious declaration of political principles. It comes to be regarded as a means of winning elections rather than a statement of what the party is obligated to accomplish. . . .

A government which limits the power of the majority might promote the general interests of society more effectually than one controlled by the majority, if the checks were in the hands of a class of superior wisdom and virtue. But in practice such a government, instead of being better than those for whom it exists, is almost invariably worse. The complex and confusing system of checks, with the consequent diffusion of power and absence of direct and definite responsibility, is much better adapted to the purposes of a self-seeking, corrupt minority than to the ends of good government. The evils of such a system which are mainly those of minority domination must be carefully distinguished from those which result from majority control. The critics of American political institutions have as a rule ignored the former or constitutional aspect of our political evils, and have held majority rule accountable for much that our system of checks has made the majority powerless to prevent. The evils of our party system, having their roots in the lack of popular control over the party machine, are thus largely a consequence of the checks on the power of the majority contained in the Constitution itself. In other words, they are the outcome, not of too much, but of too little democracy.

The advocates of political reform have directed their attention mainly to the party machine. They have assumed that control of the party organization by the people would give them control of the government. If this view were correct, the evils which exist could be attributed only to the ignorance, want of public spirit and lack of capacity for effective political cooperation on the part of the people. But as a matter of fact this method of dealing with the problem is open to the objection that it mistakes the effect for the cause. It should be clearly seen that a system of constitutional checks, which hedges about the power of the majority on every side, is incompatible with majority rule; and that even if the majority controlled the party organization, it could control the policy of the government only by breaking down and sweeping away the barriers which the Constitution has erected against it. It follows that all attempts to establish the majority in power by merely reforming the party must be futile.

Under any political system which recognizes the right of the majority to rule, responsibility of the government to the people is the end and aim of all that the party stands for. Party platforms and popular elections are not ends in themselves, but only means by which the people seek to make the government responsive to public opinion. Any arrangement of constitutional checks, then, which defeats popular control, strikes down what is most vital and fundamental in party government. And since the party under our system can not enforce public opinion, it is but natural that the people should lose interest in party affairs. . . .

The party machine can not serve the purpose of those interests which give it financial support and at the same time allow the people to nominate its candidates and formulate its political creed. Nevertheless, the semblance of popular control must be preserved. The outward appearance of the party organization, the external forms which catch the popular eye, must not reveal too clearly the secret methods and cunningly devised arrangements by which an effective minority control is maintained over the nomination of candidates and the framing of party platforms. The test of fitness for office is not fidelity to the rank and file of the people who vote the party ticket, but subserviency to those interests which dominate the party machine. The choice of candidates is largely made in the secret councils of the ruling minority and the party conventions under color of making a popular choice of candidates merely ratify the minority choice already made. Popular elections under such a system do not necessarily mean that the people have any real power of selecting public officials. They merely have the privilege of voting for one or the other of two lists of candidates neither of which may be in any true sense representative of the people or their interests. . . .

The plan for depriving the minority of the power to control the selection of public officials, which is now rapidly gaining adherents among the advocates of political reform, is the direct primary. That some such change in our method of nominating candidates is necessary to make the so-called popular election of public officials anything more than an empty form is apparent to any intelligent student of American politics. But any proposal to deprive the minority of this power must encounter the determined opposition of the party machine and the various private interests which now prosper at the expense of the people. These opponents of political reform are continually declaiming against the corruption and incapacity of the people and trying to make it appear that a government can be no better than its source—those who elect the public officials. That a government is not likely to be better than the people whom it represents may be admitted. But this is aside from the question. Our present system in its practical operation is not a democracy. It is not truly representative, but misrepresentative. To prevent this evil—this betrayal of public trust in the interest of the minority— is the aim of the direct primary. That it will go far toward breaking the power of the machine may be safely predicted, and that it will be generally adopted as soon as the people realize its significance there is scarcely room for doubt. . . .

It must be admitted, when we review the course of our political development, that much progress has been made. But the evolution has been toward a direct rather than toward a representative democracy. The reason for this is not far to seek. The system of checks which limited the power of the majority made the legislature largely an irresponsible body; and since it could not be trusted, it was necessary to take out of its hands the powers it was most likely to abuse. . . . The prevalent lack of confidence in our state legislatures is no indication of hostility to the principle of representative government; for representative government in the true sense means government that is responsible to the people. The popular movement has in modifying our state and municipal governments merely taken the line of least resistance, and that has involved the transfer of legislative powers to the people themselves.

Just how far this movement will go it is impossible to foresee. A government of the representative type, if responsive to public sentiment, would answer all the requirements of a democratic state. It would at the same time be merely carrying out in practice what has long been the generally accepted, if mistaken, view of our political system. The adoption of some effective plan of direct nomination and recall of officials would accomplish much in the way of restoring confidence in legislative bodies. To this extent it would check the tendency to place the law-making power directly in the hands of the people. Popular ratification of all important laws would be unnecessary, if our legislative bodies were really responsible to the people.

## 2

Wilson's awareness of the need for party responsibility was demonstrated in his own writings as well as in the works of his fellow political scientists. Above all else he saw that the old nineteenth-century decentralized system of political management was too irresponsible to serve a nation geared to the tempo of twentieth-century industrial life. As early as 1900, in the preface to one of the many editions of his classic work on *Congressional Government,* Wilson saw in the unprecedented power recently garnered by the speaker of the House of Representatives an imperfect response to an undoubted need. Some leadership, he felt, was better than no leadership at all:[2]

. . . The power of the Speaker has of late years taken on new phases. He is now, more than ever, expected to guide and control the whole course of business in the House,—if not alone, at any rate through the instrumentality of the small Committee on Rules, of which he is chairman. That committee is expected not only to refor-

[2] Selection from Woodrow Wilson's *Congressional Government* (15th ed., 1900), pp. ix-xi, by permission of the publishers, Houghton Mifflin Company.

mulate and revise from time to time the permanent Rules of the House, but also to look closely to the course of its business from day to day, make its programme, and virtually control its use of its time. The committee consists of five members; but the Speaker and the two other members of the committee who represent the majority in the House determine its action; and its action is allowed to govern the House. It in effect regulates the precedence of measures. Whenever occasion requires, it determines what shall, and what shall not, be undertaken. It is like a steering ministry,—without a ministry's right to speak for both houses. It is a private piece of party machinery within the single chamber for which it acts. The Speaker himself—not as a member of the Committee on Rules, but by the exercise of his right to "recognize" on the floor—undertakes to determine very absolutely what bills individual members shall be allowed to bring to a vote, out of the regular order fixed by the rules or arranged by the Committee on Rules.

This obviously creates, in germ at least, a recognized and sufficiently concentrated leadership within the House. The country is beginning to know that the Speaker and the Committee on Rules must be held responsible in all ordinary seasons for the success or failure of the session, so far as the House is concerned. The congressional caucus has fallen a little into the background. It is not often necessary to call it together, except when the majority is impatient or recalcitrant under the guidance of the Committee on Rules. To this new leadership, however, as to everything else connected with committee government, the taint of privacy attaches. It is not leadership upon the open floor, avowed, defended in public debate, set before the view and criticism of the country. It integrates the House alone, not the Senate; does not unite the two houses in policy; affects only the chamber in which there is the least opportunity for debate, the least chance that responsibility may be properly and effectively lodged and avowed. It has only a very remote and partial resemblance to genuine party leadership.

## 3

An equally convincing description of party irresponsibility was made by Elihu Root, lawyer and prominent Republican leader, in a speech delivered before the New York Constitutional Convention on August 30, 1915. So long as actual power and responsibility rested in party bosses rather than in elected officials, he held, there could be no true democracy in the United States:[3]

I am going to discuss a subject now that goes back to the beginning of the political life of the oldest man in this Convention, and one to which we cannot close our eyes, if we keep the obligations of our oath. We talk about the government of the Constitution. We have spent many days in discussing the powers of this and that and the other officer. What is the government of this State? What has it been during the forty years of my acquaintance with it? The government of the Constitution? Oh, no; not half the time, or half way. When I ask what do the people find wrong in our State government, my mind goes back to those periodic fits of public rage in which the people rouse up and tear down the political leader, first of one party and then of the other party. It goes on to the public feeling of resentment against the control of party organizations, of both parties and of all parties.

Now, I treat this subject in my own mind not as a personal question to any man. I am talking about the system. From the days of Fenton, and Conkling, and Arthur and Cornell, and Platt, from the days of David B. Hill, down to the present time the government of the State has presented two different lines of activity, one

of the constitutional and statutory officers of the State, and the other of the party leaders,—they call them party bosses. They call the system—I don't coin the phrase, I adopt it because it carries its own meaning—the system they call "invisible government." For I don't remember how many years, Mr. Conkling was the supreme ruler in this State; the Governor did not count, the legislatures did not count; comptrollers and secretaries of state and what not, did not count. It was what Mr. Conkling said, and in a great outburst of public rage he was pulled down.

Then Mr. Platt ruled the State; for nigh upon twenty years he ruled it. It was not the Governor; it was not the Legislature; it was not any elected officers; it was Mr. Platt. And the capitol was not here; it was at 49 Broadway; Mr. Platt and his lieutenants. It makes no difference what name you give, whether you call it Fenton or Conkling or Cornell or Arthur or Platt, or by the names of men now living. The ruler of the State during the greater part of the forty years of my acquaintance with the State government has not been any man authorized by the Constitution or by the law; and, sir, there is throughout the length and breadth of this State a deep and sullen and long-continued resentment at being governed thus by men not of the people's choosing. The party leader is elected by no one, accountable to no one, bound by no oath of office, removable by no one. Ah! My friends here have talked about this bill's creating an autocracy. The word points with admirable facility the very opposite reason for the bill. It is to destroy autocracy and restore power so far as may be to the men elected by the people, accountable to the people, removable by the people. I don't criticise the men of the invisible government. How can I? I have known them all, and among them have been some of my dearest friends. I can never forget the deep sense of indignation that I felt in the abuse that was heaped upon Chester A. Arthur,

[3] *Record of the Constitutional Convention of the State of New York* (Albany, 1915), III, 3387-3389.

whom I honored and loved, when he was attacked because he held the position of political leader. But it is all wrong. It is all wrong that a government not authorized by the people should be continued superior to the government that is authorized by the people.

How is it accomplished? How is it done? Mr. Chairman, it is done by the use of patronage, and the patronage that my friends on the other side of this question have been arguing and pleading for in this Convention is the power to continue that invisible government against that authorized by the people. Everywhere, sir, that these two systems of government coexist, there is a conflict day by day, and year by year, between two principles of appointment to office, two radically opposed principles. The elected officer or the appointed officer, the lawful officer who is to be held responsible for the administration of his office, desires to get men into the different positions of his office who will do their work in a way that is creditable to him and his administration. Whether it be a president appointing a superintendent of public works, whatever it may be, the officer wants to make a success, and he wants to get the man selected upon the ground of his ability to do the work.

How is it about the boss? What does the boss have to do? He has to urge the appointment of a man whose appointment will consolidate his power and preserve the organization. The invisible government proceeds to build up and maintain its power by a reversal of the fundamental principle of good government, which is that men should be selected to perform the duties of the office; and to substitute the idea that men should be appointed to office for the preservation and enhancement of power of the political leader. The one, the true one, looks upon appointment to office with a view to the service that can be given to the public. The other, the false one, looks upon appointment to office with a view to what can be gotten out of it. Gentlemen of the Convention, I appeal to your knowledge of facts. Every one of you knows that what I say about the use of patronage under the system of invisible government is true. Louis Marshall told us the other day about the appointment of wardens in the Adirondacks, hotel keepers and people living there, to render no service whatever. They were appointed not for the service that they were to render to the State; they were appointed for the service they were to render to promote the power of a political organization. Mr. Chairman, we all know that the halls of this capitol swarm with men during the session of the Legislature on pay day. A great number, seldom here, rendering no service, are put on the payrolls as a matter of patronage, not of service, but of party patronage. Both parties are alike; all parties are alike. The system extends through all. Ah, Mr. Chairman, that system finds its opportunity in the division of powers, in a six headed executive, in which, by the natural workings of human nature there shall be opposition and discord and the playing of one force against the other, and so, when we refuse to make one Governor elected by the people the real chief executive, we make inevitable the setting up of a chief executive not selected by the people, not acting for the people's interest, but for the selfish interest of the few who control the party, whichever party it may be. Think for a moment of what this patronage system means. How many of you are there who would be willing to do to your private client, or customer, or any private trust, or to a friend or neighbor, what you see being done to the State of New York every year of your lives in the taking of money out of her treasury without service? We can, when we are in a private station, pass on without much attention to inveterate abuses. We can say to ourselves, I know it is wrong. I wish it could be set right; it cannot be set right, I will do nothing. But here, here, we face the duty, we cannot escape it, we are bound to do our work, face to face, in clear recognition of the truth, unpalatable, deplorable as it may be and the truth is that what the unerring instinct of the democracy of our State has seen in this government is that a different standard of morality is applied to the conduct of affairs of States than that which is applied in private affairs. I have been told forty times since this Convention met that you cannot change it. We can try, can't we? I deny that we cannot change it. I repel that cynical assumption which is born of the lethargy that comes from poisoned air during all these years. I assert that this perversion of democracy, this robbing democracy of its virility, can be changed as truly as the system under which Walpole governed the commons of England, by bribery, as truly as the atmosphere which made the *crédit mobilier* scandal possible in the Congress of the United States has been blown away by the force of public opinion. We cannot change it in a moment, but we can do our share. We can take this one step toward, not robbing the people of their part in government, but toward robbing an irresponsible autocracy of its indefensible and unjust and undemocratic control of government, and restoring it to the people to be exercised by the men of their choice and their control.

Observations such as these profoundly influenced Woodrow Wilson. Leadership, he saw, was needed to translate the will of the majority into legislation. The political parties had failed to provide that leadership in Congress. Therefore the President must assume a new role in American life. Through personal influence, control of the patronage, and direct participation in congressional deliberations he must assume a position comparable to that of England's prime minister. This was Wilson's most important discovery. By applying the principle of executive responsibility he made his administration one of the most fruitful in history.

## INSURGENCY AND THE DEMOCRATS

### 4

Progressive Republicans gave Wilson a chance to apply his theories, for only their rebellion against the conservative majority within their party placed him in the White House. The Republican split began in 1910, when Taft's reactionary policies proved more than Republican progressives could stomach; that year they and the Democrats staged a dramatic legislative battle to strip the Republican Speaker of the House of his autocratic power over committee appointments and legislative practices. Having shown their hand, the "insurgents" realized that they would be driven out of the party unless they could wrest leadership from the conservative majority. With this in mind, they met to organize on January 21, 1911, at the home of their leader, Senator Robert La Follette of Wisconsin. Under the name of the National Progressive Republican League, they issued the following declaration of principles:[4]

We, the undersigned, associate ourselves together as The National Progressive Republican League.

The object of the League is the promotion of popular government and progressive legislation.

Popular government in America has been thwarted and progressive legislation strangled by the special interests, which control caucuses, delegates, conventions, and party organizations; and, through this control of the machinery of government, dictate nominations and platforms, elect administrations, legislatures, representatives in Congress, United States Senators, and control cabinet officers.

Under existing conditions legislation in the public interest has been baffled and defeated. This is evidenced by the long struggle to secure laws but partially effective for the control of railway rates and

[4] *La Follette's Autobiography: A Personal Narrative of Political Experiences* by Robert M. La Follette, pp. 495-496. The Robert M. La Follette Company, Madison, Wisconsin, 1913.

services, the revision of the tariff in the interest of the producer and consumer, statutes dealing with trusts and combinations, based on sound economic principles, as applied to modern industrial and commercial conditions; wise, comprehensive and impartial reconstruction of banking and monetary laws, the conservation of coal, oil, gas, timber, water-powers, and other natural resources belonging to the people, and for the enactment of all legislation solely for the common good.

Just in proportion as popular government has in certain states superseded the delegate convention system, and the people have assumed control of the machinery of government, has government become responsive to the popular will, and progressive legislation been secured.

The Progressive Republican League believes that popular government is fundamental to all other questions. To this end it advocates:

(1) The election of United States Senators by direct vote of the people.

(2) Direct primaries for the nomination of elective officials.

(3) The direct election of delegates to national conventions with opportunity for the voter to express his choice for President and Vice-President.

(4) Amendment to state constitutions providing for the Initiative, Referendum and Recall.

(5) A thoroughgoing corrupt practices act.

## 5

The Republican insurgents' declaration struck deep at a fundamental problem: how could legislators and judges be made to shift their views with changes in the popular will? The Progressives had the answer; they would allow the people a more positive voice in elections by adopting direct primaries, then use the initiative, referendum, and recall to override or remove officials who refused to obey the majority. Taft, Root, and conservative Republicans objected to this panacea. Believ-

ing sincerely in the sanctity of constitutional law as much as in the sanctity of representative government, they felt that certain areas of government should be removed from popular control. President Taft summarized their views on August 22, 1911, when he vetoed the enabling act that would have admitted Arizona to statehood under a constitution authorizing the recall of judges:[5]

This provision of the Arizona constitution, in its application to county and State judges, seems to me so pernicious in its effect, so destructive of independence in the judiciary, so likely to subject the rights of the individual to the possible tyranny of a popular majority, and, therefore, to be so injurious to the cause of free government, that I must disapprove a constitution containing it. . . .

A government is for the benefit of all the people. . . . Now, as the government is for all the people, and is not solely for a majority of them, the majority in exercising control either directly or through its agents is bound to exercise the power for the benefit of the minority as well as the majority. But all have recognized that the majority of a people, unrestrained by law, when aroused and without the sobering effect of deliberation and discussion, may do injustice to the minority or to the individual when the selfish interest of the majority prompts. Hence arises the necessity for a constitution by which the will of the majority shall be permitted to guide the course of the government only under controlling checks that experience has shown to be necessary to secure for the minority its share of the benefit to the whole people that a popular government is established to bestow. A popular government is not a government of a majority, by a majority, for a majority of the people. It is a government of the whole people, by a majority of the whole people, under such rules and

---

[5] *Congressional Record,* 62nd Cong., 1st Sess., pp. 3964-3966.

checks as will secure a wise, just, and beneficient government for all the people. It is said you can always trust the people to do justice. If that means all the people and they all agree, you can. But ordinarily they do not all agree, and the maxim is interpreted to mean that you can always trust a majority of the people. This is not invariably true; and every limitation imposed by the people upon the power of the majority in their constitutions is an admission that it is not always true. No honest, clear-headed man, however great a lover of popular government, can deny that the unbridled expression of the majority of a community converted hastily into law or action would sometimes make a government tyrannical and cruel. Constitutions are checks upon the hasty action of the majority. They are the self-imposed restraints of a whole people upon a majority of them to secure sober action and a respect for the rights of the minority, and of the individual in his relation to other individuals, and in his relation to the whole people in their character as a state or government. . . .

By the recall in the Arizona constitution it is proposed to give to the majority power to remove arbitrarily, and without delay, any judge who may have the courage to render an unpopular decision. By the recall it is proposed to enable a minority of 25 per cent of the voters of the district or State, for no prescribed cause, after the judge has been in office six months, to submit the question of his retention in office to the electorate. The petitioning minority must say on the ballot what they can against him in 200 words, and he must defend as best he can in the same space. Other candidates are permitted to present themselves and have their names printed on the ballot, so that the recall is not based solely on the record or the acts of the judge, but also on the question whether some other and more popular candidate has been found to unseat him. Could there be a system more ingeniously devised to

subject judges to momentary gusts of popular passion than this? We can not be blind to the fact that often an intelligent and respectable electorate may be so roused upon an issue that it will visit with condemnation the decision of a just judge, though exactly in accord with the law governing the case, merely because it affects unfavorably their contest. Controversies over elections, labor troubles, racial or religious issues as to the construction or constitutionality of liquor laws, criminal trials of popular or unpopular defendants, the removal of county seats, suits by individuals to maintain their constitutional rights in obstruction of some popular improvement—these and many other cases could be cited in which a majority of a district electorate would be tempted by hasty anger to recall a conscientious judge if the opportunity were open all the time. No period of delay is interposed for the abatement of popular feeling. The recall is devised to encourage quick action, and to lead the people to strike while the iron is hot. The judge is treated as the instrument and servant of a majority of the people and subject to their momentary will, not after a long term in which his qualities as a judge and his character as a man have been subjected to a test of all the varieties of judicial work and duty so as to furnish a proper means of measuring his fitness for continuance in another term. On the instant of an unpopular ruling, while the spirit of protest has not had time to cool and even while an appeal may be pending from his ruling in which he may be sustained, he is to be haled before the electorate as a tribunal, with no judicial hearing, evidence, or defense, and thrown out of office, and disgraced for life because he has failed, in a single decision, it may be, to satisfy the popular demand. Think of the opportunity such a system would give to unscrupulous political bosses in control, as they have been in control not only of conventions but elections! Think of the enormous power for evil given to the sensational, muckraking portion of the press in rousing prejudice against a just judge by false charges and insinuations, the effect of which in the short period of an election by recall it would be impossible for him to meet and offset! Supporters of such a system seem to think that it will work only in the interest of the poor, the humble, the weak and the oppressed; that it will strike down only the judge who is supposed to favor corporations and be affected by the corrupting influence of the rich. Nothing could be further from the ultimate result. The motive it would offer to unscrupulous combinations to seek to control politics in order to control judges is clear. Those would profit by the recall who have the best opportunity of rousing the majority of the people to action on a sudden impulse. Are they likely to be the wisest or the best people in a community? Do they not include those who have money enough to employ the firebrands and slanderers in a community and the stirrers-up of social hate? Would not self-respecting men well hesitate to accept judicial office with such a sword of Damocles hanging over them? What kind of judgments might those on the unpopular side expect from courts whose judges must make their decisions under such legalized terrorism? The character of the judges would deteriorate to that of trimmers and time-servers, and independent judicial action would be a thing of the past. As the possibilities of such a system pass in review, is it too much to characterize it as one which will destroy the judiciary, its standing, and its usefulness? . . .

Again judicial recall is advocated on the ground that it will bring the judges more into sympathy with the popular will and the progress of ideas among the people. It is said that now judges are out of touch with the movement toward a wider democracy and a greater control of governmental agencies in the interest and for the benefit of the people. The righteous and just course for a judge to pursue is ordinarily fixed by statute or clear principles of law, and the cases in which his judgment may be affected by his political, economic, or social views are infrequent. But even in such cases, judges are not removed from the people's influence. Surround the judiciary with all the safeguards possible, create judges by appointment, make their tenure for life, forbid diminution of salary during their term, and still it is impossible to prevent the influence of popular opinion from coloring judgments in the long run. Judges are men, intelligent, sympathetic men, patriotic men, and in those fields of the law in which the personal equation unavoidably plays a part, there will be found a response to sober popular opinion as it changes to meet the exigency of social, political, and economic changes. Indeed this should be so. Individual instances of a hidebound and retrograde conservatism on the part of courts in decisions which turn on the individual economic or sociological views of the judges may be pointed out; but they are not many, and do not call for radical action. In treating of courts we are dealing with a human machine, liable like all the inventions of man to err, but we are dealing with a human institution that likens itself to a divine institution because it seeks and preserves justice. It has been the corner stone of our gloriously free government in which the rights of the individual and of the minority have been preserved, while governmental action of the majority has lost nothing of beneficent progress, efficacy, and directness. This balance was planned in the Constitution by its framers and has been maintained by our independent judiciary.

## 6

With the line clearly drawn between progressives and conservatives within the Republican party, an open break was inevitable. This came when the party regulars, more conscious of patronage than of the popular will, renominated Taft in 1912 over the bitter protests of the insurgents. Seething with indignation, the progressives began laying plans for a new party. They were aided by the ever-popular Theodore Roosevelt, who threw his hat into the political arena at once, then came bounding in himself. In a vigorous speech delivered at Columbus, Ohio, on February 21, 1912, Roosevelt had already aligned himself with the insurgents by coming out flatfootedly for judicial recall:[6]

I do not believe in adopting the recall save as a last resort, when it has become clearly evident that no other course will achieve the desired result. But either the recall will have to be adopted or else it will have to be made much easier than it now is to get rid, not merely of a bad judge, but of a judge who, however virtuous, has grown so out of touch with social needs and facts that he is unfit longer to render good service on the bench. It is nonsense to say that impeachment meets the difficulty. In actual practice we have found that impeachment does not work, that unfit judges stay on the bench in spite of it, and indeed because of the fact that impeachment is the only remedy that can be used against them. Where such is the actual fact it is idle to discuss the theory of the case. Impeachment as a remedy for the ills of which the people justly complain is a complete failure. A quicker, a more summary, remedy is needed; some remedy at least as summary and as drastic as that embodied in the Massachusetts constitution. And whenever it be found in actual practice that such remedy does not give the needed results, I would unhesitatingly adopt the recall.

But there is one kind of recall in which I very earnestly believe, and the immediate adoption of which I urge. There are sound reasons for being cautious about the recall of a good judge who has rendered an unwise and improper decision. Every public servant, no matter how valuable—and not omitting Washington or Lincoln or Marshall—at times makes

mistakes. Therefore we should be cautious about recalling the judge, and we shall be cautious about interfering in any way with the judge in decisions which he makes in the ordinary course as between individuals. But when a judge decides a constitutional question, when he decides what the people as a whole can or cannot do, the people should have the right to recall that decision if they think it wrong. We should hold the judiciary in all respect; but it is both absurd and degrading to make a fetish of a judge or of any one else. . . .

When the supreme court of the State declares a given statute unconstitutional, because in conflict with the State or the National Constitution, its opinion should be subject to revision by the people themselves. Such an opinion ought always to be treated with great respect by the people, and unquestionably in the majority of cases would be accepted and followed by them. But actual experience has shown the vital need of the people reserving to themselves the right to pass upon such opinion. If any considerable number of the people feel that the decision is in defiance of justice, they should be given the right by petition to bring before the voters at some subsequent election, special or otherwise, as might be decided, and after the fullest opportunity for deliberation and debate, the question whether or not the judges' interpretation of the Constitution is to be sustained. If it is sustained, well and good. If not, then the popular verdict is to be accepted as final, the decision is to be treated as reversed, and the construction of the Constitution definitely decided—subject only to action by the Supreme Court of the United States.

## 7

With the dynamic Roosevelt on their side, the Republican insurgents hesitated no longer. Meeting in a separate convention, they organized the Progressive party, with the bull moose as their emblem and Theodore Roose-

[6] *Senate Documents,* 62nd Cong., 2nd Sess., Doc. No. 348, pp. 14-15.

velt as their standard-bearer. The Progressive platform of 1912 symbolized the liberalism of the era:[7]

The conscience of the people, in a time of grave national problems, has called into being a new party, born of the nation's sense of justice. We of the Progressive party here dedicate ourselves to the fulfillment of the duty laid upon us by our fathers to maintain the government of the people, by the people and for the people whose foundations they laid. . . .

### The Old Parties

Political parties exist to secure responsible government and to execute the will of the people.

From these great tasks both of the old parties have turned aside. Instead of instruments to promote the general welfare, they have become the tools of corrupt interests which use them impartially to serve their selfish purposes. Behind the ostensible government sits enthroned an invisible government owing no allegiance and acknowledging no responsibility to the people.

To destroy this invisible government, to dissolve the unholy alliance between corrupt business and corrupt politics is the first task of the statesmanship of the day.

The deliberate betrayal of its trust by the Republican party, the fatal incapacity of the Democratic party to deal with the new issues of the new time, have compelled the people to forge a new instrument of government through which to give effect to their will in laws and institutions.

Unhampered by tradition, uncorrupted by power, undismayed by the magnitude of the task, the new party offers itself as the instrument of the people to sweep away old abuses, to build a new and nobler commonwealth. . . .

---

[7] Kirk Porter (ed.), *National Party Platforms* (New York, 1924), pp. 334-349.

### The Rule of the People

In particular, the party declares for direct primaries for the nomination of State and National officers, for nation-wide preferential primaries for candidates for the presidency; for the direct election of United States Senators by the people; and we urge on the States the policy of the short ballot, with responsibility to the people secured by the initiative, referendum and recall. . . .

### Equal Suffrage

The Progressive party, believing that no people can justly claim to be a true democracy which denies political rights on account of sex, pledges itself to the task of securing equal suffrage to men and women alike.

### Corrupt Practices

We pledge our party to legislation that will compel strict limitation of all campaign contributions and expenditures, and detailed publicity of both before as well as after primaries and elections.

### Publicity and Public Service

We pledge our party to legislation compelling the registration of lobbyists; publicity of committee hearings except on foreign affairs, and recording of all votes in committee; and forbidding federal appointees from holding office in State or National political organizations, or taking part as officers or delegates in political conventions for the nomination of elective State or National officials.

### The Courts

The Progressive party demands such restriction of the power of the courts as shall leave to the people the ultimate authority to determine fundamental questions of social welfare and public policy. To secure this end, it pledges itself to provide:

1. That when an Act, passed under the police power of the State, is held uncon-

stitutional under the State Constitution, by the courts, the people, after an ample interval for deliberation, shall have an opportunity to vote on the question whether they desire the Act to become law, notwithstanding such decision.

2. That every decision of the highest appellate court of a State declaring an Act of the Legislature unconstitutional on the ground of its violation of the Federal Constitution shall be subject to the same review by the Supreme Court of the United States as is now accorded to decisions sustaining such legislation. . . .

### Administration of Justice

We believe that the issuance of injunctions in cases arising out of labor disputes should be prohibited when such injunctions would not apply when no labor disputes existed.

We believe also that a person cited for contempt in labor disputes, except when such contempt was committed in the actual presence of the court or so near thereto as to interfere with the proper administration of justice, should have a right to trial by jury.

### Social and Industrial Justice

The supreme duty of the Nation is the conservation of human resources through an enlightened measure of social and industrial justice. We pledge ourselves to work unceasingly in State and Nation for:

Effective legislation looking to the prevention of industrial accidents, occupational diseases, overwork, involuntary unemployment, and other injurious effects incident to modern industry;

The fixing of minimum safety and health standards for the various occupations, and the exercise of the public authority of State and Nation, including the Federal Control over interstate commerce, and the taxing power, to maintain such standards;

The prohibition of child labor;

Minimum wage standards for working women, to provide a "living wage" in all industrial occupations;

The general prohibition of night work for women and the establishment of an eight hour day for women and young persons;

One day's rest in seven for all wage workers;

The eight hour day in continuous twenty-four-hour industries;

The abolition of the convict contract labor system; substituting a system of prison production for governmental consumption only; and the application of prisoners' earnings to the support of their dependent families;

Publicity as to wages, hours and conditions of labor; full reports upon industrial accidents and diseases, and the opening to public inspection of all tallies, weights, measures and check systems on labor products;

Standards of compensation for death by industrial accident and injury and trade disease which will transfer the burden of lost earnings from the families of working people to the industry, and thus to the community;

The protection of home life against the hazards of sickness, irregular employment and old age through the adoption of a system of social insurance adapted to American use;

The development of the creative labor power of America by lifting the last load of illiteracy from American youth and establishing continuation schools for industrial education under public control and encouraging agricultural education and demonstration in rural schools;

The establishment of industrial research laboratories to put the methods and discoveries of science at the service of American producers;

We favor the organization of the workers, men and women, as a means of protecting their interests and of promoting their progress. . . .

## Currency

The issue of currency is fundamentally a Government function and the system should have as basic principles soundness and elasticity. The control should be lodged with the Government and should be protected from domination or manipulation by Wall Street or any special interests.

We are opposed to the so-called Aldrich currency bill, because its provisions would place our currency and credit system in private hands, not subject to effective public control. . . .

## Conservation

We believe that the remaining forests, coal and oil lands, water powers and other natural resources still in State or National control (except agricultural lands) are more likely to be wisely conserved and utilized for the general welfare if held in the public hands.

In order that consumers and producers, managers and workmen, now and hereafter, need not pay toll to private monopolies of power and raw material, we demand that such resources shall be retained by the State or Nation, and opened to immediate use under laws which will encourage development and make to the people a moderate return for benefits conferred.

## 8

The Republicans' quarrel was the Democrats' opportunity. Sensing the strong current of liberalism in American thought, they realized that they could win the election by choosing a candidate who would attract not only Democrats but Republicans unwilling to squander their votes on a divided party. Their happy choice was Woodrow Wilson, whose record as a reforming governor of New Jersey attested to his progressivism, as did such preconvention speeches as that delivered in Richmond, Virginia, on February 1, 1912:[8]

[8] *Congressional Record,* 62nd Cong., 2nd Sess., pp. 3919-3922.

I was trying to analyze the other day what a Republican is. (Laughter.) I do not want to say anything about that great body of my fellow-countrymen in various parts of America who have formed the bad habit of voting the Republican ticket. They are not the men I am talking about, but the Republican leaders, the men who establish the ideals and policies of that party, how would you describe them? Why, I would say that they are men who actually believe that the only men whose advice it is safe to take with regard to the happiness and prosperity of America are the men who have the biggest material stake in the enterprises of America. They believe, therefore, that America ought to be governed by trustees—(applause)—and that those trustees are the managers of the oldest and greatest "vested interests" of the country. That is a workable theory, that is a theory that has obtained time out of mind. It happens, though these gentlemen have forgotten it, that America was established to get rid of it, but, having forgotten that, reading only the older books, I dare say, reading back of the birth of America, they say that there are only a few men with grasp enough of affairs and knowledge enough of what are the bases of prosperity to run a big, complicated government like this.

Now, as a Democrat—(applause)—I define myself by absolutely protesting against that view of public affairs. I will not live under trustees if I can help it. (Applause.) No group of men less than the majority has a right to tell how I have got to live in America. I will submit to the majority, because I have been trained to do it, though I may have my private opinion even of the majority; but, being a dyed-in-the-wool Democrat, I am proud to submit my judgment to that majority of my fellow-citizens.

I know that there are some gum-shoe politicians in both camps who do not agree with that theory at all. They say, "You need not say much about it out loud, but we have got to run these people; this enterprise of free government has to be personally conducted"—(applause)—"that the people want this or that we do not deny, but they do not know what is good for them."

So there are two theories of trusteeship, a trusteeship of the big interests and a trusteeship of the machine. I do not see my way to subscribe to either kind of trusteeship. Not that I am an insurgent, because I believe in organization; I believe that party success is impossible without organization; but I make this distinction between organization and the machine—organization is a systematic coöperation of men for a common purpose, while the machine is a systematic coöperation of men for a private purpose. (Great applause.) I know what I am talking about, because we have a perfect specimen in New Jersey.

Now I know what supports the machine, because I have seen them eat out of a spoon. It is a golden spoon, and I have seen the nurse that fed them, and I have seen that nurse absolutely impartial as between the Republican machine and the Democratic machine—(laughter and applause)—and the price of the food, the price of the nutrition, is that the machine will be good, that it will see that nothing is done that will hurt the nurse, that nothing is done which will interfere with the private understanding that is established in the nursery.

## 9

The Democrats chose wisely. Trained in governmental theory during his twelve years as professor of political science at Princeton University, in administration during his career as president of that institution, and in politics during his two years as governor of New Jersey, Woodrow Wilson was equipped to launch one of the most stirring administrations in history. His sincere and thoughtful liberalism was apparent in both his actions and his numerous writings. His basic philosophy, expressed in his important book, *The*

*New Freedom* (1913), heartened Americans who believed in true democracy:[9]

. . . one of the interesting things that Mr. Jefferson said in those early days of simplicity which marked the beginnings of our government was that the best government consisted in as little governing as possible. And there is still a sense in which that is true. It is still intolerable for the government to interfere with our individual activities except where it is necessary to interfere with them in order to free them. But I feel confident that if Jefferson were living in our day he would see what we see: that the individual is caught in a great confused nexus of all sorts of complicated circumstances, and that to let him alone is to leave him helpless as against the obstacles with which he has to contend; and that, therefore, law in our day must come to the assistance of the individual. It must come to his assistance to see that he gets fair play; that is all, but that is much. Without the watchful interference, the resolute interference, of the government, there can be no fair play between individuals and such powerful institutions as the trusts. Freedom to-day is something more than being let alone. The program of a government of freedom must in these days be positive, not negative merely.

Well, then, in this new sense and meaning of it, are we preserving freedom in this land of ours, the hope of all the earth? Have we, inheritors of this continent and of the ideals to which the fathers consecrated it,—have we maintained them, realizing them, as each generation must, anew? Are we, in the consciousness that the life of man is pledged to higher levels here than elsewhere, striving still to bear aloft the standards of liberty and hope, or, disillusioned and defeated, are we feeling the disgrace of having had a free field in

[9] Woodrow Wilson, *The New Freedom* (New York, 1913), pp. 283-294. Reprinted by permission of Doubleday and Company, Inc., publishers.

which to do new things and of not having done them?

The answer must be, I am sure, that we have been in a fair way of failure,—tragic failure. And we stand in danger of utter failure yet except we fulfil speedily the determination we have reached, to deal with the new and subtle tyrannies according to their deserts. Don't deceive yourselves for a moment as to the power of the great interests which now dominate our development. They are so great that it is almost an open question whether the government of the United States can dominate them or not. Go one step further, make their organized power permanent, and it may be too late to turn back. The roads diverge at the point where we stand. They stretch their vistas out to regions where they are very far separated from one another; at the end of one is the old tiresome scene of government tied up with special interests; and at the other shines the liberating light of individual initiative, of individual liberty, of individual freedom, the light of untrammeled enterprise. I believe that that light shines out of the heavens itself that God has created. I believe in human liberty as I believe in the wine of life. There is no salvation for men in the pitiful condescensions of industrial masters. Guardians have no place in a land of freemen. Prosperity guaranteed by trustees has no prospect of endurance. Monopoly means the atrophy of enterprise. If monopoly persists, monopoly will always sit at the helm of the government. I do not expect to see monopoly restrain itself. If there are men in this country big enough to own the government of the United States, they are going to own it; what we have to determine now is whether we are big enough, whether we are men enough, whether we are free enough, to take possession again of the government. . . .

So we must put heart into the people by taking the heartlessness out of politics, business, and industry. We have got to make politics a thing in which an honest man can take his part with satisfaction because he knows that his opinion will count as much as the next man's, and that the boss and the interests have been dethroned. Business we have got to untrammel, abolishing tariff favors, and railroad discrimination, and credit denials, and all forms of unjust handicaps against the little man. Industry we have got to humanize, —not through the trusts,—but through the direct action of law guaranteeing protection against dangers and compensation for injuries, guaranteeing sanitary conditions, proper hours, the right to organize, and all the other things which the conscience of the country demands as the workingman's right. We have got to cheer and inspirit our people with the sure prospects of social justice and due reward, with the vision of the open gates of opportunity for all. We have got to set the energy and the initiative of this great people absolutely free, so that the future of America will be greater than the past, so that the pride of America will grow with achievement, so that America will know as she advances from generation to generation that each brood of her sons is greater and more enlightened than that which preceded it, know that she is fulfilling the promise that she has made to mankind.

She is the vision of some of us who now come to assist in its realization. For we Democrats would not have endured this long burden of exile if we had not seen a vision. We could have traded; we could have got into the game; we could have surrendered and made terms; we could have played the role of patrons to the men who wanted to dominate the interests of the country,—and here and there gentlemen who pretended to be of us did make those arrangements. They couldn't stand privation. You never can stand it unless you have within you some imperishable food upon which to sustain life and courage, the food of those visions of the spirit where a table is set before us laden with palatable fruits, the fruits of hope, the fruits of imagination, those invisible things of the spirit which are the only things upon which we can sustain ourselves through this weary world without fainting. We have carried in our minds, after you had thought you had obscured and blurred them, the ideals of those men who first set their foot upon America, those little bands who came to make a foothold in the wilderness, because the great teeming nations that they had left behind them had forgotten what human liberty was, liberty of thought, liberty of religion, liberty of residence, liberty of action.

Since their day the meaning of liberty has deepened. But it has not ceased to be a fundamental demand of the human spirit, a fundamental necessity for the life of the soul. And the day is at hand when it shall be realized on this consecrated soil,—a New Freedom,—a Liberty widened and deepened to match the broadened life of man in modern America, restoring to him in every truth the control of his government, throwing wide all gates of lawful enterprise, unfettering his energies, and warming the generous impulses of his heart,—a process of release, emancipation, and inspiration, full of a breath of life as sweet and wholesome as the airs that filled the sails of the caravels of Columbus and gave the promise and boast of magnificent Opportunity in which America *dare not fail.*

## THE PROGRESSIVISM OF THE DEMOCRATS

## 10

When Wilson entered the White House, three staggering legislative problems demanded solution. He must revise the nation's tariff policy, readjust the currency system to the needs of the day, and check the dangerous trend toward industrial monopoly that threatened consumer and small businessman alike. Particularly pressing was the tariff question. Taft as president had honestly tried to live up to his campaign promises of

extensive revision, but the special session of Congress that he called for this purpose succumbed so completely to pressure from lobbyists that the Payne-Aldrich Tariff of 1909 was regarded as one of the worst in history. Public sentiment against the tariff reached its height in the fall of 1909 when Taft, on a speaking tour that carried him to Winona, Minnesota, declared it "the best tariff bill that the Republican party ever passed":[10]

Now . . . in the campaign, I did not promise that everything should go downward. What I promised was, that there should be many decreases, and that in some few things increases would be found to be necessary; but that on the whole I conceived that the change of conditions would make the revision necessarily downward—and that, I contend, under the showing which I have made, has been the result of the Payne bill. I did not agree, nor did the Republican party agree, that we would reduce rates to such a point as to reduce prices by the introduction of foreign competition. That is what the free traders desire. That is what the revenue tariff reformers desire; but that is not what the Republican platform promised, and it is not what the Republican party wished to bring about. To repeat the statement with which I opened this speech, the proposition of the Republican party was to reduce rates so as to maintain a difference between the cost of production abroad and the cost of production here, insuring a reasonable profit to the manufacturer on all articles produced in this country. . . .

With respect to the wool schedule, I agree that it probably represents considerably more than the difference between the cost of production abroad and the cost of production here. The difficulty about the woolen schedule is that there were two contending factions early in the history of Republican tariffs, to wit, wool-

[10] *Senate Documents,* 61st Cong., 2nd Sess., Doc. No. 164, pp. 7-12.

growers and the woolen manufacturers, and that finally, many years ago, they settled on a basis by which wool in the grease should have 11 cents a pound, and by which allowance should be made for the shrinkage of the washed wool in the differential upon woolen manufactures. The percentage of duty was very heavy—quite beyond the difference in the cost of production, which was not then regarded as a necessary or proper limitation upon protective duties. . . .

On the whole, however, I am bound to say that I think the Payne tariff bill is the best tariff bill that the Republican party ever passed. . . .

If the country desires free trade, and the country desires a revenue tariff and wishes the manufacturers all over the country to go out of business, and to have cheaper prices at the expense of the sacrifice of many of our manufacturing interests, then it ought to say so and ought to put the Democratic party in power if it thinks that party can be trusted to carry out any affirmative policy in favor of a revenue tariff. Certainly in the discussions in the Senate there was no great manifestation on the part of our Democratic friends in favor of reducing rates on necessities. They voted to maintain the tariff rates on everything that came from their particular sections. If we are to have free trade, certainly it can not be had through the maintenance of Republican majorities in the Senate and House and a Republican administration.

## 11

Sharing popular dislike of the Payne-Aldrich Tariff, Wilson, upon assuming the presidency, promptly called Congress into special session to revise the measure. That Wilson's training in politics equipped him for the tasks ahead was demonstrated when the congressmen assembled. He knew that leadership was needed to prod legislators into action and to make battles in Congress an honest expression of avowed party principles. Hence the president must become a spokesman for the majority. This was in his mind when Wilson

abandoned a custom, dating back to the days of Thomas Jefferson, of sending his message; instead, he appeared before the lawmakers to read it in person. His first address dramatized the need for genuine reform:[11]

. . . I have called the Congress together in extraordinary session because a duty was laid upon the party now in power at the recent elections which it ought to perform promptly, in order that the burden carried by the people under existing law may be lightened as soon as possible, and in order, also, that the business interests of the country may not be kept too long in suspense as to what the fiscal changes are to be to which they will be required to adjust themselves. It is clear to the whole country that the tariff duties must be altered. They must be changed to meet the radical alteration in the conditions of our economic life which the country has witnessed within the last generation. While the whole face and method of our industrial and commercial life were being changed beyond recognition the tariff schedules have remained what they were before the change began, or have moved in the direction they were given when no large circumstance of our industrial development was what it is to-day. Our task is to square them with the actual facts. The sooner that is done the sooner we shall escape from suffering from the facts and the sooner our men of business will be free to thrive by the law of nature— the nature of free business—instead of by the law of legislation and artificial arrangement.

We have seen tariff legislation wander very far afield in our day—very far indeed from the field in which our prosperity might have had a normal growth and stimulation. No one who looks the facts squarely in the face or knows anything that lies beneath the surface of action can fail to perceive the principles upon which recent tariff legislation has been based. We

[11] *Congressional Record,* 63rd Cong., 1st Sess., p. 130.

long ago passed beyond the modest notion of "protecting" the industries of the country and moved boldly forward to the idea that they were entitled to the direct patronage of the Government. For a long time—a time so long that the men now active in public policy hardly remember the conditions that preceded it—we have sought in our tariff schedules to give each group of manufacturers or producers what they themselves thought that they needed in order to maintain a practically exclusive market as against the rest of the world. Consciously or unconsciously, we have built up a set of privileges and exemptions from competition behind which it was easy by any, even the crudest, forms of combination to organize monopoly; until at last nothing is normal, nothing is obliged to stand the tests of efficiency and economy, in our world of big business, but everything thrives by concerted arrangement. Only new principles of action will save us from a final hard crystallization of monopoly and a complete loss of the influences that quicken enterprise and keep independent energy alive.

It is plain what those principles must be. We must abolish everything that bears even the semblance of privilege or of any kind of artificial advantage, and put our business men and producers under the stimulation of a constant necessity to be efficient, economical, and enterprising, masters of competitive supremacy, better workers and merchants than any in the world. Aside from the duties laid upon articles which we do not, and probably can not, produce, therefore, and the duties laid upon luxuries and merely for the sake of the revenues they yield, the object of the tariff duties henceforth laid must be effective competition, the whetting of American wits by contest with the wits of the rest of the world.

## 12

Undaunted by Wilson's demand for tariff revision, lobbyists swarmed over Washington as soon as Congress assembled, confident that their pressure on individual congressmen would be as effective as in the past. The President sized up the situation at once. Spokesmen for manufacturers, he saw, were organized and in a better position to make effective demands on legislators than could the inarticulate general public that wanted a "competitive tariff." As the champion of the people he must act. Using the presidential weapon of publicity, he issued a statement to the press on May 26, 1913, that denounced the tariff lobby and mobilized opinion behind his demand for reform:[12]

I think that the public ought to know the extraordinary exertions being made by the lobby in Washington to gain recognition for certain alterations of the Tariff bill. Washington has seldom seen so numerous, so industrious or so insidious a lobby. The newspapers are being filled with paid advertisements calculated to mislead the judgment of public men not only, but also the public opinion of the country itself. There is every evidence that money without limit is being spent to sustain this lobby and to create an appearance of a pressure of opinion antagonistic to some of the chief items of the Tariff bill.

It is of serious interest to the country that the people at large should have no lobby and be voiceless in these matters, while great bodies of astute men seek to create an artificial opinion and to overcome the interests of the public for their private profit. It is thoroughly worth the while of the people of this country to take knowledge of this matter. Only public opinion can check and destroy it.

The Government in all its branches ought to be relieved from this intolerable burden and this constant interruption to the calm progress of debate. I know that in this I am speaking for the members of the two Houses who would rejoice as much as I would to be released from this unbearable situation.

---

[12] *The New York Times*, May 27, 1913. Quoted with permission of *The New York Times*.

## 13

Wilson's dramatic appeal for popular support stiffened the congressional backbone and allowed the enactment of the moderate Underwood Tariff of 1913. Equally successful was his drive for more modern revenue and currency laws. Attached to the tariff act was the first income tax under the new amendment to the Constitution; and before the end of 1913 Congress went on to create the Federal Reserve System, which freed the nation's monetary system from complete dependence on the gold standard. As dear to Wilson's heart was the attack on the trusts. Insisting that "private monopoly is indefensible and intolerable," he favored new legislation to plug the loopholes that corporation lawyers had found in the Sherman Antitrust Act. As early as 1910, in an address to the American Bar Association, he advanced the challenging thesis that monopolists and corporate wrongdoers should be made personally liable for their harmful actions:[13]

We have witnessed in modern business the submergence of the individual within the organization, and yet the increase to an extraordinary degree of the power of the individual—of the individual who happens to control the organization. Most men are individuals no longer so far as their business, its activities or its moralities, is concerned. They are not units, but fractions; with their individuality and independence of choice in matters of business they have lost also their individual choice within the field of morals. They must do what they are told to do, or lose their connection with modern affairs. They are not at liberty to ask whether what they are told to do is right or wrong. They cannot get at the men who ordered it—have no access to them. They have no voice of counsel or of protest. They are mere cogs in a machine which has men for its parts. And yet there are men here and there with whom the whole choice

lies. There are men who control the machine as a whole and the men who compose it. There are men who use it with an imperial freedom of design, whose power and whose individuality overtop whole communities. There is more individual power than ever, but those who exercise it are few and formidable, and the mass of men are mere pawns in the game. . . .

Corporations do not do wrong. Individuals do wrong, the individuals who direct and use them for selfish and illegitimate purposes, to the injury of society and the serious curtailment of private rights. Guilt, as has been very truly said, is always personal. You cannot punish corporations. Fines fall upon the wrong persons; more heavily upon the innocent than upon the guilty; as much upon those who knew nothing whatever of the transactions for which the fine is imposed as upon those who originated and carried them through—upon the stockholders and the customers rather than upon the men who direct the policy of the business. . . .

I regard the corporation as indispensable to modern business enterprise. I am not jealous of its size or might, if you will but abandon at the right points the fatuous, antiquated, and quite unnecessary fiction which treats it as a legal person; if you will but cease to deal with it by means of your law as if it were a single individual not only, but also—what every child may perceive it is not—a responsible individual. . . .

The corporation now overshadows partnerships altogether. Still more does it overshadow all individuals engaged in business on their own capital and separate responsibility. It is an arrangement by which hundreds of thousands of men who would in days gone by have set up in business for themselves put their money into a single huge accumulation and place the entire direction of its employment in the hands of men they have never seen, with whom they never confer. These

---

[13] *The Public Papers of Woodrow Wilson, College and State* (Harper & Brothers, New York, 1925), II, 253-261, 266-267. Quotation by permission of Mrs. Woodrow (Edith Bolling) Wilson, owner of the copyright.

men, these quite autocratic managers, are thereby made, as it were, multiple individuals. In them are concentrated the resources, the choices, the opportunities, in brief, the power of thousands. They could never of themselves, of their own effort and sagacity, have accumulated the vast capital they employ, and employ as if it were their own; and yet they have not the full legal responsibilities of those who supplied them with it. . . .

Society cannot afford to have individuals wield the power of thousands without personal responsibility. It cannot afford to let its strongest men be the only men who are inaccessible to the law. Modern democratic society, in particular, cannot afford to constitute its economic undertakings upon the monarchical or aristocratic principle and adopt the fiction that the kings and great men thus set up can do no wrong which will make them personally amenable to the law which restrains smaller men: that their kingdoms, not themselves, must suffer for their blindness, their follies, and their transgressions of right.

It does not redeem the situation that these kings and chiefs of industry are not chosen upon the hereditary principle (sometimes, alas! they are) but are men who have risen by their own capacity, sometimes from utter obscurity, with the freedom of self-assertion which should characterize a free society. Their power is none the less arbitrary and irresponsible when obtained. That a peasant may become king does not render the kingdom democratic. . . .

. . . Money and men must be massed in order to do the things that must be done for the support and facilitation of modern life. Whether energy or economy be your standard, it is plain enough that we cannot go back to the old competitive system under which individuals were the competitors. . . . We can have corporations, can retain them in unimpaired efficiency, without depriving law of its an-

cient searching efficacy, its inexorable mandate that men, not societies, must suffer for wrongs done. The major premise of all law is moral responsibility, the moral responsibility of individuals for their acts and conspiracies; and no other foundation can any man lay upon which a stable fabric of equitable justice can be reared.

I call your attention to the fact, therefore, that it is perfectly possible to have corporations . . . and yet dispense with a large part of the quite outworn and now in many respects deeply demoralizing fiction that a corporation is an indivisible person. . . .

The managers of corporations themselves always know the men who originated the acts charged against them as done in contravention of the law; is there no means by which their names may be disclosed to the officers of justice? Every act, every policy in the conduct of the affairs of a corporation originates with some particular officer, committee, or board. The officer, the committee, the board which orders an act or originates a policy contrary to the law of the land or intended to neutralize or contravene it is an insurgent against society; the man or men who originate any such act or policy should be punished, and they alone. It is not necessary that the corporation should be broken up. It is not fair that the stockholders should be mulcted in damages. If there are damages to be paid they should be paid out of the private means of the persons who are really guilty. An analysis of the guilt is perfectly feasible. It is the duty of lawyers, of all lawyers, to assist the makers of law and the reformers of abuses by pointing out the best and most effective way to make it. . . .

. . . We have allowed ourselves to be ridiculously limited and embarrassed by the theory that a corporation is an indivisible person not only, but that nobody outside of it, no matter how intimate his use and control, may be brought into the suit by any genteel lawyer bred in the orthodox schools of law. A corporation is merely a convenient instrument of business and we may regulate its use as we please, and those who use it. Here is merely an artificial, a fictitious person, whom God did not make or endow, which we ourselves have made with our own hands and can alter as we will. I see no law of nature in our way, but only some laws of evidence and of corporate theory which we have outgrown.

You will say that in many instances it is not fair to pick out for punishment the particular officer who ordered a thing done, because he really had no freedom in the matter: that he is himself under orders, exercises no individual liberty of choice, is a dummy manipulated from without. I reply that society should permit no man to carry out orders which are against law and public policy, and that, if you will but put one or two conspicuous dummies in the penitentiary, there will be no more dummies for hire. . . .

. . . The indivisible unit of society is the individual. He is also the indigestible unit. He cannot be merged or put into combination without being lost to liberty, because lost to independence. Make of him a fraction instead of an integer, and you have broken his spirit, cut off the sources of his life. That is why I plead so earnestly for the individualization of responsibility within the corporation, for the establishment of the principle by law that a man has no more right to do wrong as a member of a corporation than as an individual. Establish that principle, cut away the undergrowth of law that has sprung up so rankly about the corporation and made of it an ambush and covert, and it will give every man the right to say No again, to refuse to do wrong, no matter who orders him to do it. . . .

## 14

There was ample opportunity for reform in the nation's corporate structure when Wilson entered the White House. Despite Roosevelt's big-stick waving and Taft's less spectacular trust busting, the trend toward monopoly in manufacturing, banking, and transportation had continued through the Progressive Era. This was demonstrated by a congressional subcommittee led by Arsene P. Pujo, which was authorized in February, 1912, to investigate the country's financial system. The Pujo Report, which was released just before the election of 1912, not only helped elect Wilson but strengthened the support that he needed for his attack on the trusts:[14]

### Section 2—Fact of Increasing Concentration Admitted

The resources of the banks and trust companies of the city of New York on 1911 were $5,121,245,175, which is 21.73 per cent of the total banking resources of the country as reported to the Comptroller of the Currency. This takes no account of the unknown resources of the great private banking houses whose affiliations to the New York financial institutions we are about to discuss.

That in recent years concentration of control of the banking resources and consequently of credit by the group to which we will refer has grown apace in the city of New York is defended by some witnesses and regretted by others, but acknowledged by all to be a fact.

As appears from statistics compiled by accountants for the committee, in 1911, of the total resources of the banks and trust companies in New York City, the 20 largest held 42.97 per cent; in 1906, the 20 largest held 38.24 per cent of the total; in 1901, 34.97 per cent.

### Section 3—Processes of Concentration

This increased concentration of control of money and credit has been effected principally as follows:

First, through consolidations of competitive or potentially competitive banks and trust companies, which consolidations

---

[14] *House Reports,* 62nd Cong., 3rd Sess., Doc. No. 1593, pp. 55-56, 86-90.

in turn have recently been brought under sympathetic management.

Second, through the same powerful interest becoming large stockholders in potentially competitive banks and trust companies. This is the simplest way of acquiring control, but since it requires the largest investment of capital, it is the least used, although the recent investments in that direction for that apparent purpose amount to tens of millions of dollars in present market values.

Third, through the confederation of potentially competitive banks and trust companies by means of the system of interlocking directorates.

Fourth, through the influence which the more powerful banking houses, banks, and trust companies have secured in the management of insurance companies, railroads, producing and trading corporations, and public utility corporations, by means of stockholdings, voting trusts, fiscal agency contracts, or representation upon their boards of directors, or through supplying the money requirements of railway, industrial, and public utilities corporations and thereby being enabled to participate in the determination of their financial and business policies.

Fifth, through partnership or joint account arrangements between a few of the leading banking houses, banks, and trust companies in the purchase of security issues of the great interstate corporations, accompanied by understandings of recent growth—sometimes called "banking ethics"—which have had the effect of effectually destroying competition between such banking houses, banks, and trust companies in the struggle for business or in the purchase and sale of large issues of such securities.

## Section 4—Agents of Concentration

It is a fair deduction from the testimony that the most active agents in forwarding and bringing about the concentration of control of money and credit through one

or another of the processes above described have been and are—

J. P. Morgan & Co.
First National Bank of New York
National City Bank of New York
Lee, Higginson & Co., of Boston and
  New York
Kidder, Peabody & Co., of Boston and
  New York
Kuhn, Loeb & Co.

. . . . . . .

*Combined Power of Morgan & Co., the First National, and National City Banks.*— In earlier pages of the report the power of these three great banks was separately set forth. It is now appropriate to consider their combined power as one group.

First, as regards banking resources:

The resources of Morgan & Co. are unknown; its deposits are $163,000,000. The resources of the First National Bank are $150,000,000 and those of its appendage, the First Security Co., at a very low estimate, $35,000,000. The resources of the National City Bank are $274,000,000; those of its appendage, the National City Co., are unknown, though the capital of the latter is alone $10,000,000. Thus, leaving out of account the very considerable part which is unknown, the institutions composing this group have resources of upward of $632,000,000, aside from the vast individual resources of Messrs. Morgan, Baker, and Stillman.

Further, as heretofore shown, the members of this group, through stockholdings, voting trusts, interlocking directorates, and other relations, have become in some cases the absolutely dominant factor, in others the most important single factor, in the control of the following banks and trust companies in the city of New York:

| | | |
|---|---|---|
| (a) Bankers Trust Co., resources | $250,000,000 |
| (b) Guaranty Trust Co., resources | 232,000 000 |
| (c) Astor Trust Co., resources | 27,000,000 |
| (d) National Bank of Commerce, resources | 190,000,000 |
| (e) Liberty National Bank, resources | 29,000,000 |

(f) Chase National Bank,
resources         150,000,000
(g) Farmers Loan & Trust Co.,
resources         135,000,000
in all, 7, with total resources of    968,000,000
which, added to the known
resources of members of the
group themselves, makes     $1,600,000,000
as the aggregate of known
banking resources in the city
of New York under their control
or influence.

If there be added also the resources
of the Equitable Life Assurance
Society controlled through stock
ownership of J. P. Morgan      504,000,000
the amount becomes·      $2,104,000,000

. . . Third, as regards the greater producing and trading corporations.

(a) Amalgamated Copper Co.: One member of the group took part in the organization of the company, still has one leading director in common with it, and markets its securities.

(b) American Can Co.: Members of the group have two directors in common with this company.

(c) J. I. Case Threshing Machine Co.: The president of one member of the group is a voting trustee of this company and the group also has one representative in its directorate and markets its securities.

(d) William Cramp Ship & Engine Building Co.: Members of the group absolutely control this company through a voting trust.

(e) General Electric Co.: A member of the group was one of the organizers of the company, is a stockholder, and has always had two representatives in its directorate, and markets its securities.

(f) International Harvester Co.: A member of the group organized the company, named its directorate and the chairman of its finance committee, directed its management through a voting trust, is a stockholder, and markets its securities.

(g) Lackawanna Steel Co.: Members of the group have four directors in common with the company and, with associates, marketed its last issue of securities.

(h) Pullman Co.: The group has two representatives, Mr. Morgan and Mr. Baker, in the directorate of this company.

(i) United States Steel Corporation: A member of the group organized this company, named its directorate, and the chairman of its finance committee (which also has the powers of an executive committee) is its sole fiscal agent and a stockholder, and has always controlled its management. . . .

*Summary of Directorships Held by These Members of the Group.*— . . . [The Appendix] shows the combined directorships in the more important enterprises held by Morgan & Co., the First National Bank, the National City Bank, and the Bankers and Guaranty Trust Cos., which latter two, as previously shown, are absolutely controlled by Morgan & Co. through voting trusts. It appears there that firm members or directors of these institutions together hold:

One hundred and eighteen directorships in 34 banks and trust companies having total resources of $2,679,000,000 and total deposits of $1,983,000,000.

Thirty directorships in 10 insurance companies having total assets of $2,293,-000,000.

One hundred and five directorships in 32 transportation systems having a total capitalization of $11,784,000,000 and a total mileage (excluding express companies and steamship lines) of 150,200.

Sixty-three directorships in 24 producing and trading corporations having a total capitalization of $3,339,000,000.

Twenty-five directorships in 12 public utility corporations having a total capitalization of $2,150,000,000.

In all, 341 directorships in 112 corporations having aggregate resources or capitalization of $22,245,000,000.

The members of the firm of J. P. Morgan & Co. hold 72 directorships in 47 of the greater corporations: George F. Baker, chairman of the board, F. L. Hine, president, and George F. Baker, Jr., and C. D.

Norton, vice presidents, of the First National Bank of New York, hold 46 directorships in 37 of the greater corporations; and James Stillman, chairman of the board, Frank A. Vanderlip, president, and Samuel McRoberts, J. T. Talbert, W. A. Simonson, vice-presidents, of the National City Bank of New York, hold 32 directorships in 26 of the greater corporations; making in all for these members of the group 150 directorships in 110 of the greater corporations.

## 15

The Pujo Report revealed an intricate web of controls that allowed Wall Street financial interests to dominate the country's industries, banking, and transportation. Its impressive columns of figures, however, meant little to the average man in the street. Not until a number of popularizers translated its statistics into more understandable language did antitrust sentiment reach a boiling point. Of the many writers whose words brought the Pujo Report to life, none was more influential than Louis D. Brandeis, a brilliant young lawyer. His important book, *Other People's Money* (1914), set a high standard of accuracy and influence:[15]

The practice of interlocking directorates is the root of many evils. It offends laws human and divine. Applied to rival corporations, it tends to the suppression of competition and to violation of the Sherman law. Applied to corporations which deal with each other, it tends to disloyalty and to violation of the fundamental law that no man can serve two masters. In either event it tends to inefficiency; for it removes incentive and destroys soundness of judgment. It is undemocratic, for it rejects the platform: "A fair field and no favors,"—substituting the pull of privilege for the push of manhood. It is the most potent instrument of the Money Trust. Break the control so exercised by the investment bankers over railroads, public-

service and industrial corporations, over banks, life insurance and trust companies, and a long step will have been taken toward attainment of the New Freedom.

The term "Interlocking directorates" is here used in a broad sense as including all intertwined conflicting interests, whatever the form, and by whatever device effected. The objection extends alike to contracts of a corporation whether with one of its directors individually, or with a firm of which he is a member, or with another corporation in which he is interested as an officer or director or stockholder. The objection extends likewise to men holding the inconsistent position of director in two potentially competing corporations, even if those corporations do not actually deal with each other.

A single example will illustrate the vicious circle of control—the endless chain —through which our financial oligarchy now operates:

J. P. Morgan (or a partner), a director of the New York, New Haven & Hartford Railroad, causes that company to sell to J. P. Morgan & Co. an issue of bonds. J. P. Morgan & Co. borrow the money with which to pay for the bonds from the Guaranty Trust Company, of which Mr. Morgan (or a partner) is a director. J. P. Morgan & Co. sell the bonds to the Penn Mutual Life Insurance Company, of which Mr. Morgan (or a partner) is a director. The New Haven spends the proceeds of the bonds in purchasing steel rails from the United States Steel Corporation, of which Mr. Morgan (or a partner) is a director. The United States Steel Corporation spends the proceeds of the rails in purchasing electrical supplies from the General Electric Company, of which Mr. Morgan (or a partner) is a director. The General Electric sells supplies to the Western Union Telegraph Company, a subsidiary of the American Telephone and Telegraph Company; and in both Mr. Morgan (or a partner) is a director. The Telegraph Company has an exclusive wire

---

[15] Louis D. Brandeis, *Other People's Money* (New York, 1914), pp. 51-54. Reprinted by permission of Susan Brandeis Gilbert.

contract with the Reading, of which Mr. Morgan (or a partner) is a director. The Reading buys its passenger cars from the Pullman Company, of which Mr. Morgan (or a partner) is a director. The Pullman Company buys (for local use) locomotives from the Baldwin Locomotive Company, of which Mr. Morgan (or a partner) is a director. The Reading, the General Electric, the Steel Corporation and the New Haven, like the Pullman, buy locomotives from the Baldwin Company. The Steel Corporation, the Telephone Company, the New Haven, the Reading, the Pullman and the Baldwin Companies, like the Western Union, buy electrical supplies from the General Electric. The Baldwin, the Pullman, the Reading, the Telephone, the Telegraph and the General Electric companies, like the New Haven, buy steel products from the Steel Corporation. Each and every one of the companies last named markets its securities through J. P. Morgan & Co.; each deposits its funds with J. P. Morgan & Co.; and with these funds of each, the firm enters upon further operations.

## 16

The Pujo Report and its popularizers aroused such public indignation that Wilson realized the time was ripe for action. On January 20, 1914, he read a special message to Congress, urging enactment of laws that would stamp out harmful monopolies and outlaw corrupt business practices. Among other things he urged the congressmen to create a federal trade commission to serve as a watchdog against business marauders. Such a commission, he hoped, would not only kill monopoly at birth, but allow small businessmen to operate as successfully as big businessmen. The Federal Trade Commission Act was passed by Congress and approved by the President on September 26, 1914:[16]

That a commission is hereby created and established, to be known as the Federal Trade Commission (hereinafter re-

[16] *United States Statutes at Large*, XXXVIII, 717-721.

ferred to as the commission), which shall be composed of five commissioners, who shall be appointed by the President, by and with the advice and consent of the Senate. Not more than three of the commissioners shall be members of the same political party. The first commissioners appointed shall continue in office for terms of three, four, five, six, and seven years, respectively, from the date of the taking effect of this Act, the term of each to be designated by the President, but their successors shall be appointed for terms of seven years. . . .

SECTION 5. That unfair methods of competition in commerce are hereby declared unlawful.

The commission is hereby empowered and directed to prevent persons, partnerships, or corporations, except banks, and common carriers subject to the Acts to regulate commerce, from using unfair methods of competition in commerce.

Whenever the commission shall have reason to believe that any such person, partnership, or corporation has been or is using any unfair method of competition in commerce, . . . it shall issue and serve upon such person, partnership, or corporation a complaint stating its charges in that respect, and containing a notice of a hearing upon a day and at a place therein fixed at least thirty days after the service of said complaint. The person, partnership, or corporation so complained of shall have the right to appear at the place and time so fixed and show cause why an order should not be entered by the commission requiring such person, partnership, or corporation to cease and desist from the violation of the law so charged in said complaint. . . . If upon such hearing the commission shall be of the opinion that the method of competition in question is prohibited by this Act, it shall make a report in writing in which it shall state its findings as to the facts, and shall issue and cause to be served on such person, partnership, or corporation an order requiring such person, partnership, or corporation to cease and desist from using such method of competition. . . .

SEC. 6. That the commission shall also have power—

(a) To gather and compile information concerning and to investigate from time to time the organization, business, conduct, practices, and management of any corporation engaged in commerce, excepting banks and common carriers subject to the Act to regulate commerce, and its relation to other corporations and to individuals, associations, and partnerships.

(b) To require . . . corporations engaged in commerce . . . to file with the commission in such form as the commission may prescribe annual or special, or both annual and special, reports or answers in writing to specific questions, furnishing to the commission such information as it may require as to the organization, business, conduct, practices, management, and relation to other corporations, partnerships, and individuals of the respective corporations filing such reports. . . .

(c) Whenever a final decree has been entered against any defendant corporation in any suit brought by the United States to prevent and restrain any violation of the antitrust Acts, to make investigation . . . of the manner in which the decree has been or is being carried out, . . . it shall be its duty to make such investigation. It shall transmit to the Attorney General a report embodying its findings and recommendations as a result of any such investigation, and the report shall be made public in the discretion of the commission.

## 17

A more important measure growing out of Wilson's recommendations to Congress was the Clayton Antitrust Act, which was designed to strengthen business regulation by defining unfair practices. Although the lawmakers disappointed the President by refusing to outlaw holding companies or punish

violators as individuals, the measure went far toward satisfying those who wanted government regulation rather than the abolition of all trusts. The act was signed by the President on October 15, 1914:[17]

SECTION 2. That it shall be unlawful for any person engaged in commerce, in the course of such commerce, either directly or indirectly to discriminate in price between different purchasers of commodities which commodities are sold for use, consumption, or resale within . . . the jurisdiction of the United States, where the effect of such discrimination may be to substantially lessen competition or tend to create a monopoly in any line of commerce: . . .

SEC. 3. That it shall be unlawful for any person engaged in commerce, to lease or make a sale of goods, . . . or other commodities, . . . for use, consumption or resale within . . . the jurisdiction of the United States, or fix a price charged therefor, or discount from, or rebate upon, such price, on the condition, . . . that the lessee or purchaser thereof shall not use or deal in the goods, . . . or other commodities of a competitor or competitors of the lessor or seller, where the effect of such lease, sale, or contract for sale or such condition, agreement, or understanding may be to substantially lessen competition or tend to create a monopoly in any line of commerce. . . .

SEC. 6. That the labor of a human being is not a commodity or article of commerce. Nothing contained in the anti-trust laws shall be construed to forbid the existence and operation of labor, agricultural, or horticultural organizations, instituted for the purposes of mutual help, and not having capital stock or conducted for profit, or to forbid or restrain individual members of such organizations from lawfully carrying out the legitimate objects thereof; nor shall such organizations, or the members

---

[17] *Ibid.,* pp. 730-738.

thereof, be held or construed to be illegal combinations or conspiracies in restraint of trade, under the anti-trust laws.

SEC. 7. That no corporation engaged in commerce shall acquire, directly or indirectly, the whole or any part of the stock or other share capital of another corporation engaged also in commerce, where the effect of such acquisition may be to substantially lessen competition between the corporation whose stock is so acquired and the corporation making the acquisition. . . .

This section shall not apply to corporations purchasing such stock solely for investment and not using the same by voting or otherwise to bring about, or in attempting to bring about, the substantial lessening of competition. . . .

SEC. 8. That from and after two years from the date of the approval of this act no person shall at the same time be a director or other officer or employee of more than one bank, banking association or trust company, organized or operating under the laws of the United States, either of which has deposits, capital, surplus, and undivided profits aggregating more than $5,000,000; and no private banker or person who is a director in any bank or trust company, organized and operating under the laws of a State, having deposits, capital, surplus, and undivided profits aggregating more than $5,000,000, shall be eligible to be a director in any bank or banking association organized or operating under the laws of the United States. . . .

That from and after two years from the date of the approval of this Act no person at the same time shall be a director in any two or more corporations, any one of which has capital, surplus, and undivided profits aggregating more than $1,000,000, engaged in whole or in part in commerce, other than banks, banking associations, trust companies and common carriers . . . if such corporations are or shall have been theretofore, by virtue of their business and location of operation, competitors, so that

the elimination of competition by agreement between them would constitute a violation of . . . the anti-trust laws. . . .

SEC. 20. That no restraining order or injunction shall be granted by any court of the United States, or a judge or the judges thereof, in any case between an employer and employees or between employers and employees, or between employees, or between persons employed and persons seeking employment, involving, or growing out of, a dispute concerning terms or conditions of employment, unless necessary to prevent irreparable injury to property, or to a property right, of the party making the application, for which injury there is no adequate remedy at law, and such property or property right must be described with a particularity in the application, which must be in writing and sworn to by the applicant or by his agent or attorney.

And no such restraining order or injunction shall prohibit any person or persons, whether singly or in concert, from terminating any relation of employment, or from ceasing to perform any work or labor, or from recommending, advising, or persuading others by peaceful means so to do; or from attending at any place where any such person or persons may lawfully be, for the purpose of peacefully obtaining or communicating information, or from peacefully persuading any person to work or to abstain from working; or from ceasing to patronize or to employ any party to such dispute, or from recommending, advising, or persuading others by peaceful and lawful means so to do; or from paying or giving to, or withholding from, any person engaged in such dispute, any strike benefits or other moneys or things of value; or from peaceably assembling in a lawful manner, and for lawful purposes; or from doing any act or thing which might lawfully be done in the absence of such dispute by any party thereto; nor shall any of the acts specified in this paragraph be considered or held to be violations of any law of the United States.

Progressivism reached its high-water mark with the Federal Trade Commission Act and the Clayton Antitrust Act. Wilson's second administration was concerned less with domestic reform than with the war in Europe that broke out in 1914; yet progress continued, though more haltingly. As the nation awakened to the fact that the health of society in a machine civilization depended on the health of all its units, increasing attention was paid to the depressed elements in the social order. No story of the Progressive Era would be complete without an account of the remarkable gains achieved by workers and farmers during those fruitful years.

# THE ENIGMA OF LABOR AND AGRICULTURE

### 1900—1920

The progressivism of Theodore Roosevelt and Woodrow Wilson satisfied the millions of middle-class Americans who were only indirectly affected by industrial monopoly; they could placidly accept the assurances of heralds of the New Freedom who told them that the problems of living in a mechanized world had been solved. Those more immediately in touch with Big Business—the workers and farmers—were less sure. Roosevelt might tell them that his swinging big stick had smashed the trusts, but laborers barred from unions by "yellow-dog" contracts or forced from their jobs by employer agreements knew better. Wilson might proclaim the end of selfish practices in industry, but farmers who bought plows at inflated prices from a farm-machinery trust and sold their grain at deflated values to a monopolistic elevator operator were not convinced. Their valiant efforts to remedy their own situation, with little aid from the government, profoundly influenced the politics of the Progressive Era.

## CAPITAL AND LABOR

### 1

The plight of the worker was due partially to public indifference. For a generation, middle-class Americans had been told that union men were irresponsible anarchists, with a revolutionary pamphlet in one hand and a bomb in the other, who deserved neither sympathy nor understanding. Hence the rise of Progressivism aroused little popular support for Labor; instead, the usual reaction during periods of industrial conflict was "a plague on both your houses." This attitude was reflected in the writings of Herbert Croly, a leading social theorist. Croly was heart and soul a Progressive, but his *Promise of American Life* (1909) pleased neither selfish capitalists nor strong-arm labor leaders:[1]

. . . In spite of the flood of alien immigration the American laborer has been able to earn an almost constantly increasing wage, and he devoutly thinks that his unions have been the chief agency of his stronger economic position. He believes in unionism, consequently, as he believes in nothing else. He is, indeed, far more aggressively preoccupied with his class, as contrasted with his individual interests,

than are his employers. He has no respect for the traditional American individualism as applied to his own social and economic standing. Whenever he has had the power, he has suppressed competition as ruthlessly as have his employers. Every kind of contumelious reproach is heaped on the heads of the working men who dare to replace him when he strikes; and he does not scruple to use under such conditions weapons more convincing than the most opprobrious epithets. His own personality is merged in that of the union. No individual has any rights as opposed to the interests of the union. He fully believes, of course, in competition among employers, just as the employers are extremely enthusiastic over the individual liberty of the working man. But in his own trade he has no use for individuality of any kind. The union is to be composed of so many equal units who will work the same number of hours for the same wages, and no one of whom is to receive more pay even for more work. The unionist, that is, has come to depend upon his union for that material prosperity and advancement which, according to the American tradition, was to be the inevitable result of American political ideas and institutions. His attachment to his union has come to be the most important attachment of his

---

[1] From Herbert Croly, *The Promise of American Life*, pp. 127-128, 130-131, 385-388. Copyright 1909 by The Macmillan Company. Used by permission of The Macmillan Company, publishers.

life—more important in most cases than his attachment to the American ideal and to the national interest.

Some of the labor unions, like some of the corporations, have taken advantage of the infirmities of local and state governments to become arrogant and lawless. On the occasion of a great strike the strikers are often just as disorderly as they are permitted to be by the local police. When the police prevent them from resisting the employment of strike-breakers by force, they apparently believe that the political system of the country has been pressed into the service of their enemies; and they begin to wonder whether it will not be necessary for them to control such an inimical political organization. . . .

. . . The unionist leaders frequently offer verbal homage to the great American principle of equal rights, but what they really demand is the abandonment of that principle. What they want is an economic and political order which will discriminate in favor of union labor and against non-union labor; and they want it on the ground that the unions have proved to be the most effective agency on behalf of the economic and social amelioration of the wage-earner. The unions, that is, are helping most effectively to accomplish the task, traditionally attributed to the American democratic political system—the task of raising the general standard of living; and the unionists claim that they deserve on this ground recognition by the state and active encouragement. . . .

. . . The millionaire and the professional politician want above all things to be let alone, and to be allowed to enjoy the benefit of their conquests. But the labor organizations cannot exercise the power necessary in their opinion to their interests without certain radical changes in the political and economic order; and inasmuch as their power is likely to increase rather than diminish, the American people are confronted with the prospect of persistent, unscrupulous, and increasing agitation on behalf of an economic and political reorganization in favor of one class of citizens.

The large corporations and the unions occupy in certain respects a similar relation to the American political system. Their advocates both believe in associated action for themselves and in competition for their adversaries. They both demand governmental protection and recognition, but resent the notion of efficient governmental regulation. . . . Here, of course, the parallelism ends and the divergence begins. The corporations have apparently the best of the situation, because existing institutions are more favorable to the interests of the corporations than to the interests of the unionists; but on the other hand, the unions have the immense advantage of a great and increasing numerical strength. . . .

. . . The necessity for the formulation of some constructive policy in respect to labor is as patent as is that for the formulation of a similar policy in respect to corporate wealth. Any progress in the solution of the problem of the better distribution of wealth will, of course, have a profound indirect effect on the amelioration of the condition of labor; but such progress will be at best extremely slow, and in the meantime the labor problem presses for some immediate and direct action. As we have seen, American labor has not been content with the traditional politico-economic optimism. Like all aggressive men alive to their own interest, the laborer soon decided that what he really needed was not equal rights, but special opportunities. . . .

. . . The labor unions, consequently, like the big corporations, need legal recognition; and this legal recognition means in their case, also, substantial discrimination by the state in their favor. Of course, the unionist leaders appeal to public opinion with the usual American cant. According to their manifestoes they demand nothing but "fair play"; but the demand for fair play is as usual merely the hypocritical exterior of a demand for substantial favoritism. Just as there can be no effective competition between the huge corporation controlling machinery of production which cannot be duplicated and the small manufacturer in the same line, so there can be no effective competition between the individual laborer and the really efficient labor union. To recognize the labor union, and to incorporate it into the American legal system, is equivalent to the desertion by the state of the non-union laborer. It means that in the American political and economic system the organization of labor into unions should be preferred to its disorganized separation into competing individuals. . . .

An admission that the recognition of labor unions amounts to a substantial discrimination in their favor would do much to clear up the whole labor question. So far as we declare that the labor unions ought to be recognized, we declare that they ought to be favored; and so far as we declare that the labor union ought to be favored, we have made a great advance towards the organization of labor in the national interest. The labor unions deserve to be favored, because they are the most effective machinery which has as yet been forged for the economic and social amelioration of the laboring class. They have helped to raise the standard of living, to mitigate the rigors of competition among individual laborers, and in this way to secure for labor a larger share of the total industrial product. A democratic government has little or less reason to interfere on behalf of the non-union laborer than it has to interfere in favor of the small producer. As a type the non-union laborer is a species of industrial derelict. He is the laborer who has gone astray and who either from apathy, unintelligence, incompetence, or some immediately pressing need prefers his own individual interest to the joint interests of himself and his fellow-laborers. From the point of view

of a constructive national policy he does not deserve any special protection. . . .

. . . Our attitude towards the non-union laborer must be determined by our opinion of the results of his economic action. In the majority of discussions of the labor question the non-union laborer is figured as the independent working man who is asserting his right to labor when and how he prefers against the tyranny of the labor union. . . . The organization and policy of the contemporary labor union being what they are, cases will occasionally and even frequently occur in which the non-union laborer will represent the protest of an individual against injurious restrictions imposed by the union upon his opportunities and his work. But such cases are rare compared to the much larger number of instances in which the non-union laborer is to be considered as essentially the individual industrial derelict. . . . Men of this kind, either because of irresponsibility, unintelligence, or a total lack of social standards and training, are continually converting the competition of the labor market into a force which degrades the standard of living and prevents masses of their fellow-workmen from obtaining any real industrial independence. . . . From any comprehensive point of view union and not non-union labor represents the independence of the laborer, because under existing conditions such independence must be bought by association.

## 2

Middle-class Progressives such as Herbert Croly might damn capital and labor with equal gusto, but perceptive observers saw a broader importance to conflicts between the two. In every industrial dispute, they realized, the public was directly concerned; crippling strikes that stopped the free flow of goods involved consumers as well as producers. If this was the case, the obvious duty of the people, operating through their government, was to intervene in the interests of labor peace. This concept was accepted, at least in theory, by

Theodore Roosevelt in a speech delivered at Columbus, Ohio, in 1910:[2]

In all great labor struggles, not only are the capitalists and the employees parties in interest, but there is another party, and that third party is the people as a whole. You here are the party in interest, and peculiarly so in a controversy like the present, where a public service corporation is involved which has a peculiar and special connection with the government and with the people.

Now, then, your first duty is, as I have said, to see that law and order obtain. It is the duty of your representatives in public life to demand it of the lawbreaker, not as a favor, but as a right, which you will punish him for failing to fulfill; and it is to the interest of all of you to demand it, but, most of all, it is to the interest of the wage workers. But your duty does not stop there. It has only just begun. There can be no justice without law and order; but law and order are well-nigh valueless unless used as a foundation upon which justice is built up as a superstructure.

As I have said to you, conflicting statements have been made to me as to the original cause of the trouble [in Columbus, Ohio]. It has been alleged to me by reputable men that originally the trouble began because of the discharge of certain men who asked for an increase in wages. It has been alleged to me that the struggle has been continued because of the open or covert determination of the employers not to permit a union to exist among their employees. Both allegations have been denied, and I have no facts before me which enable me to decide whether or not they are correct.

As to the first allegation, it would be an act so infamous to discharge a man because he asked for an increase in wages, that I can hardly believe it can have occurred. But it would be almost as bad to discharge a man because he belonged to, or was preparing to enter, or organize, a union. I am an honorary member of a union myself. If I were a wage worker, I should certainly join a union; but when I was in I would remember that I was first of all an American citizen. Uncle Sam comes on top in everything. I would certainly join a union. In our modern industrial system the union is just as necessary as the corporation, and in the modern field of industrialism it is often an absolute necessity that there should be collective bargaining by the employees with the employers; and such collective bargaining is but one of the many benefits conferred by wisely and honestly organized unions that act properly. Of course, it is outrageous to force a man to join a union, just as it is outrageous to take part in, or encourage, the so-called secondary boycott; but it is no less an outrage to discriminate against him because he wishes to have a union, or to refuse to deal with a union when organized. The union has the same right to exist that the corporation has, and it is as unfair to refuse to deal with it as it is to refuse to deal with the corporation. Show your willingness to give the union its full rights, and you will be stronger when you set your faces like flint, as I have set mine, against the union when it is wrong. So that as soon as law and order have been obtained, it becomes your duty, you, the people, through your municipal or through your state authorities, to insist upon a thorough investigation by competent and disinterested authorities who will put before us an authoritative statement of the rights and wrongs of both sides; and then demand a thoroughgoing remedy for any wrong.

A case like this should be always a matter for mediation or arbitration. If such is refused by either party, shape your laws so that mediation and arbitration can be secured.

[2] Theodore Roosevelt, *The New Nationalism* (New York, 1910), pp. 222-225. Used by permission of Charles Scribner's Sons, publishers, and the Trustees of the Estate of Theodore Roosevelt.

## 3

The nation's business leaders were quick to recognize the implications of former President Roosevelt's stand. His views, they realized, must inevitably lead to governmental interference in the relationship between employers and employees whenever a labor dispute threatened the public welfare. To this most industrial magnates were unalterably opposed. They sincerely believed that complete freedom in contractual relationship was necessary to preserve the "American Way" as they understood it. This was the attitude especially of the leading association of employers, the National Association of Manufacturers, which had been formed in 1895 but became a power only during these years. Its views, as reflected in its publications during the Progressive Era, were summarized by Clarence E. Bonnett, a contemporary writer on economics:[3]

. . . The leaders of the Association have attempted numerous times to state its attitude towards organized labor, with the result that we have the following declarations:

"The National Association of Manufacturers is not primarily a labor-busting organization. It is true we have done much preventive work along that line, but we claim to be and are a boosting organization.". . . [*American Industries,* Dec., 1911.] . . .

"We believe in organized labor. It is the methods of organized labor that we oppose, and some of those methods are damnable." [*Proceedings,* Annual Convention, 1909.]

"We are not opposed to good unionism, if such exists anywhere. The American brand of unionism, however, is un-American, illegal and indecent, because their constitution is simply based on the plan that 'we will rule you or ruin you.' The manufacturer, therefore, has a perfect right to discriminate against an employee who is affiliated directly or indirectly with an organization that resorts to these meth-

ods.". . . [*American Industries,* Aug., 1904.] . . .

"Our Government cannot stand, nor its free institutions endure if the Gompers-Debs ideals of liberty and freedom of speech and press are allowed to dominate. . . . This Government cannot permanently endure if it permits a part, even though it be a small part, of its people to continue in open, organized rebellion against its institutions and its laws; if it continues to permit a defiant labor trust machine to ride rough shod over the rights of its citizens.". . . [*Where Do You Stand?* 1920.] . . .

"We must co-operate—we must get together and stick together to uphold our honor and honesty, we manufacturers and merchants, or rampant labor men, socialists and demagogues will be our undoing. All these new fangled ideas about the initiative, referendum and recall, and all these attacks on capital, no matter how honestly obtained, are for the sole and only purpose of putting more power into the hands of the papers and politicians. In fact, I think the greatest menace that our country has today is a so-called 'free press,' bidding for popularity with the thoughtless mob.". . . [*American Industries,* Aug., 1913.] . . .

If we take these statements in connection with the Declaration of Principles, given above, we may conclude that the Association stands for individualism, the rights of private property, and the maintenance of these by the Government; and that anything contrary to the property right, as it defines it, of the employer to employ whomever he pleases on whatever terms he pleases, is unconstitutional, and no union or legislative body can legally change such property rights. The thousands of pages of the literature of the Association abound with statements to confirm this, and only rarely is a dissenting sentence found. So we should expect this Association as a matter of course to oppose legislation restricting property rights, or

---

[3] From Clarence E. Bonnett, *Employers' Associations in the United States,* pp. 302-303, 306-309. Copyright 1922 by The Macmillan Company. Used by permission of The Macmillan Company, publishers.

curtailing the employer's liberty to manage his business as he sees fit, and in such opposition to engage in politics. Such is the case. In fact, "The Association was created to influence legislation." [*Proceedings,* Annual Convention, 1903.] . . .

. . . The Association with its subsidiary organizations, has been the most prominent opponent of labor legislation, such as eight-hour and anti-injunction bills, all of which it has characterized as class legislation. From 1902 to 1912, it successfully opposed the enactment of a federal eight-hour law applying to work done under government contract, and while its opposition could not prevent the passage of the law in 1912, it secured amendments to the law that limited somewhat the applications of that law. Its stand on this measure is thus stated in its pamphlet on "Eight Hours By Act of Congress". . . : "The National Association is committed to an unrelenting opposition to this vicious, needless, and in every way preposterous proposition, and we ask you to read and preserve the following pages as evidence, if such should ever be desired, that the worst that can be said of it is none too bad." The Association in the same manner has opposed all bills tending to lessen the power of the courts in the issue of injunctions in labor disputes. Its opposition began in 1902, became strong in 1904, and continued with complete success until the enactment of the Clayton Anti-Trust Law of 1914, an act which its leaders say does not materially lessen the power of the courts in the matter of punishing for conspiracy, although it clearly contains provisions that the Association has fought strenuously as anti-injunction measures. It has opposed even harmless anti-injunction measures on the ground that such bills serve as accusations of the justice of our courts. It has fought amendments to the Sherman-Anti-Trust Act and provisos in appropriation bills whereby labor unions were exempted from prosecution under the Sherman Anti-Trust Act by funds appropriated for its enforcement, although it demanded that the Sherman-Clayton Acts be so revised as to permit "collective economic action in business transactions," "beneficial to the public interest." [*Proceedings,* Annual Convention, 1908, 1910, 1913, 1918, 1919.] It has opposed vigorously bills defining property rights, in which the right to do business was defined as a personal right and not a property right, and in which the good-will of business was characterized as not being property. Bills for jury trials in contempt-of-court cases in labor disputes have been combated by the Association, as have bills allowing federal employees to affiliate with the American Federation of Labor. Its activities have been distinctly unfavorable to the Seamen's Bill and to legislation tending to check the use of scientific management, or efficiency measures. Its opposition to the Seamen's Act did not cease when that bill became a law, but continues to the present in the form of demands for the repeal or serious modification of the Act. It has condemned compulsory sickness insurance as a menace. It has protested against the labor provisions of the Versailles Peace Treaty. It opposed at first, then sought modifications and now demands the repeal of the excess-profits tax. It denounced the passage of the Adamson Eight Hour Law. It opposed the National Child Labor Law, and has not been favorable to minimum-wage laws.

4

That the philosophy underlying the program of the National Association of Manufacturers was unacceptable to the majority of the people was amply demonstrated during the Progressive Era. Instead, a generation already committed to the conservation of the nation's natural resources gradually awakened to the need of preserving its human resources. Forward-looking men, both in and out of Washington, saw that this could be done—and the United States kept on an even economic keel—only by assuring labor as much power as capital. One means of achieving such a balance was to dissolve industrial monopolies; with a number of competing units operating in each field of production, the law of supply and demand would force prices down, and collective bargaining would keep wages up. The New Freedom, as Wilson defined it, was designed "to break every kind of monopoly, and to set men free, upon a footing of equality." To this end Wilson's appointees to a United States Commission on Industrial Relations explored the causes of industrial conflicts. Perhaps the most farseeing advice received by the Commission was given in 1915 by Louis D. Brandeis, a noted lawyer destined to gain fame as a Supreme Court justice:[4]

Mr. BRANDEIS. My observation leads me to believe that while there are many contributing causes to unrest, that there is one cause which is fundamental. That is the necessary conflict—the contrast between our political liberty and our industrial absolutism. We are as free politically, perhaps, as free as it is possible for us to be. . . . .

On the other hand, in dealing with industrial problems the position of the ordinary worker is exactly the reverse. The individual employee has no effective voice or vote. And the main objection, as I see it, to the very large corporation is, that it makes possible—and in many cases makes inevitable—the exercise of industrial absolutism. It is not merely the case of the individual worker against employer which, even if he is a reasonably sized employer, presents a serious situation calling for the interposition of a union to protect the individual. But we have the situation of an employer so potent, so well-organized, with such concentrated forces and with such extraordinary powers of reserve and the ability to endure against strikes and other efforts of a union, that the relatively loosely organized masses of even strong unions are unable to cope with the situation . . . The

result, in the cases of these large corporations, may be to develop a benevolent absolutism, but it is an absolutism all the same; and it is that which makes the great corporation so dangerous. There develops within the State a state so powerful that the ordinary social and industrial forces existing are insufficient to cope with it.

I noted, Mr. Chairman, that the question you put to me concerning the employees of these large corporations related to their physical condition. Their mental condition is certainly equally important. Unrest, to my mind, never can be removed—and fortunately never can be removed—by mere improvement of the physical and material condition of the workingman. If it were possible we should run great risk of improving their material condition and reducing their manhood. We must bear in mind all the time that however much we may desire material improvement and must desire it for the comfort of the individual, that the United States is a democracy, and that we must have, above all things, men. It is the development of manhood to which any industrial and social system should be directed. We Americans are committed not only to social justice in the sense of avoiding things which bring suffering and harm, like unjust distribution of wealth; but we are committed primarily to democracy. The social justice for which we are striving is an incident of our democracy, not the main end. It is rather the result of democracy—perhaps its finest expression—but it rests upon democracy, which implies the rule by the people. And therefore the end for which we must strive is the attainment of rule by the people, and that involves industrial democracy as well as political democracy. That means that the problem of a trade should be not longer the problems of the employer alone. The problems of his business, and it is not the employer's business alone, are the problems of all in it. The union can not shift upon the employer the responsibility for conditions, nor can the

---

[4] United States Commission on Industrial Relations, *Final Report and Testimony*, VIII (1916), 7659-7660, 7667-7669. (*Senate Documents*, 64th Cong., 1st Sess., Doc. No. 415.)

employer insist upon determining, according to his will, the conditions which shall exist. The problems which exist are the problems of the trade; they are the problems of employer and employee. Profit sharing, however liberal, can not meet the situation. That would mean merely dividing the profits of business. Such a division may do harm, or it might do good, dependent on how it is applied.

There must be a division not only of profits, but a division also of responsibilities. The employees must have the opportunity of participating in the decisions as to what shall be their condition and how the business shall be run. They must learn also in sharing that responsibility that they must bear [too] the suffering arising from grave mistakes, just as the employer must. But the right to assist in making the decisions, the right of making their own mistakes, if mistakes there must be, is a privilege which should not be denied to labor. We must insist upon labor sharing the responsibilities for the result of the business. . . .

Commissioner WEINSTOCK. Exactly. Now, for the information of the commission, will you be good enough to point out, Mr. Brandeis, what you have observed to be the mistakes of employers in dealing with labor. Will you brief them?

Mr. BRANDEIS. I think the main mistake that the employers have made has been a failure to acquire understanding of the conditions and facts concerning labor. There has been ignorance in this respect on the part of employers—ignorance due in large part to lack of imagination. Employers have not been able to think themselves into the labor position. They do not understand labor and many successful business men have never recognized that labor presents the most important problem in the business. One of the ablest business men I ever came in contact with, and who later made some very important advances in dealing with labor problems, said to me when I first had occasion to dis-

cuss a pressing labor problem with him "I want to take up the labor question when I get around to it." He had been proceeding for years with a reorganization of his business in all other respects—in respect to distribution, in respect to financing and factory organization—but he postponed taking up the labor question until he should be through with all the other problems. . . .

The other cause of employers' difficulties is a failure to think clearly. The employers' refusal to deal with a union is ordinarily due to erroneous reasoning or false sentiment. The man who refuses to deal with the union acts ordinarily from a good motive. He is impressed with "union dictation." He is apt to think "this is my business and the American has the right of liberty of contract." He honestly believes that he is standing up for a high principle and is willing often to run the risk of having his business ruined rather than abandon that principle. They have not thought out clearly enough that liberty means exercising one's rights consistently with a like exercise of rights by other people; that liberty is distinguished from license in that it is subject to certain restrictions, and that no one can expect to secure liberty in the sense in which we recognize it in America without having his rights curtailed in those respects in which it is necessary to limit them in the general public interest. The failure of many employers to recognize these simple truths is a potent reason why employers have not been willing to deal with unions. I think our employers, as a rule, are kind hearted; they mean to do right; they mean to be just; and there is no difference between the men who have fought the hardest against labor unions and those who have yielded to and dealt with labor unions in that respect, except that the former have not had that education which comes from actual active cooperation with unions in the solution of these problems.

I had my first practical experience in

dealing with labor problems while acting for manufacturers in the effort to settle or prevent strikes. I found if I wanted to bring about a settlement it was absolutely necessary that the head of the business be brought into the conference. If the employer was a large corporation, nothing less than the president would do, and on the other hand we required the president of the international union to deal with the man in real authority. My effort was to bring these two men together and make each understand the problems of the other. And when I could bring that about, when I could make the union understand the employers' problem and the employer the union's problem, a settlement was almost certain. The next step was to make the individual employee feel that whatever the system of dealing, either through superintendents or otherwise, that there was no individual in that employ who was so insignificant but that if he believed a wrong was done him, he could, in the last analysis, appeal to the highest official of the corporation. When once that principle was established the danger of a rupture between employer and employee was usually passed. The labor men felt faith; they felt that they could deal with the employer in full confidence; and under these circumstances I found that the laboring man would accept the definite statement of the corporation as to what they could afford to pay and what they could not afford to pay. I offered the union representative the opportunity of going through the employer's books; offered them every facility to learn the actual facts and requested their suggestions. They withdrew manfully from the opposition, for they were convinced that they were being dealt with fairly, and that the rights of each individual laboring man were recognized as important as those of the biggest official. The corporation operated many factories, but the president was not burdened with numerous appeals. The fact that he recognized that there was nothing more important than the rights of the individual laboring man to human treatment was all the assurance needed.

Commissioner WEINSTOCK. On the other hand, Mr. Brandeis, what are the mistakes of organized labor, as you see them?

Mr. BRANDEIS. Well, in many ways they are similar—they are the correlative of the mistakes of the employers.

I think in the first place the commonest mistake is a belief that the employer is earning a tremendous amount of money at the expense of labor. Taking all things into consideration, the employer rarely earns "a tremendous amount of money.". . . Very few workmen appreciate how necessary it is that there should sometimes be large profits in order to set off the losses. Few people care to advertise their losses, but the profits are advertised freely, and very often are exaggerated.

Now, what the employer needs most is to have proper representatives of labor understand the problems of his business; how serious they are, how great is the chance of losing money, how relatively small is the chance of making large profits, and how great is the percentage of failures. Put a competent representative of labor on your board of directors; make him grapple with the problems whether to do or not to do a specific thing, and undertake to balance the advantages and disadvantages presented, and he will get a realizing sense of how difficult it is to operate a business successfully and what the dangers are of the destruction of the capital in the business. A few years ago, when union leaders were demanding from my client an increase in wages, and I asked them: "How much do you think the employer ought to earn before he increases your wages"? they named a figure which was far above his actual earnings, and I said to them, "Gentlemen, the books are open. If you can find either that more is being earned, or can show any way in which the employer can earn more than he is earning, the balance shall go to you." That put the responsibilities upon the labor leaders; they came to realize the difficulties under which the employer was laboring and acquiesced in the situation. The second cause of discord is the natural distrust felt by labor due largely to their lack of knowledge and of opportunities for knowledge.

The third cause is the sense of being subject to the power of the employer. That feeling of subjection can not be removed without changing the conditions under which industry is being carried on. Perhaps the greatest of labor's mistakes is the practice, in many trades or communities, of restricting production. That is a very serious difficulty. Nothing would do so much to win the employer to collective bargaining as action on the part of the labor leaders favoring increased production. If employers could be satisfied that unionism meant increased production and better discipline and that the unions were striving for that result, a large part of the apprehension of employers would be removed and collective bargaining would be wisely extended.

## 5

The final report of Wilson's Commission on Industrial Relations, delivered in eleven fat volumes during 1915 and 1916, emphasized the failure of existing laws to check industrial monopoly. The Commission's conclusions contained both a sad recital of the current state of affairs and healthy suggestions for improving the situation:[5]

. . . Political freedom can exist only where there is industrial freedom; political democracy only where there is industrial democracy.

Such industrial democracy has been established in a greater or less degree in certain American industries or for certain classes of employees. But between conditions of industrial democracy and industrial feudalism there are almost infinite gradations marking the stages of evolution

which have been reached. In every case, however, investigation has shown that the degree of political freedom and democracy which exists is conditioned by the industrial status of the citizens who form the majority of the community.

The problems of industrial relations, therefore, demand the attention of Congress, not only because they determine the life, security, and happiness of the 25,000,000, citizens of the United States who occupy the position of wage earners but because they affect for good or evil the government of localities and States and to a smaller degree that of the Nation itself. What each of these wage earners shall eat, what he shall wear, where he shall live, and how long and under what conditions he shall labor are determined by his industrial status and by his relation, individually or collectively, to the person or corporation employing him. Similarly and almost as directly, this relationship determines whether the machinery of government shall be used for or against his welfare; whether his vote shall count for or against his own interest; whether he shall be tried by a jury of his peers or a jury selected in collusion with the employing company, or, under conditions of so-called martial law, by no jury whatever; whether, in fact, he shall be a free man or be deprived of every right guaranteed by Federal and State constitutions, imprisoned without warrant for the commission of crimes of which he may be innocent or forcibly deported from the community or State in which he has made his home. . . .

The wealth of the country between 1890 and 1912 increased from sixty-five to one hundred and eighty-seven billions, or 188 per cent, whereas the aggregate income of wage earners in manufacturing, mining, and transportation has risen between 1889 and 1909 only 95 per cent, from two thousand five hundred and sixteen millions in 1889 to four thousand nine hundred and sixteen millions in 1909. Furthermore, the wage earners' share of the net product of

---

[5] *Ibid.*, I (1916), 18, 21-23. (*Senate Documents*, 64th Cong., 1st Sess., Doc. No. 415.)

industry in the case of manufactures was only 40.2 per cent in 1909, as compared with 44.9 per cent in 1889. . . .

. . . At this point it is sufficient to call attention to the results of the most exhaustive and sweeping official investigation of recent years, that of the Immigration Commission, which reported to Congress in 1909. This investigation secured detailed information regarding the daily or weekly earnings of 619,595 employees of all classes in our basic manufacturing industries and in coal mining, and information regarding income and living conditions for 15,726 families.

It was found that the incomes of almost two-thirds of these families (64 per cent) were less than $750 per year and of almost one-third (31 per cent) were less than $500, the average for all being $721. The average size of these families was 5.6 members. Elaborate studies of the cost of living made in all parts of the country at the same time have shown that the very least that a family of five persons can live upon in anything approaching decency is $700. It is probable that, owing to the fact that the families investigated by the Immigration Commission were, to a large extent, foreign born, the incomes reported are lower than the average for the entire working population; nevertheless, even when every allowance is made for that fact, the figures show conclusively that between one-half and two-thirds of these families were living below the standards of decent subsistence, while about one-third were living in a state which can be described only as abject poverty.

American society was founded and for a long period existed upon the theory that the family should derive its support from the earnings of the father. How far we have departed from this condition is shown by the fact that 79 per cent of the fathers of these families earned less than $700 per year. In brief, only one-fourth of these fathers could have supported their families on the barest subsistence level without the earnings of other members of the family or income from outside sources.

Other facts collected in this investigation show conclusively that a very large proportion of these families did not live in decency and comfort. Thirty per cent kept boarders and lodgers, a condition repugnant to every ideal of American family life, especially in the crowded tenements or tiny cottages in which the wage earners of America characteristically live. Furthermore, in 77 per cent of the families two or more persons occupied each sleeping room, in 37 per cent three or more persons, and in 15 per cent four or more persons. . . .

The terrible effects of such poverty may be outlined in a few paragraphs, but their far-reaching consequences could not be adequately shown in a volume.

Children are the basis of the State; as they live or die, as they thrive or are ill nourished, as they are intelligent or ignorant, so fares the State. How do the children of American workers fare?

It has been proved by studies here and abroad that there is a direct relation between poverty and the death rate of babies; but the frightful rate at which poverty kills was not known, at least for this country, until very recently, when through a study made in Johnstown, Pa., by the Federal Children's Bureau, it was shown that the babies whose fathers earned less than $10 per week died during the first year at the appalling rate of 256 per 1,000. On the other hand, those whose fathers earned $25 per week or more died at the rate of only 84 per 1,000. The babies of the poor died at three times the rate of those who were in fairly well-to-do families. The tremendous significance of these figures will be appreciated when it is known that one-third of all the adult workmen reported by the Immigration Commission earned less than $10 per week, even exclusive of time lost. On the showing of Johnstown these workmen may expect one out of four of their babies to die during the first year of life.

The last of the family to go hungry are the children, yet statistics show that in six of our largest cities from 12 to 20 per cent of the children are noticeably underfed and ill nourished.

The minimum amount of education which any child should receive is certainly the grammar school course, yet statistics show that only one-third of the children in our public schools complete the grammar school course, and less than 10 per cent finish high school. . . .

## 6

Dissolving monopolies was one method advocated by Progressives to assure better relations between capital and labor. The other was direct government action. They argued that laws forcing manufacturers to provide better working conditions, shorter hours, and more pay would ensure labor peace. Once they began exploring the possibilities of this solution, however, they found themselves face to face with constitutional obstacles. State laws placing a ceiling over working hours or a floor under wages apparently violated the Fourteenth Amendment, which forbade the states to deprive any person of property without due process of law; federal laws concerning production seemingly lay beyond the powers delegated to Congress by the Constitution. During the Progressive Period efforts were made to sweep away both these objections. The right of states to interfere in contractual relationships between employers and employees was upheld in two important Supreme Court cases. The first was *Muller* v. *Oregon* (1908), which placed the stamp of approval on an Oregon statute setting a ten-hour day for women in industry:[6]

It is the law of Oregon that women, whether married or single, have equal contractual and personal rights with men. . . .

It thus appears that, putting to one side the elective franchise, in the matter of personal and contractual rights they stand on the same plane as the other sex. Their rights in these respects can no more be infringed than the equal rights of their brothers. We held in *Lochner* v. *New York*, 198 U. S. 45, that a law providing that no laborer shall be required or permitted to work in a bakery more than sixty hours in a week or ten hours in a day was not as to men a legitimate exercise of the police power of the State, but an unreasonable, unnecessary, and arbitrary interference with the right and liberty of the individual to contract in relation to his labor, and as such was in conflict with, and void under, the federal Constitution. That decision is invoked by plaintiff in error as decisive of the question before us. But this assumes that the difference between the sexes does not justify a different rule respecting a restriction of the hours of labor. . . .

It may not be amiss, in the present case, before examining the constitutional question, to notice the course of legislation, as well as expressions of opinion from other than judicial sources. In the brief filed by Mr. Louis D. Brandeis for the defendant in error is a very copious collection of all these matters. . . .

The legislation and opinions referred to . . . may not be, technically speaking, authorities, and in them is little or no discussion of the constitutional question presented to us for determination, yet they are significant of a widespread belief that woman's physical structure, and the functions she performs in consequence thereof, justify special legislation restricting or qualifying the conditions under which she should be permitted to toil. Constitutional questions, it is true, are not settled by even a consensus of present public opinion, for it is the peculiar value of a written constitution that it places in unchanging form limitations upon legislative action, and thus gives a permanence and stability to popular government which otherwise would be lacking. At the same time, when a question of fact is debated and debatable, and the extent to which a special constitutional limitation goes is affected by the

---

[6] *United States Reports*, 208 U.S. 418-423.

truth in respect to that fact, a widespread and long-continued belief concerning it is worthy of consideration. We take judicial cognizance of all matters of general knowledge. . . .

That woman's physical structure and the performance of maternal functions place her at a disadvantage in the struggle for subsistence is obvious. This is especially true when the burdens of motherhood are upon her. Even when they are not, by abundant testimony of the medical fraternity continuance for a long time on her feet at work, repeating this from day to day, tends to injurious effects upon the body, and, as healthy mothers are essential to vigorous offspring, the physical well-being of woman becomes an object of public interest and care in order to preserve the strength and vigor of the race. . . .

Differentiated by these matters from the other sex, she is properly placed in a class by herself, and legislation designed for her protection may be sustained, even when like legislation is not necessary for men, and could not be sustained. It is impossible to close one's eyes to the fact that she still looks to her brother and depends upon him. Even though all restrictions on political, personal, and contractual rights were taken away, and she stood, so far as statutes are concerned, upon an absolutely equal plane with him, it would still be true that she is so constituted that she will rest upon and look to him for protection; that her physical structure and a proper discharge of her maternal functions—having in view not merely her own health, but the well-being of the race—justify legislation to protect her from the greed as well as the passion of man. The limitations which this statute places upon her contractual powers, upon her right to agree with her employer as to the time she shall labor, are not imposed solely for her benefit, but also largely for the benefit of all. Many words cannot make this plainer. The two sexes differ in structure of body, in the

functions to be performed by each, in the amount of physical strength, in the capacity for long continued labor, particularly when done standing, the influence of vigorous health upon the future well-being of the race, the self-reliance which enables one to assert full rights, and in the capacity to maintain the struggle for subsistence. This difference justifies a difference in legislation, and upholds that which is designed to compensate for some of the burdens which rest upon her. . . .

For these reasons, and without questioning in any respect the decision in *Lochner* v. *New York,* we are of the opinion that it cannot be adjudged that the act in question is in conflict with the federal Constitution, so far as it respects the work of a female in a laundry, and the judgment of the supreme court of Oregon is

Affirmed.

## 7

More sweeping was the second decision, also involving an Oregon statute passed in 1913. This set a ten-hour day for all workers and provided that overtime work must be limited to three hours daily and paid for at one and one half times the regular rate. The Supreme Court upheld the law in *Bunting* v. *Oregon* (1917):[7]

The consonance of the Oregon law with the Fourteenth Amendment is the question in the case, and this depends upon whether it is a proper exercise of the police power of the State, as the supreme court of this State decided that it is.

That the police power extends to health regulations is not denied, but it is denied that the law has such purpose or justification. It is contended that it is a wage law, not a health regulation, and takes the property of plaintiff in error without due process. . . .

There is a certain verbal plausibility in the contention that it was intended to permit thirteen hours' work if there be fif-

[7] *Ibid.,* 243 U.S. 434-439.

teen and one-half-hours' pay, but the plausibility disappears upon reflection. The provision for overtime is permissive, in the same sense that any penalty may be said to be permissive. Its purpose is to deter by its burden, and its adequacy for this was a matter of legislative judgment under the particular circumstances. . . . We cannot know all of the conditions that impelled the law or its particular form. The supreme court, nearer to them, describes the law as follows: "It is clear that the intent of the law is to make ten hours a regular day's labor in the occupations to which reference is made. Apparently the provisions permitting labor for the overtime on express conditions were made in order to facilitate the enforcement of the law, and in the nature of a mild penalty for employing one not more than three hours overtime. It might be regarded as more difficult to detect violations of the law by an employment for a shorter time than for a longer time. This penalty also goes to the employee in case the employer avails himself of the overtime clause." . . .

But passing general considerations and coming back to our immediate concern, which is the validity of the particular exertion of power in the Oregon law, our judgment of it is that it does not transcend constitutional limits. . . .

There is a contention made that the law, even regarded as regulating hours of service, is not either necessary or useful "for preservation of the health of employees in mills, factories and manufacturing establishments." The record contains no facts to support the contention, and against it is the judgment of the legislature and the supreme court, which said: "In view of the well-known fact that the custom in our industries does not sanction a longer service than 10 hours per day, it cannot be held, as a matter of law, that the legislative requirement is unreasonable or arbitrary as to hours of labor. Statistics show that the average daily working time among workingmen in different countries

is, in Australia, 8 hours; in Great Britain, 9; in the United States, 9¾; in Denmark, 9¾; in Norway, 10; Sweden, France, and Switzerland, 10½; Germany, 10¼; Belgium, Italy, and Austria, 11; and in Russia, 12 hours."

## 8

The halting efforts to establish state power over working conditions were paralleled by attempts to extend federal authority into the same realm. Here the constitutional obstacles were harder to hurdle. Nowhere, employers argued, did the Constitution give Congress authority to interfere with manufacturing; as its powers were only those specifically delegated, its hands were tied. Progressives refused to accept this strict-construction argument. Instead, they insisted that under broad construction the congressional power over interstate commerce did allow action. Not until September, 1916, was Congress bold enough to follow their advice. The Adamson Act, passed at that time, set an eight-hour day for all workers in interstate commerce, thus forestalling what threatened to be a disastrous strike of the four brotherhoods of railroad workers:[8]

*Be it enacted,* That beginning January first, nineteen hundred and seventeen, eight hours shall, in contracts for labor and service, be deemed a day's work and the measure or standard of a day's work for the purpose of reckoning the compensation for services of all employees who are now or may hereafter be employed by any common carrier by railroad, except railroads independently owned and operated not exceeding one hundred miles in length, electric street railroads, and electric interurban railroads, which is subject to the provisions of the Act of February 4, 1887, entitled "An Act to regulate commerce," as amended, and who are now or may hereafter be actually engaged in any capacity in the operation of trains used for the transportation of persons or property on railroads . . . from any State or

[8] *United States Statutes at Large,* XXXIX, 721-722.

Territory of the United States or the District of Columbia to any other State or Territory of the United States or the District of Columbia or from one place in a Territory to another place in the same Territory or from any place in the United States to an adjacent foreign country, or from any place in the United States through a foreign country to any other place in the United States; *Provided,* That the above exceptions shall not apply to railroads though less than one hundred miles in length whose principal business is leasing or furnishing terminal or transfer facilities to other railroads, or are themselves engaged in transfers of freight between railroads or between railroads and industrial plants. . . .

## COLLECTIVE BARGAINING AND THE COURTS

### 9

Despite heroic Progressive efforts to end labor disputes by dissolving industrial monopolies and placing a ceiling over working hours, the principal weapons of the laboring man were still the strike and the boycott. The Progressive Era, for all its liberalism, witnessed a concentrated attack on these two devices through the agency of the courts. Justices might give grudging consent to state ten-hour laws, but their opinion of unions was so hostile that during these years they served as practical allies of employers. In case after case they negated national and state laws favoring unionization, denied legal recognition to unions, upheld the use of yellow-dog contracts, and wielded the injunction against strikers with a cold disregard for both human and legal rights. Outstanding among the Supreme Court's antilabor decisions was *Adair* v. *United States* (1908), which held invalid the 10th section of an 1898 law forbidding railroads to discriminate against union members when hiring workers:[9]

May Congress make it a criminal offense against the United States—as by the 10th section of the Act of 1898 it does—for an

[9] *United States Report,* 208 U.S. 171-180.

agent or officer of an interstate carrier, . . . to discharge an employee from service simply because of his membership in a labor organization? . . .

The first inquiry is whether the part of the 10th section of the Act of 1898 upon which the first count of the indictment is based is repugnant to the 5th Amendment of the Constitution, declaring that no person shall be deprived of liberty or property without due process of law. In our opinion that section in the particular mentioned is an invasion of the personal liberty, as well as of the right of property, guaranteed by that Amendment. Such liberty and right embrace the right to make contracts for the purchase of the labor of others, and equally the right to make contracts for the sale of one's own labor; each right, however, being subject to the fundamental condition that no contract, whatever its subject-matter, can be sustained which the law, upon reasonable grounds, forbids as inconsistent with the public interest, or as hurtful to the public order, or as detrimental to the common good. . . . It is sufficient in this case to say that, as agent of the railroad company, and, as such, responsible for the conduct of the business of one of its departments, it was the defendant Adair's right—and that right inhered in his personal liberty, and was also a right of property—to serve his employer as best he could, so long as he did nothing that was reasonably forbidden by law as injurious to the public interest. It was the right of the defendant to prescribe the terms upon which the services of Coppage would be accepted, and it was the right of Coppage to become or not, as he chose, an employee of the railroad company upon the terms offered to him. . . .

In every case that comes before this court, therefore, where legislation of this character is concerned, . . . the question necessarily arises: Is this a fair, reasonable, and appropriate exercise of the police power of the state, or is it an unreasonable, unnecessary, and arbitrary interference with the right of the individual to his personal liberty or to enter into those contracts in relation to labor which may seem to him appropriate or necessary for the support of himself and his family? . . .

While . . . the right of liberty and property guaranteed by the Constitution against deprivation without due process of law is subject to such reasonable restraints as the common good or the general welfare may require, it is not within the functions of government . . . to compel any person in the course of his business and against his will, to accept or retain the personal services of another, or to compel any person, against his will, to perform personal services for another. . . .

As the relations and the conduct of the parties towards each other was not controlled by any contract other than a general agreement on one side to accept the services of the employee and a general agreement on the other side to render services to the employer,—no term being fixed for the continuance of the employment,—Congress could not, consistently with the 5th Amendment, make it a crime against the United States to discharge the employee because of his being a member of a labor organization.

But it is suggested that the authority to make it a crime . . . can be referred to the power of Congress to regulate interstate commerce, without regard to any question of personal liberty or right of property arising under the 5th Amendment. This suggestion can have no bearing, in the present discussion unless the statute, in the particular just stated, is, within the meaning of the Constitution, a regulation of commerce among the States. If it be not, then clearly the government cannot invoke the commerce clause of the Constitution as sustaining the indictment against Adair. . . .

Looking alone at the words of the statute for the purpose of ascertaining its scope and effect, and of determining its validity, we hold that there is no such connection between interstate commerce and membership in a labor organization as to authorize Congress to make it a crime against the United States for an agent of an interstate carrier to discharge an employee because of such membership on his part. . . .

It results, on the whole case, that the provision of the statute under which the defendant was convicted must be held to be repugnant to the 5th Amendment and as not embraced by nor within the power of Congress to regulate interstate commerce, but, under the guise of regulating commerce, and as applied to this case, it arbitrarily sanctions an illegal invasion of the personal liberty as well as the right of property of the defendant Adair.

## 10

The archaic doctrine accepted by the majority in the Adair Case was disputed in a ringing dissent by Oliver Wendell Holmes, who had recently been appointed to the bench by President Roosevelt:[10]

As we all know, there are special labor unions of men engaged in the service of carriers. These unions exercise a direct influence upon the employment of labor in that business, upon the terms of such employment, and upon the business itself. Their very existence is directed specifically to the business, and their connection with it is, at least, as intimate and important, as that of safety couplers, and, I should think, as the liability of master to servant, —matters which, it is admitted, Congress might regulate so far as they concerned commerce among the states. I suppose that it hardly would be denied that some of the relations of railroads with unions of railroad employees are closely enough connected with commerce to justify legislation by Congress. If so, legislation to prevent the exclusion of such unions from employment is sufficiently near.

[10] *Ibid.*, pp. 190-192.

The ground on which this particular law is held bad, is not so much that it deals with matters remote from commerce among the states, as that it interferes with the paramount individual rights secured by the 5th Amendment. The section is, in substance, a very limited interference with freedom of contract, no more. It does not require the carriers to employ anyone. It does not forbid them to refuse to employ anyone, for any reason they deem good, even where the notion of a choice of persons is a fiction and wholesale employment is necessary upon general principles that it might be proper to control. The section simply prohibits the more powerful party to exact certain undertakings, or to threaten dismissal or unjustly discriminate on certain grounds against those already employed. I hardly can suppose that the grounds on which a contract lawfully may be made to end are less open to regulation than other terms. So I turn to the general question whether the employment can be regulated at all. I confess that I think that the right to make contracts at will that has been derived from the word "liberty" in the Amendments, has been stretched to its extreme by the decisions; but they agree that sometimes the right may be restrained. Where there is, or generally is believed to be, an important ground of public policy for restraint, the Constitution does not forbid it, whether this court agrees or disagrees with the policy pursued. It cannot be doubted that to prevent strikes and, so far as possible, to foster its scheme of arbitration, might be deemed by Congress an important point of policy, and I think it impossible to say that Congress might not reasonably think that the provision in question would help a good deal to carry its policy along. But suppose the only effect really were to tend to bring about the complete unionizing of such railroad laborers as Congress can deal with, I think that object alone would justify the act. I quite agree that the question what and how much good labor

unions do, is one on which intelligent people may differ; I think that laboring men sometimes attribute to them advantages, as many attribute to combinations of capital, disadvantages, that really are due to economic conditions of a far wider and deeper kind; but I could not pronounce it unwarranted if Congress should decide that to foster a strong union was for the best interests, not only of the men, but of the railroads and the country at large.

## 11

Despite Justice Holmes's vigorous protest, the opinion of the majority in the Adair Case was upheld in two subsequent decisions by the Supreme Court: *Coppage* v. *Kansas* (1915), and *Hitchman Coal and Coke Company* .v. *Mitchell et al.* (1917). A biting comment on the Court's line of reasoning in these three cases was written at the time by Thomas Reed Powell, witty student of constitutional law, then a professor at Columbia University:[11]

In three important cases a majority of the United States Supreme Court has thwarted efforts of labor unions to increase their numbers. . . . *Adair* v. *United States* annulled an act of Congress which prohibited interstate carriers from discharging an employee because of his membership in a labor union. *Coppage* v. *Kansas* declared invalid a state law which forbade any employer to require of employees or of persons seeking employment an agreement not to become or remain a member of a labor union. The third decision is *Hitchman Coal and Coke Company* v. *Mitchell et al.,* handed down last December. It deals with a situation created by the type of agreement which Kansas sought unsuccessfully to forbid. Officers of a labor union were restrained by injunction

[11] Reprinted from *The Political Science Quarterly,* Volume XXXIII, No. 3, September 1918, pp. 642-647, "Collective Bargaining before the Supreme Court," by Thomas Reed Powell, published by the Academy of Political Science, Columbia University, New York City.

from securing secret promises to join the union from employees who had agreed to relinquish their employment in case they became members.

Each of these decisions was rendered in the name of freedom and liberty. . . .

This question of the disturbance of the equality between employer and employed receives further discussion in the opinions in the Coppage case. The majority in that case insist that a statute which forbids an employer to require of a laborer, as a condition of obtaining or remaining in employment, an agreement not to become or to remain a member of a labor union is as vicious as one which forbids dismissal because of membership in a union. If the employer must remain free to discharge an employee for any reason that seems to him good, he must be permitted to announce in advance what reasons he will deem sufficient for discharge. "Granted the equal freedom of both parties to the contract of employment, has not each party the right to stipulate upon what terms only he will consent to the inception, or to the continuance, of that relationship?". . . .

. . . In a dissent which takes only a paragraph he [Justice Holmes] says:

In present conditions a workman not unnaturally may believe that only by belonging to a union can he secure a contract that shall be fair to him. If that belief, whether right or wrong, may be held by a reasonable man, it seems to me that it may be enforced by law in order to establish the equality of position between the parties in which liberty of contract begins. Whether in the long run it is wise for the workingmen to enact legislation of this sort is not my concern, but I am strongly of opinion that there is nothing in the Constitution of the United States to prevent it. . . .

Thus Mr. Justice Holmes regards the statute as a promoter of liberty and equality. The majority regard it as an interference with both. . . .

To the minority liberty and equality mean something actual and concrete. Mr.

Justice Day says of the Kansas statute, "I think that the Act now under consideration, and kindred ones, are intended to promote the same liberty of action for the employee, as the employer confessedly enjoys." It is a step towards making them equal in bargaining power. It prohibits "coercive attempts" on the part of employers to deprive employees "of the free right of exercising privileges which are theirs within the law." To the argument of the majority that there is no element of coercion in offering an employee a choice between his union and his job, Mr. Justice Day says that this neglects the facts as to the relative positions of employer and employed. The choice legally open to the employee is not actually open to him. He cannot enjoy his legal right to be a member of a union if he is hampered thereby in working for his living in the occupation for which he is best fitted. . . .

. . . The majority is correct in its assertion that the state has interfered with a previous legal liberty of employers. The issue is whether the former is a justification for the latter.

The majority, in seeking for possible justifications, find none. Other interferences with liberty which have been judicially sanctioned have been "fairly deemed necessary to secure some object directly affecting the public welfare." But of the statute in question, putting aside the question of coercion, Mr. Justice Pitney says:

. . . there is no object or purpose, expressed or implied, that is claimed to have reference to health, safety, morals, or public welfare, beyond the supposed desirability of leveling inequalities of fortune by depriving one who has property of some part of what is characterized as his "financial independence." In short, an interference with the normal exercise of personal liberty and property rights is the primary object of the statute, and not an incident to the advancement of the general welfare.

This is to say that the object of the statute is to promote equality of actual opportunity, solely for the sake of that equality —a result which could not promote the general welfare. Moreover, the Constitution is regarded as having been designed to prevent the legislature from promoting equality of opportunity. Inequality is the necessary result of the institution of private property. . . .

Constitutional liberty of contract, therefore, is not "freedom of action." It is freedom from legislative interference with action. This is freedom for employer and employee alike, even though for the employee it is but the wraith of genuine freedom. Equality between employer and employee is not approximate evenness of bargaining position. It exists only when both are equally let alone by the legislature. The state may not, as Mr. Justice Holmes contends, "establish the equality of position in which liberty of contract begins." It must not interfere with that inequality of position which enables the one with superior position to drive a hard bargain. The owner of property must be guaranteed an advantage in all his dealings with those who have less than he. In the words of Mr. Justice Pitney:

Indeed, a little reflection will show that wherever the right of private property and the right of free contract coexist, each party when contracting is inevitably more or less influenced by the question whether he has much property or little or none; for the contract is made to the very end that each may gain something he needs or desires more urgently than that which he proposes to give in exchange.

To him that hath shall be given protection not only of that which he hath but of every leverage which his possessions give him in acquiring more. To him that hath not shall be given the solace that he is free and unrestrained by law as to the bargains he shall make. He may be influenced as much as he likes by the fact that he has little property or none. He lives in a land of freedom and equality.

This is where we should arrive by uniting an absolute conception of liberty of contract with an absolute conception of property, and then regarding the marriage as indissoluble. . . .

## 12

Less temperate than Professor Powell's comment, but equally well-reasoned, was labor's own reaction to a series of decisions that virtually enshrined the yellow-dog contract. Typical of the editorials that blossomed in every union publication whenever a new case was decided was the following from the *Granite Cutters' Journal*:[12]

The individual contract used by anti-union employers is contemptuously referred to as "yellow dog" by trade unionists.

To secure employment where this contract operates the worker must pledge not to join a trade union or encourage the formation of same while so employed.

The United States Supreme Court upheld this contract (Hitchman v. Mine Workers) and sustained an injunction against unionists who were charged by a West Virginia coal company with interfering with one of the "yellow dogs."

The acknowledged basis of a contract is free and voluntary action by both parties.

Courts invariably void contracts when made by duress, pressure, or coercion.

What choice has the worker seeking employment with hungry babes in his home when an employer offers him a job if he signs away his lawful right to join a trade union?

How much free will has this worker when his family is threatened with eviction because he is unable to pay the rent?

What self-control has he when he knows that if he stands on his legal rights and refused to accept employment under this agreement, others will suffer because he is alone in his fight for right?

[12] "Individual Contract," *Granite Cutters' Journal* (June, 1921), p. 5.

What respect can workers have for courts that defend the "yellow dog" on the ground of "sacredness of contract"?

Contracts are based on freedom of action, but when one of the parties uses his unequal power to force the other to accept, the first principle of contracts is outraged.

It may be said that a worker can seek work elsewhere.

That is no answer to the question. Whether he gets work elsewhere or whether he does not has nothing to do with courts throwing the power of government in favor of a contract that forces men not to do a thing that they have a legal right to do.

What kind of a public policy is it to acknowledge that workers have the legal right to join a trade union and then permit injunction judges to assist employers to annul that right?

A contract should be based on mutuality. The "yellow dog" is based on force by one of the parties and on necessity by the other.

## 13

As destructive of labor's ambitions as yellow-dog contracts were injunctions. These restraining orders, which allowed an employer to enlist the state or national police forces against strikers, were eagerly sought after and freely granted by the courts all through the Progressive Era. Indeed, the injunction was applied against such a wide variety of labor practices that strikes and boycotts were virtually outlawed. A modern student of the law, Charles O. Gregory, has described the way in which injunctions operated:[13]

. . . As soon as the labor injunction became established in the late 1880's almost anyone with an interest in obstructing the activities of labor unions could promptly secure temporary restraining orders for the asking. Continuance of a

[13] Reprinted from *Labor and the Law* by Charles O. Gregory, pp. 99-104, by permission of W. W. Norton & Company, Inc. Copyright 1946 by W. W. Norton & Company, Inc.

strike or boycott, after a restraining order or injunction was issued against it, brought down on the heads of the offenders the vengeance of the court through the exercise of its contempt power, unrelieved by the tender mercies of a jury. Hence, strikes, picket lines and boycotts were easily broken up almost before they were begun.

An employer with a strike or other union pressure on his hands went to a judge, regardless of whether or not he was actually sitting on the bench at the time, submitted to him affidavits made out by his own agents to the effect that the strikers or other union folk were about to commit or were committing, and would continue to commit, alleged unlawful acts at his plant, all of which would cause irreparable damage to his property, and prayed for a restraining order pending suit for a permanent injunction. Judges usually issued such orders on request, frequently in the absence of anyone representing the persons to be enjoined. Sometimes these orders were directed at named individuals, but frequently they were not. And in any event they all purported to restrain everyone "whomsoever," in a vague but grand manner. Obviously not much care was devoted in these transactions to legal theory or even to what was actually transpiring around the plant. And by the time the matter was set for the trial which was to determine whether or not the employer was justified in securing protection of this sort, the strike was broken up, either through the obedience of the union leaders or because they were in jail for disobedience.

As a rule, judges behaved in the same casual fashion after the trial between the two parties, when they had to decide whether or not they should grant formal injunctions and, if they decided to do so, how far they should go in preventing what kind of conduct by whom. At these trials, of course, both sides were represented and the judges took testimony, affording opportunity for cross examination. These proceedings took place before judges without juries. Frequently the evidence indicated actual or imminent violence and other unlawful conduct on the part of union members. But whether it did or did not, too many judges got into the habit of making findings of actual or threatened violence and other specifically unlawful conduct where nothing of the sort had occurred or was imminent. In these injunction suits it was customary to serve a summons only upon the leaders of the unions involved, although the injunctions were issued virtually against the world in general. Consequently, anyone violating the broad and comprehensive terms of such injunctions was punished for contempt, whether or not he had been served as a party in the suit, had had the injunction called to his attention by service of its provisions on him, or had ever heard of the injunction at all. . . .

. . . Too often the judges signing these injunctions did not draft them personally but followed the prevailing custom—perfectly proper in litigation involving less contentious issues—of permitting counsel for the complaining employers to prepare them instead. Unfortunately such injunctions left little, if any, scope for even peaceful economic coercive activity on the part of unions. And the harm occasioned to unions by this summary suppression was not undone even when appellate courts, as they seldom but occasionally did, set aside or modified injunctions because they were against the weight of the evidence adduced or contrary to established law. By that time months had passed, the possible effect of the strike or boycott was long since neutralized, and the union's investment of time, effort and money to organize the pressure was lost.

Even leading conservatives of the early 1900's inveighed against the manner in which courts issued injunctions against organized labor. They were genuinely terrified by the power judges assumed and exercised in these proceedings with such a free hand. Somewhat reasonably, they compared this sweeping exercise of power with the function of legislatures. It was perceived that judges issuing broad and general injunctions against all people whomsoever, regardless of whether or not they had been served with a summons to appear and defend, were virtually promulgating little statutes which declared in advance the illegality of anything done in the premises which the judges did not wish to be done. And they condemned the fashion in which these judges used their contempt power to punish all persons failing to comply with their injunctions, regardless of whether or not such persons had ever been served with a summons originally or had ever had the injunctions brought to their attention. . . .

But perhaps the most alarming feature of the labor injunction, less obvious than the shortcomings just discussed, was the ease with which its use increasingly tempted judges to dispense with any well-founded independent theory of illegality. After all, the injunction was originally supposed to be a kind of remedy. And judicial remedies were supposed to operate as a control of some sort of illegal conduct, actual or threatened. But many courts using the injunction against the activities of labor unions fell into the bad habit of overlooking the need for proof of specific and independently unlawful conduct, either already committed or only threatened, on which to base their injunctive orders. They came to look at much of organized labor's economic coercive activity as enjoinable in itself, without bothering to find or to state in their opinions that it was also unlawful. This was an unfortunate tendency which fed on itself. It seemed to lead many courts to grant sweeping injunctions on the basis of personal or class dislike of organized labor's economic program instead of in accordance with settled standards of law. . . .

. . . In this way too many judges began

to think of labor union activity as something enjoinable in itself. And since union leaders could not anticipate the vagaries of the judicial mind, they could not define for themselves or their followers the area of permissible economic conduct within which they were legally free to act. This unwholesome state of affairs, where labor unionists never knew just where they stood under the shadow of a brooding and undefined judicial power, involved an almost certain threat of suppression to most of organized labor's bargaining and organizational program, without benefit of any legislative declaration of policy or, indeed, of any rules of the game that might be called law. . . .

## 14

The wholesale use of injunctions was possible only because they were openly favored by many governmental leaders. Typical of the conservative attitude toward them was the view expressed by William Howard Taft in his inaugural address of March 4, 1909:[14]

Another labor question has arisen which has awakened the most excited discussion. That is in respect to the power of the federal courts to issue injunctions in industrial disputes. As to that, my convictions are fixed. Take away from the courts, if it could be taken away, the power to issue injunctions in labor disputes, and it would create a privileged class among the laborers and save the lawless among their number from a most needful remedy available to all men for the protection of their business against lawless invasion. The proposition that business is not a property or pecuniary right which can be protected by equitable injunction is utterly without foundation in precedent or reason. The proposition is usually linked with one to make the secondary boycott lawful. Such a proposition is at variance with the American instinct, and will find no support, in my judgment, when submitted to the American people. The secondary boycott

is an instrument of tyranny, and ought not to be made legitimate.

The issue of a temporary restraining order without notice has in several instances been abused by its inconsiderate exercise, and to remedy this the platform upon which I was elected recommends the formulation in a statute of the conditions under which such a temporary restraining order ought to issue. A statute can and ought to be framed to embody the best modern practice, and can bring the subject so closely to the attention of the court as to make abuses of the process unlikely in the future. The American people, if I understand them, insist that the authority of the courts shall be sustained, and are opposed to any change in the procedure by which the powers of a court may be weakened and the fearless and effective administration of justice be interfered with.

## 15

Leaders more liberal than William Howard Taft, fearful lest the widespread use of the injunction would undermine the economic democracy on which the nation's political democracy rested, refused to follow his advice. Instead, they rallied behind Woodrow Wilson and wrote into the Clayton Antitrust Act a provision designed to relieve labor unions of this burden. Carefully as the section was worded, it failed to survive the assault of company lawyers and their judicial allies. The methods used to circumvent the clear intention of Congress were illustrated in the case of *Duplex Printing Press Company* v. *Deering* (1921). A strike at the Duplex Printing Press Company plant in Battle Creek, Michigan, led to the discharge of fourteen members of the International Association of Machinists. New York members of the union thereupon instituted a boycott against the Duplex Company's product. When the company sought an injunction against the boycott, charging interference with interstate commerce, the Supreme Court reasoned in this way:[15]

The substance of the matters here complained of is an interference with complainant's interstate trade intended to have coercive effect upon complainant, and produced by what is commonly known as a "secondary boycott"; that is, a combination not merely to refrain from dealing with complainant, or to advise or by peaceful means persuade complainant's customers to refrain ("primary boycott") but to exercise coercive pressure. . . .

The principal reliance is upon sec. 20 (of Clayton Act). . . . The second paragraph declares that "no such restraining order or injunction" shall prohibit certain conduct specified,—manifestly still referring to a "case between an employer and an employee, . . . involving, or growing out of, a dispute concerning terms or conditions of employment," as designated in the first paragraph. It is very clear that the restriction upon the use of the injunction is in favor only of those concerned as parties to such a dispute as is described. . . .

The majority of the Circuit Court of Appeals appear to have entertained the view that the words "employers and employees" as used in sec. 20 should be treated as referring to "the business class or clan to which the parties litigant respectively belong"; and that, . . . sec. 20 operated to permit members of the Machinists' Union elsewhere—some 60,000 in number,—although standing in no relation of employment under complainant, past, present, or prospective, to make that dispute their own, and proceed to instigate sympathetic strikes, picketing, and boycotting against employers wholly unconnected with complainant's factory, and having relations with complainant only in the way of purchasing its product in the ordinary course of interstate commerce,—and this where there was no dispute between such employers and their employees respecting terms or conditions of employment.

We deem this construction altogether inadmissible. . . .

The emphasis placed on the words "lawful" and "lawfully," "peaceful" and "peace-

fully," and the references to the dispute and the parties to it, strongly rebut a legislative intent to confer a general immunity for conduct violative of the Anti-Trust laws, or otherwise unlawful. The subject of the boycott is dealt with specifically in the "ceasing to patronize" provision, and by the clear force of the language employed the exemption is limited to pressure exerted upon a "party to such dispute" by means of "peaceful and *lawful*" influence upon neutrals. There is nothing here to justify defendants or the organizations they represent in using either threats or persuasion to bring about strikes or a cessation of work on the part of employees of complainant's customers or prospective customers, or of the trucking company employed by the customers, with the object of compelling such customers to withdraw or refrain from commercial relations with complainant, and of thereby constraining complainant to yield the matter in dispute. To instigate a sympathetic strike in aid of a secondary boycott cannot be deemed "peaceful and lawful" persuasion. . . .

The question whether the bill legalized a secondary boycott having been raised (in the House), it was emphatically and unequivocally answered . . . in the negative. The subject . . . was under consideration when the bill was framed, and the section as reported was carefully prepared with the settled purpose of excluding the secondary boycott, and confining boycotting to the parties to the dispute, allowing parties to cease to patronize and to ask others to cease to patronize a party to the dispute; it was the opinion of the committee that it did not legalize the secondary boycott; it was not their purpose to authorize such a boycott; not a member of the committee would vote to do so; clarifying amendment was unnecessary; the section as reported expressed the real purpose so well that it could not be tortured into a meaning authorizing the secondary boycott. . . .

There should be an injunction against

defendants and the associations represented by them.

## THE I.W.W.

### 16

The unyielding conservatism of the courts led inevitably to retaliation. As capital took refuge in increasing reaction, radical leaders preached the doctrine that reform could not be secured through legal channels, persuading a number of unions to desert the middle-of-the-road liberalism usual in the American labor movement. Illustrative of the emotional depth of rebellion were the social writings of Jack London, whose excoriation of "The Scab" was often circulated by the San Francisco waterfront workmen he knew so well:[16]

After God had finished the rattlesnake, the toad and the vampire, He had some awful substance left with which He made a SCAB. A SCAB is a two-legged animal with a corkscrew soul, a waterlogged brain and a combination backbone made of jelly and glue. Where others have hearts he carries a tumor of rotten principles.

When a SCAB comes down the street men turn their backs and angels weep in heaven, and the devil shuts the gates of hell to keep him out. No man has a right to SCAB so long as there is a pool of water deep enough to drown his body in, or a rope long enough to hang his carcass with. Judas Iscariot was a gentleman compared with a SCAB. For betraying his Master, he had character enough to hang himself. A SCAB HASN'T!

Esau sold his birthright for a mess of pottage. Judas Iscariot sold his Savior for thirty pieces of silver. Benedict Arnold sold his country for a promise of a commission, in the British Army. The modern strikebreaker sells his birthright, his country, his wife, his children, and his fellow-men for an unfulfilled promise from his employer, trust or corporation.

Esau was a traitor to himself. Judas Iscariot was a traitor to his God. Benedict Arnold was a traitor to his country. A STRIKEBREAKER IS A TRAITOR TO HIS GOD, HIS COUNTRY, HIS FAMILY, AND HIS CLASS.

### 17

The small percentage of American workers who lost hope for legal reform found an outlet for their energies in the Industrial Workers of the World, a hard-boiled, left-wing union organized in 1905. Its purpose was to organize a radical labor movement that would wrest supremacy from the cautious older unions. Proclaiming a war of the classes as did Jack London, it won occasional successes by its militant tactics and fighting philosophy. Its revolutionary designs were expressed in a "Preamble of the Industrial Workers of the World" adopted in Chicago in 1919:[17]

The working class and the employing class have nothing in common. There can be no peace so long as hunger and want are found among millions of working people and the few, who make up the employing class, have all the good things of life.

Between these two classes a struggle must go on until the workers of the world organize as a class, take possession of the earth and the machinery of production and abolish the wage system.

We find that the centering of the management of industries into fewer and fewer hands makes the trade unions unable to cope with the ever growing power of the employing class. The trade unions foster a state of affairs which allows one set of workers to be pitted against another set of workers in the same industry, thereby helping defeat one another in wage wars. Moreover the trade unions aid the employing class to mislead the workers into the belief that the working class have interests in common with their employers.

These conditions can be changed and the interest of the working class upheld

---

[16] Philip S. Foner (ed.), *Jack London; American Rebel* (New York, 1947), pp. 57-59. For a slight variant, see an early reproduction in Jack London's Saloon, Oakland, California. Reprinted by permission of Mrs. Charmian K. London.

[17] P. F. Brissenden, *The I.W.W., A Study of American Syndicalism* (New York, 1919), p. 351.

only by an organization formed in such a way that all its members in any one industry, or in all industries if necessary, cease work whenever a strike or lockout is on in any department thereof, thus making an injury to one an injury to all.

Instead of the conservative motto, "A fair day's wage for a fair day's work," we must inscribe on our banner the revolutionary watchword, "Abolition of the wage system." It is the historic mission of the working class to do away with capitalism. The army of production must be organized not only for the everyday struggle with capitalists, but also to carry on production when capitalism shall have been overthrown. By organizing industrially we are forming the structure of the new society within the shell of the old.

## 18

The I.W.W. proved ephemeral but left a heritage. Its labor songs by Joe Hill became part of the folklore of American workers. One of his best-known songs urged labor to seek something more immediate than "pie in the sky":[18]

### The Preacher and the Slave

(*Tune:* "Sweet Bye and Bye")

Long-haired preachers come out every
    night,
Try to tell you what's wrong and what's
    right;
But when asked how 'bout something to
    eat
They will answer with voices so sweet:

### Chorus

You will eat, bye and bye,
In that glorious land above the sky;
Work and pray, live on hay,
You'll get pie in the sky when you die.

And the starvation army they play,
And they sing and they clap and they
    pray.

[18] *Songs of the Workers* (Chicago, 14th ed., 1918).

Till they get all your coin on the drum,
Then they'll tell you when you're on the
    bum:

Holy Rollers and jumpers come out,
And they holler, they jump and they shout.
"Give your money to Jesus," they say,
"He will cure all diseases today."

If you fight hard for children and wife—
Try to get something good in this life—
You're a sinner and bad man, they tell,
When you die you will sure go to hell.

Workingmen of all countries, unite,
Side by side we for freedom will fight:
When the world and its wealth we have
    gained
To the grafters we'll sing this refrain:

### Last Chorus

You will eat, bye and bye,
When you've learned how to cook and to
    fry
Chop some wood, 'twill do you good,
And you'll eat in the sweet bye and bye.

## FARMERS IN A CHANGING WORLD

## 19

Unlike the workers, American farmers enjoyed a period of comparative prosperity during the first two decades of the twentieth century. Adequate rainfall, expanding markets, and the artificial demand created by World War I caused them to forget the grievances that had fostered Populism during the 1890's. Yet their position was by no means secure. The mounting demand for grains, meat, and cereals transformed the farmer during these years into a commercial producer as he increasingly specialized in the crops best suited to his soil. No longer self-sufficient, he sold in the national and world markets all that he produced, then bought what he needed for his family. His old-time independence was gone; he was tied to the market, to industry, and to the city, subject as never before to the economic hurricanes that swept around the globe. This was realized, if not by the farmer, at least by progressive government leaders. Woodrow Wilson particularly capitalized on the long tradition of government aid for agriculture to prepare the farmers for the bad times that must certainly come with any slackening of demand for their produce. His success in expanding the functions of the Department of Agriculture was proudly described in 1916 by Carl Vrooman, the assistant secretary of agriculture:[19]

During the last three years, for the first time in its history, the Department of Agriculture has had at its head an economist. Under the direction of Secretary Houston it has achieved a new point of view and a new conception of its mission. For half a century the department has used its utmost endeavors to show the farmer how to fight the chinch-bug and the army-worm, the cattle tick and the Hessian fly and other insect pests, but had not even so much as attempted to show him how to protect himself from the yearly toll levied upon the fruits of his toil by such human pests as the usurer, commercial pirates posing as legitimate middlemen, and the other business parasites of the agricultural world.

The farmer who makes two blades of grass grow where only one grew before may be a good agronomist, but if he cannot sell his second blades at a profit, he is a poor farmer. In other words, farming is primarily a business. Very few practical farmers till the soil to demonstrate principles of agronomy. They produce crops to live rather than live to produce crops. Even more than large production they want *profitable* production. Upon the realization of this fundamental fact is founded the agricultural renaissance which recently has been begun.

It seems strange that a fact as simple as this should have been overlooked for many years. Every farmer, at one time or another, has been brought face to face with the paradox of big crops and small returns.

He has often been forced to the conclusion that the larger crops you raise the less money you make. . . .

In order to find a solution for this and a host of other problems in agricultural economics that involve the farmers' financial success or failure, the present administration created a new bureau, called the Office of Markets and Rural Organization. It has been in operation only two years, and has not yet solved any large number of these problems, but the very fact of its creation, the fact that the Department of Agriculture at last has undertaken the stupendous task of charting for the farmer the treacherous and tempestuous economic sea and of pointing out to him the shoals and reefs, the tides and undertows which have brought shipwreck to many thousands in the past, is a matter of historic moment. . . .

In addition to the creation of the Office of Markets and Rural Organization in the Department of Agriculture, Congress has passed a number of laws, and is now in process of passing several more, dealing with the farmers' economic and business problems. Among these may be mentioned the Cotton Futures Act. Before this law went into effect the producer was virtually at the mercy not only of the local buyer, but also of the big operators on the cotton exchanges, who were able to boost or depress the market at will through the exertion of undue influence within the exchange. . . .

Among the important measures in the interest of the farmer now pending in Congress that probably will be enacted into law during the present session, the most important is the so-called Rural Credits Bill, providing for the establishment of a system of land banks. This law does not attempt to provide additional personal credit facilities for farmers. That is a distinctly different problem, and one which ought to be and no doubt will be taken up by Congress at its next session. The Rural Credits Bill has a definite ob-

[19] Carl Vrooman, "The Agricultural Revolution," *Century Magazine*, XCIII (November, 1916), 112-115. Reprinted by permission of the author, Carl Vrooman.

ject, to furnish the farmer having the proper security to offer, first, more money, secondly, money on longer time loans, and thirdly, money at a lower rate of interest than he has been able to get it in the past. Every farmer will realize the vital importance of these three features of the bill. Every farmer will realize that a bill which furnishes him with these three things is an invaluable single step in the direction of a complete system of rural credits.

Another highly important piece of legislation now pending in Congress is the Good Roads Bill. If enacted into law, this measure will do more to provide our country with good roads than has all past legislation on that subject put together. This is a matter of primary economic importance to the farmer. At present it costs the average farmer more to haul his produce to his local market than to ship it to the nearest terminal market. The heaviest tax he pays is the penalty extorted from him for having bad roads. . . .

. . . Fewer than a dozen years ago the Department of Agriculture was almost as far removed from actual contact with the masses of our farmers as the State Department or the Coast and Geodetic Survey. No wide-spread, continuous, and systematic effort has yet been made to carry agricultural education to the farmer by word of mouth or by demonstration; the Office of Farm Management was a minor appendage of one of the older bureaus; the publications of the department were lucky if they escaped being still-born, so little was the effort made to popularize them and to interest the farmers in them by means of the press. . . .

An even more important popular educational movement has been instituted by means of the Smith-Lever Bill. This bill has set in motion a plan which within a few years will place in every county in the United States that is willing to cooperate with the State and Federal governments an agricultural county agent, an official who is really a species of deputy secretary

of agriculture. This work is modeled on the agricultural demonstration work started several years ago by the late Seaman A. Knapp in the Southern States, and within a very few years will result in an annual expenditure of anywhere from ten to twenty million dollars, and is planning to bring the latest and most successful scientific methods directly to the door of the American farmers. This is the greatest university extension campaign the would has ever seen. It is learning democratized, learning brought out of the laboratories and the libraries, out of the experiment fields and the bulletins, adapted to local conditions, mixed with horse-sense and business gumption, and explained to the individual farmer by a man who lives in his community and understands intimately the needs both of its soil and of its people.

I was told the other day by a banker from central New York that in two short years one of our county agents located in his county had done more for the farmers of that county than the entire Department of Agriculture had done during the fifty years preceding. . . .

## 20

County agents, rural credit, and better roads all helped the farmer, but there were other areas where aid was just as essential. Vast sections of rural America were ravaged by disease—disease that singled out the hired hand or the share cropper, yet scarcely affected the wealthier planter or city dweller. Was there some connection between farm poverty and epidemics? Here was an avenue for investigation that attracted the interest of an infant government agency, the United States Public Health Service. The epic battle of one of its agents, Dr. Joseph Goldberger, against the plague of red death—pellagra—has been described by Paul de Kruif in his classic work on *Hunger Fighters:*[20]

There now began to be published, in American medical journals, reports of per-

---

[20] Adapted from *Hunger Fighters* by Paul de Kruif, pp. 335-346, 362-363, copyright, 1928, by Harcourt, Brace and Company, Inc.

sons with sore mouths, with rashes that broke out looking only like a mild sunburn, but that turned into sores to make them look like lepers. And some of these people died gibbering, insane, and certainly thirty to forty out of every hundred that came to clinics and hospitals with pellagra died, one way or another. "Like a mushroom pellagra is coming up overnight, spreading everywhere," wrote one of Goldberger's mates of the Public Health Service, the able Lavinder. Lavinder toiled at it, showed how terribly prevalent this plague was below the Mason and Dixon line—but explain it? Who had learned anything about this evil mystery, in two hundred years?

The doctors of the South were many of them sure this was a contagious pestilence, for here were villages, that seemed to be suddenly swept by it. . . .

In 1914 Joseph Goldberger got orders from the red brick laboratory on the hill over the Potomac in Washington, to take the train down South, to be in charge of pellagra investigations. . . .

He made a tour of State Insane Asylums. . . .

. . . Here were plenty of demented folks, made still more miserable by this breaking-out, by this what-is-it that gnawed at their skins, by the evil that turned their bowels to water: and again he asked questions, and after preliminary politenesses, talked of nothing but pellagra with the Georgia doctors. And he argued:

"From what the best books say, and from what I've seen," said Goldberger, "the big difference between folks that die of pellagra and those that never get it, is that pellagrins are poor!"

Possibly true, answered the Georgia doctors, but still, there were cases. . . .

"No—here's something more," persisted Goldberger. "The big difference between rich and poor is that the poor don't get the right stuff to eat!". . .

. . . And the gaunt Goldberger watched the trays of food, crowned with a cloud of steam, come up from the kitchen. He saw the waiters fill the plates of the patients from the identical trays that furnished their own grub—but he saw something more.

Goldberger caught what ninety-nine searchers out of a hundred would have said was an insignificant nothing, noticed an event you yourself would say was absolutely unimportant, and he nabbed this truth because he was first of all a human being, alive to human kinks and quirks, aware of human weaknesses. He looked down those rows of crazy ones, then he turned to Lorenz, with his very small, quick smile.

"You're right, Goldberger," said Lorenz, excited. "See! By George! You're right—who'd have thought it?"

Goldberger was right. It was the attendants, the nurses, who got the nice cuts of meat, the glasses of milk. "And look," said Lorenz, "a lot of those patients aren't even eating the gristly meat they get!". . .

. . . He hit the trail once more—back to Jackson, Mississippi. He pulled up at a desolate little Baptist Orphanage there, presented his credentials. One hundred and thirty of those fatherless, motherless young ones could at this place be set down as pellagrous. He went down to a poverty-stricken Methodist Orphanage, and here seventy-nine of those homeless brats were down with the red ailment that made them so listless. . . .

It was the summer of 1914, a year when 1,192 persons are recorded to have died of pellagra in the State of Mississippi—and in that state the records of the cause of death were not then too complete. . . . And in those records there appeared a fact —it was certainly surprising—and that fact was this: that the children between the ages of six and twelve—and hardly a soul among the older or younger ones—were down with pellagra. He mulled over it, got nowhere. . . .

These orphanages were a hurly-burly of lisping tots, mischievous brats, and boys and girls already past puberty—all in a heap, overcrowded was no word for them. Everybody had a splendid chance to catch this pellagra, but only this one bunch had it. But food—the kind of food—what is it they're eating? . . .

Sidewise from his brown eyes he saw this fifteen-year-old boy sneak a long swig of milk from the cow he'd just been milking.

He got growing-up girls to confess they stole into the pantry, nights after supper, for milk and a piece of meat, maybe—and who could blame them?

He watched the older children at their suppers and dinners: the older ones all had some kind of little job to do to earn their keep—and these actually were served fresh meat several times a week.

And here was something nice, something the trustees of this poor waifs' home were to be congratulated upon: the tots, those up to five or six, got a couple of good mugs of fresh milk a day—little youngsters must have their milk, and the authorities could afford to keep just enough cows to see that they got it. . . .

Goldberger started his first experiment. These orphanages were maintained in a reasonably dirty and miserable condition, for want of funds to pay for help. Crowded was a polite name to call them, but he didn't try to change their sanitation at all. He simply went to the grave trustees of poor children's homes, and spoke soft to them!

"Would you object to feeding fresh meat and plenty of fresh milk to *all* of your children here—if the Government, if the United States Public Health Service, pays for it?"

The grave trustees looked at the hawk-face as if he were Santa Claus: "Would they object?" Just let Dr. Goldberger try them!

So, in the middle of the month of September, 1914, those youngsters began to have the luxury of two seven-ounce cups of milk each day. They began to live like

so many little lords—on nice cuts of fresh meat four times each week. Every child under twelve had at least one egg a day—for breakfast. And they were to have beans and peas all winter. And they did. And it was like Christmas all the time for them.

The next year, 1915, was the very devil of a year for pellagra, and 1,535 souls in Mississippi are down in the records as having died from it—and who can tell how many perished forgotten? But let's go to those orphanages. Here is Joseph Goldberger, that big doctor who got them the meat and the milk, walking among the children at the Baptist and the Methodist orphanages, and they're always tickled to see him. And Goldberger and Waring go over every single one of those kids, their faces, their hands, the young skin of their naked bodies, and it is beautiful:

At the Methodist home, where seventy-nine last year suffered from the flaming rash—not a single youngster has so much as a sign of it.

At the Baptist home where one hundred and thirty last year were red-skinned, listless, one lone child has a possible touch of it. . . .

. . . Well-off folks hadn't ever heard of Goldberger; prosperous folks, thank heaven, didn't have to see those sufferers. He lived among these unknown thousands who were dying from pellagra, starving to a red· death though they were eating plenty—on tenant farms, in mill villages. Is it any wonder that Goldberger lay awake, one hot southern night after another? This grotesque fact faced him, leered at him: "The surer it is that pellagra is only a hidden hunger, the more hopeless it seems to try to wipe it out."

For two years he went up and down through seven drab mill villages in the South Carolina cotton country, with the help of Wheeler, and the encouragement of that statistical shark, Edgar Sydenstricker. They spent two years at proving what they were already sure of: Well-off, prosperous families, with good incomes of, say, a thousand dollars a year or a little better, have none of this red-skinned death! There was a mockery in this, that you give the most ignorant imaginable folks an extra dollar, and they'll buy fresh meat, never worry, and milk for their kids, and themselves; and give them a little land and a little daylight in the evenings—and they'll make a fist at raising a truck garden. But where were the dollars, and where was the daylight? . . .

. . . There were plenty of hard-boiled people who'd tell you that if those poor whites down there amounted to a row of pins they'd get out of those villages and go where they could earn more and so get the right grub. . . . And myself I've sat listening while men of science told me Goldberger was foolish to try to find a cure for such low-down folks; they had bad heredity; it were better they be left to die—to be cut down by the natural selection that uses this red death as a scythe.

## 21

Despite health services and increased government aid to agriculture, significant segments of the rural population were still enmeshed in a backward system. Improvement of rural credit benefited the more solvent farm owners. New concern for agricultural workers and farmers who were not owners was suggested in the report of the United States Commission on Industrial Relations (1916):[21]

1. Tenancy in the Southwestern States is already the prevailing method of cultivation and is increasing at a very rapid rate. In 1880 Texas had 65,468 tenant families, comprising 37.6 per cent of all farms in the State. In 1910 tenant farmers had increased to 219,571 and operated 53 per cent of all farms in the State. Reckoning on the same ratio of increase that was maintained between 1900 and 1910, there

[21] United States Commission on Industrial Relations, *Final Report and Testimony*, I (1916), 86-89. (*Senate Documents*, 64th Cong., 1st Sess., Doc. No. 415.)

should be in Texas in the present year (1915) at least 236,000 tenant farmers. A more intensive study of the field, however, shows that in the 82 counties of the State where tenancy is highest the average percentage of tenants will approximate 60.

For Oklahoma we have not adequate census figures so far back, but at the present time the percentage of farm tenancy in the State is 54.8, and for the 47 counties where the tenancy is highest the percentage of tenancy is 68.13.

2. Tenancy, while inferior in every way to farm ownership from a social standpoint, is not necessarily an evil if conducted under a system which protects the tenants and assures cultivation of the soil under proper and economical methods, but where tenancy exists under such conditions as are prevalent in the Southwest, its increase can be regarded only as a menace to the Nation.

3. The prevailing system of tenancy in the Southwest is share tenancy, under which the tenant furnishes his own seed, tools, and teams and pays the landlord one-third of the grain and one-fourth of the cotton. There is, however, a constant tendency to increase the landlord's share through the payment either of cash bonuses or of a higher percentage of the product. Under this system tenants as a class earn only a bare living through the work of themselves and their entire families. Few of the tenants ever succeed in laying by a surplus. On the contrary, their experiences are so discouraging that they seldom remain on the same farm for more than a year, and they move from one farm to the next, in the constant hope of being able to better their condition. Without the labor of the entire family the tenant farmer is helpless. As a result, not only is his wife prematurely broken down, but the children remain uneducated and without the hope of any condition better than that of their parents. The tenants having no interest in the results beyond the crops of a single year, the soil is being rapidly ex-

hausted and the conditions, therefore, tend to become steadily worse. Even at present a very large proportion of the tenants' families are insufficiently clothed, badly housed, and underfed. Practically all of the white tenants are native born. As a result of these conditions, however, they are deteriorating rapidly, each generation being less efficient and more hopeless than the one preceding.

4. A very large proportion of the tenants are hopelessly in debt and are charged exorbitant rates of interest. Over 95 per cent of the tenants borrow from some source, and about 75 per cent borrow regularly year after year. The average interest rate on all farm loans is 10 per cent, while small tenants in Texas pay 15 per cent or more. In Oklahoma the conditions are even worse, in spite of the enactment of laws against usury. Furthermore, over 80 per cent of the tenants are regularly in debt to the stores from which they secure their supplies, and pay exorbitantly for this credit. The average rate of interest on store credit is conservatively put at 20 per cent and in many cases ranges as high as 60 per cent.

5. The leases are largely in the form of oral contracts which run for only one year and which make no provision for compensation to the tenant for any improvements which may be made upon the property. As a result, tenants are restrained from making improvements, and in many cases do not properly provide for the upkeep of the property.

6. Furthermore, the tenants are in some instances the victims of oppression on the part of landlords. This oppression takes the form of dictation of character and amount of crops, eviction without due notice, and discrimination because of personal and political convictions. The existing law provides no recourse against such abuses.

7. As a result both of the evils inherent in the tenant system and of the occasional oppression by landlords, a state of acute unrest is developing among the tenants and there are clear indications of the beginning of organized resistance which may result in civil disturbances of a serious character.

8. The situation is being accentuated by the increasing tendency of the landlords to move to the towns and the cities, relieving themselves not only from all productive labor, but from direct responsibility for the conditions which develop. Furthermore, as a result of the increasing expenses incident to urban life there is a marked tendency to demand from the tenant a greater share of the products of his labor.

9. The responsibility for the existing conditions rests not upon the landlords, but upon the system itself. The principal causes are to be found in the system of short leases, the system of private credit at exorbitant rates, the lack of a proper system of marketing, the absence of educational facilities, and last but not least the prevalence of land speculation.

10. A new factor is being introduced into the agricultural situation through the development of huge estates owned by corporations and operated by salaried managers upon a purely industrial system. The labor conditions on such estates are subject to grave criticism. The wages are extremely low, 80 cents per day being the prevailing rate on one large estate which was thoroughly investigated; arbitrary deductions from wages are made for various purposes; and a considerable part of the wages themselves are paid in the form of coupons, which are in all essential particulars the same as the "scrip" which has been the source of such great abuse. Furthermore, the communities existing on these large estates are subject to the complete control of the land-owning corporation, which may regulate the lives of citizens to almost any extent. There is an apparent tendency toward the increase of these large estates, and the greatest abuses may be expected if they are allowed to develop unchecked.

11. Prompt and effective action on the part of the States and Nation is necessary if any alleviation of the conditions which have been described is to be achieved.

It is suggested that the commission recommend:

1. The development through legislation of longer time farm leases that will make for fair rents, security of tenure, and protection of the interests of the tenant in the matter of such improvements as he may make on a leasehold in his possession. Such legislation should look forward to leasing systems that will increase tillage, improve the yielding powers of the soil and maintain a greater population.

In order to secure this desired end it is suggested that the commission further recommend the creation of:

2. National and State land commissions with powers—

(a) To act as land courts with powers to hear evidence given by landlord and tenants as to questions that have to do with fair rents, fixity of tenure and improvements made by tenants on landlords' property; to gather evidence, independently of both parties, that will the better enable such land courts to arrive at the true facts in each case; and to render judgment that will be mandatory for such time as the contractual relationship may be determined to hold. . . .

3. The development of better credit facilities through the assistance of the Government and cooperative organization of farmers and tenants. No single measure can be recommended; the results must be achieved through the development of a sound rural-credit system, the development of land banks, mortgage associations and credit unions. Foreign experience shows that through these means the rate of interest can be greatly reduced and the security of both the borrower and the lender can be increased.

4. The general introduction of modernized rural schools and compulsory education of children. The functions of the

school system should extend beyond education to the social service of the entire rural community, assisting in the organization of farmers and tenants for cooperative purposes, and promoting other measures looking to the community's welfare.

5. The revision of the taxation system so as to exempt from taxation all improvements and tax unused land at its full rental value. . . .

## 22

President Wilson's earnest efforts to better the lot of farmers were not confined to reform of the Department of Agriculture and extension of the Public Health Service. Instead, government agencies dealing with agriculture were strengthened, new ones were created, and Congress was prodded into passing laws beneficial to rural areas. Wilson summed up the progress that had been made in a letter written in 1916 to A. F. Lever, chairman of the Committee on Agriculture:[22]

MY DEAR MR. LEVER:

It has given me much satisfaction to approve to-day the bill making appropriations for the Department of Agriculture for the fiscal year ending June 30, 1917, and for other purposes, because the bill not only makes very generous provision for the improvement of farm production in the Nation and for investigations and demonstrations in the field of marketing of farm crops and of the organization of rural life, but also contains three well-conceived measures designed to improve market practices and the storage and financing of staple crops. As the passage of this bill marks the practical completion of an important part of the program for the betterment of rural life which was mapped out at the beginning of the administration, I feel that I cannot let the occasion pass without conveying to you and your associates in both Houses my appreciation of the great service rendered

[22] *Congressional Record*, 64th Cong., 1st Sess., appendix, pp. 1762-1763.

to the nation in strengthening its great agricultural foundations.

The record, legislative as well as administrative, is a remarkable one. It speaks for itself and needs only to be set forth.

1. Appreciation of the importance of agriculture has been shown through greatly and intelligently increased appropriations for its support.

2. Particular pains have been taken to foster production by every promising means, and careful thought has been given especially to the matter of increasing the meat supply of the Nation.

3. Greatly increased provision has been made, through the enactment of the cooperative agricultural extension act, for conveying agricultural information to farmers, and for inducing them to apply it. This piece of legislation is one of the most significant and far-reaching measures for the education of adults ever adopted by any Government. It provides for cooperation between the States and the Federal Government. This is a highly important and significant principle. When the act is in full operation there will be expended annually under its terms, from Federal and State sources alone, a total of over $8,600,000 in the direct education of the farmer; this amount is being and will be increasingly supplemented by contributions from local sources. It will permit the placing in each of the 2,850 rural counties of the Nation two farm demonstrators and specialists, who will assist the demonstrators in the more difficult problems confronting them.

4. Systematic provision for the first time has been made for the solution of problems in that important half of agriculture which concerns distribution, marketing, rural finance, and rural organization.

5. Provision was made promptly for the creation of an Office of Markets and Rural Organization, and the appropriations for this office, including those for enforcing new laws designed to promote better marketing, have been increased to $1,200,000.

The more difficult problems of marketing are being investigated and plans are in operation for furnishing assistance to producers of perishables through a market news service. A similar service for the livestock interest will be inaugurated during the year.

6. The problem of securing the uniform grading of staple crops, of regulating dealings and traffic in them, of developing a better system of warehouses, and of providing more available collateral for farm loans has been successfully dealt with.

7. Under the cotton-futures act standards for cotton have been established, the operations of the future exchanges have been put under supervision, and the sale of cotton has been placed on a firmer basis.

8. The United States grain-standards act will secure uniformity in the grading of grain, enable the farmer to obtain fairer prices for his product, and afford him an incentive to raise better grades of grain.

9. The United States warehouse act will enable the Department of Agriculture to license bonded warehouses in the various States. It will lead to the development of better storage facilities for staple crops and will make possible the issuance of reliable warehouse receipts which will be widely and easily negotiable.

10. Of no less importance for agriculture and for national development is the Federal Aid road act. This measure will conduce to the establishment of more effective highway machinery in each State, strongly influence the development of good road building along right lines, stimulate larger production and better marketing, promote a fuller and more attractive rural life, add greatly to the convenience and economic welfare of all the people, and strengthen the national foundations. The act embodies sound principles of road legislation and will safeguard the expenditure of funds arising under the act not only, but will also result

in the more efficient use of the large additional sums made available by States and localities.

11. The Federal Reserve Act benefits the farmer, as it does all the other people of the Nation, by guaranteeing better banking, safeguarding the credit structure of the country, and preventing panics. It takes particular note of the special needs of the farmer by making larger provision for loans through national banks on farm mortgages and by giving farm paper a maturity period of six months.

12. It was essential, however, that banking machinery be devised which would reach intimately into the rural districts, that it should operate on terms suited to the farmer's needs, and should be under sympathetic management. The need was for machinery which would introduce business methods into farm finance, bring order out of chaos, reduce the cost of handling farm loans, place upon the market mortgages which would be a safe investment for private funds, attract into agricultural operations a fair share of the capital of the Nation, and lead to a reduction of interest. These needs and these ideals have been met by the enactment of the Federal farm-loan act.

The Progressive Era witnessed a noticeable improvement in the lot of both farmer and worker. During those years both state and national governments, stirred by an awakening public conscience, enacted laws designed to restore a more equitable balance between Big Business and the toilers of field and factory. Yet the victory was far from won when World War I brought an end to the wave of reform. Not until the Great Depression of the 1930's brought the plight of the nation's masses into sharper relief did the United States carry to a conclusion the battle for justice begun by the prophets of progressivism.

# THE WORLD'S ILLUSION

## 1900-1917

Domestic progressivism did not alter the course of American foreign policy. Between 1900 and 1917 a newly imperialistic United States moved into the world arena, with strength as its justification and colonies as its prize. That the forces America was seeking to democratize at home should foster imperialism abroad was both tragic and understandable. Ignoring the fact that the nineteenth-century technological revolutions had created an interdependent world, statesmen were impressed, instead, with the knowledge that industry gave strength to the strong. Arrogantly conscious of their country's power, they succumbed to false prophets, who told them that external possessions were a mark of great nations, that aggressive diplomacy meant more dollars for all, and that racial destiny demanded rule over "backward" peoples of the world. Yet before the Progressive Era came to a close they were tragically reminded that the end product of nationalism was war.

## THE FALL OF LIBERAL NATIONALISM

### 1

The liberal nationalism of Adam Smith and the nineteenth century had looked to a co-operative world, to be achieved by reducing trade barriers and blurring economic boundaries. The nationalism of Theodore Roosevelt and the twentieth century looked, instead, to a divided world of independent nations, each protected by its strength and each economically supreme within its own sphere of influence. In such a world each powerful country must surround itself with a ring of satellites; in return for protection these weak dependencies would serve as defensive outposts as well as markets for goods of the guardian nation. Jingoistic writers began to urge Americans to enter the race for colonies —already well under way in Europe—during the first years of the century. Most influential was Admiral Alfred Thayer Mahan, who compactly summarized twenty years of his own writings in an article "The Place of Force in International Relations," published in 1912:[1]

It is often asserted that the existence of the armed forces of Europe, one over against the other, is provocative of war. They might be, they probably would be, if during negotiation or in a moment of

[1] From *Armaments and Arbitration* by A. T. Mahan. Copyright, 1912, by Harper & Brothers. Copyright, 1940, by Lyle Evans Mahan.

excitement they were paraded in threatening manner. Sensible men, however, know well that other sensible men will avoid a known danger, unless circumstances are such that avoidance may be taken to show a yielding to fear; and therefore, unless desirous of collision for specific reasons, as Bismarck was in 1870, they prefer to carry their point by discussion, in which the factor of force is ignored, yet understood.

Can then force, broadly considered, be regarded as an inevitable factor in international adjustments and in the maintenance of the general international balances? . . .

In this country we have recently been passing through, and have not yet emerged from, a period in which force, astutely managed and directed, has largely controlled the business relations of the entire community. The force of concentrated capital is as real and as material as the force of an organized army, and it has the same advantage over a multitude of unorganized competitors that an army has over a mob. . . .

The States of the world of European civilization, in which America is included, in their organized national activities represent among themselves an international community of competing business organizations. They recognize that the general benefit depends ultimately upon the welfare of each and all; but nevertheless the aim of each is to compass for itself—that is, for its people—the utmost preponderance of advantage possible to be secured. Of this aim and effort, Protection, technically so called, is the most evident and the crudest manifestation. Protection is simply the use of force, of national power recognized as legal, to secure commercial advantage; but it becomes immediately apparent that, so far as the system is economically sound, the greater the area that can be embraced within it—that is, the larger the concentration—the more effective is the operation.

Hence results inevitably the attempt to enlarge the national boundaries, in order to include and to administer to the national advantage as much territory at least as can be securely held and profitably exploited. The motives thereto, though not purely economical, are largely so; but undoubtedly there does co-operate the perfectly human and universal motive of enjoyment in mere possession. This must be taken into account, as a real and influential national factor. It is a mistake to argue that because nations and peoples are largely animated by self-interest, self-interest alone moves them; . . .

The extension of national control in order to further national advantage, or to flatter national self-esteem, is a natural outcome of Protection. That the same disposition is observed in the great non-protectionist State—Great Britain—shows how deeply the fundamental idea of Protection is rooted in human nature. But here enters that other universally recognized factor—that forces take the line of least resistance. Probably no State in Europe at the present time seriously contemplates the acquisition by force of the European territory of a rival. . . . The armaments of European States now are not so much for protection against conquest as to secure to themselves the utmost possible share of the unexploited, or imperfectly exploited, regions of the world; the outlying markets, or storehouses of raw material, which under national control shall minister to national emolument. The case is much like that of the ownership of ore-fields by the Steel Trust of which we have heard so much; the natural, and certainly not unwise, wish of the manufacturer to command his own sources of fuel and raw materials.

But while the scene of such acquisition is elsewhere than in Europe, it is in Europe that the battle is fought. . . . Even the author of *The Great Illusion* holds that co-operation in the subjugation of the planet, the utilization of its resources, is the true warfare of man, and, if I rightly understand him, admits that communities which do not contribute to this may be taken in hand gently and administered temporarily to that end. But what decides which among several competitors shall be the administrator? Force simply; not only the military force of organized armies and navies, but force of position, or of previous incidents which have given one or another a certain priority of intervention, or advantage of neighborhood, as of France against Germany in the Morocco imbroglio. In the adjustments which take place, armed force, and that in distant Europe itself, has the casting vote, either to maintain or to reserve; and in Europe, not in the remote dependency, would collision take place. . . .

In short, competition for control is extending its sphere from the scene of European civilization to that of extra-European, and exists not only between the European peoples themselves in these exterior regions, but between the present occupants and the intruders. It is a competition not merely of nations, as in Europe and in America, but of civilizations; and of the religions which have stamped their essential characteristics upon the nations professing them. Of the Christian religion the great constituent is power; which in another shape, easily assumed, becomes force. Force is power in action. We are prone to assume, because the personal ideal of the individual Christian, exemplified above all in the Master, is abnegation of self, that therefore power and force are alien from the Christian scheme of character. The history of the Master Himself refutes this. . . .

. . . To right what is amiss, to convert, to improve, to develop, is of the very essence of the Christian ideal. Without man's responsive effort, God Himself is—not powerless—but deprived of the instrument through which alone He wills to work. Hence the recognition that, if force is necessary, force must be used for the benefit of the community, of the commonwealth of the World. This fundamental proposition is not impaired by the fact that force is best exercised through law, when adequate law exists. Except as the expression of right, law is an incubus.

To such a view aggression, in its primary sense of onward movement, is inevitable. Those who will not move must be swept aside. . . .

## 2

Admiral Mahan's words were parroted by a legion of imperialistic writers in the United States and abroad. The arguments that they employed to justify the junglelike aggressions of the great powers were admirably summarized by George William Nasmyth, an American sociologist and Wilsonian Democrat, in his *Social Progress and the Darwinian Theory* (1916):[2]

The entrance of the United States of America upon an Imperialistic career by the annexation of Hawaii, and later, of the Philippines, marks the extension of the competition to the Western Hemisphere.

This unprecedented growth of Imperialism among all the great powers contributed powerfully to the spread of the philosophy of force. On the one hand,

[2] George W. Nasmyth, *Social Progress and the Darwinian Theory* (1916), pp. 46-50. Courtesy of G. P. Putnam's Sons.

"social Darwinism" was enlisted to justify the methods of force which were used so extensively in this process of conquest and subjugation; on the other hand, the results of Imperialism were pointed to as the proofs of the process of the survival of the fittest and the inevitable dominance of the higher civilization, thus contributing to the spread of the pseudo-scientific doctrine.

Even sociologists have shown themselves eager in some cases to accept the philosophy of force as the sufficient justification of Imperialism, and to apply it to defend the necessity, the utility, and even the righteousness of continuing the physical struggle between the races and types of civilization to the point of complete subjugation or extermination. Thus Professor Karl Pearson maintains that a constant struggle with other groups or races is demanded for the maintenance and progress of a race or nation. If you abate the necessity of struggle, the vigour of the race flags and perishes. It is to the real interest of a vigorous race, he says, to be "kept up to a high pitch of external efficiency by contest, chiefly by way of war with inferior races, and with equal races by the struggle for trade routes and for the sources of raw material and of food supply. This is the natural history view of mankind, and I do not think you can in its main features subvert it."

By others, who take a wider, cosmic view, the argument has been put on the ground of "social efficiency." "Human progress," so runs the argument, "requires the maintenance of the race struggle, in which the weakest races shall go under, while the 'socially efficient' races survive and flourish; we are the socially efficient race; therefore our nation must take up the 'white man's burden' and enter upon an Imperialistic career." The principle of social efficiency is described as being "as indisputable as the law of gravitation" by Edmund Demolins, who enunciates it as follows:

"When one race shows itself superior to another in the various externals of domestic life, it *inevitably* in the long run gets the upper hand in public life and establishes its predominance. Whether this predominance is asserted by peaceable means or feats of arms, it is none the less, when the proper time comes, officially established, and afterwards unreservedly acknowledged. I have said that this law is the only thing which accounts for the history of the human race and the revolutions of empires, and that, moreover, it explains and justifies the appropriation by Europeans of territories in Asia, Africa, and Oceania, and the whole of our colonial development."

The gospel of Imperialism, as embodied in the career of Hubert Hervey of the British South African Chartered Company, has been summed up by his fellow-adventurer, Earl Grey, as follows:

"Probably every one would agree that an Englishman would be right in considering his way of looking at the world and at life better than that of the Maori or Hottentot, and no one will object in the abstract to England doing her best to impose her better and higher view on those savages. But the same idea will carry you much further. In so far as an Englishman differs in essentials from a Swede or a Belgian, he believes that he represents a more perfectly developed standard of general excellence. Yes, and even those nations nearest to us in mind and sentiment—German and Scandinavian—we regard on the whole as not so excellent as ourselves, comparing their typical characteristics with ours. Were this not so, our energies would be directed to becoming what they are. Without doing this, however, we may well endeavour to pick out their best qualities and add them to ours, believing that our compound will be superior to the foreign stock.

"It is the mark of an independent nation that it should feel thus. How far such a feeling is, in any particular case, justified, history alone decides. But it is essential that each claimant for the first place should put forward his whole energy to prove his right. This is the moral justification for international strife and for war, and a great change must come over the world and over men's minds before there can be any question of everlasting universal peace, or the settlement of all international differences by arbitration. More especially must the difficulty caused by the absence of a generally recognized standard of justice be felt in the case of contact between civilized and uncivilized races. Is there any likelihood of the gulf between the white and the black man being bridged within any period of time that we can foresee? Can there be any doubt that the white man must, and will, impose his superior civilization on the coloured races? The rivalry of the principal European countries in extending their influence over other continents should lead naturally to the evolution of the highest attainable type of government of subject races by the superior qualities of their rulers."

This is an excellent statement of the scientific basis of Imperialism, including in its survey the physical struggle between white races, the subjugation of lower races by the white race, the necessity and the utility of this struggle and this subjugation, and finally the right of domination based upon this necessity. The white man believes he is a more excellent type than any other man; he believes he is better able to assimilate any special virtues others may have; he believes that this character gives him a right to rule which no other can possess. Thus, starting from natural history, the doctrine soon takes on the outer garments of ethical and even religious sanctions, and we soon reach the elevated atmosphere of "Imperial Christianity," the "mission of civilization," in which our nation is called upon to teach the "arts of good government," the "dignity of labour."

## AMERICAN EXPANSION AND POWER POLITICS

### 3

The United States applied in two different ways the advice offered by prophets of imperialism. In the Caribbean region and northern Latin America its policy was one of open preponderance, seeking to convert the small republics there into American satellites. In the Pacific and the Far East, on the other hand, it adopted a modified balance-of-power technique designed to secure commercial privileges for its nationals by preventing the European powers from making outright territorial grabs. This course was deemed necessary after 1895 when Japan, recognizing the deterioration of the ancient Chinese empire, seized the island of Formosa, which lay strategically close to the Philippines. As other nations began the "scramble for concessions" in China, Secretary of State John Hay realized that America's commercial toehold in the Orient would soon be rendered worthless. Rejecting a British proposal for joint action to preserve the *status quo*, he formulated instead the Open-Door policy. This was announced in a circular note to the interested powers on September 6, 1899:[3]

SIR: At the time when the Government of the United States was informed by that of Germany that it had leased from His Majesty the Emperor of China the port of Kiao-chao and the adjacent territory in the province of Shantung, assurances were given to the ambassador of the United States at Berlin by the Imperial German minister for foreign affairs that the rights and privileges insured by treaties with China to citizens of the United States would not thereby suffer or be in anywise impaired within the area over which Germany had thus obtained control.

More recently, however, the British Government recognized by a formal agreement with Germany the exclusive right of the latter to enjoy in said leased area and the

contiguous "sphere of influence or interest" certain privileges, more especially those relating to railroads and mining enterprises; but, as the exact nature and extent of the rights thus recognized have not been clearly defined, it is possible that serious conflicts of interest may at any time arise, not only between British and German subjects within said area, but that the interests of our citizens may also be jeopardized thereby.

Earnestly desirous to remove any cause of irritation and to insure at the same time to the commerce of all nations in China the undoubted benefits which should accrue from a formal recognition by the various powers claiming "spheres of interest" that they shall enjoy perfect equality of treatment for their commerce and navigation within such "spheres," the Government of the United States would be pleased to see His German Majesty's Government give formal assurances and lend its coöperation in securing like assurances from the other interested powers that each within its respective sphere of whatever influence—

*First.* Will in no way interfere with any treaty port or any vested interest within any so-called "sphere of interest" or leased territory it may have in China.

*Second.* That the Chinese treaty tariff of the time being shall apply to all merchandise landed or shipped to all such ports as are within said "sphere of interest" (unless they be "free ports"), no matter to what nationality it may belong, and that duties so leviable shall be collected by the Chinese Government.

*Third.* That it will levy no higher harbor dues on vessels of another nationality frequenting any port in such "sphere" than shall be levied on vessels of its own nationality, and no higher railroad charges over lines built, controlled, or operated within its "sphere" on merchandise belonging to citizens or subjects of other nationalities transported through such "sphere" than shall be levied on similar

---

[3] *Papers Relating to the Foreign Relations of the United States, 1899* (Washington, 1901), pp. 129-130.

merchandise belonging to its own nationals transported over equal distances.

The liberal policy pursued by His Imperial German Majesty in declaring Kiaochao a free port and in aiding the Chinese Government in the establishment there of a custom-house are so clearly in line with the proposition which this Government is anxious to see recognized that it entertains the strongest hope that Germany will give its acceptance and hearty support.

The recent ukase of His Majesty the Emperor of Russia declaring the port of Talien-wan open during the whole of the lease under which it is held from China, to the merchant ships of all nations, coupled with the categorical assurances made to this Government by His Imperial Majesty's representative at this capital at the time, and since repeated to me by the present Russian ambassador, seem to insure the support of the Emperor to the proposed measure. Our ambassador at the Court of St. Petersburg has, in consequence, been instructed to submit it to the Russian Government and to request their early consideration of it. A copy of my instruction on the subject to Mr. Tower is herewith inclosed for your confidential information.

The commercial interests of Great Britain and Japan will be so clearly served by the desired declaration of intentions, and the views of the Governments of these countries as to the desirability of the adoption of measures insuring the benefits of equality of treatment of all foreign trade throughout China are so similar to those entertained by the United States, that their acceptance of the propositions herein outlined and their cooperation in advocating their adoption by the other powers can be confidently expected. . . .

## 4

Possession of the Philippines and maneuvers to increase American trade in the Far East involved the United States in the secret diplomacy by which European powers extended their sway. Secretary Hay in 1900, soon after sponsoring the Open Door, secretly sought Japanese assent to acquisition of a coaling station from China for the use of the United States Navy, only to be politely rebuffed on grounds that it would violate the Open Door:[4]

*The Secretary of State to Minister Buck*

[Telegram]

DEPARTMENT OF STATE
WASHINGTON, December 7, 1900

The Navy greatly desires a coaling station at Samsah Inlet north of Fuchow. Ascertain informally and discreetly whether Japanese Government would see any objection to our negotiating for this with China.

HAY

*The Japanese Foreign Office to the Japanese Minister*

[Copy handed to the Secretary of State by the Japanese Minister, December 11, 1900.]

. . . The Imperial Government harbor no territorial designs upon China; their policy, on the contrary, is directed to the maintenance of her territorial integrity; and they have noted with entire satisfaction the declaration made on several occasions by the Secretary of State that the United States were also anxious to preserve the territorial entity of that Empire. That desired end may be, in the opinion of the Imperial Government, best attained by those Powers which entertain similar views refraining from accepting any advantages which might give other Powers a pretext for territorial demands.

For these reasons, which are suggested with the frankness and sincerity fully justified by the good relations subsisting between the two Governments, the Imperial Government confidently hope that the United States Government will definitely abandon their above-mentioned project.

[4] *Ibid., 1915* (Washington, 1924), pp. 113-115.

You are hereby instructed to present to the Secretary of State an answer in the above sense.

## 5

Having entered the game of power politics in the Far East, the United States was intimately concerned in 1904 when Japan went to war with Russia to prevent Russian penetration through Manchuria into the ancient kingdom of Korea. American sympathy was completely with the Japanese, partly because that tiny nation seemed the underdog, partly because Nippon's expansion was expected to favor business interests. Mixed motives of Americans, reflecting the new position of the United States in affairs of great powers, were vigorously expressed in a series of editorials in the *New York Times,* which went so far as to condone the sneak attack by which the Japanese sank the Russian fleet:[5]

Editorial, February 9, 1904: "Why Should Russia Fight."

. . . A great part of Asia, including the whole of the Chinese Empire, is destined apparently to be the future field of commercial exploitation by Europe and America. . . . Our Manchurian trade has, under Russian occupation, sunk from a very promising beginning to a condition which has brought American mills to bankruptcy. . . . The instance is typical. It shows that whereas whatever is gained by Japan is gained for mankind, whatever is gained by Russia is lost to mankind.

Editorial, February 10, 1904: "Japan's First Blow."

. . . By the successful attack of the Japanese torpedo boats at Port Arthur yesterday morning the numerical superiority is shifted in favor of Japan. . . . As a matter of naval strategy and tactics, this prompt, enterprising, and gallant feat of the Japanese arms will be memorable. . . . But the first blow came unexpectedly. The result is that the naval superiority in the

[5] *The New York Times,* February 9-12, 1904. Quoted with permission of *The New York Times.*

Far East is now unquestionably with Japan. . . .

Editorial, February 11, 1904: "The Responsibility."

It seems hardly to become the dignity of the ruler of a great nation to complain that he has been struck before he was quite ready. . . . If Russia has been caught unprepared the fault is surely her own. . . . To impute treachery to the Japanese because they took the promptest possible advantage . . . was a gloss reserved for the publicists of St. Petersburg and of Paris.

Editorial, February 12, 1904: "The Neutrality of China."

. . . Her [Japan's] best defense against the Muscovite menace is the preservation of the Chinese Empire in its integrity. . . . Japan for her own preservation must make the independence of China and Korea a fundamental part of her policy. The irritation manifested in St. Petersburg at the openly expressed sympathy of the Americans for the Japanese cause is perfectly natural. But it is also natural for us to sympathize with that one of the belligerents who is fighting for the attainment of ends of very great value and importance to us, and whose ultimate triumph would serve our National interests. . . . We are aware of no sentimental considerations which would outweigh these very practical considerations of commerce in determining the placing of our sympathies. . . .

## 6

A secret diplomatic conversation of 1905, unexpectedly made known through a Japanese newspaper, led to a charge that Roosevelt made the United States a "silent partner" in the Anglo-Japanese alliance. Secretary of War Taft, visiting Tokyo immediately after Roosevelt had arranged for a peace conference between Russia and Japan at Portsmouth, conferred with the Japanese premier, Count Katsura. The confidential "Taft-Katsura Memorandum" (July, 1905) accurately reflected the motives for Roosevelt's approval of Japanese penetration of Korea:[6]

. . . First, in speaking of some pro-Russians in America who would have the public believe that the victory of Japan would be a certain prelude to her aggression in the direction of the Philippine Islands, . . . [the American] observed that Japan's only interest in the Philippines would be, in his opinion, to have these islands governed by a strong and friendly nation like the United States, and not to have them placed either under the misrule of the natives, yet unfit for self-government, or in the hands of some unfriendly European Power. Count Katsura confirmed in the strongest terms the correctness of his views on the point and positively stated that Japan does not harbor any aggressive designs whatever on the Philippines; adding that all the insinuations of the yellow peril type are nothing more or less than malicious and clumsy slanders calculated to do mischief to Japan.

Second, Count Katsura observed that the maintenance of general peace in the extreme East forms the fundamental principle of Japan's international policy. Such being the case, he was very anxious to exchange views with . . . [the American] as to the most effective means for insuring this principle. In his own opinion the best, in fact the only, means for accomplishing the above object would be to form good understanding between the three governments of Japan, the United States, and Great Britain which have common interests in upholding the principle of eminence [sic]. The Count well understands the traditional policy of the United States in this respect and perceives fully the impossibility of their entering into a formal alliance of such nature with foreign nations, but in view of our common interests he could [not] see why some good under-

standing or an alliance in practice if not in name, should not be made between these three nations, in so far as respects the affairs in the Far East. With such understanding firmly formed, general peace in these regions would be easily maintained to the great benefit of all Powers concerned.

. . . [The American] said that it was difficult, indeed impossible, for the President of the United States of America to enter even to any understanding amounting in effect to a confidential informal agreement, without the consent of the Senate, but that he felt sure that without any agreement at all the people of the United States was [sic] so fully in accord with the people of Japan and Great Britain in the maintenance of peace in the Far East that whatever occasion arose appropriate action of the Government of the United States, in conjunction with Japan and Great Britain, for such a purpose could be counted on by them quite as confidently as if the United States were under treaty obligations to take [it].

Third, in regard to the Korean question, Count Katsura observed that Korea being the direct cause of our war with Russia, it is a matter of absolute importance to Japan that a complete solution of the peninsula question should be made as the logical consequence of the war. If left to herself after the war Korea will certainly draw back to her habit of entering into any agreements or treaties with other Powers, thus resuscitating the same international complications as existed before the war. In view of the foregoing circumstances Japan feels absolutely constrained to take some definite step with a view to precluding the possibility of Korea falling back into her former condition and of placing us again under the necessity of entering upon another foreign war.

. . . [The American] fully admitted the justness of the Count's observations and remarked to the effect that, in his personal opinion, the establishment by Japanese

[6] Printed in Tyler Dennett, *Roosevelt and the Russo-Japanese War* (New York, 1925), pp. 112-114.

troops of a suzerainty over Korea to the extent of requiring that Korea enter into no foreign treaties without the consent of Japan was the logical result of the present war and would directly contribute to permanent peace in the East. His judgment was that the President would concur in his view in this regard, although he had no authority to give assurance of this; indeed, . . . [the American] added that he felt much delicacy in advancing the views he did for he had no mandate for the purpose from the President. . . . He could not, however, in view of Count Katsura's courteous desire to discuss the question, decline to express his opinions. . . .

### 7

The United States gained little by endorsing Japan's cause in the Russo-Japanese War. When President Roosevelt used his good offices to bring peace, the Nipponese grumbled that without his intervention their share of Russian and Chinese loot would have been still larger. To make matters worse, ill feeling between the two powers was heightened by mounting anti-Japanese sentiment within the United States. This centered in California, where laws were passed requiring the segregation of Japanese school children, while Congress threatened to expand the earlier exclusion of immigrants from China to include all Orientals. Only when President Roosevelt persuaded the Californians to repeal their nativistic laws did Japan's haughty rulers consent to the "Gentleman's Agreement" (1907) which temporarily eased the growing tension:[7]

In order that the best results might follow from an enforcement of the regulations, an understanding was reached with Japan that the existing policy of discouraging emigration of its subjects of the laboring classes to continental United States should be continued, and should by co-operation with the governments, be made as effective as possible. This understanding contemplates that the Japanese government shall issue passports to continental United States only to such of its subjects as are non-laborers or are laborers who, in coming to the continent, seek to resume a formerly acquired domicile, to join a parent, wife, or children residing there, or to assume active control of an already possessed interest in a farming enterprise in this country, so that the three classes of laborers entitled to receive passports have come to be designated "former residents," "parents, wives, or children of residents," and "settled agriculturists." With respect to Hawaii, the Japanese government of its own volition stated that, experimentally at least, the issuance of passports to members of the laboring classes proceeding thence would be limited to "former residents" and "parents, wives, or children of residents." The said government has also been exercising a careful supervision over the subject of emigration of its laboring class to foreign contiguous territory.

### 8

The "Gentleman's Agreement" could not heal the international breach caused by American nativists. Intensely proud, the Japanese were far from ready to forget the insulting implications of California's hasty action. The hurt that they experienced was revealed in an open letter to the Japanese Foreign Minister from Julius Kumpei Matsumoto, an American-educated member of Japan's parliament, which was republished in the *Review of Reviews* in 1907:[8]

The fundamental cause of the political and social ostracism to which the Japanese are condemned in America is the fact that they have not the privilege of naturalization. If the Japanese had that privilege, and within three years after naturalization they had the rights to vote as the Italians,

---

[7] "Report of the Commissioner-General of Immigration," Department of Commerce and Labor, *Reports*, 1908 (Washington, 1909), pp. 221-222.

[8] "A Japanese M.P. on American Citizenship for His Countrymen," *American Monthly Review of Reviews*, XXXV (March, 1907), 341-342.

the Irish, the Germans, and other nationalities have, the voice of Japanese exclusion would never have been raised in politics or in society in America. . . . In perusing the Constitution of the United States I find that the races that are allowed to be naturalized are two: the white and the negro. The Supreme Court of the United States interprets this portion of the Constitution and says in relation to Japanese: "The Japanese are neither of the white race, nor of the negro race, but they are of the Mongolian race. Therefore, the Japanese have not the privilege of naturalization." The court thinks this is a just interpretation of the Constitution, and has no compunction about declaring its opinion. . . . Setting aside the question of justice of the matter, such is an indisputable fact of the law as it stands. When persons who come from Italy, Germany, Ireland, Russia, Spain, Portugal, and other countries have the privilege of naturalization, it is an insult to the Japanese to deny the privilege to them alone. The Japanese call themselves an enlightened race. They class themselves as a nation among the strongest civilized powers of the world. But in the United States they are not accorded the right which even the people of poor and minor nations of Europe have. If the United States Government denies the Japanese the same right to become citizens that it gives to the Europeans, where is the sincerity of the American people? Naturalization, viewed from the standpoint of international private laws, is a special privilege of the people of civilized nations on equal terms. The Americans may be naturalized in Japan. The Japanese cannot be naturalized in America. It is against the principle of reciprocity embodied in international law. . . . We owe much to America for our civilization and progress. Our countrymen are all grateful. We look up to America as our real guide in civilization, as our propitious friend, and as more than our ally. In spite of this relationship, America

still looks down upon the Japanese as an inferior race, denies even the privilege of naturalization, and takes an attitude of seclusion and exclusiveness. This is indeed a lamentable affair for the Americans who are proud of being the champion of the cause of humanity.

## 9

More troublesome than Japanese relations was the status of the Philippines, wrested from Spain in the Spanish-American War. Should they be administered as colonies in the best tradition of imperialism, or should they be granted the oft-acclaimed democratic institutions of their new master? This was the question placed before a Philippine Commission, with William Howard Taft at its head, which reported in October, 1901. Although the commission suggested a colonial government with slightly less home rule than England granted America before 1776, even this mild degree of representation for the Filipinos was unpalatable to Senate expansionists. A student of that day, Charles B. Elliott, recorded both the Taft recommendations and the reaction to them:[9]

. . . It was recommended "That Congress be requested to confirm the legislation of the commission already enacted, and vest by Congressional enactment in the civil governor and commission and their successors to be appointed by the President the authority heretofore exercised by them under the instructions of the President, with the limitations therein contained, until January 1, 1904; and that provision be made in such legislation for a government to begin January 1, 1904, and to be composed of a governor and the heads of four executive departments, to be appointed by the President; of an Executive Council, to consist of the governor and the four heads of departments, and four others to be appointed by the Presi-

[9] From *The Philippines. To the End of the Commission Government,* by Charles B. Elliott, pp. 8-9, 13-14. Copyright 1917. Used by special permission of the publishers, The Bobbs-Merrill Company.

dent (the Executive Council to consist both of Americans and Filipinos),, and of a popular assembly of not exceeding thirty representatives to be elected from districts to be determined after a census of the Filipino population in the islands; that in such government the members of the popular assembly shall serve for a term of two years, and the popular assembly shall be limited to an annual session of three months, from the first of January to the first of April, except as this may be extended by call of the governor for a definite period in extra session; that the power of the popular assembly shall be that of a coordinate branch of the legislature, except that in the case of appropriation bills, if the popular assembly shall fail to vote the appropriations required by law during its regular session of three months the right to vote such necessary appropriations shall vest in the executive council; that the governor shall have the power to veto the legislation of the two chambers unless the same shall be again passed by a two-thirds vote of both houses; that Congress shall have full power to abrogate all legislation, and that by a joint vote of the popular assembly and the Executive Council two delegates, who shall be residents of the islands, shall be elected to represent the interests of these islands and the Filipino people before Congress and the Executive at Washington, their expenses and salaries to be paid from the insular treasury.". . .

Secretary Root and many of the leading supporters of the administration doubted the advisability of creating the Philippine Assembly until the natives had shown more evidence of capacity and a stronger disposition to accept American sovereignty. They believed that the practical native control of the provincial and municipal governments and large participation in the executive work was sufficient for the time being. However, Secretary Root yielded to the arguments of Mr. Taft and consented to the insertion in the law of the provision

for the assembly. The Senate struck it out of the bill which it passed, but in deference to the demands of the House of Representatives, the provision for a bicameral legislature was finally adopted and the Filipinos given equal power in the lawmaking body.

The Democratic members objected not to the policy of providing a native legislative assembly but to the conditions precedent to its being etstablished. They wished it established at once. To their suspicious minds it seemed that the calling of the election would be indefinitely postponed. Senator Patterson, for instance, was certain that the bill did not hold out the shadow of a reasonable hope of any sort of a legislative body even in the distant future. He had no expectation that there would ever be a general peace in the islands and if such a desirable condition should occur he was sure that the designing people in charge of the government would find an excuse for denying it in order to prevent the assembly from being instituted. As Senator Culbertson expressed it, they were opposed to the bill because it did not fix the political *status* of the Filipinos, and did not state the ultimate purpose of the United States government with reference to the islands, and also because under its other provisions all of the property of the people would be disposed of, mortgaged or pledged, long before the Filipinos would have any substantial share in the government.

## 10

The irrepressible Finley Peter Dunne, whose barbed comments sobered thoughtful Americans while tickling the national funny bone, had the last word on "The Philippine Peace" as on all others. His friendly bartender, Mr. Dooley, "quoted" Mr. Taft's explanation of American policy toward the Filipinos in 1902 to the patient Mr. Hennessy:[10]

[10] Finley Peter Dunne, *Observations by Mr. Dooley* (New York, 1902), pp. 118-120. Reprinted by permission of Charles Scribner's Sons, publishers.

"'Passin' to th' pollytical situation, I will say it is good. Not perhaps as good as ye'ers or mine, but good. Ivry wanst in a while whin I think iv it, an iliction is held. Unforchnitly it usually happens that those ilicted have not yet surrindhered. In th' Ph'lippeens th' office seeks th' man, but as he is also pursooed be th' sojery, it is not always aisy to catch him an' fit it on him. Th' counthry may be divided into two parts, pollytically,—where th' insurrection continues an' where it will soon be. Th' brave but I fear not altogether cheery army conthrols th' insurrected parts be martiyal law, but th' civil authorities are supreme in their own house. Th' diff'rence between civil law an' martiyal law in th' Ph'lippeens is what kind iv coat th' judge wears. Th' raysult is much th' same. Th' two branches wurruks in perfect harmony. We bag thim in th' city an' they round thim up in th' counthry.

"'It is not always nicessry to kill a Filipino American right away. Me desire is to idjacate thim slowly in th' ways an' customs iv th' counthry. We ar-re givin' hundherds iv these pore benighted haythen th' well-known, ol'-fashioned American wather cure. Iv coorse, ye know how 'tis done. A Filipino, we'll say, niver heerd iv th' histhry iv this counthry. He is met be wan iv our sturdy boys in black an' blue iv th' Macabebee scouts who asts him to cheer f'r Abraham Lincoln. He rayfuses. He is thin placed upon th' grass an' given a dhrink, a baynit bein' fixed in his mouth so he cannot rejict th' hospitality. Undher th' inflooence iv th' hose that cheers but does not inebriate, he soon warrums or perhaps I might say swells up to a ralization iv th' granjoor iv his adoptive counthry. One gallon makes him give three groans f'r th' constitchoochion. At four gallons, he will ask to be wrapped in th' flag. At th' dew pint he sings Yankee Doodle. Occasionally we run acrost a stubborn an' rebellyous man who wud sthrain at me idee iv human rights an' swallow th' Passyfic Ocean, but I mus' say mos' iv these little

fellows is less hollow in their pretintions. Nachrally we have had to take a good manny customs fr'm th' Spanyard, but we have improved on thim. I was talkin' with a Spanish gintleman th' other day who had been away f'r a long time an' he said he wudden't know th' counthry. Even th' faces iv th' people on th' sthreets had changed. They seemed glad to see him. Among th' mos' useful Spanish customs is reconcenthration. Our reconcenthration camps is among th' mos' thickly popylated in th' wurruld. But still we have to rely mainly on American methods. They are always used fin'lly in th' makin' iv a good citizen, th' garotte sildom.

"'I have not considhered it advisable to inthrajooce anny fads like thrile be jury iv ye'er peers into me administhration. Plain sthraight-forward dealin's is me motto. A Filipino at his best has on'y larned half th' jooty iv mankind. He can be thried but he can't thry his fellow man. It takes him too long. But in time I hope to have thim thrained to a pint where they can be good men an' thrue at th' inquest.

"'I hope I have tol' ye enough to show ye that th' stories iv disordher is greatly exagerated. Th' counthry is pro-gressin' splindidly, th' ocean still laps th' shore, th' mountains are there as they were in Bivridge's day, quite happy apparently; th' flag floats free an' well guarded over th' govermint offices, an' th' cherry people go an' come on their errands—go out alone an' come back with th' throops. Ivrywhere happiness, contint, love iv th' sthepmother counthry, excipt in places where there ar-re people. Gintlemen, I thank ye.'"

"An' there ye ar-re, Hinnissy. I hope this here lucid story will quite th' waggin' tongues iv scandal an' that people will let th' Ph'lippeens stew in their own happiness."

"But sure they might do something f'r thim," said Mr. Hennessy.

"They will," said Mr. Dooley. "They'll give thim a measure iv freedom."

"But whin?"

"Whin they'll sthand still long enough to be measured," said Mr. Dooley.

## EMPIRE IN THE AMERICAS

### 11

Geographically closer than the Orient, but equally remote from the consciousness of the average American citizen, were the Caribbean republics. The United States staked out its claims in the Western Hemisphere during the Spanish-American War, acquiring ownership of Puerto Rico and an integral interest in other islands. Particularly perplexing was the fate of Cuba. Although humanitarians had preached the need of war to free the Cubans from the yoke of Spain, more materially minded Americans were reluctant to abandon the rich island when the war was over. Their unhappy solution was embodied in the Platt Amendment, drafted by Secretary of War Elihu Root, and attached by Congress to an army appropriation bill in 1901, then embodied in a treaty with Cuba signed on May 22, 1903:[11]

ARTICLE I. The Government of Cuba shall never enter into any treaty or other compact with any foreign power or powers which will impair or tend to impair the independence of Cuba, nor in any manner authorize or permit any foreign power or powers to obtain by colonization or for military or naval purposes, or otherwise, lodgement in or control over any portion of said island.

ART. II. The Government of Cuba shall not assume or contract any public debt to pay the interest upon which, and to make reasonable sinking-fund provision for the ultimate discharge of which, the ordinary revenues of the Island of Cuba, after defraying the current expenses of the Government, shall be inadequate.

ART. III. The Government of Cuba consents that the United States may exercise the right to intervene for the preservation of Cuban independence, the maintenance of a government adequate for the protec-

tion of life, property, and individual liberty, and for discharging the obligations with respect to Cuba imposed by the treaty of Paris on the United States, now to be assumed and undertaken by the government of Cuba.

ART. IV. All Acts of the United States in Cuba during its military occupancy thereof are ratified and validated, and all lawful rights acquired thereunder shall be maintained and protected.

ART. V. The Government of Cuba will execute, and as far as necessary extend, the plans already devised or other plans to be mutually agreed upon, for the sanitation of the cities of the island, to the end that a recurrence of epidemics and infectious diseases may be prevented thereby assuring protection to the people and commerce of Cuba, as well as to the commerce of the southern ports of the United States and the people residing therein.

ART. VI. The Isle of Pines shall be omitted from the boundaries of Cuba, specified in the Constitution, the title thereto being left to future adjustment by treaty.

ART. VII. To enable the United States to maintain the independence of Cuba, and to protect the people thereof, as well as for its own defense, the government of Cuba will sell or lease to the United States lands necessary for coaling or naval stations at certain specified points to be agreed upon with the President of the United States.

### 12

The growing interest in the Caribbean area which fostered the Platt Amendment cannot be explained purely in terms of dollar diplomacy. In that day of mounting nationalism, defense was more and more in the consciousness of strategists. To those of the United States, this meant not only control of adjacent seas and islands, but a canal between the Atlantic and Pacific oceans; this was essential, they insisted, if the fleet were to guard both coasts. They agreed, too, that the canal should be built across the Isthmus of

---

[11] *United States Statutes at Large,* XXXIII, 2251-2253.

Panama. When the Republic of Colombia rejected a treaty leasing the area to the United States, the American government determined to secure the isthmus by fair means or foul, The result was a more brazen repudiation of the ethical principles underlying the Monroe Doctrine than any European incursion in Latin America, save only Napoleon III's abortive venture with Maximilian in Mexico. The methods employed were revealed in a series of telegrams between Washington officials and representatives in the field:[12]

DEPARTMENT OF STATE
WASHINGTON, June 9, 1903

The Colombian Government apparently does not appreciate the gravity of the situation. The canal negotiations were initiated by Colombia, and were energetically pressed upon this Government for several years. The propositions presented by Colombia, with slight modifications, were finally accepted by us. In virtue of this agreement our Congress reversed its previous judgment and decided upon the Panama route. If Colombia should now reject the treaty or unduly delay its ratification, the friendly understanding between the two countries would be so seriously compromised that action might be taken by the Congress next winter which every friend of Colombia would regret. Confidential. Communicate substance of this verbally to the minister of foreign affairs. If he desires it, give him a copy in form of memorandum.

HAY

*Mr. Beaupré to Mr. Hay*

[Telegram]

BOGOTÁ, August 12, 1903
(Received 15.)

August 12, 7 P.M. The treaty was rejected by the Senate to-day in its entirety . . .

BEAUPRÉ

[12]*Senate Documents*, 58th Cong., 2nd Sess., Doc. No. 51, pp. 18, 51, 97-98, 104.

DEPARTMENT OF STATE
WASHINGTON, November 3, 1903
(Sent 3:40 P.M.)

Uprising on Isthmus reported. Keep Department promptly and fully informed.

LOOMIS, *Acting*

*Mr. Ehrman to Mr. Hay*

PANAMA, November 3, 1903
(Received 8:15 P.M.)

No uprising yet. Reported will be in the night. Situation is critical.

EHRMAN

*Mr. Ehrman to Mr. Hay*

[Telegram]

PANAMA, November 3, 1903
(Received 9:50 P.M.)

Uprising occurred to-night, 6; no bloodshed. Army and navy officials taken prisoners. Government will be organized to-night, consisting three consuls, also cabinet. Soldiers changed. Supposed same movement will be effected in Colon. Order prevails so far. Situation serious. Four hundred soldiers landed Colon to-day Barranquilla.

EHRMAN

*Mr. Loomis to Mr. Ehrman*

[Telegram]

DEPARTMENT OF STATE
WASHINGTON, November 3, 1903
(Sent 11:18 P.M.)

Message sent to *Nashville* to Colon may not have been delivered. Accordingly see that following message is sent to *Nashville* immediately:

*Nashville,* COLON:

In the interests of peace make every effort to prevent Government troops at Colon from proceeding to Panama. The transit of the Isthmus must be kept open and order maintained. Acknowledge. (*Signed*) DARLING, *Acting.*

Secure special train, if necessary. Act promptly.

LOOMIS, *Acting*

*Mr. Hay to Mr. Ehrman*

[Telegram]

DEPARTMENT OF STATE
WASHINGTON, November 6, 1903
(Sent 12:51 P.M.)

The people of Panama have, by an apparently unanimous movement, dissolved their political connection with the Republic of Colombia and resumed their independence. When you are satisfied that a de facto government, republican in form, and without substantial opposition from its own people, has been established in the State of Panama, you will enter into relations with it as the responsible government of the territory and look to it for all due action to protect the persons and property of citizens of the United States and to keep open the isthmian transit in accordance with the obligations of existing treaties governing the relation of the United States to that territory.

Communicate above to Malmros, who will be governed by these instructions in entering into relations with the local authorities.

HAY

## 13

With the recognition of the new Republic of Panama, the building of the canal could begin. From that date, America's interest in the Caribbean was both strategic and economic: the canal must be kept open at all costs to allow the fleet to shuttle between Atlantic and Pacific, and European powers must be prevented from getting a foothold near by. Determined to keep the Caribbean an American lake, Roosevelt announced his famous corollary to the Monroe Doctrine in a message to Congress in December, 1904:[13]

It is not true that the United States feels any land hunger or entertains any projects as regards the other nations of the Western Hemisphere save such as are

for their welfare. All that this country desires is to see the neighboring countries stable, orderly, and prosperous. Any country whose people conduct themselves well can count upon our hearty friendship. If a nation shows that it knows how to act with reasonable efficiency and decency in social and political matters, if it keeps order and pays its obligations, it need fear no interference from the United States. Chronic wrongdoing, or an impotence which results in a general loosening of the ties of civilized society, may in America, as elsewhere, ultimately require intervention by some civilized nation, and in the Western Hemisphere the adherence of the United States to the Monroe Doctrine may force the United States, however reluctantly, in flagrant cases of such wrongdoing or impotence, to the exercise of an international police power. If every country washed by the Caribbean Sea would show the progress in stable and just civilization which with the aid of the Platt amendment Cuba has shown since our troops left the island, and which so many of the republics in both Americas are constantly and brilliantly showing, all question of interference by this Nation with their affairs would be at an end. Our interests and those of our southern neighbors are in reality identical. They have great natural riches, and if within their borders the reign of law and justice obtains, prosperity is sure to come to them. While they thus obey the primary laws of civilized society they may rest assured that they will be treated by us in a spirit of cordial and helpful sympathy. We would interfere with them only in the last resort, and then only if it became evident that their inability or unwillingness to do justice at home and abroad had violated the rights of the United States or had invited foreign aggression to the detriment of the entire body of American nations. It is a mere truism to say that every nation, whether in America or anywhere else, which desires to maintain its freedom, its

[13] *Congressional Record,* 58th Cong., 3rd Sess., p. 19.

independence, must ultimately realize that the right of such independence can not be separated from the responsibility of making good use of it.

## 14

Acting under the self-granted authority of the Roosevelt Corollary, the United States assumed the role of policeman for the entire Caribbean area. Any revolution there, any political upheaval, any financial shakiness, was certain to arouse American interest—and often inspired American intervention, always with the excuse that interference was necessary to forestall action by European powers. At the same time the State Department encouraged investment there to prevent economic penetration by other nations. The process was illustrated when continuing revolutions in Haiti so threatened American investments that Marines were landed in July, 1915. After forcing the government to accept a new constitution which gave the United States virtual control of that Republic, a treaty was signed in 1916 to legalize the proceedings:[14]

ARTICLE II. The President of Haiti shall appoint, upon nomination by the President of the United States, a General Receiver and such aids and employees as may be necessary, who shall collect, receive and apply all customs duties on imports and exports accruing at the several custom houses and ports of entry of the Republic of Haiti.

The President of Haiti shall appoint, upon nomination by the President of the United States, a Financial Adviser, who shall be an officer attached to the Ministry of Finance, to give effect to whose proposals and labours the Minister will lend efficient aid. The Financial Adviser shall devise an adequate system of public accounting, aid in increasing the revenues and adjusting them to the expenses, inquire into the validity of the debts of the Republic, enlighten both Governments with reference to all eventual debts, rec-

ommend improved methods of collecting and applying the revenues, and make such other recommendations to the Minister of Finance as may be deemed necessary for the welfare and prosperity of Haiti.

ART. III. The Government of the Republic of Haiti will provide by law or appropriate decrees for the payment of all customs duties to the General Receiver, and will extend to the Receivership, and to the Financial Adviser, all needful aid and full protection in the execution of the powers conferred and duties imposed herein; and the United States on its part will extend like aid and protection.

ART. IV. Upon the appointment of the Financial Adviser, the Government of the Republic of Haiti, in co-operation with the Financial Adviser, shall collate, classify, arrange and make full statement of all the debts of the Republic, the amounts, character, maturity and condition thereof, and the interest accruing and the sinking fund requisite to their final discharge.

ART. V. All sums collected and received by the General Receiver shall be applied, first, to the payment of the salaries and allowances of the General Receiver, his assistants and employees and expenses of the Receivership, including the salary and expenses of the Financial Adviser, which salaries will be determined by previous agreement; second, to the interest and sinking fund of the public debt of the Republic of Haiti; and, third, to the maintenance of the constabulary referred to in Article X, and then the remainder to the Haitian Government for purposes of current expenses. . . .

ART. VII. The General Receiver shall make monthly reports of all collections, receipts and disbursements to the appropriate officer of the Republic of Haiti and to the Department of State of the United States, which reports shall be open to inspection and verification at all times by the appropriate authorities of each of the said Governments.

The Republic of Haiti shall not increase

---

[14] *United States Statutes at Large,* XXXIX, 1654-1660.

its public debt except by previous agreement with the President of the United States, and shall not contract any debt or assume any financial obligation unless the ordinary revenues of the Republic available for that purpose, after defraying the expenses of the Government, shall be adequate to pay the interest and provide a sinking fund for the final discharge of such debt. . . .

ART. IX. The Republic of Haiti will not without a previous agreement with the President of the United States, modify the customs duties in a manner to reduce the revenues therefrom; and in order that the revenues of the Republic may be adequate to meet the public debt and the expenses of the Government, to preserve tranquillity and to promote material prosperity, the Republic of Haiti will co-operate with the Financial Adviser in his recommendations for improvement in the methods of collecting and disbursing the revenues and for new sources of needed income.

## 15

Protectorates over Haiti and other islands built up a veiled American empire in the Caribbean, but in Puerto Rico the responsibility was more immediate. That the United States failed to bring either political freedom or economic opportunity to the natives was one of the tragedies of the age. The financial interests that exploited the Puerto Ricans were the frequent targets of one of the anti-imperialists of the era, Senator R. F. Pettigrew of South Dakota. In his *Triumphant Plutocracy* (1921) he described his efforts, as chairman of the Committee on Insular Affairs, to block concessions for English, French, and Spanish landlords—and later developments:[15]

. . . When my term of office expired in 1901 these foreign highwaymen, waiting to prey upon the people of Porto Rico, returned to Washington and secured the legislation they desired. They also secured

control of the Government of Porto Rico, and made arrangements for a large armed police force to preserve law and order. They also appealed to Congress to put a duty on Cuban sugar in order to prevent it from competing with Porto Rican sugar. They then returned to the islands and began their work of "economic development."

About the first thing they did was to cancel the leases of the inhabitants who occupied the land. Then they compelled them to work for wages, raising sugar and tobacco, and they refused them the use of any land to raise yams, bananas, pigs and chickens, and they fixed the wages at 50 cents a day in silver. Little provision was made for the education of the people, and the wages were so low that, with their large families, the laborers found it impossible to buy adequate food and clothing. Consequently, their children grew up without clothes—ran naked in the fields and even in the towns—and were put to work as soon as they grew old enough to be of use.

Shortly after this beautiful plan of "economic development" was put in effect, the owners of Porto Rico began to boast of the great things they had done for the people. They told how they had furnished employment; had put up the mills and factories and brought in the machinery to make the sugar out of the raw cane, and to manufacture the tobacco, so that Porto Rico exported $150,000,000 worth of the product per annum to the United States. With it all, the miserable peons of Porto Rico went naked and starving in one of the richest spots of the whole world.

After the first few crops had been harvested, the laborers of Porto Rico went on strike, leaving the cane to sour in the field. Thereupon these foreign pirates, the English, the Spanish, the French and the American planters, called in the police force and the armed men of the United States and shot up the strikers and arrested them and put them back to work in the

[15] R. F. Pettigrew, *Triumphant Plutocracy* (New York, 1921), pp. 354-360.

fields—those they had not wounded or murdered. Thus, economic development pursued its imperial course in Porto Rico, where conditions are as bad today as they were when we took possession of the island twenty-two years ago, and always will remain as bad until the system of exploitation at home and abroad is abandoned and labor is given its just reward.

Lest anyone should think that I am exaggerating, I should like to call attention to a report recently published by the United States Department of Labor, giving a full description of the working and living conditions in Porto Rico. (Labor Conditions in Porto Rico, by Joseph Marcus, Washington, 1919.) The special investigator who wrote the report for the Labor Department, as a result of a careful study of conditions, states that:

The American flag has been flying over the island of Porto Rico for twenty years, yet the percentage of illiteracy is still abnormally high. During the years 1917 and 1918 "only 142,846 children out of a total of 427,666 of school age actually enrolled in the public schools." "The difficulty," says Mr. Marcus, "lies in the bad economic condition" in which the worker finds himself. "Porto Rico is an island of wealthy land proprietors and of landless workers. There is a law in Porto Rico prohibiting any single individual from owning more than 500 acres of land. . . . With the American occupation the price of cane land rose very high—from thirty to three hundred dollars per acre—and this induced many a small holder to sell his land and join the ranks of the laborers." Under the circumstances, the law limiting land holdings was not enforced, and at the present time "of the best land of Porto Rico, 537,-193 acres are owned and 229,203 acres are leased by 477 individuals, partnerships, or corporations from the United States, Spain, France and other countries." The total wealth of the island is in the hands of fifteen per cent of the population. Fourteen per cent of the wealth is in the hands of

native Porto Ricans. Sixty-seven per cent is owned by Americans. . . . "Throughout the island thousands of children of the ages from one to seven years go naked, in the towns as well as in the rural districts."

When the laborer is at work he and his family share the following diet:

Breakfast—Black coffee, without milk, and quite often without sugar.
Lunch—Rice and beans, or rice and codfish, or codfish and plantins.
Supper—The same as lunch.

This diet holds good while the laborer has steady work, but, during a large part of the year—five or six months—there is no work. "How he pulls through the slow season is a mystery to many who are interested in the welfare of the laborer."

The Porto Rican laborer is a sick man. "Hookworm disease, anemia, etc., are very widespread.". . .

The investigation upon which Mr. Marcus bases his report was made during the year 1919. At that time machinists in the sugar mills received about one dollar per day. Laborers in the busy season were paid ninety cents per day; in the slow season seventy cents. The working day is from ten to twelve hours. On the tobacco plantations men's wages during the busy season are from sixty to eighty cents a day and, during the dull season, from forty to sixty cents a day. Women receive from thirty-five to forty-five cents a day in the busy season and from twenty-five to thirty-five a day in the dull season. On the coffee plantations wages are lower. Men receive from fifty to sixty cents per day in the busy season and from thirty-five to forty-five cents per day in the dull season. . . .

Detailed descriptions are given of living and working conditions in these and other industries. Enough has been said here to indicate very clearly that the American people, having assumed the responsibility for directing the lives of 1,118,012 Porto Ricans, are far behind the standard of "health and decency" which civilization prescribes as the minimum below which human beings cannot be expected to live and to work.

## WILSONIAN DEMOCRACY AND INTEGRAL NATIONALISM

### 16

Even the election of the liberal Woodrow Wilson in 1912 did not stem the tide of nationalism and imperialism. During his first administration, American military forces dominated Caribbean republics as they had before, while economic penetration into Latin America increased rather than diminished. Moreover, nationalistic fervor reached new heights at home, where native Americans looked with increasing suspicion on all aliens whose race or religion did not conform to the majority pattern. The spirit of ethnic nationalism was fostered by a flood of allegedly scientific works which paraded "evidence" to show the superiority of Nordic Protestants over swarthy skinned immigrants from Eastern and Southern Europe. Typical was Madison Grant's *The Passing of the Great Race* (1916), which declared "inequality and not equality" to be the law of nature, and in the first edition—deleted in the second—decried the "multiplication of the inferior classes fostered and aided by the noble but fatuous philanthropy of the well-to-do":[16]

In America we have nearly succeeded in destroying the privilege of birth; that is, the intellectual and moral advantage a man of good stock brings into the world with him. We are now engaged in destroying the privilege of wealth; that is, the reward to successful intelligence and industry and in some quarters there is developing a tendency to attack the privilege of intellect and to deprive a man of the advantage gained from an early and thorough classical education. . . .

There exists today a widespread and fatuous belief in the power of environment,

as well as of education and opportunity to alter heredity, which arises from the dogma of the brotherhood of man, derived in its turn from the loose thinkers of the French Revolution and their American mimics. Such beliefs have done much damage in the past and if allowed to go uncontradicted, may do even more serious damage in the future. . . .

. . . The cross between a white man and an Indian is an Indian; the cross between a white man and a Negro is a Negro; the cross between a white man and a Hindu is a Hindu; and the cross between any of the three European races and a Jew is a Jew. . . .

Where altruism, philanthropy or sentimentalism intervene [*sic*] with the noblest purpose and forbid nature to penalize the unfortunate victims of reckless breeding, the multiplication of inferior types is encouraged and fostered. Indiscriminate efforts to preserve babies among the lower classes often result in serious injury to the race. . . .

. . . When it becomes thoroughly understood that the children of mixed marriages between contrasted races belong to the lower type, . . . to bring halfbreeds into the world will be regarded as a social and racial crime of the first magnitude. The laws against miscegenation must be greatly extended if the higher races are to be maintained. . . .

. . . Negroes have demonstrated throughout recorded time that they are a stationary species and that they do not possess the potentiality of progress or initiative from within. . . .

The result of unlimited immigration is showing plainly in the rapid decline in the birth rate of native Americans. . . . The man of the old stock is being crowded out of many country districts by these foreigners just as he is today being literally driven off the streets of New York City by the swarms of Polish Jews. These immigrants adopt the language of the native American, they wear his clothes, they steal

---

[16] Madison Grant, *The Passing of the Great Race* (1918 edn.), pp. 6, 16, 18, 48, 60, 77, 91, 222, 228. Reprinted by permission of Charles Scribner's Sons, publishers.

his name and they are beginning to take his women, but they seldom adopt his religion or understand his ideals and while he is being elbowed out of his own home the American looks calmly abroad and urges on others the suicidal ethics which are exterminating his own race. . . .

Race feeling may be called prejudice by those whose careers are cramped by it but it is a natural antipathy which serves to maintain the purity of type. . . .

The Nordics are, all over the world, a race of soldiers, sailors, adventurers and explorers, but above all, of rulers, organizers and aristocrats in sharp contrast to the essentially peasant and democratic character of the Alpines. The Nordic race is domineering, individualistic, self-reliant and jealous of their personal freedom both in political and religious systems and as a result they are usually Protestants. Chivalry and knighthood and their still surviving but greatly impaired counterparts are peculiarly Nordic traits and feudalism, class distinctions and race pride among Europeans are traceable for the most part to the north.

## 17

Congress succumbed to propaganda of this sort in 1915 when it adopted a literacy test for immigrants. Long favored by custodians of the mythical "national character," similar measures had been passed twice before but vetoed by Presidents Cleveland and Taft. Wilson followed his predecessors' example in a message that pointed up the class discrimination against the "new immigrants" and its departure from the democratic cosmopolitanism of the American tradition:[17]

In two particulars of vital consequence this bill embodies a radical departure from the traditional and long established policy of this country, a policy in which our people have conceived the very character of their Government to be expressed, the very mission and spirit of the Nation in

[17] *Congressional Record*, 63rd Cong., 3rd Sess., pp. 2481-2482.

respect of its relations to the peoples of the world outside their borders. It seeks to all but close entirely the gates of asylum which have always been open to those who could find nowhere else the right and opportunity of constitutional agitation for what they conceived to be the natural and inalienable rights of men; and it excludes those to whom the opportunities of elementary education have been denied, without regard to their character, their purposes, or their natural capacity.

Restrictions like these, adopted earlier in our history as a Nation, would very materially have altered the course and cooled the humane ardors of our politics. The right of political asylum has brought to this country many a man of noble character and elevated purpose who was marked as an outlaw in his own less fortunate land, and who has yet become an ornament to our citizenship and to our public councils. The children and compatriots of these illustrious Americans must stand amazed to see the representatives of their Nation now resolved, in the fullness of our national strength and at the maturity of our great institutions, to risk turning such men back from our shores without test of quality or purpose. It is difficult for me to believe that the full effect of this feature of the bill was realized when it was framed and adopted, and it is impossible for me to assent to it in the form in which it is here cast.

The literacy test and the tests and restrictions which accompany it constitute an even more radical change in the policy of the Nation. Hitherto we have generously kept our doors open to all who were not unfitted by reason of disease or incapacity for self-support or such personal records and antecedents as were likely to make them a menace to our peace and order or to the wholesome and essential relationships of life. In this bill it is proposed to turn away from tests of character and of quality and impose tests which exclude and restrict; for the laws here embodied are not tests of quality or of character or of personal fitness, but tests of opportunity. Those who come seeking opportunity are not to be admitted unless they have already had one of the chief of the opportunities they seek, the opportunity of education. The object of such provisions is restriction, not selection.

If the people of this country have made up their minds to limit the number of immigrants by arbitrary tests and so reverse the policy of all the generations of Americans that have gone before them, it is their right to do so. I am their servant and have no license to stand in their way. But I do not believe that they have. I respectfully submit that no one can quote their mandate to that effect. Has any political party ever avowed a policy of restriction in this fundamental matter, gone to the country on it, and been commissioned to control its legislation? Does this bill rest upon the conscious and universal assent and desire of the American people? I doubt it. It is because I doubt it that I make bold to dissent from it. I am willing to bide by the verdict, but not until it has been rendered. Let the platforms of parties speak out upon this policy and the people pronounce their wish. The matter is too fundamental to be settled otherwise.

I have no pride of opinion in this question. I am not foolish enough to profess to know the wishes and ideals of America better than the body of her chosen representatives know them. I only want instruction direct from those whose fortunes with ours, and all men's are involved.

## 18

Undaunted by President Wilson's words, congressmen in 1917 re-enacted the literacy test for immigrants, and this time passed the measure over a second veto. Both the terms and the actual purpose of the bill were described in a later report of the Commissioner-General of Immigration:[18]

---

[18] Bureau of Immigration, *Annual Report of the Commissioner-General of Immigration, 1923* (Washington, 1923), pp. 2-3.

The immigration act of 1882, which . . . was the first general law upon the subject, provided for the exclusion from the United States of the following classes only: Convicts, lunatics, idiots, and persons likely to become a public charge. This law underwent more or less important revisions in 1891, 1893, 1903, 1907, and 1917, until the last-mentioned act, which is the present general immigration law, denies admission to many classes of aliens, including the following: Idiots, imbeciles, feeble-minded persons, epileptics, insane persons; persons who have had one or more attacks of insanity at any time previously; persons of constitutional psychopathic inferiority; persons with chronic alcoholism; paupers; professional beggars; vagrants; persons afflicted with tuberculosis in any form or with a loathsome or dangerous contagious disease; persons certified by the examining physician as being mentally or physically defective, such physical defect being of a nature which may affect the ability of the alien to earn a living; persons who have been convicted of or admit having committed a felony or other crime or misdemeanor involving moral turpitude; polygamists, or persons who practice polygamy or believe in or advocate the practice of polygamy; anarchists and similar classes; immoral persons and persons coming for an immoral purpose; contract laborers; persons likely to become a public charge; persons seeking admission within one year of date of previous debarment or deportation; persons whose ticket or passage is paid for with the money of another or who are assisted by others to come, unless it is affirmatively shown that such persons do not belong to one of the foregoing excluded classes; persons whose ticket or passage is paid for by any corporation, association, society, municipality, or foreign government, either directly or indirectly; stowaways; children under 16 years of age unless accompanied by one or both of their parents; persons who are natives of certain geographically defined territory; aliens over

16 years of age who are unable to read some language or dialect; certain accompanying aliens, as described in the last proviso of section 18 of the act; and persons who have arrived in Canada or Mexico by certain steamship lines. Persons who fail to meet certain passport requirements were added to the excluded classes in subsequent legislation.

Obviously it would be difficult to find, or even to invent, many other terms denoting individual undesirability which might be added to the foregoing list, but, as already pointed out, the general law is essentially selective in theory, for even its most rigid application with respect to the excludable classes above enumerated could not be depended upon to prevent the coming of unlimited numbers of aliens who were able to meet the tests imposed.

Even a casual survey of congressional discussions of the immigration problem during the past quarter of a century demonstrates very clearly that while the law makers were deeply concerned with the mental, moral, and physical quality of immigrants, there developed as time went on an even greater concern as to the fundamental racial character of the constantly increasing numbers who came. The record of alien arrivals year by year had shown a gradual falling off in the immigration of northwest European peoples, representing racial stocks which were common to America even in colonial days, and a rapid and remarkably large increase in the movement from southern and eastern European countries and Asiatic Turkey. Immigration from the last-named sources reached an annual average of about 750,000 and in some years nearly a million came, and there seems to have been a general belief in Congress that it would increase rather than diminish. At the same time no one seems to have anticipated a revival of the formerly large influx from the "old sources," as the countries of northwest Europe came to be known.

This remarkable change in the sources and racial character of our immigrants led to an almost continuous agitation of the immigration problem both in and out of Congress, and there was a steadily growing demand for restriction, particularly of the newer movement from the south and east of Europe. During the greater part of this period of agitation the so-called literacy test for aliens was the favorite weapon of the restrictionists, and its widespread popularity appears to have been based quite largely on a belief, or at least a hope, that it would reduce to some extent the stream of "new" immigration, about one-third of which was illiterate, without seriously interfering with the coming of the older type, among whom illiteracy was at a minimum.

## INVOLVEMENT IN WORLD WAR

### 19

The spirit of integral nationalism that fostered antialien laws in the United States was world-wide. As the nations of Europe reared economic and ideological barriers between themselves during the opening decades of the twentieth century, observers realized that only an incident was needed to translate mounting antagonism into open conflict. This was provided in 1914, when the assassination of an Austrian archduke sent the nations of half the world flying at each other's throats. The United States could not hope to remain aloof, for the submarine campaign of the Central Powers profoundly shocked every decent-minded American citizen. The sinking of the "Lusitania" on May 7, 1915, brought war near; a year later, the crisis was renewed with the torpedoing of the steamer "Sussex" in the channel. Correctly gauging American opinion, President Wilson solemnly warned Congress that continued submarine warfare would force him to sever diplomatic relations between the United States and Germany:[19]

The Government of the United States has been very patient. At every stage of this distressing experience of tragedy after

---

[19] *Congressional Record*, 64th Cong., 1st Sess., pp. 6448-6449.

tragedy in which its own citizens were involved, it has sought to be restrained from any extreme course of action or of protest by a thoughtful consideration of the extraordinary circumstances of this unprecedented war, and actuated in all that it said or did by the sentiments of genuine friendship which the people of the United States have always entertained and continue to entertain towards the German nation. It has of course accepted the successive explanations and assurances of the Imperial German Government as given in entire sincerity and good faith, and has hoped, even against hope, that it would prove to be possible for the German Government so to order and control the acts of its naval commanders as to square its policy with the principles of humanity as embodied in the law of nations. It has been willing to wait until the significance of the facts became absolutely unmistakable and susceptible of but one interpretation.

That point has now unhappily been reached. The facts are susceptible of but one interpretation. The Imperial German Government has been unable to put any limits or restraints upon its warfare against either freight or passenger ships. It has therefore become painfully evident that the position which this Government took at the very outset is inevitable, namely, that the use of submarines for the destruction of an enemy's commerce is, of necessity, because of the very character of the vessels employed and the very methods of attack which their employment of course involves, incompatible with the principles of humanity, the long established and incontrovertible rights of neutrals, and the sacred immunities of noncombatants.

I have deemed it my duty, therefore, to say to the Imperial German Government, that if it is still its purpose to prosecute relentless and indiscriminate warfare against vessels of commerce by the use of submarines, notwithstanding the now demonstrated impossibility of conducting that warfare in accordance with what the Gov-

ernment of the United States must consider the sacred and indisputable rules of international law and the universally recognized dictates of humanity, the Government of the United States is at last forced to the conclusion that there is but one course it can pursue; and that unless the Imperial German Government should now immediately declare and effect an abandonment of its present methods of warfare against passenger and freight carrying vessels this Government can have no choice but to sever diplomatic relations with the Government of the German Empire altogether.

This decision I have arrived at with the keenest regret; the possibility of the action contemplated I am sure all thoughtful Americans will look forward to with unaffected reluctance. But we cannot forget that we are in some sort and by the force of circumstances the responsible spokesmen of the rights of humanity, and that we cannot remain silent while those rights seem in process of being swept utterly away in the maelstrom of this terrible war. We owe it to a due regard for our own rights as a nation, to our sense of duty as a representative of the rights of neutrals the world over, and to a just conception of the rights of mankind to take this stand now with the utmost solemnity and firmness.

## 20

Germany responded to Wilson's pressure by announcing, on May 4, 1916, that no merchant vessels would be sunk without warning unless they offered resistance. Hopes for peace soon went glimmering, however. Desperation drove the Central Powers to resume unrestricted submarine warfare in January, 1917, while a series of other incidents increased tension. Most electrifying among these was the release by the State Department on March 1, 1917, of an intercepted note from German Foreign Secretary Zimmermann to the German minister in Mexico:[20]

[20] J. B. Scott (ed.), *Diplomatic Correspondence between the United States and Germany* (New York, 1918), p. 338.

BERLIN, January 19, 1917

On the first of February we intend to begin submarine warfare unrestricted. In spite of this it is our intention to keep neutral the United States of America.

If this attempt is not successful we propose an alliance on the following basis with Mexico: That we shall make war together and together make peace. We shall give general financial support, and it is understood that Mexico is to reconquer the lost territory in New Mexico, Texas, and Arizona. The details are left for your settlement.

You are instructed to inform the President of Mexico of the above in the greatest confidence as soon as it is certain there will be an outbreak of war with the United States, and we suggest that the President of Mexico on his own initiative should communicate with Japan suggesting adherence at once to this plan; at the same time offer to mediate between Germany and Japan.

Please call to the attention of the President of Mexico that the employment of ruthless submarine warfare now promises to compel England to make peace in a few months.

ZIMMERMANN

## 21

By the spring of 1917 the American people were convinced that the Zimmermann plot and such crimes against humanity as unrestricted submarine warfare must not go unpunished. Yet revenge was only one motive driving them along the road to war. Underlying their action was a deep-seated faith in the better world that must emerge from the conflict. They knew—for their President had told them—that American participation would assure a just peace, dedicated to the cause of humanity and international good will. Wilson planted this hopeful concept in the minds of his countrymen by delivering a series of idealistic addresses on the war's objectives to Congress and the people. Typical

was his message to the Senate on January 22, 1917:[21]

On the eighteenth of December last I addressed an identic note to the governments of the nations now at war requesting them to state, more definitely than they had yet been stated by either group of belligerents, the terms upon which they would deem it possible to make peace. I spoke on behalf of humanity and of the rights of all neutral nations like our own, many of whose most vital interests the war puts in constant jeopardy. The Central Powers united in a reply which stated merely that they were ready to meet their antagonists in conference to discuss terms of peace. The Entente Powers have replied much more definitely and have stated, in general terms, indeed, but with sufficient definiteness to imply details, the arrangements, guarantees, and acts of reparation which they deem to be the indispensable conditions of a satisfactory settlement. We are that much nearer a definite discussion of the peace which shall end the present war. We are that much nearer the discussion of the international concert which must thereafter hold the world at peace. In every discussion of the peace that must end this war it is taken for granted that that peace must be followed by some definite concert of power which will make it virtually impossible that any such catastrophe should ever overwhelm us again. Every lover of mankind, every sane and thoughtful man, must take that for granted. . . .

The equality of nations upon which peace must be founded if it is to last must be an equality of rights; the guarantees exchanged must neither recognize nor imply a difference between big nations and small, between those that are powerful and those that are weak. Right must be based upon the common strength, not upon the

---

[21] *Papers Relating to the Foreign Relations of the United States, 1917, Supplement 1* (Washington, 1931), pp. 24-29.

individual strength, of the nations upon whose concert peace will depend. Equality of territory or of resources there of course cannot be; nor any other sort of equality not gained in the ordinary peaceful and legitimate development of the peoples themselves. But no one asks or expects anything more than an equality of rights. Mankind is looking now for freedom of life, not for equipoises of power.

And there is a deeper thing involved than even equality of right among organized nations. No peace can last, or ought to last, which does not recognize and accept the principle that governments derive all their just powers from the consent of the governed, and that no right anywhere exists to hand peoples about from sovereignty to sovereignty as if they were property. . . .

It is a problem closely connected with the limitation of naval armaments and the cooperation of the navies of the world in keeping the seas at once free and safe. And the question of limiting naval armaments opens the wider and perhaps more difficult question of the limitation of armies and of all programmes of military preparation. Difficult and delicate as these questions are, they must be faced with the utmost candour and decided in a spirit of real accommodation if peace is to come with healing in its wings, and come to stay. Peace cannot be had without concession and sacrifice. There can be no sense of safety and equality among the nations if great preponderating armaments are henceforth to continue here and there to be built up and maintained. The statesmen of the world must plan for peace and nations must adjust and accommodate their policy to it as they have planned for war and made ready for pitiless contest and rivalry. The question of armaments, whether on land or sea, is the most immediately and intensely practical question connected with the future fortunes of nations and of mankind. . . .

I am proposing, as it were, that the nations should with one accord adopt the doctrine of President Monroe as the doctrine of the world: that no nation should seek to extend its polity over any other nation or people, but that every people should be left free to determine its own polity, its own way of development, unhindered, unthreatened, unafraid, the little along with the great and powerful.

I am proposing that all nations henceforth avoid entangling alliances which would draw them into competitions of power, catch them in a net of intrigue and selfish rivalry, and disturb their own affairs with influences intruded from without. There is no entangling alliance in a concert of power. When all unite to act in the same sense and with the same purpose all act in the common interest and are free to live their own lives under a common protection.

I am proposing government by the consent of the governed; that freedom of the seas which in international conference after conference representatives of the United States have urged with the eloquence of those who are convinced disciples of liberty; and that moderation of armaments which makes of armies and navies a power for order merely, not an instrument of aggression or of selfish violence.

These are American principles, American policies. We could stand for no others. And they are also the principles and policies of forward-looking men and women everywhere, of every modern nation, of every enlightened community. They are the principles of mankind and must prevail.

## 22

Thus prepared, the American people felt more relief than sorrow when President Wilson appeared before the members of Congress on April 2, 1917, to ask that a state of war be declared between the United States and the Central Powers. His message, attacking secret diplomacy and the monarchical systems that deflected the will of peace-loving peoples, called for a world planted upon the tested foundations of political liberty:[22]

With a profound sense of the solemn and even tragical character of the step I am taking and of the grave responsibilities which it involves, but in unhesitating obedience to what I deem my constitutional duty, I advise that the Congress declare the recent course of the Imperial German Government to be in fact nothing less than war against the Government and people of the United States; that it formally accept the status of belligerent which has thus been thrust upon it; and that it take immediate steps not only to put the country in a more thorough state of defense, but also to exert all its power and employ all its resources to bring the Government of the German Empire to terms and end the war. . . .

Neutrality is no longer feasible or desirable where the peace of the world is involved and the freedom of its peoples, and the menace to that peace and freedom lies in the existence of autocratic Governments, backed by organized force which is controlled wholly by their will, not by the will of their people. We have seen the last of neutrality in such circumstances. We are at the beginning of an age in which it will be insisted that the same standards of conduct and of responsibility for wrong done shall be observed among nations and their Governments that are observed among the individual citizens of civilized States.

We have no quarrel with the German people. We have no feeling toward them but one of sympathy and friendship. It was not upon their impulse that their Government acted in entering this war. It was not with their previous knowledge or approval. It was a war determined upon as wars used to be determined upon in the

old, unhappy days, when peoples were nowhere consulted by their rulers and wars were provoked and waged in the interest of dynasties or of little groups of ambitious men who were accustomed to use their fellowmen as pawns and tools.

Self-governed nations do not fill their neighbor States with spies or set the course of intrigue to bring about some critical posture of affairs which will give them an opportunity to strike and make conquest. Such designs can be successfully worked out only under cover and where no one has the right to ask questions. Cunningly contrived plans of deception or aggression, carried, it may be, from generation to generation, can be worked out and kept from the light only within the privacy of courts or behind the carefully guarded confidences of a narrow and privileged class. They are happily impossible where public opinion commands and insists upon full information concerning all the Nation's affairs.

A steadfast concert for peace can never be maintained except by a partnership of democratic nations. No autocratic Government could be trusted to keep faith within it or observe its covenants. It must be a league of honor, a partnership of opinion. Intrigue would eat its vitals away; the plottings of inner circles who could plan what they would and render account to no one would be a corruption seated at its very heart. Only free peoples can hold their purpose and their honor steady to a common end and prefer the interests of mankind to any narrow interest of their own.

Does not every American feel that assurance has been added to our hope for the future peace of the world by the wonderful and heartening things that have been happening within the last few weeks in Russia? Russia was known by those who knew it best to have been always in fact democratic at heart, in all the vital habits of her thought, in all the intimate relationships of her people that spoke their natural instinct, their habitual attitude toward life.

[22] *Congressional Record,* 65th Cong., 1st Sess., pp. 102-104.

The autocracy that crowned the summit of her political structure, long as it had stood and terrible as was the reality of its power, was not in fact Russian in origin, character, or purpose; and now it has been shaken off and the great, generous Russian people have been added, in all their native majesty and might, to the forces that are fighting for freedom in the world, for justice, and for peace. Here is a fit partner for a league of honor.

One of the things that has served to convince us that the Prussian autocracy was not and could never be our friend is that from the very outset of the present war it has filled our unsuspecting communities, and even our offices of government, with spies and set criminal intrigues everywhere afoot against our National unity of counsel, our peace within and without, our industries and our commerce. Indeed, it is now evident that its spies were here even before the war began; and it is unhappily not a matter of conjecture, but a fact proved in our courts of justice, that the intrigues, which have more than once come perilously near to disturbing the peace and dislocating the industries of the country, have been carried on at the instigation, with the support, and even under the personal direction of official agents of the Imperial Government, accredited to the Government of the United States.

Even in checking these things and trying to extirpate them we have sought to put the most generous interpretation possible upon them because we knew that their source lay, not in any hostile feeling or purpose of the German people toward us (who were, no doubt, as ignorant of them as we ourselves were), but only in the selfish designs of a Government that did what it pleased and told its people nothing. But they have played their part in serving to convince us at last that the Government entertains no real friendship for us, and means to act against our peace and security at its convenience. That it means to stir up enemies against us at our very

doors the intercepted note to the German Minister at Mexico City is eloquent evidence.

We are accepting this challenge of hostile purpose because we know that in such a Government, following such methods, we can never have a friend; and that in the presence of its organized power, always lying in wait to accomplish we know not what purpose, can be no assured security for the democratic Governments of the world. We are now about to accept the gage of battle with this natural foe to liberty and shall, if necessary, spend the whole force of the nation to check and nullify its pretensions and its power. We are glad, now that we see the facts with no veil of false pretense about them, to fight thus for the ultimate peace of the world and for the liberation of its peoples, the German people included; for the rights of nations, great and small, and the privilege of men everywhere to choose their way of life and of obedience. The world must be made safe for democracy. Its peace must be planted upon the tested foundations of political liberty.

We have no selfish ends to serve. We desire no conquest, no dominion. We seek no indemnities for ourselves, no material compensation for the sacrifices we shall freely make. We are but one of the champions of the rights of mankind. We shall be satisfied when those rights have been made as secure as the faith and the freedom of nations can make them.

Just because we fight without rancor and without selfish object, seeking nothing for ourselves but what we shall wish to share with all free peoples, we shall, I feel confident, conduct our operations as belligerents without passion and ourselves observe with proud punctilio the principles of right and of fair play we profess to be fighting for.

I have said nothing of the Governments allied with the Imperial Government of Germany because they have not made war upon us or challenged us to defend our right and our honor. The Austro-Hungarian Government has, indeed, avowed its unqualified endorsement and acceptance of the reckless and lawless submarine warfare, adopted now without disguise by the Imperial German Government, and it has therefore not been possible for this Government to receive Count Tarnowski, the Ambassador recently accredited to this Government by the Imperial and Royal Government of Austria-Hungary; but that Government has not actually engaged in warfare against citizens of the United States on the seas, and I take the liberty, for the present at least, of postponing a discussion of our relations with the authorities at Vienna. We enter this war only where we are clearly forced into it because there are no other means of defending our right.

It will be all the easier for us to conduct ourselves as belligerents in a high spirit of right and fairness because we act without animus, not with enmity toward a people or with the desire to bring any injury or disadvantage upon them, but only an armed opposition to an irresponsible Government which has thrown aside all considerations of humanity and of right and is running amuck. We are, let me say again, the sincere friends of the German people, and shall desire nothing so much as the early reëstablishment of intimate relations of mutual advantage between us, however hard it may be for them for the time being to believe that this is spoken from our hearts. We have borne with their present Government through all these bitter months because of that friendship, exercising a patience and forbearance which would otherwise have been impossible. We shall, happily, still have an opportunity to prove that friendship in our daily attitude and actions toward the millions of men and women of German birth and native sympathy who live among us and share our life, and we shall be proud to prove it toward all who are in fact loyal to their neighbors and to the Government in the hour of test. They are most of them as true

and loyal Americans as if they had never known any other fealty or allegiance. They will be prompt to stand with us in rebuking and restraining the few who may be of a different mind and purpose. If there should be disloyalty, it will be dealt with with a firm hand of stern repression; but, if it lifts its head at all, it will lift it only here and there and without countenance except from a lawless and malignant few.

It is a distressing and oppressive duty, gentlemen of the Congress, which I have performed in thus addressing you. There are, it may be, many months of fiery trial and sacrifice ahead of us. It is a fearful thing to lead this great, peaceful people into war, into the most terrible and disastrous of all wars, civilization itself seeming to be in the balance. But the right is more precious than peace, and we shall fight for the things which we have always carried nearest our hearts—for democracy, for the right of those who submit to authority to have a voice in their own Governments, for the rights and liberties of small nations, for a universal dominion of right by such a concert of free peoples as shall bring peace and safety to all nations and make the world itself at last free.

## NATIONALIST CHAOS AND THE SEARCH FOR SANITY

### 23

Behind Wilson's statement of war aims was the terrifying realization that there could be no neutrality in an industrialized world united by the revolutions in technology and transportation. Any one nation could remain at peace only by helping assure peace for all. For some time before 1917 thoughtful men and women had sought a formula for a successful international organization that would remove the causes of war. A bold pronouncement of the aims of these internationalists was issued by the Massachusetts legislature in 1915:[23]

[23] Commonwealth of Massachusetts, *Senate Journal* (Boston, 1915), p. 361.

RESOLUTIONS

Requesting Congress to invite All the Nations to Unite in the Formation of a World State.

WHEREAS, The incalculable cost and calamity of the European war have caused a strong public sentiment for the end of all war, therefore be it

*Resolved,* That the general court of Massachusetts hereby respectfully requests the Congress of the United States to make a declaration in substance as follows:

The United States of America affirms the political unity of all mankind.

It affirms the supremacy of world sovereignty over national sovereignty.

It promises loyal obedience to that sovereignty.

It believes that the time has come for the organization of the world government, with legislative, judicial and executive departments.

It invites all nations to join with it in the formal establishment of the government. . . .

## 24

Others had gone beyond the Massachusetts legislature in their efforts to implement the vague dream of a world government. To these President Wilson turned for advice as his thoughts strayed to the subject of peace while the United States was engaged in war. Of the counsel that he received, none was more arresting than that offered by Frederick Jackson Turner, historian and leading student of American sectionalism:[24]

The following is an *abstract* of suggestions (derived from the study of the history of American sectionalism and the geography of American political parties) upon the bearing of American experience on the problems of a League of Nations. The conclusion is reached that in such a

[24] Frederick Jackson Turner, "International Political Parties in a Durable League of Nations," *American Historical Review,* XLVII (April, 1942), 547-551. Reprinted by permission of *The American Historical Review.*

League there should be a Legislative body, with substantial, but at first limited, functions, as well as a Court, or Council of Nations, and particularly that the *operation of international political parties in connection with such a Legislature* would promote the permanence of the League. . . .

The weakness inherent in a League of Nations is that it is exposed to intrigues by one or more of its component nations. . . . The danger lies partly in the European habit of diplomacy, the traditions and the training of her statesmen, and the analogy of a Congress of Nations to the historic Congresses of diplomats, and partly in the economic interests and ambitions of the nations under old-time leaders.

On the other hand, American ideas as so nobly set forth by the President, have found a quicker response among the European laboring classes than elsewhere, and in the passion for democratic peace among the masses lies the hope of the peace of the World internationally. What light does American experience cast upon the possibility of so using the masses as to promote international unity?

1. The area of the United States is about that of Europe; its geographic provinces or sections are comparable in area and in resources to Nations of Europe; in some respects these sections have cultural features clearly distinguishing each. Nevertheless, the history of the United States offers a sharp contrast to that of Europe in that *these sections have not become rival nations.*

2. Although *in form the federal aspect* of the United States is that of a union of *States,* in fact such States have acted in *sectional groups,* or have acted with the knowledge that they were backed by a common sectional sympathy. *Actually the federation has been between sections,* concealing their operation for the most part under the form of state action, or under the form of votes in Congress, in National political conventions, or in the distribution of votes in Presidential elections. A rather

careful study of such material has shown that such votes are much more often evidences of sectional rather than mere party action than is usually realized. . . .

3. In short, *the section is the imperfect image of a nation in the European sense, deprived of those attributes of a European nation which have been productive of war.* Except for the tragedy of the Civil War, there has been a *Pax Americana between these sections stretched across a continent* for a period of over a century and a quarter. This has not been because there was an absence of grounds for sectional antagonisms, or of those antagonisms themselves. . . .

5. Divergent as are the conditions and the development of Europe the very freedom of this country from some of the complexities of Europe, the large lines in which her simpler story has run, may be helpful, not only as a warning, but as a constructive contribution to the new order. . . .

We have given evidence that immigrants from all nations of the world can live together peacefully under a single government that does justice. *In our political institutions also are elements worthy of consideration.*

Notice has already been taken of the utility of the provision of the Constitution which assigns to the federal government a direct relation to the individual in important assigned spheres of jurisdiction. This may not be at first practicable in a League of Nations. But it is important to call attention to the *significance of the American national political parties, operating upon the whole Union, not confined to a section. The last tie that snapped before the Civil War, was the party tie.* This has, perhaps, in its working, been *the most effective single political institution for the prevention of sectional disunion.*

In a region as diversified in some respects as Europe itself, and as large, the *national political parties ran across all sections, evoked intersectional or nonsectional party loyalty,* checked the *exclusive* claim of the section to a vote in the interest of the section, furnished the dissenting minority within the section *an organic connection with party associates in other sections, at the same time that this connection was dependent upon just recognition of the special section* in which the minority lived. It was an *elastic bond, but one that was strong. It ran horizontal cross-sections of party ties across the vertical lines of sectional division.* It *enabled the voter to act continentally,* and it compelled the statesman to act on lines of policy that transcended his section, if he would secure a continental following strong enough to bring success.

6. There is a distinct advantage in utilizing this party system in a League of nations, if it does not carry with it counter-availing disadvantages grave enough to lead to its rejection. In essence it means the utilization of that body of internationalism already in evidence not only in such organizations as radical political parties, such as the International, the I.W.W., Socialists generally, etc., but also the opposite tendencies seen in international business combinations, scientific and educational international organizations, and conservative forces generally. The class struggle, so called, is in fact not a national but an international struggle. If party organization of the radical element alone exists, and if this organization is also dominated and shaped by some one or two nations, as Germany or Russia, it will be extended, as it has been, to other countries in the form of secret, or intriguing societies, proceeding by revolutionary methods, with little or no regard for the separate interests of the nation into which it is introduced as an alien, and with its helmsman operating from the outside, and steering a course which almost necessarily involves adhesion to the primary interest of the country in which such a party is recognized as a powerful element in the determination of the policy.

Is it better to try to exclude these international political forces from the organization of the new order, or to utilize their internationalizing tendencies by enabling them to operate upon an international legislative body, responsive to play of parties? Is it worth while to use the fact of class consciousness to diminish the violence of national consciousness?

There can be little doubt that the common people, whether of the extreme radical wing of socialists, or of the conservative party groups, were reluctant to enter the war, and are now in Germany and Austria-Hungary the severest critics of the autocratic group which deceived them and misled them. The labor groups have been more responsive to the policy of internationalism than, as yet, the other groups. At critical junctures their support, in England and France, has been important to the policy of President Wilson. They have a measure of international self-consciousness, partly because they have international organizations. There is no reason why similar organization on an international basis might not be given to conservative parties.

7. One recoils from any suggestion of adding a party loyalty international in its appeal to the loyalty to the individual nation. But the very idea of a League of Nations involves some diminution of the national feeling, some cultivation of international loyalty. If one could keep the Bolsheviki serpent out of the American Eden, he would hesitate to admit any international party organization which permitted such organization.

But in the reconstruction and the ferment which will follow the return of peace, there will be doubts about the existence of Edens anywhere, and the Bolsheviki serpent will creep in under whatever fence be attempted. May it not be safer to give him a job of international legislation rather than to leave him to strike from dark corners, and with no sense of responsibility?

On these questions, I am not sure. Consideration might be given to the probable actual vote possible, considering the estimated strength of political parties in the component nations of such a League, before assigning legislative functions in detail. We should have at least a rough estimate of the probable power and probable policies of the various groups. This I have not. So far as the special interests of the United States, however, operate on the decision, she has less to lose by an improvement in the conditions of labor and wages in Europe or Asia than she has to gain. If such a central legislative body, therefore, should gain even the power to standardize labor conditions, it must standardize them upward to avoid revolution, and this result, desirable in itself does not diminish but rather increases the power of the United States to develop international commerce, etc., and makes plain our relatively higher standards.

8. For the operation of international parties as a check upon nationalism, there is requisite a Legislative body in the League, with limited but real powers. The evils of combining class struggles with national feeling would be apparent in a mere judicial or executive tribunal with international coercion as its sanction. The League should take to itself a field of legislation.

At first this might be merely certain fiscal subjects, funds for supporting the League activities. Its action might be required precedent to the use of force either by a component state, or by the League as a sanction to its decisions. The kind of economic pressure to be placed upon a delinquent state might be there determined. Principles to apply to the internationally controlled areas might be determined. International tariff legislation might be assigned to it. Legislation upon labor questions as advocated by some of the international labor congresses might even be finally confided to such an organization. Possibly at first its power in such matters might be recommendatory, the formulation of bills or policies to be urged upon national legislatures.

There is an abundant field from which to select. The choice should be made with two ideas prominent: first that progress should be made carefully, without hazarding the system by too sudden a construction, liable to fail by its newness and radical nature; and second that unless some real powers are conferred upon such a legislature, it will fail to call out international parties to affect its action, these parties will be under the domination of special states where their influence will be greatest, and the unifying influence of non-national party organization will not be secured.

I have no doubt that all things considered the international party would tend toward unity in such a league as the intersectional parties did in the United States. . . . It might conceivably be used by [an] ultraconservative majority to restrain re-

form in a particular nation. But similar difficulties will‧ exist in the charges of special combinations within a League equipped only with judicial tribunals or consultative congresses, or with administrative organizations. There will be sectional jealousy and suspicion in any League, with whatever form of political organization. It is inherent in its nature. The problem is the introduction of checks and antidotes to this tendency.

Idealists who dreamed of the better world that would emerge from World War I faced a rude awakening. What awaited them was the inevitable aftermath of all wars, an era of nationalism and conservatism, of bitterness and disillusionment. Amidst the "normalcy" of the 1920's the internationalism of Woodrow Wilson was temporarily forgotten.

# NATIONALISM AND NORMALCY

## 1918–1932

The postwar reactions of the American people help explain the twentieth century's tragedies. Twice they marched off to wage a holy crusade for justice, democracy, and eternal peace. Twice they were sorely disillusioned by the brutalities of war and the sordidness of diplomacy. Each time many people concluded that their sacrifice was in vain and the world not worth saving. Bitterly disappointed, they succumbed (in differing degree) to false prophets who told them that the path to security stretched backward rather than forward; that the road to peace followed isolationism rather than internationalism. Nationalism and conservatism twice in the twentieth century became the dominant intellectual forces in American life, with internationalism repudiated and liberalism eclipsed. The reactionary period that followed World War I lasted from the end of hostilities to the Great Depression of 1929.

## SOVEREIGNTY TRIUMPHANT

### 1

America's reaction at the end of World War I caused a rapid deflation of the hopes that had been pitched so high under the leadership of Woodrow Wilson. An idealist to the core, Wilson assured his countrymen again and again as fighting went on that this was no ordinary war: this was a crusade that would bring justice to downtrodden humanity, make the world safe for democracy, and culminate in such a just peace that future wars would be unnecessary. He laid down blueprints for the better world of the future in a series of notable addresses, the most important being that of January 8, 1918, where he listed the Fourteen Points essential to any lasting peace:[1]

We entered this war because violations of right had occurred which touched us to the quick and made the life of our own people impossible unless they were corrected and the world secured once for all against their recurrence. What we demand in this war, therefore, is nothing peculiar to ourselves. It is that the world be made fit and safe to live in; and particularly that it be made safe for every peace-loving nation which, like our own, wishes to live its own life, determine its own institutions, be assured of justice and fair dealing by the other peoples of the world as against force and selfish aggression. All the peoples of the world are in effect partners in this interest, and for our own part we see very clearly that unless justice be done to others it will not be done to us. The program of the world's peace, therefore, is our program; and that program, the only possible program, as we see it, is this:

I. Open covenants of peace, openly arrived at, after which there shall be no private international understandings of any kind but diplomacy shall proceed always frankly and in the public view.

II. Absolute freedom of navigation upon the seas, outside territorial waters, alike in peace and in war, except as the seas may be closed in whole or in part by international action for the enforcement of international covenants.

III. The removal, so far as possible, of all economic barriers and the establishment of an equality of trade conditions among all the nations consenting to the peace and associating themselves for its maintenance.

IV. Adequate guarantees given and taken that national armaments will be reduced to the lowest point consistent with domestic safety.

V. A free, open-minded, and absolutely impartial adjustment of all colonial claims, based upon a strict observance of the prin-

[1] *Congressional Record*, 65th Cong., 2nd Sess., pp. 680-681.

ciple that in determining all such questions of sovereignty the interests of the populations concerned must have equal weight with the equitable claims of the government whose title is to be determined.

VI. The evacuation of all Russian territory and such a settlement of all questions affecting Russia as will secure the best and freest coöperation of the other nations of the world in obtaining for her an unhampered and unembarrassed opportunity for the independent determination of her own political development and national policy and assure her of a sincere welcome into the society of free nations under institutions of her own choosing; and, more than a welcome, assistance also of every kind that she may need and may herself desire. The treatment accorded Russia by her sister nations in the months to come will be the acid test of their good will, of their comprehension of her needs as distinguished from their own interests, and of their intelligent and unselfish sympathy.

VII. Belgium, the whole world will agree, must be evacuated and restored, without any attempt to limit the sovereignty which she enjoys in common with all other free nations. No other single act will serve as this will serve to restore confidence among the nations in the laws which they have themselves set and determined for the government of their relations with one another. Without this healing act the whole structure and validity of international law is forever impaired.

VIII. All French territory should be freed and the invaded portions restored, and the wrong done to France by Prussia in 1871 in the matter of Alsace-Lorraine, which has unsettled the peace of the world for nearly fifty years, should be righted, in order that peace may once more be made secure in the interest of all.

IX. A readjustment of the frontiers of Italy should be effected along clearly recognizable lines of nationality.

X. The peoples of Austria-Hungary, whose place among the nations we wish to see safeguarded and assured, should be accorded the freest opportunity of autonomous development.

XI. Rumania, Serbia, and Montenegro should be evacuated; occupied territories restored; Serbia accorded free and secure access to the sea; and the relations of the several Balkan states to one another determined by friendly counsel along historically established lines of allegiance and nationality; and international guarantees of the political and economic independence and territorial integrity of the several Balkan states should be entered into.

XII. The Turkish portions of the present Ottoman Empire should be assured a secure sovereignty, but the other nationalities which are now under Turkish rule should be assured an undoubted security of life and an absolutely unmolested opportunity of autonomous development, and the Dardanelles should be permanently opened as a free passage to the ships and commerce of all nations under international guarantees.

XIII. An independent Polish state should be erected which should include the territories inhabited by indisputably Polish populations, which should be assured a free and secure access to the sea, and whose political and economic independence and territorial integrity should be guaranteed by international covenant.

XIV. A general association of nations must be formed under specific covenants for the purpose of affording mutual guarantees of political independence and territorial integrity to great and small states alike.

In regard to these essential rectifications of wrong and assertions of right we feel ourselves to be intimate partners of all the governments and peoples associated together against the Imperialists. We cannot be separated in interest or divided in purpose. We stand together until the end. . . .

We have spoken now, surely, in terms too concrete to admit of any further doubt or question. An evident principle runs through the whole program I have outlined. It is the principle of justice to all peoples and nationalities, and their right to live on equal terms of liberty and safety with one another, whether they be strong or weak. Unless this principle be made its foundation no part of the structure of international justice can stand. The people of the United States could act upon no other principle; and to the vindication of this principle they are ready to devote their lives, their honor, and everything that they possess.

## 2

Wilson's hopes were shaken but not shattered when he met with other Allied statesmen at Versailles to draft the treaties to end World War I. Confronted with cold blooded balance-of-power politics, he was forced to back down on point after point. Yet he was not discouraged, for he believed that the people of the world were behind him. Eventually their voices, expressed through the League of Nations, would wipe out the influence of professional diplomats. Firmly convinced that a better world was within the grasp of mankind, Wilson returned to the United States to tell his own people that salvation lay in the League. One of his most eloquent pleas was contained in an address to the Senate on July 10, 1919:[2]

. . . It was our duty to do everything that it was within our power to do to make the triumph of freedom and of right a lasting triumph in the assurance of which men might everywhere live without fear.

Old entanglements of every kind stood in the way,—promises which Governments had made to one another in the days when might and right were confused and the power of the victor was without restraint. Engagements which contemplated any dispositions of territory, any extensions of sovereignty that might seem to be to the interest of those who had the power to insist upon them, had been entered into without thought of what the peoples concerned might wish or profit by; and these could not always be honorably brushed aside. It was not easy to graft the new order of ideas on the old, and some of the fruits of the grafting may, I fear, for a time be bitter. But with very few exceptions, the men who sat with us at the peace table desired as sincerely as we did to get away from the bad influences, the illegitimate purposes, the demoralizing ambitions, the international counsels and expedients out of which the sinister designs of Germany had sprung as a natural growth. . . .

The atmosphere in which the Conference worked seemed created, not by the ambitions of strong governments, but by the hopes and aspirations of small nations and of peoples, hitherto under bondage to the power that victory had shattered and destroyed. . . .

And out of the execution of these great enterprises of liberty sprang opportunities to attempt what statesmen had never found the way before to do; an opportunity to throw safeguards about the rights of racial, national and religious minorities by solemn international covenant; an opportunity to limit and regulate military establishments where they were most likely to be mischievous; an opportunity to effect a complete and systematic internationalization of waterways and railways which were necessary to the free economic life of more than one nation and to clear many of the normal channels of commerce of unfair obstructions of law or of privilege; and the very welcome opportunity to secure for labor the concerted protection of definite international pledges of principle and practice. . . .

. . . The promises governments were making to one another about the way in which labor was to be dealt with, by law not only but in fact as well, would remain a mere humane thesis if there was to be no common tribunal of opinion and judgment to which liberal statesmen could resort for the influences which alone

---

[2] *Ibid.*, 66th Cong., 1st Sess., pp. 2336-2339.

might secure their redemption. A league of free nations had become a practical necessity. . . .

And so the most practical, the most skeptical among them turned more and more to the League as the authority through which international action was to be secured, the authority without which, as they had come to see it, it would be difficult to give assured effect either to this treaty or to any other international understanding upon which they were to depend for the maintenance of peace. . . .

. . . War had lain at the heart of every arrangement of the Europe,—of every arrangement of the world,—that preceded the war. Restive peoples had been told that fleets and armies, which they toiled to sustain, meant peace; and they now knew that they had been lied to: that fleets and armies had been maintained to promote national ambitions and meant war. They knew that no old policy meant anything else but force, force,—always force. And they knew that it was intolerable. Every true heart in the world, and every enlightened judgment demanded that, at whatever cost of independent action, every government that took thought for its people or for justice or for ordered freedom should lend itself to a new purpose and utterly destroy the old order of international politics. Statesmen might see difficulties, but the people could see none and could brook no denial. A war in which they had been bled white to beat the terror that lay concealed in every Balance of Power must not end in a mere victory of arms and a new balance.

### 3

Wilson might have forged an instrument that placed international rule above selfish nationalism, but he still had to reckon with a powerful minority at home. Nationalists abhorred any limitation on American sovereignty; yet few of the senators who opposed the League were honest enough openly to join the irreconcilable isolationists. Sensing that a majority of the people favored Ameri-

can adherence, they set out to obscure the issues by tactics of obstruction and misrepresentation. Their skill at issue-clouding was exemplified in the speech delivered by Senator Warren G. Harding of Ohio on November 19, 1919, just after the Senate had acted unfavorably on one point:[3]

. . . I have not liked this treaty; I think, as originally negotiated, it is a colossal blunder of all time, but, recognizing the aspirations of our own people and the people of the world to do something toward international cooperation for the promotion and preservation of peace and a more intimate and better understanding between nations, I have wished to make it possible to accept this covenant. I could, however, no more vote to ratify this treaty without reservations which make sure America's independence of action, which make sure the preservation of American traditions, which make sure and certain our freedom in choosing our course of action, than I could participate in a knowing betrayal of this Republic. . . .

We are content to give you your league of nations, doubtful as we are about the wisdom of the great experiment. . . .

If this ratification is made with the reservations which have been adopted, there remains the skeleton of a league on which the United States can, if it deems it prudent, proceed in deliberation and calm reflection toward the building of an international relationship which shall be effective in the future.

The trouble with the whole league covenant is that it was hastily negotiated to be made the foundation of a treaty of peace, when there ought to have been a treaty of peace negotiated with a league of nations created in the deliberate aftermath.

Under these circumstances, recognizing conditions, without discussing the partisan phase of it or any political advantage, we have this arrangement, and we must meet it as it exists; and those on the majority

[3] *Ibid.*, 66th Cong., 1st Sess., pp. 8791-8792.

ide, those against it irreconcilably, and those for the league want these reservations to go to the nations of the Old World to assert and make certain America's freedom of action in the future, and leave a semblance of a league on which to build. . . .

I know, Mr. President, that in this covenant we have originally bartered American independence in order to create a league. We have traded away America's freedom of action in order to establish a supergovernment of the world, and it was never intended to be any less. I speak for one who is old-fashioned enough to believe that the Government of the United States of America is good enough for me. In speaking my reverence for the Government of the United States of America, Senators, I want the preservation of those coordinate branches of government which were conceived and instituted by the fathers, and if there is nothing else significant in the action of this day, you can tell to the people of the United States of America and to the world that the Senate of the United States has once more reasserted its authority, and representative government abides. . . .

## 4

The senators who opposed the League of Nations finally agreed on a series of reservations proposed by Senator Henry Cabot Lodge of Massachusetts. After the defeat of the ratification of the Covenant as Wilson recommended it, the Lodge reservations were tacked on. Then, by a vote of 49 yeas and 35 nays, the Senate in March, 1920, failed to give the League the two-thirds majority that would have meant American participation. That internationalists of the Woodrow Wilson school joined with a few diehard isolationists in voting against the treaty with the reservations added was understandable; Lodge's additions effectively negated the lofty ambitions of those who looked forward to a better world of international co-operation:[4]

1. The United States so understands and construes article 1 that in case of notice of withdrawal from the League of Nations . . . the United States shall be the sole judge as to whether all its international obligations and all its obligations under the said covenant have been fulfilled. . . .

2. The United States assumes no obligation to preserve the territorial integrity or political independence of any other country by the employment of its military or naval forces, its resources, or any form of economic discrimination, or to interfere in any way in controversies between nations . . . under the provisions of article 10, or to employ the military or naval forces of the United States, under any article of the treaty for any purpose, unless in any particular case the Congress . . . so provide.

3. No mandate shall be accepted by the United States . . . except by action of the Congress of the United States.

4. The United States reserves to itself exclusively the right to decide what questions are within its domestic jurisdiction and declares that all domestic and political questions relating wholly or in part to its internal affairs, including immigration, labor, coast-wise traffic, the tariff, commerce, the suppression of traffic in women and children and in opium and other dangerous drugs, and all other domestic questions, are solely within the jurisdiction of the United States and are not under this treaty to be submitted in any way either to arbitration or to the consideration of the council or of the assembly of the League of Nations, or any agency thereof, or to the decision or recommendation of any other power.

5. The United States will not submit to arbitration or to inquiry by the assembly or by the council of the League of Nations, provided for in said treaty of peace, any questions which in the judgment of the United States depend upon or relate to its long-established policy, commonly known as the Monroe doctrine; said doctrine is to be interpreted by the

---

*Ibid.,* 2nd Sess., pp. 4599-4600.

United States alone and is hereby declared to be wholly outside the jurisdiction of said League of Nations and entirely unaffected by any provision contained in the said treaty of peace with Germany. . . .

8. The United States understands that the reparation commission will regulate or interfere with exports from the United States to Germany, or from Germany to the United States, only when the United States by act or joint resolution of Congress approves such regulation or interference.

9. The United States shall not be obligated to contribute to any expenses of the League of Nations . . . or for the purpose of carrying out the treaty provisions, unless and until an appropriation of funds available for such expenses shall have been made by the Congress of the United States. . . .

10. No plan for the limitation of armaments proposed by the council of the League of Nations under the provisions of article 8 shall be held as binding the United States until the same shall have been accepted by Congress, and the United States reserves the right to increase its armament without the consent of the council whenever the United States is threatened with invasion or engaged in war.

11. The United States reserves the right to permit, in its discretion, the nations of a covenant-breaking State, as defined in article 16 of the covenant of the League of Nations, residing within the United States or in countries other than such covenant-breaking State, to continue their commercial, financial, and personal relations with the nationals of the United States. . . .

14. Until Part I, being the covenant of the League of Nations, shall be so amended as to provide that the United States shall be entitled to cast a number of votes equal to that which any member of the League and its self-governing dominions, colonies, or parts of empire, in the aggregate shall be entitled to cast, the United States assumes no obligation to be bound, except in cases where Congress has previously given its consent, by any election, decision, report, or finding of the council or assembly in which any member of the league and its self-governing dominions, colonies, or parts of empire, in the aggregate have cast more than one vote.

The United States assumes no obligation to be bound by any decision, report, or finding of the council or assembly arising out of any dispute between the United States and any member of the league if such member, or any self-governing dominion, colony, empire, or part of empire united with it politically has voted.

15. In consenting to the ratification of the treaty with Germany the United States adheres to the principle of self-determination and to the resolution of sympathy with the aspirations of the Irish people for a government of their own choice adopted by the Senate June 6, 1919, and declares that when such government is attained by Ireland, a consummation it is hoped is at hand, it should promptly be admitted as a member of the League of Nations.

## 5

The League of Nations issue was hopelessly lost after 1920, but internationalists still hoped to salvage something from the wreckage of Wilsonian idealism by winning American adherence to the World Court of International Justice. Authorized in the Covenant of the League and formally organized in 1921, this judicial body was acclaimed by both the Democratic and the Republican party as a necessary instrument for peace and international understanding. Despite bipartisan support, nationalists in 1926 insisted on attaching the following reservations to the bill authorizing participation, then defeated the bill altogether:[5]

*Resolved* (two-thirds of the Senators present concurring), That the Senate advise and consent to the adherence on the part of the United States to the said protocol of December 16, 1920, and the adjoined

---

[5] *Ibid.*, 69th Cong., 1st Sess., pp. 2824-2825.

statute for the Permanent Court of International Justice (without accepting or agreeing to the optional clause for compulsory jurisdiction contained in said statute), and that the signature of the United States be affixed to the said protocol, subject to the following reservations and understandings, which are hereby made a part and condition of this resolution, namely:

1. That such adherence shall not be taken to involve any legal relation on the part of the United States to the League of Nations or the assumption of any obligations by the United States under the treaty of Versailles.

2. That the United States shall be permitted to participate, through representatives designated for the purpose and upon an equality with the other states, members, respectively, of the Council and Assembly of the League of Nations, in any and all proceedings of either the council or the assembly for the election of judges or deputy judges of the Permanent Court of International Justice or for the filling of vacancies.

3. That the United States will pay a fair share of the expenses of the court, as determined and appropriated from time to time by the Congress of the United States.

4. That the United States may at any time withdraw its adherence to the said protocol and that the statute for the Permanent Court of International Justice adjoined to the protocol shall not be amended without the consent of the United States.

5. That the court shall not render any advisory opinion except publicly after due notice to all states adhering to the court and to all interested states and after public hearing or opportunity for hearing given to any state concerned; nor shall it, without the consent of the United States, entertain any request for an advisory opinion touching any dispute or question in which the United States has or claims an interest.

The signature of the United States to the said protocol shall not be affixed until the powers signatory to such protocol shall have indicated, through an exchange of notes, their acceptance of the foregoing reservations and understandings as a part and a condition of adherence by the United States to the said protocol.

*Resolved further,* As a part of this act of ratification that the United States approve the protocol and statute hereinabove mentioned, with the understanding that recourse to the Permanent Court of International Justice for the settlement of differences between the United States and any other state or states can be had only by agreement thereto through general or special treaties concluded between the parties in dispute; and

*Resolved further,* That adherence to the said protocol and statute hereby approved shall not be so construed as to require the United States to depart from its traditional policy of not intruding upon, interfering with, or entangling itself in the political questions of policy or internal administration of any foreign state; nor shall adherence to the said protocol and statute be construed to imply a relinquishment by the United States of its traditional attitude toward purely American questions.

# 6

With the United States holding itself steadfastly aloof, both the League of Nations and the World Court were powerless. Even the most sanguine internationalists realized by the middle 1920's that something more was needed to preserve peace; unless world ties were strengthened, individual nations would not trust each other to hold back the dogs of war. Seeking to build mutual confidence, Europe's leading nations agreed at the Locarno Conference (1925) never to fight each other again. Three years later this pious promise was expanded to a global scale when Secretary of State Frank B. Kellogg, in the Kellogg-Briand Pact (1928), broadened a French offer to outlaw war:[6]

---

[6] *United States Statutes at Large,* XLVII, 2343.

ARTICLE I. The high contracting parties solemnly declare in the names of their respective peoples that they condemn recourse to war for the solution of international controversies, and renounce it as an instrument of national policy in their relations with one another.

ART. 2. The high contracting parties agree that the settlement or solution of all disputes or conflicts of whatever nature or of whatever origin they may be, which may arise among them, shall never be sought except by pacific means.

## CONSERVATISM AND CONSTITUTIONAL LAW

### 7

The nationalism responsible for such an ineffective "international kiss" as the Kellogg-Briand Pact was paralleled by a conservatism that stifled domestic progress. For twelve years—between 1920 and 1932—the lessons of the Progressive Era were forgotten as prosperity dulled the social consciences of the American people, allowing a materialistic-minded minority to gain control. Leading this retreat from liberalism were the justices of the Supreme Court, whose conservatism was mirrored in a series of decisions that threatened to undo all the gains made under Theodore Roosevelt and Woodrow Wilson. Typical of their attitude was the majority opinion in the case of *Hammer* v. *Daggenhart et al.* (1918), which invalidated a child labor law passed in 1916:[7]

The attack upon the act rests upon three propositions: *First*. It is not a regulation of interstate and foreign commerce. *Second*. It contravenes the Tenth Amendment to the Constitution. *Third*. It conflicts with the Fifth Amendment to the Constitution.

The controlling question for decision is: Is it within the authority of Congress in regulating commerce among the States to prohibit the transportation in interstate commerce of manufactured goods, the product of a factory in which, within thirty days prior to their removal therefrom, children under the age of fourteen have been employed or permitted to work, or children between the ages of fourteen and sixteen years have been employed or permitted to work more than eight hours in any day, or more than six days in any week, or after the hour of 7 o'clock P.M. or before the hour of 6 o'clock A.M.?

The power essential to the passage of this act, the government contends, is found in the commerce clause of the Constitution which authorizes Congress to regulate commerce with foreign nations and among the States. . . .

The thing intended to be accomplished by this statute is the denial of the facilities of interstate commerce to those manufacturers in the States who employ children within the prohibited ages. The act in its effect does not regulate transportation among the States, but aims to standardize the ages at which children may be employed in mining and manufacturing within the States. The goods shipped are of themselves harmless. The act permits them to be freely shipped after thirty days from the time of their removal from the factory. When offered for shipment, and before transportation begins, the labor of their production is over, and the mere fact that they were intended for interstate commerce transportation does not make their production subject to federal control under the commerce power.

Commerce "consists of intercourse and traffic . . . and includes the transportation of persons and property, as well as the purchase, sale and exchange of commodities." The making of goods and the mining of coal are not commerce, nor does the fact that these things are to be afterwards shipped, or used in interstate commerce, make their production a part thereof.

Over interstate transportation, or its incidents, the regulatory power of Congress is ample, but the production of articles intended for interstate commerce is a mat-

[7] *United States Reports*, 247 U.S. 269-277.

ter of local regulation. . . . If it were otherwise, all manufacture intended for interstate shipment would be brought under federal control to the practical exclusion of the authority of the states, a result certainly not contemplated by the framers of the Constitution. . . .

It is further contended that the authority of Congress may be exerted to control interstate commerce in the shipment of child-made goods because of the effect of the circulation of such goods in other States where the evil of this class of labor has been recognized by local legislation, and the right to thus employ child labor has been more rigorously restrained than in the state of production. In other words, that the unfair competition thus engendered may be controlled by closing the channels of interstate commerce to manufacturers in those States where the local laws do not meet what Congress deems to be the more just standard of other States.

There is no power vested in Congress to require the States to exercise their police power so as to prevent possible unfair competition. Many causes may coöperate to give one State, by reason of local laws or conditions, an economic advantage over others. The commerce clause was not intended to give to Congress a general authority to equalize such conditions. In some of the States laws have been passed fixing minimum wages for women, in others the local law regulates the hours of labor of women in various employments. Business done in such States may be at an economic disadvantage when compared with States which have no such regulation; surely, this fact does not give Congress the power to deny transportation in interstate commerce to those who carry on business where the hours of labor and the rate of compensation for women have not been fixed by a standard in use in other States and approved by Congress.

The grant of power to Congress over the subject of interstate commerce was to enable it to regulate such commerce, and not to give it authority to control the States in their exercise of the police power over local trade and manufacture.

The grant of authority over a purely federal matter was not intended to destroy the local power always existing and carefully reserved to the States in the Tenth Amendment to the Constitution. . . .

In interpreting the Constitution it must never be forgotten that the nation is made up of states, to which are entrusted the powers of local government. And to them and to the people the powers not expressly delegated to the national government are reserved. . . .

In our view the necessary effect of this act is, by means of a prohibition against the movement in interstate commerce of ordinary commercial commodities, to regulate the hours of labor of children in factories and mines within the States, a purely state authority. Thus the act in a twofold sense is repugnant to the Constitution. It not only transcends the authority delegated to Congress over commerce, but also exerts a power as to a purely local matter to which the federal authority does not extend. The far-reaching result of upholding the act cannot be more plainly indicated than by pointing out that if Congress can thus regulate matters intrusted to local authority by prohibition of the movement of commodities in interstate commerce, all freedom of commerce will be at an end, and the power of the states over local matters may be eliminated, and thus our system of government be practically destroyed.

For these reasons we hold that this law exceeds the constitutional authority of Congress. It follows that the decree of the district court must be affirmed.

## 8

The conservatives' defense of child labor was paralleled by a bitter attack on freedom of speech. This began during the war but did not reach its height until the postwar years, when utterances of socialists or pacifists were distorted into threats to the national security by overvigilant federal officials. As harmless idealists were hustled away to jail for voicing opinions that did not jibe with those of the majority, a few calm voices were raised in protest, a few thoughtful men reminded a hysterical people of the forgotten First Amendment to their Constitution. Among these none was more eloquent than Justice Oliver Wendell Holmes, whose ringing dissenting opinions set a high standard of sincerity and logic. His dissent in the case of *Abrams* v. *United States* (1919) will be considered a classic wherever men treasure their liberties:[8]

In this case sentences of twenty years imprisonment have been imposed for the publishing of two leaflets that I believe the defendants had as much right to publish as the Government has to publish the Constitution of the United States now vainly invoked by them. Even if I am technically wrong and enough can be squeezed from these poor and puny anonymities to turn the color of legal litmus paper; I will add, even if what I think the necessary intent were shown; the most nominal punishment seems to me all that possibly could be inflicted, unless the defendants are to be made to suffer not for what the indictment alleges but for the creed that they avow—a creed that I believe to be the creed of ignorance and immaturity when honestly held, as I see no reason to doubt that it was held here, but which, although made the subject of examination at the trial, no one has a right even to consider in dealing with the charges before the Court.

Persecution for the expression of opinions seems to me perfectly logical. If you have no doubt of your premises or your power and want a certain result with all your heart you naturally express your wishes in law and sweep away all opposition. To allow opposition by speech seems to indicate that you think the speech impotent, as when a man says that he has squared the circle, or that you do not care

whole-heartedly for the result, or that you doubt either your power or your premises. But when men have realized that time has upset many fighting faiths, they may come to believe even more than they believe the very foundations of their own conduct that the ultimate good desired is better reached by free trade in ideas—that the best test of truth is the power of the thought to get itself accepted in the competition of the market, and that truth is the only ground upon which their wishes safely can be carried out. That at any rate is the theory of our Constitution. It is an experiment, as all life is an experiment. Every year if not every day we have to wager our salvation upon some prophecy based upon imperfect knowledge. While that experiment is part of our system I think that we should be eternally vigilant against attempts to check the expression of opinions that we loathe and believe to be fraught with death, unless they so imminently threaten immediate interference with the lawful and pressing purposes of the law that an immediate check is required to save the country. I wholly disagree with the argument of the Government that the First Amendment left the common law as to seditious libel in force. History seems to me against the notion. I had conceived that the United States through many years had shown its repentence for the Sedition Act of 1798, by repaying fines that it imposed. Only the emergency that makes it immediately dangerous to leave the correction of evil counsels to time warrants making any exception to the sweeping command, "Congress shall make no law . . . abridging the freedom of speech." Of course I am speaking only of expressions of opinion and exhortations, which were all that were uttered here, but I regret that I cannot put into more impressive words my belief that in their conviction upon this indictment the defendants were deprived of their rights under the Constitution of the United States.

[8] *Ibid.*, 250 U.S. 629-631.

## 9

Judicial conservatism during the 1920's opened new vistas to industrialists. Correctly judging the temper of the judges, they saw that the time was ripe to negate the Clayton Antitrust Act, just as an earlier generation of tycoons had made the Sherman Antitrust Act a dead letter. Their success was nowhere better demonstrated than in the case of the *United States* v. *United States Steel Corporation* (1920). The price leadership of this billion-dollar holding company held prices rigid; steel rails, for example, sold at $28 a ton from 1901 to 1916, and again—after the Court's favorable decision in 1920—at a postwar price of $43 a ton for a solid decade. The government maintained that a combination capable of controlling markets and prices was a substantial monopoly injurious to the public; the Court held that it was not:[9]

[In the opinion of two judges in a lower court] testimony did "not show that the Corporation, in and of itself, ever possessed or exerted sufficient power when acting alone to control prices. . . ." Its power was efficient only when in co-operation with its competitors, and hence it concerted with them in the expedients of pools, associations, trade meetings, and finally in a system of dinners inaugurated in 1907 by the president of the company, E. H. Gary, and called "the Gary dinners.". . . They were instituted first in "stress of panic," but . . . were afterwards called to control prices "in periods of industrial calm.". . .

. . . Indeed, it is said in many ways and illustrated that "instead of relying upon its own power to fix and maintain prices, the Corporation, at its very beginning, sought and obtained the assistance of others." It combined the power with that of its competitors. . . . Its offense, therefore, such as it was, was not different from theirs, and was distinguished from "theirs only in the leadership it assumed in promulgating and perfecting the policy. . . ."

. . . We have seen that the judges of the District Court unanimously concurred in the view that the Corporation did not achieve monopoly, and such is our deduction. . . . Monopoly, therefore, was not achieved, and competitors had to be persuaded by pools, associations, and trade meetings, all of them, it may be, violations of the law. . . . They were scattered through the years from 1901 . . . until 1911, but . . . abandoned nine months before this suit. . . .

What, then, can now be urged against the Corporation?

. . . The company's officers, and, as well, its competitors and customers, testified that its competition was genuine. . . . No practical witness was produced by the Government in opposition. . . . Counsel say, "They [the Corporation is made a plural] called . . . two hundred witnesses out of some forty thousand customers, and they expect with that evidence to overcome the whole train of price movement since the Corporation was formed.". . .

. . . the opinion of an editor of a trade journal is adduced, and that of an author and teacher of economics whose philosophical deductions had, perhaps, fortification from experience as Deputy Commissioner of Corporations and as an employee in the Bureau of Corporations. His deduction was that when prices are constant through a definite period an artificial influence is indicated. . . . It has become an aphorism that there is danger of deception in generalities, and in a case of this importance we should have something surer for judgment than speculation,—something more than a deduction . . . even though the facts it rests on or asserts were not contradicted. . . .

. . . Against it competitors, dealers, and customers of the Corporation testify in multitude that . . . prices . . . varied according to natural conditions. . . .

. . . The Corporation is undoubtedly of impressive size, and it takes an effort of resolution not to be affected by it or to exaggerate its influence. But . . . the law

[9] *Ibid.*, 251 U.S. 440-452.

does not make mere size an offense or the existence of unexerted power an offense. . . .

. . . The Steel Corporation by its formation united under one control competing companies, and thus, it is urged, a condition was brought about in violation of the statute. . . .

. . . We have seen whatever there was of wrong intent could not be executed; whatever there was of evil effect was discontinued before this suit was brought; and this, we think, determines the decree.

## 10

When the Court narrowed the commerce power by rejecting the first child labor law, the Wilson administration won congressional approval for a new measure (1919) which exercised the government's taxing power to cripple firms that persisted in hiring children. When this act was contested in the case of *Bailey* v. *Drexel Furniture Company* (1922), Chief Justice William H. Taft not only branded the law as unconstitutional but seriously restricted the congressional taxing power:[10]

The law is attacked on the ground that it is a regulation of the employment of child labor in the States—an exclusively state function under the Federal Constitution and within the reservations of the Tenth Amendment. . . . It provides a heavy exaction for a departure from a detailed and specified course of conduct in business. That course of business is that employers shall employ in mines and quarries, children of an age greater than sixteen years; in mills and factories, children of an age greater than fourteen years, and shall prevent children of less than sixteen years in mills and factories from working more than eight hours a day or six days in the week. If an employer departs from this prescribed course of business, he is to pay to the Government one-tenth of his entire net income in the business for a full year. . . .

[10] *Ibid.*, 259 U.S. 36-38.

. . . The good sought in unconstitutional legislation is an insidious feature because it leads citizens and legislators of good purpose to promote it without thought of the serious breach it will make in the ark of our covenant or the harm which will come from breaking down recognized standards. In the maintenance of local self government, on the one hand, and the national power on the other, our country has been able to endure and prosper for near a century and a half.

Out of a proper respect for the acts of a co-ordinate branch of the Government, this court has gone far to sustain taxing acts as such, even though there has been ground for suspecting from the weight of the tax it was intended to destroy its subject. But in the act before us the presumption of validity cannot prevail, because the proof of the contrary is found on the very face of its provisions. Grant the validity of this law, and all that Congress would need to do, hereafter, in seeking to take over to its control any one of the great number of subjects of public interests, jurisdiction of which the States have never parted with, and which are reserved to them by the Tenth Amendment, would be to enact a detailed measure of complete regulation of the subject and enforce it by a so-called tax upon departures from it. To give such magic to the word "tax" would be to break down all constitutional limitation of the powers of Congress and completely wipe out the sovereignty of the State.

## 11

Minimum-wage laws also aroused judicial ire during the 1920's. The principal case, *Adkins* v. *Children's Hospital* (1923), dealt with a congressional statute fixing minimum wages for women and minors in the District of Columbia. Such workers, the law stated, should be paid enough to provide decent, healthful, and moral living conditions. The majority of the Court spoke with finality against the measure, although a dissenting opinion by Justice Oliver Wendell Holmes prophetically noted that men in other lands made no such bogey of liberty of contract:[11]

The judicial duty of passing upon the constitutionality of an act of Congress is one of great gravity and delicacy. . . . This court, by an unbroken line of decisions from Chief Justice Marshall to the present day, has steadily adhered to the rule that every possible presumption is in favor of the validity of an act of Congress until overcome beyond rational doubt. But if, by clear and indubitable demonstration, a statute be opposed to the Constitution, we have no choice but to say so. . . .
. . . The statute now under consideration is attacked upon the ground that it authorizes an unconstitutional interference with the freedom of contract included within the guaranties of the due process clause of the 5th Amendment. That the right to contract about one's affairs is a part of the liberty of the individual protected by this clause is settled by the decisions of this Court and is no longer open to question. Within this liberty are contracts of employment of labor. In making such contracts, generally speaking, the parties have an equal right to obtain from each other the best terms they can as the result of private bargaining. . . .
. . . It is simply and exclusively a price-fixing law, confined to adult women (for we are not now considering the provisions relating to minors), who are legally as capable of contracting for themselves as men. It forbids two parties having lawful capacity—under penalties as to the employer—to freely contract with one another in respect of the price for which one shall render service to the other in a purely private employment where both are willing, perhaps anxious, to agree. . . .
The standard furnished by the statute for the guidance of the board is so vague as to be impossible of practical application with any reasonable degree of accuracy.

What is sufficient to supply the necessary cost of living for a woman worker and maintain her in good health and protect her morals is obviously not a precise or unvarying sum—not even approximately so. The amount will depend upon a variety of circumstances: the individual temperament, habits of thrift, care, ability to buy necessaries intelligently, and whether the woman live alone or with her family. . . .
. . . It cannot be shown that well paid women safeguard their morals more carefully than those who are poorly paid. Morality rests upon other considerations than wages; and there is, certainly, no such prevalent connection between the two as to justify a broad attempt to adjust the latter with reference to the former. . . . For these reasons, and others which might be stated, the inquiry in respect of the necessary cost of living and of the income necessary to preserve health and morals, presents an individual and not a composite question, and must be answered for each individual considered by herself and not by a general formula prescribed by a statutory bureau. . . .
The law takes account of the necessities of only one party to the contract. It ignores the necessities of the employer by compelling him to pay not less than a certain sum, not only whether the employee is capable of earning it, but irrespective of the ability of his business to sustain the burden, generously leaving him, of course, the privilege of abandoning his business as an alternative for going on at a loss. . . .
Finally, it may be said that if, in the interest of the public welfare, the police power may be invoked to justify the fixing of a minimum wage, it may, when the public welfare is thought to require it, be invoked to justify a maximum wage. The power to fix high wages connotes, by like reasoning, the power to fix low wages. If, in the face of the guaranties of the 5th Amendment, this form of legislation shall be legally justified, the field for the operation of the police power will have been

---

[11] *Ibid.*, 261 U.S. 544-562, 567-571.

widened to a great and dangerous degree. . . .

It follows from what has been said that the act in question passes the limit prescribed by the Constitution, and, accordingly, the decrees of the court below are Affirmed. . . .

. . . HOLMES, J., dissenting: The question in this case is the broad one, whether Congress can establish minimum rates of wages for women in the District of Columbia, with due provision for special circumstances, or whether we must say that Congress has no power to meddle with the matter at all. . . . When so many intelligent persons who have studied the matter more than any of us can, have thought that the means are effective and are worth the price, it seems to me impossible to deny that the belief reasonably may be held by reasonable men. . . . But, in the present instance, the only objection that can be urged is founded in the vague contours of the 5th Amendment, prohibiting the depriving any person of liberty or of property without due process of law. To that I turn.

The earlier decisions upon the same words in the 14th Amendment began within our memory, and went no farther than an unpretentious assertion of the liberty to follow the ordinary callings. Later that innocuous generality was expanded into the dogma Liberty of Contract. Contract is not specially mentioned in the text that we have to construe. It is merely an example of doing what you want to do, embodied in the word "liberty." But pretty much all law, consists in forbidding men to do some things that they want to do, and contract is no more exempt from law than other acts. . . .

The criterion of constitutionality is not whether we believe the law to be for the public good. We certainly cannot be prepared to deny that a reasonable man reasonably might have that belief, in view of the legislation of Great Britain, Victoria, and a number of the states of this Union.

The belief is fortified by a very remarkable collection of documents submitted on behalf of the appellants, material here, I conceive, only as showing that the belief reasonably may be held. . . .

## 12

That judicial hewing to the conservative line aroused little resentment, even from liberals, was due to the idealization of the courts in American folklore. Scarcely a loyal citizen could be found in the 1920's who did not accept unquestioningly certain propositions: (1) that the Constitution must never be questioned, and (2) that the Supreme Court was the sole judge of the meaning of the Constitution. Of the few who realized that judicial finality was often a means of frustrating the popular will, none was more outspoken than Harvard's witty professor of law, Thomas Reed Powell. His good-humored attack on those who enshrined the Constitution and worshiped the Supreme Court was illustrated in his review of a book by James M. Beck, *The Constitution of the United States* (1925), which was guilty of those very traits that Professor Powell most deplored:[12]

I never knew what the Constitution really is until I read Mr. Beck's book. He says that "it is something more than a written formula of government—it is a great spirit. It is a high and noble assertion, and, indeed, vindication, of the morality of government." It is splendid to have a Constitution like that and to know, as Mr. Beck tells us, that "to the succeeding ages, the Constitution will be a flaming beacon." This is not all that it is, for Mr. Beck says also:

I have elsewhere likened the Constitution to a Gothic cathedral, like that of Rheims. Its foundations seem secure, even though some of its buttresses may be weakened and its statuary mutilated. Nevertheless it remains a noble and serviceable temple of Liberty and Justice. Let us hope that, with the present indiffer-

[12] Thomas Reed Powell, "Constitutional Metaphors," *The New Republic,* XLI (February 11, 1925), 314-315. Quoted by permission from *New Republic,* February 11, 1925.

ence of the masses to the Constitution and the spirit of innovation of this restless and impatient age, that the time will not come that the Constitution will be as the Cathedral of Rheims when the author saw it in the summer of 1916. Rheims was a noble but pitiful ruin. Its high altar had been overthrown, and its glorious rose windows hopelessly shattered.

The high altar of the Constitution is the self-restraint which the American people of 1787 were wise enough to impose upon themselves, and their posterity, and the rose windows are those great traditions of Liberty which we have gained at an infinite sacrifice of treasure and life from our English-speaking ancestry.

It helps us to know what the Constitution is if we know what it is not. It is a beacon and a Gothic cathedral, but it is not a rock and it is not a beach. Instead of these things, it is a floating dock. Mr. Beck puts it very beautifully when he says:

The Constitution is neither, on the one hand, a Gibraltar rock, which wholly resists the ceaseless washing of time and circumstance, nor is it, on the other hand, a sandy beach, which is slowly destroyed by the erosion of the waves. It is rather to be likened to a floating dock, which, while firmly attached to its moorings, and not therefore at the caprice of the waves, yet rises and falls with the tide of time and circumstance.

You might think that a Constitution which is all these wonderful things would be sure to last forever without any help from anything else. But this is not so. Mr. Beck says that it would not have lasted so long as it has if it had not been for the Supreme Court which he says is the "balance wheel of the Constitution." He has a whole chapter which he calls The Balance Wheel and this chapter ends up by saying:

But always the Supreme Court stands as a great lighthouse and even when the waves beat upon it with terrific violence (as in the Civil War, when it was shaken to its very

foundation), yet after they have spent their fury, the great lamp of the Constitution—as that of another Pharos—illumines the troubled face of the waters with the benignant rays of those immutable principles of liberty and justice, which alone can make a nation free as well as strong.

It makes you see how marvelous the Supreme Court really is when it can be a balance wheel at the beginning of a chapter and a lighthouse at the end.

Even if you are not interested in the Constitution for its own sake, you will like to read what Mr. Beck says about it because he is such a lovely writer. He is the kind of writer who likes to write just for the sake of writing. He shows how he loves his work. He is not one of those writers who have to stop in their writing while they are making up their minds what to say. You can read him right along because he is so simple in his thoughts. He does not get you all mixed up the way so many writers do, but he brings up in your mind beautiful pictures of the Constitution as a temple and a beacon and a floating dock and he lets you see the Supreme Court shining and balancing in a very wonderful way. I have read a great many books about the Constitution, but there is no other book that has given me just the same kind of pleasure that this one has.

You will have a very happy feeling while you are reading Mr. Beck's book, until you come to the last three chapters. Then you begin to feel sad. The ending is not a happy ending. It tells of dangers that will hurt our country if we do not look out. It is not enough to have a Gothic cathedral with a balance wheel. We must all be wise and good men who will not make changes. This is like so many books that have a moral lesson at the end. On his very last page Mr. Beck tells what we should do. He says that when the Constitution came out of the safe in the State Department a few years ago, "the ink, in which it had been engrossed nearly one hundred and thirty-seven years ago, was found to have faded." He hopes that this is not a bad sign. This is what he means when he says that "all who believe in constitutional government must hope that this is not a portentous symbol"; just hoping will not help any, and it would not do any good to put fresh ink on top of the ink that is fading. We must do something different from that. Mr. Beck tells us very plainly what we should do when he says that "the American people must write the compact, not with ink upon a parchment, but with 'letters of living light'—to use Webster's phrase—upon their hearts." That must be a very hard way to write, and I should think it would be a good thing to write the ink letters, as well as the light letters, because the light might go out before the ink had all faded.

## NATIONALISM AND NORMALCY

### 13

Both the nationalism of senators and the conservatism of justices rested on a firm popular foundation. Perhaps some Americans during the 1920's still clung to Wilsonian progressivism and internationalism, but far more were thoroughly disillusioned by the realities of the peace and the terrors of reconstruction. When they found that, despite their wartime sacrifices, tyranny, persecutions, and conflict still continued throughout the world, they simply lost faith in reform. As the swelling prosperity of the postwar years stimulated individualism, they retreated into their shells, forsaking both the world and society. Material gain, personal success, the almighty dollar—those were their goals, rather than a better social order. Nothing was more expressive of this comfortable philosophy than a best-selling biography of Christ, *The Man Nobody Knows* (1924), from the pen of Bruce Barton, a New York advertising man. Widely distributed by business firms to their executives and salesmen, this amazing volume sought to dignify Jesus by portraying in Him the qualities of a successful American businessman: aggressive self-confidence, per-

sonal magnetism, organizing ability, and a capacity to pick men:[13]

### How It Came to Be Written

The little boy's body sat bolt upright in the rough wooden chair, but his mind was very busy.

This was his weekly hour of revolt.

The kindly lady who could never seem to find her glasses would have been terribly shocked if she had known what was going on inside the little boy's mind.

"You must love Jesus," she said every Sunday, "and God.". . .

. . . Jesus was the "lamb of God." The little boy did not know what that meant, but it sounded like Mary's little lamb. Something for girls—sissified. Jesus was also "meek and lowly," a "man of sorrows and acquainted with grief." He went around for three years telling people not to do things. . . .

Years went by and the boy grew up and became a business man.

He began to wonder about Jesus.

He said to himself: "Only strong magnetic men inspire great enthusiasm and build great organizations. Yet Jesus built the greatest organization of all. It is extraordinary."

The more sermons the man heard and the more books he read the more mystified he became.

One day he decided to wipe his mind clean of books and sermons.

He said, "I will read what the men who knew Jesus personally said about him. I will read about him as though he were a new historical character, about whom I had never heard anything at all."

The man was amazed.

A physical weakling! Where did they get that idea? Jesus pushed a plane and swung an adze; he was a successful car-

---

[13] From *The Man Nobody Knows* by Bruce Barton, pp. 1, 18-20, 23, copyright 1924, used by special permission of the publishers, The Bobbs-Merrill Company.

penter. He slept outdoors and spent his days walking around his favorite lake. His muscles were so strong that when he drove the money-changers out, nobody dared to oppose him!

A kill-joy! He was the most popular dinner guest in Jerusalem! The criticism which proper people made was that he spent too much time with publicans and sinners (very good fellows, on the whole, the man thought) and enjoyed society too much. They called him a "wine bibber and a gluttonous man."

A failure! He picked up twelve men from the bottom ranks of business and forged them into an organization that conquered the world.

When the man had finished his reading he exclaimed, "This is a man nobody knows.

"Some day," said he, "some one will write a book about Jesus. Every business man will read it and send it to his partners and his salesmen. For it will tell the story of the founder of modern business."

So the man waited for some one to write the book, but no one did. Instead, more books were published about the "lamb of God" who was weak and unhappy and glad to die.

The man became impatient. One day he said, "I believe I will try to write that book, myself."

And he did.

### The Executive

. . . Success is always exciting; we never grow tired of asking what and how. What, then, were the principal elements in his power over men? How was it that the boy from a country village became the greatest leader?

First of all he had the voice and manner of the leader—the personal magnetism which begets loyalty and commands respect . . . The essential element in personal magnetism is a consuming sincerity

—an overwhelming faith in the importance of the work one has to do. . . .

Most of us go through the world mentally divided against ourselves. We wonder whether we are in the right jobs, whether we are making the right investments, whether, after all, anything is as important as it seems to be. Our enemies are those of our own being and creation. Instinctively we wait for a commanding voice, for one who shall say authoritatively, "I have the truth. This way lies happiness and salvation." There was in Jesus supremely that quality of conviction. . . .

In any crowd and under any circumstances the leader stands out. By the power of his faith in himself he commands, and men instinctively obey.

This blazing conviction was the first and greatest element in the success of Jesus. The second was his wonderful power to pick men, and to recognize hidden capacities in them.

## 14

Bruce Barton's interpretation of the Gospel recorded the temper of the 1920's. So did the presidents who sat in the White House during those years. Warren G. Harding, Calvin Coolidge, and Herbert Hoover all expressed undying faith in rugged individualism, the inevitability of continued material progress, and the perfection of business leadership. Technological improvements, they honestly believed, had solved the problems of the machine age; "two chickens in every pot" and "two cars in every garage" would be the reward of the most humble wage earner as a business civilization showered blessings on all who worshiped at the altar of gain. The philosophy of the country's leaders was expressed by Hoover in a campaign speech delivered on October 22, 1928, in New York City:[14]

. . . During one hundred and fifty years we have builded up a form of self-government and a social system which is

---

[14] *The New York Times,* October 23, 1928. Quoted with permission of *The New York Times.*

peculiarly our own. It differs essentially from all others in the world. It is the American system. It is just as definite and positive a political and social system as has ever been developed on earth. It is founded upon a particular conception of self-government in which decentralized local responsibility is the very base. . . .

When the war closed, the most vital of all issues both in our own country and throughout the world was whether governments should continue their wartime ownership and operation of many instrumentalities of production and distribution. We were challenged with a peace-time choice between the American system of rugged individualism and a European philosophy of diametrically opposed doctrines—doctrines of paternalism and state socialism. The acceptance of these ideas would have meant the destruction of self-government through centralization of government. It would have meant the undermining of the individual initiative and enterprise through which our people have grown to unparalleled greatness.

The Republican Party from the beginning resolutely turned its face away from these ideas and these war practices. . . . When the Republican Party came into full power it went at once resolutely back to our fundamental conception of the state and the rights and responsibilities of the individual. Thereby it restored confidence and hope in the American people, it freed and stimulated enterprise, it restored the government to its position as an umpire instead of a player in the economic game. . . .

There has been revived in this campaign, however, a series of proposals, which, if adopted, would be a long step toward the abandonment of our American system and a surrender to the destructive operation of governmental conduct of commercial business. Because the country is faced with difficulty and doubt over certain national problems—that is prohibition, farm relief, and electrical power—our opponents propose that we must thrust government a long way into the businesses which give rise to these problems. In effect, they abandon the tenets of their own party and turn to state socialism as a solution for the difficulties presented by all three. . . .

I should like to state to you the effect that this projection of government in business would have upon our system of self-government and our economic system. That effect would reach to the daily life of every man and woman. It would impair the very basis of liberty and freedom not only for those left outside the fold of expanded bureaucracy but for those embraced within it.

Let us first see the effect upon self-government. When the Federal Government undertakes to go into commercial business it must at once set up the organization and administration of that business, and it immediately finds itself in a labyrinth, every alley of which leads to the destruction of self-government.

Commercial business requires a concentration of responsibility. Self-government requires decentralization and many checks and balances to safeguard liberty. Our Government to succeed in business would need to become in effect a despotism. There at once begins the destruction of self-government. . . .

Government, in order to avoid the possible incompetence, corruption and tyranny of too great authority in individuals entrusted with commercial business, inevitably turns to boards and commissions. To make sure that there are checks and balances, each member of such boards and commissions must have equal authority. Each has his separate responsibility to the public, and at once we have the conflict of ideas and the lack of decision which would ruin any commercial business. It has contributed greatly to the demoralization of our shipping business. Moreover, these commissions must be representative of different sections and different political parties, so that at once we have an entire blight upon coordinated action within their ranks which destroys any possibility of effective administration. . . .

It is a false liberalism that interprets itself into the government operation of commercial business. Every step of bureaucratizing of the business of our country poisons the very roots of liberalism —that is, political equality, free speech, free assembly, free press, and equality of opportunity. It is the road not to more liberty, but to less liberty. Liberalism should be found not striving to spread bureaucracy but striving to set bounds to it. . . .

Liberalism is a force truly of the spirit, a force proceeding from the deep realization that economic freedom cannot be sacrificed if political freedom is to be preserved. Even if Governmental conduct of business could give us more efficiency instead of less efficiency, the fundamental objection to it would remain unaltered and unabated. It would destroy political equality. It would increase rather than decrease abuse and corruption. It would stifle initiative and invention. It would undermine the development of leadership. It would cramp and cripple the mental and spiritual energies of our people. It would extinguish equality and opportunity. It would dry up the spirit of liberty and progress. For these reasons primarily it must be resisted. For a hundred and fifty years liberalism has found its true spirit in the American system, not in the European systems.

I do not wish to be misunderstood in this statement. I am defining a general policy. It does not mean that our Government is to part with one iota of its national resources without complete protection to the public interest. I have already stated that where the government is engaged in public works for purposes of flood control, of navigation, of irrigation, of scientific research or national defense, or in pioneering a new art, it will at times necessarily

produce power or commodities as a by-product. But they must be a by-product of the major purpose, not the major purpose itself.

Nor do I wish to be misinterpreted as believing that the United States is free-for-all and devil-take-the-hindmost. The very essence of equality of opportunity and of American individualism is that there shall be no domination by any group or combination in this republic, whether it be business or political. On the contrary, it demands economic justice as well as political and social justice. It is no system of laissez faire. . . .

By adherence to the principles of decentralized self-government, ordered liberty, equal opportunity, and freedom to the individual, our American experiment in human welfare has yielded a degree of well-being unparalleled in all the world. It has come nearer to the abolition of poverty, to the abolition of fear of want, than humanity has ever reached before. Progress of the past seven years is the proof of it. This alone furnishes the answer to our opponents, who ask us to introduce destructive elements into the system by which this has been accomplished. . . .

## 15

The philosophy of rugged individualism determined the political atmosphere of the 1920's. Hewing strictly to the laissez-faire line, both the presidents and the Congress stood aside while business followed its own path toward greater production and more lavish profits. As profits spiraled upward (and wages followed haltingly) a few observers detected a flaw in the economic structure: farm prices were steadily declining while industrial prices remained rigid. Although almost no one had the good sense to recognize the inevitable effect of vanishing agrarian markets on industrial sales, the farmers were sufficiently aroused to demand a change. Acting through a bipartisan congressional "Farm Bloc," they pushed through the McNary-Haugen Bill, designed to bolster agricultural prices by government support of farm exports. President Coolidge's veto of the measure in

1927 was chiefly inspired by dislike for "government in business":[15]

Clearly this legislation involves government fixing of prices. It gives the proposed Federal board almost unlimited authority to fix prices on the designated commodities. This is price fixing, furthermore, on some of the Nation's basic foods and materials. Nothing is more certain than that such price fixing would upset the normal exchange relationships existing in the open market and that it would finally have to be extended to cover a multitude of other goods and services. Government price fixing, once started, has alike no justice and no end. It is an economic folly from which this country has every right to be spared.

This legislation proposes, in effect, that Congress shall delegate to a Federal Farm Board, nominated by farmers, the power to fix and collect a tax, called an equalization fee, on certain products produced by those farmers. That certainly contemplates a remarkable delegation of the taxing power. The purpose of that tax, it may be repeated, is to pay the losses incurred in the disposition of the surplus products in order to raise the price on that portion of the products consumed by our own people.

This so-called equalization fee is not a tax for purposes of revenue in the accepted sense. It is a tax for the special benefit of particular groups. As a direct tax on certain of the vital necessaries of life it represents the most vicious form of taxation. Its real effect is an employment of the coercive powers of Government to the end that certain special groups of farmers and processors may profit temporarily at the expense of other farmers and of the community at large. . . .

A board of 12 men are granted almost unlimited control of the agricultural industry and can not only fix the price which

[15] *Congressional Record*, 69th Cong., 2nd Sess., pp. 4771-4776.

the producers of five commodities shall receive for their goods, but can also fix the price which the consumers of the country shall pay for these commodities. The board is expected to obtain higher prices for the American farmer by removing the surplus from the home market and dumping it abroad at a below-cost price. To do this, the board is given the authority by implication to fix the domestic price level, either by means of contracts which it may make with processors or cooperatives, or by providing for the purchase of the commodities in such quantities as will bring the prices up to the point which the board may fix. . . .

. . . The granting of any such arbitrary power to a Government board is to run counter to our traditions, the philosophy of our Government, the spirit of our institutions, and all principles of equity. . . .

The effect of this plan will be continuously to stimulate American production and to pile up increasing surpluses beyond the world demand. We are already overproducing. . . . With such increased surpluses dumped from the United States on to foreign markets the world prices will be broken down and with them American prices upon which the premium is based will likewise be lowered to the point of complete disaster to American farmers. It is impossible to see how this bill can work.

Several of our foreign markets have agriculture of their own to protect and they have laws in force which may be applied to dumping and we may expect reprisals from them against dumping agricultural products which will even more diminish our foreign markets.

The bill is essentially a price-fixing bill, because in practical working the board must arrive in some way at the premium price which will be demanded from the American consumer, and it must fix these prices in the contracts at which it will authorize purchases by flour millers, packers, other manufacturers, and such cooperatives as may be used, for the board must formulate a basis upon which the board will pay losses on the export of their surplus. . . .

This measure is so long and involved that it is impossible to discuss it without going into many tiresome details. Many other reasons exist why it ought not to be approved, but it is impossible to state them all without writing a book. The most decisive one is that it is not constitutional. This feature is discussed in an opinion of the Attorney General, herewith attached and made a part hereof, so that I shall not consider the details of that phase of my objections. . . .

# 16

The unshaken faith of popular leaders in what they chose to call the "American system" boded ill for all who dared raise dissenting voices. Reformers who had commanded respect a few years before suddenly found themselves branded as "radicals," internationalists were labeled "pacifists," and mild socialists became dangerous "agitators." Most abhorrent to advocates of the *status quo* were Marxists, for the success of the Communist Revolution in Russia terrified conservatives on both sides of the Atlantic. The extent of hysterical fear was shown in January, 1920, when the New York Legislature refused to seat five legally elected Socialist assemblymen. The episode has been described by Zechariah Chafee, Jr., Harvard professor of law, who was one of the few consistent advocates of freedom of speech in that undemocratic era:[16]

The Socialist Party of New York was a legally recognized party under the Election Law, so that its candidates had as much right on the ballot as Democrats or Republicans. . . . And on this day, in 1920, the five members took office without interference, swearing that they would support the Constitution of the United

States and that of New York, and discharge the duties of their office to the best of their ability, and that they had not influenced votes by bribe or promise. The New York Constitution, Article XIII, prescribes this oath and makes it all-sufficient:

No other oath, declaration or test shall be required as a qualification for any office of public trust.

They occupied their seats and for upwards of two hours entered into all the business of the day.

Suddenly the newly-elected Speaker, without notice or motion, directed the Sergeant-at-Arms to present the five Socialist members before the bar of the House. The surprised men were paraded down into the well of the Assembly chamber in front of the Speaker's rostrum, in full view of their fellow-members and hundreds of guests, who crowded the galleries and the floor to witness the ceremonies of the opening day. There they were lined up with the Sergeant-at-Arms on guard, while the Speaker addressed them:

You are seeking seats in this body, you who have been elected on a platform that is absolutely inimical to the best interests of the State of New York and of the United States.

He then declared that the Socialist Party was not truly a political party, but a subversive and unpatriotic organization, and informed them that if the House should adopt a resolution declaring their places vacant they would be given an opportunity to appear before a tribunal to prove their rights to sit in the Assembly.

Next a resolution was presented to the Assembly, which had been drafted by the Attorney General as counsel for the Lusk Committee. Probing committees seem indigenous to New York. They had one in 1780 to detect and defeat conspiracies of Loyalists. On March 26, 1919, the Legislature set up a joint committee of

---

[16] Reprinted by permission of the publishers from Zechariah Chafee, Jr., *Free Speech in the United States* (1941), Cambridge, Mass.: Harvard University Press, 1941, pp. 269-282.

six under the chairmanship of Senator Lusk to investigate seditious activities and report to the legislature. Although in no sense a body for the prosecution of crime, it proceeded to conduct a series of spectacular illegal raids on the offices of the Rand School and other radical organizations, instigate prosecutions of radical leaders like Gitlow, and fill the press with a flow of terrorizing descriptions of the Red menace. And now it was the moving spirit in ousting the Socialist Assemblymen.

The Lusk Committee's resolution did not even recite that the members were charged with certain offenses, but stated facts as if already proved, an Alice-in-Wonderland performance of "sentence first—verdict afterwards.". . . The roll-call was then taken and the five Socialists were called upon to vote as members. After the passage of the resolution they were hustled by the Sergeant-at-Arms out of the chamber, where their seats remained vacant for the remainder of the session, to the disfranchisement of sixty thousand voters of the City of New York. . . .

On January 20th the investigation of the five members began before the Judiciary Committee, which was appointed by the Speaker who had taken such a definite stand against them. At the outset the Bar Association committee appeared, with Mr. Hughes as its chairman, but was not allowed to participate in the proceedings. Before withdrawing it filed a brief and these recommendations:

That the Judiciary Committee at once report to the Assembly that there is no question properly before the Judiciary Committee of any disqualification on the part of these members; that no charges against these members of any constitutional disqualification, or of any misconduct in office or of any violation of law on their part have been properly made, that the members under suspension should at once be restored to the privileges of their seats and that if it be desired to present any charges against them of any violation of law, such charges should be properly formulated,

and that until such charges, properly laid, have been established by proof, after due opportunity to be heard, these members shall enjoy all the privileges of their seats in recognition of their own rights and of the rights of their constituencies.

This position was conclusively established by the Bar Association in its brief. . . . Secondly, the five Socialists were not charged with violating any law. They had been convicted of no crime, they were accused of no crime which could conceivably be a bar to office. They were proscribed for their beliefs and their membership in the Socialist Party. . . .

No person who followed with any intelligence the proceedings of the Socialist Party at the convention of September, 1919, or May, 1920, could doubt that that party was as much divided into factions as any other. Nevertheless, the five members were held responsible on the principle just stated, not merely for the statements in the party platform, but also for the Debs speech at Canton, Ohio; for statements in the Moscow manifesto; for extracts from a book in Yiddish published by the Jewish Socialist Federation of America; for all the articles contributed to the *American Socialist;* for everything that was said by speakers at meetings at which one of the Socialist assemblymen was present; as well as for statements made in a letter by an organization to which he was bitterly opposed. This was guilt by association with a vengeance.

When such testimony and arguments were admitted, the result was a foregone conclusion. The Committee recommended expulsion, the Assembly characteristically waited until April 1st, which was too late for a reelection, and then expelled the five members by an overwhelming vote. The Legislature next enacted several bills drafted by the triumphant Lusk Committee, which throttled the Rand School and excluded from the ballot any organization which advocated "doctrines or policies that tend, if carried into effect, to the destruction, subversion, or endangering of the existing governments" of the state and nation, "and of the rights, privileges and institutions secured under such constitutions." Governor Alfred E. Smith vetoed all these Lusk bills in stinging messages. And then, leaving the Governor's welfare bills untouched, the New York Legislature adjourned, and Speaker Sweet proclaimed the session "a victory for undivided Americanism."

## 17

Amidst the postwar hysteria, popular wrath was turned against harmless foreigners or even Americans whose race or religion did not coincide with the majority pattern. Particularly feared were aliens who might spread "foreign" ideologies among the people, or who might "weaken" the American stock with "inferior breeds." To stop their coming, and to protect the United States from a postwar immigrant flood that would engulf the labor market, Congress rushed to close America's gates. The most important of a series of laws designed to end migration was adopted on May 26, 1924. Its terms were explained in a proclamation issued by President Coolidge:[17]

Whereas it is provided in the act of Congress approved May 26, 1924, entitled "An act to limit the immigration of aliens into the United States, and for other purposes" that—

"The annual quota of any nationality shall be two per centum of the number of foreign-born individuals of such nationality resident in continental United States as determined by the United States census of 1890, but the minimum quota of any nationality shall be 100 (Sec. 11(a)). . . .

"The Secretary of State, the Secretary of Commerce, and the Secretary of Labor, jointly, shall, as soon as feasible after the enactment of this act, prepare a statement showing the number of individuals of the various nationalities resident in continental United States as determined by the United States census of 1890, which statement shall be the population basis for the purposes of subdivision (a) of section 11 (sec. 12(b)).

"Such officials shall, jointly, report annually to the President the quota of each nationality under subdivision (a) of section 11, together with the statements, estimates, and revisions provided for in this section. The President shall proclaim and make known the quotas so reported." (Sec. 12(e)).

Now, therefore, I, Calvin Coolidge, President of the United States of America acting under and by virtue of the power in me vested by the aforesaid act of Congress, do hereby proclaim and make known that on and after July 1, 1924, and throughout the fiscal year 1924-1925, the quota of each nationality provided in said Act shall be as follows:

Country or Area of Birth

| Country or Area of Birth | Quota 1924-1925 |
|---|---|
| Afghanistan | 100 |
| Albania | 100 |
| Andorra | 100 |
| Arabian peninsula (1, 2) | 100 |
| Armenia | 124 |
| Australia, including Papua, Tasmania, and all islands appertaining to Australia (3, 4) | 121 |
| Austria | 785 |
| Belgium (5) | 512 |
| Bhutan | 100 |
| Bulgaria | 100 |
| Cameroon (proposed British mandate) | 100 |
| Cameroon (French mandate) | 100 |
| China | 100 |
| Czechoslovakia | 3,073 |
| Danzig, Free City of | 228 |
| Denmark (5, 6) | 2,789 |
| Egypt | 100 |
| Esthonia | 124 |
| Ethiopia (Abyssinia) | 100 |
| Finland | 471 |
| France (1, 5, 6) | 3,954 |
| Germany | 51,227 |

[17] Department of Labor, *Annual Report of the Commissioner-General of Immigration, 1924* (Washington, 1924), pp. 24-27.

|  | Quota 1924-1925 |
|---|---|
| Great Britain and Northern Ireland (1, 3, 5, 6) | 34,007 |
| Greece | 100 |
| Hungary | 473 |
| Iceland | 100 |
| India (3) | 100 |
| Iraq (Mesopotamia) | 100 |
| Irish Free State (3) | 28,567 |
| Italy, including Rhodes, Dodecanesia, and Castellorizzo (5) | 3,845 |
| Japan | 100 |
| Latvia | 142 |
| Liberia | 100 |
| Liechtenstein | 100 |
| Lithuania | 344 |
| Luxemburg | 100 |
| Monaco | 100 |
| Morocco (French and Spanish Zones and Tangier) | 100 |
| Muscat (Oman) | 100 |
| Nauru (proposed British mandate) (4) | 100 |
| Nepal | 100 |
| Netherlands (1, 5, 6) | 1,648 |
| New Zealand (including appertaining islands) (3, 4) | 100 |
| Norway (5) | 6,453 |
| New Guinea, and other Pacific Islands under proposed Australian mandate (4) | 100 |
| Palestine (with Trans-Jordan, proposed British mandate) | 100 |
| Persia (1) | 100 |
| Poland | 5,982 |
| Portugal (1, 5) | 503 |
| Ruanda and Urundi (Belgium mandate) | 100 |
| Rumania | 603 |
| Russia, European and Asiatic (1) | 2,248 |
| Samoa, Western (4) (proposed mandate of New Zealand) | 100 |
| San Marino | 100 |
| Siam | 100 |
| South Africa, Union of (3) | 100 |
| South West Africa (proposed mandate of Union of South Africa) | 100 |
| Spain (5) | 131 |
| Sweden | 9,561 |
| Switzerland | 2,081 |
| Syria and The Lebanon (French mandate) | 100 |
| Tanganyika (proposed British mandate) | 100 |

|  | Quota 1924-1925 |
|---|---|
| Togoland (proposed British mandate) | 100 |
| Togoland (French mandate) | 100 |
| Turkey | 100 |
| Yap and other Pacific islands (under Japanese mandate) | 100 |
| Yugoslavia | 671 |

1. (a) Persons born in the portions of Persia, Russia, or the Arabian peninsula situated within the barred zone, and who are admissible under the immigration laws of the United States as quota immigrants, will be charged to the quotas of these countries; and (b) persons born in the colonies, dependencies, or protectorates, or portions thereof, within the barred zone, of France, Great Britain, the Netherlands, or Portugal, who are admissible under the immigration laws of the United States as quota immigrants, will be charged to the quota of the country to which such colony or dependency belongs or by which it is administered as a protectorate. . . .

3. Quota immigrants born in the British self-governing dominions or in the Empire of India, will be charged to the appropriate quota rather than to that of Great Britain and Northern Ireland. There are no quota restrictions for Canada and Newfoundland. . . .

5. Quota immigrants eligible to citizenship in the United States, born in a colony, dependency, or protectorate of any country to which a quota applies will be charged to the quota of that country.

6. In contrast with the law of 1921, the immigration act of 1924 provides that persons born in the colonies or dependencies of European countries situated in Central America, South America, or the islands adjacent to the American continents (except Newfoundland, Labrador and Canada), will be charged to the quota of the country to which such colony or dependency belongs.

## 18

The race consciousness that helped inspire the Immigration Act of 1924 was more disgracefully expressed in the success of the Ku Klux Klan. Riding to triumph after triumph on their platform of "100 per cent Americanism," the members of this intolerant society won some five million converts by the middle of the decade. Their open enmity toward Negroes, Catholics, and Jews was no more truly American than their program of flogging, lynching, and terrorism, yet an indifferent nation watched with scarcely a protest as Klansmen persecuted innocent victims in state after state. A contemporary observer recorded their acts of violence in one section of the nation during the month of July, 1921:[18]

July 1, 1921.—At Forth Worth, Texas, a white man whose name was not printed was taken from his home at 9 P.M. and given twenty lashes for alleged mistreatment of his wife.

July 4, 1921.—At Austin, Texas, Governor Heff, chief executive of the State in an address before the Rotary Club said that a crime wave had struck the State and that "the entire administration of the criminal code had broken down." On the same day warnings of the Ku Klux Klan were posted on the State Capitol grounds.

July 5, 1921.—At Fort Worth, Texas, Benny Pinto was tarred and feathered and ordered out of town. A woman found with him in his automobile was taken home by his abductors.

July 8, 1921.—At Glidden, Texas, Harry Adams, a gardener, was beaten and choked by masked armed men. Then found to be the wrong man, he was released.

July 12, 1921.—At Enid, Okla., Walter Billings, a motion-picture operator, was given a coating of cotton and crude oil, after being whipped by masked men.

July 14, 1921.—One hundred masked

men gathered at the jail at Greeneville, Texas, and unsuccessfully attempted to lynch Matt Olizen, negro, charged with killing Orbie Standlee.

July 14, 1921.—A delegation from Duncanville, Texas, warned the Dallas authorities that if Archie Holsome, charged with attacking a white woman was released, he would be lynched.

July 16, 1921.—At Tenaha, Texas, Mrs. Beulah Johnson, a white woman, was seized from the porch of a hotel, taken to the woods, stripped of her clothing, tarred and feathered preceding which her hair was clipped. Masked men wearing white uniforms attacked her, the woman said. They drove up to the hotel in three automobiles. Mrs. Johnson had been arrested on a charge of bigamy at Center, Texas, and was out on bond when she was seized.

July 17, 1921.—At Nacogdoches, Texas, J. M. McKnight was beaten by masked men.

July 17, 1921.—At Miami, Fla. At the close of his evening services, eight masked men waylaid the Rev. Philip S. Irwin, archdeacon of the English Episcopal Church, and head of the work of that church among South Florida negroes, carried him into the woods, whipped him, and then applied a coat of tar and feathers to his body. He was placed in a sack and taken in an automobile to a spot in the center of the town and dumped into the street. The following Tuesday, in response to a telegram from Rev. R. T. Phillips, rector of Trinity Church, Right Reverend Cameron Mann, Bishop of Southern Florida reached Miami and conferred with several officials, also appearing before the Grand Jury in order to make a statement as to Archdeacon Irwin's work. In his report to the Presiding Bishop of the Protestant Episcopal Church of the United States, Bishop Mann said:

"About the middle of the afternoon, while I was consulting with the mayor

---

[18] From *The Modern Ku Klux Klan* by Henry P. Fry, pp. 188-191: copyright 1922 by Small, Maynard and Company: used by permission of Bruce Humphries, Inc.

and the circuit judge, the commander of the local post of the American Legion came in and stated that he had reliable information that if Archdeacon Irwin remained in the city he would be lynched, and that in all probability church property would be burned and numerous lives lost. He therefore asked that Archdeacon Irwin should agree to leave the city that afternoon."

The charge made by the mob against the clergyman was that he had preached "race equality" and "inter-marriage." Bishop Mann declared unequivocally that Archdeacon Irwin does not hold to social or political equality for negroes in the United States, has never taught it, and in his missionary work has incurred disfavor with some negroes by his opposition to societies and movements which upheld the doctrine.

It was reported in the papers that the judge who brought the case to the attention of the Grand Jury told that body that, while the right of free speech is guaranteed, strangers should not defy the sentiments and traditions of the public.

July 16, 1921.—At Bay City, Tex., W. M. Hoopengarner, a banker, was tarred and feathered and beaten. The reason alleged was domestic infidelity.

July 18, 1921.—G. C. Benson beaten at Dickinson, Tex.

July 18, 1921.—E. H. Peters, of Athens, Tex., was dragged from his room, beaten, dumped out of an automobile and seriously hurt.

July 19, 1921.—At Tenaha, Tex., J. W. McKnight was seized a second time by masked men.

July 19, 1921.—Declaring that he had information that fifty per cent of the members of the Oklahoma City police department belonged to the Ku Klux Klan, Mayor John C. Welton directed Chief Glitsch to investigate and to discharge every police officer who did not resign immediately from the Klan. On July 24, Mayor Welton was called on the telephone, and was told: "We warn you to lay off the Ku Klux Klan, or we will have to wait on you." The mayor paid no attention to the warning.

July 22, 1921.—At Hillsboro, Tex., a note from the Ku Klux Klan was received and published in the local paper as a "warning to some married men who should spend more time with their own wives."

July 26, 1921.—At Topeka, Kan., a warning was sent to Senator Capper's newspaper to "leave the Ku Klux Klan alone."

July 29, 1921.—Ben Wiley, of Lufkin, Tex., was put into a sack and tarred and feathered.

In the State of Missouri, a farmer aged sixty-eight years, was taken from his bed at night, removed out of doors and severely beaten by masked men; and a woman in Birmingham, Ala., was also maltreated by a mob composed of the same sort of individuals.

## 19

To a later generation of liberals, the high-water mark of intolerance during the 1920's was reached in the trial of Bartolomeo Vanzetti and Nicola Sacco. Both men were anarchists and foreigners. They were charged with the murder of a paymaster for a South Braintree, Massachusetts, shoe factory on April 15, 1920. Despite questionable evidence and a world-wide insistence that they were being persecuted because of their social views, the two men were executed in 1927. Vanzetti, a harmless agitator whose philosophy was one of freedom rather than force, spoke some unforgettable words after receiving his sentence:[19]

If it had not been for these thing, I might have live out my life talking at street corners to scorning men. I might have die, unmarked, unknown, a failure. Now we are not a failure. This is our

[19] Marion D. Frankfurter and Gardner Jackson, *The Letters of Sacco and Vanzetti* (The Viking Press, New York, 1928), p. v.

career and our triumph. Never in our full
live could we hope to do such work for
tolerance, for joostice, for man's onder-
standing of man as now we do by accident.
Our words—our lives—our pains—nothing! The taking of our lives—lives of a
good shoemaker and a poor fish-peddler
—all! That last moment belongs to us—
that agony is our triumph.

## THE END OF AN ERA, 1929–1932

## 20

The golden prosperity that accompanied the
individualism and intolerance of the 1920's
came to an abrupt end with the stock market
crash of 1929. As panic swept the nation in
the wake of vanishing paper profits, a numb-
ing depression slowly paralyzed the economic
structure. Herbert Hoover, who entered the
White House only six months before the col-
lapse, found himself faced with the task of
restoring a shattered national economy in a
world of shattered economies. His answer,
and the answer of the Republican majority in
Congress, was a new tariff to protect American industry from imagined foreign competition. Even businessmen were uncertain that
this was the solution; a revived world trade
would, many believed, benefit producers more
than a doubtful market at home. Despite this
advice, Congress went doggedly ahead with
the measure that came to be known as the
Smoot-Hawley Tariff of 1930. As usual it was
framed largely by representatives of pressure
groups whose concern was individual profits
rather than national well-being. A monograph by E. E. Schattschneider indicates the
extent to which members of Congress and
business spokesmen acted upon the theory of
representation of vested interests:[20]

. . . To an amazing degree the hearings
were permitted to take whatever direction
was given to them by the witnesses themselves, who were in most cases allowed to
give what information they chose in the
form most agreeable to their own sense of
propriety. No attempt was made to check

[20] Reprinted by permission of Prentice-Hall, Inc.
from *Politics, Pressures and the Tariff* by E. E.
Schattschneider, pp. 38-44. Copyright, 1935, by
Prentice-Hall, Inc.

briefs . . . and no statements were au-
dited, nor were witnesses required to show
the sources of the statistical information
they presented. No books or papers were
requisitioned. There was little close scru-
tiny of testimony. . . . In a very large proportion of the cases the hearings established only the precise terms of the changes
in the law desired by the petitioners. . . .

Furthermore, the questions asked were
remarkably tender to the sensibilities of
protected interests. Inquiries into profits,
capitalization, bond issues, dividends, stock
dividends, ownership of corporations,
monopolistic trade practices, and labor
policies were rarely made. . . .

Senator King, who interested himself in
the monopoly practices of petitioners,
ownership of corporations, and a few
other matters generally slightly taboo,
examined Mr. F. B. Richards, spokesman
for the producers of pig iron, concerning
their profits and asked him to submit in
writing data which he seemed unable to
supply orally. The rest of the committee,
however, did not support Mr. King with
much vigor. . . . In fact, Senator King
was fortunate not to encounter the active
opposition of the rest of the committee to
his course of examination. At one stage of
a vigorous examination Senator Reed intervened to explain to the witness, "All
right, Mr. Kimball. We do not regard
prosperity as a crime." . . . In one instance Senator King asked for a statement
showing the assets and liabilities, the
property and profits or losses, output, and
prices of the manufacturers of umbrella
frames. Mr. Oscar I. Meyer, speaking for
this group, replied,

I do not know whether they would be willing to do that, but, if I did, and they were
willing to, it would have no bearing on this
case.

This feeling of the impropriety of questions about profits was shared by most
members of the committees. Even Mr.
Rainey, who was exceptionally interested

in the subject, prefaced an inquiry concerning dividends with "If it is a fair question . . . ," and another with "Would you be willing . . . ?" Senator Sackett went out of his way to make his question innocuous.

. . . what has been the reputation in the trade as to the success, financially, of cordage companies in this country?

Senator Reed likewise appreciated the delicacy of the subject and, on one of few occasions on which he mentioned it at all, introduced it as inoffensively as possible.

Have you any objection to talking about the finances of your company? . . .

Indeed, the language of the hearings often was not what one might expect to find in communications between a sovereign state and its citizens, nor was it, in many instances, that of an inquiry by a governmental body into the merits of a public policy. It was, rather, in the style and manner of equals engaged in negotiation. The representatives of economic groups addressed the committee in the language of the quotations below:

If your committee will grant us relief in paragraph 385 . . . we would agree in turn to have the duty on our finished products . . . reduced. . . .

. . . we are willing to take that.

The manufacturers are willing to accept the duty on raw materials contained in paragraph 1001.

. . . we have consented to a reduction of 10 or 12 cents a pound in the duties of this group. . . .

This will be in accordance with our original understanding and will be giving us what we expected to receive.

I said (to the Finance Committee in 1913), "In view of the political exigencies of the situation, we will accept some form of reduction, or something to save the face of the party in power if they wish to make this reduction. We will come down to 20 per cent if we can

continue in the United States of America, but below that we can not continue here and we shall have to go abroad."

The group I represent would accept a duty of 10 per cent on hides provided leather carried a duty of 20 per cent. . . .

. . . we accept, in so far as they go, the provisions of paragraph 1530. . . .

I am perfectly willing to modify that.

I am willing to accept a flat import duty of 10 per cent. . . .

. . . I am willing to accept. . . .

Members of the committees addressed the spokesmen of economic interests in the same manner:

Would it suit you if there were a specific duty of $1\frac{1}{2}$ cents . . . ?

But you are perfectly satisfied with the duties levied in 302?

Do I understand you to say that if this camel's hair is placed on the free list you would consent to the rewriting of paragraph 1109?

Would you be satisfied if Congress should adopt this in principle . . . ?

You would not mind, then, if we made an exception . . . ?

You would be willing that it be stricken out of the bill, would you not?

You will accept it but you do not want it.

The business of the hearings was, in this way, expedited by the spirit in which it was conducted, for agreements may be reached speedily in a friendly proceeding in which every major premise of the petitioners is conceded in advance.

## 21

Tactics such as these, although acceptable in the past, were certain to arouse protest when a deepening economic depression quickened men's interest in politics and society. Many were moved to question the wisdom of higher tariffs when thirty-six countries made diplomatic protests to the United States before the Smoot-Hawley Bill had even passed Congress. The most effective objection was levied by 1,028 American economists, whose last-minute appeal to President Hoover for a veto attracted wide attention—but no presidential response:[21]

The undersigned American economists and teachers of economics strongly urge that any measure which provides for a general upward revision of tariff rates be denied passage by Congress, or if passed, be vetoed by the President. . . .

Our export trade, in general, would suffer. Countries cannot permanently buy from us unless they are permitted to sell to us, and the more we restrict the importation of goods from them by means [of] ever higher tariffs, the more we reduce the possibility of our exporting to them.

This applies to such exporting industries as copper, automobiles, agricultural machinery, typewriters and the like fully as much as it does to farming. The difficulties of these industries are likely to be increased still further if we pass a higher tariff.

There are already many evidences that such action would inevitably provoke other countries to pay us back in kind by levying retaliatory duties against our goods. There are few more ironical spectacles than that of the American Government as it seeks, on the one hand, to promote exports through the activity of the Bureau of Foreign and Domestic Commerce, while, on the other hand, by increasing tariffs it makes exportation ever more difficult.

We do not believe that American manufacturers, in general, need higher tariffs. The report of the President's Committee on Recent Economic Changes has shown that industrial efficiency has increased, that costs have fallen, that profits have grown with amazing rapidity since the end of the World War. Already our factories supply our people with over 96 per cent of the manufactured goods which they consume, and our producers look to foreign markets to absorb the increasing output of their machines.

Further barriers to trade will serve them not well, but ill.

Many of our citizens have invested their money in foreign enterprises. The Department of Commerce has estimated that such investments, entirely aside from the war debts, amounted to between $12,555,000,-000 and $14,555,000,000 on Jan. 1, 1929. These investors, too, would suffer if restrictive duties were to be increased, since such action would make it still more difficult for their foreign debtors to pay them the interest due them.

America is now facing the problem of unemployment. The proponents of higher tariffs claim that an increase in rates will give work to the idle. This is not true. We cannot increase employment by restricting trade. American industry, in the present crisis, might well be spared the burden of adjusting itself to higher schedules of duties.

Finally, we would urge our government to consider the bitterness which a policy of higher tariffs would inevitably inject into our international relations. The United States was ably represented at the world economic conference which was held under the auspices of the League of Nations in 1927. This conference adopted a resolution announcing that "the time has come to put an end to the increase in tariffs and to move in the opposite direction."

The higher duties proposed in our pending legislation violate the spirit of this agreement and plainly invite other nations to compete with us in raising further barriers to trade. A tariff war does not furnish good soil for the growth of world peace.

## 22

Despite his insistence on a higher tariff as an aid to business, President Hoover was reluctant to allow the giant force of government to be used against the depression. Industry, he insisted, must lift itself back to prosperity by its own bootstraps; "recovery without re-

---

[21] *The New York Times,* May 5, 1930. Quoted with permission of *The New York Times.*

form" might well have been the slogan of his administration. His unwavering faith in private enterprise was demonstrated anew when Congress, goaded by popular pressure, decided in 1931 that the electric power and nitrate plants built in wartime at Muscle Shoals on the Tennessee River should be operated by the government to produce cheap fertilizer. Hoover vetoed the bill on March 3, 1931, in a message that asserted again his distrust of "government in business":[22]

The plants at Muscle Shoals were originally built for a production of nitrates for use in war explosives. I am advised by the War Department that the very large development in the United States by private enterprise in the manufacture of synthetic nitrogen now affords an ample supply covering any possible requirements of war. It is therefore unnecessary to maintain this plant for any such purposes.

This bill provides that the President for a period of 12 months may negotiate a lease of the nitrate plants for fertilizer manufacture under detailed limitations, but in failure to make such a lease the bill makes it mandatory upon the Government to manufacture nitrogen fertilizers at Muscle Shoals by the employment of existing facilities or by modernizing existing plants. . . .

I am firmly opposed to the Government entering into any business the major purpose of which is competition with our citizens. There are national emergencies which require that the Government should temporarily enter the field of business, but they must be emergency actions and in matters where the cost of the project is secondary to much higher considerations. There are many localities where the Federal Government is justified in the construction of great dams and reservoirs, where navigation, flood control, reclamation or stream regulation are of dominant importance, and where they are beyond the capacity or purpose of private or local

government capital to construct. In these cases power is often a by-product and should be disposed of by contract or lease. But for the Federal Government deliberately to go out to build up and expand an occasion to the major purpose of a power and manufacturing business is to break down the initiative and enterprise of the American people; it is destruction of equality of opportunity of our people; it is the negation of the ideals upon which our civilization has been based.

This bill raises one of the important issues confronting our people. That is squarely the issue of Federal Government ownership and operation of power and manufacturing business not as a minor by-product but as a major purpose. Involved in this question is the agitation against the conduct of the power industry. The power problem is not to be solved by the project in this bill. The remedy for abuses in the conduct of that industry lies in regulation and not by the Federal Government entering upon the business itself. I have recommended to the Congress on various occasions that action should be taken to establish Federal regulation of interstate power in cooperation with State authorities. This bill would launch the Federal Government upon a policy of ownership and operation of power utilities upon a basis of competition instead of by the proper Government function of regulation for the protection of all the people. I hesitate to contemplate the future of our institutions, of our country if the preoccupation of its officials is to be no longer the promotion of justice and equal opportunity but is to be devoted to barter in the markets. That is not liberalism, it is degeneration.

This proposal can be effectively opposed upon other and perhaps narrower grounds. The establishment of a Federal-operated power business and fertilizer factory in the Tennessee Valley means Federal control from Washington with all the vicissitudes of national politics and the tyrannies of remote bureaucracy imposed upon the

---

[22] *Congressional Record*, 71st Cong., 3rd Sess., pp. 7046-7048.

people of that valley without voice by them in their own resources, the overriding of State and local government, the undermining of State and local responsibility. The very history of this project over the past 10 years should be a complete demonstration of the ineptness of the Federal Government to administer such enterprise and of the penalties which the local community suffers under it.

This bill distinctly proposes to enter the field of powers reserved to the States. It would deprive the adjacent States of the right to control rates . . . and would invade and weaken the authority of local government. . . .

The real development of the resources and the industries of the Tenessee Valley can only be accomplished by the people in that valley themselves. Muscle Shoals can only be administered by the people upon the ground, responsible to their own communities, directing them solely for the benefit of their communities and not for purposes of pursuit of social theories or national politics. Any other course deprives them of liberty. . . .

The United States was ready for a change in leadership by the autumn of 1932. Hoover's program of "recovery without reform" aroused more disdain than anger, but its fatal weakness was lack of results. As the depression deepened, as bread lines grew, as firms slid into bankruptcy, as unkempt Hoovervilles sprouted on the edge of cities, as banks closed their doors, the national mood grew increasingly dangerous. Clearly reform was needed to forestall something more revolutionary. Amidst these tragic scenes, Americans prepared to repudiate the rugged individualism of the past for the social planning of the future.

# THE ROOSEVELT REVOLUTION

## 1933-1940

The election of 1932 inaugurated that stirring epoch in recent history that is known as the "Roosevelt Revolution." Turning his back on the political philosophy which had prevailed in the 1920's, Franklin Delano Roosevelt held that the government's duty included positive steps to establish and maintain the general welfare of the people. With strong backing from both nation and Congress, his "New Deal" included general reform for the country's economic system as well as relief for the poverty-stricken and recovery for industry and agriculture. His dramatic party leadership not only won him four terms in the White House but was responsible for more progressive legislation than had been crowded into all the nation's history before 1933.

## SOCIAL TENSIONS AND REFORM

### 1

For those who could read the signs of the times, the popular mandate for the New Deal in 1932 came as no surprise; the ground swell of progressivism was forming beneath the surface long before it burst into the open on election day. One indication of the liberalizing effect of the depression on popular thought was the social gospel avowed by the Federal Council of Churches at its meeting in 1932:[1]

. . . The Christian social ideal is one of a good life, abundant, progressive, and generously devoted to human welfare—a life lived "under the eye and by the strength of God." It implies satisfaction in work as in leisure. Deadening and injurious occupations and conditions of work are inconsistent with it; so also are stultifying, stupefying, injurious indulgences in time of leisure. In economic terms, the Christian ideal demands a basic standard of living for the masses of the people, adequate to assure security and freedom for the development of spiritual values. It means sound education both of mind and will, so that one may know the better and choose it; so that one may know what is the higher good and prefer it. The Christian religion has many precious aids to

finding and living the good life; but even the most devout Christian can make progress in the good life only by the constant use of intelligent and critical judgment. He must have an appreciation of values and learn from his own experience and that of others. A high standard of living implies opportunity for growth in this process of choice and judgment. . . .

The churches have a definite obligation to resist the lower standards and to promote the ideal of the good life as inherent in the gospel, both by social and educational activities of their own and by fruitful cooperation with one another and with voluntary or governmental agencies created for the purpose, such as schools, libraries, museums, welfare societies, health centers, cooperative associations, and labor unions. . . .

Our social life becomes ever more complex, and it offers ever enlarging areas for cooperation. The religious passion of love meets the challenge of these new demands by calling to its aid increasingly the techniques of science for analysis of the factors involved. It demands that our developing resources shall be so organized as to minister to the life of all people and to brotherly relations among them; that a world organization shall be built which will not only renounce war but make for increasing fellowship among the peoples of all nations and races; and that our educational forces shall be so conceived and used as to train

[1] "Social Ideals of the Churches"; printed in Federal Council of the Churches of Christ in America, *Quadrennial Report, 1932* (New York, 1933), pp. 59-65, 69.

human beings for participation in a world increasingly complex and increasingly rich in opportunity for cooperative enterprise. The churches have an obligation to prepare their members for world citizenship both by increasing their knowledge and by developing the necessary changes of attitude. . . .

### Economic Relations

The teachings of Christ which bear on economics are not expressed in technical terms; but deal primarily with motives and human values. They are therefore the more searching and timeless. They center upon the priceless worth of the humblest human being. . . .

The present economic organization of society is complicated and cannot be accurately described in easy general phrases. That our present economic system breaks down, however, at vital points, will not be denied. The evidences are unmistakable.

First of these are the recurring depressions with severe and prolonged unemployment. The industrial mechanism does not function in the use of the natural resources and the productive capacity of the nation in such a way as to meet obvious human needs adequately or even fairly.

Next in evidence are the shocking inequalities of income. No doubt there is a relation between these two phenomena. Too large a share of the national income goes to those who must invest it, if it is to be profitable to them, in activities which are already over-developed and over-capitalized. Too small a share goes to those who would use it for food, clothing, housing, and other necessities or comforts of life. Ultimate consumers, if they had more income, would create an effective demand for commodities which are useful but which cannot be sold.

The Christian ideal calls for hearty support of a planned economic system in which maximum social values shall be sought. It demands that cooperation shall supplant competition as the fundamental

method. It assumes the principle that the personalities of human beings are of more value than their labor power and deserve prior consideration. . . .

The economic order of today, whether we like the fact or not, is fundamentally international. Tariffs, international debts, foreign investments may have far-reaching internal consequences. No lasting beneficial progress can be made which fails to recognize that all nations, however diverse and self-dependent they may seem to be, are in essential respects bound together in an emerging world order. . . .

Industrial democracy is a goal comparable to that of political democracy. Both are relative terms. There is more than one way of making progress toward their realization. In one stage of development, cooperation through collective agreements between the representatives of management and of workers, counseled by technical experts, may be the most advantageous. Even in this elementary form of industrial relations, the right of workers to organize and to be represented by counsel or agents of their own free choice must be recognized as fundamental. In another stage, participation of workers in management may be possible and desirable; in another, workers might provide their own capital and assume full responsibility; in still another, the government might assume and exercise the powers of ownership, control, and management for the common good.

In any case industry should bear the costs of the problems which it creates. Unemployment, for example, is incident to the development of our present industrial system. Security against want due to illness, to permanent disability from invalidism, and to old age, is an elementary condition for a sound economic system, but is still lacking. Heretofore in America we have expected workers to find such security for themselves, relying upon high wages and cheap land to furnish the means. We have not recognized that unemployment and occupational disease are familiar aspects of the prevailing industrial system; and that, even though skilled workers have on the whole larger real incomes than before, there is no real possibility that all can provide against such contingencies from their own earnings, and that therefore the need for systems of insurance, socially administered, is urgent. . . .

### Race Relations

Relations between races have often been characterized by prejudice, antagonism, fear, cruelty, injustice, exploitation. But racial differences need have none of these consequences. The likenesses between races—the characteristics which the majority in each group have in common with those of other groups—are more numerous and more important than their differences.

### 2

Equally indicative of the growing social consciousness of the American people was the increasing attention paid the progressive wing of the Supreme Court. The little group of judges who regularly recorded dissenting opinions during the 1920's found themselves popular idols in the early 1930's; thousands viewed them as symbols of the attack on vested property rights which were held responsible for the depression. Among those spotlighted was Louis Brandeis, whose broad social concepts were expressed in his dissent in the case of *New State Ice Company* v. *Liebmann* (1932):[2]

. . . The notion of a distinct category of business "affected with a public interest," employing property "devoted to a public use," rests upon historical error. The consequences which it is sought to draw from those phrases are belied by the meaning in which they were first used centuries ago, and by the decision of this Court, in *Munn* v. *Illinois,* 94 U. S. 113, which first introduced them into the law of the Constitution. In my opinion, the true principle is that the State's power extends to every regulation of any business reasonably required and appropriate for the public protection. I find in the due process clause no other limitation upon the character or the scope of regulation permissible. . . .

The people of the United States are now confronted with an emergency more serious than war. Misery is widespread, in a time, not of scarcity, but of overabundance. The long-continued depression has brought unprecedented unemployment, a catastrophic fall in commodity prices, and a volume of economic losses which threatens our financial institutions. . . . But rightly or wrongly, many persons think that one of the major contributing causes has been unbridled competition. Increasingly, doubt is expressed whether it is economically wise, or morally right, that men should be permitted to add to the producing facilities of an industry which is already suffering from over-capacity. . . . Many insist there must be some form of economic control. There are plans for proration. There are many proposals for stabilization. And some thoughtful men of wide business experience insist that all projects for stabilization and pro-ration must prove futile unless, in some way, the equivalent of the certificate of public convenience and necessity is made a prerequisite to embarking new capital in an industry in which the capacity already exceeds the production of schedules.

Whether that view is sound nobody knows. The objections to the proposal are obvious and grave. The remedy might bring evils worse than the present disease. The obstacles to success seem insuperable. The economic and social sciences are largely uncharted seas. We have been none too successful in the modest essays in economic control already entered upon. The new proposal involves a vast extension of the area of control. . . .

Some people assert that our present plight is due, in part, to the limitations set

---

[2] *United States Reports,* 285 U.S. 302-303, 306-311.

by courts upon experimentation in the fields of social and economic science; and to the discouragement to which proposals for betterment there have been subjected otherwise. There must be power in the states and the nation to remould, through experimentation, our economic practices and institutions to meet changing social and economic needs. I cannot believe that the framers of the Fourteenth Amendment, or the states which ratified it, intended to deprive us of the power to correct the evils of technological unemployment and excess productive capacity which have attended progress in the useful arts.

To stay experimentation in things social and economic is a grave responsibility. Denial of the right to experiment may be fraught with serious consequences to the nation. It is one of the happy incidents of the federal system that a single courageous State may, if its citizens choose, serve as a laboratory, and try novel social economic experiments without risk to the rest of the country. This Court has the power to prevent an experiment. We may strike down the statute which embodies it on the ground that, in our opinion, the measure is arbitrary, capricious, or unreasonable. We have power to do this, because the due process clause has been held by the Court applicable to matters of substantive law as well as to matters of procedure. But, in the exercise of this high power, we must be ever on our guard, lest we erect our prejudices into legal principles. If we would guide by the light of reason, we must let our minds be bold.

### 3

But the liberal ground swell was not the product of theorists and humanitarians alone. The Roosevelt Revolution was engineered by the little men of America—the apple sellers, the occupants of Hoovervilles, the dust-bowl farmers, the share croppers, the haunters of bread lines, the unemployed workers, the Okies—those of the dispossessed whose security had been snatched away by forces they never pretended to understand. Their plight

—the human side of the great dislocation that brought on the Roosevelt Revolution—was chronicled in the novels of social protest that appeared during the 1930's. *The Grapes of Wrath* by John Steinbeck gave urban Americans a better understanding of the grim migrations that went on in the Southwest as hungry men sought the right to work—and live:[3]

And then the dispossessed were drawn west—from Kansas, Oklahoma, Texas, New Mexico; from Nevada and Arkansas families, tribes, dusted out, tractored out. Carloads, caravans, homeless and hungry; twenty thousand and fifty thousand and a hundred thousand and two hundred thousand. They streamed over the mountains, hungry and restless—restless as ants, scurrying to find work to do—to lift, to push, to pull, to pick, to cut—anything, any burden to bear, for food. The kids are hungry. We got no place to live. Like ants scurrying for work, for food, and most of all for land. . . .

And the dispossessed, the migrants, flowed into California, two hundred and fifty thousand, and three hundred thousand. Behind them new tractors were going on the land and the tenants were being forced off. And new waves were on the way, new waves of the dispossessed and the homeless, hardened, intent, and dangerous.

And while the Californians wanted many things, accumulation, social success, amusement, luxury, and a curious banking security, the new barbarians wanted only two things—land and food; and to them the two were one. And whereas the wants of the Californians were nebulous and undefined, the wants of the Okies were beside the roads, lying there to be seen and coveted: the good fields with water to be dug for, the good green fields, earth to crumble experimentally in the hand, grass to smell, oaten stalks to chew

---

[3] From *The Grapes of Wrath* by John Steinbeck, pp. 317-321. Copyright 1939 by John Steinbeck. Reprinted by permission of The Viking Press, Inc.

until the sharp sweetness was in the throat. A man might look at a fallow field and know, and see in his mind that his own bending back and his own straining arms would bring the cabbages into the light, and the golden eating corn, the turnips and carrots.

And a homeless hungry man, driving the roads with his wife beside him and his thin children in the back seat, could look at the fallow fields which might produce food but not profit, and that man could know how a fallow field is a sin and the unused land a crime against the thin children. And such a man drove along the roads and knew temptation at every field, and knew the lust to take these fields and make them grow strength for his children and a little comfort for his wife. The temptation was before him always. The fields goaded him, and the company ditches with good water flowing were a goad to him.

And in the south he saw the golden oranges hanging on the trees, the little golden oranges on the dark green trees; and guards with shotguns patrolling the lines so a man might not pick an orange for a thin child, oranges to be dumped if the price was low.

He drove his old car into a town. He scoured the farms for work. Where can we sleep the night?

Well, there's Hooverville on the edge of the river. There's a whole raft of Okies there.

He drove his old car to Hooverville. He never asked again, for there was a Hooverville on the edge of every town.

The rag town lay close to water; and the houses were tents, and weed-thatched enclosures, paper houses, a great junk pile. The man drove his family in and became a citizen of Hooverville—always they were called Hooverville. The man put up his own tent as near to water as he could get; or if he had no tent, he went to the city dump and brought back cartons and built a house of corrugated paper. And when the rains came the house melted and

washed away. He settled in Hooverville and he scoured the countryside for work, and the little money he had went for gasoline to look for work. In the evening the men gathered and talked together. Squatting on their hams they talked of the land they had seen.

There's thirty thousan' acres, out west of here. Layin' there. Jesus, what I could do with that, with five acres of that! Why, hell, I'd have ever'thing to eat.

Notice one thing? They ain't no vegetables nor chickens nor pigs at the farms. They raise one thing—cotton, say, or peaches, or lettuce. 'Nother place'll be all chickens. They buy the stuff they could raise in the dooryard.

Jesus, what I could do with a couple pigs!

Well, it ain't yourn, an' it ain't gonna be yourn.

What we gonna do? The kids can't grow up this way.

In the camps the word would come whispering. There's work at Shafter. And the cars would be loaded in the night, the highways crowded—a gold rush for work. At Shafter the people would pile up, five times too many to do the work. A gold rush for work. They stole away in the night, frantic for work. And along the roads lay the temptations, the fields that could bear food.

That's owned. That ain't our'n.

Well, maybe we could get a little piece of her. Maybe—a little piece. Right down there—a patch. Jimson weed now. Christ, I could git enough potatoes off'n that little patch to feed my whole family!

It ain't our'n. It got to have Jimson weeds.

## 4

Nor was the plight of John Steinbeck's Okies exaggerated. That the horrors of reality were as terrifying as the horrors of fiction was demonstrated by the news dispatches that chronicled the growing spirit of rebellion among the common people in the dark days just before Roosevelt's inauguration. A sampling of those reports, compiled by Mauritz A. Hallgren in his *Seeds of Revolt* (1933), revealed a nation on the verge of open rebellion:[4]

England, Arkansas, January 3, 1931. The long drought that ruined hundreds of Arkansas farms last summer had a dramatic sequel late today when some 500 farmers, most of them white men and many of them armed, marched on the business section of this town. . . . Shouting that they must have food for themselves and their families, the invaders announced their intention to take it from the stores unless it were provided from some other source without cost. (N. Y. *Herald Tribune*.)

Detroit, July 9, 1931. An incipient riot by 500 unemployed men turned out of the city lodging house for lack of funds was quelled by police reserves in Cadillac Square tonight. (United Press.) . . .

Indiana Harbor, Indiana, August 15, 1931. Fifteen hundred jobless men stormed the plant of the Fruit Growers Express Company here, demanding that they be given jobs to keep from starving. The company's answer was to call the city police, who routed the jobless with menacing clubs. (Federated Press.) . . .

Boston, November 10, 1931. Twenty persons were treated for injuries, three were hurt so seriously that they may die, and dozens of others were nursing wounds from flying bottles, lead pipe, and stones after clashes between striking longshoremen and Negro strikebreakers along the Charlestown-East Boston waterfront. (Federated Press.)

Detroit, November 28, 1931. A mounted patrolman was hit on the head with a stone and unhorsed and one demonstrator was arrested during a disturbance in Grand Circus Park this morning when

[4] Reprinted from *Seeds of Revolt* by Mauritz A. Hallgren, pp. 165-170, by permission of Alfred A. Knopf, Inc. Copyright 1933 by Mauritz A. Hallgren.

2,000 men and women met there in defiance of police orders. (Associated Press.)

Chicago, April 1, 1932. Five hundred school children, most with haggard faces and in tattered clothes, paraded through Chicago's downtown section to the Board of Education offices to demand that the school system provide them with food. (Federated Press.) . . .

Philadelphia, April 30, 1932. More than twenty persons were injured today when police broke up a proposed march on City Hall as it was started from two mobilization points. A dozen marchers were arrested, fifteen were treated or held at hospitals for observation, and five policemen were injured sufficiently to require hospital treatment. (N. Y. *Times*.)

Boston, June 3, 1932. Twenty-five hungry children raided a buffet lunch set up for Spanish War veterans during a Boston parade. Two automobile-loads of police were called to drive them away. (Federated Press.) . . .

Cleveland, August 2, 1932. When a local grocery advertised for its opening that it would give away free baskets of food to the first 1,500 persons to enter the store, 6,000 people jammed the surrounding sidewalk. The crowd began to gather at midnight and at 9 A.M. there was a riot. Fifty-two people were injured. (Federated Press.) . . .

Detroit, August 26, 1932. Police were keeping a watchful eye today on the 5100 block on Springwells Avenue, where a clash between 1,000 civilians and 300 policemen as the aftermath of a frustrated eviction resulted in injuries to ten persons yesterday. (Associated Press.) . . .

Vacaville, California, December 5, 1932. Six reputed leaders of a strike which has disrupted fruit picking in Vaca Valley were kidnaped from Vacaville Jail early today, whisked away in automobiles and reported painted red, beaten, and told never to return to this vicinity. (Associated Press.)

New York, January 21, 1933. Several

hundred jobless surrounded a restaurant just off Union Square today demanding they be fed without charge. Their demands were presented by a delegation of five which attacked the restaurant manager when he refused their request. Police riot squads arrived to find the manager stabbed and the several hundred milling outside the restaurant entrance. (N. Y. *Evening Post.*) . . .

Rochester, New York, February 14, 1933. Menaced by nightsticks and tear gas bombs in the hands of 100 police reserves summoned by radio from every precinct in the city, 400 men and women rioting in a Welfare Bureau station were quickly subdued today after two policemen had been slightly injured. (Associated Press.)

Seattle, February 16, 1933. A two-day siege of the County-City Building, occupied by an army of about 5,000 unemployed, was ended early tonight, deputy sheriffs and police evicting the demonstrators after nearly two hours of effort. (Associated Press.)

Ottawa, Illinois, April 6, 1933. Eleven hundred unemployed relief demonstrators on the way to the state capitol at Springfield were turned back toward their homes today by a barrage of tear gas. (Associated Press.) . . .

Seattle, April 27, 1933. Fifteen demonstrators were under arrest here today on open charges, while Sheriff Claude G. Bannick and eight of his deputies nursed broken bones and severe cuts and bruises, the outgrowth of a riot during eviction of a family. (Associated Press.)

New Orleans, May 1, 1933. Mounted police arrested about twelve men and dispersed a crowd of unemployed who staged a demonstration in front of the City Hall here today. (Associated Press.)

## 5

Those of the dispossessed who looked to Franklin Roosevelt for a "New Deal" were not to be disappointed. His inaugural address soberly estimated the magnitude of the crisis and gave courage to the millions by bold promises of energetic action:[5]

This is a day of national consecration, and I am certain that my fellow-Americans expect that on my induction into the Presidency I will address them with a candor and a decision which the present situation of our nation impels. . . .

So first of all let me assert my firm belief that the only thing we have to fear is fear itself—nameless, unreasoning, unjustified terror which paralyzes needed efforts to convert retreat into advance.

In every dark hour of our national life a leadership of frankness and vigor has met with that understanding and support of the people themselves which is essential to victory. I am convinced that you will again give that support to leadership in these critical days.

In such a spirit on my part and on yours we face our common difficulties. They concern, thank God, only material things. Values have shrunken to fantastic levels; taxes have risen; our ability to pay has fallen, government of all kinds is faced by serious curtailment of income; the means of exchange are frozen in the currents of trade; the withered leaves of industrial enterprise lie on every side; farmers find no markets for their produce; the savings of many years in thousands of families are gone.

More important, a host of unemployed citizens face the grim problem of existence, and an equally great number toil with little return. Only a foolish optimist can deny the dark realities of the moment.

Yet our distress comes from no failure of substance. We are stricken by no plague of locusts. . . . Plenty is at our doorstep, but a generous use of it languishes in the very sight of the supply.

Primarily, this is because the rulers of the exchange of mankind's goods have failed through their own stubbornness and

[5] *Congressional Record*, 73rd Cong., Special Sess., pp. 5-6.

their own incompetence, have admitted their failure and abdicated. Practices of the unscrupulous money changers stand indicted in the court of public opinion, rejected by the hearts and minds of men. . . .

Stripped of the lure of profit by which to induce our people to follow their false leadership, they have resorted to exhortations, pleading tearfully for restored confidence. They know only the rules of a generation of self-seekers. . . .

The measure of the restoration lies in the extent to which we apply social values more noble than mere monetary profit. . . .

Recognition of the falsity of material wealth as the standard of success goes hand in hand with the abandonment of the false belief that public office and high political position are to be valued only by the standards of pride of place and personal profit; and there must be an end to a conduct in banking and in business which too often has given to a sacred trust the likeness of callous and selfish wrongdoing. . . .

Restoration calls, however, not for changes in ethics alone. This nation asks for action, and action now.

Our greatest primary task is to put people to work. This is no unsolvable problem if we face it wisely and courageously.

It can be accomplished in part by direct recruiting by the government itself, treating the task as we would treat the emergency of a war, but at the same time, through this employment, accomplishing greatly needed projects to stimulate and reorganize the use of our natural resources. . . .

The task can be helped by definite efforts to raise the values of agricultural products and with this the power to purchase the output of our cities.

It can be helped by preventing realistically the tragedy of the growing loss, through foreclosure, of our small homes and our farms. . . .

It can be helped by the unifying of relief activities which today are often scattered, uneconomical and unequal. It can be helped by national planning for and supervision of all forms of transportation and of communication and other utilities which have a definitely public character. . . .

Finally, in our progress toward a resumption of work we require two safeguards against a return of the evils of the old order; there must be a strict supervision of all banking and credits and investments; there must be an end to speculation with other people's money, and there must be provision for an adequate but sound currency. . . .

Our international trade relations, though vastly important, are, in point of time and necessity, secondary to the establishment of a sound national economy.

I favor as a practical policy the putting of first things first. I shall spare no effort to restore world trade by international economic readjustment, but the emergency at home cannot wait on that accomplishment.

The basic thought that guides these specific means of national recovery is not narrowly nationalistic. . . .

In the field of world policy I would dedicate this nation to the policy of the good neighbor—the neighbor who resolutely respects himself and, because he does so, respects the rights of others—the neighbor who respects his obligations and respects the sanctity of his agreements in and with a world of neighbors.

If I read the temper of our people correctly, we now realize as we have never before, our interdependence on each other; that we cannot merely take, but we must give as well; that if we are to go forward we must move as a trained and loyal army willing to sacrifice for the good of a common discipline, because, without such discipline, no progress is made, no leadership becomes effective.

We are, I know, ready and willing to

submit our lives and property to such discipline because it makes possible a leadership which aims at a larger good.

This I propose to offer, pledging that the larger purposes will bind upon us all as a sacred obligation with a unity of duty hitherto evoked only in time of armed strife.

With this pledge taken, I assume unhesitatingly the leadership of this great army of our people, dedicated to a disciplined attack upon our common problems.

Action in this image and to this end is feasible under the form of government which we have inherited from our ancestors. . . .

It is to be hoped that the normal balance of executive and legislative authority may be wholly adequate to meet the unprecedented task before us. But it may be that an unprecedented demand and need for undelayed action may call for temporary departure from that normal balance of public procedure.

I am prepared under my constitutional duty to recommend the measures that a stricken nation in the midst of a stricken world may require.

These measures, or such other measures as the Congress may build out of its experience and wisdom, I shall seek, within my constitutional authority, to bring to speedy adoption.

But in the event that the Congress shall fail to take one of these two courses, and in the event that the national emergency is still critical, I shall not evade the clear course of duty that will then confront me.

I shall ask the Congress for the one remaining instrument to meet the crisis— broad executive power to wage a war against the emergency as great as the power that would be given me if we were in fact invaded by a foreign foe.

For the trust reposed in me I will return the courage and the devotion that befit the time. I can do no less.

We face the arduous days that lie before

us in the warm courage of national unity; with the clear consciousness of seeking old and precious moral values; with the clean satisfaction that comes from the stern performance of duty by old and young alike.

We aim at the assurance of a rounded and permanent national life.

We do not distrust the future of essential democracy. The people of the United States have not failed. In their need they have registered a mandate that they want direct, vigorous action.

They have asked for discipline and direction under leadership. They have made me the present instrument of their wishes. In the spirit of the gift I take it. . . .

## SOCIAL PLANNING AND PRIVATE ENTERPRISE

### 6

President Roosevelt's assault on both the depression and the economic maladjustments responsible for the hard times set a new standard in the history of executive leadership. Within a year, relief agencies were aiding the unemployed, business was mobilizing under the National Recovery Administration, agriculture was slowly reviving under the Agricultural Adjustment Administration, loans from the Reconstruction Finance Corporation were reopening closed factories, the Home Owners Loan Corporation was rescuing citizens from mortgage foreclosures, the Federal Deposit Insurance Corporation was allowing closed banks to reopen, and a host of other agencies were attacking deflation with an energy that sent new hope surging through the United States. Frances Perkins, a distinguished social worker who became secretary of labor in Roosevelt's first cabinet, described the social ideals of the New Deal in her book, *People at Work* (1934):[6]

The economic situation at which we looked in 1932 and 1933 was like an interesting and complicated machine, well designed and perfect in all its parts, but it

---

[6] Frances Perkins, *People at Work*, pp. 282-287. John Day Company, New York, 1934.

did not go, and wealth, money and income being what they are, movement of the machine was essential. Static, it is useless and hideously expensive, since by the technique of interest we have, through the recent centuries, agreed to pay for use of the savings of many people invested in the plant and structure of an industry, and even on idle plant and structure. Interest charge goes on and on. The desperate problem before the American people and its government in the Spring of 1933 was to make this economic machine start going again.

To any person who has repaired his automobile or fixed the plumbing by the experimental use of whatever gadgets or personal belongings have taken the place of the hairpin, the conception of consciously tinkering with the economic machine to restore the flow of income, exchange, production and consumption is not difficult.

A great deal is said about what this new beginning growing under our eyes is doing to the wage-worker—how it is turning him into a better market. But the Labor Department is always dealing with men and women of flesh and bone. The Department of Labor is the one great department of the government all the activities of which deal in human welfare. We have come to a point of view under the discipline of American opinion and feeling where we demand an industrial life good in human terms as well as in terms of complicated economic formulae. The winter's coal, the plumbing, the interest on the mortgage, a good diet, the baby's milk, marriage, and cultural needs, even soda waters and rides on the pony in the park must always precede generalized abstract theory in our own thinking. We are chiefly concerned with men and women in the process of living and working. To make them complete members of a civilized world, to humanize the laws which affect them, is the purpose which must

form the background of everything a department of labor does. The Department of Labor which this nation has set up to promote human welfare, has a conscious and deliberate dedication to human needs —to understand if it can and to listen with a concentrated ear to what people need and hope. The labor of the human being is not a commodity, nor an article of commerce, and the world does not consist of buying power and efficiency and sound investment.

The Government must establish and maintain certain human standards. Industrial leaders have a larger opportunity and they have often done great things in this country in the improvement of machinery, of techniques, of method. Sometimes out of those improvements in technique and production have come great improvements in the circumstances of the human beings working under these improved conditions. An important duty of a Government Department, segregated for the purpose of emphasizing the interests and needs of labor in our civic life, would seem to be to make itself into a sort of a bureau of standards for the purely human factors in industry. The Bureau of Standards at Washington, serves a valuable purpose with reference to material and machines. Labor Departments should serve a similar purpose for establishing high standard practices for environment and opportunities for the men and women in industry. Having set up such minimum standards, to see that they are really adopted becomes a matter for education, persuasion, direction and enforcement by legislation, for at least the minimum which must be required by law in the public interest.

Through achieving a balance in our industrial life, and creating a situation in which the concern of the whole is the welfare of the many, business may gain a new sense that it is fraught with public interest and may become a great and honored profession—a profession devoted primarily as are all the other great professions, medicine, and law, teaching and the clergy, to the promotion of human welfare.

In these years of economic misery, we have come to realize that progress toward social justice does not rest on law alone. It rests on law, plus custom, plus insistence, from those who feel the effects of social injustice. A sense of brotherhood and co-operation greatly eases and glorifies this inevitable path to right relationships.

Most people function as better people in a group. Many of the higher virtues, notably the power to co-operate, grow out of group life. Government is an instrument for transferring this group achievement into the general good. That is the way democracy gets into action. On post office corners, in grocery stores, at soda fountains, in clubs today, at sewing circles, at dinners, in learned societies, in church societies and union meetings, America is discussing the country, building up by this group thinking and projection into common action the desired pattern of life in the American to be. The advancing partnership of the public takes all elements of the community into conference for the solution of any human problem. Human beings have a power and a desire for association and co-operation which has never yet been completely realized. When practiced nobly it represents a close human approach to that which men call the kingdom of heaven.

Democracy mobilizes this power of association and co-operation, giving it expression in activities for human fulfillment. Government in a democracy is a service agency for these essential activities of human co-operation. The labor departments of the Federal Government and States are a specialized service for co-operation in achieving the fulfillment of human aspirations toward the best possible situation for workers in relation to their labor. It is the people and their life which is of real importance, and our industries and the profits

from them will never be either safe or sound until they provide an environment and opportunity for the people who work in them which is as good as human ingenuity can devise and fit for children of God.

Last summer a threatened strike in practically the only industrial activity of one of our manufacturing towns promised a stoppage of work for hundreds of workers. In those early days of recovery, it was highly desirable that there should be no deadlock in a going industry. The workers were on strike against the conditions of their work. The employer had reached a high state of excitement and antagonism. One of our great industrialists working under the NRA was assigned to this problem and went over to this town to see what he could do to settle its trouble. After long negotiations, a basis of agreement seemed to have been reached, and a vote of the workers was about to be taken, when suddenly the employer sprang to his feet.

"But why should they vote?" he said. "It's my factory, isn't it? I pay their wages, don't I? Why should they vote, I ask you?"

"Why should they vote?" echoed the negotiator thoughtfully. "Yes, why should they vote? . . . Well, I suppose just because this is AMERICA!"

## 7

Why did Franklin Roosevelt choose a frontal attack on the nation's economic problems rather than aid business to recover its own equilibrium in the progressive tradition of a generation before? The answer can be found partly in the changed state of American industry, partly in the shifting pattern of social thought. Certainly the nation's industrial organization in 1933 bore little resemblance to that of 1912. The decline of competition and the growth of absentee ownership during the 1920's forced Roosevelt to adopt a revised concept of private property and the purpose of public controls. An influential government document by the economist Gardiner

C. Means, analyzed the change from the old economy to the new:[7]

### Introduction

. . . There are two essentially different types of market in operation—the traditional market in which supply and demand are equated by a flexible price and the administered market in which production and demand are equated at an inflexible administered price. In the first type of market economic adjustments are brought about primarily by fluctuations in price. In the second type of market economic adjustments are brought about primarily by changes in volume of production, while price changes are of secondary significance in producing adjustment.

The difference between market prices and administered prices is clear. A market price is one which is made in the market as the result of the interaction of buyers and sellers. The prices of wheat and cotton are market prices as are many other agricultural products. This is the type of price around which traditional economic theory has been built.

An administered price is essentially different. It is a price which is set by administrative action and held constant for a period of time. We have an administered price when a company maintains a posted price at which it will make sales or simply has its own prices at which buyers may purchase or not as they wish. Thus, when the General Motors management sets its wholesale price for a particular model and holds that price for 6 months or a year the price is an administered price. Many wholesale and most retail prices are administered rather than market prices. For administered prices the price is rigid, at least for a period of time, and sales (and usually production) fluctuate with the demand at the rigid price. . . .

---

[7] Gardiner C. Means, "Industrial Prices and Their Relative Inflexibility," *Senate Documents,* 74th Cong., 1st Sess., Doc. No. 13, pp. 1, 8, 10-12, 27-28.

One can make the broad generalization, having of course many exceptions, that for industries in which prices dropped most during the depression production tended to drop least, while for those in which prices were maintained the drop in production was usually greatest. Indeed, the whole depression might be described as a general dropping of prices at the flexible end of the price scale and a dropping of production at the rigid end with intermediate effects between. . . .

### Part I. The Basic Cause for the Failure of a Laissez Faire Policy

.     .     .     .     .     .     .

12. The presence of administered prices, while it does not indicate monopoly, does mean that the number of concerns competing in the market has been reduced to the point that the individual concern has a significant power to choose within limits between changing its prices and changing its volume of production or sales. When any small drop in demand occurs, it is in a position to hold its price and reduce its production without losing all its business. As a result it tends to hold up price and reduce volume of production for the industry as a whole.

13. But this means that individuals have a direct power over industrial policy which they exercise in making business policy for their own enterprise.

14. The distinction drawn here between industrial policy and business policy is of the greatest importance.

15. According to laissez faire principles, industrial policy was supposed to result from the interaction in the market of the business policies of a large number of independent units, no one of which had any significant power. . . . Prior to A.A.A., agricultural products, such as wheat and cotton, were produced and marketed under these conditions.

16. Where the number of competing units in a particular industry have been reduced to a relatively small handful, in-

dustrial policy is no longer made wholly by the market but in part by individuals. Industrial policy becomes subject to administrative control even through there is no monopoly or collusion between the separate enterprises.

17. But when the business man has the power to affect industrial policy, he almost necessarily makes wrong industrial decisions. The very position, experience and training of the business man which lead him to make the correct decisions on business policy tend to force him to make the wrong decisions on industrial policy in spite of the utmost public spirit which he, as an individual, may seek to exercise. The fact that his decisions are wrong from the point of view of the public interest is no necessary reflection on either his character or his intelligence, but arises from the nature of the situation within which he operates and the functions which he performs.

18. The business man is expected to make business policy in a way to maximize the profits of his own enterprise. When he has the power to choose between lowering price and lowering production, good business policy frequently requires him in the presence of falling demand to hold price and curtail his production even though this means idle men and idle machines. . . . The fact that he can lay off his workers enables him to cut production without having to carry the burden of idle workers as he does that of idle machines. His interest dictates lowering price only when he is able to squeeze his costs, particularly his labor costs. At best, it is an even choice whether he will choose to maintain profits or minimize losses by seeking a relatively large profit margin on a reduced volume or a small margin on a maintained volume of sales, and in such a situation the easier device, and the one involving the lesser risk, is the device of holding price and accepting curtailed volume. It is only because this holding of prices has become widespread

and customary that the term "price chiseler" could be a term of opprobrium in an economy supposed to be coordinated through flexible prices.

19. The net effect of business control over industrial policy is, therefore, to aggravate any fluctuations in economic activity and prevent any necessary readjustments. An initial drop in demand would result, not in price readjustment, but in maintained prices and curtailment of production, thus throwing workers and machines out of employment, reducing money income and spending power, and further reducing demand. . . .

. . . . . . . .

## Appendix E

In the modern corporation, "private property" in the traditional sense, i.e., in the sense that an "owner" has power over, responsibility for, and interest in his property, does not exist, for the interests and controls which have been combined to constitute traditional ownership have become lodged in different hands. In the modern corporation, most of the ownership interests are in the hands of stockholders, but where stock is widely dispersed, power does not lie with the stockholders but with the directors and officers of the corporation. The ordinary stockholder can do as he pleases with his share of stock—sell it, hold it, or burn it up—but over the corporate enterprise as such, and over its physical property, he has practically no control. The control exercised by corporate management, on the other hand, does not rest on ownership, for in most of the great corporations the controlling group holds a negligible proportion of the stock. . . .

The separation of control from interest in respect to ownership is only one of the ways in which modern economic organization has made this separation between interest and control. Under the factory system, the worker surrenders much of the control over his own activity during

working hours. So long as the factory
enterprise was small and one of a large
number competing for the services of
workers, the worker still retained an important measure of control, for he could
always transfer to some other enterprise.
But as the administrative units have become ever larger, the direct control of the
worker over the conditions under which
he works has become less and less. To
some extent this loss in direct control has
been counterbalanced by a measure of control through labor organization, but, for
the most part, workers have ceased to be
in a position to exercise an important element of control.

The consumer, likewise, has lost much
of the control which he had through bargaining as the business units with which
he deals have become less numerous and
more powerful.

Thus, the shift of large segments of economic activity from coordination through
the market to coordination through administered activity has gradually sucked
controls over industrial activity away from
the three parties mainly at interest, the
security holders, the workers, and the
consumers. It has placed this control in
the hands of administrators, nominally
responsible to the one group, the security
holders, but factually responsible in all too
many cases to no one. Such a concentration of controls leaves the investors, the
workers, and the consumers with great
and basic interests in industrial activity
but with a minimum of control over it.

## 8

Relief and recovery were essential ingredi-
ents of the New Deal, but President Roosevelt's principal concern was with long-range
plans to reform the American economy.
Without these, he knew, the maladjustments
responsible for 1929 would recur in later
years. Of the countless measures that he
pushed through Congress, three held the
greatest implications for the future: the law
creating the Tennessee Valley Authority, the
Social Security Act, and the National

Labor Relations Act. The first, passed in
1933, authorized a bold experiment in government planning. The TVA's director, David
E. Lilienthal, explained in his *TVA: Democracy on the March* how blueprints for the
future, applied to a great river system, involved human resources, conservation, farm
relief, industry, and all aspects of community
interdependence:[8]

. . . The message of President Roosevelt urging approval of the Norris bill
(which became a law with his signature
on May 18, 1933) boldly proposed a new
and fundamental change in the development of our country's resources. . . .

It is clear [the message read] that the
Muscle Shoals development is but a small
part of the potential public usefulness of the
entire Tennessee River. Such use, if envisioned in its entirety, transcends mere power
development: it enters the wide fields of flood
control, soil erosion, afforestation, elimination
from agricultural use of marginal lands, and
distribution and diversification of industry.
In short, this power development of war days
leads logically to national planning for a
complete river watershed involving many
states and the future lives and welfare of
millions. It touches and gives life to all forms
of human concerns.

The President then suggested

legislation to create a Tennessee Valley Authority—a corporation clothed with the power
of government but possessed of the flexibility
and initiative of a private enterprise. It should
be charged with the broadest duty of planning for the proper use, conservation, and
development of the natural resources of the
Tennessee River drainage basin and its adjoining territory for the general social and
economic welfare of the Nation. This authority should also be clothed with the necessary
power to carry these plans into effect. Its duty
should be the rehabilitation of the Muscle
Shoals development and the coordination of it
with the wider plan.

Many hard lessons have taught us the

[8] From *TVA: Democracy on the March* by David
E. Lilienthal, pp. 47-50, 53, 55, 56. Copyright,
1944, by David E. Lilienthal.

human waste that results from lack of planning. Here and there a few wise cities and counties have looked ahead and planned. But our Nation has "just grown." It is time to extend planning to a wider field, in this instance comprehending in one great project many States directly concerned with the basin of one of our greatest rivers. . . .

The TVA Act was nothing inadvertent or impromptu. It was rather the deliberate and well-considered creation of a new national policy. For the first time in the history of the nation, the resources of a river were not only to be "envisioned in their entirety"; they were to be developed *in that unity with which nature herself regards her resources*—the waters, the land, and the forests together, a "seamless web"—just as Maitland saw "the unity of all history," of which one strand cannot be touched without affecting every other strand for good or ill.

Under this new policy, the opportunity of creating wealth for the people from the resources of this valley was to be faced as a single problem. To integrate the many parts of that problem into a unified whole was to be the responsibility of one agency. The Tennessee Valley's resources were not to be dissected into separate bits that would fit into the jurisdictional pigeon-holes into which the instrumentalities of government had by custom become divided. It was not conceded that at the hour of Creation the Lord had divided and classified natural resources to conform to the organization chart of the federal government. The particular and limited concerns of private individuals or agencies in the development of this or that resource were disregarded and rejected in favor of the principle of unity. What God had made one, man was to develop as one.

"Envisioned in its entirety" this river, like every river in the world, had many potential assets. It could yield hydro-electric power for the comfort of the people in their homes, could promote prosperity on their farms and foster the development of industry. But the same river by the very same dams, if they were wisely designed, could be made to provide a channel for navigation. The river could also be made to provide fun for fishermen and fish for food, pleasure from boating and swimming, a water supply for homes and factories. But the river also presented an account of liabilities. It threatened the welfare of the people by its recurrent floods; pollution from industrial wastes and public sewage diminished its value as a source of water supply and for recreation; its current carried to the sea the soil of the hills and fields to be lost there to men forever.

To a single agency, the TVA, these potentialities of the river for good and evil were entrusted. But the river was to be seen as part of the larger pattern of the region, one asset of the many that in nature are interwoven: the land, the minerals, the waters, the forests—and all of these as one—in their relation to the lives of the valley's people. It was the total benefit to all that was to be the common goal and the new agency's responsibility. . . .

That is not the way public resource development had heretofore been undertaken in this country. Congress in creating TVA broke with the past. No single agency had in this way ever been assigned the unitary task of developing a river so as to release the total benefit from its waters for the people. Not far from where I write are other rivers developed by private interests or public agencies. They will serve to illustrate the contrast. On these rivers it is the common practice in public projects as well as private to build a single dam without first having fixed upon a general plan that will ultimately insure the full use of the whole river as a unit. There are dams built for the single purpose of power development. Such individual dams, in order to yield an immediate return in power,

impair or destroy the river's full development of power at other sites, for they were
not designed or built with the whole river
thought of as it is in nature, a unit. These
power dams are not built or operated to
control floods, and do not provide a continuous navigable channel. The full usefulness of that river is lessened. Similarly,
hundreds of millions of dollars in public
funds have been expended for the single
purpose of navigation on some of our
rivers, but most of the dams constructed
will not control the rivers' floods or create
electric energy. They now stand as mas-
sive barriers against the erection of multi-
purpose structures.

Over a long period of years scores of
millions of dollars have been spent for
levees to hold the waters back on the lower
reaches of some of our rivers, but at the
headwaters there were no reservoir dams
that could make local levee protection
effective.

And through the long years there has
been a continuing disregard of nature's
truth: that in any valley of the world
what happens on the *river* is largely determined by what happens on the *land*—
by the kind of crops that farmers plant
and harvest, by the type of machines they
use, by the number of trees they cut down.
The full benefits of stream and of soil
cannot be realized by the people if the
water and the land are not developed in
harmony.

If the soil is exposed, unprotected from
the rains by cover and by roots, the people
will be poor and the river will be muddy,
heavy with the best soil of the fields. And
as a consequence each year the farmers
will be forced more and more to use their
land in ways that speed up this cycle of
ruin, until the cover and then the top soil
itself are wholly gone. When that day
comes, as in the great reaches of China's
sorrowful Yellow River Valley, then the
rains run off the land almost as rapidly as
water runs from a pavement. Even a mod-

erate rainfall forces the river from its
banks, and every downpour brings disastrous floods, destroying crops and homes
and bridges and highways, not only where
the land is poor, but down the river's
length, down in the areas where people
are more prosperous, where the soil is
still protected and factories have been
built at the river's bend. Industries and
railroads will be interrupted, farms flooded
out, towns and villages destroyed, while
heavy silt deposits fill the power reservoirs and stop up the channels of navigation. . . .

How industry came to Ducktown in
the mountains of eastern Tennessee a
generation ago is one such story. Copper
ore was discovered; mining began; a
smeltery was built. One of the resources
of this remote region was being developed; it meant new jobs, income to supplement farming and forestry. But the
developers had only copper in their plans.
The magnificent hardwood forests to a
distance of seven miles were cut and
burned as fuel for the smelter's roasting
ovens. The sulphur fumes from the stacks
destroyed the thin cover that remained;
not only the trees but every sign of living
vegetation was killed and the soil became
poison to life.

The dead land, shorn of its cover of
grass and trees was torn mercilessly by
the rains; and the once lovely and fruitful
earth was cut into deep gullies that widened into desolate canyons twenty and
more feet deep. No one can look upon
this horror as it is today without a shud-
der. Silt, swept from unprotected slopes,
filled the streams and destroyed fish life.
The water was robbed of its value for
men, for animals, and for industry, while
farther down the stream a reservoir of a
private power company was filling with
silt. One of Ducktown's resources, copper,
had been developed. But all its other resources had been destroyed in the process.

The people and their institutions suffered in the end. . . .

The effect of large supplies of low-cost electricity upon industrialization illustrates the modern hazard. For electricity is not freed of these dangers simply because it is publicly owned, as some single-track enthusiasts would appear to imply. . . . For the stimulation of industrial development by large supplies of electricity, unless the principles of unity govern, can hasten the destruction of natural resources and bring closer the day of decline. . . .

For when a people or a region rely almost exclusively for their living upon the extraction of raw materials—the cutting of lumber, the growing of wheat, the mining of coal or iron—and depend little upon the processing, by manufacture, of those raw materials, these natural resources are put under a severe drain to support a growing population. The income which comes to a region from cutting trees or growing cotton and bringing them to a point of transportation is only a small fraction of the income, the "value added," when those trees have been processed into paper or the cotton into overalls. If a region depends—as most "colonial" regions are forced to do—almost entirely upon the income from cutting the lumber or growing the cotton, and hardly at all upon making the paper, the textiles, the furniture, or any of the other articles manufactured from the raw resources, then the pressure to "mine" the fertility of the soil, to devastate the forests for lumber, to deplete the oil fields and coal reserves becomes very great indeed.

That pressure to deplete resources can be lessened by the growth of the industries which electric power encourages. But if the industry is only exploitative, if it does not *sustain* the productivity of the resources upon which all of us depend, industry can exhaust a region and hurt its people's chances of security and happiness. The "how" of industrial development, like the "how" of developing a river or the land or the forests, is the all-important point.

## 9

As far reaching in importance as the TVA was the Social Security Act of 1935. In framing this measure to provide a minimum of old-age and unemployment insurance for workers, as well as health benefits for children, the blind, and the aged, President Roosevelt sought to steer a middle course between the do-nothing policy of conservatives and the overambitious programs of such false prophets as Huey Long and Dr. F. E. Townsend. The principal provisions of the act promised benefits to the overaged and the unemployed:[9]

SECTION 1. For the purpose of enabling each State to furnish financial assistance, as far as practicable under the conditions in such State, to aged needy individuals, there is hereby authorized to be appropriated for the fiscal year ending June 30, 1936, the sum of $49,750,000, and there is hereby authorized to be appropriated for each fiscal year thereafter a sum sufficient to carry out the purposes of this title. The sums made available under this section shall be used for making payments to States which have submitted, and had approved by the Social Security Board established by Title VII, State plans for old-age assistance.

SEC. 2. (a) A State plan for old-age assistance must (1) provide that it shall be in effect in all political subdivisions of the State, and, if administered by them, be mandatory upon them; (2) provide for financial participation by the State; (3) either provide for the establishment or designation of a single State agency to administer the plan, or provide for the establishment or designation of a single State agency to supervise the administration of the plan; (4) provide for granting to any individual, whose claim for old-age assistance is denied, an opportunity for

---

[9] *United States Statutes at Large*, XLIX, 620-648.

a fair hearing before such State agency; (5) provide such methods of administration (other than those relating to selection, tenure of office, and compensation of personnel) as are found by the Board to be necessary for the efficient operation of the plan; (6) provide that the State agency will make such reports, in such form and containing such information, as the Board may from time to time require, and comply with such provisions as the Board may from time to time find necessary to assure the correctness and verification of such report. . . .

SEC. 201. (a) There is hereby created an account in the Treasury of the United States to be known as the "Old-Age Reserve Account.". . .

SEC. 202. (a) Every qualified individual shall be entitled to receive, with respect to the period beginning on the date he attains the age of sixty-five, or on January 1, 1942, whichever is the later, and ending on the date of his death, an old-age benefit (payable as nearly as practicable in equal monthly installments) as follows:

(1) If the total wages determined by the Board to have been paid to him, with respect to employment after December 31, 1936, and before he attained the age of sixty-five, were not more than $3,000, the old-age benefit shall be at a monthly rate of one-half of 1 per centum of such total wages;

(2) If such total wages were more than $3,000, the old-age benefit shall be at a monthly rate equal to the sum of the following:

(A) One-half of 1 per centum of $3,000; plus

(B) One-twelfth of 1 per centum of the amount by which such total wages exceeded $3,000 and did not exceed $45,000; plus

(C) One-twenty-fourth of 1 per centum of the amount by which such total wages exceeded $45,000.

(b) In no case shall the monthly rate computed under subsection (a) exceed $85. . . .

SEC. 302. (a) The Board shall from time to time certify to the Secretary of the Treasury for payment to each State which has an unemployment compensation law approved by the Board under Title IX, such amounts as the Board determines to be necessary for the proper administration of such law during the fiscal year in which such payment is to be made. The Board's determination shall be based on (1) the population of the State; (2) an estimate of the number of persons covered by the State law and of the cost of proper administration of such law; and (3) such other factors as the Board finds relevant. The Board shall not certify for payment under this section in any fiscal year a total amount in excess of the amount appropriated therefor for such fiscal year. . . .

SEC. 303. (a) The Board shall make no certification for payment to any State unless it finds that the law of such State, approved by the Board under Title IX, includes provisions for—

(1) Such methods of administration (other than those relating to selection, tenure of office, and compensation of personnel) as are found by the Board to be reasonably calculated to insure full payment of unemployment compensation when due; and

(2) Payment of unemployment compensation solely through public employment offices in the State or such other agencies as the Board may approve; and

(3) Opportunity for a fair hearing, before an impartial tribunal, for all individuals whose claims for unemployment compensation are denied; and

(4) The payment of all money received in the unemployment fund of such State, immediately upon such receipt, to the Secretary of the Treasury to the credit of the Unemployment Trust Fund established by section 904; and

(5) Expenditure of all money requisitioned by the State agency from the Un-

employment Trust Fund, in the payment of unemployment compensation, exclusive of expenses of administration; and

(6) The making of such reports, in such form and containing such information, as the Board may from time to time require, and compliance with such provisions as the Board may from time to time find necessary to assure the correctness and verification of such reports; and

(7) Making available upon request to any agency of the United States charged with the administration of public works or assistance through public employment, the name, address, ordinary occupation and employment status of each recipient of unemployment compensation, and a statement of such recipient's rights to further compensation under such law.

(b) Whenever the Board, after reasonable notice and opportunity for hearing to the State agency charged with the administration of the State law, finds that in the administration of the law there is—

(1) a denial, in a substantial number of cases, of unemployment compensation to individuals entitled thereto under such law; or

(2) a failure to comply substantially with any provision specified in subsection (a);

the Board shall notify such State agency that further payments will not be made to the State until the Board is satisfied that there is no longer any such denial or failure to comply. Until it is so satisfied it shall make no further certification to the Secretary of the Treasury with respect to such State. . . .

SEC. 801. In addition to other taxes, there shall be levied, collected, and paid upon the income of every individual a tax equal to the following percentages of the wages (as defined in section 811) received by him after December 31, 1936, with respect to employment (as defined in section 811) after such date:

(1) With respect to employment during the calendar years 1937, 1938, and 1939, the rate shall be 1 per centum.

(2) With respect to employment during the calendar years 1940, 1941, and 1942, the rate shall be 1½ per centum. . . .

SEC. 802. (a) The tax imposed by section 801 shall be collected by the employer of the taxpayer, by deducting the amount of the tax from the wages as and when paid. . . .

SEC. 804. In addition to other taxes, every employer shall pay an excise tax, with respect to having individuals in his employ, equal to the following percentages of the wages (as defined in section 811) paid by him after December 31, 1936, with respect to employment (as defined in section 811) after such date:

(1) With respect to employment during the calendar years 1937, 1938, and 1939, the rate shall be 1 per centum.

(2) With respect to employment during the calendar years 1940, 1941, and 1942, the rate shall be 1½ per centum. . . .

SEC. 811. When used in this title—. . .

(b) The term "employment" means any service, of whatever nature, performed within the United States by an employee for his employer, except—

(1) Agricultural labor;

(2) Domestic service in a private home;

(3) Casual labor not in the course of the employer's trade or business;

(4) Service performed by an individual who has attained the age of sixty-five;

(5) Service performed as an officer or member of the crew of a vessel documented under the laws of the United States or of any foreign country;

(6) Service performed in the employ of the United States Government or of an instrumentality of the United States;

(7) Service performed in the employ of a State, a political subdivision thereof, or an instrumentality of one or more States or political subdivisions;

(8) Service performed in the employ of a corporation, community chest, fund, or foundation, organized and operated exclusively for religious, charitable, scientific, literary, or educational purposes, or for the prevention of cruelty to children or animals, no part of the net earnings of which inures to the benefit of any private shareholder or individual. . . .

SEC. 903. (a) The Social Security Board shall approve any State law submitted to it, within thirty days of such submission, which it finds provides that—

(1) All compensation is to be paid through public employment offices in the State or such other agencies as the Board may approve;

(2) No compensation shall be payable with respect to any day of unemployment occurring within two years after the first day of the first period with respect to which contributions are required;

(3) All money received in the unemployment fund shall immediately upon such receipt be paid over to the Secretary of the Treasury to the credit of the Unemployment Trust Fund. . . .

(5) Compensation shall not be denied in such State to any otherwise eligible individual for refusing to accept new work under any of the following conditions: (A) If the position offered is vacant due directly to a strike, lockout, or other labor dispute; (B) if the wages, hours, or other conditions of the work offered are substantially less favorable to the individual than those prevailing for similar work in the locality; (C) if as a condition of being employed the individual would be required to join a company union or to resign from or refrain from joining any bona fide labor organization.

SEC. 904. (a) There is hereby established in the Treasury of the United States a trust fund to be known as the "Unemployment Trust Fund, . . ."

(b) It shall be the duty of the Secretary of the Treasury to invest such portion of the Fund as is not, in his judgment, required to meet current withdrawals. Such investment may be made only in interest bearing obligations of the United States or in obligations guaranteed as to both principal and interest by the United States.

## 10

The National Labor Relations Act, known generally as the Wagner Act because of the sponsorship of Senator Robert F. Wagner of New York, was also designed to effect long-range adjustments in the American economic system. Realizing that workers were consumers as well as laborers, President Roosevelt believed that they must be well enough organized to wring adequate wages from employers. Should these not be forthcoming, he feared, underconsumption would lead to overproduction and a recurrence of the depression. The Wagner Act was intended to assure workers the right to join unions of their own choosing, and to bring the pressure of numbers against their employers:[10]

SECTION 1. The denial by employers of the right of employees to organize and the refusal by employers to accept the procedure of collective bargaining lead to strikes and other forms of industrial strife or unrest, which have the intent or the necessary effect of burdening or obstructing commerce by (a) impairing the efficiency, safety, or operation of the instrumentalities of commerce; (b) occurring in the current of commerce; (c) materially affecting, restraining, or controlling the flow of raw materials or manufactured or processed goods from or into the channels of commerce, or the prices of such materials or goods in commerce; or (d) causing diminution of employment and wages in such volume as substantially to impair or disrupt the market for goods flowing from or into the channels of commerce.

The inequality of bargaining power between employees who do not possess full

[10] *Ibid.,* pp. 449-457.

freedom of association or actual liberty of contract, and employers who are organized in the corporate or other forms of ownership association substantially burdens and affects the flow of commerce, and tends to aggravate recurrent business depressions, by depressing wage rates and the purchasing power of wage earners in industry and by preventing the stabilization of competitive wage rates and working conditions within and between industries.

Experience has proved that protection by law of the right of employees to organize and bargain collectively safeguards commerce from injury, impairment, or interruption, and promotes the flow of commerce by removing certain recognized sources of industrial strife and unrest, by encouraging practices fundamental to the friendly adjustment of industrial disputes arising out of differences as to wages, hours, or other working conditions, and by restoring equality of bargaining power between employers and employees.

It is hereby declared to be the policy of the United States to eliminate the causes of certain substantial obstructions to the free flow of commerce and to mitigate and eliminate these obstructions when they have occurred by encouraging the practice and procedure of collective bargaining and by protecting the exercise by workers of full freedom of association, self-organization, and designation of representatives of their own choosing, for the purpose of negotiating the terms and conditions of their employment or other mutual aid or protection. . . .

SEC. 3. (a) There is hereby created a board, to be known as the "National Labor Relations Board," which shall be composed of three members, who shall be appointed by the President, by and with the advice and consent of the Senate. One of the original members shall be appointed for a term of one year, one for a term of three years, and one for a term of five years, but their successors shall be appointed for terms of five years each, except

that any individual chosen to fill a vacancy shall be appointed only for the unexpired term of the member whom he shall succeed. The President shall designate one member to serve as chairman of the Board. Any member of the Board may be removed by the President, upon notice and hearing, for neglect of duty or malfeasance in office, but for no other cause. . . .

SEC. 7. Employees shall have the right of self-organization, to form, join, or assist labor organizations, to bargain collectively through representatives of their own choosing, and to engage in concerted activities, for the purpose of collective bargaining or other mutual aid or protection.

SEC. 8. It shall be an unfair labor practice for an employer—

(1) To interfere with, restrain, or coerce employees in the exercise of the rights guaranteed in section 7.

(2) To dominate or interfere with the formation or administration of any labor organization or contribute financial or other support to it: *Provided,* That subject to rules and regulations made and published by the Board pursuant to section 6 (a), an employer shall not be prohibited from permitting employees to confer with him during working hours without loss of time or pay.

(3) By discrimination in regard to hire or tenure of employment or any term or condition of employment to encourage or discourage membership in any labor organization: *Provided,* That nothing in this Act, or in the National Industrial Recovery Act (U.S.C., Supp. VII, title 15, secs. 701-712), as amended from time to time, or in any code or agreement approved or prescribed thereunder, or in any other statute of the United States, shall preclude an employer from making an agreement with a labor organization (not established, maintained, or assisted by any action defined in this Act as an unfair labor practice) to require as a condition of employment membership therein, if such labor organization is the representative of the em-

ployees as provided in section 9 (a), in the appropriate collective bargaining unit covered by such agreement when made.

(4) To discharge or otherwise discriminate against an employee because he has filed charges or given testimony under this Act.

(5) To refuse to bargain collectively with the representatives of his employees, subject to the provisions of Section 9 (a).

SEC. 9. (a) Representatives designated or selected for the purposes of collective bargaining by the majority of the employees in a unit appropriate for such purposes, shall be the exclusive representatives of all the employees in such unit for the purposes of collective bargaining in respect to rates of pay, wages, hours of employment, or other conditions of employment: *Provided,* That any individual employee or a group of employees shall have the right at any time to present grievances to their employer.

(b) The Board shall decide in each case whether, in order to insure to employees the full benefit of their right to self-organization and to collective bargaining, and otherwise to effectuate the policies of this Act, the unit appropriate for the purposes of collective bargaining shall be the employer unit, craft unit, plant unit, or subdivision thereof.

(c) Whenever a question affecting commerce arises concerning the representation of employees, the Board may investigate such controversy and certify to the parties, in writing, the name or names of the representatives that have been designated or selected. In any such investigation, the Board shall provide for an appropriate hearing upon due notice, either in conjunction with a proceeding under section 10 or otherwise, and may take a secret ballot of employees, or utilize any other suitable method to ascertain such representatives. . . .

SEC. 10. (a) The Board is empowered, as hereinafter provided, to prevent any person from engaging in any unfair labor practice (listed in section 8) affecting commerce. This power shall be exclusive, and shall not be affected by any other means of adjustment or prevention that has been or may be established by agreement, code, law, or otherwise.

(b) Whenever it is charged that any person has engaged in or is engaging in any such unfair labor practice, the Board, or any agent or agency designated by the Board for such purposes, shall have power to issue and cause to be served upon such person a complaint stating the charges in that respect, and containing a notice of hearing before the Board or a member thereof, or before a designated agent or agency, at a place therein fixed, not less than five days after the serving of said complaint. Any such complaint may be amended by the member, agent, or agency conducting the hearing or the Board in its discretion at any time prior to the issuance of an order based thereon. The person so complained of shall have the right to file an answer to the original or amended complaint and to appear in person or otherwise and give testimony at the place and time fixed in the complaint. In the discretion of the member, agent or agency conducting the hearing or the Board, any other person may be allowed to intervene in the said proceeding and to present testimony. In any such proceeding the rules of evidence prevailing in courts of law or equity shall not be controlling. . . .

## 11

The methods used by the National Labor Relations Board as it struggled to prevent the industrial coercion of workers and to assure labor equality of bargaining power were illustrated in its relations with one of the nation's giant holding companies. A press release, issued by the board on June 18, 1938, revealed both the effectiveness of its efforts and the need for such an agency:[11]

[11] "Labor Organization Ordered Disestablished in Utah Copper Mills." Release of June 18, 1938, National Labor Relations Board (Washington, 1938).

The National Labor Relations Board today ordered Kennecott Copper Corporation, New York City, and its wholly owned subsidiary, Utah Copper Company, Salt Lake City, Utah, to disestablish Employees' General Committee, Department of Mills, as representative of any employees at the companies' Arthur and Magna mills, located near the town of Magna, in Salt Lake County, Utah. . . .

The Board found that the committee was entirely company-supported. It collected no dues, and levied no assessments upon the employees. The only requirement for participation in committee elections was non-supervisory employment at the mills. Rules governing the committee's activities could be changed only with the consent of the management. Committee members were paid by the companies for attending committee meetings. The committee had no final authority over the disposition of grievances coming before it, and no method of arbitration was provided. No general meetings of employees were held to permit the employees to present a collective expression of opinion on matters affecting their wages, hours, or other conditions of employment. . . .

Following an organizing campaign initiated by the union among employees at the Arthur and Magna mills in May 1937, the companies impressed their hostility to the union upon their employees by acts and statements, and by discrimination against union members, the Board found. . . .

Supervisory officials at one time or another made the following statements to employees:

That the men "should not get into the C.I.O."

That the C.I.O. was "causing a lot of trouble back east."

That "If you want to get ahead with the company, you will be better off if you are not affiliated with the C.I.O."

That if Utah Copper was ever unionized its president would close the place down,

and "would never stand for it a minute."

That the speaker "didn't see why the men wanted a union around there."

## 12

President Roosevelt recognized that permanent recovery could be secured only by effecting an equitable balance between the economy of differing occupational groups: industrialists, workers, and farmers. The Wagner Act and the agricultural program were designed to assure laborers and farmers a larger share of the profits hitherto absorbed by industry. In the same way, he sought to bring the nation's geographic sections into better balance. This involved the rehabilitation of the South, "the Nation's No. 1 economic problem." The need for action was revealed by the report of a Special Committee on Farm Tenancy (February, 1937), which laid bare the social and human consequences of the share-cropping system:[12]

### Consequences of Fee-Simple Ownership

The land policy adopted by this country, under which title to practically all of the agricultural land of the Nation passed to private owners in fee simple absolute, has proved defective as a means of keeping the land in the ownership of those who work it. Fee-simple ownership has also implied that the right to unrestricted use was also a right to abuse of the land. The fact that a large number of owners have been concerned chiefly with early sale has militated against permanence of occupancy by themselves or in tenant contracts that would assure stability. Policies for disposing of the public domain have permitted the acquisition of large areas, mostly for speculative purposes, by those who had no intention of farming them. Periodic booms and depressions, especially the extreme rise in land values culminating in 1920, and the subsequent drastic decline, have caused many farmers to lose their farms and sink to the status of tenants or even migratory laborers.

[12] *House Documents,* 75th Cong., 1st Sess., Doc. No. 149, pp. 1, 6-13.

## Erosion of Our Soil

The defectiveness of past and present policies of land tenure can be measured in terms of what has happened to the Nation's chief natural asset, the soil. The correlation between soil erosion and tenant occupancy is very striking. The reasons are obvious. The tenant whose occupancy is uncertain at best, and ordinarily does not average more than 2 years, can ill afford to plant the farm to any but cash crops. "The shorter the operator's time on the farm, the higher the percentage of crop land in corn tends to be, and consequently the higher the degree of erosion," says an Iowa Experiment Station bulletin. The tenant who has no assurance of permanent occupancy can rarely afford to apply fertilizers beyond the amount which will give him most immediate return, or to plant soil-building crops. . . .

## Erosion of Our Society

Erosion of our soil has its counterpart in erosion of our society. The one wastes natural resources; the other, human resources. Instability and insecurity of farm families leach the binding elements of rural community life.

## Shifting Citizens

We find the unwholesome spectacle of men, women, and children, especially among the tenant families, moving from farm to farm each year. This social erosion not only wears down the fiber of the families themselves; it saps the resources of the entire social order. In the spring of 1935 there were more than a third (34.2 percent) of the 2,865,000 tenant farmers of the Nation who had occupied their present farms only 1 year. In many areas the proportion exceeded 50 percent. White tenants move more frequently than do colored tenants. The incessant movement of tenant and cropper families and of migratory laborers from farm to farm and from community to community deprives these

families of normal social participation. It lays a heavy hand upon the large numbers of rural children caught in this current, who find their schooling periodically interrupted, if not made impossible; they suffer from mental as well as economic insecurity.

## Their Standard of Living

The extreme poverty of one-fifth to one-fourth of the farm population reflects itself in a standard of living below any level of decency.

Large families of tenants or croppers, or hired farm laborers, are living in houses of two or three rooms. The buildings are frequently of poor construction, out of alinement, weather-beaten, and unsightly. The doors and windows are rarely screened. Often the roofs are leaky. The surroundings of such houses are bleak and unattractive. Many have even no outside toilet, or if available, it is highly unsanitary.

Many of these families are chronically undernourished. They are readily subject to diseases. Pellagra, malaria, and the hookworm and other parasites exact heavy tolls in life and energy. Suitable provision for maintaining health and treating disease among these families is lacking or inadequate in many localities.

Clothing is often scarcely sufficient to afford protection to the body, much less to help maintain self-respect.

Farm and city well-being are closely interrelated. Low standards of living in the country limit production in the city. The use which is made of America's industrial productive capacity in part depends on the purchasing power of agriculture. And the extent to which American industry is active in turn affects the capacity of the farm population to find more jobs for its people and markets for its products. . . .

## Land for Tenants

The Committee recommends a program of land purchase by the Federal Government and disposition of the land under long-term contracts of sale to operating farmers. It is recommended that the Secretary of Agriculture, through the proposed Farm Security Corporation, be authorized to acquire suitable farm land, subdivide or otherwise create from it the various types of holdings hereafter recommended, and provide for requisite improvements.

Contracts of sale should not be undertaken until after a trial lease period not to exceed 5 years. The trial period should be terminable as soon as the farmer demonstrates his integrity, industry, and capacity as a potential owner. At the termination of the trial period the Corporation should enter into a contract of sale under which the purchaser may pay up all the principal and obtain a deed any time after 20 years. At the minimum rate of repayment, a deed would be obtained at the end of 40 years. . . .

The purpose of initial purchase by the Government would be to put the Nation in a position to assert its right to discourage subdivision of economic units, wastage of natural resources, reckless speculation, and absentee landlordism and tenancy. Except for restrictions on his freedom to engage in such practices the purchaser would have virtually all the other rights and privileges enjoyed by landowners in fee simple absolute.

## THE REVOLUTION IN CONSTITUTIONAL LAW

## 13

The Roosevelt Revolution was scarcely begun before it encountered a formidable obstacle. Sitting in judgment on every law passed by Congress were the nine justices of the Supreme Court. Between them and the President there was no basis for compromise. Roosevelt insisted that the government must protect the welfare of its people within the broad framework of powers granted or implied by the Constitution; the Court contended that each enactment must be tested by the hoary precedents of constitutional law.

Among a series of defeats for the believers in broad construction was the NRA decision in the case of *Schechter Poultry Corp.* v. *U.S.* (1935):[13]

In determining how far the federal government may go in controlling intrastate transactions upon the ground that they "affect" interstate commerce, there is a necessary and well-established distinction between direct and indirect effects. The precise line can be drawn only as individual cases arise, but the distinction is clear in principle. . . .

The question of chief importance relates to the provisions of the Code as to the hours and wages of those employed in defendants' slaughterhouse markets. It is plain that these requirements are imposed in order to govern the details of defendants' management of their local business. The persons employed in slaughtering and selling in local trade are not employed in interstate commerce. Their hours and wages have no direct relation to interstate commerce. The question of how many hours these employees should work and what they should be paid differs in no essential respect from similar questions in other local businesses which handle commodities brought into a State and there dealt in as a part of its internal commerce. This appears from an examination of the considerations urged by the Government with respect to conditions in the poultry trade. Thus, the Government argues that hours and wages affect prices; that slaughterhouse men sell at a small margin above operating costs; that labor represents 50 to 60 per cent of these costs; that a slaughterhouse operator paying lower wages or reducing his cost by exacting long hours of work, translates his saving into lower prices; that this results in demands for a cheaper grade of goods; and that the cutting of prices brings about demoralization of the price structure. Similar conditions may be adduced in relation to

---

[13] *United States Reports*, 295 U.S. 546-551.

other businesses. The argument of the Government proves too much. If the federal government may determine the wages and hours of employees in the internal commerce of a State, because of their relation to cost and prices and their indirect effect upon interstate commerce, it would seem that a similar control might be exerted over other elements of cost, also affecting prices, such as the number of employees, rents, advertising, methods of doing business, etc. All the processes of production and distribution that enter into cost could likewise be controlled. If the cost of doing an intrastate business is in itself the permitted object of federal control, the extent of the regulation of cost would be a question of discretion and not of power.

The Government also makes the point that efforts to enact state legislation establishing high labor standards have been impeded by the belief that unless similar action is taken generally, commerce will be diverted from the States adopting such standards, and that this fear of diversion has led to demands for federal legislation on the subject of wages and hours. The apparent implication is that the federal authority under the commerce clause should be deemed to extend to the establishment of rules to govern wages and hours in intrastate trade and industry generally throughout the country, thus overriding the authority of the States to deal with domestic problems arising from labor conditions in their internal commerce.

It is not the province of the Court to consider the economic advantages or disadvantages of such a centralized system. It is sufficient to say that the Federal Constitution does not provide for it. . . . The same answer must be made to the contention that is based upon the serious economic situation which led to the passage of the Recovery Act,—the fall in prices, the decline in wages and employment, and the curtailment of the market for commodities. Stress is laid upon the great importance of maintaining wage distribu-

tions which would provide the necessary stimulus in starting "the cumulative forces making for expanding commercial activity." Without in any way disparaging this motive, it is enough to say that the recuperative efforts of the federal government must be made in a manner consistent with the authority granted by the Constitution.

We are of the opinion that the attempt through the provisions of the Code to fix the hours and wages of employees of defendants in their intrastate business was not a valid exercise of federal power. . . .

On both the grounds we have discussed, the attempted delegation of legislative power, and the attempted regulation of intrastate transactions which affect interstate commerce only indirectly, we hold the code provisions here in question to be invalid and that the judgment of conviction must be reversed.

## 14

As one New Deal measure after another reached the Supreme Court, the slim conservative majority of justices branded each unconstitutional with a regularity that suggested prejudice rather than reason. Realizing that action was needed to save his whole program from judicial emasculation, President Roosevelt on March 9, 1937, proposed to Congress a sweeping change in the nation's court system:[14]

. . . In 1933 you and I knew that we must never let our economic system get completely out of joint again—that we could not afford to take the risk of another great depression.

We also became convinced that the only way to avoid a repetition of those dark days was to have a government with power to prevent and to cure the abuses and the inequalities which had thrown that system out of joint.

We then began a program of remedying those abuses and inequalities—to give

---

[14] *Senate Reports,* 75th Cong., 1st Sess., Doc. No. 711, pp. 41-45.

balance and stability to our economic system—to make it bombproof against the causes of 1929. . . .

The courts, however, have cast doubts on the ability of the elected Congress to protect us against catastrophe by meeting squarely our modern social and economic conditions. . . .

Last Thursday I described the American form of government as a three-horse team provided by the Constitution to the American people so that their field might be plowed. The three horses are, of course, the three branches of government—the Congress, the executive, and the courts. Two of the horses are pulling in unison today; the third is not. Those who have intimated that the President of the United States is trying to drive that team overlook the simple fact that the President, as Chief Executive, is himself one of the three horses. . . .

It is the American people themselves who expect the third horse to pull in unison with the other two. . . .

For nearly 20 years there was no conflict between the Congress and the Court. Then, in 1803, Congress passed a statute which the Court said violated an express provision of the Constitution. The Court claimed the power to declare it unconstitutional and did so declare it. But a little later the Court itself admitted that it was an extraordinary power to exercise and through Mr. Justice Washington laid down this limitation upon it: "It is but a decent respect due to the wisdom, the integrity, and the patriotism of the legislative body, by which any law is passed, to presume in favor of its validity until its violation of the Constitution is proved beyond all reasonable doubt."

But since the rise of the modern movement for social and economic progress through legislation, the Court has more and more often and more and more boldly asserted a power to veto laws passed by the Congress and State legislatures in complete disregard of this original limitation.

In the last 4 years the sound rule of giving statutes the benefit of all reasonable doubt has been cast aside. The Court has been acting not as a judicial body, but as a policy-making body. . . .

That is not only my accusation. It is the accusation of most distinguished Justices of the present Supreme Court. I have not the time to quote to you all the language used by dissenting Justices in many of these cases. But in the case holding the Railroad Retirement Act unconstitutional, for instance, Chief Justice Hughes said in a dissenting opinion that the majority opinion was "a departure from sound principles," and placed "an unwarranted limitation upon the commerce clause." And three other Justices agreed with him.

In the case holding the A.A.A. unconstitutional, Justice Stone said of the majority opinion that it was a "tortured construction of the Constitution." And two other Justices agreed with him.

In the case holding the New York Minimum Wage Law unconstitutional, Justice Stone said that the majority were actually reading into the Constitution their own "personal economic predilections," and that if the legislative power is not left free to choose the methods of solving the problems of poverty, subsistence, and health of large numbers in the community, then "government is to be rendered impotent." And two other Justices agreed with him.

In the face of these dissenting opinions, there is no basis for the claim made by some members of the Court that something in the Constitution has compelled them regretfully to thwart the will of the people.

In the face of such dissenting opinions, it is perfectly clear that as Chief Justice Hughes has said, "We are under a Constitution, but the Constitution is what the judges say it is."

The Court in addition to the proper use of its judicial functions has improperly set itself up as a third House of the

Congress—a superlegislature, as one of the Justices has called it—reading into the Constitution words and implications which are not there, and which were never intended to be there.

We have, therefore, reached the point as a Nation where we must take action to save the Constitution from the Court and the Court from itself. We must find a way to take an appeal from the Supreme Court to the Constitution itself. . . .

When I commenced to review the situation with the problem squarely before me, I came by a process of elimination to the conclusion that short of amendments the only method which was clearly constitutional, and would at the same time carry out other much-needed reforms, was to infuse new blood into all our courts. We must have men worthy and equipped to carry out impartial justice. But at the same time we must have judges who will bring to the courts a present-day sense of the Constitution—judges who will retain in the courts the judicial functions of a court and reject the legislative powers which the courts have today assumed. . . .

What is my proposal? It is simply this: Whenever a judge or justice of any Federal court has reached the age of 70 and does not avail himself of the opportunity to retire on a pension, a new member shall be appointed by the President then in office, with the approval, as required by the Constitution, of the Senate of the United States.

That plan has two chief purposes: By bringing into the judicial system a steady and continuing stream of new and younger blood, I hope, first, to make the administration of all Federal justice speedier and therefore less costly; secondly, to bring to the decision of social and economic problems younger men who have had personal experience and contact with modern facts and circumstances under which average men have to live and work. This plan will save our National Constitution from hardening of the judicial arteries. . . .

Why was the age fixed at 70? Because the laws of many States, the practice of the civil service, the regulations of the Army and Navy, and the rules of many of our universities and of almost every great private business enterprise commonly fix the retirement age at 70 years or less. . . .

Those opposing this plan have sought to arouse prejudice and fear by crying that I am seeking to "pack" the Supreme Court and that a baneful precedent will be established.

What do they mean by the words "packing the Court"? . . .

If by that phrase "packing the Court" it is charged that I wish to place on the bench spineless puppets who would disregard the law and would decide specific cases as I wished them to be decided, I make this answer: That no President fit for his office would appoint, and no Senate of honorable men fit for their office would confirm, that kind of appointees to the Supreme Court.

But if by that phrase the charge is made that I would appoint and the Senate would confirm Justices worthy to sit beside present members of the Court who understand these modern conditions; that I will appoint Justices who will not undertake to override the judgment of the Congress on legislative policy; that I will appoint Justices who will act as Justices and not as legislators—if the appointment of such Justices can be called "packing the Courts" —then I say that I, and with me the vast majority of the American people, favor doing just that thing—now. . . .

A very large percentage of newspaper publishers, chambers of commerce, bar associations, manufacturers' associations, who are trying to give the impression that they really do want a constitutional amendment, would be the first to exclaim as soon as an amendment was proposed: "Oh, I was for an amendment all right, but this amendment that you have proposed is not the kind of an amendment that I was thinking about. I am, therefore, going to spend my time, my efforts, and my money to block that amendment, although I would be awfully glad to help get some other kind of amendment ratified."

Two groups oppose my plan on the ground that they favor a constitutional amendment. The first includes those who fundamentally object to social and economic legislation along modern lines. That is the same group who during the campaign last fall tried to block the mandate of the people. . . .

The other group is composed of those who honestly believe the amendment process is the best and who would be willing to support a reasonable amendment if they could agree on one. . . .

Even if an amendment were passed, and even if in the years to come it were to be ratified, its meaning would depend upon the kind of Justices who would be sitting on the Supreme Court bench. An amendment like the rest of the Constitution is what the Justices say it is rather than what its framers or you might hope it is.

## 15

No measure introduced by President Roosevelt during his first two administrations aroused such resentment and controversy as his court reorganization bill. Amidst charges that he was trying to "pack the Court," conservatives of both parties banded together in opposition, vowing that passage of the act would mean the end of constitutional government in the United States. Their arguments were summarized in the report of the Senate Committee on the Judiciary, which recommended defeat for the President's proposal:[15]

This bill is an invasion of judicial power such as has never before been attempted in this country. It is true that in the closing days of the administration of John Adams, a bill was passed creating 16 new circuit

judges while reducing by one the number of places on the Supreme Court. It was charged that this was a bill to use the judiciary for a political purpose by providing official positions for members of a defeated party. The repeal of that law was the first task of the Jefferson administration.

Neither the original act nor the repealer was an attempt to change the course of judicial decision. And never in the history of the country has there been such an act. The present bill comes to us, therefore, wholly without precedent.

It is true that the size of the Supreme Court has been changed from time to time, but in every instance after the Adams administration, save one, the changes were made for purely administrative purposes in aid of the Court, not to control it. . . .

Shall we now, after 150 years of loyalty to the constitutional ideal of an untrammeled judiciary, duty bound to protect the constitutional rights of the humblest citizen even against the Government itself, create the vicious precedent which must necessarily undermine our system? The only argument for the increase which survives analysis is that Congress should enlarge the Court so as to make the policies of this administration effective.

We are told that a reactionary oligarchy defies the will of the majority, that this is a bill to "unpack" the Court and give effect to the desires of the majority; that is to say, a bill to increase the number of Justices for the express purpose of neutralizing the views of some of the present members. In justification we are told, but without authority, by those who would rationalize this program, that Congress was given the power to determine the size of the Court so that the legislative branch would be able to impose its will upon the judiciary. This amounts to nothing more than the declaration that when the Court stands in the way of a legislative enactment, the Congress may reverse the ruling by enlarging the Court. When such

---

[15] *Ibid.*, pp. 11-14, 23.

a principle is adopted, our constitutional system is overthrown!

This, then, is the dangerous precedent we are asked to establish. When proponents of the bill assert, as they have done, that Congress in the past has altered the number of Justices upon the Supreme Court and that this is reason enough for our doing it now, they show how important precedents are and prove that we should now refrain from any action that would seem to establish one which could be followed hereafter whenever a Congress and an executive should become dissatisfied with the decisions of the Supreme Court.

This is the first time in the history of our country that a proposal to alter the decisions of the court by enlarging its personnel has been so boldly made. Let us meet it. Let us now set a salutary precedent that will never be violated. Let us, of the Seventy-fifth Congress, in words that will never be disregarded by any succeeding Congress, declare that we would rather have an independent Court, a fearless Court, a Court that will dare to announce its honest opinions in what it believes to be the defense of the liberties of the people, than a Court that, out of fear or a sense of obligation to the appointing power, or factional passion, approves any measure we may enact. We are not the judges of the judges. We are not above the Constitution.

Even if every charge brought against the so-called "reactionary" members of this Court be true, it is far better that we await orderly but inevitable change of personnel than that we impatiently overwhelm them with new members. Exhibiting this restraint, thus demonstrating our faith in the American system, we shall set an example that will protect the independent American judiciary from attack as long as this Government stands. . . .

We recommend the rejection of this bill as a needless, futile, and utterly dangerous abandonment of constitutional principle.

It was presented to the Congress in a most intricate form and for reasons that obscured its real purpose.

It would not banish age from the bench nor abolish divided decisions.

It would not affect the power of any court to hold laws unconstitutional nor withdraw from any judge the authority to issue injunctions.

It would not reduce the expense of litigation nor speed the decision of cases.

It is a proposal without precedent and without justification.

It would subjugate the courts to the will of Congress and the President and thereby destroy the independence of the judiciary, the only certain shield of individual rights.

It contains the germ of a system of centralized administration of law that would enable an executive so minded to send his judges into every judicial district in the land to sit in judgment on controversies between the Government and the citizen.

It points the way to the evasion of the Constitution and establishes the method whereby the people may be deprived of their right to pass upon all amendments of the fundamental law.

It stands now before the country, acknowledged by its proponents as a plan to force judicial interpretation of the Constitution, a proposal that violates every sacred tradition of American democracy.

Under the form of the Constitution it seeks to do that which is unconstitutional.

Its ultimate operation would be to make this Government one of men rather than one of law, and its practical operation would be to make the Constitution what the executive or legislative branches of the Government choose to say it is—an interpretation to be changed with each change of administration.

It is a measure which should be so emphatically rejected that its parallel will never again be presented to the free representatives of the free people of America.

## 16

The President lost his battle to reform the courts, but he won the war. Beating a hasty retreat from conservatism, the justices of the Supreme Court suddenly discovered that a more liberal interpretation of New Deal laws was entirely constitutional. During the 168 days that Congress considered the reorganization bill, they upheld the Social Security Act, state minimum-wage laws, a federal farm-mortgage-moratorium act, and numerous others. Their most momentous decision upheld the Wagner Act. In the case of *National Labor Relations Board* v. *Jones and Laughlin Steel Corporation* (1937), the Court accepted the proposition that the production of goods could be regulated by Congress under its commerce power:[16]

Respondent says that whatever may be said of employees engaged in interstate commerce, the industrial relations and activities in the manufacturing department of respondent's enterprise are not subject to federal regulation. The argument rests upon the proposition that manufacturing in itself is not commerce. . . .

The Government distinguishes these cases. The various parts of respondent's enterprise are described as interdependent and as thus involving "a great movement of iron ore, coal and limestone along well-defined paths to the steel mills, thence through them, and thence in the form of steel products into the consuming centers of the country—a definite and well-understood course of business." It is urged that these activities constitute a "stream" or "flow" of commerce, of which the Aliquippa manufacturing plant is the focal point, and that industrial strife at that point would cripple the entire movement. Reference is made to our decision sustaining the Packers and Stockyards Act. The Court found that the stockyards were but a "throat" through which the current of commerce flowed and the transactions which there occurred could not be separated from that movement. . . .

We do not find it necessary to determine whether these features of defendant's business dispose of the asserted analogy to the "stream of commerce" cases. The congressional authority to protect interstate commerce from burdens and obstructions is not limited to transactions which can be deemed to be an essential part of a "flow" of interstate or foreign commerce. Burdens and obstructions may be due to injurious action springing from other sources. The fundamental principle is that the power to regulate commerce is the power to enact "all appropriate legislation" for "its protection and advancement"; to adopt measures "to promote its growth and insure its safety"; "to foster, protect, control and restrain." That power is plenary and may be exerted to protect interstate commerce "no matter what the source of the dangers which threaten it." Although activities may be intrastate in character when separately considered, if they have such a close and substantial relation to interstate commerce that their control is essential or appropriate to protect that commerce from burdens and obstructions, Congress cannot be denied the power to exercise that control. Undoubtedly the scope of this power must be considered in the light of our dual system of government and may not be extended so as to embrace effects upon interstate commerce so indirect and remote that to embrace them, in view of our complex society, would effectually obliterate the distinction between what is national and what is local and create a completely centralized government. The question is necessarily one of degree. . . .

That intrastate activities, by reason of close and intimate relation to interstate commerce, may fall within federal control demonstrated in the case of carriers who are engaged in both interstate and intrastate transportation. There federal control has been found essential to secure the freedom of interstate traffic from interference or unjust discrimination and to pro-

---

[16] *United States Reports*, 301 U.S. 34-49.

mote the efficiency of the interstate service. It is manifest that intrastate rates deal *primarily* with a local activity. But in rate-making they bear such a close relation to interstate rates that effective control of the one must embrace some control over the other. Under the Transportation Act, 1920, Congress went so far as to authorize the Interstate Commerce Commission to establish a state-wide level of intrastate rates in order to prevent an unjust discrimination against interstate commerce. Other illustrations are found in the broad requirements of the Safety Appliance Act and the Hours of Service Act. It is said that this exercise of federal power has relation to the maintenance of adequate instrumentalities of interstate commerce. But the agency is not superior to the commerce which uses it. The protective power extends to the former because it exists as to the latter.

The close and intimate effect which brings the subject within the reach of federal power may be due to activities in relation to productive industry although the industry when separately viewed is local. This has been abundantly illustrated in the application of the federal Anti-Trust Act. . . .

Upon the same principle, the Anti-Trust Act has been applied to the conduct of employees engaged in production. . . .

It is thus apparent that the fact that the employees here concerned were engaged in production is not determinative. The question remains as to the effect upon interstate commerce of the labor practice involved. . . .

Giving full weight to respondent's contention with respect to a break in the complete continuity of the "stream of commerce" by reason of respondent's manufacturing operations, the fact remains that the stoppage of those operations by industrial strife would have a most serious effect upon interstate commerce. In view of respondent's far-flung activities, it is idle to say that the effect would be indirect or remote. It is obvious that it would be im-

mediate and might be catastrophic. We are asked to shut our eyes to the plainest facts of our national life and to deal with the question of direct and indirect effects in an intellectual vacuum. Because there may be but indirect and remote effects upon interstate commerce in connection with a host of local enterprises throughout the country, it does not follow that other industrial activities do not have such a close and intimate relation to interstate commerce as to make the presence of industrial strife a matter of the most urgent national concern. When industries organize themselves on a national scale, making their relation to interstate commerce the dominant factor in their activities, how can it be maintained that their industrial labor relations constitute a forbidden field into which Congress may not enter when it is necessary to protect interstate commerce from the paralyzing consequences of industrial war? We have often said that interstate commerce itself is a practical conception. It is equally true that interferences with that commerce must be appraised by a judgment that does not ignore actual experience.

Experience has abundantly demonstrated that the recognition of the right of employees to self-organization and to have representatives of their own choosing for the purpose of collective bargaining is often an essential condition of industrial peace. Refusal to confer and negotiate has been one of the most prolific causes of strife. This is such an outstanding fact in the history of labor disturbances that it is a proper subject of judicial notice and requires no citation of instances. But with respect to the appropriateness of the recognition of self-organization and representation in the promotion of peace, the question is not essentially different in the case of employees in industries of such a character that interstate commerce is put in jeopardy from the case of employees of transportation companies. And of what avail is it to protect the facility of transportation, if interstate conmmerce is throttled with respect to the commodities to be transported! . . .

Our conclusion is that the order of the Board was within its competency and that the Act is valid. . . .

## DEMOCRACY AND PARTY LOYALTY

### 17

The battle over court reorganization cost President Roosevelt heavily. For some time, malcontents within his party had shown resentment at his liberal legislative program, his strong executive leadership, and the declining role of Congress. When these Democratic conservatives found themselves aligned with Republicans in the fight over the court bill, they hesitated to relinquish a partnership that gave them such power. From then on they worked with the opposition party on a loose bipartisan basis. Controlling key committees, they were in a position to block the will of both the President and congressional majorities. Roosevelt, endorsing a small-scale "purge" of obstructionist Democrats in the elections of 1938, used a press conference and a public speech to propound the concept of party government and majority rule that he had learned from Lord Bryce and Woodrow Wilson:[17]

*Press Conference, August 16, 1938*

THE PRESIDENT: I knew that somebody would ask the question so I have a perfectly good statement here. . . .

Q. Will you read it slowly, sir?

THE PRESIDENT: Yes. It is entitled, "Why the President 'Interferes.'" (*Laughter*)

And the first sentence is in quotes— you will see why afterwards. The first sentence is this: (*Reading*) "The President of the United States ought not to interfere in party primaries." And then the second sentence is not in quotes. (*Reading*)

That statement, in one form or another, is appearing these days throughout the Tory Press.

The idea is that the President should be aloof from such sordid considerations as who wins the primaries in his own party. But actually these primaries will determine to a large extent the makeup of the next Congress. And that, in turn, will determine whether or not the President can keep his campaign promises to the people.

Campaign promises are supposed to be the responsibility of the whole party. At least that's the theory. But in practice the head of the party alone is held responsible for them.

In American politics any one can attach himself to a political party whether he believes in its program or not.

That is a hot one.

We hear the phrase "read out of the party," but it doesn't mean anything. No one is read out of the Democratic or the Republican Party. There are many prominent Democrats today who are heart and soul against everything the Democratic Party has stood for since 1932. And those men are still in the party.

What's worse, not one of them was candid enough to oppose the renomination of Franklin D. Roosevelt in 1936, although after four years there was no doubt whatever as to the program Franklin D. Roosevelt was pursuing.

The same hidden opposition, after giving the New Deal lip-service in 1936, turned around and knifed it in Congress in 1937 and 1938.

Now that election time has come around again, the hidden opposition hides the ax behind its back and prepares to give the President lip-service once more.

In those circumstances there is nothing for the President to do—as the responsible head of the New Deal—but to publicly repudiate those who have betrayed the New Deal in the past and will again.

If men like Senator Tydings of Maryland said frankly: "I no longer believe in the platform of the Democratic Party as expressed in the New Deal; I'm running for re-election as a member of the Republican opposition to the New Deal," then there would be no reason and no excuse

[17] From *The Public Papers and Addresses of Franklin D. Roosevelt, 1938*, pp. 488-489, 516-517. Copyright, 1941 by Franklin Delano Roosevelt. Used by permission of The Macmillan Company, publishers.

for President Roosevelt to intervene against them.

The issue would be clear. The voter could take his choice between the New Deal and Tydings' record of consistent opposition to it. But Tydings tells the voters he supports the "bone and sinew" of the New Deal. He wants to run with the Roosevelt prestige and the money of his conservative Republican friends both on his side.

In that case it becomes the President's right and duty to tell the people what he thinks of Millard Tydings.

That's why we welcome the report that Roosevelt help is going to be given to Tydings' opponent, Representative David J. Lewis, and to James H. Fay, candidate for the nomination in the Sixteenth Congressional District of New York.

Fay is running against Representative John J. O'Connor, one of the most effective obstructionists in the lower house. Week in and week out O'Connor labors to tear down New Deal strength, pickle New Deal legislation.

Why shouldn't the responsible head of the New Deal tell the people just that?

Q. That is very mild. (*Laughter*)

Q. It reads as though it was an editorial.

THE PRESIDENT: Yes, it was an editorial, but it is my statement now.

### Address at Denton, Maryland, September 5, 1938

I ran across an interesting thing the other day. Lord Bryce, in the last edition of his great work on the American Commonwealth, had this to say: "An eminent journalist remarked to me in 1908 that the two great parties were like two bottles. Each bore a label denoting the kind of liquor it contained, but each was empty. This at any rate may be said, that the parties may seem to have erred . . . by neglecting to discover and work out any principles capable of solving the problems which now perplex the country. . . . The duty of a great party is to face these, to find answers and remedies, applying to the facts of the hour the doctrines it has lived by, so far as they are still applicable, and

when they have ceased to be applicable, thinking out new doctrines conformable to the main principles and tendencies which it represents."

That has been my conception of the obligations and ideals of the Democratic Party, for the Democratic Party has always been a party of ideas rather than money, and it has always failed when it has only been one of two empty bottles.

Yes, why should not we be frank with each other? The Democratic Party will live and continue to receive the support of the majority of Americans just so long as it remains a liberal party. If it reverts to the situation of thirty or forty years ago, which Lord Bryce described, it will fail.

As the leader of that party, I propose to try to keep it liberal. As President of the United States, I conceive that course to be in the best interests not only of Democrats but also of those millions of American men and women who are affiliated with other parties or with no party at all. And I have the right, in sincerity and honesty, to make that statement in any state, in any county and in any community of the United States of America.

Democratic majorities were returned in the elections of 1938; but Republicans made gains, and the continued bipartisan opposition slowed the tempo of the Roosevelt Revolution. The crowded years from 1933 to 1938 in which so many and so far-reaching social and economic reforms won popular acceptance were without parallel in the history of the nation. The New Deal, stopping short of nationalization and European "social democracy," pursued traditional objectives of American liberalism; but it broke new ground with the important concept of governmental intervention to keep the economy at full production. The reform impulse was to emerge again in less than a decade; but meanwhile, as Roosevelt rounded out the New Deal, he became increasingly concerned with forbidding developments in Asia and Europe. War clouds were on the horizon, and the American people were ill prepared for earth-shaking events that rapidly outmoded traditional ideas.

XXVI

# DEMOCRACY VS. NATIONALISM

## 1933–1945

If the decade of the 1920's indicated that each great war strengthened modern nationalism, the decade of the 1930's revealed that a world-wide depression gave even greater power to extreme nationalists. In Europe and in Asia a new Caesarism, deifying the martial leader, sprang from failures in the economic system. As democracy's leaders rallied to stem the rising tide of totalitarianism, the United States sloughed off the last relics of its outworn isolationism to join in the all-out war against the absolutism of Germany, Italy, and Japan. The new internationalism of the American people was attested when they overwhelmingly supported the United Nations, the world-wide organization that emerged from the struggle, and expanded the earlier "Good Neighbor Policy" to a global scale, playing a leading role in the economic and political reconstruction of battered Europe.

## RECESSION FROM NATIONALISM

### 1

The depression of the 1930's, tempting people everywhere to look after their own interests, fed the spirit of nationalism throughout the world. In the United States, Congress succumbed sufficiently to pass the so-called Neutrality Acts, but neither President Roosevelt nor a healthy minority of influential leaders forsook the internationalist cause. Their constant stress on world responsibilities did much to offset the clamor of isolationists. One who understood the need for world economic and political co-operation was Henry A. Wallace, secretary of agriculture in Roosevelt's cabinet, whose widely read pamphlet, *America Must Choose* (1934), stressed the importance of planned international trade in the nation's economy:[1]

. . . I see the seeds of war alike in *laissez-faire* accumulating pressing surpluses at home, and in seeking by hook or crook to thrust such surpluses abroad. Whether such a system is permitted freely to secrete and discharge its own poison within national borders or about the world at large, the pressure of ungoverned surpluses seems to me an equal stimulant to ruination and slaughter, before and during wars. . . .

[1] Henry A. Wallace, *America Must Choose* (New York, 1934), pp. 19-23, 30, 33. Reprinted by permission of the Foreign Policy Association and World Peace Foundation, Inc.

A clean-cut program of planned international trade or barter would be far less likely to get us into war, I think, than the attempts to function internationally as sellers, yet nationalistically as buyers, inaugurated under Presidents Harding and Coolidge, and followed by President Hoover. Such tactics pursued in the past by older nations led to bloody foreclosure proceedings, at the point of guns. . . .

It comes to this: If we insist upon selling without buying, we have to lend our surplus to foreign countries, and never take it back. It stays abroad. But we think we still own it, and that makes us figure out ways and means of keeping the investment safe. We must have some security that transcends the good faith of the borrower. There is no surer path to war.

The method of reciprocal trade, on the other hand, leads to peace. It makes no sales without providing opportunities for the buyers to pay the bill. Since the bill does not remain outstanding indefinitely, and does not have to be collected at the point of a gun, it makes new business easy to get and profitable. . . .

Creditor countries under normal conditions tend to have "unfavorable" balances of trade. Before the war Great Britain, France, Germany, the Netherlands and Switzerland had unfavorable balances.

474

They were rich creditor countries, with capital invested all over the world. This capital returned payments to them in goods —payments of interest and principal. It was an important factor in giving them an excess of imports over exports. Orthodox economic theory holds that an unfavorable trade balance, when it comes from payments on successful foreign investments, should not hurt a country. Paradoxically, however, all countries in that position try to escape from it as soon as they can. They strive to offset the rising flood of imports with a rising flood of exports. . . .

Germany was not alone in cherishing the desire to sell without receiving payment immediately, to export as much as possible and import as little as possible, to lend and seek reimbursement in world power rather than in goods. The nations with whom it fought, including the United States, were possessed of the same illusion that it is possible endlessly to sell without buying. Where they accepted unfavorable balances of trade they did so unwillingly, and did everything possible to get out of it. Most nations still cherish the illusion that wealth comes from selling without buying; and the notion can do us as much harm in the future as it has in the past. . . .

Enduring social transformation such as our New Deal seeks is impossible of realization without changed human hearts. The classical economists, most orthodox scientists, and the majority of practical business men question whether human nature can be changed. I think it can be changed because it has been changed many times in the past.

It is a belief often expressed nowadays that men are born greedy, with a strong self-seeking strain of meanness inherent in their make-up; and that you can't change human nature. I cannot believe it. It sounds to me like a sheltering modern rationalization built from the despised and all but forgotten Puritan concept that only man is vile. The real need now is not to change human nature but to give it a new chance. And in trying to simplify to myself the change of ways by which we may all, as a people, come in time to personal freedom, personal security, and to the sort of self-respect which makes life worth living, I keep coming back to the question of fear.

If we could rid the general mass of our people of that paralyzing fear which breeds and grows at a bare sustenance level of wages and prices, and which spreads in time to infect the whole of business and society, it is conceivable that we could proceed in time from an economy of denied plenty, with heaping surpluses next door to bitter hunger, to an economy of potential abundance developed to the uttermost and ungrudgingly shared. It is mean and niggardly in a land so wide and rich as this one, and many others, to stem the currents of production, and to deflect the things all men desire into channels so limited, for a privileged few. It is bad management. Perhaps we can evolve in this country an economy that deals in potentialities instead of in denial. Perhaps in time we shall be able safely to unleash the productive capacities of all our industries, including agriculture, and turn out for the widest distribution imaginable the kind of goods which Americans, and people throughout the world in general, so achingly desire. . . .

That an enforced meanness has throughout modern society become a real menace, no one can deny. The breadlines testify to this reality; a million forced sales of farms in this country tell another part of the wretched story; and then you have only begun to take count of all the millions the world over who live in constant and degrading fear that the same thing may happen to them tomorrow.

Unless, not with words, but in better wages and prices, we can remove that fear from the minds and hearts of those great masses of people who farm or work for wages, our New Deal will be a thing of words alone. We must implant security, and a full confidence in continued security, throughout the base of our new structure, if we want it to stand up better than the one that fell down on us after 1929.

In our big city press every day now, I see frantic calls for the American government to give new assurances to business. The demand is that we "restore confidence" in Wall Street and on the Loop. Day after day this entreaty is repeated, in headlines which in themselves whimper and cry of fear. I think we have a right to expect more than that from our American business men. . . .

In an age when an advanced technology pours forth goods in a smothering abundance, fear of freezing to death and starving to death should be removed as a matter of common decency from the lives of civilized people as a whole. This is not a cloudy idealism which has no basis in facts. Only those really close to science can know the abundance that could be ours with even-handed justice and a generous distribution between groups. . . .

It should be recognized that our surplus problems here in the United States, and the resulting necessity of keeping parts of our factories idle and withdrawing acreage, or of widening foreign markets, or of doing these things in combination, is really part of a world surplus problem. This country has more industrial as well as more agricultural capacity than it needs for home consumption. Surplus capacity in industry shows up mainly in unemployment, rather than in a persistent accumulation of commodities; but in all branches of our economic life there is an identical tendency for production to outrun consumption. Other nations have just the same trouble, as we know from the prevalence of unemployment and dole systems throughout the world. . . .

Now, it is this discrepancy between production-power and domestic consumption which makes all nations wish to sell more abroad than they buy abroad, and gives rise to economic nationalism in its most determined forms. There can be little doubt that the trouble traces, in whole or in part, to a maldistribution of income. That doctrine is implicit in our New Deal, which seeks to compensate for falling markets by building up purchasing power at home.

On a national and on a world scale alike, the tendency of old-time opportunist capitalism to pile up surpluses and to polarize wealth leads to disaster. Planned production and plans for a better distribution of income are essential to safe and decent business within nations and among nations. Whether you are an extreme free trader, in principle, or an extreme isolationist, maldistribution will kill any attempt toward plenty, security and release. . . .

The nationalist rests his case on the idea that we cannot expect any longer to trade with the world as we used to. He does not expect an adequate natural revival of foreign demand, and believes it would be folly for us to stimulate the demand artificially by loans.

The internationalist position, on the other hand, is less pessimistic about natural foreign trade prospects. The internationalist does not regard loans as the only means of brightening those prospects and enlarging them. He holds that there is no possible way of making loans eventually secure unless we become import-minded. He would rather trust to tariff concessions and other means of developing trade reciprocally. He considers the pains of this course to be less than those of a nationalist program.

I lean to the international solution. But it is no open and shut question. It needs study, and above all dispassionate discussion. Unfortunately, those arguments which appeal to fear, to suspicion of neighbor nations, to narrow self-interest, and to ingrained hatred of change are the arguments which will be most loudly invoked. I want to see the whole question examined by our people in a new spirit.

## 2

These sentiments were translated into a broad program of action by the Roosevelt administration. Particularly effective was the assault on economic nationalism. Only a month after he became president, Roosevelt announced his determination to sweep away trade barriers, a resolve that was realized when Congress adopted his Reciprocal Trade Agreements Act in 1934. This measure authorized the executive to negotiate bilateral trade agreements with other nations, and empowered him to reduce specific tariffs as much as 50 per cent in return for similar favored treatment accorded American goods:[2]

*Be it enacted* . . . That the Tariff Act of 1930 is amended by adding at the end of the Title III the following:

"SECTION 350. (a) For the purpose of expanding foreign markets for the products of the United States (as a means of assisting in the present emergency in restoring the American standard of living, in overcoming domestic unemployment and the present economic depression, in increasing the purchasing power of the American public, and in establishing and maintaining a better relationship among various branches of American agriculture, industry, mining, and commerce) by regulating the admission of foreign goods into the United States in accordance with the characteristics and needs of various branches of American production so that foreign markets will be made available to those branches of American production which require and are capable of developing such outlets by affording corresponding market opportunities for foreign products in the United States, the President, whenever he finds as a fact that any existing duties or other import restrictions of the United States or any foreign country are unduly burdening and restricting the foreign trade of the United States and that the pur-

pose above declared will be promoted by the means hereinafter specified, is authorized from time to time—

"(1) To enter into foreign trade agreements with foreign governments or instrumentalities thereof; and

"(2) To proclaim such modifications of existing duties and other import restrictions, or such additional import restrictions, or such continuance, and for such minimum periods, of existing customs or excise treatment of any article covered by foreign trade agreements, as are required or appropriate to carry out any foreign trade agreement that the President has entered into hereunder. No proclamation shall be made increasing or decreasing by more than 50 per centum any existing rate of duty or transferring any article between the dutiable and free lists. The proclaimed duties and other import restrictions shall apply to articles the growth, produce, or manufacture of all foreign countries, whether imported directly, or indirectly: *Provided,* That the President may suspend the application to articles the growth, produce, or manufacture of any country because of its discriminatory treatment of American commerce or because of other acts or policies which in his opinion tend to defeat the purposes set forth in this section; and the proclaimed duties and other import restrictions shall be in effect from and after such time as is specified in the proclamation. The President may at any time terminate any such proclamation in whole or in part. . . ."

SEC. 2. (c) The authority of the President to enter into foreign trade agreements under section 1 of this Act shall terminate on the expiration of three years from the date of the enactment of this Act. . . .

SEC. 4. Before any foreign trade agreement is concluded . . . reasonable public notice . . . shall be given in order that any

[2] *United States Statutes at Large,* XLVIII, 943-945.

interested person may have an opportunity to present his views to the President, or to such agency as the President may designate. . . .

## 3

A necessary corollary to the internationalism of the Roosevelt administration was a retreat from the imperialism of the past. Having tasted the glories of empire and found them wanting, the United States by 1933 was ready to grant freedom to its colonies whenever their people seemed equipped for self-government. A noteworthy demonstration was a law of March 24, 1934, to release the Philippines from colonial bondage. Congressional support for the Philippine Independence Act was, however, inspired by mixed motives. The terms of the measure indicated that some, at least, among those who espoused independence were anxious to place Philippine goods and the Filipinos themselves outside the American tariff and immigration walls:[3].

SECTION 1. The Philippine Legislature is hereby authorized to provide for the election of delegates to a constitutional convention, which shall meet . . . at such time as the Philippine Legislature may fix, but not later than October 1, 1934, to formulate and draft a constitution for the government of the Commonwealth of the Philippine Islands, subject to the conditions and qualifications prescribed. . . .

SEC. 8. (a) Effective upon the acceptance of this Act by concurrent resolution of the Philippine Legislature or by a convention called for that purpose, as provided in section 17—

(1) For the purposes of the Immigration Act of 1917, the Immigration Act of 1924 (except section 13 (c)), this section, and all other laws of the United States relating to the immigration, exclusion, or expulsion of aliens, citizens of the Philippine Islands who are not citizens of the United States shall be considered as if they were aliens. For such purposes the Philippine Islands shall be considered as a separate

country and shall have for each fiscal year a quota of fifty. . . .

SEC. 10. (a) On the 4th day of July immediately following the expiration of a period of ten years from the date of the inauguration of the new government under the constitution provided for in this Act the President of the United States shall by proclamation withdraw and surrender all right of possession, supervision, jurisdiction, control, or sovereignty then existing and exercised by the United States in and over the territory and people of the Philippine Islands, including all military and other reservations of the Government of the United States in the Philippines (except such naval reservations and fueling stations as are reserved under section 5), and, on behalf of the United States, shall recognize the independence of the Philippine Islands as a separate and self-governing nation and acknowledge the authority and control over the same of the government instituted by the people thereof, under the constitution then in force. . . .

SEC. 13. After the Philippine Islands have become a free and independent nation there shall be levied, collected, and paid upon all articles coming into the United States from the Philippine Islands the rates of duty which are required to be levied, collected, and paid upon like articles imported from other foreign countries. . . .

SEC. 14. Upon the final and complete withdrawal of American sovereignty over the Philippine Islands the immigration laws of the United States . . . shall apply to persons who were born in the Philippine Islands to the same extent as in the case of other foreign countries.

## 4

Roosevelt's internationalism was most effectively applied to the Latin-American republics, under the happy phrase, the "Good Neighbor policy." In rapid succession the President transformed the Monroe Doctrine from a unilateral to a multilateral instrument

---

[3] *Ibid.,* pp. 456-465.

against external aggression, withdrew financial receiverships from the Caribbean islands, and reopened South American trade through reciprocal trading agreements. Important as these steps were, they engendered less good will than the abrogation of the Platt Amendment. In a dramatic gesture, this relic of an earlier day was wiped from the statute books on May 29, 1934:[4]

ARTICLE I. The Treaty of Relations which was concluded between the two contracting parties on May 22, 1903, shall cease to be in force, and is abrogated, from the date on which the present treaty goes into effect.

ART. II. All the acts effected in Cuba by the United States of America during its military occupation of the island, up to May 20, 1902, the date on which the Republic of Cuba was established, have been ratified and held as valid; and all rights legally acquired by virtue of those acts shall be maintained and protected.

ART. III. Until the two contracting parties agree to the modification or abrogation of the stipulations of the agreement in regard to the lease to the United States of America of lands in Cuba for coaling and naval stations signed by the President of the Republic of Cuba on February 16, 1903, and by the President of the United States of America on the 23rd day of the same month and year, the stipulations of that agreement with regard to the naval station of Guantanamo shall continue in effect. The supplementary agreement in regard to naval or coaling stations signed between the two governments on July 2, 1903, shall continue in effect in the same form and on the same conditions with respect to the naval station at Guantanamo. So long as the United States of America shall not abandon the said naval station of Guantanamo or the two governments shall not agree to a modification of its present limits, the station shall continue to have the territorial area that it now has,

with the limits that it has on the date of the signature of the present treaty.

ART. IV. If at any time in the future a situation should arise that appears to point to an outbreak of contagious disease in the territory of either of the contracting parties, either of the two governments shall, for its own protection, and without its act being considered unfriendly, exercise freely and at its discretion the right to suspend communications between those of its ports that it may designate and all or part of the territory of the other party, and for the period that it may consider to be advisable. . . .

## 5

The impressive results of the Good Neighbor policy were summarized by President Roosevelt in a speech given at Chautauqua, New York, on August 14, 1936:[5]

. . . Long before I returned to Washington as President of the United States, I had made up my mind that, pending what might be called a more opportune moment on other continents, the United States could best serve the cause of peaceful humanity by setting an example. That was why on the 4th of March, 1933, I made the following declaration:

In the field of world policy I would dedicate this nation to the policy of the good neighbor—the neighbor who resolutely respects himself and because he does so, respects the rights of others—the neighbor who respects his obligations and respects the sanctity of his agreements in and with a world of neighbors.

This declaration represents my purpose; but it represents more than a purpose, for it stands for a practice. To a measurable degree it has succeeded; the whole world now knows that the United States cherishes no predatory ambitions. We are strong; but less powerful nations know

---

[4] *Ibid.*, pp. 1682-1685.

[5] *Peace and War: United States Foreign Policy, 1931-1941* (Washington, 1943), pp. 323-329.

that they need not fear our strength. We seek no conquest; we stand for peace.

In the whole of the Western Hemisphere our good neighbor policy has produced results that are especially heartening.

The noblest monument to peace and to neighborly economic and social friendship in all the world is not a monument in bronze or stone but the boundary which unites the United States and Canada—3,000 miles of friendship with no barbed wire, no gun or soldier, and no passport on the whole frontier.

Mutual trust made that frontier—to extend the same sort of mutual trust throughout the Americas was our aim.

The American republics to the south of us have been ready always to cooperate with the United States on a basis of equality and mutual respect, but before we inaugurated the good neighbor policy there was among them resentment and fear, because certain administrations in Washington had slighted their national pride and their sovereign rights.

In pursuance of the good neighbor policy, and because in my younger days I had learned many lessons in the hard school of experience, I stated that the United States was opposed definitely to armed intervention.

We have negotiated a Pan-American convention embodying the principle of non-intervention. We have abandoned the Platt amendment which gave us the right to intervene in the internal affairs of the Republic of Cuba. We have withdrawn American marines from Haiti. We have signed a new treaty which places our relations with Panama on a mutually satisfactory basis. We have undertaken a series of trade agreements with other American countries to our mutual commercial profit. At the request of two neighboring republics, I hope to give assistance in the final settlement of the last serious boundary dispute between any of the American nations.

Throughout the Americas the spirit of the good neighbor is a practical and living fact. The twenty-one American republics are not only living together in friendship and in peace; they are united in the determination so to remain. . . .

We seek to dominate no other nation. We ask no territorial expansion. We oppose imperialism. We desire reduction in world armaments.

We believe in democracy; we believe in freedom; we believe in peace. We offer to every nation of the world the handclasp of the good neighbor. Let those who wish our friendship look us in the eye and take our hand.

## TOTALITARIAN NATIONALISM

### 6

While the United States moved forward along the road to internationalism, the totalitarian states during the 1930's retreated backward toward greater nationalism. Their guide and inspiration was Adolf Hitler's Germany. The National Socialism of that doomed nation was not socialism, nor did its Nazi leaders have any sympathy for international cooperation or democracy. Instead, lacking a majority in the legislature as they marched to power, they showed their true nature by extinguishing rival parties. The German "Law Creating a One-Party State" was not a law but a cabinet decree; a decree of death to the basic democratic liberty; the right to oppose and the right to win a majority:[6]

The German Cabinet has resolved the following law. . . .

ARTICLE 1. The National Socialist German Workers' Party constitutes the only political party in Germany.

ART. 2. Whoever undertakes to maintain . . . another political party or to form a new political party will be punished with penal servitude up to three years or with imprisonment of from six months to three years, if the deed is not subject to a greater penalty according to other regulations.

[6] Raymond E. Murphy *et al.* (eds.), *National Socialism* (Washington, 1943), p. 220.

## 7

Contemptuous alike of democratic ideals and international good will, Nazi business leaders and their totalitarian backers cunningly developed German foreign policy into a world-wide system for enrichment of themselves by preying on the labor and resources of others. *You Can't Do Business with Hitler* (1941), a best-selling book by the American commercial attaché at Berlin, Douglas Miller, opened the eyes of many isolationists to Germany's cynical economic war on innocent countries:[7]

When exchange control was introduced in Germany in July 1931, it was considered an emergency measure to stop the drain on Germany's gold and foreign exchange reserves and to bring the nation's balance of trade and balance of payments into proper alignment. Only after the re-emergence of Dr. Schacht in the Reichsbank during the spring of 1933 did it appear evident that the Nazis had made a virtue of necessity and were using the totalitarian control of foreign commerce transactions as an offensive as well as a defensive weapon.

Foreign exchange control sets up a wall around the country at the frontier and insures that no currency, negotiable instruments, or other securities can pass that frontier without a special permit from the authorities. . . .

. . . On September 24, 1934, Dr. Schacht's new plan was put into operation; this stopped all possibility of imports, except under specific permit from the government.

Twenty-five import-control offices, allocated according to commodities, administered the new regulations and allowed permits for the importation of necessities. By 1935 necessities were defined as goods of military significance. . . .

The foreign-trade permit system led to

---

[7] Douglas Miller, *You Can't Do Business with Hitler,* pp. 68-85. Copyright 1941, by Little, Brown and Company.

monopolies in the imported articles, and the monopolists were not slow to take advantage of their favorable situation by price increases. To counteract such tendencies, the government was forced to set up a price control governing imported commodities, and later on was forced to control the prices of goods made from imported raw materials. A logical extension of this system forced controlled prices throughout German economy.

As a necessary corollary of controlled prices, it was found expedient to allocate production among domestic firms. Production in both agriculture and industry was put upon a quota basis. Some time previously, wages had also been set at fixed levels by thirteen labor trustees, appointed by the government under the National Labor Law of 1934. Wages were in general set at the 1932 levels, with certain provisions for bonuses in defense industries. Finally, the control of wages and the control of production led in 1938 to the control of jobs.

Even before the present war started, German employees were frozen at their existing desks or workbenches. It was assumed that everyone was a soldier taking a part in the national effort and should not be allowed to seek other employment merely because it paid better or seemed more suitable. . . .

But a greater wonder was in store. Dr. Schacht and his colleagues slowly evolved a system by which Germany's economic difficulties were turned into advantages and a new type of economic pressure developed which has proved successful in most parts of the world since 1934 . . . They realized the implications of the well-known fact that a dishonest debtor has all the advantage over his creditor and that international trading is not enforced by the sanction of any court.

The broad lines of Schacht's economic policy were, first, to segregate Germany's trade relations from participation in any international network of commercial and financial transactions, establishing a series of independent bilateral relations with individual foreign countries. Or in other words, Germany's foreign trade was no longer to be international trade but a system of parallel but separate relations with other states. . . .

Such clearing agreements, frequently revised and amended, covered the bulk of German transactions. They were divided into state-arranged clearings, set up by foreign treaty arrangements between governments, and central bank-clearing agreements, regulated by the German Reichsbank on one side and central banks abroad on the other. . . .

In practice, however, bilateral trade between any pair of countries almost never results in an exact balance. One or the other country has an excess of exports. Its balance must be carried forward into the next year and certain exporters must wait for payment out of new import transactions. . . . Finally, there is pressure put upon trade circles in the exporting country to hold down shipments to equal or cut under current imports from the debtor country. If this proves successful, the other country retaliates by reducing its balance, both nations jockeying for position and each attempting to hold down its exports below its imports through fear of delays in payments and eventual losses.

It was not long before most of my commercial attaché colleagues in Berlin, whose countries were working under clearings, spent a great part of their efforts in preventing shipments from their own countries to Germany, since they were fearful of running up too big a credit and finally being forced to take a loss. . . .

The Germans on their part were bursting with optimism and big ideas. They were willing to negotiate for the entire crops of smaller countries at attractive prices, and blandly explained that of courses they were not paying cash, but that the little country could certainly obtain from Germany in payment a wide variety of suitable articles well designed to meet its needs.

The small one-crop countries of Latin America and Eastern Europe proved to be easy meat for the Germans. Most of these nations had been suffering from the stagnation of world trade, and marketing of their main crops in an era of low prices was their principal economic headache. Now mighty Germany, a consuming unit of nearly 70,000,000 persons, appeared willing to buy the whole crop. All marketing problems were at an end. The pressure of producing groups upon the local governments bested any skeptical fears about the suitability or availability of German goods in exchange; furthermore, most of these producers' groups were better organized and more vigorous than the remaining mass of people. They knew what they wanted—quick sales at a high price, reimbursement out of the funds of their central bank; and they were perfectly willing to let their government hold the bag and collect from Germany as best it could. . . .

In this way the German negotiators incurred a huge commodity indebtedness with the outside world . . . Dr. Schacht had realized that an honest debtor worries about his obligations and desires to keep them at a minimum; a dishonest debtor lets his creditors do the worrying for him and tries to run up his obligations as high as possible, because he is not planning to pay anyhow.

The German Ministry of Economics then began to see other advantages to be derived from this system. The Nazis could get rid of unsalable stocks of merchandise on long-term credits to individual merchants in foreign countries. It was easy for them to extend credit to any foreign merchant in a country which operated a clearing because the local government was holding the bag, not the Germans. Another device was to use commodities obtained under the clearing for resale in cash markets. The price didn't particularly matter, because the goods were obtained on credit, sold for cash; the cash could be used for propaganda, the purchase of war materials, and other urgent needs, and the final bills would not be paid anyway until they were finally obliterated in the next war. In this way Germans resold Brazilian coffee, Bulgarian tobacco, Greek currants, and obtained cash for airplane parts from the United States and Great Britain.

Naturally, such tactics began to upset the world market for the commodities of the unfortunate one-crop countries. They could only squirm and wriggle but could not escape from the new economy in which they were enmeshed. Instead of breaking off trade with Germany, their inability to sell in other markets made them more dependent upon their bulk customer. They were forced to sell an even larger proportion of their crop to Germany than before.

In this way the Nazi economists believed that Germany could make herself the world's middleman and that overseas buyers would have to come to Berlin for all sorts of foreign commodities. In fact, before the present war, American buyers of Oriental tobacco and similar products found that they could buy for cash in Berlin more cheaply than any place else in the world. In these negotiations, the Germans seemed quite unmindful of considerations which would ordinarily limit a commercial transaction. . . .

. . . Nations which were either situated close to the German frontier or had a large part of their trade with the Reich were forced to adjust their own methods of doing business in order to fit it to the Nazi picture. It was necessary for them to maintain two sectors of their economy— one semi-controlled to work with the controlled economy of Germany, and the other relatively uncontrolled which maintained ordinary trade relations with the Western democratic powers. There is an innate tendency for measures of control to spread over a larger area, and the experience of the years before the recent war showed a constant tendency for the totalitarian trade

methods to extend themselves into countries supposed to be operating on a free economy. Single firms are unable to buck a totalitarian machine. They called for help from their own governments and in this way a certain measure of totalitarian economic control was set up even in countries which professed to eschew such methods.

Furthermore, German commercial policy continually aimed at expanding its share of the world. Germans insisted that they needed more living space. This apparently means a larger area of land for German people to live in, as well as an increasing block of subsidiary states acting as markets and suppliers of raw materials. High pressure methods were constantly at work to enlarge this area. To put it in simpler terms, the Germans, together with their Axis allies, would suddenly approach a small neighboring country, already closely enmeshed in totalitarian trade schemes, with a demand somewhat as follows: "The new order is now doing 60 per cent of your foreign business. We are your largest market and largest source of supply. You must choose whether to join us completely or lose every bit of this existing business." In practically every case these demands were successful. In this way smaller nations were steadily brought into the enlarged orbit of the totalitarians. The addition of each new nation created a greater economic block and enlarged the possibilities of pressure on the next neighboring states. This had the effect of gradually narrowing the area of free economy in the world, causing tremendous fluctuations in prices, rapid movements of commodities, and cable transfers of funds from one center to another. London, Paris, Amsterdam, and even New York, began to feel that their world was shrinking.

## 8

The Nipponese "New Order" in the East posed the same problem as Hitler's unlimited ambitions in the West. In 1937, Japan launched her drive into China; and in November, 1938, notified the United States that the Open Door was no longer applicable to the "new situation." The reply to Japan in the note of December 31, 1938, maintained the historic American position:[8]

In the light of facts and experience the Government of the United States is impelled to reaffirm its previously expressed opinion that imposition of restrictions upon the movements and activities of American nationals who are engaged in philanthropic, educational, and commercial endeavors in China has placed and will, if continued, increasingly place Japanese interests in a preferred position and is, therefore, unquestionably discriminatory, in its effect, against legitimate American interests. Further, with reference to such matters as exchange control, compulsory currency circulation, tariff revision, and monopolistic promotion in certain areas of China, the plans and practices of the Japanese authorities imply an assumption on the part of those authorities that the Japanese Government or the regimes established and maintained in China by Japanese armed forces are entitled to act in China in a capacity such as flows from rights of sovereignty and, further, in so acting to disregard and even to declare non-existent or abrogated the established rights and interests of other countries, including the United States. . . .

In the concluding portion of its note under reference, the Japanese Government states that it is firmly convinced that "in the face of the new situation, fast developing in East Asia, any attempt to apply to the conditions of to-day and to-morrow inapplicable ideas and principles of the past neither would contribute toward the establishment of a real peace in East Asia nor solve the immediate issues," and that "as long as these points are understood, Japan has not the slightest inclination to

oppose the participation of the United States and other Powers in the great work of reconstructing East Asia along all lines of industry and trade."

The Government of the United States in its note of 6 October requested, in view of the oft-reiterated assurances proffered by the Government of Japan of its intention to observe the principle of equality of opportunity in its relations with China, and in view of Japan's treaty obligations so to do, that the Government of Japan abide by these obligations and carry out these assurances in practice. The Japanese Government in its reply appears to affirm that it is its intention to make its observance of that principle conditional upon an understanding by the American Government and by other governments of a "new situation" and a "new order" in the Far East as envisaged and fostered by Japanese authorities. . . .

This country's adherence to and its advocacy of the principle of equality of opportunity do not flow solely from a desire to obtain the commercial benefits which naturally result from the carrying out of that principle. They flow from a firm conviction that observance of that principle leads to economic and political stability, which are conducive both to the internal well-being of nations and to mutually beneficial and peaceful relationships between and among nations; from a firm conviction that failure to observe that principle breeds international friction and ill-will, with consequences injurious to all countries, including in particular those countries which fail to observe it; and from an equally firm conviction that observance of that principle promotes the opening of trade channels, thereby making available the markets, the raw materials, and the manufactured products of the community of nations on a mutually and reciprocally beneficial basis. . . .

It is known to all the world that various of the parties to treaties concluded for the purpose of regulating contacts in the Far

---

[8] *Peace and War: United States Foreign Policy, 1931-1941* (Washington, 1943), pp. 442-447.

East and avoiding friction therein and therefrom—which treaties contained, for those purposes, various restrictive provisions—have from time to time, and by processes of negotiation and agreement, contributed, in the light of changed situations, toward the removal of restrictions and toward the bringing about of further developments which would warrant, in the light of further changes, in the situation, further removals of restrictions. By such methods and processes, early restrictions upon the tariff autonomy of all countries in the Far East were removed. By such methods and processes, the rights of extraterritorial jurisdiction once enjoyed by Occidental countries in relations with countries in the Far East have been given up in relations with all of those countries except China; and in the years immediately preceding and including the year 1931, countries which still possess those rights in China, including the United States, were actively engaged in negotiations—far advanced—looking toward surrender of those rights. All discerning and impartial observers have realized that the United States and other of the "treaty Powers" have not, during recent decades, clung tenaciously to their so-called "special" rights and privileges in countries of the Far East, but on the contrary have steadily encouraged the development in those countries of institutions and practices in the presence of which such rights and privileges may safely and readily be given up and all observers have seen those rights and privileges gradually being surrendered voluntarily, through agreement, by the Powers which have possessed them. On one point only has the Government of the United States, along with several other governments, insisted: namely, that new situations must have developed to a point warranting the removal of "special" safeguarding restrictions and that the removals be effected by orderly processes. . . .

Meanwhile, this Government reserves all rights of the United States as they exist and does not give assent to any impairment of any of those rights.

## THE END OF ISOLATION

### 9

Few in the United States were able to see the handwriting on the wall as the expanding aggressivism of the totalitarian powers brought the world closer and closer to war. Instead, Congress in January, 1937, prohibited arms shipments to war-torn Spain, failing to see that a triumph for fascism over democracy there would encourage dictators everywhere. A few months later, in May, 1937, the Third Neutrality Act was passed with the expressed purpose of making American isolation from Europe "permanent." Both these measures were applauded by a majority of the people, despite President Roosevelt's reiterated insistence that they reflect upon realities and adopt a wiser course. Notable among his appeals was his "Quarantine" speech, delivered in Chicago on October 5, 1937:[9]

. . . The political situation in the world, which of late has been growing progressively worse, is such as to cause grave concern and anxiety to all the peoples and nations who wish to live in peace and amity with their neighbors.

Some 15 years ago the hopes of mankind for a continuing era of international peace were raised to great heights when more than 60 nations solemnly pledged themselves not to resort to arms in furtherance of their national aims and policies. The high aspirations expressed in the Briand-Kellogg Peace Pact and the hopes for peace thus raised have of late given away to a haunting fear of calamity. The present reign of terror and international lawlessness began a few years ago.

It began through unjustified interference in the internal affairs of other nations or the invasion of alien territory in violation of treaties and has now reached a stage where the very foundations of civilization are seriously threatened. The land-

[9] *Ibid.*, pp. 383-387.

marks and traditions which have marked the progress of civilization toward a condition of law, order, and justice are being wiped away.

Without a declaration of war and without warning or justification of any kind, civilians, including women and children, are being ruthlessly murdered with bombs from the air. In times of so-called peace ships are being attacked and sunk by submarines without cause or notice. Nations are fomenting and taking sides in civil warfare in nations that have never done them any harm. Nations claiming freedom for themselves deny it to others.

Innocent peoples and nations are being cruelly sacrificed to a greed for power and supremacy which is devoid of all sense of justice and human consideration. . . .

If those things come to pass in other parts of the world let no one imagine that America will escape, that it may expect mercy, that this Western Hemisphere will not be attacked, and that it will continue tranquilly and peacefully to carry on the ethics and the arts of civilization. . . .

If those days are not to come to pass— if we are to have a world in which we can breathe freely and live in amity without fear—the peace-loving nations must make a concerted effort to uphold laws and principles on which alone peace can rest secure.

The peace-loving nations must make a concerted effort in opposition to those violations of treaties and those ignorings of humane instincts which today are creating a state of international anarchy and instability from which there is no escape through mere isolation or neutrality.

Those who cherish their freedom and recognize and respect the equal right of their neighbors to be free and live in peace, must work together for the triumph of law and moral principles in order that peace, justice, and confidence may prevail in the world. There must be a return to a belief in the pledged word, in the value of a signed treaty. There must be recogni-

tion of the fact that national morality is as vital as private morality. . . .

There is a solidarity and interdependence about the modern world, both technically and morally, which makes it impossible for any nation completely to isolate itself from economic and political upheavals in the rest of the world, especially when such upheavals appear to be spreading and not declining. There can be no stability or peace either within nations or between nations except under laws and moral standards adhered to by all. International anarchy destroys every foundation for peace. . . .

It seems to be unfortunately true that the epidemic of world lawlessness is spreading.

When an epidemic of physical disease starts to spread, the community approves and joins in a quarantine of the patients in order to protect the health of the community against the spread of the disease.

It is my determination to pursue a policy of peace and to adopt every practicable measure to avoid involvement in war. It ought to be inconceivable that in this modern era, and in the face of experience, any nation could be so foolish and ruthless as to run the risk of plunging the whole world into war by invading and violating in contravention of solemn treaties the territory of other nations that have done them no real harm and which are too weak to protect themselves adequately. Yet the peace of the world and the welfare and security of every nation is today being threatened by that very thing.

No nation which refuses to exercise forbearance and to respect the freedom and rights of others can long remain strong and retain the confidence and respect of other nations. No nation ever loses its dignity or good standing by conciliating its differences and by exercising great patience with and consideration for the rights of other nations. . . .

If civilization is to survive the principles of the Prince of Peace must be restored.

Shattered trust between nations must be revived.

Most important of all, the will for peace on the part of peace-loving nations must express itself to the end that nations that may be tempted to violate their agreements and the rights of others will desist from such a cause. There must be positive endeavors to preserve peace. . . .

## 10

Deaf to President Roosevelt's entreaties, the bipartisan isolationist bloc in Congress continued to base its hopes for peace on the "neutrality" acts. The Nazi blitz of Poland in September, 1939, first awakened the public. Opinion polls showed that a growing majority of Americans were no longer content to skulk behind the Atlantic barrier while England and France shouldered the burden of defending democracy. Impressed by this shift in sentiment, and goaded on by the President, Congress on November 4, 1939, repealed the arms embargo, making possible the shipment of essential war materials to fascism's foes. Repeal was embodied in the Fourth Neutrality Act, which still crippled American efforts to aid those who were resisting aggressors:[10]

. . . SECTION 2. (a) Whenever the President shall have issued a proclamation under the authority of section 1 (a) it shall thereafter be unlawful for any American vessel to carry any passengers or any other articles or materials to any state named in such proclamation. . . .

(c) Whenever the President shall have issued a proclamation under the authority of section 1 (a) it shall thereafter be unlawful to export . . . any articles or materials until all right, title, and interest therein shall have been transferred to some foreign government, agency, . . . corporation, or national. . . .

SEC. 7. (a) Whenever the President shall have issued a proclamation under the authority of section 1 (a), it shall thereafter be unlawful for any person within the

United States to purchase, sell, or exchange bonds, securities, or other obligations of the government of any state named in such proclamation . . . or to make any loan or extend any credit (other than necessary credits accruing in connection with the transmission of telegraph, cable, wireless and telephone services) to any such government, political subdivision, or person.

## 11

Once the congressional dam was broken with repeal of the arms embargo, President Roosevelt was able to expand his program for aiding the democracies. During the next year his leadership won from a reluctant Congress passage of the Lend-Lease Bill, a Selective Service Act, military and naval appropriations, and other vital defense measures. Although an increasing majority of the people favored each new step, Roosevelt's policy survived congressional onslaughts by the narrowest of margins. A caustic editorial in *The New York Times* summarized the record:[11]

Since the beginning of the war there have been four votes in Congress on questions of critical importance. These votes came on repeal of the arms embargo, on passage of the lease-lend bill, on adoption of the Selective Service Act and on the proposal to extend the period of training under that legislation. Every one of these measures was of vital importance to the defense of the United States. Every one of them was of intense interest to our friends and enemies abroad: to the Latin-American nations which count on our assistance in case of trouble; to the democracies of Europe and Asia which are fighting in defense of their own freedom; to the dictators who believe that democracy is out-of-date—bewildered, disunited and ripe for plucking.

The record shows that every one of these four measures was adopted solely because the President received the support

---

[10] *Ibid.*, pp. 495, 500.

[11] *The New York Times*, August 14, 1941. Quoted with permission of *The New York Times*.

of a large majority of his own party. Not one of them would be law today if the decision had been left to the Republicans in Congress. The tally of Republican votes runs as follows:

On repeal of the arms embargo—
 Senate: 8 in favor, 15 against.
 House: 21 in favor, 143 against.
On the passage of the lease-lend bill—
 Senate: 10 in favor, 17 against.
 House: 24 in favor, 135 against.
On adoption of the Selective Service Act—
 Senate: 7 in favor, 10 against.
 House: 46 in favor, 88 against.
On extension of the period of training—
 Senate: 7 in favor, 13 against.
 House: 21 in favor, 133 against.

The Republicans in Congress have achieved, in short, a perfect record of opposition to these measures recommended by the President, by the Secretary of State and by the Army's Chief of Staff.

It is true that the Republicans in Congress have received less cooperation from the President than they were entitled to receive. He has failed to take them into his confidence as fully as he should. He has made the enormous mistake of not consulting their leaders in advance of the submission of such important measures as the lease-lend bill. It is also true that it is the duty of the Republicans to vote according to their convictions and their own best judgment, and no doubt some of them have been sincerely opposed on principle to the adoption of these measures.

But when all this has been said, it is impossible to dismiss the element of plain party politics from votes so heavily one-sided as these. Crisis or no crisis, the Republicans in Congress are still "fighting Roosevelt," still jockeying for position, still trying to write a record which they can turn to profit if and when there occurs that long-delayed "reaction" on which they have built their political hopes.

This may be legitimate strategy in time of peace. But in time of crisis the record

they are actually writing is one that will help them only if the Lindbergh-Wheeler version of the war is right and the Lindbergh-Wheeler prophecies come true. This is a fact which a great many rank-and-file Republicans throughout the country must find distasteful.

## ARSENAL OF DEMOCRACY

### 12

Frightening events bearing out previous warnings by the President of the unlimited ambitions of the aggressors and the limitless scope of modern war placed isolationists on the defensive. In an address to Congress on January 6, 1941, Roosevelt urged conversion of the United States into an arsenal of democracy. Proposing a lend-lease law, the President expressed the high purpose of assuring victory for the democracies and the Four Freedoms for all:[12]

New circumstances are constantly begetting new needs for our safety. I shall ask this Congress for greatly increased new appropriations and authorizations to carry on what we have begun.

I also ask this Congress for authority and for funds sufficient to manufacture additional munitions and war supplies of many kinds, to be turned over to those nations which are now in actual war with aggressor nations. . . .

The time is near when they will not be able to pay for them in ready cash. We cannot, and will not, tell them they must surrender, merely because of present inability to pay for the weapons which we know they must have.

I do not recommend that we make them a loan of dollars with which to pay for these weapons—a loan to be repaid in dollars. . . .

For what we sent abroad, we shall be repaid, within a reasonable time following the close of hostilities, in similar materials, or, at our option, in other goods of many

---

[12] *Peace and War: United States Foreign Policy, 1931-1941* (Washington, 1943), p. 611.

kinds which they can produce and which we need. . . .

In the future days, which we seek to make secure, we look forward to a world founded upon four essential human freedoms.

The first is freedom of speech and expression—everywhere in the world.

The second is freedom of every person to worship God in his own way—everywhere in the world.

The third is freedom from want—which, translated into world terms, means economic understandings which will secure to every nation a healthy peacetime life for its inhabitants—everywhere in the world.

The fourth is freedom from fear—which, translated into world terms, means a world-wide reduction of armaments to such a point and in such a thorough fashion that no nation will be in a position to commit an act of physical aggression against any neighbor—anywhere in the world.

## 13

The Lend-Lease Act of March 11, 1941, put an end to isolation and permitted the flow from American farms and factories of the food, planes, tanks, guns, and ammunition that allowed the hard-pressed British and Russians to hold out against the Nazi juggernaut:[13]

SECTION 3. (a) Notwithstanding the provisions of any other law, the President may, from time to time, when he deems it in the interest of national defense, authorize the Secretary of War, the Secretary of the Navy, or the head of any other department òr agency of the Government—

(1) To manufacture in arsenals, factories, and shipyards under their jurisdiction, or otherwise procure, to the extent to which funds are made available therefor, or contracts are authorized from time to time by the Congress, or both, any defense article for the government of any country whose defense the President deems vital to the defense of the United States.

(2) To sell, transfer title to, exchange, lease, lend, or otherwise dispose of, to any such government any defense article. . . .

(b) The terms and conditions upon which any such foreign government receives any aid authorized under subsection (a) shall be those which the President deems satisfactory, and the benefit to the United States may be payment or repayment in kind or property, or any other direct or indirect benefit which the President deems satisfactory. . . .

## 14

President Roosevelt's success in wringing Lend-Lease aid from Congress strengthened the Allies; but democracy could not be defended by munitions alone. Pronouncement of the Four Freedoms heartened friends of democracy everywhere. Before 1941 was over, the basic principles underlying Roosevelt's declaration were supplemented by the Atlantic Charter, signed jointly by the President and by England's prime minister, Winston Churchill. Further clarifying the issues of World War II, this dramatic document gave comfort to the oppressed and hope to fascism's foes:[14]

*Joint declaration of the President of the United States of America and the Prime Minister, Mr. Churchill, representing His Majesty's Government in the United Kingdom, being met together, deem it right to make known certain common principles in the national policies of their respective countries on which they base their hopes for a better future for the world.*

First, their countries seek no aggrandizement, territorial or other;

Second, they desire to see no territorial changes that do not accord with the freely expressed wishes of the peoples concerned;

Third, they respect the right of all peo-

---

[13] *United States Statutes at Large,* LV, 31-32.

[14] *Peace and War: United States Foreign Policy, 1931-1941* (Washington, 1943), pp. 718-719.

ples to choose the form of government under which they will live; and they wish to see sovereign rights and self-government restored to those who have been forcibly deprived of them;

Fourth, they will endeavor, with due respect for their existing obligations, to further the enjoyment by all states, great or small, victor or vanquished, of access, on equal terms, to the trade and to the raw materials of the world which are needed for their economic prosperity;

Fifth, they desire to bring about the fullest collaboration between all nations in the economic field with the object of securing, for all, improved labor standards, economic advancement, and social security;

Sixth, after the final destruction of the Nazi tyranny, they hope to see established a peace which will afford to all nations the means of dwelling in safety within their own boundaries, and which will afford assurance that all the men in all the lands may live out their lives in freedom from fear and want;

Seventh, such a peace should enable all men to traverse the high seas and oceans without hindrance;

Eighth, they believe that all of the nations of the world, for realistic as well as spiritual reasons, must come to the abandonment of the use of force. Since no future peace can be maintained if land, sea, or air armaments continue to be employed by nations which threaten, or may threaten, aggression outside of their frontiers, they believe, pending the establishment of a wider and permanent system of general security, that the disarmament of such nations is essential. They will likewise aid and encourage all other practicable measures which will lighten for peace-loving peoples the crushing burden of armaments.

## 15

With America's entry into the war after Japan's sneak attack on Pearl Harbor (December 7, 1941), the principles embodied in the Atlantic Charter were embraced by all loyal citizens. The United States, Republicans and Democrats alike agreed, could never again neglect its global responsibilities in a world united by steam and electricity. Instead, the nation must lead in building a better world, dedicated to the Four Freedoms and united through some form of international organization. None better understood this necessity than Wendell Willkie, inspiring presidential candidate of the Republican party in 1940. His best-selling book, *One World* (1943), awakened all save die-hard isolationists to America's role in the future:[15]

If our withdrawal from world affairs after the last war was a contributing factor to the present war and to the economic instability of the past twenty years—and it seems plain that it was—a withdrawal from the problems and responsibilities of the world after this war would be sheer disaster. Even our relative geographical isolation no longer exists.

At the end of the last war, not a single plane had flown across the Atlantic. Today that ocean is a mere ribbon, with airplanes making regular scheduled flights. The Pacific is only a slightly wider ribbon in the ocean of the air, and Europe and Asia are at our very doorstep.

America must choose one of three courses after this war: narrow nationalism, which inevitably means the ultimate loss of our own liberty; international imperialism, which means the sacrifice of some other nation's liberty; or the creation of a world in which there shall be an equality of opportunity for every race and every nation. I am convinced the American people will choose, by overwhelming majority, the last of these courses. To make this choice effective, we must win not only the war, but also the peace, and we must start winning it now.

To win this peace three things seem to

[15] Wendell Willkie, *One World*, pp. 202-206. Copyright, 1943, by Wendell L. Willkie. Reprinted by permission of Simon and Schuster, publishers.

me necessary—first, we must plan now for peace on a world basis; second, the world must be free, politically and economically, for nations and for men, that peace may exist in it; third, America must play an active, constructive part in freeing it and keeping its peace.

When I say that peace must be planned on a world basis, I mean quite literally that it must embrace the earth. Continents and oceans are plainly only parts of a whole, seen, as I have seen them, from the air. England and America are parts. Russia and China, Egypt, Syria and Turkey, Iraq and Iran are also parts. And it is inescapable that there can be no peace for any part of the world unless the foundations of peace are made secure throughout all parts of the world.

This cannot be accomplished by mere declarations of our leaders, as in an Atlantic Charter. Its accomplishment depends primarily upon acceptance by the peoples of the world. For if the failure to reach international understanding after the last war taught us anything it taught us this: even if war leaders apparently agree upon generalized principles and slogans while the war is being fought, when they come to the peace table they make their own interpretations of their previous declarations. So unless today, while the war is being fought, the people of the United States and of Great Britain, of Russia and of China, and of all the other United Nations, fundamentally agree on their purposes, fine and idealistic expressions of hope such as those of the Atlantic Charter will live merely to mock us as have Mr. Wilson's Fourteen Points. The Four Freedoms will not be accomplished by the declarations of those momentarily in power. They will become real only if the people of the world forge them into actuality.

When I say that in order to have peace this world must be free, I am only reporting that a great process has started which no man—certainly not Hitler—can

stop. Men and women all over the world are on the march, physically, intellectually, and spiritually. After centuries of ignorant and dull compliance, hundreds of millions of people in eastern Europe and Asia have opened the books. Old fears no longer frighten them. They are no longer willing to be Eastern slaves for Western profits. They are beginning to know that men's welfare throughout the world is interdependent. They are resolved, as we must be, that there is no more place for imperialism within their own society than in the society of nations. The big house on the hill surrounded by mud huts has lost its awesome charm.

Our Western world and our presumed supremacy are now on trial. Our boasting and our big talk leave Asia cold. Men and women in Russia and China and in the Middle East are conscious now of their own potential strength. They are coming to know that many of the decisions about the future of the world lie in their hands. And they intend that these decisions shall leave the peoples of each nation free from foreign domination, free for economic, social, and spiritual growth.

Economic freedom is as important as political freedom. Not only must people have access to what other peoples produce, but their own products must in turn have some chance of reaching men all over the world. There will be no peace, there will be no real development, there will be no economic stability, unless we find the method by which we can begin to break down the unnecessary trade barriers hampering the flow of goods. Obviously, the sudden and uncompromising abolition of tariffs after the war could only result in disaster. But obviously, also, one of the freedoms we are fighting for is freedom to trade. I know there are many men, particularly in America, where our standard of living exceeds the standard of living in the rest of the world, who are genuinely alarmed at such a prospect, who believe that any such process will only lessen our own standard of living. The reverse of this is true.

Many reasons may be assigned for the amazing economic development of the United States. The abundance of our national resources, the freedom of our political institutions, and the character of our population have all undoubtedly contributed. But in my judgment the greatest factor has been the fact that by the happenstance of good fortune there was created here in America the largest area in the world in which there were no barriers to the exchange of goods and ideas.

And I should like to point out to those who are fearful one inescapable fact. In view of the astronomical figures our national debt will assume by the end of this war, and in a world reduced in size by industrial and transportation developments, even our present standard of living in America cannot be maintained unless the exchange of goods flows more freely over the whole world. It is also inescapably true that to raise the standard of living of any man anywhere in the world is to raise the standard of living by some slight degree of every man everywhere in the world.

Finally, when I say that this world demands the full participation of a self-confident America, I am only passing on an invitation which the peoples of the East have given us. They would like the United States and the other United Nations to be partners with them in this grand adventure. They want us to join them in creating a new society of independent nations, free alike of the economic injustices of the West and the political malpractices of the East. But as partners in that great new combination they want us neither hesitant, incompetent, nor afraid. They want partners who will not hesitate to speak out for the correction of injustice anywhere in the world.

Our allies in the East know that we intend to pour out our resources in this war. But they expect us now—not after the war—to use the enormous power of our giving to promote liberty and justice. Other peoples, not yet fighting, are waiting no less eagerly for us to accept the most challenging opportunity of all history —the chance to help create a new society in which men and women the world around can live and grow invigorated by independence and freedom.

## 16

World War II united Americans as never before; but the same patriotic urgency made the public impatient if strikes threatened to interrupt production. The bipartisan conservative bloc in Congress seized the opportunity to assail the Wagner Act. Virtually all unions lived up to a no-strike pledge made at the beginning of hostilities, but John L. Lewis, the boss of the United Mine Workers, took a different attitude. A confirmed isolationist and "Roosevelt-hater," he called a number of strikes during the spring of 1943 and threatened another even more crippling during the fall. His action aroused such antilabor sentiment that congressional conservatives successfully passed the Smith-Connally Labor Disputes Act (June 25, 1943) over Roosevelt's veto:[16]

SECTION 3. Section 9 of the Selective Training and Service Act of 1940 is hereby amended by adding at the end thereof the following new paragraph:

"The power of the President under the foregoing provisions of this section to take immediate possession of any plant upon a failure to comply with any such provisions, and the authority granted by this section for the use and operation by the United States or in its interests of any plant of which possession is so taken, shall also apply as hereinafter provided to any plant, mine, or facility equipped for the manufacture, production, or mining of any articles or materials which may be required for the war effort or which may be useful in connection therewith. Such power and authority may be exercised by

---

[16] *United States Statutes at Large*, LVII, 163-168.

the President through such department or agency of the Government as he may designate, and may be exercised with respect to any such plant, mine, or facility whenever the President finds, after investigation, and proclaims that there is an interruption of the operation of such plant, mine, or facility as a result of a strike or other labor disturbance, that the war effort will be unduly impeded or delayed by such interruption, and that the exercise of such power and authority is necessary to insure the operation of such plant, mine, or facility in the interest of the war effort.". . .

Sec. 6. (a) Whenever any plant, mine, or facility is in the possession of the United States, it shall be unlawful for any person (1) to coerce, instigate, induce, conspire with, or encourage any person, to interfere, by lock-out, strike, slow-down, or other interruption, with the operation of such plant, mine, or facility, or (2) to aid any such lock-out, strike, slow-down, or other interruption interfering with the operation of such plant, mine, or facility by giving direction or guidance in the conduct of such interruption, or by providing funds for the conduct or direction thereof or for the payment of strike, unemployment, or other benefits to those participating therein. No individual shall be deemed to have violated the provisions of this section by reason only of his having ceased work or having refused to continue to work or to accept employment. . . .

Sec. 8. (a) In order that the President may be apprised of labor disputes which threaten seriously to interrupt war production, and in order that employees may have an opportunity to express themselves, free from restraint or coercion, as to whether they will permit such interruptions in wartime—

(1) The representative of the employees of a war contractor, shall give to the Secretary of Labor, the National War Labor Board, and the National Labor Relations Board, notice of any such labor dispute involving such contractor and employees, together with a statement of the issues giving rise thereto.

(2) For not less than thirty days after any notice under paragraph (1) is given, the contractor and his employees shall continue production under all the conditions which prevailed when such dispute arose, except as they may be modified by mutual agreement or by decision of the National War Labor Board.

(3) On the thirtieth day after notice under paragraph (1) is given by the representative of the employees, unless such dispute has been settled, the National Labor Relations Board shall forthwith take a secret ballot of the employees in the plant, plants, mine, mines, facility, facilities, bargaining unit, or bargaining units, as the case may be, with respect to which the dispute is applicable on the question whether they will permit any such interruption of war production. The National Labor Relations Board shall include on the ballot a concise statement of the major issues involved in the dispute and of the efforts being made and the facilities being utilized for the settlement of such dispute. The National Labor Relations Board shall by order forthwith certify the results of such balloting, and such results shall be open to public inspection. The National Labor Relations Board may provide for preparing such ballot and distributing it to the employees at any time after such notice has been given. . . .

Sec. 9. Section 313 of the Federal Corrupt Practices Act, 1925, is amended to read as follows:

"Sec. 313. It is unlawful for any national bank, or any corporation organized by authority of any law of Congress, to make a contribution in connection with any election to any political officer, or for any corporation whatever, or any labor organization to make a contribution in connection with any election at which

Presidential and Vice Presidential electors or a Senator or Representative in, or a Delegate or Resident Commissioner to Congress are to be voted for, or for any candidate, political committee, or other person to accept or receive any contribution prohibited by this section."

## 17

Buckling to the task of achieving an orderly world, the Allied nations forced the aggressors into retreat in 1943 and went on to victory after victory in 1944 and 1945. Allied triumph was due to no one factor: the unexpected strength of Russia, the inspired might of free peoples, and the miracle of production within the United States all contributed. The importance of the last was revealed in 1944 by the report of a congressional investigating committee headed by Senator Harry S. Truman:[17]

War production is now firmly established on a successful working basis. Our armies are active on every fighting front, equipped with American-made weapons and secure in the knowledge that an uninterrupted flow of materials is assured. In contrast to the First World War, in which our own troops abroad obtained from our allies many of the most important items of equipment, including substantially all of their artillery and aircraft, we are supplying in this war substantially all of our own needs and an important portion of the needs of all of the other United Nations. . . .

Industry, labor, and Government deserve credit for the job of providing war matériel of excellent quality and quantity worthy of the use which the fighting forces are giving it.

The figures on production have properly been made public. In addition to guns, tanks, and regular equipment and clothing of all sorts for more than 10,000,000 men, we produced in 1941, 1942, and 1943, 153,061 airplanes, 746 combatant naval vessels, 1,899 Liberty ships with a total deadweight capacity of 20,450,800 tons, 702 commercial ships of other types, 1,567,940 military trucks, and 28,286 subsidiary naval vessels, including 23,867 landing craft.

We have constructed housing and training facilities for more than 10,000,000 men, and airfields and bases in all quarters of the world.

We have constructed nearly 20 billion dollars worth of the best and most modern plant facilities in the world equipped with the finest machine tools that can be designed. These plants are producing vast quantities of new materials, such as butadiene, synthetic rubber, and 100-octane gasoline, and have greatly increased our former capacity to produce basic commodities such as alloy steels, aluminum and magnesium. With them we can make fabulous quantities of engines, gears, turbines, valves, bearings and all the other articles necessary for mass production of the most complicated engines of destruction that man can devise.

To make all this possible our workers engaged in manufacturing, mining, and agriculture contributed nearly 45 percent more man-days of work in 1943 than in 1939, despite the fact that more than 10,000,000 men were withdrawn from the labor pool for the armed forces. In manufacturing alone, our workmen contributed 89.6 percent more man-days in 1943 than in 1939.

This astounding performance exceeds anything of its kind ever achieved in the history of the world. The results obtained are the best answer to the critics of the home front. They do not indicate perfection, but they do evidence accomplishment of a high order.

All Americans who have participated can be justly proud, because the success is due to the accumulated efforts of the millions of people who have each done their share rather than to any miraculous planning of a few experts at the top. Women in particular deserve credit for filling the huge gap created by manpower

---

[17] *Senate Reports,* 78th Cong., 2nd Sess., No. 10, Pt. 16 (1944), pp. 2-4, 12.

requirements of the armed services. Older men who had retired from active work have returned to their jobs and because of their experience are among the most valuable of workers. The job that has been done not only assures that victory will be won, but it assures that it will be won more quickly and with fewer casualties. Our armed forces have more and better equipment than our foes.

This committee has noted many decisions that were hastily and sometimes foolishly made, and many mistakes that were continued long after they should have been rectified. The committee unhesitatingly has urged corrective action to be taken. There are few informed citizens, whether they be soldiers, workmen, or businessmen, who have not personally seen instances of waste and inefficiency....

In presenting these facts, the committee does not intend in any way to condone the many mistakes that have been made. The war program has been burdened by many incompetent, selfish, and even dishonest men in all ranks of industry, labor, and government, and the committee frequently has noted a stubborn refusal, usually in isolated although important instances, to profit by the mistakes of the past. The committee has been and will continue to be insistent upon corrective action....

It is self-evident that the largest possible portion of the economy should be devoted to war production up to the point where the actual needs of the armed services are filled. Once the requirements of the fighting forces are met, the Army and Navy can best be supported by strengthening the home economy. This does not entail waste or soft, luxurious living.

The military has had trouble understanding this proposition. Prior to December 1941, it failed to proceed quickly enough to convert industry from civilian to war production, in part because of the fragmentary and indefinite understanding of what they would need and how to go about getting it. Thereafter it showed too

great zeal to curtail the civilian economy to bare necessities. The guiding principle should be curtailment where, but only where, the military benefits exceed the detriment resulting from disarrangement of the economy.

From its inception early in 1941, this committee sought to create an awareness of the necessity of converting some of our basic industries from civilian to war production in order to conserve materials that were going to be scarce, and in order to get mass war production sooner. However, this committee never favored carrying this policy to extremes by cutting civilian production beyond the point that would produce tangible returns in the form of increased war production.

Had the advice of the military in 1942 to eliminate the production of all items except bare necessities been followed, it is very doubtful that we would have been able to maintain our transportation system and to provide machinery and equipment for agriculture. The confusion and loss that would have followed would have been very great.

## UNITED NATIONS

### 18

Statesmen of the caliber of Willkie shared with the President the deep conviction that peace must be secured and organized on a global basis that men might be free. Mindful of the stubborn opposition in the Senate that defeated the League of Nations, a bipartisan group launched a drive during 1943 to commit Congress to the support of an international organization. Token of the rising public demand, the Fulbright and Connally resolutions passed the House and Senate in September and November, 1943:[18]

#### The Fulbright Resolution

*Resolved* by the House of Representatives (the Senate concurring), That the Congress hereby expresses itself as favoring the creation of appropriate interna-

---

[18] *Congressional Record*, 78th Cong., 1st Sess., pp. 7725, 9222.

tional machinery with power adequate to establish and to maintain a just and lasting peace, among the nations of the world, and as favoring participation by the United States therein through its constitutional processes.

### The Connally Resolution

*Resolved,* That the war against all our enemies be waged until complete victory is achieved.

That the United States cooperate with its comrades-in-arms in securing a just and honorable peace.

That the United States, acting through its constitutional processes, join free and sovereign nations in the establishment and maintenance of international authority with power to prevent aggression and to preserve the peace of the world.

That the Senate recognize the necessity of there being established at the earliest practicable date a general international organization, based on the principle of the sovereign equality of all peace-loving states, and open to membership by all such states, large and small, for the maintenance of international peace and security.

## 19

With American support assured, planners felt free to blueprint a world organization. At a conference in Moscow during the autumn of 1943, the foreign secretaries of England, Russia, and the United States united to endorse "a general international organization, based on the principle of the sovereign equality of all peace-loving nations." Russian delegates attended the Dumbarton Oaks Conference in the United States in 1944, where a blueprint was made; and in February, 1945, Roosevelt, Churchill, and Stalin met at Yalta to consider the problems of the fast-approaching peace. Among the important results of the Yalta Conference was an invitation to the Allied Powers, asking them to meet at San Francisco to draft a constitution for the United Nations:[19]

[19] Department of State, *Bulletin,* XII, No. 295 (February 18, 1945), 214-215.

### The Occupation and Control of Germany

We have agreed on common policies and plans for enforcing the unconditional surrender terms which we shall impose together on Nazi Germany after German armed resistance has been finally crushed. These terms will not be made known until the final defeat of Germany has been accomplished. Under the agreed plan, the forces of the three powers will each occupy a separate zone of Germany. Coordinated administration and control has been provided for under the plan through a central control commission consisting of the Supreme Commanders of the three powers with headquarters in Berlin. It has been agreed that France should be invited by the three powers, if she should so desire, to take over a zone of occupation, and to participate as a fourth member of the control commission. The limits of the French zone will be agreed by the four governments concerned through their representatives on the European Advisory Commission. . . .

### United Nations Conference

We are resolved upon the earliest possible establishment with our allies of a general international organization to maintain peace and security. We believe that this is essential, both to prevent aggression and to remove the political, economic and social causes of war through the close and continuing collaboration of all peace-loving peoples.

The foundations were laid at Dumbarton Oaks. On the important question of voting procedure, however, agreement was not there reached. The present Conference has been able to resolve this difficulty.

We have agreed that a conference of United Nations should be called to meet at San Francisco in the United States on April 25, 1945, to prepare the charter of such an organization, along the lines proposed in the informal conversations at Dumbarton Oaks. . . .

*Declaration on Liberated Europe*

The Premier of the Union of Soviet Socialist Republics, the Prime Minister of the United Kingdom, and the President of the United States of America have consulted with each other in the common interests of the peoples of their countries and those of liberated Europe. They jointly declare their mutual agreement to concert during the temporary period of instability in liberated Europe the policies of their three governments in assisting the peoples liberated from the domination of Nazi Germany and the peoples of the former Axis satellite states of Europe to solve by democratic means their pressing political and economic problems.

The establishment of order in Europe and the rebuilding of national economic life must be achieved by processes which will enable the liberated peoples to destroy the last vestiges of Nazism and Fascism and to create democratic institutions of their own choice. This is a principle of the Atlantic Charter—the right of all peoples to choose the form of government under which they will live—the restoration of sovereign rights and self-government to those peoples who have been forcibly deprived of them by the aggressor nations.

To foster the conditions in which the liberated peoples may exercise these rights, the three governments will jointly assist the people in any European liberated state or former Axis satellite state in Europe where in their judgment conditions require (A) to establish conditions of internal peace; (B) to carry out emergency measures for the relief of distressed peoples; (C) to form interim governmental authorities broadly representative of all democratic elements in the population and pledged to the earliest possible establishment through free elections of governments responsive to the will of the people; and (D) to facilitate where necessary the holding of such elections. . . .

## 20

The deadlock on voting procedure was resolved at Yalta by a secret agreement on a Big Power veto, not announced until the month before the San Francisco Conference:[20]

1. Each member of the Security Council should have one vote.
2. Decisions of the Security Council on procedural matters should be made by an affirmative vote of seven members.
3. Decisions of the Security Council on all matters should be made by an affirmative vote of seven members, including the concurring votes of the permanent members. . . .

## 21

Pursuant to the summons issued at Yalta, delegates from the Allied Powers, large and small, assembled at San Francisco in April, 1945. Despite the disagreements usual in the making of a peace, they eventually settled upon the Charter of the United Nations, which was subsequently ratified by the Senate of the United States without reservations. Although President Roosevelt, principal architect of the global enterprise, did not live to see its acceptance, the United Nations Participation Act passed the Senate by a vote of 65 to 7 and the House by 344 to 15, and was signed by President Truman on December 20, 1945:[21]

SECTION 2. (a) The President, by and with the advice and consent of the Senate, shall appoint a representative of the United States at the seat of the United Nations who shall have the rank and status of envoy extraordinary and ambassador plenipotentiary, shall receive annual compensation of $20,000, and shall hold office at the pleasure of the President. Such representative shall represent the United States in the Security Council of the United Nations and shall perform such other functions in connection with the participation of the United States in the United Nations

---

[20] *Ibid.*, No. 298 (March 11, 1945), p. 394.
[21] *United States Statutes at Large,* LIX, 619-621.

as the President may from time to time direct. . . .

(c) The President, by and with the advice and consent of the Senate, shall designate from time to time to attend a specified session or specified sessions of the General Assembly of the United Nations not to exceed five representatives of the United States and such number of alternatives as he may determine consistent with the rules of procedure of the General Assembly. . . .

SEC. 3. The representatives provided for in section 2 hereof, when representing the United States in the respective organs and agencies of the United Nations, shall, at all times, act in accordance with the instructions of the President transmitted by the Secretary of State. . . .

SEC. 4. The President shall, from time to time as occasion may require, but not less than once a year, make reports to the Congress of the activities of the United Nations and of the participation of the United States therein. . . .

SEC. 5. (a) Notwithstanding the provisions of any other law, whenever the United States is called upon by the Security Council to apply measures which said Council has decided, pursuant to article 41 of said Charter, are to be employed to give effect to its decisions under said Charter, the President may, to the extent necessary to apply such measures, through any agency which he may designate, and under such orders, rules, and regulations as may be prescribed by him, investigate, regulate, or prohibit, in whole or in part, economic relations or rail, sea, air, postal, telegraphic, radio, and other means of communication between any foreign country or any national thereof or any person therein and the United States or any person subject to the jurisdiction thereof, or involving any property subject to the jurisdiction of the United States. . . .

SEC. 6. The President is authorized to negotiate a special agreement or agreements with the Security Council which shall be subject to the approval of the Congress by appropriate Act or joint resolution, providing for the numbers and types of armed forces, their degree of readiness and general location, and the nature of facilities and assistance, including rights of passage, to be made available to the Security Council on its call for the purpose of maintaining international peace and security in accordance with article 43 of said Charter. The President shall not be deemed to require the authorization of the Congress to make available to the Security Council on its call in order to take action under article 42 of said Charter and pursuant to such special agreement or agreements the armed forces, facilities, or assistance provided for therein: *Provided,* That nothing herein contained shall be construed as an authorization to the President by the Congress to make available to the Security Council for such purpose armed forces, facilities or assistance in addition to the forces, facilities, and assistance provided for in such special agreement or agreements.

The gigantic conflict which had swept virtually the whole human race into global war came to an end in 1945 just as the die was being cast for American participation as a member of the United Nations. Germany capitulated on May 5, 1945; on August 6 the first atomic bomb fell on Japan; eight days later the Nipponese bowed in unconditional surrender. Statesmen faced again, as in 1919 but in more formidable circumstances, the problem of peace or power—a peace among equals or a peace based on power. Nor was that all; war-weary victors now shouldered responsibility for occupied countries, the problem of Germany, restoration of self-government and economic recovery—the Herculean tasks of world reconstruction.

# WORLD RECONSTRUCTION

## 1945–1950

Victory in World War II left a legacy of clashes of nationalism, generating fears of a war to come. Although the hope of disarmament faded, the world vision of the American people did not die. Nor did postwar nationalism and a renewed Red scare indicate duplication of the 1920's. In both postwar eras there were people who groped vainly for a "normalcy" that never was and never would be; yet the step backward was less marked after World War II than twenty years before. Reaction produced no widespread vigor in the revived Ku Klux Klan, no such flare-up of anti-Semitism or lynch law, no such ruthless smashing of labor unions. And in 1948 the Roosevelt ideal of positive government for a welfare state showed continued vitality when Harry S. Truman won re-election by campaigning for a "Fair Deal" that in many ways went beyond the original "New Deal." Above all else, the 1940's witnessed no wholesale return to isolation; for the American people had finally and painfully learned that their fate was the world's, and the world's fate was theirs.

## MILITARY GOVERNMENT

### 1

Upon the strongest power rested the greatest responsibility. Victory in 1945 brought the United States face to face with the staggering problem of reconstruction. Not only was half the world devastated by the most destructive war in history, but defeated enemies equally with victors were in need of rehabilitation. Germans, Italians, and Japanese had lived for a generation under dictators whose absolutism stifled initiative and glorified obedience; now they must be reintroduced to the principles of democracy. Here indeed was a test of global sanity. The enormity of the task was soon illustrated in Japan. There, under the military occupation directed by General Douglas MacArthur, the United States not only spent American dollars freely to rebuild the nation physically, but launched a precarious experiment in democratic education. Institutions for self-government, the subordination of the emperor, freedom of religious worship, and the dissolution of industrial monopolies were among the specifications to fit the Japanese into the One World of the future. Typical of the occupation decrees was one of October 4, 1945, restoring civil liberties to the people:[1]

1. In order to remove restrictions on political, civil and religious liberties and dis-

crimination on grounds of race, nationality, creed or political opinion, the Imperial Japanese Government will:

a. Abrogate and immediately suspend the operation of all provisions of all laws, decrees, orders, ordinances and regulations which:

(1) Establish or maintain restrictions on freedom of thought, of religion, of assembly and of speech, including the unrestricted discussion of the Emperor, the Imperial Institution and the Imperial Japanese Government.

(2) Establish or maintain restrictions on the collection and dissemination of information.

(3) By their terms or their applications, operate unequally in favor of or against any person by reason of race, nationality, creed or political opinion. . . .

c. Release immediately all persons now detained, imprisoned, under "protection or surveillance," or whose freedom is restricted in any other manner who have been placed in that state of detention, imprisonment, "protection and surveillance," or restriction of freedom:

(1) Under the enactments referred to in Para 1 a and b above.

(2) Without charge.

(3) By charging them technically with a minor offense, when, in reality, the

<hr>

[1] Department of State, *Bulletin,* XIII, No. 332 (November 4, 1945), 730-732.

reason for detention, imprisonment, "Protection and Surveillance," or restriction of freedom, was because of their thought, speech, religion, political beliefs, or assembly. The release of all such persons will be accomplished by 10 October 1945.

d. Abolish all organizations or agencies created to carry out the provisions of the enactments referred to in Para 1 a and b above and that part of, or functions of, other offices or subdivisions of other civil departments or organs which supplement or assist them in the execution of such provisions. These include, but are not limited to:

(1) All secret police organs.

(2) Those departments in the Ministry of Home Affairs, such as the Bureau of Police, charged with supervision of publications, supervision of public meetings and organizations, censorship of motion pictures, and such other departments concerned with the control of thought, speech, religion or assembly.

(3) Those departments, such as the special higher police (Tokubetsu, Koto, Keisatsu Bu), in the Tokyo Metropolitan Police, the Osaka Metropolitan Police, and other Metropolitan Police, the Police of the Territorial Administration of Hokkaido and the various prefectural police charged with supervision of publication, supervision of public meetings and organizations, censorship of motion pictures, and such other departments concerned with the control of thought, speech, religion or assembly.

(4) Those departments, such as the Protection and Surveillance Commission, and all Protection and Surveillance Stations responsible thereto, under the Ministry of Justice charged with protection and surveillance and control of thought, speech, religion, or assembly.

e. Remove from office and employment the Minister of Home Affairs, the Chief of the Bureau of Police of the Ministry of Home Affairs, the Chief of the Tokyo Metropolitan Police Board, the Chief of Osaka Metropolitan Police Board, the Chief of any other Metropolitan Police, the Chief of Police of the Territorial Administration of Hokkaido, the Chiefs of each prefectural police department, the entire personnel of the special higher police of all metropolitan, territorial and prefectural police departments, the guiding and protecting officials and all other personnel of the Protection and Surveillance Commission and of the Protection and Surveillance Stations. None of the above persons will be reappointed to any position under the Ministry of Home Affairs, the Ministry of Justice or any police organ in Japan. Any of the above persons whose assistance is required to accomplish the provisions of this directive will be retained until the directive is accomplished and then dismissed.

f. Prohibit any further activity of police officials, members of police forces, and other government, national or local, officials or employees which is related to the enactments referred to in Para 1 a and b above and to the organs and functions abolished by Para 1 d above.

g. Prohibit the physical punishment and mistreatment of all persons detained, imprisoned, or under protection and surveillance under any and all Japanese enactments, laws, decrees, orders, ordinances and regulations. All such persons will receive at all times ample sustenance.

h. Ensure the security and preservation of all records and any and all other materials of the organs abolished in Para 1 d. These records may be used to accomplish the provisions of this directive, but will not be destroyed, removed, or tampered with in any way. . . .

2. All officials and subordinates of the Japanese Government affected by the terms of this directive will be held personally responsible and strictly accountable for compliance with and adherence to the spirit and letter of this directive.

## 2

America's position in Japan was clearly defined, for its individual conquest of the Japanese gave ascendancy to its military government after victory. The rehabilitation of Germany, occupied and held jointly by the armed forces of England, Russia, and the United States, proved more difficult. The postwar fate of that nation was decided at the Potsdam Conference, held in late July, 1946, with President Truman, Prime Minister Attlee, and Generalissimo Stalin in attendance:[2]

### A. Political Principles

1. In accordance with the agreement on control machinery in Germany, supreme authority in Germany is exercised, on instructions from their respective Governments, by the commanders in chief of the armed forces of the United States of America, the United Kingdom, the Union of Soviet Socialist Republics and the French Republic, each in his own zone of occupation, and also jointly, in matters affecting Germany as a whole, in their capacity as members of the Control Council.

2. So far as is practicable, there shall be uniformity of treatment of the German population throughout Germany.

3. The purposes of the occupation of Germany by which the Control Council shall be guided are:

(I) The complete disarmament and demilitarization of Germany and the elimination or control of all German industry that could be used for military production. To these ends:

(a) All German land, naval and air forces, the SS, SA, SD and Gestapo, with all their organizations, staffs and institutions, including the General Staff, the Officers' Corps, Reserve Corps, military schools, war veterans' organizations and all other military and semi-military organizations, together with all clubs and associations which serve to keep alive the military tradition in Germany, shall be

completely and finally abolished in such manner as permanently to prevent the revival or reorganization of German militarism and Nazism;

(b) All arms, ammunition and implements of war and all specialized facilities for their production shall be held at the disposal of the Allies or destroyed. The maintenance and production of all aircraft and all arms, ammunition and implements of war shall be prevented.

(II) To convince the German people that they have suffered a total military defeat and that they cannot escape responsibility for what they have brought upon themselves, since their own ruthless warfare and the fanatical Nazi resistance have destroyed German economy and made chaos and suffering inevitable.

(III) To destroy the National Socialist party and its affiliated and supervised organizations, to dissolve all Nazi institutions, to insure that they are not revived in any form and to prevent all Nazi and militarist activity or propaganda.

(IV) To prepare for the eventual reconstruction of German political life on a democratic basis and for eventual peaceful cooperation in international life by Germany.

4. All Nazi laws which provide the basis of the Hitler regime or established discriminations on grounds of race, creed, or political opinion shall be abolished. No such discriminations, whether legal, administrative or otherwise, shall be tolerated.

5. War criminals and those who have participated in planning or carrying out Nazi enterprises involving or resulting in atrocities or war crimes shall be arrested and brought to judgment. Nazi leaders, influential Nazi supporters and high officials of Nazi organizations and institutions and any other persons dangerous to the occupation or its objectives shall be arrested and interned.

6. All members of the Nazi party who

[2] *Ibid.*, No. 319 (August 5, 1945), pp. 154-157.

have been more than nominal participants in its activities and all other persons hostile to Allied purposes shall be removed from public and semi-public office and from positions of responsibility in important private undertakings. Such persons shall be replaced by persons who, by their political and moral qualities, are deemed capable of assisting in developing genuine democratic institutions in Germany.

7. German education shall be so controlled as completely to eliminate Nazi and militarist doctrines and to make possible the successful development of democratic ideas.

8. The judicial system will be reorganized in accordance with the principles of democracy, of justice under law and of equal rights for all citizens without distinction of race, nationality or religion.

9. The administration in Germany should be directed toward the decentralization of the political structure and the development of local responsibility. To this end:

(I) Local self-government shall be restored throughout Germany on democratic principles and in particular through elective councils as rapidly as is consistent with military security and the purposes of military occupation;

(II) All democratic political parties with rights of assembly and of public discussion shall be allowed and encouraged throughout Germany;

(III) Representative and elective principles shall be introduced into regional, provincial and state (Land) administration as rapidly as may be justified by the successful application of these principles in local self-government;

(IV) For the time being, no central German Government shall be established. Notwithstanding this, however, certain essential central German administrative departments, headed by state secretaries shall be established, particularly in the fields of finance, transport, communications, foreign trade and industry. Such

departments will act under the direction of the Control Council.

10. Subject to the necessity for maintaining military security, freedom of speech, press and religion shall be permitted, and institutions shall be respected. Subject likewise to the maintenance of military security, the formation of free trade unions shall be permitted.

B. Economic Principles

11. In order to eliminate Germany's war potential, the production of arms, ammunition and implements of war as well as all types of aircraft and sea-going ships shall be prohibited and prevented. Production of metals, chemicals, machinery and other items that are directly necessary to a war economy shall be rigidly controlled and restricted to Germany's approved postwar peacetime needs to meet the objectives stated in Paragraph 15. Productive capacity not needed for permitted production shall be removed in accordance with the reparations plan recommended by the Allied Commission on reparations and approved by the Governments concerned, or if not removed, shall be destroyed.

12. At the earliest practicable date, the German economy shall be decentralized for the purpose of eliminating the present excessive concentration of economic power as exemplified in particular by cartels, syndicates, trusts and other monopolistic arrangements. . . .

15. Allied controls shall be imposed upon the German economy, but only to the extent necessary:

(a) To carry out programs of industrial disarmament and demilitarization, of reparations, and of approved exports and imports.

(b) To assure the production and maintenance of goods and services required to meet the needs of the occupying forces and displaced persons in Germany and essential to maintain in Germany average living standards not exceeding the average of the standards of living of European countries. (European countries means all European countries, excluding the 'United Kingdom and the U.S.S.R.)

(c) To insure in the manner determined by the Central Council the equitable distribution of essential commodities between the several zones so as to produce a balanced economy throughout Germany and reduce the need for imports.

(d) To control German industry and all economic and financial international transactions, including exports and imports, with the aim of preventing Germany from developing a war potential and of achieving the other objectives named herein.

(e) To control all German public and private scientific bodies, research and experimental institutions, laboratories, etc., connected with economic activities.

16. In the imposition and maintenance of economic controls established by the Control Council, German administrative machinery shall be created and the German authorities shall be required to the fullest extent practicable to proclaim and assume administration of such controls. Thus it should be brought home to the German people that the responsibility for the administration of such controls and any breakdown in these controls will rest with themselves. Any German controls which may run counter to the objectives of occupation will be prohibited. . . .

19. Payment of reparations should leave enough resources to enable the German people to subsist without external assistance. In working out the economic balance of Germany, the necessary means must be provided to pay for imports approved by the Control Council in Germany. The proceeds of exports from current production and stocks shall be available in the first place for payment for such imports.

The above clause will not apply to the equipment and products referred to in Paragraphs 4 (a) and 4 (b) of the reparations agreement.

*III. Reparations from Germany*

1. Reparation claims of the U.S.S.R. shall be met by removals from the zone of Germany occupied by the U.S.S.R. and from appropriate German external assets.

2. The U.S.S.R. undertakes to settle the reparation claims of Poland from its own share of reparations.

3. The reparation claims of the United States, the United Kingdom and other countries entitled to reparations shall be met from the Western zones and from appropriate German external assets.

4. In addition to the reparations to be taken by the U.S.S.R. from its own zone of occupation, the U.S.S.R. shall receive additionally from the Western zones:

(a) 15 per cent of such usable and complete industrial capital equipment, in the first place from the metallurgical, chemical and machine manufacturing industries as is unnecessary for the German peace economy and should be removed from the Western zones of Germany, in exchange for an equivalent value of food, coal, potash, zinc, timber, clay products, petroleum products and such other commodities as may be agreed upon.

(b) 10 per cent of such industrial capital equipment as is unnecessary for the German peace economy and should be removed from the Western zones, to be transferred to the Soviet Government on reparations account without payment or exchange of any kind in return.

Removals of equipment as provided in (a) and (b) above shall be made simultaneously.

# COLD WAR

## 3

Science and technology destroyed old geographical barriers upon which peace-loving countries had relied for defense. Even before clashes in sessions of the United Nations revealed the chasm between the Russian idea of economic democracy and the Western idea of political democracy, Americans in high places shared the growing fear and distrust that spread over the world, eventually to result in diplomatic crises amounting to a "cold war." General Marshall's report at the end of hostilities in 1945 drew the conclusion that security must be based upon military strength:[3]

. . . The Nation is just emerging from one of its greatest crises. This generation of Americans can still remember the black days of 1942 when the Japanese conquered all of Malaysia, occupied Burma, and threatened India while the German armies approached the Volga and the Suez. In those hours Germany and Japan came so close to complete domination of the world that we do not yet realize how thin the thread of Allied survival had been stretched.

In good conscience this Nation can take little credit for its part in staving off disaster in those critical days. It is certain that the refusal of the British and Russian peoples to accept what appeared to be inevitable defeat was the great factor in the salvage of our civilization. Of almost equal importance was the failure of the enemy to make the most of the situation. . . .

There can be no doubt that the greed and the mistakes of the war-making nations as well as the heroic stands of the British and Soviet peoples saved the United States a war on her own soil. The crisis had come and passed at Stalingrad and El Alamein before this Nation was able to gather sufficient resources to participate in the fight in a determining manner. Had the U.S.S.R. and the British Army of the Nile been defeated in 1942, as they well might if the Germans, Japanese, and Italians had better coordinated their plans and resources and successive operations, we should have stood today in the western hemisphere confronted by enemies who controlled a greater part of the world.

[3] Biennial Report of the Chief of Staff of the Army, printed in *United States News*, XIX, No. 16 (Extra Number, October 10, 1945), 1, 4, 6.

Our close approach to that terrifying situation should have a sobering influence on Americans for generations to come. Yet, this is only a prelude of what can be expected so long as there are nations on earth capable of waging total war.

. . . There is no easy way to safeguard the nation or preserve the peace. In the immediate years ahead the United Nations will unquestionably devote their sincere energies to the effort to establish a lasting peace. To my mind there is now greater chance of success in this effort than ever before in history. Certainly the implications of atomic explosion will spur men of judgment as they have never before been pressed to seek a method whereby the peoples of earth can live in peace and justice.

However, these hopes are by no means certainties. If man does find the solution for world peace it will be the most revolutionary reversal of his record we have ever known. Our own responsibilities to these efforts are great. Our diplomacy must be wise and it must be strong. Nature tends to abhor weakness. The principle of the survival of the fit is generally recognized. If our diplomacy is not backed by a sound security policy, it is, in my opinion, forecast to failure. We have tried since the birth of our nation to promote our love of peace by a display of weakness. This course has failed us utterly, cost us millions of lives and billions of treasure. The reasons are quite understandable. The world does not seriously regard the desires of the weak. Weakness presents too great a temptation to the strong, particularly to the bully who schemes for wealth and power.

We must, if we are to realize the hopes we may now dare have for lasting peace, enforce our will for peace with strength. We must make it clear to the potential gangsters of the world that if they dare break our peace they will do so at their great peril.

This Nation's destiny clearly lies in a

sound permanent security policy. In the War Department's proposals there are two essentials: (1) Intense scientific research and development; (2) a permanent peacetime citizen army. I will discuss these essentials in detail later in this report. The importance of scientific research is the most obvious to the civilian, but the importance of a peacetime citizen army based on universal military training is of greater importance, in my opinion. . . .

## 4

Inevitable conflicts arising out of the administration of divided Germany contributed to the ill feeling that developed among the former allies during the late 1940's. Traditionally suspicious of communist Russia, the Western Powers viewed with alarm that nation's creation of "satellite" states and encouragement of communism throughout Europe. Many Americans became convinced that Russia's totalitarianism threatened democratic institutions in the 1940's, as had Germany's in the 1930's. This feeling was intensified when English and American attempts to restore a monarchical regime in Greece led to an armed rebellion which, it was generally believed, was communist-inspired. The parallels between Russia's alleged activities in Greece and Germany's in Czechoslovakia were sufficiently apparent to arouse a popular outcry against appeasement and a second Munich Pact. The President responded to this pressure by enunciating the "Truman Doctrine" in a message to Congress on March 12, 1947:[4]

The gravity of the situation which confronts the world today necessitates my appearance before a joint session of the Congress. The foreign policy and the national security of this country are involved.

One aspect of the present situation, which I wish to present to you at this time for your consideration and decision, concerns Greece and Turkey.

The United States has received from the Greek Government an urgent appeal for

[4] *Congressional Record*, 80th Cong., 1st Sess., pp. 1980-1981.

financial and economic assistance. Preliminary reports from the American Economic Mission now in Greece and reports from the American Ambassador in Greece corroborate the statement of the Greek Government that assistance is imperative if Greece is to survive as a free nation.

I do not believe that the American people and the Congress wish to turn a deaf ear to the appeal of the Greek Government. . . .

The very existence of the Greek state is today threatened by the terrorist activities of several thousand armed men, led by Communists, who defy the Government's authority at a number of points, particularly along the northern boundaries. A commission appointed by the United Nations Security Council is at present investigating disturbed conditions in Northern Greece and alleged border violations along the frontiers between Greece on the one hand and Albania, Bulgaria and Yugoslavia on the other.

Meanwhile, the Greek Government is unable to cope with the situation. The Greek Army is small and poorly equipped. It needs supplies and equipment if it is to restore the authority to the Government throughout Greek territory.

Greece must have assistance if it is to become a self-supporting and self-respecting democracy. The United States must supply this assistance. We have already extended to Greece certain types of relief and economic aid but these are inadequate. There is no other country to which democratic Greece can turn. No other nation is willing and able to provide the necessary support for a democratic Greek Government.

The British Government, which has been helping Greece, can give no further financial or economic aid after March 31. Great Britain finds itself under the necessity of reducing or liquidating its commitments in several parts of the world, including Greece.

We have considered how the United

Nations might assist in this crisis. But the situation is an urgent one requiring immediate action, and the United Nations and its related organizations are not in a position to extend help of the kind that is required.

It is important to note that the Greek Government has asked for our aid in utilizing effectively the financial and other assistance we may give to Greece, and in improving its public administration. It is of the utmost importance that we supervise the use of any funds made available to Greece, in such manner that each dollar spent will count toward making Greece self-supporting, and will help to build an economy in which a healthy democracy can flourish.

No government is perfect. One of the chief virtues of a democracy, however, is that its defects are always visible and under democratic processes can be pointed out and corrected. The Government of Greece is not perfect. Nevertheless, it represents 85 per cent of the members of the Greek Parliament who were chosen in an election last year. Foreign observers, including 692 Americans, considered this election to be a fair expression of the views of the Greek people.

The Greek Government has been operating in an atmosphere of chaos and extremism. It has made mistakes. The extension of aid by this country does not mean that the United States condones everything that the Greek Government has done or will do. We have condemned in the past, and we will condemn now, extremist measures of the right or the left. We have in the past advised tolerance, and we advise tolerance now.

Greece's neighbor, Turkey, also deserves our attention. The future of Turkey as an independent and economically sound state is clearly no less important to the freedom-loving peoples of the world than the future of Greece. The circumstances in which Turkey finds itself today are considerably different from those of Greece.

Turkey has been spared the disasters that have beset Greece. And during the war, the United States and Great Britain furnished Turkey with material aid. Nevertheless, Turkey now needs our support.

Since the war Turkey has sought additional financial assistance from Great Britain and the United States for the purpose of effecting that modernization necessary for the maintenance of its national integrity. That integrity is essential to the preservation of order in the Middle East.

The British Government has informed us that, owing to its own difficulties, it can no longer extend financial or economic aid to Turkey. As in the case of Greece, if Turkey is to have the assistance it needs, the United States must supply it. We are the only country able to provide that help.

I am fully aware of the broad implications involved if the United States extends assistance to Greece and Turkey, and I shall discuss these implications with you at this time.

One of the primary objectives of the foreign policy of the United States is the creation of conditions in which we and other nations will be able to work out a way of life free from coercion. This was a fundamental issue in the war with Germany and Japan. Our victory was won over countries which sought to impose their will, and their way of life, upon other nations.

To ensure the peaceful development of nations, free from coercion, the United States has taken a leading part in establishing the United Nations. The United Nations is designed to make possible lasting freedom and independence for all its members. We shall not realize our objectives, however, unless we are willing to help free peoples to maintain their free institutions and their national integrity against aggressive movements that seek to impose on them totalitarian regimes. This is no more than a frank recognition that totalitarian regimes imposed on free peoples, by direct or indirect aggression, undermine the foundations of international peace and hence the security of the United States.

The peoples of a number of countries of the world have recently had totalitarian regimes forced upon them against their will. The Government of the United States has made frequent protests against coercion and intimidation, in violation of the Yalta Agreement, in Poland, Rumania and Bulgaria. I must also state that in a number of other countries there have been similar developments.

At the present moment in world history nearly every nation must choose between alternative ways of life. The choice is too often not a free one.

One way of life is based upon the will of the majority, and is distinguished by free institutions, representative government, free elections, guarantees of individual liberty, freedom of speech and religion, and freedom from political oppression.

The second way of life is based upon the will of the minority forcibly imposed upon the majority. It relies upon terror and oppression, a controlled press and radio, fixed elections, and the suppression of personal freedoms.

I believe that it must be the policy of the United States to support free peoples who are resisting attempted subjugation by armed minorities or by outside pressures.

I believe that we must assist free peoples to work out their own destinies in their own way.

I believe that our help should be primarily through economic and financial aid which is essential to economic stability and orderly political processes.

The world is not static, and the status quo is not sacred. But we cannot allow changes in the status quo in violation of the charter of the United Nations by such methods as coercion, or by such subterfuges as political infiltration. In helping free and independent nations to maintain their freedom, the United States will be giving effect to the principles of the charter of the United Nations. . . .

Should we fail to aid Greece and Turkey in this fateful hour, the effect will be far reaching to the west as well as to the east. We must take immediate and resolute action.

I therefore ask the Congress to provide authority for assistance to Greece and Turkey in the amount of $400,000,000 for the period ending June 30, 1948.

In addition to funds, I ask the Congress to authorize the detail of American civilian and military personnel to Greece and Turkey, at the request of those countries, to assist in the tasks of reconstruction, and for the purpose of supervising the use of such financial and material assistance as may be furnished. I recommend that authority also be provided for the instruction and training of selected Greek and Turkish personnel.

Finally, I ask that the Congress provide authority which will permit the speediest and most effective use, in terms of needed commodities, supplies, and equipment, of such funds as may be authorized.

This is a serious course upon which we embark. I would not recommend it except that the alternative is much more serious. . . .

The seeds of totalitarian regimes are nurtured by misery and want. They spread and grow in the evil soil of poverty and strife. They reach their full growth when the hope of a people for a better life has died. We must keep that hope alive. The free peoples of the world look to us for support in maintaining their freedoms.

If we falter in our leadership, we may endanger the peace of the world—and we shall surely endanger the welfare of this nation. . . .

## 5

The "Truman Doctrine," with its promise to support free states against "totalitarian regimes," became one bulwark in America's defense against world-wide communism. The other was the economic reconstruction of Europe, for the administration believed that a poverty-stricken people would succumb more readily to Russian propaganda. The blueprint for European aid was sketched by Secretary of State George C. Marshall in an address at the Harvard University commencement on June 5, 1947. The "Marshall plan" was based on the belief that Europe was an economic unit which could enjoy full recovery only when all countries were again functioning normally:[5]

In considering the requirements for the rehabilitation of Europe, the physical loss of life, the visible destruction of cities, factories, mines, and railroads was correctly estimated, but it has become obvious during recent months that this visible destruction was probably less serious than the dislocation of the entire fabric of European economy. For the past 10 years conditions have been highly abnormal. The feverish preparation for war and the more feverish maintenance of the war effort engulfed all aspects of national economies. Machinery has fallen into disrepair or is entirely obsolete. Under the arbitrary and destructive Nazi rule, virtually every possible enterprise was geared into the German war machine. Long-standing commercial ties, private institutions, banks, insurance companies and shipping companies disappeared, through loss of capital, absorption through nationalization or by simple destruction. In many countries, confidence in the local currency has been severely shaken. The breakdown of the business structure of Europe during the war was complete. Recovery has been seriously retarded by the fact that 2 years after the close of hostilities a peace settlement with Germany and Austria has not been agreed upon. But even given a more prompt solution of these difficult problems, the rehabilitation of the economic structure of Europe quite evidently will require a much longer time and greater effort than had been foreseen. . . .

[5] Department of State, *Bulletin*, XVI, No. 415 (June 15, 1947), 1159-1160.

The truth of the matter is that Europe's requirements for the next 3 or 4 years of foreign food and other essential products—principally from America—are so much greater than her present ability to pay that she must have substantial additional help, or face economic, social, and political deterioration of a very grave character.

The remedy lies in breaking the vicious circle and restoring the confidence of the European people in the economic future of their own countries and of Europe as a whole. The manufacturer and the farmer throughout wide areas must be able and willing to exchange their products for currencies the continuing value of which is not open to question.

Aside from the demoralizing effect on the world at large and the possibilities of disturbances arising as a result of the desperation of the people concerned, the consequences to the economy of the United States should be apparent to all. It is logical that the United States should do whatever it is able to do to assist in the return of normal economic health in the world, without which there can be no political stability and no assured peace. Our policy is directed not against any country or doctrine but against hunger, poverty, desperation, and chaos. Its purpose should be the revival of a working economy in the world so as to permit the emergence of political and social conditions in which free institutions can exist. Such assistance, I am convinced, must not be on a piecemeal basis as various crises develop. Any assistance that this Government may render in the future should provide a cure rather than a mere palliative. Any government that is willing to assist in the task of recovery will find full cooperation, I am sure, on the part of the United States Government. Any government which maneuvers to block the recovery of other countries cannot expect help from us. Furthermore, governments, political parties, or groups which seek to perpetuate human misery in order to profit therefrom politically or otherwise will encounter the opposition of the United States.

It is already evident that, before the United States Government can proceed much further in its efforts to alleviate the situation and help start the European world on its way to recovery, there must be some agreement among the countries of Europe as to the requirements of the situation and the part those countries themselves will take in order to give proper effect to whatever action might be undertaken by this Government. It would be neither fitting nor efficacious for this Government to undertake to draw up unilaterally a program designed to place Europe on its feet economically. This is the business of the Europeans. The initiative, I think, must come from Europe. The role of this country should consist of friendly aid in the drafting of a European program and of later support of such a program so far it may be practical for us to do so. The program should be a joint one, agreed to by a number, if not all European nations.

An essential part of any successful action on the part of the United States is an understanding on the part of the people of America of the character of the problem and the remedies to be applied. Political passion and prejudice should have no part. With foresight, and a willingness on the part of our people to face up to the vast responsibility which history has clearly placed upon our country, the difficulties I have outlined can and will be overcome.

## 6

Angered by the Truman Doctrine and the Marshall plan, the Russians retreated behind their "iron curtain" while suspicion mounted on both sides. Only joint efforts in the United Nations maintained a limited co-operation; economic collaboration did not materialize, and political friction committed both sides to a course of nationalistic action that meant a risk of war. At a meeting of the American Academy of Political and Social Science in 1948, James P. Warburg, a thoughtful inter-

nationalist, discussed long-range factors underlying the crisis:[6]

Make no mistake about it—there is going to be one world. There is going to be one world no matter what foreign policy we pursue. The only question is by which of three possible means our world is going to be unified. We shall shortly see either a Russian-dominated world, or an American-dominated world, or a world united under world law and governed peacefully on the federal principle. . . .

At present, our policy makers apparently see only the threat of a Russian-dominated world—which, as things are going now, is a very real threat and a most unpleasant one to contemplate. But, in seeking to forestall this danger, the makers of United States policy are unfortunately thinking in purely negative terms—in terms of "How to Stop Russia." This means, in effect, that they are consciously or unconsciously thinking of an American-dominated world as the sole alternative. And this, in turn, means a rapid approach to a trial of physical strength between the United States and the Union of Soviet Socialist Republics. . . .

. . . I should now like to submit to you that, whatever the wrongs committed by the Soviet Union and whatever the true motivation and present purpose of Russian policy, the world crisis and the present threat to world peace are caused by four major factors, three of which have nothing whatsoever to do with the Soviet Union. . . .

The first factor, as I see it, is that we are in a technological revolution, at least as far-reaching in its implications upon human society as the industrial revolution of the late eighteenth century. This tech-

[6] James P. Warburg, "The United States and the World Crisis," *Annals of the American Academy of Political and Social Science*, CCLVIII (July, 1948), 112, 119-121. Reprinted by permission of the American Academy of Political and Social Science.

nological revolution has shrunk a world formerly divided by oceans, mountains, and deserts into one world—one little world in which there can be neither peace nor prosperity for any people unless there is peace and prosperity for all peoples.

The technological revolution has also vastly increased the problem of feeding the world's population, because it has greatly prolonged human life, has eliminated to some extent the occasional mass slaughter by pestilence, and has in general decreased the death rate far more rapidly in the world's backward areas than higher living standards have so far reduced the birth rate. Finally, the technological revolution has made war between nations into a threat of genocide. . . .

The second great factor is that we are living in a socioeconomic revolution, accelerated and sharpened by the destruction wrought by two great wars. The whole Eastern Hemisphere is suffering from shortages. Its machinery of production has been worn out or destroyed, its raw materials depleted, its populations exhausted, its managerial power groups dispersed or dispossessed. The middle-class structure of Europe has been undermined by a series of expropriations, by the depreciation of currencies, and by an almost total inhibition of the formation of new private capital.

Similarly, the colonial and feudal structure of society in the world's backward areas, and especially the traditional structure of Asia, is tottering. Colonial empires are in the process of liquidation, giving rise to new problems for both the peoples emerging into freedom and the peoples whose living standards were in the past supported by colonial exploitation. In other words, a large part of the world is in a state of fundamental and far-reaching change. . . .

The third factor in the current crisis is that an accelerated process of elimination among the great powers has caused the world's military, political, and eco-nomic power to become concentrated in only two poles of super-power—the Soviet Union and the United States. . . .

A balance of power is, in the long run, impossible without room for maneuver among the nation-states. There can be no room for maneuver when power is polarized in only two nation-states. There is then room only for an armament race between the two rival powers. This means that we have come to the end of the long period of international anarchy—that we have come to the end of that part of human history in which men could live within nations under law while nations lived among each other in a state of jungle lawlessness.

These, as I see it, are the three primary causes of the present crisis in world affairs. None of them has anything whatever to do with the nature or intentions of the Soviet Union. We should be in a world-wide technological, social, and economic revolution if Marx and Lenin had never lived or written. We should be living in a state of no longer tolerable international anarchy if power had become concentrated in any two super-powers other than Russia and the United States. . . .

I do not for one moment deny that there is a fourth and very important cause of the present world crisis. The Soviet Union has without doubt been cynically fishing in troubled waters. It has exploited the world-wide socioeconomic revolution in order to propagate the Communist ideology. It has exploited the existence of international anarchy among the sovereign nation-states in order to gain every possible advantage for itself. . . .

The trouble is that our Government sees only the Soviet Union's contribution to the present state of world affairs. It does not see its own contribution, nor that of others. Above all, it fails to recognize that the most important causes of the present crisis are no one's fault in particular but are to be sought in the historical developments of the time in which we live. . . .

In the recent past, this had led us to ally ourselves with the forces of reaction throughout the world instead of allying ourselves with the forces of progress. We have driven the masses of Asia toward Communism because we have backed anti-democratic and corrupt feudal regimes which oppose land reform, thus giving the Communists a monopoly on the one great magnet of political attraction in that teeming continent. We have driven the peasants of eastern Europe in the same direction by the same foolish means. And we have alienated the urban industrial workers of Europe by looking askance at democratic socialism, fearing it as a step toward totalitarian dictatorship and seeking to restore discarded systems and dispossessed and discredited power groups.

Thus, we have left to the Soviet Union the exploitation of the world-wide aspiration for a new and better future. Thus, we have failed to destroy the illusion that Communist totalitarianism is the road to a better future. Thus, in our anxiety to stop the spread of Communism, we have actually been helping the Soviet Union to fertilize the soil for its growth.

In the same way we have, by default, left to the Soviet Union the inestimable advantage of exploiting the existing condition of international anarchy. We, who have nothing to lose and everything to gain from strengthening the United Nations and building it into a world government, have undermined the United Nations, have lacked faith in it, have failed to infuse it with our own great strength, and have not—even at this late date—made up our minds to achieve one world as once we made up our minds to achieve one nation.

## 7

Although communist countries did not co-operate, recovery in Western Europe was assisted by the Marshall plan. The early stages of the contest between East and West had been political and economic; but the Truman Doctrine had also proposed military assistance, on the supposition that tension between Russia and the United States increased the probability of resort to force. Belief by the State Department that Western Europe was vital to American security and that the Soviet threat was primarily military led, in 1949, to the signing of the North Atlantic Pact:[7]

The Parties to this Treaty reaffirm their faith in the purposes and principles of the Charter of the United Nations and their desire to live in peace with all peoples and all governments.

They are determined to safeguard the freedom, common heritage and civilization of their peoples, founded on the principles of democracy, individual liberty and the rule of law.

They seek to promote stability and well-being in the North Atlantic area.

They are resolved to unite their efforts for collective defense and for the preservation of peace and security.

They therefore agree to this North Atlantic Treaty:

1. The Parties undertake, as set forth in the Charter of the United Nations, to settle any international disputes in which they may be involved by peaceful means in such a manner that international peace and security, and justice, are not endangered, and to refrain in their international relations from the threat or use of force in any manner inconsistent with the purposes of the United Nations.

2. The Parties will contribute toward the further development of peaceful and friendly international relations by strengthening their free institutions, by bringing about a better understanding of the principles upon which these institutions are founded, and by promoting conditions of stability and well-being. They will seek to eliminate conflict in their international economic policies and will encourage eco-

---

[7] Department of State, *Bulletin*, XX, No. 507 (March 20, 1949), 339-341.

nomic collaboration between any or all of them.

3. In order more effectively to achieve the objectives of this Treaty, the Parties, separately and jointly, by means of continuous and effective self-help and mutual aid, will maintain and develop their individual and collective capacity to resist armed attack.

4. The Parties will consult together whenever, in the opinion of any of them, the territorial integrity, political independence or security of any of the Parties is threatened.

5. The Parties agree that an armed attack against one or more of them in Europe or North America shall be considered an attack against them all; and consequently they agree that, if such an armed attack occurs, each of them, in exercise of the right of individual or collective self-defense recognized by Article 51 of the Charter of the United Nations, will assist the Party or Parties so attacked by taking forthwith, individually and in concert with the other Parties, such action as it deems necessary, including the use of armed force, to restore and maintain the security of the North Atlantic area.

Any such armed attack and all measures taken as a result thereof shall immediately be reported to the Security Council. Such measures shall be terminated when the Security Council has taken the measures necessary to restore and maintain international peace and security.

6. For the purpose of Article 5 an armed attack on one or more of the Parties is deemed to include an armed attack on the territory of any of the Parties in Europe or North America, on the Algerian departments of France, on the occupation forces of any Party in Europe, on the islands under the jurisdiction of any Party in the North Atlantic area north of the Tropic of Cancer or on the vessels or aircraft in this area of any of the Parties.

7. This Treaty does not affect, and shall not be interpreted as affecting, in any way

the rights and obligations under the Charter of the Parties which are members of the United Nations, or the primary responsibility of the Security Council for the maintenance of international peace and security.

8. Each Party declares that none of the international engagements now in force between it and any other of the Parties or any third state is in conflict with the provisions of this Treaty, and undertakes not to enter into any international engagement in conflict with this Treaty.

9. The Parties hereby establish a council, on which each of them shall be represented, to consider matters concerning the implementation of this Treaty. The council shall be so organized as to be able to meet promptly at any time. The council shall set up such subsidiary bodies as may be necessary; in particular it shall establish immediately a defense committee which shall recommend measures for the implementation of Articles 3 and 5.

10. The Parties may, by unanimous agreement, invite any other European state in a position to further the principles of this Treaty and to contribute to the security of the North Atlantic area to accede to this Treaty. Any state so invited may become a party to the Treaty by depositing its instrument of accession with the Government of the United States of America. The Government of the United States of America will inform each of the Parties of the deposit of each such instrument of accession.

11. This Treaty shall be ratified and its provisions carried out by the Parties in accordance with their respective constitutional processes. The instruments of ratification shall be deposited as soon as possible with the Government of the United States of America, which will notify all the other signatories of each deposit. The Treaty shall enter into force between the states which have ratified it as soon as the ratifications of the majority of the signatories, including the ratifications of Belgium,

Canada, France, Luxembourg, the Netherlands, the United Kingdom and the United
States, have been deposited and shall come
into effect with respect to other states on
the date of the deposit of their ratifications.

12. After the Treaty has been in force
for ten years, or at any time thereafter, the
Parties shall, if any of them so requests,
consult together for the purpose of reviewing the Treaty, having regard for
the factors then affecting peace and security in the North Atlantic area, including
the development of universal as well as
regional arrangements under the Charter
of the United Nations for the maintenance
of international peace and security.

13. After the Treaty has been in force
for twenty years, any Party may cease to
be a party one year after its notice of denunciation has been given to the Government of the United States of America,
which will inform the Governments of the
other Parties of the deposit of each notice
of denunciation.

### 8

Prolonged negotiations brought no general
peace settlement; and a crisis in Germany
followed the breakdown of the Potsdam
agreement. The blockade of Berlin, countered
by the Anglo-American airlift, was abandoned
by Russia in 1949; but meanwhile Germany
in effect was partitioned between East and
West. American policy toward Germany and
the steps leading to organization of a West
German Republic were explained in an address made on April 28, 1949, by Secretary
of State Acheson:[8]

This Government made earnest efforts
for two and a half years after the war to
resolve the major issues arising from the
defeat of Germany and to achieve a general settlement. During that period we
participated in the four-power machinery
for control of Germany established by international agreement in 1945.

By the end of 1947 it appeared that the
Soviet Union was seeking to thwart any

settlement which did not concede virtual
Soviet control over German economic and
political life. This was confirmed in two
futile meetings of the Council of Foreign
Ministers in Moscow and London. It was
emphasized in the Allied Control Authority in Berlin, where the Soviet veto power
was exercised three times as often as by
the three Western Powers combined.

The resultant paralysis of interallied policy and control created an intolerable situation. Germany became divided into disconnected administrative areas and was
rapidly being reduced to a state of economic chaos, distress, and despair. Disaster
was averted primarily by American economic aid.

The German stalemate heightened the
general European crisis. The European
Recovery Program could not succeed without the raw materials and finished products which only a revived German economy could contribute.

By 1948 it became clear that the Western
Powers could no longer tolerate an im-
passe which made it impossible for them
to discharge their responsibilities for the
organization of German administration
and for the degree of German economic
recovery that was essential for the welfare
of Europe as a whole. These powers determined to concert their policies for the
area of Germany under their control,
which embraced about two thirds of the
territory and three fourths of the population of occupied Germany.

These common policies were embodied
in the London agreements, announced on
June 1, 1948. This joint program, I wish
to emphasize, is in no sense a repudiation
of our international commitments on Germany, embodied in the Potsdam protocol
and other agreements. It represents a sincere effort to deal with existing realities
in the spirit of the original Allied covenants pertaining to Germany.

The London agreements constitute a set
of arrangements for the coordinated administration of Germany pending a de-

---

[8] *Ibid.*, No. 514 (May 8, 1949), pp. 586-588.

finitive peace settlement. The execution of this program, now in progress, should restore stability and confidence in Western Germany while protecting the vital interests of Germany's neighbors. It seeks to insure cooperation among the Western nations in the evolution of a policy which can and should lead to a peaceful and fruitful association of Germany with Western Europe. It is a provisional settlement which in no way excludes the eventual achievement of arrangements applicable to all of Germany.

The London agreements established a basic pattern for future action in the West. The bizonal area, formed by economic merger of the American and British zones in 1947, and the French zone were to be coordinated and eventually merged. The Western zones were to participate fully in the European Recovery Program. An International Authority for the Ruhr was to be created to regulate the allocation of coal, coke, and steel between home and foreign consumption, to insure equitable international access to Ruhr resources, and safeguard against remilitarization of Ruhr industry.

The Germans were authorized to establish a provisional government, democratic and federal in character, based upon a constitution of German inception. It would be subject, in accordance with an occupation statute, to minimum supervision by the occupation authorities in the interest of the general security and of broad Allied purposes for Germany. Coordinated three-power control was to be established, with the virtual abolition of the zonal boundaries.

Of exceptional importance were the guarantees of security against a German military revival, a point sometimes overlooked in present-day talk about the hazards inherent in rebuilding German economic and political life. The London agreements provide that there is to be consultation among the three occupying powers in the event of any threat of German military resurgence; that their armed forces are to remain in Germany until the peace of Europe is secure; that a joint Military Security Board should be created with powers of inspection to insure against both military and industrial rearrangement; that all agreed disarmament and demilitarization measures should be maintained in force; and that long-term demilitarization measures should be agreed upon prior to the end of the occupation. It should be observed that these far reaching safeguards are to accompany the more constructive aspects of the program and assure that the new powers and responsibilities assumed by the Germans may not be abused.

During the last 10 months notable progress has been made in Western Germany, which is apparent to all the world. An entirely new atmosphere of hope and creative activity has replaced the lethargy and despair of a year ago. Much of the London program is well on the way to realization. An agreement establishing the International Authority for the Ruhr has been drafted and approved. The Military Security Board has been established. The bizone and French zone are participating fully in the European Recovery Program. Agreements have been reached with respect to such difficult and controverted issues as the protection of foreign property rights in Germany, the revision of lists of plants scheduled for dismantling on reparations account, and determination of restricted and prohibited industries. . . .

The agreement in Washington on the text of an occupation statute has removed one of the major obstacles to the establishment of the German Federal Republic. The Parliamentary Council met at Bonn on September 1, and has been working diligently to draft a basic law or provisional constitution for a Federal German Government. . . .

Provision is made in the occupation statute for a review of its terms after a year in force.

In accordance with the statute, the action

of the German Government authorities generally does not require affirmative Allied approval. This means that the day-to-day operations of the German Government cannot be thwarted by the veto of one occupying power or by Allied disagreement. German Government authorities will be at liberty to take administrative and legislative action, and such action will be valid if not disapproved by Allied authorities.

There is one important element in the Washington agreements on the economic side that I want to stress because it is a good indication of our intent. As you know, this Government has expended in Germany since the cessation of hostilities large sums of appropriated funds in order to feed the German people and support the German economy. These sums were carried in the Army budget. Since the commencement of economic cooperation aid, the bizonal area and the French zone have been receiving ECA funds and the Military Governors of the bizonal and the French zone concluded bilateral ECA agreements with the United States Government.

It has now been agreed that with the establishment of the German Federal Republic, funds provided by the United States Government to the German economy will be made available through the Economic Cooperation Administration. The German Federal Republic would itself execute a bilateral ECA agreement with the United States Government, and would likewise become a party to the convention for European Economic Cooperation and participate as a full member in the Organization for European Economic Cooperation.

The German economy has responded energetically to the currency reform of last June and to the recovery assistance already received. The German workshop is beginning again to produce, for itself, for its Western European neighbors, and for other cooperating countries. The Germans now, under the foreseen arrangements, will have an opportunity through their own government to become a responsible partner in the European Recovery Program.

The Washington agreements envisage at the time of the establishment of the German Federal Republic the termination of Military Government and its replacement by an Allied High Commissioner of civilian character. Military functions will continue to be exercised by military commanders, but each of the Allied establishments in Germany, aside from occupation forces, will come under the direction of a High Commissioner. The functions of the Allied authorities are to become mainly supervisory.

## ISSUES AT HOME

### 9

War scares and a revived spirit of nationalism weakened renewed efforts to carry on at home where the New Deal left off. President Truman's struggle for enactment of housing and public health reforms and the like met with partial success. A Full Employment law, a Congressional Reorganization Act, recommendations for administrative reform sponsored by a bipartisan commission headed by former President Hoover, and recommendation by the President's Committee on Civil Rights, all attested the continuing battle for progressivism. But there was matching vigor in the resurgence of nationalism and conservatism. Wartime controls were thrown off rapidly, as after World War I, and again inflated prices, strikes, and shortages jangled the public nerves. Antilabor sentiment mounted rather than declined when war was over. Thirteen states prohibited union shops; while on the national stage a shift in power opened the way for repeal of the Wagner Act. After Republican capture of Congress in 1946, the bipartisan conservative coalition mustered the votes to override President Truman's veto and pass the Taft-Hartley Act (1947):[9]

---

[9] *United States Statutes at Large*, LXI, 136-162.

Section 101. The National Labor Relations Act is hereby amended to read as follows: . . . .

"Sec. 7. Employees shall have the right to self-organization, to form, join, or assist labor organizations, to bargain collectively through representatives of their own choosing, and to engage in other concerted activities for the purpose of collective bargaining or other mutual aid or protection, and shall also have the right to refrain from any or all of such activities except to the extent that such right may be affected by an agreement requiring membership in a labor organization as a condition of employment as authorized in section 8 (a) (3).

Sec. 8. (a) It shall be an unfair labor practice for an employer—"(1) to interfere with, restrain, or coerce employees in the exercise of the rights guaranteed in section 7; . . . .

"(3) by discrimination in regard to hire or tenure of employment or any term or condition of employment to encourage or discourage membership in any labor organization: *Provided,* That nothing in this Act, or in any other statute of the United States, shall preclude an employer from making an agreement with a labor organization (not established, maintained, or assisted by any action defined in section 8 (a) of this Act as an unfair labor practice) to require as a condition of employment membership therein on or after the thirtieth day following the beginning of such employment or the effective date of such agreement, whichever is the later, (i) if such labor organization is the representative of the employees as provided in section 9 (a), in the appropriate collective-bargaining unit covered by such agreement when made; and (ii) if, following the most recent election held as provided in section 9 (e) the Board shall have certified that at least a majority of the employees eligible to vote in such election have voted to authorize such labor organization to make such an agreement. . . .

"(b) It shall be an unfair labor practice for a labor organization or its agents—

"(1) to restrain or coerce (A) employees in the exercise of the rights guaranteed in section 7: *Provided,* That this paragraph shall not impair the right of a labor organization to prescribe its own rules with respect to the acquisition or retention of membership therein; or (B) an employer in the selection of his representatives for the purposes of collective bargaining or the adjustment of grievances; . . .

"(4) To engage in, or to induce or encourage the employees of any employer to engage in, a strike or a concerted refusal in the course of their employment to use, manufacture, process, transport, or otherwise handle or work on any goods, articles, materials, or commodities or to perform any services, where an object thereof is: . . .

(D) forcing or requiring any employer to assign particular work to employees in a particular labor organization or in a particular trade, craft, or class rather than to employees in another labor organization or in another trade, craft, or class. . . .

"(5) to require of employees covered by an agreement authorized under subsection (a) (3) the payment, as a condition precedent to becoming a member of such organization, of a fee in an amount which the Board finds excessive or discriminatory under all the circumstances. In making such a finding, the Board shall consider, among other relevant factors, the practices and customs of labor organizations in the particular industry, and the wages currently paid to the employees affected; and

"(6) to cause or attempt to cause an employer to pay or deliver or agree to pay or deliver any money or other thing of value, in the nature of an exaction, for services which are not performed or not to be performed.

"(c) The expressing of any views, argument, or opinion, or the dissemination thereof, whether in written, printed, graphic, or visual form, shall not constitute or be evidence of an unfair labor practice under any of the provisions of this Act, if such expression contains no threat of reprisal or force or promise of benefit. . . .

"Sec. 9. (a) Representatives designated or selected for the purposes of collective bargaining by the majority of the employees in a unit appropriate for such purposes, shall be the exclusive representatives of all the employees in such unit for the purposes of collective bargaining in respect to rates of pay, wages, hours of employment, or other conditions of employment: *Provided,* That any individual employee or a group of employees shall have the right at any time to present grievances to their employer and to have such grievances adjusted, without the intervention, of the bargaining representative, as long as the adjustment is not inconsistent with the terms of a collective-bargaining contract or agreement then in effect: *Provided further,* That the bargaining representative has been given opportunity to be present at such adjustment. . . ."

Sec. 206. Whenever in the opinion of the President of the United States, a threatened or actual strike or lock-out affecting an entire industry or a substantial part thereof engaged in trade, commerce, transportation, transmission, or communication among the several States or with foreign nations, or engaged in the production of goods for commerce, will, if permitted to occur or to continue, imperil the national health or safety, he may appoint a board of inquiry to inquire into the issues involved in the dispute and to make a written report to him within such time as he shall prescribe. Such report shall include a statement of the facts with respect to the dispute, including each party's statement of its position but shall not contain any recommendations. . . .

Sec. 208. (a) Upon receiving a report from a board of inquiry the President may direct the Attorney General to petition any district court of the United States

having jurisdiction of the parties to enjoin such strike or lock-out or the continuing thereof, and if the court finds that such threatened or actual strike or lock-out—

(i) affects an entire industry or a substantial part thereof engaged in trade, commerce, transportation, transmission, or communication among the several States or with foreign nations, or engaged in the production of goods for commerce; and

(ii) if permitted to occur or to continue, will imperil the national health or safety, it shall have jurisdiction to enjoin any such strike or lock-out, or the continuing thereof, and to make such other orders as may be appropriate.

(b) In any case, the provisions of the Act of March 23, 1932, entitled "An Act to amend the Judicial Code and to define the limit the jurisdiction of courts sitting in equity, and for other purposes," shall not be applicable. . . .

Sec. 301. (a) Suits for violation of contracts between an employer and a labor organization representing employees in an industry affecting commerce as defined in this Act, or between any such labor organizations, may be brought in any district court of the United States having jurisdiction of the parties, without respect to the amount in controversy or without regard to the citizenship of the parties.

(b) Any labor organization which represents employees in an industry affecting commerce as defined in this Act and any employer whose activities affect commerce as defined in this Act shall be bound by the acts of its agents. Any such labor organization may sue or be sued as an entity and in behalf of the employees whom it represents in the courts of the United States. Any money judgment against a labor organization in a district court of the United States shall be enforceable only against the organization as an entity and against its assets, and shall not be enforceable against any individual member or his assets. . . .

(e) For the purposes of this section, in

determining whether any person is acting as an "agent" of another person so as to make such other person responsible for his acts, the question of whether the specific acts performed were actually authorized or subsequently ratified shall not be controlling. . . .

# 10

That organized labor should object to the Taft-Hartley Act was inevitable; its Republican authors became the target of a concentrated union attack that was partially responsible for the Democratic victory in 1948. Also significant was the bipartisan liberal opposition that the measure aroused. Republican Senator Wayne Morse, who had had years of experience in dealing with relations of employers and employees, was one of the principal critics. His views were expressed in an article, "How I Would Change the Taft-Hartley Law," published in 1948:[10]

Many, many people seem to forget this curious fact: Throughout the long history of the labor movement in this country every demand made by the nation's workers has met with consistent and often violent opposition. Then, after each gain had been won, historians and people generally looked back and agreed that labor's so-called "demands" were just and necessary.

Go back as far as you like, the story is always the same. Even labor's long fight for free education was bitterly denounced. As for the right to organize and bargain collectively, there is still a powerful minority of labor-hating employers who want no part of it. Unfortunately their attitude is reflected in sections of the Taft-Hartley Act.

And I want to remind you also that collective bargaining now plays a vital part in our economy. Today some 50,000 union contracts protect the wages and living

standards of 15 million workers and their families. The arithmetic of these contracts is the arithmetic of democracy.

Neither the letter of the Taft-Hartley law nor the spirit in which it was written recognizes these fundamental realities. How would I amend this statute?

The ideal way to amend the Taft-Hartley law would be to repeal it and then consider new labor legislation based on entirely different principles and procedures. As a practical matter, however, I look for less drastic action in Congress—action aimed at correction of it, rather than outright repeal.

It is common knowledge on Capitol Hill that many of the men who voted for this bill admitted that it contains a number of unsound provisions which must be changed. A rather sorry confession to come from supposedly responsible legislators engaged in passing a law which effects [*sic*] the welfare of countless workers throughout the nation.

It is also common knowledge that the Taft-Hartley bill was designed not only to curb certain abuses but to weaken labor's position at the bargaining table. In other words, this law's faults go far beyond the enactment of unworkable provisions. It weights the economic scales against those millions of Americans who depend on wages and salaries for their livelihood. Does any fair-minded person believe we need a law which loads the dice against our working people? Do we want to raise once more the whole issue of labor injunctions and shift the adjudication of labor disputes into the field of common law courts?

The Taft-Hartley bill does both. It ignores the realities of labor relations and threatens to undermine the economic stability which we so desperately need in the months ahead.

Here are some of the more glaring imperfections in this legislative hodge-podge.

It invites a return to government by injunction. That phrase may not mean much to some, but behind it lies a long history

---

[10] Senator Wayne Morse, "How I Would Change the Taft-Hartley Law," *Everybody's Digest*, VII (March, 1948), 5-9. Reprinted by permission of *Everybody's Digest*, March, 1948, issue.

of strike-breaking edicts and restraints upon the legitimate rights of working people. Not so long ago, injunctions were widely used to block not only collective bargaining but even labor's right to organize. These abuses culminated in the passage of the Norris-La Guardia Act. Today many of the safeguards provided in that act are seriously endangered.

Consider, for example, the Taft-Hartley bill's definition of the term "agent." Apologists call it a "minor" amendment. But in reality this change makes a labor organization subject to civil suits and unfair labor practice charges because of the misconduct of any *steward or organizer in the plant* —even though the union had never authorized or approved the acts in question. This leaves the way open for anti-labor employers to ring in labor spies, company stooges and all the strong-arm methods which were exposed by the La Follette investigations. That period before the Wagner Act was an ugly, violent era. We cannot afford to repeat it. . . .

. . . Under the detailed registration requirements of the Taft-Hartley Act the National Labor Relations Board cannot proceed upon the merits of any dispute until they first find that the union has met all the registration requirements of the Act.

Because this section of the bill is so loaded down with detailed technical requirements, employers can delay Board action almost indefinitely. So far as the unions go, this is like telling a citizen whose house is being burglarized that he cannot have any police protection because his taxes are in arrears.

Such legislation is neither fair nor workable—though it will provide a field day for lawyers. There are so many grounds for litigation under this act that hostile employers can keep a union treasury bankrupt. Add the inevitable delays that legal procedures involve and you have a perfect formula for industrial unrest. The Taft-Hartley law lays down special

rules of procedure and evidence to be applied only to the National Labor Relations Board. This is class legislation with a vengeance, for it singles out this Board as an exception to the Administrative Procedures Act, passed by Congress in 1946. Thus the NLRB is subject to rules which do not apply to the railroads under the Interstate Commerce Commission or to industry generally under the Federal Trade Commission or to the radio industry under its Commission. . . .

The Taft-Hartley law attempts to force the settlement of these social and economic issues into the straight-jackets [*sic*] of court procedures and legal technicalities. The whole history of the American labor movement shows that both free workers and free employers have always opposed such attempts. Now more than ever, we need to preserve and strengthen the basic principle of voluntary action which must and should characterize employer-employee relationships.

We do not want the government or the courts to dominate that relationship, a relationship traditionally based on give and take between free groups.

Another very dubious provision of the Taft-Hartley law discriminates against both labor and those employers who are located in certain states—states which maintain good labor standards. To see how this two-edged sword may cut, you must remember that the only jurisdiction that Congress has over labor relations grows out of its constitutional authority to regulate interstate commerce. Now it is obvious that any Federal rule regulating labor should apply equally throughout the United States. But under the Taft-Hartley Act, if one state passes a more stringent labor control, that measure in effect supersedes the Federal law in that state.

This is bound to produce conflicting and often contradictory labor policies among the different states. And that lack of uniformity will breed strikes and industrial unrest. It will also cause unfair competition from states which enact laws to beat down labor and encourage sweat shops. It is a backward step for employers and employees alike.

Now it is time to consider that ticklish and very controversial subject: jurisdictional disputes. Nothing better illustrates the vindictive and mistaken philosophy behind the Taft-Hartley Act. Instead of providing machinery for settling these family quarrels, the Act declared them to be illegal. As if that edict could possibly prevent the honest differences of opinion that arise between labor organizations over which union is entitled to perform certain work.

It would be just as sensible to pass a law making it illegal for two property owners to quarrel over their boundary line.

There is nothing unlawful about a jurisdictional dispute. In our complex industrial structure with production methods and materials undergoing constant change, disputes are inevitable.

What is needed for their settlement is a decision as to the rights of the disputants based on the merits of the controversy. The decision should be rendered by experts in the field of labor relations who know a great deal about the history and practices of work assignments among crafts and unions.

Surely arbitration, rather than court action, is the fairest and most workable solution to the problem of jurisdictional strikes. I made that proposal, calling for compulsory arbitration of such disputes. This procedure was generally recognized as the most severe that can be imposed. I believe it is necessary if innocent employers and the public are to be protected from these family quarrels within the house of labor.

Instead, the new rules governing such cases now provide for (1) a hearing before a staff member of the Board (NLRB) on the merits of the jurisdictional dispute with (2) review of his recommendations by the Board followed by (3) efforts to obtain compliance with the determination of the Board, which if not forthcoming is followed by (4) a hearing on the unfair labor practice charge with (5) a review by the Board and (6) judicial review of the entire proceeding on the wide basis now allowed by the statute. No such proceeding could be completed short of two years!

A good many qualified observers agree that this routine should be called six steps to industrial chaos.

There is plenty of mischief, too, in the remedy for contract violations—haul the union into court. As everyone familiar with labor relations knows, many union agreements are rather loosely drawn and the terms may be subject to different interpretations. Our courts are not well equipped to decide these issues. The vast majority of such cases should go before an administrative agency like the National Labor Relations Board. I made that proposal, but this common sense remedy was rejected in favor of court action. . . .

Yes, I would repeal the Taft-Hartley law. But while it is on the statute books, let us enforce it. Strict enforcement will show how far this measure fails to meet the social and economic needs of a free people.

## 11

Despite the drift toward normalcy after World War II, the struggle for enlightenment continued. Its advocates were middle-class liberals, workers, and humanitarians drawn from both parties; its purpose the achievement of those human rights proclaimed as mankind's right in the Four Freedoms. An immediate goal of liberals in the middle 1940's was to prevent a revival of the racism that had marred the 1920's. A distinguished Committee on Civil Rights, authorized by President Truman, illustrated in its 1947 report that progress was being made toward a global brotherhood of man:[11]

[11] *To Secure These Rights. The Report of the President's Committee on Civil Rights* (Simon and Schuster, New York, 1947), pp. 139-141, 144-147.

## The Moral Reason

We have considered the American heritage of freedom at some length. We need no further justification for a broad and immediate program than the need to reaffirm our faith in the traditional American morality. The pervasive gap between our aims and what we actually do is creating a kind of moral dry rot which eats away at the emotional and rational bases of democratic beliefs. There are times when the difference between what we preach about civil rights and what we practice is shockingly illustrated by individual outrages. There are times when the whole structure of our ideology is made ridiculous by individual instances. And there are certain continuing, quiet, omnipresent practices which do irreparable damage to our beliefs.

As examples of "moral erosion" there are the consequences of suffrage limitations in the South. The fact that Negroes and many whites have not been allowed to vote in some states has actually sapped the morality underlying universal suffrage. Many men in public and private life do not believe that those who have been kept from voting are capable of self rule. They finally convince themselves that disfranchised people do not really have the right to vote. . . .

*The United States can no longer countenance these burdens on its common conscience, these inroads on its moral fiber.*

## The Economic Reason

One of the principal economic problems facing us and the rest of the world is achieving maximum production and continued prosperity. The loss of a huge, potential market for goods is a direct result of the economic discrimination which is practiced against many of our minority groups. A sort of vicious circle is produced. Discrimination depresses the wages and income of minority groups. As a result, their purchasing power is curtailed

and markets are reduced. Reduced markets result in reduced production. This cuts down employment, which of course means lower wages and still fewer job opportunities. Rising fear, prejudice, and insecurity aggravate the very discrimination in employment which sets the vicious circle in motion. . . .

Discrimination imposes a direct cost upon our economy through the wasteful duplication of many facilities and services required by the "separate but equal" policy. That the resources of the South are sorely strained by the burden of a double system of schools and other public services has already been indicated. Segregation is also economically wasteful for private business. Public transportation companies must often provide duplicate facilities to serve majority and minority groups separately. Places of public accommodation and recreation reject business when it comes in the form of unwanted persons. Stores reduce their sales by turning away minority customers. Factories must provide separate locker rooms, pay windows, drinking fountains, and washrooms for the different groups.

Discrimination in wage scales and hiring policies forces a higher proportion of some minority groups onto relief rolls than corresponding segments of the majority. A study by the Federal Emergency Relief Administration during the depression of the Thirties revealed that in every region the percentage of Negro families on relief was far greater than white families:

| | PER CENT OF FAMILIES ON RELIEF (May, 1934) | |
| | Negro | White |
|---|---|---|
| Northern cities | 52.2 | 13.3 |
| Border state cities | 51.8 | 10.4 |
| Southern cities | 33.7 | 11.4 |

Similarly, the rates of disease, crime, and fires are disproportionately great in areas which are economically depressed as compared with wealthier areas. Many of the prominent American minorities are confined—by economic discrimination, by law, by restrictive covenants, and by social pressure—to the most dilapidated, undesirable locations. Property in these locations yields a smaller return in taxes, which is seldom sufficient to meet the inordinately high cost of public services in depressed areas. The majority pays a high price in taxes for the low status of minorities.

To the costs of discrimination must be added the expensive investigations, trials, and property losses which result from civil rights violations. In the aggregate, these attain huge proportions. The 1943 Detroit riot alone resulted in the destruction of two million dollars in property.

Finally, the cost of prejudice cannot be computed in terms of markets, production, and expenditures. Perhaps the most expensive results are the least tangible ones. No nation can afford to have its component groups hostile toward one another without feeling the stress. People who live in a state of tension and suspicion cannot use their energy constructively. The frustrations of their restricted existence are translated into aggression against the dominant group. Myrdal says:

Not only occasional acts of violence, but most laziness, carelessness, unreliability, petty stealing and lying are undoubtedly to be explained as concealed aggression. . . . The truth is that *Negroes generally do not feel they have unqualified moral obligations to white people.* . . . The voluntary withdrawal which has intensified the isolation between the two castes is also an expression of Negro protest under cover.

It is not at all surprising that a people relegated to second-class citizenship should behave as second-class citizens. This is true, in varying degrees, of all of our minorities. What we have lost in money, production, invention, citizenship, and leadership as the price for damaged,

thwarted personalities—these are beyond estimate.

*The United States can no longer afford this heavy drain upon its human wealth, its national competence.*

### The International Reason

Our position in the postwar world is so vital to the future that our smallest actions have far-reaching effects. We have come to know that our own security in a highly interdependent world is inextricably tied to the security and well-being of all people and all countries. Our foreign policy is designed to make the United States an enormous, positive influence for peace and progress throughout the world. We have tried to let nothing, not even extreme political differences between ourselves and foreign nations, stand in the way of this goal. But our domestic civil rights shortcomings are a serious obstacle.

In a letter to the Fair Employment Practice Committee on May 8, 1946, the Honorable Dean Acheson, then Acting Secretary of State, stated that:

. . . the existence of discrimination against minority groups in this country has an adverse effect upon our relations with other countries. We are reminded over and over by some foreign newspapers and spokesmen, that our treatment of various minorities leaves much to be desired. While sometimes these pronouncements are exaggerated and unjustified, they all too frequently point with accuracy to some form of discrimination because of race, creed, color, or national origin. Frequently we find it next to impossible to formulate a satisfactory answer to our critics in other countries; the gap between the things we stand for in principle and the facts of a particular situation may be too wide to be bridged. An atmosphere of suspicion and resentment in a country over the way a minority is being treated in the United States is a formidable obstacle to the development of mutual understanding and trust between the two countries. We will have better international relations when these reasons for suspicion and resentment have been removed. I think it is quite obvious . . . that the existence of discriminations against minority groups in the United States is a handicap in our relations with other countries. The Department of State, therefore, has good reason to hope for the continued and increased effectiveness of public and private efforts to do away with these discriminations.

The people of the United States stem from many lands. Other nations and their citizens are naturally intrigued by what has happened to their American "relatives." Discrimination against, or mistreatment of, any racial, religious or national group in the United States is not only seen as our internal problem. The dignity of a country, a continent, or even a major portion of the world's population, may be outraged by it. A relatively few individuals here may be identified with millions of people elsewhere, and the way in which they are treated may have world-wide repercussions. We have fewer than half a million American Indians; there are 30 million more in the Western Hemisphere. Our Mexican American and Hispano groups are not large; millions in Central and South America consider them kin. We number our citizens of Oriental descent in the hundreds of thousands; their counterparts overseas are numbered in hundreds of millions. Throughout the Pacific, Latin America, Africa, the Near, Middle, and Far East, the treatment which our Negroes receive is taken as a reflection of our attitudes toward all dark-skinned peoples.

In the recent war, citizens of a dozen European nations were happy to meet Smiths, Cartiers, O'Haras, Schultzes, di Salvos, Cohens, and Sklodowskas and all the others in our armies. Each nation could share in our victories because its "sons" had helped win them. How much of this good feeling was dissipated when they found virulent prejudice among some of our troops is impossible to say.

We cannot escape the fact that our civil rights record has been an issue in world politics. The world's press and radio are full of it. This Committee has seen a mul-

titude of samples. We and our friends have been, and are, stressing our achievements. Those with competing philosophies have stressed—and are shamelessly distorting—our shortcomings. They have not only tried to create hostility toward us among specific nations, races, and religious groups. They have tried to prove our democracy an empty fraud, and our nation a consistent oppressor of underprivileged people. This may seem ludicrous to Americans, but it is sufficiently important to worry our friends. The following United Press dispatch from London proves that (*Washington Post,* May 25, 1947):

Although the Foreign Office reserved comment on recent lynch activities in the Carolinas, British diplomatic circles said privately today that they have played into the hands of Communist propagandists in Europe. . . . Diplomatic circles said the two incidents of mob violence would provide excellent propaganda ammunition for Communist agents who have been decrying America's brand of "freedom" and "democracy." News of the North Carolina kidnaping was prominently displayed by London papers. . . .

The international reason for acting to secure our civil rights now is not to win the approval of our totalitarian critics. We would not expect it if our record were spotless; to them our civil rights record is only a convenient weapon with which to attack us. Certainly we would like to deprive them of that weapon. But we are more concerned with the good opinion of the peoples of the world. Our achievements in building and maintaining a state dedicated to the fundamentals of freedom have already served as a guide for those seeking the best road from chaos to liberty and prosperity. But it is not indelibly written that democracy will encompass the world. We are convinced that our way of life—the free way of life—holds promise of hope for all people. We have what is perhaps the greatest responsibility ever placed upon a people to keep this promise alive. Only still greater achievements will do it.

*The United States is not so strong, the final triumph of the democratic ideal is not so inevitable that we can ignore what the world thinks of us or our record.*

## 12

Although President Truman won re-election in his own right by his Fair Deal campaign, he faced a stiff battle against the coalition of Republicans and conservative Democrats when he outlined his program in his "State of the Union" message (1949):[12]

During the last 16 years the American people have been creating a society which offers new opportunities for every man to enjoy his share of the good things of life.

In this society we are conservative about the values and principles which we cherish; but we are forward-looking in protecting those values and principles and in extending their benefits. We have rejected the discredited theory that the fortunes of the Nation should be in the hands of a privileged few. [Applause.] We have abandoned the "trickle down" concept of national prosperity. Instead, we believe that our economic system should rest on a democratic foundation and that wealth should be created for the benefit of all. [Applause.]

The recent election shows that the American people are in favor of this kind of society and want to go on improving it. [Applause.]

The American people have decided that poverty is just as wasteful and just as unnecessary as preventable disease. We have pledged our common resources to help one another in the hazards and struggles of individual life. We believe that no unfair prejudice or artificial distinction should bar any citizen of the United States from an education, or from good health, or from

[12] *Congressional Record*, 81st Cong., 1st Sess., pp. 66-69.

a job that he is capable of performing. [Applause.]. . . .

Reinforced by these policies, our private enterprise system has reached new heights of production. Since the boom year of 1929, while our population has increased by only 20 percent, our agricultural production has increased by 45 percent, and our industrial production has increased by 75 percent. We are turning out far more goods and more wealth per worker than we have ever done before. . . .

But, great as our progress has been, we still have a long way to go.

As we look around the country, many of our shortcomings stand out in bold relief.

We are suffering from excessively high prices.

Our production is still not large enough to satisfy our demands.

Our minimum wages are far too low.

Small business is losing ground to growing monopoly.

Our farmers still face an uncertain future. And too many of them lack the benefits of our modern civilization.

Some of our natural resources are still being wasted.

We are acutely short of electric power, although the means for developing such power are abundant.

Five million families are still living in slums and firetraps. Three million families share their homes with others.

Our health is far behind the progress of medical science. Proper medical care is so expensive that it is out of reach of the great majority of our citizens.

Our schools, in many localities, are utterly inadequate.

Our democratic ideals are often thwarted by prejudice and intolerance.

Each of these shortcomings is also an opportunity—an opportunity for the Congress and the President to work for the good of the people.

Our first great opportunity is to protect

enact the provisions for low-rent
housing, slum clearance, farm hous-
and housing research which I have re-
dly recommended. The number of
ent public housing units provided
the legislation should be increased to
,000 units in the next 7 years. [Ap-
se.] Even this number of units will
begin to meet our need for new hous-

Iost of the houses we need will have to
built by private enterprise, without pub-
subsidy. By producing too few rental
ts and too large a proportion of high-
ced houses, the building industry is
idly pricing itself out of the market.
ilding costs must be lowered. [Ap-
ause.] . . .

The driving force behind our progress is
ur faith in our democratic institutions.
hat faith is embodied in the promise of
qual rights and equal opportunities which
he founders of our Republic proclaimed
o their countrymen and to the whole
world.

The fulfillment of this promise is among
the highest purposes of government. The
civil rights proposals I made to the Eight-
ieth Congress, I now repeat to the Eighty-
first Congress. [Applause.] They should
be enacted in order that the Federal Government may assume the leadership and
discharge the obligations clearly placed
upon it by the Constitution. . . .

As the troubled decade of the 1940's drew
to a close, world-wide tensions and mounting
political friction seemed to indicate a blurring
in the minds of leaders, in the West as well
as in the East, of the ideals proclaimed in the
Four Freedoms, the Atlantic Charter, and
the Human Rights declarations of the United
Nations. Once more, as in the 1920's, postwar
nationalism threatened to undo the noble
work of planners who built the United Nations that men might know peace. Yet the
scene was not as gloomy as pessimistic observers or fire-eating orators would have people believe. For in two ways the 1940's differed from the 1920's. One was the changed
attitude of the American people; refusing to
return to nationalism and normalcy, they
gladly shouldered their share of the world's
problems and continued to be sympathetic to
progressive endeavors at home. The other
was the changed attitude of the people everywhere; unmoved by warmongering politicians, they dedicated themselves soberly to
the task of reconstruction and refused to
accept war and reaction as an answer to the
friction so common among nations. In their
calm devotion to the cause of peace and human progress was hope for the future. In
their growing power was an indication that
this might yet become the century of the
common man.

our economy against the evils of "boom and bust.". . .

The Employment Act of 1946 pledges the Government to use all its resources to promote maximum employment, production, and purchasing power. This means that the Government is firmly committed to protect business and the people against the dangers of recession and against the evils of inflation. This means that the Government must adapt its plans and policies to meet changing circumstances. . . .

If we want to keep our economy running in high gear, we must be sure that every group has the incentive to make its full contribution to the national welfare. At present, the working men and women of the Nation are unfairly discriminated against by a statute that abridges their rights, curtails their constructive efforts, and hampers our system of free collective bargaining. That statute is the Labor-Management Relations Act of 1947, sometimes called the Taft-Hartley Act.

That act should be repealed. [Applause.]

The Wagner Act should be reenacted. However, certain improvements, which I recommended to the Congress, 2 years ago, are needed. Jurisdictional strikes and unjustifiable secondary boycotts should be prohibited. The use of economic force to decide issues arising out of the interpretation of existing contracts should be prevented. Without endangering our democratic freedoms, means should be provided for setting up machinery for preventing strikes in vital industries which affect the public interest. [Applause.] . . .

We should strengthen our anti-trust laws by closing those loopholes that permit monopolistic mergers and consolidations. [Applause.]

Our national farm program should be improved—not only in the interest of the farmers but for the lasting prosperity of the whole Nation. Our goals should be abundant farm production and parity of income for agriculture. [Applause.] Stand-

ards of living on the
as good as anywhere

Farm price supports
of our program to achie
supports should be use
price declines which are
general price levels, to
ments in production to co
and to promote good land

We must push forward w
ment of our rivers for po
navigation, and flood contr
We should apply the lesson
nessee Valley experience to o
river basins. [Applause.]

I again recommend that ac
by the Congress to approve t
rence seaway and power pr
plause.]

This is about the fifth tir
recommended it. . . .

The present coverage of t
security laws is altogether inadeq
benefit payments are too low. On
our workers are not covered. Th
receive old age and survivors ir
benefits receive an average payn
only $25 a month. Many others w
not work because they are physical
abled are left to the mercy of charit
should expand our social-security pro
both as to size of benefits and exte
coverage, against the economic haz
due to unemployment, old age, sickn
and disability. [Applause.]

We must spare no effort to raise t
general level of health in this country. In
nation as rich as ours, it is a shocking fac
that tens of millions lack adequate medical care. We are short of doctors, hospitals,
and nurses. We must remedy these shortages. Moreover, we need—and we must
have without further delay—a system of
prepaid medical insurance which will
enable every American to afford good
medical care. [Applause.] . . .

The housing shortage continues to be
acute. As an immediate step, the Congress

# BIBLIOGRAPHY

The following bibliography includes recent works that treat aspects of the subjects touched upon in the readings and documents reproduced above.

## CHAPTER XIII
## THE ROAD TO REUNION
### 1865–1876

The course of reconstruction is set forth in J. G. Randall, *The Civil War and Reconstruction* (1937) and interpreted by Charles and Mary Beard in *The Rise of American Civilization* (1930). P. H. Buck, *The Road to Reunion* (1937) is provocative; H. K. Beale, *The Critical Year* (1930), a significant analysis of 1866, is also illuminating for the period as a whole. Henry Adams makes many penetrating observations in *The Education of Henry Adams* (1927).

R. W. Shugg, *Origins of the Class Struggle in Louisiana* (1939) offers insights into southern conditions generally. R. W. Winston, *Andrew Johnson, Plebian and Patriot* (1928) and L. P. Stryker, *Andrew Johnson: A Study in Courage* (1929) are two studies of Lincoln's successor. P. S. Pierce, *The Freedman's Bureau* (1904) is standard. H. E. Flack, *The Adoption of the Fourteenth Amendment* (1908) is comprehensive. The Negro as a free man is the subject of C. S. Johnson, *The Negro in American Civilization* (1930) and C. H. Wesley, *Negro Labor in the United States* (1927) cover the materials implied by the title. D. M. DeWitt, *Impeachment and Trial of Andrew Johnson* (1903) is authoritative. J. C. Lester and D. L. Wilson, *Ku Klux Klan: Its Origin, Growth, and Disbandment* (1905) is the best discussion of the Klan available.

## CHAPTER XIV
## THE BANKRUPTCY OF POLITICS
### 1865–1874

E. E. Edwards discusses agricultural history in *Farmers in a Changing World* in *Yearbook of Agriculture, 1940* (1940) while the relationships between railroad building and western lands are expertly set forth in J. B. Hedges, *Henry Villard and the Railways of the Northwest* (1930) and P. W. Gates, *The Illinois Central and Its Colonization Work* (1934). V. L. Parrington, *Main Currents in American Thought*, 3 v. (1927, 1930) III, contains many valuable suggestions on the bankruptcy of politics and morals. E. Stanwood, *American Tariff Controversies in the Nineteenth Century* (1903) and F. W. Taussig, *Tariff History of the United States* (1931) cover the topic fully, as A. B. Hepburn, *History of Coinage and Currency in the United States* (1915) and D. R. Dewey, *Financial History of the United States* (1903) do theirs.

P. L. Haworth, *The Hayes-Tilden Election* (1927) is the standard work on the disputed election. John Bigelow is the author of *Samuel J. Tilden*, 2 v. (1895), and C. R. Williams has written a biography of his successful opponent *The Life of Rutherford B. Hayes*, 2 v. (1914). W. B. Hesseltine has made a study of General Grant, *Ulysses S. Grant Politician* (1935). K. G. Crawford, *The Pressure Boys* (1939) and Mathew Josephson, *The Politicos, 1865-1900* (1938) present materials which illumine the topics treated in this chapter. D. S. Muzzey, *James G. Blaine* (1934) and Allan Nevins, *Grover Cleveland: A Study in Courage* (1932) deal with two other leading figures.

The most important volume on democracy and party theory is E. E. Schattschneider, *Party Government* (1942). Woodrow Wilson, *Congressional Government* (1885) is a classic which everyone concerned with democracy and politics should read. K. H. Porter, *National Party Platforms* (1924) contains essential source materials.

CHAPTER XV
WESTWARD EXPANSION
AND RURAL DISLOCATION
1865–1890

R. A. Billington, *Westward Expansion* (1949) is the most recent survey of the whole subject. Mining is covered in T. A. Rickard, *A History of American Mining* (1932) and W. J. Trimble, *The Mining Advance into the Inland Empire* (1914). F. A. Shannon, *The Farmer's Last Frontier* (1945) treats many of the topics covered in this section. E. S. Osgood, *The Day of the Cattleman* (1929) is the work of a specialist and P. A. Rollins, *The Cowboy* (1922) is an admirable supplementary book. L. B. Priest, *Uncle Sam's Stepchildren* (1942) tells the story of the Indians in rich but selected detail. A significant volume is W. P. Webb, *The Great Plains* (1931).

The farmers and the railroads are discussed in the works of Gates, Hedges, and Shannon already cited. Helpful material will also be found in Webb, Osgood, and, Billington.

CHAPTER XVI
INDUSTRY AND URBAN LIFE
1865–1890

A. M. Schlesinger, *The Rise of the City 1878-1898* (1933) is a pioneer study of urbanism and basic for an understanding of its influence. Lewis Mumford, *The Culture of Cities* (1938) covers the theme on a much larger scale. A. I. Abell, *The American Impact on American Protestantism 1865-1900* appraises a vital aspect of the process.

E. A. Hecker, *A Short History of Women's Rights* (1911) and Thomas Woody, *A History of Women's Education in the United States*, 2 v. (1929), discuss two important aspects of the emancipation of women. While the materials are ill-

digested, there are many suggestive points made in A. W. Calhoun, *A Social History of the American Family* (1919) III.

The impact of the doctrine of evolution is analyzed in B. J. Loewenberg, "Darwinism Comes to America," *Mississippi Valley Historical Review*, XXVIII (1941), while a different phase is explored in Richard Hofstadter, *Social Darwinism in American Thought, 1860-1915* (1944). C. H. Hopkins, *The Rise of the Social Gospel in American Protestantism 1865-1915* (1940) is a thorough study.

M. R. Davie, *World Immigration* (1936) is the only single volume written from a global view. Two useful studies are C. F. Wittke, *We Who Built America* (1939) and G. M. Stephenson, *A History of American Immigration, 1820-1924* (1926). Edith Abbott has edited an extensive collection of documents: *Historical Aspects of the Immigration Problem: Select Documents* (1926).

CHAPTER XVII
SINS OF SOCIETY
1865–1890

E. A. Ross, *Sin and Society* (1907) remains the best short account. Thorstein Veblen, *The Theory of Business Enterprise* (1927) is incomparable as an introduction. E. C. Kirkland, *A History of American Economic Life* (1939), F. A. Shannon, *America's Economic Growth* (1940), and H. U. Faulkner, *American Economic History* (1927), are general summaries helpful at all points. H. W. Odum, *Southern Regions of the United States* (1936) is a fundamental book.

Contemporary accounts, however, convey a sense of drama which the conventional monograph seldom recaptures. H. D. Lloyd, *Wealth against Commonwealth* (1894), R. T. Ely, *The Labor Movement in America* (1886), J. A. Riis, *How the Other Half Lives* (1890), Jane Addams, *Democracy and Social Ethics* (1902), and

John Spargo, *The Bitter Cry of the Children* (1906) are particularly notable.

## CHAPTER XVIII
## DISSENT AND FRUSTRATION
### 1885–1900

The prevailing social and economic codes are clearly defined in M. E. Curti, *Growth of American Thought* (1943) and in R. H. Gabriel, *The Course of American Democratic Thought* (1940). Hofstadter, cited above, traces the specific relation of Darwinian ideas and laissez faire. W. Z. Ripley (ed.), *Trusts, Pools and Corporations* (1905) is still a valuable compendium.

N. J. Ware, *The Labor Movement in the United States 1860-1895* accords the Knights of Labor full treatment; L. L. Lorwin, *The American Federation of Labor* (1933) discusses that organization comprehensively, and F. T. Carlton, *The History and Problems of Organized Labor* (1920) is one of many excellent general treatises on the labor movement. Samuel Yellen, *American Labor Struggles* (1936) is an exciting account of a number of important clashes in American labor history. J. R. Commons, *Legal Foundations of Capitalism* (1924) is an exceedingly worthwhile study, and Charles Warren, *Supreme Court in United States History*, 2 v. (1926) is a good general introduction. C. B. Swisher, *The Growth of Constitutional Power in the United States* (1946) is a recent analysis by an outstanding authority. The student will find E. S. Corwin, *The Constitution and What It Means Today* (1938 and later editions) an excellent guide.

The political protest of agriculture has been investigated by Nathan Fine, *Labor and Farmer Parties in the United States, 1828-1928* (1928). S. J. Buck, *The Agrarian Crusade* (1921) dwells on the agrarian alone but covers the whole movement from the Civil War period. J. D. Hicks, *The Populist Revolt* (1931) describes this special phase of the farmer's protest. C. M. Destler, *American Radicalism, 1865-1901* (1947) reveals the importance of urban dissent.

## CHAPTER XIX
## THE SHRINKING WORLD
### 1865–1900

T. A. Bailey, *A Diplomatic History of the American People* (1940) and S. F. Bemis, *Diplomatic History of the United States* (1936) are comprehensive surveys which deal with all the items covered by this section. A highly rewarding study, which cuts across formal diplomatic history, is A. K. Weinberg, *Manifest Destiny: A Study in Nationalist Expansion in American History* (1935), and the expert analysis of D. Perkins, *Hands Off: A History of the Monroe Doctrine* (1941) should be frequently consulted. Allan Nevins, *Grover Cleveland* (1934) and the same author's *Hamilton Fish* (1936) treat most of the diplomatic incidents exhaustively.

J. B. Pratt, *Expansionists of 1898* (1936) covers the Cuban episode and involvement with Spain, and W. L. Langer, *The Diplomacy of Imperialism*, 2 v. (1935) makes the important world relations understandable. Walter Millis, *The Martial Spirit* (1931) is a provocative study of the background of the war. The struggle for ratification of the treaty is presented in W. S. Holt, *Treaties Defeated by the Senate* (1933).

## CHAPTER XX
## THE RISE OF PROGRESSIVISM
### 1900–1912

Much of the color of Theodore Roosevelt's era was caught in the early volumes of Mark Sullivan, *Our Times* (1926-1935). Social and economic trends are excellently summarized in T. C. Cochran and William Miller, *The Age of Enterprise* (1942) and, with more factual detail, in H. U. Faulkner, *The Quest for Social Justice* (1931). The literature of exposure is examined in C. C. Regier, *The Era of the Muckrakers* (1932) and Louis Filler, *Crusaders for American Liberalism* (1939). Well-balanced introductions to progressive thought are the analyses in Merle Curti, *The Growth of American Thought* (1943), Ralph H. Gabriel, *The Course of American Democratic Thought* (1940), and E. R. Lewis, *American Political Thought* (1937). More detailed on the same subject is John Chamberlain, *Farewell to Reform* (1932). Helpful on politics under two presidents are the biographies by Henry Pringle, *Theodore Roosevelt* (1931) and *William Howard Taft* (1939). The rise of Republican insurgency is traced in Robert M. La Follette, *Autobiography* (1913) and Claude G. Bowers, *Beveridge and the Progressive Era* (1932). The best recent account of politics of the era is George E. Mowry, *Roosevelt and the Progressive Movement* (1946). Judicial resistance to social and economic legislation is the theme of E. S. Bates, *The Story of the Supreme Court* (1936). Antitrust decisions are traced in H. R. Seager and C. A. Gulick, *Trust and Corporation Problems* (1929).

## CHAPTER XXI
## WILSONIAN DEMOCRACY
### 1912–1916

Creakings of the party system in the age of Roosevelt, Taft, and Wilson are analyzed in J. Allen Smith, *The Spirit of American Government* (1907) and T. K. Finletter, *Can Representative Government Do the Job?* (1945). The power of political machines to resist reform receives penetrating analysis in E. E. Schattschneider, *Party Government* (1942). On Wilsonian regulation of business, H. R. Seager and C. A. Gulick, *Trust and Corporation Problems* (1929) is useful, as is also A. T.

Mason, *Brandeis* (1933). F. L. Paxson, *The Pre-War Years, 1913-1917* (1936) covers Wilson's first administration. More exhaustive are the volumes of R. S. Baker, *Woodrow Wilson, Life and Letters* (1927-1939) and the current scholarly study by Arthur Link, of which the first published volume is *Wilson, The Road to the White House* (1947). Of shorter accounts, the best political appraisal is W. E. Dodd, *Woodrow Wilson and His Work* (1920), and the best personal evaluation is H. C. F. Bell, *Woodrow Wilson and the People* (1945). Other biographies that cast light on battles for social and economic legislation are Alfred Lief, *Democracy's Norris* (1939), R. L. Neuberger and S. B. Kahn, *Integrity, Life of George Norris* (1937), Alfred Lief, *Brandeis* (1936), and the readable account of Justice Holmes, C. D. S. Bowen, *Yankee from Olympus* (1944). The hardening of the constitutional doctrine of vested rights and protests against it receive scholarly analysis in C. G. Haines, *The American Doctrine of Judicial Supremacy* (1932) and E. S. Corwin, *Liberty against Government* (1948).

## CHAPTER XXII
## THE ENIGMA OF LABOR AND AGRICULTURE
### 1900–1920

Standard accounts of the labor movement are Selig Perlman and Philip Taft, *Labor Movements, 1896-1932* (1935) and L. L. Lorwin, *The American Federation of Labor* (1933). A readable new survey is F. R. Dulles, *Labor in America* (1949). Noteworthy for analysis of social forces and trends is N. J. Ware, *Labor in Modern Industrial Society* (1935). The story of strikebreaking and industrial violence is traced vividly in Louis Adamic, *Dynamite* (1934) and Edward Levinson, *I Break Strikes* (1935). Important strikes are covered in Samuel Yellen, *American Labor Struggles* (1936). Factual data on conditions of living can be gleaned from pioneer studies such as R. C. Chapin, *The Standard of Living among Workingmen's Families in New York City* (1909). International and American standards in social legislation are compared in J. R. Commons and J. B. Andrews, *Principles of Labor Legislation* (1920). Revolutionary radicalism, as well as reform agitations, is traced in Lillian Symes and Travers Clement, *Rebel America* (1934). No satisfactory history of agrarianism exists, although Nathan Fine, *Labor and Farmer Parties in the United States, 1828-1928* (1928), H. E. Gaston, *The Nonpartisan League* (1920), and Arthur Capper, *The Farm Bloc* (1922) provide useful information. A provocative analysis of subordination of agriculture to industry is L. M. Hacker, *The Farmer Is Doomed* (1933). *Farmers in a Changing World,* which appeared as *The Yearbook of Agriculture, 1940* (1940), contains valuable interpretive articles and historical data on all aspects of rural life. Searching sociological analysis of rural readjustment to urban civilization appears in J. M. Williams, *Our Rural Heritage* (1925) and W. H. Wilson, "Country versus City," *Papers and Proceedings, American Sociological Society, 1915,* reprinted in W. Thorp, Merle Curti, and C. Baker, *American Issues: The Social Record* (1941).

## CHAPTER XXIII
## THE WORLD'S ILLUSION
### 1900–1917

American foreign policy in the Progressive Era is competently surveyed in T. A. Bailey, *A Diplomatic History of the American People* (1942). A well-organized documentary volume with concise introductions is R. J. Bartlett (ed.), *The Record of American Diplomacy* (1947). P. T. Moon, *Imperialism and World Politics* (1926) and F. L. Schuman, *International Politics* (1948) are penetrating accounts

of the nationalism and imperialism that culminated in war. American indoctrination in racist and imperialist ideas is treated in Merle Curti, *The Growth of American Thought* (1943), Richard Hofstadter, *Social Darwinism in American Thought* (1944), and R. H. Gabriel, *The Course of American Democratic Thought* (1940). Far Eastern relations are studied in Tyler Dennett, *John Hay* (1933) and T. A. Bailey, *Theodore Roosevelt and the Japanese-American Crisis* (1934). A long-range general account is A. W. Griswold, *The Far Eastern Policy of the United States* (1938). For Caribbean penetration, a general survey is W. H. Callcott, *The Caribbean Policy of the United States, 1890-1920* (1942). Special phases are examined in D. C. Miner, *The Fight for the Panama Route* (1940), L. H. Jenks, *Our Cuban Colony* (1928), M. M. Knight, *The Americans in Santo Domingo* (1928), B. W. and J. W. Diffie, *Porto Rico: A Broken Pledge* (1931), Carleton Beals, *Banana Gold* (1930), J. F. Rippy, *The United States and Mexico* (1931), and J. M. Callahan, *American Foreign Policy in Mexican Relations* (1932). An expert treatment of the aggressive twist given to the Monroe Doctrine is Dexter Perkins, *Hands Off* (1941). Economic penetration is the theme of B. H. Williams, *Economic Foreign Policy of the United States* (1929). C. H. Haring, *South America Looks at the United States* (1928) portrays the reaction to American policy. Among controversial explanations of war with Germany, Charles Seymour, *American Neutrality, 1914-1917* (1935) stresses submarine violations, while C. C. Tansill, *America Goes to War* (1938) places emphasis on Allied propaganda and economic entanglement. The most recent general account of the United States and the war is F. L. Paxson, *American Democracy and the World War: America at War* (1939). The peace movement before and during the war is traced in Merle Curti, *War or Peace, the American Struggle: 1636-1936* (1936).

## CHAPTER XXIV
## NATIONALISM AND NORMALCY
### 1918–1932

Paul Birdsall, *Versailles Twenty Years After* (1941) corrects earlier isolationist bias regarding the making of the peace; as also, in a lucid, broad survey, does Sigmund Neumann, *The Future in Perspective* (1946). A factual account of defeat of the League is D. L. Fleming, *The United States and the League of Nations* (1932). A critical but informative book on Lodge is Karl Schriftgiesser, *The Gentleman from Massachusetts* (1944). Hostile to Wilson but scholarly are two books by T. A. Bailey, *Woodrow Wilson and the Lost Peace* (1944) and *Woodrow Wilson and the Great Betrayal* (1945). F. L. Allen, *Only Yesterday* (1931) is a vivid description of the Age of Normalcy. More sober and recent is F. L. Paxson, *Post-War Years: Normalcy* (1948). Social history is presented in Preston Slosson, *The Great Crusade and After* (1930), while Karl Schriftgiesser, *This Was Normalcy* (1948) emphasizes political aspects. Illuminating on the conservatism of the Supreme Court is Henry Pringle, *William Howard Taft* (1939). Phases of intolerance are studied in J. M. Mecklin, *The Ku Klux Klan* (1924) and Zechariah Chafee, *Free Speech in the United States* (1941). California nativism is surveyed in Carey McWilliams, *Prejudice: Japanese-Americans* (1944). D. F. Fleming, *The United States and the World Court* (1945) treats one phase of isolationism. American economic nationalism is critically studied in B. H. Williams, *Economic Foreign Policy of the United States* (1929). Illuminating materials are reprinted in R. J. Bartlett (ed.), *The Record of American Diplomacy* (1947). Pressure groups and the tariff are carefully scrutinized in E. E. Schattschneider, *Politics, Pressures and the Tariff* (1935). L. M. Hacker, *American Problems of Today* (1938) and George Soule, *Prosperity Decade* (1947) treat economic problems. The

onset of depression is vigorously chronicled in Gilbert Seldes, *The Years of the Locust: America, 1929-1932* (1933) and F. L. Allen, *Since Yesterday* (1940).

## CHAPTER XXV
## THE ROOSEVELT REVOLUTION
### 1933–1940

Basil Rauch, *History of the New Deal* (1944) is a compact political account. An economic history, often critical of the New Deal, is Broadus Mitchell, *Depression Decade* (1948). The most satisfactory general account stressing social history is Dixon Wecter, *The Age of the Great Depression* (1948). Frances Perkins, *The Roosevelt I Knew* (1946) and Eleanor Roosevelt, *This I Remember* (1949) are revealing. Studies of special aspects include D. E. Lilienthal, *TVA: Democracy on the March* (1944), R. R. R. Brooks, *When Labor Organizes* (1937), Herbert Harris, *Labor's Civil War* (1940), and Ferdinand Pecora, *Wall Street under Oath* (1939), the last explaining the background of regulation of the stock exchange and corporation finance. The Supreme Court issue is treated (before the event) in E. S. Corwin, *Twilight of the Supreme Court* (1935) and (after the event) in R. H. Jackson, *The Struggle for Judicial Supremacy* (1941). The revolution in constitutional law is the theme of C. H. Pritchett, *The Roosevelt Court* (1948). The problem of party unity and political accountability during the New Deal is analyzed in Roland Young, *This Is Congress* (1943) and E. E. Schattschneider, *Party Government* (1942).

## CHAPTER XXVI
## DEMOCRACY vs. NATIONALISM
### 1933–1945

Sigmund Neumann, *The Future in Perspective* (1946) admirably traces the growth of world crisis. Helpful books dealing with America's relation to world problems include H. J. Tasca, *Reciprocal Trade*

*Policy of the United States* (1938), Dexter Perkins, *Hands Off* (1941), T. A. Bisson, *American Policy in the Far East, 1931-1940* (1940), Allan Nevins and L. M. Hacker (eds.), *The United States and Its Place in World Affairs* (1943), and R. J. Bartlett (ed.), *The Record of American Diplomacy* (1947). *Peace and War: United States Foreign Policy, 1931-1941* (1943) is an official collection of basic documents, while Forrest Davis and E. K. Lindley, *How War Came* (1942) is a semiofficial interpretation. International conferences and diplomacy during wartime are described in Dexter Perkins, *America and Two Wars* (1944), R. E. Sherwood, *Roosevelt and Hopkins* (1948), and W. L. Langer, *Our Vichy Gamble* (1947). Important aspects of the American war effort are treated in J. P. Baxter, *Scientists Against Time* (1946), E. R. Stettinius, *Lend-Lease: Weapon for Victory* (1944), and Donald Nelson, *Arsenal of Democracy* (1946). The initial struggle for all-out industrial mobilization is traced in E. Stein et al., *Our War Economy* (1943). Indispensable on critical stages of the war and on Anglo-American relations is the history by Winston Churchill, *The Second World War* (1948-in progress). Four series now in progress relate the story of American armed forces: S. E. Morison, *History of the United States Naval Operations in World War II* (1947-in progress); W. F. Craven and J. T. Cate (eds.), *The Army Air Forces in World War II* (1948- ); K. R. Greenfield (ed.), *United States Army in World War II* (1947- ); and W. J. Karig et al., *Battle Report,* 5 v. (1944-1949). V. M. Dean, *Four Cornerstones of Peace* (1946) deals with the evolution of the United Nations.

## CHAPTER XXVII
## WORLD RECONSTRUCTION
### 1945–1950

The development of postwar rivalry between East and West is traced in V. M. Dean, *The United States and Russia* (1947). R. E. Sherwood, *Roosevelt and Hopkins* (1948) and E. R. Stettinius (ed. by Walter Johnson), *Roosevelt and the Russians* (1949) follow diplomatic negotiations through the Yalta Conference to the end of the Roosevelt era. Controversial discussions of military strategy and diplomacy in the Truman era include: J. F. Byrnes, *Speaking Frankly* (1948), Walter Lippmann, *Cold War* (1947), Pauline Tompkins, *American-Russian Relations in the Far East* (1949), Drew Middleton, *The Struggle for Germany* (1949), and Gen. L. D. Clay, *Decision in Germany* (1950). Thoughtful criticism of American policy is presented in Sumner Welles, *Where Are We Heading?* (1946) and in two books by J. P. Warburg, *Germany, Bridge or Battleground* (1947) and *Last Call for Common Sense* (1949). Vannevar Bush, *Modern Arms and Free Men* (1949) discusses a portentous issue without sensationalism.

# DECLARATION OF INDEPENDENCE

*In Congress, July 4, 1776,*

THE UNANIMOUS DECLARATION OF
THE THIRTEEN UNITED STATES
OF AMERICA

When in the course of human events, it becomes necessary for one people to dissolve the political bands, which have connected them with another, and to assume among the powers of the earth, the separate and equal station to which the Laws of Nature and of Nature's God entitle them, a decent respect to the opinions of mankind requires that they should declare the causes which impel them to the separation.

We hold these truths to be self-evident, that all men are created equal, that they are endowed by their Creator with certain unalienable Rights, that among these are Life, Liberty and the pursuit of Happiness. That to secure these rights, Governments are instituted among Men, deriving their just powers from the consent of the governed. That whenever any Form of Government becomes destructive of these ends, it is the Right of the People to alter or to abolish it, and to institute new Government, laying its foundation on such principles and organizing its powers in such form, as to them shall seem most likely to effect their Safety and Happiness. Prudence, indeed, will dictate that Governments long established should not be changed for light and transient causes; and accordingly all experience hath shewn, that mankind are more disposed to suffer, while evils are sufferable, than to right themselves by abolishing the forms to which they are accustomed. But when a long train of abuses and usurpations, pursuing invariably the same Object evinces a design to reduce them under absolute Despotism, it is their right, it is their duty, to throw off such Government, and to provide new Guards for their future security. Such has been the patient sufferance of these Colonies; and such is now the necessity which constrains them to alter their former Systems of Government. The history of the present King of Great Britain is a history of repeated injuries and usurpations, all having in direct object the establishment of an absolute Tyranny over these States. To prove this, let Facts be submitted to a candid world.

He has refused his Assent to Laws, the most wholesome and necessary for the public good.

He has forbidden his Governors to pass Laws of immediate and pressing importance, unless suspended in their operation till his Assent should be obtained; and when so suspended, he has utterly neglected to attend to them.

He has refused to pass other Laws for the accommodation of large districts of people, unless those people would relinquish the right of Representation in the Legislature, a right inestimable to them and formidable to tyrants only.

He has called together legislative bodies at places unusual, uncomfortable, and distant from the depository of their public Records, for the sole purpose of fatiguing them into compliance with his measures.

He has dissolved Representative Houses repeatedly, for opposing with manly firmness his invasions on the rights of the people.

He has refused for a long time, after such dissolutions, to cause others to be elected; whereby the Legislative Powers, incapable of Annihilation, have returned to the People at large for their exercise; the State remaining in the mean time exposed to all the dangers of invasion from without, and convulsions within.

He has endeavoured to prevent the population of these States; for that purpose obstructing the Laws for Naturalization of Foreigners; refusing to pass others to encourage their migrations hither, and raising the conditions of new Appropriations of Lands.

He has obstructed the Administration of

Justice, by refusing his Assent to Laws for establishing Judiciary powers.

He has made Judges dependent on his Will alone, for the tenure of their offices, and the amount and payment of their salaries.

He has erected a multitude of New Offices, and sent hither swarms of Officers to harass our people, and eat out their substance.

He has kept among us, in times of peace, Standing Armies without the Consent of our legislatures.

He has affected to render the Military independent of and superior to the Civil power.

He has combined with others to subject us to a jurisdiction foreign to our constitution, and unacknowledged by our laws; giving his Assent to their Acts of pretended Legislation:

For quartering large bodies of armed troops among us:

For protecting them, by a mock Trial, from punishment for any Murders which they should commit on the Inhabitants of these States:

For cutting off our trade with all parts of the world:

For imposing Taxes on us without our Consent:

For depriving us in many cases, of the benefits of Trial by Jury:

For transporting us beyond Seas to be tried for pretended offences:

For abolishing the free System of English Laws in a neighbouring Province, establishing therein an Arbitrary government, and enlarging its Boundaries so as to render it at once an example and fit instrument for introducing the same absolute rule into these Colonies:

For taking away our Charters, abolishing our most valuable Laws, and altering fundamentally the Forms of our Governments:

For suspending our own Legislatures, and declaring themselves invested with power to legislate for us in all cases whatsoever.

He has abdicated Government here, by declaring us out of his Protection and waging War against us.

He has plundered our seas, ravaged our Coasts, burnt our towns, and destroyed the lives of our people.

He is at this time transporting large Armies of foreign Mercenaries to compleat the works of death, desolation and tyranny, already begun with circumstances of Cruelty & perfidy scarcely paralleled in the most barbarous ages, and totally unworthy the Head of a civilized nation.

He has constrained our fellow Citizens taken Captive on the high Seas to bear Arms against their Country, to become the executioners of their friends and Brethren, or to fall themselves by their Hands.

He has excited domestic insurrections amongst us, and has endeavoured to bring on the inhabitants of our frontiers, the merciless Indian Savages, whose known rule of warfare, is an undistinguished destruction of all ages, sexes and conditions.

In every stage of these Oppressions We have Petitioned for Redress in the most humble terms: Our repeated Petitions have been answered only by repeated injury. A Prince, whose character is thus marked by every act which may define a Tyrant, is unfit to be the ruler of a free People.

Nor have We been wanting in attentions to our British brethren. We have warned them from time to time of attempts by their legislature to extend an unwarrantable jurisdiction over us. We have reminded them of the circumstances of our emigration and settlement here. We have appealed to their native justice and magnanimity, and we have conjured them by the ties of our common kindred to disavow these usurpations, which would inevitably interrupt our connections and correspondence. They too have been deaf to the voice of justice and of consanguinity. We must, therefore, acquiesce in the necessity, which denounces our Separation, and hold them, as we hold the rest of mankind, Enemies in War, in Peace Friends.

We, therefore, the Representatives of the united States of America, in General Congress, Assembled, appealing to the Supreme Judge of the world for the rectitude of our intentions do, in the Name, and by Authority of the good People of these Colonies, solemnly publish and declare, That these United Colonies are, and of Right ought to be Free and Independent States; that they are Absolved from all Allegiance to the British Crown, and that all political connection between them and the State of Great Britain, is and ought to be totally dissolved; and that as Free and Independent States, they have full Power to levy War, conclude Peace, contract Alliances, establish Commerce, and to do all other Acts and Things which Independent States may of right do. And for the support of this Declaration, with a firm reliance on the Protection of Divine Providence, we mutually pledge to each other our Lives, our Fortunes and our sacred Honor.

# CONSTITUTION OF THE UNITED STATES[1]

*We the people of the United States in order to form a more perfect union, establish justice, insure domestic tranquillity, provide for the common defence, promote the general welfare and secure the blessings of liberty to ourselves and our posterity, do ordain and establish this CONSTITUTION for the United States of America.*

## ARTICLE I

Section 1. All legislative powers herein granted shall be vested in a Congress of the United States, which shall consist of a Senate and House of Representatives.

Section 2. The House of Representatives shall be composed of members chosen every second year by the people of the several States, and the electors in each State shall have the qualifications requisite for electors of the most numerous branch of the State Legislature.

No person shall be a Representative who shall not have attained to the age of twenty-five years, and been seven years a citizen of the United States, and who shall not when elected, be an inhabitant of that State in which he shall be chosen.

Representatives and direct taxes shall be apportioned among the several States which may be included within this Union, according to their respective numbers, which shall be determined by adding to the whole number of free persons, including those bound to service for a term of years, and excluding Indians not taxed, three fifths of all other persons. The actual enumeration shall be made within three years after the first meeting of the Congress of the United States, and within every subsequent term of ten years, in such manner as they shall by law direct. The number of Representatives shall not exceed one for every thirty thousand, but each State shall have at least one Representative; and until such enumeration shall be made, the State of *New Hampshire* shall be entitled to choose three, *Massachu-*

*setts* eight, *Rhode Island* and *Providence Plantations* one, *Connecticut* five, *New York* six, *New Jersey* four, *Pennsylvania* eight, *Delaware* one, *Maryland* six, *Virginia* ten, *North Carolina* five, *South Carolina* five, and *Georgia* three.

When vacancies happen in the representation from any State, the Executive authority thereof shall issue writs of election to fill such vacancies.

The House of Representatives shall choose their Speaker and other officers; and shall have the sole power of impeachment.

Section 3. The Senate of the United States shall be composed of two Senators from each State, chosen by the Legislature thereof, for six years; and each Senator shall have one vote.

Immediately after they shall be assembled in consequence of the first election, they shall be divided as equally as may be, into three classes. The seats of the Senators of the first class shall be vacated at the expiration of the second year, of the second class at the expiration of the fourth year, and of the third class at the expiration of the sixth year, so that one third may be chosen every second year; and if vacancies happen by resignation or otherwise, during the recess of the Legislature of any State, the executive thereof may make temporary appointments, until the next meeting of the Legislature, which shall then fill such vacancies.

No person shall be a Senator who shall not have attained to the age of thirty years, and been nine years a citizen of the United States, and who shall not, when elected, be an inhabitant of that State for which he shall be chosen.

The Vice President of the United States shall be President of the Senate, but shall

[1] Jonathan Elliot, *The Debates in the Several Conventions on the Adoption of the Federal Constitution* (1836), 1-21, "copied and carefully compared with the original in the Department of State. Punctuation, paragraphs, and capital letters, same as said original," p. 1.

have no vote unless they be equally divided.

The Senate shall choose their other officers, and also a President protempore, in the absence of the Vice President or when he shall exercise the office of President of the United States.

The Senate shall have the sole power to try all impeachments: when sitting for that purpose, they shall be on oath or affirmation. When the President of the United States is tried the Chief Justice shall preside: and no person shall be convicted without the concurrence of two-thirds of the members present.

Judgment in cases of impeachment shall not extend farther than to removal from office, and disqualification to hold and enjoy any office of honor, trust, or profit under the United States: but the party convicted shall nevertheless be liable and subject to indictment, trial, judgment and punishment, according to law.

Section 4. The times, places and manner of holding elections for Senators and Representatives, shall be prescribed in each State by the legislature thereof; but the Congress may at any time by law make or alter such regulations, except as to the places of choosing Senators.

The Congress shall assemble at least once in every year, and such meeting shall be on the first Monday in December unless they shall by law appoint a different day.

Section 5. Each House shall be the judge of the elections, returns and qualifications of its own members, and a majority of each shall constitute a quorum to do business; but a smaller number may adjourn from day to day, and may be authorized to compel the attendance of absent members, in such manner, and under such penalties as each House may provide.

Each House may determine the rules of its proceedings, punish its members for disorderly behavior, and, with the concurrence of two thirds, expel a member.

Each House shall keep a journal of its proceedings, and from time to time publish the same, excepting such parts as may in their judgment require Secrecy; and the yeas and nays of the members of either House on any question shall, at the desire of one-fifth of those present, be entered on the journal.

Neither House, during the Session of Congress, shall, without the consent of the other, adjourn for more than three days, nor to any other place than that in which the two Houses shall be sitting.

Section 6. The Senators and Representatives shall receive a compensation for their services, to be ascertained by law, and paid out of the Treasury of the United States. They shall in all cases except treason, felony and breach of the peace, be privileged from arrest during their attendance at the session of their respective Houses, and in going to and returning from the same; and for any speech or debate in either House, they shall not be questioned in any other place.

No Senator or Representative shall, during the time for which he was elected, be appointed to any civil office under the authority of the United States, which shall have been created, or the emoluments whereof shall have been increased during such time: and no person holding any office under the United States shall be a member of either House during his continuance in office.

Section 7. All bills for raising revenue shall originate in the House of Representatives; but the Senate may propose, or concur with, amendments, as on other bills.

Every bill which shall have passed the House of Representatives, and the Senate, shall, before it become a law, be presented to the President of the United States; if he approve he shall sign it, but if not he shall return it, with his objections to that House in which it shall have originated, who shall enter the objections at large on their journal, and proceed to reconsider it. If after such reconsideration two thirds of that House shall agree to pass the bill, it shall be sent, together with the objections, to the other House, by which it shall likewise be reconsidered, and if approved by two thirds of that House, it shall become a law. But in all such cases the votes of both Houses shall be determined by yeas and nays, and the names of the persons voting for and against the bill shall be entered on the journal of each House respectively. If any bill shall not be returned by the President within ten days (Sundays excepted), after it shall have been presented to him, the same shall be a law, in like manner as if he had signed it, unless the Congress by their adjournment prevent its return, in which case it shall not be a law.

Every order, resolution, or vote to which the concurrence of the Senate and House of Representatives may be necessary (except on a question of adjournment) shall be presented to the President of the United States; and before the same shall take effect, shall be approved by him, or, being disapproved by him, shall be repassed by two-thirds of the Senate and House of Representatives, according to the rules and limitations prescribed in the case of a bill.

Section 8. The Congress shall have power To lay and collect taxes, duties, imposts and excises, to pay the debts and provide for the common defence and general welfare of the United States; but all duties, imposts and excises shall be uniform throughout the United States;

To borrow money on the credit of the United States;

To regulate commerce with foreign nations, and among the several States, and with the Indian tribes;

To establish an uniform rule of naturalization, and uniform laws on the subject of bankruptcies throughout the United States;

To coin money, regulate the value thereof, and of foreign coin, and fix the standard of weights and measures;

To provide for the punishment of counterfeiting the securities and current coin of the United States;

To establish post offices and post roads;

To promote the progress of science and useful arts, by securing for limited times to authors and inventors the exclusive right to their respective writings and discoveries;

To constitute tribunals inferior to the supreme court;

To define and punish piracies and felonies committed on the high seas and offences against the law of nations;

To declare war, grant letters of marque and reprisal, and make rules concerning captures on land and water;

To raise and support armies, but no appropriation of money to that use shall be for a longer term than two years;

To provide and maintain a navy;

To make rules for the government and regulation of the land and naval forces;

To provide for calling forth the militia to execute the laws of the Union, suppress insurrections and repel invasions;

To provide for organizing, arming and disciplining, the militia, and for governing such part of them as may be employed in the service of the United States, reserving to the States respectively, the appointment of the officers, and the authority of training the militia according to the discipline prescribed by Congress;

To exercise exclusive legislation in all cases whatsoever over such district (not exceeding ten miles square) as may, by cession of particular States, and the acceptance of Congress, become the seat of the government of the United States, and to exercise like authority over all places purchased by the consent of the Legislature of the State in which the same shall be, for the erection of forts, magazines, arsenals, dockyards, and other needful buildings;—And

To make all laws which shall be necessary and proper for carrying into execution the foregoing powers, and all other powers vested by this constitution in the government of the United States, or in any department or officer thereof.

Section 9. The migration or importation of such persons as any of the States now existing shall think proper to admit, shall not be prohibited by the Congress prior to the year eighteen hundred and eight, but a tax or duty may be imposed on such importation, not exceeding ten dollars for each person.

The privilege of the writ of *Habeas Corpus* shall not be suspended, unless when in cases of rebellion or invasion the public safety may require it.

No bill of attainder or ex post facto law shall be passed.

No capitation, or other direct, tax shall be laid, unless in proportion to the census or enumeration herein before directed to be taken.

No tax or duty shall be laid on articles exported from any State.

No preference shall be given by any regulation of commerce or revenue to the ports of one State over those of another: nor shall vessels bound to, or from, one State, be obliged to enter, clear, or pay duties in another.

No money shall be drawn from the Treasury, but in consequence of appropriations made by law; and a regular statement and account of the receipts and expenditures of all public money shall be published from time to time.

No title of nobility shall be granted by the United States and no person holding any office of profit or trust under them, shall, without the consent of the Congress, accept of any present, emolument, office, or title, of any kind whatever, from any king, prince, or foreign State.

Section 10. No State shall enter into any treaty, alliance, or confederation; grant letters of marque and reprisal; coin money, emit bills of credit; make any thing but gold and silver coin a tender in payment of debts; pass any bill of attainder, ex post facto law; or law impairing the obligation of contracts; or grant any title of nobility.

No State shall, without the consent of the Congress, lay any imposts or duties on imports or exports, except what may be absolutely necessary for executing its inspection laws: and the net produce of all duties and imposts, laid by any State on imports or exports, shall be for the use of the Treasury of the United States; and all such laws shall be subject to the revision and control of the Congress.

No State shall, without the consent of Congress, lay any duty of tonnage, keep troops, or ships of war in time of peace, enter into any agreement or compact with another State, or with a foreign power, or engage in war, unless actually invaded, or in such imminent danger as will not admit of delay.

## ARTICLE II

Section 1. The executive power shall be vested in a President of the United States of America. He shall hold his office during the term of four years, and, together with the Vice-President, chosen for the same term, be elected as follows:

Each State shall appoint, in such manner as the Legislature thereof may direct, a number of electors equal to the whole number of Senators and Representatives to which the State may be entitled in the Congress; but no Senator or Representative, or person holding an office of trust or profit under the United States, shall be appointed an elector.

The electors shall meet in their respective States, and vote by ballot for two persons, of whom one at least shall not be an inhabitant of the same State with themselves. And they shall make a list of all the persons voted for, and of the number of votes for each; which list they shall sign and certify, and transmit sealed to the seat of the government of the United States, directed to the President of the Senate. The President of the Senate shall, in the presence of the Senate and House of Representatives, open all the certificates, and the votes shall then be counted. The person having the greatest number of votes shall be the President, if such number be a majority of the whole number of electors appointed; and if there be more than one who have such majority, and have an equal number of votes, then the House of Representatives shall immediately choose by ballot one of them for President; and if no person have a majority, then from the five highest on the list the said House shall, in like manner, choose the President. But in choosing the President, the votes shall be taken by States, the representation from each State having one vote; a quorum for this purpose shall consist of a member or members from two-thirds of the States, and a majority of all the States shall be necessary to a choice. In every case, after the choice of the President, the person having the greatest number of votes of the electors shall be the Vice-President. But if there should remain two or more who have equal votes, the Senate shall choose from them by ballot the Vice-President.

The Congress may determine the time of choosing the electors, and the day on which they shall give their votes; which day shall be the same throughout the United States.

No person except a natural born citizen, or a citizen of the United States, at the time of the adoption of this constitution, shall be eligible to the office of President; neither shall any person be eligible to that office who shall not have attained to the age of thirty-five years, and been fourteen years a resident within the United States.

In case of the removal of the President from office, or of his death, resignation or inability to discharge the powers and duties of the said office, the same shall devolve on the Vice-President, and the Congress may by law provide for the case of removal, death, resignation or inability, both of the President and Vice-President, declaring what officer shall then act as President, and such officer shall act accordingly, until the disability be removed, or a President shall be elected.

The President shall, at stated times, receive for his services, a compensation, which shall neither be increased nor diminished during the period for which he shall have been elected, and he shall not receive within that period any other emolument from the United States, or any of them.

Before he enter on the execution of his office, he shall take the following oath or affirmation: *"I do solemnly swear (or affirm) that I will faithfully execute the office of President of the United States, and will, to the best of my ability, preserve, protect, and defend the Constitution of the United States."*

Section 2. The President shall be commander in chief of the army and navy of the United States, and of the militia of the several States, when called into the actual service of the United States; he may require the opinion, in writing, of the principal officer in each of the executive departments, upon any subject relating to the duties of their respective offices; and he shall have power to grant reprieves and pardons for offences against the United States, except in cases of impeachment.

He shall have power, by and with the advice and consent of the Senate, to make treaties, provided two-thirds of the Senators present concur; and he shall nominate, and by and with the advice and consent of the Senate, shall appoint ambassadors, other public ministers and consuls, judges of the supreme court, and all other officers of the United States, whose appointments are not herein otherwise provided for, and which shall be established by law: But the Congress may by law vest the appointment of such inferior officers as they think proper, in the President alone, in the courts of law, or in the heads of departments.

The President shall have power to fill up all vacancies that may happen during the recess of the Senate, by granting commissions which shall expire at the end of their next session.

Section 3. He shall from time to time give to the Congress information of the state of the Union, and recommend to their consideration such measures as he shall judge necessary and expedient; he may, on extraordinary occasions, convene both Houses, or either of them, and, in case of disagreement between them, with respect to the time of adjournment, he may adjourn them to such time as he shall think proper; he shall receive ambassadors and other public ministers; he shall take care that the laws be faithfully executed, and shall commission all the officers of the United States.

Section 4. The President, Vice-President and all civil officers of the United States, shall be removed from office on impeachment for, and conviction of, treason, bribery, or other high crimes and misdemeanors.

## ARTICLE III

Section 1. The judicial power of the United States shall be vested in one Supreme Court, and in such inferior courts as the Congress may from time to time ordain and establish. The judges, both of the supreme and inferior courts, shall hold their offices during good behaviour, and shall, at stated times, receive for their services, a compensation, which shall not be diminished during their continuance in office.

Section 2. The judicial power shall extend to all cases in law and equity, arising under this constitution, the laws of the United States, and the treaties made, or which shall be made, under their authority; to all cases—affecting ambassadors, other public ministers, and consuls;—to all cases of admiralty and maritime jurisdiction;—to controversies to which the United States shall be a party;—to controversies between two or more States;—between a State and citizens of another State;—between citizens of different States;—between citizens of the same State, claiming lands under grants of different States, and between a State or the citizens thereof, and foreign States, citizens or subjects.

In all cases affecting ambassadors, other public ministers and consuls, and those in which a State shall be party, the supreme court shall have original jurisdiction. In all the other cases before-mentioned, the supreme court shall have appellate jurisdiction, both as to law and fact, with such exceptions, and under such regulations, as the Congress shall make.

The trial of all crimes, except in cases of impeachment, shall be by jury; and such trial shall be held in the State where the said crimes shall have been committed; but when not committed within any State, the trial shall be at such place or places as the Congress may by law have directed.

Section 3. Treason against the United States, shall consist only in levying war against them, or in adhering to their enemies, giving them aid and comfort. No person shall be convicted of treason, unless on the testimony of two witnesses to the same overt act, or on confession in open court.

The Congress shall have power to declare the punishment of treason, but no attainder of treason shall work corruption of blood, or forfeiture except during the life of the person attainted.

## ARTICLE IV

Section 1. Full faith and credit shall be given in each State to the public acts, records, and judicial proceedings of every other State. And the Congress may by general laws prescribe the manner in which such acts, records, and proceedings shall be proved, and the effect thereof.

Section 2. The citizens of each State shall be entitled to all the privileges and immunities of citizens in the several States.

A person charged in any State with treason, felony, or other crime, who shall flee from justice, and be found in another State, shall on demand of the executive authority of the State from which he fled, be delivered up, to be removed to the State having jurisdiction of the crime.

No person held to service or labor in one State, under the laws thereof, escaping into another, shall, in consequence of any law or regulation therein, be discharged from such service or labor, but shall be delivered up on claim of the party to whom such service or labor may be due.

Section 3. New States may be admitted by the Congress into this Union; but no new State shall be formed or erected within the jurisdiction of any other State; nor any State be formed by the junction of two or more States, or parts of States, without the consent of the Legislature of the States concerned as well as of the Congress.

The Congress shall have power to dispose of and make all needful rules and regulations respecting the territory or other property belonging to the United States; and nothing in this constitution shall be so construed as to prejudice any claims of the United States, or of any particular State.

Section 4. The United States shall guaranty to every State in this Union a republican form of government, and shall protect each of them against invasion; and on application of the legislature, or of the executive (when the legislature cannot be convened) against domestic violence.

## ARTICLE V

The Congress, whenever two-thirds of both Houses shall deem it necessary, shall propose amendments to this constitution, or, on the application of the legislatures of two-thirds of the several States, shall call a convention for proposing amendments, which in either case, shall be valid to all intents and purposes, as part of this constitution, when ratified by the legislatures of three-fourths of the several States, or by conventions in three-fourths thereof, as the one or the other mode of ratification may be proposed by the Congress; provided, that no amendment, which may be made prior to the year one thousand eight hundred and eight, shall in any manner affect the first and fourth clauses in the ninth section of the first article; and that no State, without its consent, shall be deprived of its equal suffrage in the Senate.

## ARTICLE VI

All debts contracted and engagements entered into, before the adoption of this constitution, shall be as valid against the United States under this constitution as under the confederation.

This constitution, and the laws of the United States which shall be made in pursuance thereof; and all treaties made, or which shall be made, under the authority of the United States, shall be the supreme law of the land; and the judges in every state shall be bound thereby, any thing in the constitution or laws of any State to the contrary notwithstanding.

The Senators and Representatives before mentioned, and the members of the several State legislatures, and all executive and judicial officers, both of the United States and of the several States shall be bound by oath or affirmation, to support this constitution: but no religious test shall ever be required as a qualification to any office or public trust under the United States.

## ARTICLE VII

The ratification of the conventions of nine states, shall be sufficient for the establishment of this constitution between the States so ratifying the same.

Done in convention by the unanimous consent of the States present the seventeenth day of September in the year of our Lord one thousand seven hundred and eighty-seven and of the independence of the United States of America the twelfth.

# THE BILL OF RIGHTS: 1791

## AMENDMENTS [2]

## ARTICLE I

Congress shall make no law respecting an establishment of religion, or prohibiting

[2] The first ten Articles declared in force December 15, 1791.

the free exercise thereof; or abridging the freedom of speech, or of the press; or the right of the people peaceably to assemble, and to petition the government for a redress of grievances.

## ARTICLE II

A well-regulated militia being necessary to the security of a free State, the right of the people to keep and bear arms shall not be infringed.

## ARTICLE III

No soldier shall, in time of peace, be quartered in any house without the consent of the owner, nor in time of war but in a manner to be prescribed by law.

## ARTICLE IV

The right of the people to be secure in their persons, houses, papers, and effects, against unreasonable searches and seizures, shall not be violated; and no warrants shall issue but upon probable cause, supported by oath or affirmation, and particularly describing the place to be searched and the persons or things to be seized.

## ARTICLE V

No person shall be held to answer for a capital or otherwise infamous crime, unless on a presentment or indictment of a grand jury, except in cases arising in the land or naval forces, or in the militia when in actual service, in time of war or public danger; nor shall any person be subject, for the same offence, to be twice put in jeopardy of life or limb, nor shall be compelled in any criminal case to be a witness against himself; nor be deprived of life, liberty, or property, without due process of law; nor shall private property be taken for public use without just compensation.

## ARTICLE VI

In all criminal prosecutions the accused shall enjoy the right to a speedy and public trial, by an impartial jury of the State

and district wherein the crime shall have been committed, which district shall have been previously ascertained by law; and to be informed of the nature and cause of the accusation; to be confronted with the witnesses against him; to have compulsory process for obtaining witnesses in his favor; and to have the assistance of counsel for his defence.

## ARTICLE VII

In suits at common law, where the value in controversy shall exceed twenty dollars, the right of trial by jury shall be preserved; and no fact tried by a jury shall be otherwise reëxamined in any court of the United States, than according to the rules of the common law.

## ARTICLE VIII

Excessive bail shall not be required, nor excessive fines imposed, nor cruel and unusual punishments inflicted.

## ARTICLE IX

The enumeration in the Constitution of certain rights shall not be construed to deny or disparage others retained by the people.

## ARTICLE X

The powers not delegated to the United States by the Constitution, nor prohibited by it to the States, are reserved to the States respectively, or to the people.

# LATER CONSTITUTIONAL AMENDMENTS

## ARTICLE XI [3]

The judicial power of the United States shall not be construed to extend to any suit in law or equity commenced or prosecuted against any one of the United States by citizens of another state, or by citizens or subjects of any foreign State.

---

[3] January 8, 1798.

## ARTICLE XII [4]

The electors shall meet in their respective States, and vote by ballot for President and Vice-President, one of whom, at least, shall not be an inhabitant of the same State with themselves; they shall name in their ballots the person voted for as President, and in distinct ballots the person voted for as Vice-President; and they shall make distinct lists of all persons voted for as President, and of all persons voted for as Vice-President, and of the number of votes for each; which lists they shall sign and certify, and transmit sealed to the seat of the government of the United States, directed to the President of the Senate; the President of the Senate shall, in the presence of the Senate and House of Representatives, open all the certificates, and the votes shall then be counted: the person having the greatest number of votes for President shall be the President, if such number be a majority of the whole number of electors appointed; and if no person have such majority, then, from the persons having the highest numbers, not exceeding three, on the list of those voted for as President, the House of Representatives shall choose, immediately, by ballot, the President. But, in choosing the President, the votes shall be taken by States, the representation from each State having one vote; a quorum for this purpose shall consist of a member or members from two-thirds of the States, and a majority of all the States shall be necessary to a choice. And if the House of Representatives shall not choose a President whenever the right of choice shall devolve upon them, before the fourth day of March next following, then the Vice-President shall act as President, as in the case of the death or other constitutional disability of the President. The person having the greatest number of votes as Vice-President shall be the Vice-President, if such number be a majority of the whole number of electors appointed; and if no person have a major-

ity, then, from the two highest numbers on the list, the Senate shall choose the Vice-President: a quorum for the purpose shall consist of two-thirds of the whole number of Senators, and a majority of the whole number shall be necessary to a choice. But no person constitutionally ineligible to the office of President, shall be eligible to that of Vice-President of the United States.

## ARTICLE XIII [5]

Section 1. Neither slavery nor involuntary servitude, except as a punishment for crime whereof the party shall have been duly convicted, shall exist within the United States, or any place subject to their jurisdiction.

Section 2. Congress shall have power to enforce this article by appropriate legislation.

## ARTICLE XIV [6]

Section 1. All persons born or naturalized in the United States, and subject to the jurisdiction thereof, are citizens of the United States and of the State wherein they reside. No State shall make or enforce any law which shall abridge the privileges or immunities of citizens of the United States; nor shall any State deprive any person of life, liberty, or property, without due process of law; nor deny to any person within its jurisdiction the equal protection of the laws.

Section 2. Representatives shall be apportioned among the several States according to their respective numbers, counting the whole number of persons in each State, excluding Indians not taxed. But when the right to vote at any election for the choice of electors for President and Vice President of the United States, Representatives in Congress, the Executive and Judicial officers of a State, or the members of the Legislature thereof, is denied to any of the male inhabitants of such State, being twenty-one years of age, and citizens of

[4] September 25, 1804.

[5] December 18, 1865.
[6] July 23, 1868.

the United States, or in any way abridged, except for participation in rebellion, or other crime, the basis of representation therein shall be reduced in the proportion which the number of such male citizens shall bear to the whole number of male citizens twenty-one years of age in such State.

Section 3. No person shall be a Senator or Representative in Congress, or elector of President and Vice President, or hold any office, civil or military, under the United States, or under any State, who, having previously taken an oath, as a member of Congress, or as an officer of the United States, or as a member of any State legislature, or as an executive or judicial officer of any State, to support the Constitution of the United States, shall have engaged in insurrection or rebellion against the same, or given aid or comfort to the enemies thereof. But Congress may by a vote of two-thirds of each House, remove such disability.

Section 4. The validity of the public debt of the United States, authorized by law, including debts incurred for payment of pensions and bounties for services in suppressing insurrection or rebellion, shall not be questioned. But neither the United States nor any State shall assume or pay any debt or obligation incurred in aid of insurrection or rebellion against the United States, or any claim for the loss or emancipation of any slave; but all such debts, obligations and claims shall be held illegal and void.

Section 5. The Congress shall have power to enforce, by appropriate legislation, the provisions of this article.

## ARTICLE XV [7]

Section 1. The right of citizens of the United States to vote shall not be denied or abridged by the United States or by any State on account of race, color, or previous condition of servitude.

Section 2. The Congress shall have power

to enforce this article by appropriate legislation.

## ARTICLE XVI [8]

The Congress shall have power to lay and collect taxes on incomes, from whatever source derived, without apportionment among the several States, and without regard to any census or enumeration.

## ARTICLE XVII [9]

The Senate of the United States shall be composed of two senators from each State, elected by the people thereof, for six years; and each Senator shall have one vote. The electors in each State shall have the qualifications requisite for electors of the most numerous branch of the State legislature.

When vacancies happen in the representation of any State in the Senate, the executive authority of such State shall issue writs of election to fill such vacancies: *Provided,* That the legislature of any State may empower the executive thereof to make temporary appointments until the people fill the vacancies by election as the legislature may direct.

This amendment shall not be so construed as to affect the election or term of any Senator chosen before it becomes valid as part of the Constitution.

## ARTICLE XVIII [10]

Section 1. After one year from the ratification of this article the manufacture, sale, or transportation of intoxicating liquors within, the importation thereof into, or the exportation thereof from the United States and all territory subject to the jurisdiction thereof for beverage purposes is hereby prohibited.

Section 2. The Congress and the several States shall have concurrent power to enforce this article by appropriate legislation.

This article shall be inoperative unless it shall have been ratified as an amend-

---

[7] March 30, 1870.

[8] February 25, 1913.
[9] May 31, 1913.
[10] January 29, 1919.

ment to the Constitution by the legislatures of the several States, as provided in the Constitution, within seven years from the date of the submission hereof to the States by the Congress.

## ARTICLE XIX [11]

The right of citizens of the United States to vote shall not be denied or abridged by the United States or by any State on account of sex.

Congress shall have power to enforce this article by appropriate legislation.

## ARTICLE XX [12]

Section 1. The terms of the President and Vice-President shall end at noon on the 20th day of January, and the terms of Senators and Representatives at noon on the 3d day of January, of the years in which such terms would have ended if this article had not been ratified; and the terms of their successors shall then begin.

Section 2. The Congress shall assemble at least once in every year, and such meeting shall begin at noon on the 3d day of January, unless they shall by law appoint a different day.

Section 3. If, at the time fixed for the beginning of the term of the President, the President elect shall have died, the Vice-President elect shall become President. If a President shall not have been chosen before the time fixed for the beginning of his term, or if the President elect shall have failed to qualify, then the Vice-President elect shall act as President until a President shall have qualified; and the Congress may by law provide for the case wherein neither a President elect nor a Vice-President elect shall have qualified,

declaring who shall then act as President, or the manner in which one who is to act shall be selected, and such person shall act accordingly until a President or Vice-President shall have qualified.

Section 4. The Congress may by law provide for the case of the death of any of the persons from whom the House of Representatives may choose a President whenever the right of choice shall have devolved upon them, and for the case of the death of any of the persons from whom the Senate may choose a Vice-President whenever the right of choice shall have devolved upon them.

Section 5. Sections 1 and 2 shall take effect on the 15th day of October following the ratification of this article.

Section 6. This article shall be inoperative unless it shall have been ratified as an amendment to the Constitution by the legislatures of three-fourths of the several States within seven years from the date of its submission.

## ARTICLE XXI [13]

Section 1. The eighteenth article of amendment to the Constitution of the United States is hereby repealed.

Section 2. The transportation or importation into any State, Territory or possession of the United States for delivery or use therein of intoxicating liquors, in violation of the laws thereof, is hereby prohibited.

Section 3. This article shall be inoperative unless it shall have been ratified as an amendment to the Constitution by conventions in the several States, as provided in the Constitution, within seven years from the date of the submission hereof to the States by the Congress.

---

[11] August 26, 1920.
[12] February 6, 1933.

[13] December 5, 1933.

# INDEX

## A

Abrams Case, Justice Holmes's dissent, 418
*Adair* v. *U.S.*, 357-358
  Justice Holmes's dissent, 358-359
Adamson Act, 356-357
Adkins Case, Justice Holmes's dissent, 420-422
A.F. of L., organization of, 217-218
Agnosticism, 152-156
Agrarian crusade: Populism, 224-227
  Sherman Silver Purchase Act, 224
Agrarian discontent, 119-121
  social bases of, 121-122
Agriculture, granger movement, 119-125
  McNary-Haugen Bill, Coolidge veto of, 427-429
  under progressivism, 367-376
  government aid, 374-376
  in South, cotton, 115-119
  sugar planters of Hawaii, 264-267
  in West, 111-115
Alabama, "Black Code," 19-20
"Alabama Claims," 251-253
*Alarm, The,* advice on dynamite, 217
American commonwealth, Lord Bryce on, 81-83
American government, Macaulay on, 187-188
"American letter" from immigrant farmer, 104-105
*Ames, Smyth* v., 238-239
Anarchism, 215-217
Antitrust Act, Clayton, 340-342, 364-366
  Supreme Court negation of, 419-420
Arms embargo, repeal of, 487
Arthur, Chester A., on Indian policy, 99-100
Association for Improvement of Condition of Poor,
  on immigration, 160-162
Atlantic Charter, 489-490

## B

Baer, George, on labor negotiations, 300
*Bailey* v. *Drexel Furniture Co.*, 420
Baker, Ray Stannard, *The Reign of Lawlessness,* 289-292
Banking trust, Brandeis on, 338-339
  Pujo Report on, 335-338
Barton, Bruce, *The Man Nobody Knows,* 424-425
Beecher, Henry Ward, "The Two Revelations," 142-145
Bell, W. A., *New Tracks in North America,* 101-102
Bellamy, Edward, *Looking Backward,* 194-195
Big business, Roosevelt, Theodore, on, 298-300
"Black Codes," 19-20
Black reconstruction, 33-34
Blaine, James G., on Pan-American Conference, 254-255
  "waving the bloody shirt," 71-73
"Bloody shirt" campaigning, 71-73
Bonnett, C. E., on National Association of Manufacturers, 347-348
Brandeis, Louis D., on industrial relations, 349-352
  *Other People's Money,* 338-339
  on social experiment, 442-443

Brewer, Justice, conservatism exemplified by, 237-238
Bryan, W. J., "Cross of Gold" speech, 233-237
Bryce, James, on American commonwealth, 81-83
Bull Moose platform, 324-327
*Bunting* v. *Oregon,* 355-356
Business, big, Theodore Roosevelt on, 298-300
  and political corruption during Grant administration, 56-59
  program after Civil War: Homestead Act, 44-45
  land speculation, 45-47
  "sound" currency, 52-56
  tariff protection for industry, 50-52
  transcontinental railroads, 48-50
  and theory of evolution, 151-152

## C

Candee, H. C., on Oklahoma rush, 105-107
Capitalism, farmers, adjustment of, 111-114
  monopoly and western agriculture, 114-115
Caribbean empire, corollary to Monroe Doctrine, 391-392
  Cuba, protectorate over, 389
  Haiti, protectorate over, 392-393
  Panama, revolution in, 389-391
  Puerto Rico, 393-395
Carnegie, Andrew, "The Advantages of Poverty," 170
  "The Bugaboo of Trusts," 171
  *The Gospel of Wealth,* 167-170
  on theology and evolution, 151-152
  on urbanization of America, 126-127
Cattle frontier, 94-95
Chafee, Zechariah, Jr., *Free Speech in the United States,* 429-431
Child labor, action after World War I, 416-417, 420
Children, results of poverty on, 182-184
Chinese Exclusion Act, 162-163
Christian Socialism, 147-151
Christianity, Social, 145-147
Cities, political machines of, 294-297
Civil rights, in Japan under occupation, 499-500
  report of committee, 1947, 520-524
Civil Rights Act, 1866, 13-15
  1875, 37-38
Civil Rights Cases, 1883, Supreme Court on, 38-39
Civil service, Hayes on, 69-71
Civil service reform, 73-75
Class war, I.W.W. on, 366-367
Clayton Antitrust Act, 340-342, 364-366
  Supreme Court negation of, 419-420
Clemens, Samuel L., *Roughing It,* 90-92
Cleveland, Grover, on annexation of Hawaii, 265-267
  on repeal of Sherman Silver Purchase Act, 229-231
  on tariff reform, 204-207
  on Venezuelan boundary dispute, 269-271
  veto of immigration-restriction bill, 165-166
  veto of social legislation, 203-204